Menu Mystique

Menu Mystique

The Diner's Guide
to Fine Food & Drink

by
NORMAN ODYA KROHN

jD | JONATHAN DAVID PUBLISHERS, INC.
MIDDLE VILLAGE, NEW YORK 11379

MENU MYSTIQUE

The Diner's Guide
to Fine Food & Drink

Jonathan David Publishers, Inc.
68-22 Eliot Avenue
Middle Village, New York 11379

10 9 8 7 6 5 4 3 2 1

Library of Congress Cataloging in Publication Data

Krohn, Norman Odya, 1920-
    Menu mystique.

    Bibliography
    1. Food—Dictionaries. I. Title.
TX349.K76   641'.03'21   81-23660
ISBN 0-8246-0280-3

Printed in the United States of America

To
HELLMUTH SCHUPP,
my mentor, confidant, and friend,
without whose encouragement, persuasion, and
help, this book would never have
come into being

Acknowledgements

My sincerest thanks go to the many friends who have helped me in my research for this book, especially Dr. Hellmuth Schupp, of Davos, Switzerland, who has been exceedingly helpful in solving many linguistic and culinary problems.

Of the many foreign associations that have generously shared with me invaluable information about their lands and cuisines, I wish to express particular thanks to the Danish, Italian, Japanese, Korean, and Polish consulates.

I am deeply indebted also to Mr. Jean Fayet, a great restaurateur and friend, who went far beyond the call of duty and friendship, sacrificing hours of his time poring over the manuscript to insure its Gallic authenticity.

A special mention must be given to my editor, Mr. David Kolatch, who by his kindness, patience, and dedicated hard work brought my thoughts to the page most clearly.

Finally, my deepest thanks to Mrs. Hannah Cohen and Mr. Philip Gutride for their encouragement and help just when I needed it.

Preface

I have been personally involved with food and the challenge of its service in hotels and restaurants for more than a quarter of a century. Although I learned the basics of cooking while attending a Swiss hotel school, I have never worked as a professional cook. Rather, I have been paid good money to assure restaurant diners, both here and abroad, of the finest food service I could muster.

As a *maître d'hôtel,* each lunch and dinner hour seemed respectively like the matinee and evening performance of some classic piece of theater, beginning with the introduction and exposition (the appetizers and soups), building up to the climax (the main course), and followed by the denouement (the dessert, coffee, and cordial), the final curtain.

My reward as host of various restaurants over the years has not been the actor's applause but the warm handclasp and smile of the satisfied guest as he or she left the dining room. It is in the guise of that same host that I have set out to write this book. By taking the mystery out of today's menus, I hope to make dining out a more pleasurable event.

Often, the English-speaking diner is presented with a cryptic menu brimming with foreign terms. Usually the foreign names of dishes give a clue as to how the dishes offered are prepared, or they tell us when, where, or by or for whom they were created. It is unfortunate, however, that foreign culinary jargon is often used incorrectly. In fact it is often used misleadingly. We are, for example, all familiar with the restaurateur who calls a mutton chop a *cotelette d'agneau,* or refers to the common flounder as "Dover sole," or labels his sauce *Hollandaise* when in fact flour has been substituted for as much as seventy percent of the sweet butter that makes a true *Hollandaise* such a delight. Only the diner well versed in culinary parlance will be able to cope with such blatant "misuse of terms," a euphemism for kitchen-skulduggery.

The uninitiated diner in a French restaurant feels utter frustration when having to wrestle with such menu expressions as *entrecôte marchand de vin, raie au beurre noir,* or *tournedos Périgourdine.* But the restaurateur is faced with a problem as well: How does he translate *cassoulet Carcassonnais* or *bouillabaisse Provençale* into appropriate English and still manage to conjure up the same mouthwatering visions that the French mother-tongue—with its tonality, rhythm, and music—is able to? A *Wiener Schnitzel,* for instance, sounds so much better than a "breaded veal cutlet." And ordering a *sashimi* from a Japanese menu will encourage digestive juices to flow much faster than just calling for "a plate of raw fish." And when compared to "stewed veal shank," the Italian equivalent, *osso bucco alla Milanese,* has all the style and grace of an operatic aria. It is natural, then, that the enterprising restaurateur—always ready to describe his fare in the most enticing way—will choose the more colorful, more musical foreign menu terms over their pedestrian English counterparts.

In keeping the name of the dish in the original foreign language, the restaurateur in a sense "promises" the diner that the dish will be prepared and served as it was when first created. However, only the sophisticated diner will know with certainty whether that promise has been fulfilled. Only the knowledgeable diner will be able to determine whether the dish he has ordered has been prepared properly.

To enjoy dining out to its fullest, one must be able to read and understand the restaurant menus of many different cuisines, for only then is one able to order a meal with confidence. While I hardly expect the diner to develop a litmus-paper palate after reading this book, it is my hope that *Menu Mystique* will help cut through the gastronomic gobbledygook so prevalent in restaurants today, that it will contribute towards the education of all those who love restaurant dining and the pleasures it can bring.

NORMAN KROHN

January 1983
Long Island City, NY

Introduction

Four middle-aged businessmen entered the Grill Room of the Four Seasons Restaurant in New York City. They had had their cocktails and ordered a simple lunch. Each ordered a steak in turn. "I'll have a sirloin, rare," said one. The next said, "Give me a *filet mignon,* also rare." The third man ordered the same. The fourth gentleman studied the menu and then gave me his order: "I'll take that steak there—the Steak Tartar—and rare!" Everyone laughed. However, when I returned with the double-ground sirloin that had been prepared for the Steak Tartar and presented it to the gentleman, asking if he wanted all of the garniture served with it, he blew his top: "I ordered a steak. That's not a steak. That's raw hamburger!" The man was so incensed that I chose not to argue that the double-ground sirloin was, indeed, the Steak Tartar that he had ordered. Instead, I returned the menu to him and pointed to the grilled steaks and chops. This is but one example—and a simple one—of how foreign menu terms can cause trouble and confusion in a restaurant.

Menu Mystique is an attempt to interpret and translate those pesky but necessary foreign phrases found on restaurant menus. The book will explain that Steak Tartar is not a grilled beefsteak but ground raw sirloin served with an equally raw egg, capers, onions, and spices; that *teriyaki* is not a former Japanese general but a special Oriental method of first marinating and then barbecuing cubes of choice beef. It will detail the differences between a *sauce Béarnaise* and a sauce *Béchamel;* it will tell what makes an omelette *baveuse* and a fillet of beef *Périgueux;* it will explain how a duck becomes a delicacy called *Peking* and what makes an East Indian hen blush a *tandoori* red.

Gastronomic Language

Although this book defines thousands of culinary terms gleaned from many languages, the official gastronomic language has come to be French—not the French we learned at school but that imaginative culinary tongue which endows the most ordinary words with an entirely different meaning. These words and phrases are "kitchen terms" that for the most part were conceived by talented chefs while caught up in the ecstasy of creating new taste thrills. The chefs often cryptically set the terms down on paper, and many of those descriptive names have confused and intimidated diners ever since. Take heart, however, for even the French have problems deciphering some of their archaic culinary terminology.

How Dishes Are Named

The name given to a specific dish may include the name of the chef who created it (Carême, Dugléré, Béchamel), or it may state the name of the restaurant where the dish was first served (Divan, Paillard, Marguery). Sometimes the name of a dish tells us how it is prepared (for example, a dish described as *au four,* "in the oven," is quite literally baked in the oven); or it may say something about the size, shape, or color of the preparation *(cardinale, chiffonade, brunoise, julienne)*. A dish may be named for the place of origin of one of its ingredients (for example, the *potage Argenteuil,* a cream of asparagus soup, is so named because the very finest asparagus in France are produced in Argenteuil, a suburb of Paris).

Of all the countries in the world, France is the only one to have honored the act of love by naming so many fine dishes after mistresses and concubines. DuBarry, Pompadour, Agnès Sorel, Maintenon, or just plain Anna are a few appellations that come immediately to mind. After mistresses follow the names of actresses, singers, composers, and statesmen: Rossini, Verdi, Melba, Metternich, Talleyrand, and of course the "Divine" Sarah Bernhardt, who, it is said, once read a menu with such feeling that she moved a whole restaurant full of diners to tears.

An interesting commentary on the times is the fact that many of those dishes that originated before the sixteenth century bear the names of saints, mythical gods, or Roman celebrities.

The Entries

The main entries in this book for the most part consist of foreign names of dishes and of foreign terms used to characterize or describe certain dishes. With this in mind, if one should want to learn how sweetbreads *poulette,* the French dish, is prepared, one would look not under "sweetbreads" but rather under *poulette,* the foreign culinary term that characterizes the dish.

The main entries are not limited exclusively to foreign terms. One will also find English-language entries for some very well-known foods. These mostly consist of popular foods about which there is something unusual or noteworthy to say, information that it is deemed will be of use to the diner. Under the entries for onion and garlic, for example, we find that these marvelous food enhancers also provide many health benefits. Under the entry for pepper we learn that this spice was once so costly a commodity that it was used to ransom the city of Rome, and later it was substituted for legal tender in the payment of bills and offered as a tempting bribe for judges with few scruples and long fingers.

There is more to dining than just eating. We, like most animals, eat to survive, to live; but when we dine, we attempt to making living an art. Interspersed among the thousands of food entries in this book, the reader will find brief descriptions of nonfood items that are important to the art of dining. Such information will help the reader derive the greatest pleasure from fine food and drink. We explain, for instance, the necessity of "decanting" a bottle of wine, a real must when the wine is a fifteen-year-old Bordeaux. Also relating to wine, we explain what features make a corkscrew an *excellent* one. Under the entry for table manners we learn that primitive man was not really so primitive after all. We trace the evolution of table manners through the age of Erasmus of Rotterdam, Charlemagne, and the Royal Court of France, and we learn about the dining customs of China and Japan. The dining etiquette espoused by Emily Post is discussed as well. All of this information will help make the diner a sophisticated one. To know, for instance, the correct method of serving wine at a Japanese dinner is a definite social plus for anyone, and the entry that familiarizes the diner with Arabic dining customs might do much to prevent him from committing a cardinal faux pas.

Subentries

Within some main entries, the reader will find one or more subentries. The subentries demonstrate other ways in which the diner is likely to see the main entry term used.

Nationality or Ethnic Origin

The nationality or ethnic origin of every dish listed as a main entry is either given parenthetically immediately following the name of the dish or it is mentioned within the first line of text of the entry. In cases where more than one nationality is associated with the dish, this is specified.

Within each entry, where it is considered of interest, the specific origin of each dish is discussed. Where important, the origin of the name of the dish, the history or lore surrounding its creation, and facts about its creator are discussed.

Alternate Spellings

Particular attention has been paid to the correct spelling of foreign menu terms. However, because there is no accepted system for transliterating Russian, Chinese, Hindi, Japanese, Arabic, Greek, Turkish, and similar languages into English, this has not always been an easy task. On restaurant menus one is apt to find as many as six different English spellings used for the same dish. It is also true that the pronunciation of the name of a dish may vary considerably from locale to locale within one country, and this accounts, at least in part, for the variety of spellings we find.

The noted Russian dish *koulibiac* is seen spelled *coulibiac, kulybyaka,* and *kulibyaka.* The Turkish *börek* is also spelled *beurreck, boerek, beurreque,* and *bourekia.* The *Kugelhopf,* a famous cake said to have been created in Vienna but brought to its ultimate greatness in Alsace, is known also as *Gougeloff, Gougloff, Guglupf, Gougelhopf,* and *Kougelhupf,* depending upon where it is being served. The Russian beet soup is called *borsch, barszcz, borsht, borscht, bortch, bartch,* with as many more et ceteras as there are languages. The spellings used in this book are those most commonly found on restaurant menus.

To add to the confusion, some American restaurants, I find, present "Italian-French" menus. These menus are a blur with main dishes whose names are basically Italian but whose sauces are primarily French. Paradoxically, it appears that in Japan today one finds in use a new Japanese system, called *katakana,* which describes English foods in half-Japanese and half-English. Restaurant menus there produce strange and often comic results. *Pain jiūsu* is *katakana* for "pineapple juice," and *hamu tōsuto* is naturally a "toasted ham sandwich," and *karēraisu* will bring "curried rice" to your table.

Preparation and Service

For each dish discussed, there is a succinct description of the traditional method used to cook or otherwise prepare the dish. This is followed by an explanation of the way the dish is served and an indication of the side dishes that are considered complementary.

The method is not written in cookbook style. Precise measurements or instructions have generally been omitted. The reason for this is simple: the procedure followed in preparing a given dish is offered not to teach the reader actually how to cook the dish but to acquaint him with the preparation, appearance, and taste of the dish so that he will better be able to identify it. Armed with this information, the restaurant diner will feel more confident to question a dish he finds to be lacking an ingredient or to be improperly prepared. For example, if a menu calls for a dish to be prepared *à la Périgourdine,* or simply *Périgueux,* the diner should expect to find the delicious black truffles adding an exquisite flavor to the dish; finely sliced black olives should not be substituted, as is sometimes the case. Likewise, if a Caesar salad is tossed in a wooden salad bowl that has not first been rubbed with a clove of fresh garlic, or if the final sprinkling of freshly grated Parmesan cheese is omitted from the dish, the salad cannot be said to be the true Caesar salad. It is a salad, but not the one ordered. Needless to say, the diner has a right to expect that the food he orders will be properly prepared.

Compatible Wines/Beverages

At the end of most entries the reader will find a listing of wines or other beverages recommended to accompany the dish in question. Should there be a series of subentries within one entry, the wines listed at the end of the series are recommended as suitable to all of the dishes in that category.

The wine recommendations that I have, in all modesty, offered throughout the book naturally follow my own particular taste. In spite of the many slogans which emphatically demand white wines to be served with light-colored meats and fish and red wines to be served with red meats, there really are no fixed rules when it comes to matching dry table wines with food. Where one diner might choose a white wine to accompany a dish, another diner might be perfectly justified to take, instead, a light red wine.

Chicken, for instance, does not inevitably demand that a white wine be served with it. If the chicken has been barbecued, basted with a spicy garlic-and-tomato sauce, a red wine would be preferred. A salmon *Chambord* that has been braised in a fish *fumet* made with red wine and glazed in a slow oven would be perfectly complemented with a red Burgundy wine. A sole *Bordelaise, Rouennaise,* or *Bourguignonne,* having been cooked in red wine, will harmonize deliciously with a Pommard, Fixin, or Châteauneuf-du-Pape. A goose can be served either with a light red wine—a Côtes du Rhône or Mercurey—or a mellow white wine—a fine German *Auslese,* a dry Sauterne, or an Alsatian Gewürztraminer. Often, it is not the type of meat or fish that determines what wine to drink, but the kind of sauce, herbs, and spices that have been used in the preparation of the dish.

Among the many wine recommendations in this book, I have rarely included rosé or Champagne. I consider Champagne vastly overrated and always overpriced, so much so that I feel it should be reserved for weddings, baptisms, Bar Mitzvahs, funerals, and launchings. Ordering Champagne with a meal is usually done for effect or just to hear the pop of the cork. A Batard-Montrachet, Vouvray, or Pouilly-Fumé from France or a Bernkasteler Doktor, Piesporter Goldtröpfchen, or Rüdesheimer from Germany would be less costly, more satisfying, and in the end leave one with more than bubbles. But before my French colleagues disown me, let me add that Champagne is one of the best *apéritifs* and most elegant and magical of stimulants at cocktail times. Drink it then.

Rosé wine is another pet bugaboo. It is usually ordered by those who want to be on the safe side. There comes to mind very few dishes that would demand a rosé over any other wine, and most of these dishes are highly spiced, so full of curry, cayenne, vinegar, or mustard that any wine drunk with them would be tasteless. In such cases one might just as well drink beer, tea, or plain water. Generally, I find rosé wines to be very bland, wishy-washy, without character. The only rosé wines that seem worth their grapes are the Lancer's from Portugal if one likes bubbles, or the Tavel rosé from France if a still wine is preferred. I have always felt that a rosé wine is best for picnics, served cool, high on a hill, under a spreading oak tree on a warm summer's day.

The thick, sweet Retsina wines of Greece (flavored with resin) demand a special palate, although Greek table wines—Marco and Tegea—would be fine if readily available. The Tokay wines from Hungary are excellent. They, too, are on the sweet side, and a good knowledge of vintage and locale is necessary to enjoy them. The many dessert wines, like port, sherry, and the three famous M's—Madeira, Marsala, and Malaga—plus the sweet Barsac and exquisite Château d'Yquem from the Bordeaux region of France and the golden *Trockenbeerenauslese* from Germany all go well with *soufflés, tortes,* and rich pastries. In my recommendations, I have concentrated on table wines from seven of the richest wine areas on the globe: Bordeaux, Burgundy, Loire, Rhône, Rhine, and California.

A Concluding Word

The United States, Canada, Australia, and England have over the years accepted peoples from all parts of the globe. As a result, the populations of these countries have been exposed to many of the great cuisines of the world. Today, in our large American cities, there are more Korean, Turkish, Pakistani, Israeli, East Indian, Armenian, yes, even Lebanese and Iranian restaurants than ever before. The famous dishes of France, Germany, Italy, Spain, and Greece have become known to a large percentage of the populace. Nonetheless, the English-speaking diner, who nowadays more and more takes his meals in restaurants, often finds himself at a loss in attempting to decipher menus laden with obscure foreign culinary terms.

In writing this book, I have tried to define those restaurant terms that might cause confusion. Reconciling conflicting information from different sources and coming to a judicious conclusion has been both time-consuming and difficult. Just the fact that a particular foreign dish is found to have six different spellings and a complete variance in its ingredients can make one take more hot baths than he needs to ease frustration. Therefore, this collection of menu terms is selective rather than comprehensive. I have included those dishes I thought to be distinctive and representative of the various cuisines of the world.

I realize that a book of this scope will undoubtedly have omissions, and I ask forgiveness if I have overlooked a favorite ethnic dish; but to accomplish the impossible—a food encyclopedia comprising ten volumes— would call for another lifetime. For me, preparing *Menu Mystique* has been a labor of love, an undefinable pleasure that I must share with you to be realized.

ABALONE This edible gastropod belongs to the same family as the sea slug and is related to the snail as well. Out of its shell it resembles a large scallop. It can flavor a soup, be sautéed with mushrooms, or be served as a salad. Overcooking results in toughness. (See BÊCHE-DE-MER)

ABBACHIO AL FORNO (Italian) A baby leg of lamb that is roasted with the magical blend of rosemary and garlic. COMPATIBLE WINES: A red wine, e.g., Margaux, Haut Médoc, Zinfandel.

ABRUZZESE (Italian) A reference to the Abruzzi region of Italy, where food is cooked with an abundance of hot red peppers.

ABURAGE (Japanese) Thickly cut pieces of *tofu* that have been fried. When filled with mixtures of fish, cooked rice, and vegetables, they are called *inarisushi*. When cooked, they become puffed up and light. (See TOFU)

AC'CENT See AJINOMOTO, MONOSODIUM GLUTAMATE

ACHIOTE See ANNATTO

ACINI DI PEPE (Italian) See PASTA

ADOBO (Polynesian) This method of cooking, also popular in the cuisine of the Philippines, is used to prepare pork, beef, fish, or chicken. The food being prepared is first simmered in a marinade of water, vinegar, garlic, and peppercorns. It is then fried in oil.

AEBELSKIVER (Danish) The name of a famous dessert which, in the process of being cooked, did not know whether to become a fritter or a doughnut but finally decided to leave the pan as a proud Danish dessert dumpling. The Danes have a special *aebelskiver* pan for cooking these dumplings on top of the stove, but a muffin pan will serve as well.

First, sour cream, milk, egg yolks, and soft butter are mixed together, then flour, sugar, baking soda, salt, and cardamom seeds are added. Egg whites are beaten and carefully folded into the mixture, then the batter is poured into buttered muffin molds, which are turned during cooking to insure even browning. The *aebelskivers* are served liberally sprinkled with powdered sugar and accompanied with a tart jam and richly aromatic hot coffee.

AEMONO (Japanese) A term for foods that are served with a sauce. These foods include vegetables, meat, seafood, and *tofu*. Seafood and mixed vegetables are usually dressed with a mixture of *miso*, soy sauce, and sesame seeds. Some vegetables—potatoes, pumpkins, and lima beans, for example—are cooked in a sugar mixture, while other vegetables are simmered in a chicken stock flavored with soy sauce,

Foods that are mixed in sauces containing vinegar fall under another category, *sunomono*. (See MISO, SUNOMONO, TOFU)

AEPPEL-FLÄSK (Swedish) A dish composed of rashers of smoked bacon cooked together with onions and apple rings and served with freshly ground pepper. COMPATIBLE BEVERAGES: Beer is preferable, but a red wine such as a Beaujolais or Médoc is acceptable.

AFFUMICATO (Italian) A culinary term meaning "smoked," used to designate foods so treated.
  Storione Affumicato Smoked sturgeon. COMPATIBLE WINES: A white wine, e.g., Montrachet, Soave, Pinot Chardonnay.

AFRICAINE, À L' (French) An attempt to cook in the African style, using eggplant, tomatoes, and sharp spices.
  Crème à l'Africaine A curried chicken soup to which cream and rice are added. It is garnished with hearts of artichokes and sliced eggplant.

  Garniture Africaine A concoction of eggplant, mushrooms, tomatoes, and *Château potatoes* that is served with roasts. When served with fish, a garnish of fried bananas simmered in a *sauce diable* is used. (See CHÂTEAU, DIABLE)
  Sauce Africaine A sauce made by adding cooked chopped onions to chopped tomatoes and peppers. Salt, paprika, garlic, parsley, bay leaf, and thyme are added, and the mixture is cooked in white wine. A rich *demi-glace* finishes the sauce. (See DEMI-GLACE)

AGAR-AGAR The name of a seaweed that swallows regurgitate and use to hold their nests together high on the sides of steep cliffs facing the China Sea. The Chinese use this paste to make their famous delicacy, bird's nest soup. The name of this gelatinous carbohydrate, *agar-agar,* stems from a Malay word meaning "jelly." Although *agar-agar* is commonly referred to as Chinese gelatin, it is actually a carbohydrate, not an animal substance. Its thin transparent strands are often used in Oriental salads and cold dishes. (See BIRD'S NEST SOUP, KANTEN)

AGEDASHI (Japanese) Deep-fried squares of soybean curd. The curd is dried, browned in hot oil, and drained. The squares of curd are then placed in individual bowls containing a sauce composed of sweet saké and soy sauce. Grated radish, grated fresh ginger, and preflaked dried bonito are added as a garnish. (See DAIKON, KATSOUBUSHI, SOBA TSUYU, TOFU) COMPATIBLE BEVERAGES: Tea, Sauterne, saké, beer.

AGEMONO (Japanese) The designation for foods that have been pan-fried or deep-fried.

AGNEAU (French) Lamb that is less than one year old. By using the word *agneau,* many restaurants will falsely indicate that the mutton they are serving is lamb, thereby giving the diner the impression that the meat will be the tenderest.

Pilaw d'Agneau Cubed lamb that is fried with chopped onions, flavored with curry and a *sauce demi-glace,* and served in a ring of cooked rice. (See DEMI-GLACE) COMPATIBLE WINES: A red wine, e.g., Beaujolais, Médoc.

AGNÈS SOREL Lovely lady that she must have been, this mistress of Charles VII of France was, alas, never aware of the many dishes that came to bear her name. How unfortunate, inasmuch as she was the one royal mistress who demanded, as the price of her favors, only the explulsion of the English from her beloved France.

Crème Agnès Sorel This rich chicken soup, made with heavy cream and a purée of mushrooms, is served garnished with a *julienne* of chicken, tongue, and mushrooms. (See JULIENNE)

Omelette Agnès Sorel A *baveuse* omelette filled with mushrooms, a purée of chicken, and smoked tongue. (See BAVEUX/BAVEUSE)

Garniture Agnès Sorel A garnish composed of pickled tongue, mushrooms, truffles, and mounds of white rice. It is served with large cuts of meat, with eggs and poultry.

AGNOLOTTI (Italian) Dough dumplings stuffed with meat and vegetables. This speciality from Turino means "little lambs." (See RAVIOLI)

AGRO DOLCE, SAUCE (Italian) This sauce is made with pistachio and pine nuts, bitter chocolate, sugar, vinegar, candied lemon and orange peel, dried currants, currant jelly, and meat gravy. The whole is simmered until melded. *Agro dolce* is served with roast meats and game. A variation is a fish sauce made from a mixture of chopped onions, basil, and parsley that is fried in olive oil and butter, seasoned with salt, pepper, and cinnamon, and finally enriched with chopped tomatoes, white wine, and sugar.

AIGLON, L' (French) The son of Napoleon Bonaparte, Francis Joseph Charles, was given the name *l'Aiglon,* meaning "little eagle." Many dishes have been named after him. (See PETIT DUC)

Filets de Sole l'Aiglon Fillets of sole are poached in a fish *fumet,* then they are arranged on a bed of puréed mushrooms, coated with a rich white wine sauce flavored with onion purée, and lightly browned in the grill. The sole is served garnished with *fleurons,* crescent-shaped pieces of puff pastry. (See FUMET) COMPATIBLE WINES: A white wine, e.g., Meursault, Bernkasteler Doktor, Montrachet, Soave, Pinot Chardonnay, Riquewihr, Dézaley, Debro.

AÏGO-SAU (French) A fish-and-vegetable soup from Provence, and being *Provençale,* the soup is heavily accented with fresh garlic.

AIGRE-DOUCE, SAUCE (French) This sweet-and-sour sauce is a'prickle with surprising taste contrasts, making each swallow a new adventure. The sauce is composed of sugar, white wine, chopped shallots, and vinegar, all cooked together. Then, just before serving, a rich *sauce demi-glace* is added and the mixture is brought to a boil. After passing the sauce through a sieve, it is garnished with softened raisins and capers. *Sauce aigre-douce* enhances the taste of steaks, chops, calf's brains, and sweetbreads. (See DEMI-GLACE)

AILLADE (French) A *Mayonnaise* prepared with crushed walnuts, hazelnuts, and garlic mixed with olive oil and egg yolks and seasoned with salt and pepper. It is served with cold fish of all kinds and is particularly suited to herb-flavored snails.

AÏOLI (French) This garlic and olive oil sauce is Italian in flavor and name only. Many believe that the sauce originated in Provence—that sunny province in the south of France so closely affiliated with Italy, both culturally and geographically, that the French spoken there rings with strong overtones of Italian. However, a sauce as powerfully pungent as the *aïoli* cannot possibly keep its true birthright veiled for very long. The fact is that in 1628, during a war between France and Spain, the Duc de Richelieu discovered a delightfully creamy sauce which the Spanish called *ali-oli*. The Duc brought this sauce to Versailles as his own, dubbing it *Mayonnaise* after the port city (Mahon) of Minorca, which he captured. But he omitted one ingredient, and that was the garlic. The *aïoli* then, is, simply a *Mayonnaise* to which garlic is added. It can be served with hardboiled eggs, poached snails, cod, cold boiled potatoes or hot baked potatoes, or with artichokes, to name a few. Serve this sauce to a garlic-lover and you will have a friend for life. (See MAYONNAISE)

AJINOMOTO (Japanese) A widely-used flavor enhancer, monosodium glutamate, prevalent in Oriental cuisine. The Chinese version is called *ve-tsin,* "essence of taste." Monosodium glutamate is commercially sold in the United States under the brand name "Ac'cent." (See AC'CENT, MONOSODIUM GLUTAMATE).

AJO (Spanish) Garlic.
Sopa de Ajo A hearty Spanish soup made from garlic, chopped and fried in oil, to which water, salt, and *Mayonnaise* are added. Tomatoes or green peppers and/or paprika are sometimes added as well. All versions are garnished with bread croutons that have been fried in oil. Another version uses diced chicken and chopped *chorizo.* (See CHORIZO, MAYONNAISE, MOJO DE AJO)

AKEE The famous Captain Bligh, of His Majesty's ship *The Bounty,* is said to have carried this fruit of the African tree *Blighia sapida* to the Island of Jamaica, where the species thrives today. The fruits of this evergreen tree resemble brains or scrambled eggs. *Akees,* which have a rather delicate flavor, are available in cans in Latin American markets. (See SALTFISH AND AKEE)

À L'/À LA (French) With, after the style of, in the fashion of.

Chicken Sautée à l'Estragon   A cut-up chicken that has been browned in butter is simmered in a mixture of dry white wine, tomato purée, and chopped tarragon leaves *(estragon)*. COMPATIBLE WINES: A white wine, e.g., Meursault, Montrachet, Pinot Chardonnay, Piesporter Goldtröpfchen.

Tiny Peas à la Française   To be done *à la Française,* in the French manner, these peas must be freshly picked and freshly shelled and all of a uniform size. The peas are cooked in a small quantity of water together with butter, parsley, tiny pearl onions, a heart of lettuce, salt, and pepper. Before serving the peas, fresh uncooked butter is added. Cooked and uncooked butter vary greatly in taste. (See BABA AU RHUM)

ALASKA, BAKED   This sensational American dessert is startling by its contrasts: a rectangle of sponge cake is covered with ice cream, then with a layer of stiffly beaten egg whites. This is thrust into a hot oven to be browned over. To add yet another contrast, the ice cream-filled Alaska can be flamed with a mixture of brandy and a flavored liqueur of choice, such as Grand Marnier or Cointreau. It was to honor America's purchase of Alaska from Russia that the great Delmonico Restaurant in New York featured the baked Alaska. However, on the Continent the dessert is called *omelette surprise, omelette Nor-végienne,* and *glace au four.*

ALBERT, SAUCE (German-English)   The creation of this popular sauce is sometimes credited to one Albrecht (Albert) Pfalzgraf, who in 1554 composed a gastronomic work including laws, practices, and recipes of food. Another legend states that the sauce was named to honor a German King, Albert I; yet another story links the name to an actress of the Parisian stage, one Madame Albert; and still another claims that the sauce was named to honor Prinz Albert von Sax-Cobourg-Gotha, consort to the dominant Queen Victoria of England, which to all contemporary gastronomes means that the sauce is definitely English.

Howsoever the sauce was born, it is made by cooking freshly grated horseradish in a consommé flavored with finely chopped shallots that have been cooked down in tarragon vinegar. To finish, the sauce is bound with egg yolks and seasoned with salt, pepper, and a touch of English mustard. *Sauce Albert* is served with platters of braised beef.

ALBUFERA (French)   After his victories in Spain, Marshal Suchet was not only made the Duke of Albufera. He was honored in France as well by the great chef Carême, who dubbed a sauce, a stuffing, and a method of roasting duck with the name *Albufera.* (See CARÊME)

Albufera, Sauce   When veal stock and pimiento-butter plus a *glace de viande* are added to a *sauce suprême,* voilà, we have *sauce Albufera.* This sauce is served with sweetbreads and with poached or braised poultry. (See GLACE DE VIANDE, SUPRÊME)

Duckling Albufera Duckling roasted with slices of ham, chopped onions, butter, herbs, and Madeira wine. COMPATIBLE WINES: A white wine, e.g., Graves, Traminer, Tokay, Keknyelu, Schloss Vollrads.

ALEC An Old Latin word, derived from the ancient Greek language, meaning "marinated herring in a brine solution."

ALEXANDRA (French) As the daughter of Christian IX, the king of Denmark, Alexandra was no more than another Danish princess who loved milk, cheese, and chicken. But when Edward VII of Great Britain took notice of her and made her his queen, many chefs named culinary creations after her.

Chicken Alexandra Breasts of chicken are poached in sweet butter, then lightly browned in the broiler. The cooking juices are diluted with white stock and reduced; a chicken *velouté,* a *Soubise purée,* cream, and butter are stirred in, strained and served over the chicken. (See POËLÉ, SOUBISE, VELOUTÉ) COMPATIBLE WINES: A white wine, e.g., Niersteiner, Gewürztraminer, Orvieto, Chenin Blanc.

Consommé Alexandra A rich chicken consommé, bound with tapioca, is garnished with a *julienne* of chicken and shredded lettuce plus small *quenelles* of chicken. (See JULIENNE, QUENELLES)

ALFONSE, SAUCE (French) Named to honor Alphonse XIII of Spain, this cream sauce is composed of meat concentrate, a *velouté,* cayenne pepper, and pimiento-butter. A sauce with a tang, it is served with roasts. (See VELOUTÉ)

ALI-OLI (Spanish) A garlic-and-oil sauce from Spain, said to be the original of the more common French *aïoli.* (See AÏOLI)

ALLEMANDE, SAUCE (French) When the famous chef Carême created this light, creamy sauce, its blond color brought to mind the light-haired, fair-complexioned German race. Accordingly, he named the sauce *Allemande,* meaning "German." Made from a *velouté,* this sauce is bound with egg yolks and cream; a touch of nutmeg is added for flavoring. *Sauce Allemande* is served with poached chicken, variety meats, eggs, and vegetables. Because of the centuries-old antipathy between France and Germany, Escoffier once tried to change the Teutonic name to something like *sauce blonde* or *sauce Parisienne,* but the original name prevailed. (See CARÊME, VELOUTÉ)

ALLSPICE The fruit of an evergreen tree *(Pimenta officinalis)* of the myrtle family, native to the West Indies and to the southern coast of North America. The globular-shaped berries, gathered when mature but still green, are set out to dry in the sun. They have an aroma similar to that of cloves and a flavor that seems to combine the tastes of cloves, cinnamon, and nutmeg—hence the name. Allspice is used either whole or ground to flavor meats, puddings, cakes, beverages, sauces, relishes, pickles, preserves, and mincemeat. The Spanish call it *pimento,* and the French *toute-épice* or *poivre de Jamaica.* The spice grows profusely in Jamaica. (See PIMENTO)

ALLU KA ACCHAR (East Indian) An exotic potato dish that is flavored with mustard oil, lime juice, and various spices. The potatoes are boiled, quartered, seasoned with salt and turmeric and kept warm. Sesame seeds are toasted and then ground in a blender together with red peppers, grated ginger, more turmeric, and salt; the ground mixture is then folded into the potatoes. In a pan, a bit of asafoetida, seeded chili peppers, and fenugreek seeds are quickly sautéed in hot mustard or vegetable oil and immediately poured over the potatoes, which are left to marinate for a half-hour before serving. (See ASAFOETIDA, FENUGREEK, TURMERIC)

ALLUMETTES (French) In culinary parlance, this word means "matches" and refers either to potatoes that are cut to resemble matchsticks and then deep-fried, or to puff pastry that is shaped similarly, covered with cheese, icing, or a paste and baked to a golden brown.

ALMENDRA ROJA, SALSA DE (Mexican) A red almond sauce made by combining sautéed white bread croutons with cooked onions, garlic, almonds, _pequin_ chili, and chicken broth and then blending the mixture until smooth. The sauce is served warm with green vegetables and cooked fish, pork, or veal dishes.

Almendra Verde This sauce is similar to the _roja_ variety. Here, however, green tomatoes are used and the _serrano_ chili is substituted for the _pequin chili._ (See CHILI)

ALSACIENNE (French) Stemming from the Alsace-Lorraine district, that strip of land along the Rhine River that is still in France but so German that the natives speak a dialect similar to the Swiss-German spoken in Basel, the term denotes the presence of sauerkraut in a dish. (See SAUERKRAUT)

Pheasant au Champagne Alsacienne Prebaked pheasant is split and then baked with sauerkraut and grated potatoes flavored with Champagne and Cognac. COMPATIBLE WINES: A white wine, e.g., Champagne, Vouvray, Tokay, Forster Jesuitengarten, Muscat d'Alsace.

AMANDINE (American) This pseudo-French culinary term is peculiar to the United States, where it is used to denote that fish or poultry have been prepared with chopped or slivered almonds, either broiled or fried.

Sole Amandine Fresh sole or flounder is pan-fried and served with slivered almonds that have been lightly browned in butter. If the fish is a Dover sole, you can be pretty sure that you are dining in the British Isles or on the Continent; the Dover sole served elsewhere has been frozen. COMPATIBLE WINES: A white wine, e.g., Chablis, Montrachet, Verdicchio, Soave, Pinot Chardonnay, Wehlener Sonnenuhr.

AMARETTI (Italian) Macaroons made from an almond paste. The Italian word *amaro* means "bitter," and the literal translation of *amaretti* is "the little bitter ones."

AMBERGRIS In ancient times this was a much sought-after product of the sperm whale. Unfortunately, it could be obtained only after the poor beast had been slain. As it is lighter than water, ambergris, normally discharged by the whale, can be found afloat in tropical seas or washed up on shore. Widely touted as an effective aphrodisiac, it was the foundation of nearly all dishes of classical antiquity. A waxlike substance with a strong but pleasant smell, today ambergris is used as a fixative in fine perfumes.

AMBIGU (Créole) This French-Créole term refers to a meal in which all dishes are placed on the table at the same time, in contrast to a meal that is served in courses. It also describes a type of buffet service observed in Louisiana.

AMÉRICAINE, HOMARD (French) Lobster (*homard*) done "the American way." The dish was invented by a French restaurateur, Pierre Fraisse, who late one evening found that he had a large party of hungry Americans yet to serve before closing for the night. Seeing that a few live lobster was all he had left in the kitchen, Fraisse cooked them together with whatever else he thought might complement the dish: tomatoes, wine, garlic, and various herbs. He flamed the lobster with good Cognac and served the Americans. When the diners, in an evident state of elation and satiety, inquired as to the name of the lovely dish, Fraisse blurted out, "Lobster *Américaine,*" and the name has been used ever since.

Fraisse knew an excellent method of putting a lobster to sleep quickly by rubbing its head gently with the thumb. This little massage relaxes the beast, thus insuring that when the spinal cord is severed the flesh remains quite tender. Plunging a live lobster into wildly boiling water, on the other hand, causes the animal to tense up as soon as it feels the exteme heat, causing the meat to become inordinately tough. COMPATIBLE WINES: A white wine, e.g., Meursault, Bernkasteler Doktor, Pouilly-Fuissé, Soave, Debro, Pinot Chardonnay.

AMÉRICAINE, SAUCE (French) A sauce prepared by pounding the shells of a lobster together with a bit of lobster meat and lobster coral until a thick purée is formed. An equal amount of rich fish *velouté* is then added. Fresh butter is stirred into the sauce just before serving. (See VELOUTÉ)

AMERICAN CUISINE With the possible exception of the Créole cooking of the State of Louisiana, America cannot boast of a national cuisine with a heritage equal to that of France, Italy, China, or Germany. However, the American food enthusiast has a vast international kitchen from which to choose. In New York, for instance, one can enjoy a Korean or a Czechoslovakian lunch; one can satisfy his hunger at dinnertime in *Schuh-Klappen* style, with *Hasenpfeffer* and oompah-music on the side, or watch a Japanese chef put on a great show, carving meat for a *sukiyaki* or raw fish for a tasty *sashimi;* or one can dine on Turkish, Armenian, Greek, or even Iranian food. Since the Second World War, the American diner has become more conversant with food specialities of all nations; more often than not, he can discuss them intelligently and with discrimination. (See CRÉOLE, HASENPFEFFER, SASHIMI, SUKIYAKI, YANKEE COOKING)

AMOURETTES The French use this delightful word to designate the marrow from the spinal cord of beef and the marrow of calves' bones. Poached and well seasoned, the marrow is used as a garnish for soups and meat dishes. Often, dipped in a batter and fried in butter, *amourettes* are served as *croquettes.* Cut into various decorative forms, they are used to set off *les grands plats,* such as *lobster en belle-vue.* (See BELLE-VUE, CROQUETTES)

ANCHOIS, SAUCE (French) To create this perky anchovy sauce, anchovy-butter is added to a *sauce Normande.* The butter is prepared by whipping a fine purée of washed and dried anchovy fillets into softened fresh butter. The sauce is served with fish dishes. (See ANCHOVY SAUCE, NORMANDE)

ANCHOVY What the famous Bombay duck does for Indian curries and chutney sauces, this tiny herringlike fish, the anchovy, does for Occidental preparations of fish, flesh, and fowl; however, it is hardly as crude or strong as its Indian counterpart. Anchovy-butter, a staple of any first-rate kitchen, is delightful when served glistening over a freshly broiled steak or when blended into a piquant sauce or salad dressing of olive oil, tarragon vinegar, mustard, egg yolks, minced parsley, chives, capers, chervil, and freshly ground pepper. This dressing goes equally well with raw oysters. The anchovy imparts a mysterious taste—mysterious only when used with discretion—to beef roasts, game, fowl, and wild birds. (See ANCHOIS, ANCHOVY SAUCE, BOMBAY DUCK)

ANCHOVY SAUCE The Italians make two versions of anchovy sauce. The first, used to complement hot dishes, is prepared by heating oil, flour, chopped anchovies, and capers and then slaking the mixture with a beef bouillon and reducing it until creamy. The sauce is refined with heavy cream, butter, and a pinch of salt. It is served with *pasta* dishes and with zucchini.

The second version is made by cooking an anchovy paste with garlic, vinegar, olive oil, mashed egg yolks, and parsley. When cool, the sauce is served with cold meat dishes and with fish. (See ANCHOIS, ANCHOVY)

ANCIENNE, À L' (French) A term denoting foods prepared "in the old style, as of yore."

Chicken à l'Ancienne In this classic creation, tiny pearl onions and button mushrooms are braised together with the chicken in a *velouté*. Truffles and rosettes of puff pastry are used as a garnish. COMPATIBLE WINES: A red wine, e.g., Margaux, Valpolicella, Beaujolais, Zinfandel, Nebbiolo.

ANDALOUSE (French) This garnish, named after the Spanish province, consists of green peppers stuffed with cooked rice, bits of sausage meat, tiny peas and minced pimiento, plus sections of eggplant that are cooked in oil and topped with parslied, diced tomatoes. *Andalouse* is served with large roasts and with poultry. (See CONSOMMÉ)

Andalouse, Sauce To make this sauce, a *velouté* is mixed with a concentrated tomato purée and finely chopped and braised sweet pimientos; it is then flavored with parsley. The sauce is served with cold meat dishes, eggs, fish, and poultry. (See PIMENTO/PIMIENTO, VELOUTÉ)

ANDOUILLES, LES (French) Chitterlings—intestine casings filled with a finely ground mixture of fat pork, lean pork, and the inner stomach of the hog. The mixture is highly seasoned with salt, pepper, allspice, mace, cloves, cayenne and chili pepper, onions, and garlic; it is flavored further with such herbs as thyme, marjoram, and parsley. These rich sausages are first boiled in water or milk that has been flavored with an herb bouquet; they are then baked briefly. *Les andouilles,* a favored delicacy of southwestern France—or chitterlings, as they are known in the southern United States—are generally served with a lentil purée and heaps of mashed potatoes. (See CHITTERLINGS)

ANGELICA Called "the herb of angels," and looking much like rhubarb, this plant is used in Europe as a vegetable: its carrotlike root is used in cooking; the stalks are peeled and eaten as celery; and in France the leaves are blanched and used in salads. Liqueurs, such as Benedictine and Chartreuse, use the root in their composition, and candied angelica stalks are added to rhubarb jam. Angelica is also made into a syrup.

ANGLAISE, À L' (French) After the French Revolution, for a time there was a kind of snob appeal in things English; there was, one might say, a veritable surge of Anglophiles. The French were much impressed by English nobility, and as many French chefs no longer had jobs (their former masters had either been deposed or beheaded), the cooks flocked to England to work in aristocratic kitchens. And, in time, many culinary creations came to be honored by these French chefs with the term *à l'Anglaise,* "in the English manner."

Garnish à l'Anglaise This garniture of carrots, turnips, beans, cauliflower, and potatoes—plainly cooked in salted water—is served with chicken.

Eels à l'Anglaise Sections of eel are poached in salted water and served with a sauce of chopped parsley cooked in butter.

Sauce Anglaise Chopped yolks of hard-boiled eggs are mashed into a *velouté* to which pepper, nutmeg, lemon juice, and anchovy-butter are added. The sauce is served with poultry. (See VELOUTÉ)

Friture à l'Anglaise Another twist of this French culinary term depicts a method of crumbing food to be fried. The food is well seasoned, whisked in olive oil, then dusted with flour, dipped in beaten eggs, rolled in breadcrumbs, and fried in hot fat or oil.

Crème à l'Anglaise A sauce made by creaming egg yolks with sugar, then combining the mixture with milk and vanilla, all of which is heated until thickened. The sauce is then passed through a sieve, after which it may be flavored with a liqueur of choice and kept refrigerated until used. *Crème à l'Anglaise* is served with sweet dishes and cakes.

ANGOSTURA BITTERS Although this great bartender helper is named after a town in Venezuela, it is made from a substance obtained from the bark of the Cusparia tree, which grows on the Island of Trinidad.

In 1824, a German doctor living in Venezuela mixed this substance with the blossoms of the blue gentian and a number of secret herbs and roots to create a tonic for his ailing wife. Legend has it that the German doctor's creation worked as a cure for malaria and other tropical diseases; sailors swore that it cured seasickness, especially when mixed with rum. Today, Angostura Bitters is used to flavor fruit compotes, ice cream, and soups, but it is best known as the essential ingredient of the popular cocktail called the "Manhattan."

ANGUILLES AU VERT (Belgian) Eels served in a green sauce. The eels are skinned and cut into segments, dusted with flour, and cooked in clarified butter until golden. Shallots, parsley, chervil, sorrel, spinach, sage, and tarragon are all chopped fine; and, together with a dry white wine, they are added to the eels. After seasoning with salt and pepper, the contents are simmered until the eels are tender; the contents are then transferred to a glass or earthenware bowl. Fish stock that has been cooked with beaten egg yolks and lemon juice until slightly thickened is now folded into the fish mixture and set in the refrigerator to cool before serving. (See CLARIFIED BUTTER) COMPATIBLE WINES: A white wine, e.g., Corton Charlemagne, Fendant, Gewürztraminer, Soave, Sauvignon Blanc.

ANIMALS ON THE MENU Throughout history, civilized people have balked at the thought of eating certain animals. In 1871, during the Siege of Paris by the Prussians, starving Parisians were forced to slaughter the animals in the Paris Zoo. Elephant trunk, for instance, was sold for 40 francs per pound, and it was often served *à la Béarnaise*. Some Parisians ate spaniel and even rat, disguised with strongly spiced sauces no doubt. Eating horse meat suddenly became socially acceptable. Even today, in Switzerland, France, and Germany there are meat markets that sell horse meat which is quite tasty. The sale of dog meat is illegal in Hong Kong, but when a Hong Kong restaurant starts to advertise "Freshly-arrived Goat Meat," one can be sure there is some spaniel or chowchow mixed in with it. Snake meat is also popular in China; it is often served with bits of chicken. But for every individual who will not eat snake or dog meat there is another who will not eat pork, or beef, even chicken.

In the United States today, a company in Lockport, Illinois supplies as much as five tons of exotic animal meat weekly to discriminating restaurants throughout the nation. Restaurant menus boast of hippo roasts and steaks, hippoburgers, camelburgers, lion steaks, and even ostrich. Rattlesnake meat is most popular made into a *pâté,* fried, or barbecued, but because of the scarcity of meat on an ostrich, it sells the slowest. (See BÉARNAISE, UNUSUAL TASTES)

ANIMELLES When this term appears on an Italian menu, it means "sweetbreads." In French, however, the very same word has quite a different meaning: "ram's testicles." The royal French chef Monconseil diligently served Louis XV his ration of *les animelles* at least once a week. These supposed asphrodisiacs are served even in the West today under the name "mountain oysters." In Spain, the testicles of brave bulls are said to provide a delightful treat when sliced, seasoned, and cooked in a fine *sauce Madère.* (See APHRODISIACS, MADÈRE, MOUNTAIN OYSTERS, SWEETBREADS)

ANISE The *Pimpinella anisum,* an annual herbaceous plant belonging to the carrot or parsley family, is native to Egypt but is also cultivated today throughout the Far East, Europe, South America, and Mexico. Dried anise fruit, commonly called "aniseed," has a pleasant aroma and taste and is used to flavor cakes, cookies, biscuits, licorice, liqueurs, and confections.

Ancient Romans and Greeks used anise not only to make relishes, seasonings, sauces and to flavor cakes, but also to sweeten the breath, to stimulate the appetite, and to get rid of moths. It was also thought to give one a youthful look, to impart sweet dreams if inhaled while sleeping, and to free the traveler from fatigue after a long voyage. Absinthe in Victorian days and Pernod today are liqueurs flavored with anise, and both act as a tonic and a pick-me-up. Hippocrates, the noted Greek physician, wrote that anise will prevent sneezing. (See STAR ANISE)

ANNA POTATOES (French) Some say this creation was invented by Dugléré, the chef of the Café Anglaise on the rue Lafitte in Paris, and that Dugléré named it after the famed Anna Deslions, a famous prostitute who resembled Cleopatra in dress and in facial make-up. The dish, as popular as was Anna, is prepared by tiering a heavy casserole with alternate layers of potatoes, sliced thin, plus clarified butter. Salt and pepper are the only seasonings used. After baking tightly-covered for some forty minutes, the contents are inverted onto another pan and baked for an additional ten minutes. The potatoes become crisp and brown, and the cooked mass is cut like a crusty cake.

ANNATTO This yellowish-red dyestuff is prepared from the pulp found around the seeds of the *Bixa orellano,* a tropical tree. The small red seeds are used as a flavoring agent in South America and in the West Indies. In Spanish, annatto is called *achiote,* but in Argentina it is called *urucú.* (See SOFRITO)

ANTIPASTO This Italian word for appetizer (plural, *antipasti*) means "before the *pasta.*" A cold *antipasto* dish consists of varieties of thinly sliced *salame,* several types of olives, air-cured ham, vegetables served in oil and vinegar, tuna, anchovies, sardines, cold fish, hard-boiled eggs, shellfish, and salad. A hot *antipasto* may consist of warm canapés of melted cheese and anchovies, fish and shellfish, cooked chicken livers, stuffed mushrooms or artichokes, and *frittate* of all kinds. (See FRITTATA, SALAME) COMPATIBLE WINES: A rosé wine or a red wine, e.g., Veltliner, Valpolicella.

ANTOJITOS (Mexican) Literally, "snacks." A general term used for such foods as *tacos, enchiladas,* and *tamales.* (See ENCHILADAS, TACOS, TAMALES)

APFELPFANNKUCHEN (German) This popular dessert, "apple pancakes," is made by first cooking finely sliced apples in butter until tender, then adding lemon rind, sugar, and cinnamon and folding this mixture into already-cooked pancakes composed of flour, milk, eggs, and salt. They are usually served sprinkled generously with powdered sugar. (See BLINI, BLINTZ, CRÊPE, PANCAKE, PLÄTTAR, TORTILLA)

APFELSCHMARRN (German) A pancake made from eggs, flour, a touch of lemon juice, and diced apples. The pancake is sprinkled with cinnamon and sugar before serving.

APFELSTRUDEL (German) This pastry, so popular in Austria and Germany, is prepared by covering sliced tart apples with a mixture of lemon juice, sugar, cinnamon, and raisins. Two different doughs are then prepared: the first, made of yeast, flour, eggs, water, and sugar, is kneaded, covered, and set aside; the second dough is merely a mixture of flour and butter that is well-kneaded and set to cool in the refrigerator. Many traditionalists insist on using only yeast dough. Now comes the "moment of truth." After the two doughs are combined and rolled out on a floured surface, the rolled-out dough is stretched out over the backs of supple hands—much like making a pizza dough—until it is paper-thin. The dough—now rectangular-shaped and stretched out on a floured tablecloth—is brushed with melted butter, sprinkled with breadcrumbs, and covered with the marinated apple slices. It is then carefully rolled lengthwise, jelly-roll fashion. The ends are sealed so that the stuffing will not ooze out, and the *Strudel* is then bent into a horseshoe shape, brushed with melted butter, and baked. *Strudel* should always be eaten as fresh from the oven as possible, while the delicious aroma can still fill the nostrils and stimulate taste buds and appetites. Once cold, it is like a long-lost love: rewarming helps but little. (See STRUDEL)

APHRODISIACS Webster defines an aphrodisiac as being anything that arouses or increases sexual desire. Since the dawn of civilization, man has sought to renew and stimulate his sexual vigor through the use of food and drink. The young wished to increase their sexual frequency; the old tried, by eating certain foods, to delay the onset of impotency and senility. In perhaps the earliest recorded reference to an aphrodisiac, the Bible mentions Reuben as having brought the necessary mandrake root to Leah, his mother, who then, after lying with Jacob, conceived his fifth son. Ancient Greeks and Romans were also aware of the aphrodisiac powers of the mandrake root; even Pliny, the noted Roman scholar, made mention of it in his writings.

Aphrodisiac foods through the ages have run the gamut from the exotic Arabian camel's milk mixed with honey and the African ground-up rhinoceros horn to the more prosaic foods such as oysters, truffles, and eggs plus such stimulant spices as saffron, pepper, cardamom, nutmeg, ginger, paprika, mace, cloves, and aromatic herbs of all kinds. It is said that garlic and onions, eaten raw, can bring two people to the heights of sexual gratification, but pleasure comes only if both have eaten the redolent vegetables. Whether the desired result of these various aphrodisiacs is due to the psychological or to the physical effect of having ingested the foods is really immaterial.

Sex and food go together; various cultures throughout history bear this out. The ancient Romans, for instance, took their food while reclining on their couches in the *triclinium*. On special occasions, one of the more amorous Louis of France had his food served conveniently in his royal bedroom: the dining table rose through the floor on an elevator from the kitchens below. But one need not go back to ancient Rome or to King Louis for examples of sex in the dining room. During the latter part of the nineteenth and well on into the twentieth century certain restaurants offered their select clientele *le cabinet particulier,* a private dining room complete with bed, towels, bidet, and flaming chafing dishes—all the comforts of a luxurious bawdy house plus excellent food and drink. The drink, actually alchoholic beverages of various strengths, readied and mellowed the participants for the *pièce de résistance* by breaking down any existing inhibitions. (See CARDAMOM, CLOVE, GARLIC, MACE, PAPRIKA, PEPPER, SAFFRON)

APRICOT The glorious apricot, said to have come from China, grows on a tree, and although it resembles the plum, its skin is as fuzzy as that of the peach. The taste and nutritional value of the apricot has remained superior throughout the centuries. In its dried state, the apricot contains a greater amount of vitamin A than the fresh fruit.

After soaking in water, dried apricots can be puréed to make compotes, puddings, exquisite fillings and toppings for cakes, a delicious jam, and a brandy with an unusual aroma.

In some cultures, the apricot is a staple food. The Hunzakuts, for instance, who live high in the Himalayas, regard the apricot tree as the staff of life. They dry their apricots for use in the winter, and the pits are broken open to reveal an almond-like kernel from which a useful oil is obtained. This oil is used in salad dressings, in cooking, and even as a skin emollient.

ARANYGALUSKA The Hungarian term for dumpling is _galuska,_ and the _aranygaluska_ is a special cake consisting of a series of dumplings. The dumplings, made from a yeast dough, are rolled first in butter and then in a mixture of finely chopped walnuts, sugar, cinnamon, and raisins. The balls of dough are set in a baking pan, left to rise, and then are sprinkled with melted butter. They are baked until golden brown. (See GALUSKA)

ARGENTEUIL Mention _Argenteuil_ to a Frenchman and he might think of the star-crossed lovers Héloise and Abelard and of the convent at Argenteuil, a suburb of Paris, where Héloise took refuge. However, the Frenchman is far more likely to envision a steaming plate of white asparagus set before him, for Argenteuil is famous for growing the finest asparagus in all of France.

Potage Argenteuil A cream soup made from puréed asparagus, heavy cream, and chervil and garnished with cooked asparagus tips.

ARLEQUIN (French) This is the French term for Harlequin, one of the most famous of the stock characters that made up the commedia dell'arte of Italy. Harlequin was ever-amorous, and his costume was as multicolored as was his wit multifaceted. The character's costume consisted of many triangular pieces of cloth sewn together and accented with sparkling red, green, and blue stones. With this in mind, the French have used the word _Arlequin_ to describe foods of many colors.

Omelette Arlequin A French dish consisting of a number of tiny individual omelettes, each filled with a food of a different color, such as spinach and tomato purées, yellow squash, or black truffles. The individual omelettes are served surrounded by a thick tomato sauce.

ARLÉSIENNE, SAUCE (French) The ancient city of Arles, for which this sauce is named, retained its Romanesque ambiance through the black days of the Middle Ages, the riotous slaughter of the French Revolution, even up to the present. Therefore, it is fitting that the sauce be composed of tiny Italian tomatoes which are first stewed in butter and then puréed. The purée is added to a finished _sauce Béarnaise,_ with just a trace of anchovy paste added to make the sauce authentically _Arlésienne._ (SEE BÉARNAISE)

ARMENIAN PALASCINTA TORTE (Armenian) A cake composed of four *palascintas,* or thin pancakes, layered with various fillings. The bottom pancake is covered with chopped walnuts and honey; the next, spread with poppy seeds and honey; the next, with thick plum preserves mixed with finely minced walnuts; and the top pancake is garnished with a mixture of chocolate, seedless raisins, candied orange peel and dark Jamaican rum. The multilayered *torte* is sprinkled with granulated sugar and melted butter before being baked for 15 minutes in a medium oven. (See PALASCINTA)

ARROSTINO ANNEGATO (Italian) This preparation consists of thick chunks of veal that are skewered, covered with rosemary, sage, salt, and pepper, fried in olive oil on all sides, and then braised in the oven with white wine, lemon juice, and brown stock. *Annegato* ("drowned") refers to the braising procedure. The dish is often served with Anna Potatoes.

Arrostino Annegato alla Milanese This version uses calf's liver cut lengthwise and rolled into a boned loin of veal. The stuffed loin is cut into slices, skewered, sautéed and braised as above. Usually served with rice. (See ANNA POTATOES) COMPATIBLE WINES: A white wine, e.g., Orvieto, Sancerre, Aigle, Sauvignon Blanc, Schloss Vollrads.

ARROSTO/ARISTA (Italian) Roasted/roast.

Arista de Vitello al Forno A delicious roast loin of veal, baked in a bit of water and white wine and flavored with herbs and seasonings. COMPATIBLE WINES: A white wine, e.g., Orvieto, Frascati, Riquewihr, Fendant, Gewürztraminer, Chenin Blanc, Beaune Blanc.

Arista Fiorentina This is the way the Florentines bake a roast loin of pork. After the rind is removed, the loin is flavored with whole cloves of garlic pressed into the meat together with rosemary and whole cloves. The surface of the meat is rubbed with salt and pepper and is then roasted until done in a bit of water, after which it is left to cool. The roast is served cold in slices. COMPATIBLE WINES: A red wine, e.g., Nebbiolo, Barbaresco, Valpolicella, Fleurie, Margaux, Zinfandel, Médoc, Mercurey, Côte Rôtie.

ARROZ (Spanish) Rice.

Arroz con Pollo This popular chicken-and-rice dish is actually a *paella* without shellfish or meat. (See PAELLA). COMPATIBLE WINES: A red wine, e.g., Rioja, Mâcon, Zinfandel, Valpolicella.

ARTICHAUTS À LA VARENNE (French) This method of preparing and cooking artichoke hearts was first introduced by La Varenne who, while working in the royal kitchens of both Henry IV and the famous Louis XIV, brought glory to French cuisine. These hearts of artichoke are first lightly simmered in salted water and lemon juice (but never in an aluminum pot, unless you want black ones). When tender, the hearts are filled with finely chopped broccoli and coated with a rich *sauce Hollandaise.* They are then browned lightly in the grill. (See HOLLANDAISE)

ARTICHOKE See JERUSALEM ARTICHOKE

ARUGULA/RUGULA/RUGOLA (Italian) There are about as many different spellings of this term as there are provinces of Italy, all stemming from the Latin word *eruca,* meaning "a type of cabbage." This flat-leaf green herb, long a favorite addition to Italian salads, has a peppery-bitter flavor and a rather coarse texture. Called "rocket" in England, in America it is known by its French name, *roquette,* which is derived from the Italian word *rochetta,* a corruption of the aforementioned Latin word *eruca.*

ASADO (Spanish) Roasted.

ASAFOETIDA This fetid gum resin is obtained from various Asiatic plants of the parsley family. In Europe in the Middle Ages it was thought that a small piece of this bad-smelling gum, when hung around a child's neck, would protect the child from disease—especially from those germs that "hated" the odor, as well as from infected playmates. The lump variety of the resin is the purest form. Under the name *hing,* it is used extensively in East Indian cooking. (See DALS)

ASSAISONNEMENT AU LARD (French) A salad dressing composed of a blending of salt, pepper, vinegar, and the rendered fat and fried cubes of bacon. It is often used as a dressing for a dandelion salad. (See PISSENLITS)

ASSIETTES PARISIENNES (French) A variety of small relishes or *hors d'oeuvre* that are served on individual small plates. (See HORS D'OEUVRE)

ASUA YAPRAGI (Turkish) Grapevine leaves, used to form the traditional rice or meat *dolmas.* They are sold in glass jars or in cans in Middle Eastern or Oriental stores. (See DOLMAS)

ATES (Mexican) A fruit paste usually made from the guava, the quince, the mango, or the papaya and served as a dessert with rich cream cheese.

AUBERGINE (French) Eggplant.

AU FOUR (French) Baked "in the oven."

AU JUS (French) An indication that the meat's own juices were reduced with stock until the roasting pan's residue was totally absorbed in the gravy.

AURORE The French have adopted the name of Aurora, the goddess of the dawn, to describe many dishes that are reddish in color.
  Sauce Aurore For this sauce, the French start with a *sauce velouté,* flavor it with chopped tarragon and shallots, and then add tomato purée for color. When prepared in this manner, the sauce is served with poultry, eggs, and sweetbreads. If the sauce is to be served with

fish, it is colored with a lobster-butter made from the eggs of lobster or other shellfish (called coral) and is then cooked in a bouillon to which fresh butter has been added. (See VELOUTÉ)

Crème Aurore This soup made from rice, barley or tapioca has consommé as its base, is enriched with cream and butter and flavored and tinted with tomato purée and seasonings. (See CONSOMMÉ)

AUSLESE (German) A word designating that a particular wine was produced from a late harvesting of specially selected "bunches" of grapes, absolutely excluding any grapes that are unripe or damaged by disease. (See BEERENAUSLESE, EISWEIN, KABINETT, SPÄTLESE, TROCKENBEERENAUSLESE)

AVGOLÉMONO SOUP (Greek) This cold chicken soup, tangy with lemon, is a delightful treat, especially in the summertime. To the rice, cooked in a rich chicken broth, a mixture of eggs and lemon juice is added; this mixture is then seasoned and cooked until slightly thick. The soup is refrigerated until serving. A Greek *pasta* called *orzo* is sometimes substituted for the rice. (See ORZO)

AWENDAW (American) A hominy-cornmeal casserole that originated in a small South Carolina coastal town bearing the same name. A simple and tasty dish, Awendaw is made by blending together hominy, beaten eggs, cornmeal, milk, salt, and butter and baking the mixture in a moderate oven. COMPATIBLE WINES: A red wine, e.g., Rioja, Chianti, Beaujolais, Zinfandel.

AZTECA, SALSA Also called *salsa ranchera* and *salsa Mexicana,* this national sauce of Mexico is so popular that just the word *salsa* (sauce) will bring it to the table. It is usually found on Mexican restaurant tables, much like catsup and A-One Sauce are in American restaurants. Seeded and stemmed chilies are ground up with tomatoes, onions, garlic, and coriander until smooth. Vinegar, olive oil, and salt are then added. The finished sauce is served with meat and vegetable dishes as well as in soups and over beans.

AZUKI (Japanese) A popular red bean that can be eaten simply boiled or, when crushed and sweetened, used as a delectable filling for Japanese cakes and sweets. (See KEKIHAN, YOKAN)

BABA (French) The word *baba,* which means "papa" or "father" in Turkish, was adopted by the French as the name for a small yeast cake. The *baba,* made for papa's pleasure, is named according to the liquor or liqueur with which it is flavored—*baba au rhum, baba au Kirsch, baba au framboise,* etc. King Stanislaus I of Poland is credited as discoverer of this treat. The king not only fathered Marie Leczinska, queen of France and wife to Louis XV, but one day, while making a *Kugelhopf* (also called *Gugelhopf, Guglhupf, Gougelhopf,* or *Kugelhupf*), he filled individual molds with *Kugelhopf* batter and saturated the baked cakes with rum. The result was the famous *babas au rhum.* These cakes, rich with sweet butter and eggs and saturated with hot syrup flavored with rum, are served topped with whipped cream. (See KUGELHOPF)

BABA GHANOUJ See EGGPLANT-BUTTER

BACALAO (Spanish) Dried, salted codfish.

Bacalao a la Vizcaina This is one of the traditional dishes of the Spanish cuisine that was born in the Basque province of Vizcaya, right on the Bay of Biscay. It is after the Basques, the inhabitants of the province, that both the bay and the dish are named.

To prepare the dish, dried cod is soaked overnight, then blanched, boned, and skinned. Chunks of cod are fried in olive oil and removed. Then, after cooking tomato purée and red peppers in one pan and tomatoes, chopped garlic, and onions in another, these well-seasoned foods are layered alternately with the chunks of codfish and rounds of potatoes. The assembled dish is baked in the oven until done. (See BACCALÀ, BRANDADE) COMPATIBLE WINES: A white wine, e.g., Riesling, Sauterne, Gewürztraminer, Anjou, Château-Grillet, Chenin Blanc, Vouvray; or a red wine, such as Côte Rôtie, Veltliner, Beaujolais, Rioja.

BACCALÀ (Italian) Dried, salted codfish. (See BACALAO, BRANDADE)

BAGATELLE This French word, from the Italian *bagatella,* meaning "a trifle," is used to describe anything that is trifling or flirtatious, a trinket.

Sole Bagatelle These rolled fillets of sole appear to be little gems or trinkets, served as they are on mounds of chopped tomatoes and mushrooms, covered with a rich *sauce Mornay,* and lightly browned under the grill. (See MORNAY) COMPATIBLE WINES: A white wine, e.g., Gewürztraminer, Corton-Charlemagne, Johannisberg, Orvieto, Dézaley.

BAGEL The bagel, native to New York, is as foreign in Dubuque as a ham-on-rye is in Kuwait. The name of this hard, chewy roll comes from the Low German *Bägel,* meaning "stirrup," and it is baked in that form. The bagel is made from flour, salt, sugar, yeast, water, and eggs. The dough is kneaded into a ball, is allowed to rise, and is then kneaded again. Pieces of dough are then formed into the bagel shape, like a doughnut, and placed under the broiler for a few minutes. Next, each bagel is dropped into wildly boiling water and cooked for 15 minutes. The bagels are then removed and baked in a hot oven for 10 minutes more, until the crust is golden brown and crisp. Now—a bagel without lox (smoked salmon) would be like Irish cabbage without corned beef, Yorkshire pudding without roast beef, French *pâté* without *foie gras,* or a Chinese dinner without rice; therefore, smoked salmon should always be served with a fine bagel. (See BUBLIKI, FOIE GRAS, LOX, PÂTÉ, YORKSHIRE PUDDING)

BAGHAR (East Indian) This method of flavoring *ghee* (clarified butter) is used by the East Indians. The butter is heated nearly to the smoking point, then the selected spices are added, and the pot is covered and removed from the heat. After a suitable time, during which the flavors of the spices are absorbed by the butter, the spiced butter is passed through a sieve. The butter is now ready to be added to whatever dish is to be served. (See GHEE, CLARIFIED BUTTER)

BAGLAWA (Syrian/Lebanese) A very popular Middle Eastern pastry, *baglawa* is made with *phyllo* dough. Buttered layers of *phyllo* pastry sheets are covered with a mixture of chopped nuts, cinnamon, and sugar. Drenched with honey and butter, they are baked in a roll or flat. In Turkey and in Greece, this treat is known as *baklava.* The sweetness of the pastry, which some diners may find cloying, can be lessened with the addition of enough fresh lemon juice. (See BAKLAVA, PHYLLO)

BAGNA CAUDA (Italian) Literally, "hot bath." This anchovy-and-garlic dip is made by bringing heavy cream to the boil, reducing it to half by cooking while simmering anchovies and chopped garlic in butter in another pot. The cream is poured into the pot with the garlic and anchovies and left to simmer until blended. The dip is served at once, hot as it is, together with a variety of raw cut vegetables, such as cucumbers, carrots, red and green peppers, celery stalks, scallions, plus whole cherry tomatoes and mushrooms. Italian breadsticks go well with this dish.

BAGOONG (Philippine) More unusual than the name *bagoong* is the fact that this dip is so similar to the ancient Roman *garum.* Old Rome obtained *garum* from the fermentation of fish viscera: livers, milt, roe, gonads. The liquid that is drained off during fermentation of the fish viscera is called *patis* by the Philippines; they use it to flavor salads. What is left is pounded, salted, and allowed to stand a bit longer. This dip, which might be enjoyed by those with an adventurous gastronomic spirit, is used as a seasoning for fish, meat, and vegetable dishes. (See GARUM)

BAGUETTES The name given by French bakers to their crisp, crunchy, long loaves of bread. *Baguette* literally means "stick, rod." At first French bread was all shaped round, but when bakers realized that their crusts were so tasty, they gave the bread more crust by making them long. Today breadlovers all over the world enjoy the crusty, yeasty French *baguette*. (See BÂTARD, BÂTONS)

BAHMI GORENG (Indonesian) The practical Dutch have adopted this dish as their very own. For this speciality, noodles are cooked in salted water then cooled in the refrigerator; in another bowl, strips of lean pork are marinated in a mixture of soy sauce, garlic, and chopped green onions. Eggs, cooked pancake-style, are sliced *à la julienne*. After the pork and noodles have rested for several hours, the pork strips are sautéed in hot oil and then set aside to cool. Onions and ginger root are likewise sautéed and set aside. Bean sprouts, Chinese cabbage, and shelled shrimp are then cooked together; and when the vegetables are tender, the cooked pork, onions, and ginger root are added, together with the soy sauce mixture, and the whole is simmered. The cooled noodles are cooked crisp and brown in very hot oil and then mixed with the pork and the shrimp. The dish is served garnished with slices of hard-boiled egg. (See JULIENNE, NASI GORENG) COMPATIBLE BEVERAGES: Tea, ale, beer, rosé or saké wines.

BAKED ALASKA See ALASKA

BAKLAVA A popular Greek and Turkish pastry. (See BAGLAWA)

BAL KABAGI KIZARTMASI (Turkish) Pumpkin chips. Paper-thin slices of pumpkin are dipped into a batter made from water, flour, salt, and pepper and then fried in hot oil. Salt is lightly strewn over the chips, which are served with a yogurt dip flavored with fresh, crushed garlic.

BALLEKES This memorable meatball dish is typically Belgian: the meat is cooked in beer. A mixture of ground pork, chopped onions, freshly grated breadcrumbs, and raw eggs is formed into meatballs and fried. They are then simmered in beer that has been flavored with garlic and various herbs. The dish is usually served with potatoes. COMPATIBLE WINES: A red wine, e.g., Côte Rôtie, Nebbiolo, Zinfandel; but the Belgian would drink the same beer in which the *ballekes* were cooked.

BALLETJES (Dutch) To prepare these rather spicy meatballs, ground veal is combined with curry, salt, pepper, eggs, and milk-soaked pieces of white bread. Meatballs are then formed and set aside. Next, a redolent assemblage of chopped onions, leeks, carrots, and celery are sautéed in butter and oil; a beef bouillon flavored with marjoram is added. The mixture is simmered until the vegetables are somewhat tender, then the meatballs are added to the pot and cooked with the other ingredients. This Dutch-style *minestrone* is served with *vermicelli,* cooked *al dente,* and topped with parsley. (See DENTE, MINESTRONE, VERMICELLI) COMPATIBLE BEVERAGES: Beer, ale.

BALLOTINE (French) An ancient culinary term for boned meat, game, fowl, or fish that is stuffed, rolled, securely fastened, and cooked. It is much like a *galantine,* but the *galantine* is always served cold, whereas the *ballotine* may be served hot. (See GALANTINE, ROULADE, ROULADEN)

BÂLOISE, À LA See BASLER ART

BAMBOO SHOOTS AND GREEN PEPPERS, MINCED BEEF WITH (Chinese) For this wok preparation, a flank steak is minced, dredged in flour, and stir-fried in hot oil flavored with ginger and cayenne pepper. Stir-fried slivers of bamboo shoots and chopped green peppers are added to the meat and cooked together with soy sauce, sugar, and rice wine (saké) or dry sherry. (See JOOK SOON) COMPATIBLE BEVERAGES: Tea, beer, or saké.

BANGA (East Indian) A preparation of tripe served with garlic, lamb, and coconut milk. Garlic and fresh ginger are puréed and boiled in water with the cut-up tripe for about four hours. After the tripe is removed, cubed lamb is cooked in the same broth until tender. Chopped onions are browned in *ghee;* to the browned onion, ground chili peppers plus the tripe, the cubed lamb, and the coconut milk are added. The ingredients are cooked uncovered until all of the coconut milk has been absorbed. The dish is served with boiled white rice. (See GHEE) COMPATIBLE BEVERAGES: Beer, ale, tea.

BANIROV BÖREGS (Armenian) *Banirov* means "with cheese," and to make these cheese-filled pastry wraps, a pastry dough is made from flour, salt, cream of tartar, butter, and water. The dough is rolled out, flattened, and refrigerated several times; it is then cut into rectangles. Cheese filling composed of eggs, grated Cheddar and Muenster cheese, parsley, salt, and mint is placed in the center of the dough rectangles, which are then folded and sealed. The pastries are brushed with beaten egg and baked until golden brown. (See BÖREKS) COMPATIBLE WINES: A red wine, e.g., Beaujolais, Côte Rôie, Valpolicella, Zinfandel, Santenay.

BANIZA (Rumanian) A layer cake with a nut filling. A *baniza* dough made from flour, butter, vinegar, salt, and oil, is rolled out into thin sheets called *phyllo.* The thin sheets of dough are then sprinkled with ground walnuts or hazelnuts, sugar, cinnamon, ground cloves, and melted butter and placed one on top of the other. The sheets of dough are then carefully rolled up, cut into portions, and baked. (See PHYLLO)

BANQUIÈRE, À LA (French) A descriptive term for foods that have been richly prepared "in a banker's style."

Garniture à la Banquière This garnish, served with beef steaks, poultry, and sweetbreads, is composed of braised *quenelles* of chicken, mushrooms, and black truffles.

Sauce à la Banquière Madeira wine and chopped truffles are added to a *sauce suprême.* This sauce complements egg and poultry dishes and those *vol-au-vent* dishes made with sweetbreads or brains. (See QUENELLE, SUPRÊME, VOL-AU-VENT)

BAOBAB TREE When Stanley, the avid newspaper reporter of the New York *Herald,* finally located Dr. Livingston near Lake Tanganyika, the good doctor told him that he considered the baobab tree to be a kind of gigantic carrot that someone had planted upside down just to be mean. Although many black Africans consider the tree to be a symbol of evil, it has been a boon to them for centuries. It grows in India as well as in Africa and is exceeded in size only by the giant Sequoia tree that grows along the coast of California and southern Oregon. The huge trunks of the baobab are hollowed out to make rude but adequate dwellings for the natives, who use the bark to fashion rope and cloth and the leaves to make condiments and medicine. Its gourd-like fruit is called "monkey bread" (not to be confused with the yeast-dough coffee cake of the same name). From the seeds, a crude type of baking powder can be made to substitute for yeast. The fruit is eaten in its natural state, and its flesh, dried and ground into a flour, is used to thicken sauces. The seeds, when dried and crushed, add flavor to stews of all kinds.

BARANKA (Russian) An unsweetened, unsalted cake that is formed in the shape of a doughnut and sprinkled with poppy seeds.

BARBACOA (Spanish) It is from this word that the English equivalent, "barbecue," derives. In America in 1695, "barbecue" first referred to a type of crude grill used for smoking or drying meat before or over a fire. Later, the barbecue method of roasting a whole animal over a hot fire was adopted. Today, of course, when we think of a barbecue, we envision a family cookout held out of doors, where pieces of chicken, various meats, fish, and even vegetables are grilled over an open fire made from charcoal; the food is periodically basted with a zesty sauce. Originally, in Mexico agave leaves or banana leaves were used to envelop the food, which was then cooked *luau*-style, in a pit. In the southern United States there is a dish popularly known as "barbecue." Composed of thinly sliced pork, the dish is cooked right on the stove and served in a spicy sauce. This dish has no relation to the barbecue method of cooking.

BARBECUE See BARBACOA

BARD A culinary term referring to the practice of surrounding or enveloping beef, veal, poultry, or game with pork fat. The fat keeps the meat moist while it cooks. The verb "to bard" is sometimes mistaken for the term "to lard," which means to insert thin strips of fat into meat, poultry, or game.

The *Châteaubriand,* when first created, was well barded, and today many chefs bard roast beef and poultry to keep the meat juicy and tender. (See CHÂTEAUBRIAND)

BÄRKRÄM (Swedish) A rich Scandinavian cream dessert made with fruit. Strawberries, raspberries, gooseberries, or currants can be used. The fruit, after being cooked in water to cover, is passed through a sieve. Corn flour is then added, and the mixture is brought to the boil; it is then left to chill. The dish is served with heavy cream. (See BAVAROISE, HEDELMÄRAHKA)

BAR-LE-DUC (French) The name of a town in the Lorraine district of France and of the red currant preserves named after it. The black currant, however, is equally famous, for it is used to manufacture the fine Cassis liqueur known all over the world. The dried currant, used in cooking, comes from the Levant (countries bordering the Mediterranean Sea). Originally, it came from Corinth, which accounts for its English name, "currant." In French the dried currant is known as *raisin de Corinthe* and the fresh currant as *groseille.*

BARODA BHURAN (East Indian) A certain Maharaja of Baroda commissioned an Indian-English cookbook, and within the pages devoted to sweets and desserts this special yogurt dessert was designated to be eaten only after dark, following an old proverb. To prepare *baroda bhuran,* the yogurt is drained of its liquid until it is quite dry. It is then whipped together with sugar until smooth and creamy. Finally, fresh chopped fruits are folded into the whipped mixture, which is then left to chill thoroughly before serving.

BARQUETTES (French) Small boat-shaped pastries that are first baked and then used to hold various fillings—meat, fish, fowl, vegetable, or fruit. (See CANAPÉS, HORS D'OEUVRE)

BASIL Though ancient Greek and Roman doctors believed that basil would grow only if its cultivators sowed the seeds while ʼscreaming wild curses and shouting unintelligibly–thereby giving rise to the French adage *semer le basilic,* "sowing the basil," used to refer to one who is "raving"—the greatest of French chefs considered this herb to be the *herbe royale,* "the royal herb." The mintlike flavor of basil will enhance the taste of bland vegetables and soups, salad dressings, and egg dishes. The French have proved it a must in the preparation of broiled tomatoes, turtle soups, and in various *ragoûts* and sauces. (See RAGOÛT)

BASLER ART/À LA BÂLOISE (Swiss) These terms—the first German, the second French—literally mean "in the fashion of the Baslers," those Swiss living in Basel, that triangle of land that pricks the belly of Germany on the Rhine. The terms refer to a sauce made from white wine or lemon juice, Worcestershire sauce, butter, paprika, and parsley. It is served with fried fish smothered with fried onion rings. (See WORCESTERSHIRE SAUCE) COMPATIBLE WINES: A white wine, e.g., Dézaley, Muscadet, Mâcon Blanc, Orvieto, Pinot Chardonnay, Quincy.

BASQUAISE, À LA (French) A descriptive term for food prepared in the Basque style, the style of those independently proud and freedom-loving people who live both in France and in Spain, on opposite slopes of the towering Pyrenees Mountains.

If a large roast of meat is garnished with fried *cèpe* mushrooms, green peppers, onions, tomatoes, molds of *Anna potatoes,* and topped with chopped ham, it can be said to be served *à la Basquaise.* The same name is given to a beef consommé that is served with chopped sweet peppers and tomatoes, cooked white rice, and chervil. (See ANNA POTATOES, CHAMPIGNONS, MUSHROOMS) COMPATIBLE WINES: A red wine, e.g., Chambertin, Chambolle-Musigny, Nuits Saint Georges, Dôle, Barolo, Pinot Noir.

BASTERMA (Armenian) Marinated dried beef. The sirloin of beef is salted, wind-dried, and then cured with a hot fenugreek paste and a mixture of various spices and herbs, including paprika, pepper, and garlic. The beef is then wind-dried again. (See BÜNDNERFLEISCH, CHARQUI, FENUGREEK) COMPATIBLE BEVERAGES: Beer, ale, rosé wine.

Basterma Shashlik A sirloin of beef, cut into cubes, is marinated in a mixture of vinegar, onions, salt, pepper, and garlic for several days. It is then threaded on skewers and broiled. Chunks of tomatoes and green peppers, broiled in the same manner, are seasoned and served with the beef. COMPATIBLE BEVERAGES: The same as for the *basterma.*

BASTILA (Arabic) This pigeon pie, complicated to make, boasts diverse textures and tastes. No great Moroccan feast, whether it be a wedding, a circumcision, or just a gathering of friends and relatives, would be complete without it. To prepare the pie, the pigeons are fried to a golden brown in fresh butter. Then they are simmered in a mixture of water, coriander, cumin, parsley, sautéed chicken hearts, gizzards and livers, ginger, red peppers, turmeric, saffron, and cinnamon. When tender, the pigeons are skinned, boned, and cut into strips. One-half of the sauce is reduced to a glaze while the other half is mixed with eggs into a curdlike mass, to which the glaze is then added.

A number of *phyllo* pastry sheets are arranged in a pan, sprinkled with an almond-sugar-cinnamon mixture, and covered with the egg mixture. The strips of pigeon are arranged over all. The whole is then topped with more of the egg mixture and fried in a large skillet until the bottom becomes well browned. The *bastila* is then inverted onto a large plate and slid back onto the skillet to be browned on the other side. Sprinkled with sugar and cinnamon, the *bastila* is cut into wedges and served warm. (See PHYLLO) COMPATIBLE BEVERAGES: Beer, hot mint tea.

BÂTARD (French) A popular bread that is a bit more than a foot in length and about three inches wide. Whether seeded or plain, it is always crusty and butter-rich. (See BAGUETTE, BÂTONS)

BÂTARDE, SAUCE This French sauce, seemingly without a sire, was mothered by a Béchamel, bound with egg yolks, flavored with lemon juice, enriched with fresh cream, and passed into the culinary world through a fine sieve. It is served with poached chicken and light-colored meats and with fish and vegetable dishes. (See BÉCHAMEL)

BATELIÈRE, À LA Since the French word for boatman is *batelier,* any dish labeled *à la batelière* bears some relation to fish or to the sea.
Garniture à la Batelière A garnish composed of mushrooms, glazed pearl onions, fried eggs, and crayfish. It is served with fish dishes.

BÂTONS (French) Long crusty breads. The *baguette* bread is thinner. (See BAGUETTE, BÂTARD)

BATTUTO When an Italian cook starts a soup or a stew by first browning chopped onions, carrots, parsley, celery, and garlic either in olive oil or in butter, this culinary prologue is called *battuto* or *soffrito,* depending on what part of Italy the chef comes from. (See SOFFRITO, SOFRITO)

BAVAROIS/BAVAROISE, CRÈME (French) this "Bavarian cream" has nothing to do with Bavaria, Munich, or Berchtesgaden for that matter. *Crème Bavaroise* is a delicate custard made from eggs, gelatin, and whipped cream and flavored with wines or liqueurs, fresh fruit, berries and/or nuts.

BAVAROISE, SAUCE (French) This sauce is as *gemütlich* as the southern German state for which it is so aptly named. It is basically a rich *sauce Hollandaise* added to a reduction of peppercorns, grated horseradish, thyme, and vinegar. This is flavored with crayfish-butter and garnished with crayfish tails. It is served with fish dishes. (See HOLLANDAISE)

BAVEUX/BAVEUSE (French) A culinary term meaning "runny, soft in consistency."
Omelette Baveuse A soft omelette. It can be served plain or with any number of fillings, such as caviar, fruit preserves, crab meat, or ham. The perfect omelette is soft in consistency, served piping hot and golden brown. Its success in large part depends upon the quality of the omelette pan used. The pan must be thick, cleaned only with salt and oil, never washed with soap, and used only to make omelettes.

BAYERISCHER LINSENTOPF (German) This Bavarian speciality consists of a casserole composed of lentils and smoked pork, flavored with herbs and spices, and baked in the oven. COMPATIBLE WINES: A red wine, e.g., Côte Rôtie, Valpolicella, Beaujolais, Zinfandel, Nebbiolo.

BAY LEAVES See LAUREL LEAVES

BAYONNAISE, À LA (French) "In the style of Bayonne," where ham (Bayonne is famous for its wine-cured ham) and other pork products are used in the preparation of many dishes.

Chicken Sauté Bayonnaise   A young broiling chicken is cut up and browned in butter with bits of chopped ham. It is then stewed in a brown sauce and served with boiled white rice. (See BROWN SAUCE) COMPATIBLE WINES: A red wine, e.g., Valpolicella, Fleurie, Moulin-à-Vent, Zinfandel.

Bayonnaise Garniture   This garnish, composed of cooked macaroni in a cream sauce, mixed with slivers of ham, is served with various meat dishes.

BEAN CURD (Chinese) Bean curd, called _fu juk_ by the Chinese, is as basic to Oriental cooking as _pasta_ is to Italian cuisine. There are many variations.

Dried bean curd is prepared from boiled soybeans. The top skin, formed by boiling, is removed each time one forms on the surface. As the skin dries, it becomes quite firm, even chewy.

Fresh bean curd is prepared from soybean flour, gypsum, and water. The mixture is left to curdle. The high-protein curdled product, which looks much like ordinary milk curd, is shaped into small square cakes. Fresh bean curd has many aliases: bean cake, bean custard, even vegetable cheese.

Red preserved bean curd is prepared by fermenting pressed soybean cakes in a mixture of saké, spices, and salt. The preparation is subsequently dyed a deep red with the addition of a red rice. The curd has a definite nutlike taste.

White preserved bean curd is prepared by fermenting soybean curd in saké and salt. The end product, similar to Camembert cheese, becomes stronger in flavor as it ages. It is also known as "white Chinese cheese" or "white bean curd cheese." (See TOFU)

BÉARNAISE, SAUCE   Although sometimes spelled _Bernaise,_ and occasionally _Bernese,_ this sauce is definitely not Swiss, nor does it come from Berne. The sauce is French, and its only connection with Béarn, the birthplace of Henry IV, is that it was invented in the kitchens of a Paris restaurant called Le Pavillon Henri IV and was dubbed _Béarnaise_ in Henry's honor.

The sauce, a classic, is made by reducing a mixture of vinegar, chopped shallots, salt, pepper, and tarragon and then straining it. After adding egg yolks, melted butter is dribbled in a bit at a time while mixing constantly over hot water until the sauce thickens. The sauce is rubbed through a fine sieve, seasoned with salt and cayenne pepper, and finished with chopped chervil and tarragon. _Sauce Béarnaise_ is served with grilled meats and poultry.

BEATRICE, SCAMPI (Italian) A shrimp preparation named to honor Beatrice, the beloved of the famous poet of "Inferno" fame, Dante Alighieri. The shrimp—shelled, deveined, and cooked—are sautéed in butter with finely chopped shallots, garlic, and mushrooms. After being flamed with Cognac, fish stock and heavy cream are added. The flavors are melded and the sauce thickened by simmering. To serve, the shrimp are spooned into the center of a ring of boiled white rice. A *sauce Hollandaise* flavored with Pernod is served on the side. (See HOLLANDAISE) COMPATIBLE WINES: A white wine, e.g., Meursault, Orvieto, Aigle, Chenin Blanc, Graacher Himmelreich.

BÉCHAMEL, SAUCE (French) No one knows how Louis de Béchamiel, the Major-Domo of Louis XIV, ever managed to produce this superb sauce. Notwithstanding the high post he enjoyed at the French court, culinary history has portrayed Béchamiel at times as having been something of a ninny and yet at other times as having been an uncompromising wheeler-dealer. He is, nevertheless, credited with having created one of the greatest of all cream sauces—a feat that no chef, strangely enough, was able to accomplish.

Today *sauce Béchamel* stands as the basis for all other cream sauces, and as such it has brought more honor to the name of Béchamiel than all the victories of Napoleon. The sauce is made from a white *roux* (equal parts of butter and flour stirred vigorously over heat) to which milk and cream (optional) are added. It can be served cold over chicken, fish, or meat or hot with fish, game, meat, or vegetable dishes. (See ROUX)

BÊCHE-DE-MER (French) This term refers to that wart-covered sea slug also known as the sea cucumber. The Chinese know it as *hoi sum*. The protein-rich *bêche-de-mer,* which grows up to two feet long, digs, scoops, and shovels its way along the sandy bottom of the sea, feeding as it goes, somewhat like Father Neptune's favorite vacuum cleaner. This creature is known to produce opal and was found to have beads of iron under its skin. Considered a great delicacy by Orientals (especially the trepang variety), its rubbery, slippery texture and medicinal taste, just like Scotch and olives, take a bit of getting used to, but once one has tried it in an abalone soup, one is hooked. (See ABALONE)

BEDEMLI MUHALLEB (Turkish) An exotic almond pudding. Milk, sugar, and salt are brought to a boil and, with the addition of a solution of cornstarch, rice flour, and water, the whole mixture is cooked, stirring constantly. Last, finely ground almonds and almond extract are added. The now-thick pudding is poured into individual heatproof bowls and browned in the grill.

BEERENAUSLESE This German word will be found on the labels of white German wines that have been made from the specially-selected, late-harvest "single grapes." This means that the grapes are not removed in bunches, but one by one. (See AUSLESE, EISWEIN, SPÄTLESE, TROCKENBEERENAUSLESE, KABINETT)

BEĞENDI (Turkish) This eggplant purée so fascinated the Empress Eugénie of France while a guest of Sultan Abdulaziz that she requested the recipe. In its preparation whole eggplants are scorched over a high flame. When the skin has turned completely black, the now-soft eggplant is skinned, seeded, and placed into a bowl containing cold water, lemon juice, and salt. The eggplant, drained of all water, is then added to a *sauce Béchamel.* Grated Gruyère cheese is added as well, and the two are mashed together and then cooked until the mixture begins to bubble. When the French Empress Eugénie first tasted this heavenly eggplant, it was served with cubed lamb that had been browned in olive oil with onions and tomatoes—a dish called *Hünkâr Beğendi,* "Sultan's Delight." (See BÉCHAMEL) COMPATIBLE WINES: A red wine, e.g., Beaujolais, Zinfandel, Nebbiolo, Savigny.

BEIGNETS (French) The term for various foods—including meats, fish, vegetables, and fruits—that are cut into pieces, dipped in a beer batter, and deep-fried. There is also the plain *beignet,* made from a dough composed of flour, sugar, butter, salt, eggs, and flavoring. The dough is formed into small balls, deep-fried, and served dusted with confectioner's sugar. (See CROMESQUI, FRITTER, TEMPURA)

Beignets de Volaille Some think that this is one of the most unfortunate accidents ever to have happened to a chicken—and in France of all places. The poached bird is diced, marinated for a time, then stirred into a batter made from flour, eggs, milk, salt, and butter. With a tablespoon, the chicken batter is dropped into hot oil and deep-fried to a golden brown. The result is uncomfortably reminiscent of those breaded clumps of similarly treated chicken displayed under glass on Coney Island's boardwalk in New York City. (See BEIGNET, CROMESQUI, FRITTER) COMPATIBLE WINES: A white wine, e.g., Orvieto, Chenin Blanc, Riesling, Château Chalon.

BEIZE (German) A pickling mixture or marinade that is usually made up of wine vinegar, onions, wine, bay leaf, cloves, thyme, juniper berries, crushed garlic, salt, and peppercorns. (See HASENPFEFFER, MARINADE, PICKLING, SAUERBRATEN)

BELEGTES BROT (German) "Open-faced sandwiches" which are usually topped with a great variety of fine sausage meats, cheese, hard-boiled eggs, and a garniture of olives and pickles. COMPATIBLE BEVERAGES: Beer, of course.

BELGIAN CUISINE Belgium, set between Holland and France, has been greatly influenced by those countries. Unlike France, Belgium uses much beer in its cooking.

BELGIAN ENDIVE See ENDIVE, CHICONS GRATINÉS

BELLE-HÉLÈNE (French) The name of an operetta by the French composer Jacques Offenbach, for which many French dishes have been named.

Pears Belle-Hélène Pears are poached in a heavy syrup flavored with vanilla and served on a mound of vanilla ice cream. A rich, hot chocolate sauce is served separately. (See CONSOMMÉ)

Tournedos Belle-Hélène   Fillets of beef are grilled and served richly garnished with shoestring potatoes, artichokes stuffed with watercress topped with *sauce Béarnaise,* mushrooms stuffed with *tomates concassées* or peas, small new carrots and *croquettes* made from asparagus tips topped with a slice of glazed truffle. (See BÉARNAISE, CONCASSER, CROQUETTES, TOURNEDOS) COMPATIBLE WINES: A red wine, e.g., Clos de La Roche, Château Lascombes, Kirwan, Barbera, Chambertin.

Poulet Belle-Hélène   Delicately sautéed chicken breasts are garnished with asparagus tips, black truffles, and a *sauce suprême.* (See SUPRÊME) COMPATIBLE WINES: A white wine, e.g., Meursault, Orvieto, Pinot Chardonnay, Pouilly-Fuissé.

BELLE-VUE, EN (French) A culinary term meaning "beautifully displayed."

Lobster en Belle-Vue   Six to eight cooked lobsters are presented on large serving trays, covered with a thin coating of aspic, and surrounded by a multitude of decorative garnishes, such as black truffles, tomato-colored aspic cut in diamond shapes, and croutons. This dish is usually served at buffet dinners and large banquets. COMPATIBLE WINES: A white wine, e.g., Chablis, Montrachet, Soave, Pinot Chardonnay, Aigle, Dézaley, Verdicchio, Debro, Wehlener Sonnenuhr.

BELUGA CAVIAR The word "caviar" comes from the Turkish word *havyar. Beluga* is the word the Russian connoisseur would use when referring to the finest white sturgeon of the Black and Caspian Seas, from which the largest eggs are obtained. To the Russians, it is *ikra;* to us, caviar.

BENEDICT, EGGS (American) One story says that a French chef invented this dish for an American honeymoon couple; another version tells of a Benedict named Sam who, seeking relief from a deadly hangover one morning, ordered this dish made to his specifications at the Waldorf-Astoria Hotel in New York City. Still another legend states that the dish was, indeed, created at the Waldorf, but by the famous *maître d'hôtel* Oscar. Whatever the precise origin, this decidedly American dish consists of toasted English muffins covered with grilled ham and poached eggs that are in turn coated with a rich *sauce Hollandaise* plus a slice of black truffle. Often, a slice of black olive is substituted for the real thing. COMPATIBLE BEVERAGES: Tea, coffee, and perhaps beer.

BÉNÉDICTINE, CRABS (French) During the Middle Ages in France, the good brothers of the black cowl had little more to do than to pray and meditate on their next meal. One such enterprising Benedictine brother selected a number of soft-shelled crabs and placed them, still alive, to frolic and splash in a bowl full of milk for three to five hours. Of course, the pot was covered. When at last the crabs were still, they were dredged in flour, dipped first in beaten egg and then in breadcrumbs, and finally fried until golden brown in hot oil. After being drained, the crabs were served on a bed of crisply-fried parsley, garnished with lemon wedges, exactly as they are served today. COMPATIBLE WINES: A white wine, e.g., Meursault, Pouilly-Fuissé, Orvieto, Sauvignon Blanc, Bernkasteler Doktor.

BENI SHOGA (Japanese) Ginger roots that have been blanched then marinated in a brine composed of salt and vinegar. A red food dye is added to deepen the natural pink color of the roots. These pickled ginger roots are a favorite Japanese garnish.

BENLØSE FUGL (Norwegian) Literally, "boneless birds." The dish consists of thin slices of round steak covered with a mixture of ground pork, salt, pepper, ginger, and cloves. The beef slices are rolled up with the filling inside, tied securely, and browned in butter. Then, swimming in a good beef stock, the "birds" are simmered until done and served coated with a thick brown sauce made from a *roux* moistened with the beef stock. (See ROUX) COMPATIBLE WINES: A red wine, e.g., Médoc, Beaujolais, Zinfandel, Petit Sirah, Lambrusco.

BERBERE This is the Ethiopian answer to the raw steak tartar. The dish consists of raw meat that is cut off in slices and served with a sauce made hot with peppers and spices. (See TARTAR) COMPATIBLE BEVERAGES: Beer, ale, stout, tea.

BERCY, SAUCE (French) Almost any course one can name has a dish flavored *Bercy:* eggs *Bercy,* steak *Bercy,* fish *Bercy,* etc. The French term honors the renowned Bercy Market in Paris and signifies a predominance of shallots in the preparation of a dish. When used with fish, the sauce is made by simmering shallots in white wine and butter, adding parsley and lemon juice and seasoning to taste. When served with grilled meats, chopped shallots and pepper are reduced in white wine, adding meat glaze and butter, and ultimately sliced marrow and parsley.

Huîtres Bercy Oysters are lightly poached in their own juices, returned to their shells and coated with a *sauce Bercy,* then lightly browned under the broiler. COMPATIBLE WINES: A white wine: e.g., Muscadet, Chablis, Soave, Wehlener Sonnenuhr, Pinot Chardonnay.

BERGÈRE (French) The term for a dish that has been prepared "in the style of a shepherdess," that is, with sweet butter, heavy cream, and mushrooms.

Chicken Sauté à la Bergère A young chicken is cut up and the pieces are sautéed in butter without browning. The pan is deglazed with a veal stock and Madeira wine; this mixture is then reduced and enriched with heavy cream. To serve, the sauce is poured over the chicken, which is garnished with shoestring potatoes and with button mushrooms that have been sautéed in butter. (See BEURRE MANIÉ,

DEGLAZE) COMPATIBLE WINES: A white wine, e.g., Dézaley, Pouilly-Fumé, Orvieto, Schloss Vollrads, Johannisberg.

BERNER PLATTE (Swiss) This German term refers to a hearty dish that is almost a national speciality in Switzerland. It consists of chunks of smoked pork, pig's feet, sausages, boiled beef, country bacon, and heaps of wine-cooked sauerkraut and boiled potatoes. COMPATIBLE WINES: A white wine, e.g., Dézaley, Gewürztraminer, Riquewihr, Neuchâtel, Sauvignon Blanc.

BETEL NUTS These hard round nuts, called *supari* by the East Indians, are really the astringent seeds of the betel palm (also called the areca palm). Since ancient times, they have been chewed throughout the Orient for their stimulating effect. After having been chewed a while, the nut softens and gives off a peculiar taste that must be acquired to be appreciated. Habitual chewing of the betel nut will stain the teeth black. (See PAAN)

BETTERAVES SCHUPP À LA CRÈME, SALADE DE (Swiss) "What can be better than uncooked fresh vegetables, tenderly treated and decoratively served?" Dr. H. Schupp, the noted Swiss chemist and dietitian, answers his own rhetorical query with this dish. Fresh beets are thoroughly cleaned, finely grated, and mixed with oatmeal, honey, lemon juice, plus a dash of Cointreau or Grand Marnier liqueur. This delicious salad is then plated, topped first with yogurt and then with a dollop of heavy whipped cream. It makes a delightful summer luncheon. COMPATIBLE BEVERAGES: Tea.

BEURRE MANIÉ (French) A thickener composed of soft butter and flour kneaded together. It is used to bind sauces, soups, and stews. The butter and flour are formed into tiny balls. These are added at the last minute to soups and sauces that require thickening. They are briskly whipped in over low heat. The mixture must never be brought to the boil.

BEURRE NOIR (French) Sweet butter that has been cooked until it has just turned a light shade of brown and to which wine vinegar, capers, and parsley are added. This "black butter" is served with skate, calf's brains, eggs, and boiled vegetables. (See CAPERS, CERVELLES, STING-AREE AU BEURRE NOIR)

BEURRE, SAUCE AU (French) A butter sauce. To prepare, boiling salted water is added to a *roux,* into which egg yolks and cold water are whisked. Then, over very low heat, sweet butter is added, a bit at a time. The sauce is seasoned, strained, and accented with a drop of lemon juice. (See BÂTARDE, ROUX)

BEURRES COMPOSÉS These French-inspired compound butters are made from a multitude of flavorful foods, condiments, and herbs. At one time the ingredients were pounded and ground mercilessly in huge mortars together with cold sweet butter and then forced through fine sieves. Today we have efficient blenders that will do the job far better and in a fraction of the time. Compound butters are added to sauces or used alone to garnish various foods. Their names come from the main ingredient used with the butter—for example, lobster-butter, anchovy-butter, parsley-butter. (See COMPOUND BUTTER)

BHAJIA See PAKORIS

BHOON (East Indian) The process of boiling or frying foods which, in themselves, may or may not possess fats or oils. (See KHEEMA WITH FRIED ONIONS)

BHUNA (East Indian) A method of sautéing food quickly in hot fat in a round-bottomed pot, to which, just as the meat or other food is about to stick to the pan, a quantity of water, yogurt, or broth is added. This system is similar to the popular Chinese stir-fry method of cooking. (See STIR-FRYING)

BIBB LETTUCE This very tender, crisp lettuce, having a cup-shaped head and a deep green color, was first cultivated in Kentucky by a man named Jack Bibb shortly after the Civil War. It is also called "limestone lettuce" because the great amount of limestone present in the ground in the section of Kentucky where it is grown adds both calcium and a special crispness to this lettuce. Bibb lettuce is an expensive, tender rarity.

BIERSUPPE Any dish that is predominantly beer must be of Nordic origin, usually German, which this soup definitely is. To prepare, a light beer is mixed into a *roux* and flavored with cinnamon, salt, pepper, and a bit of sugar. After simmering for a few minutes, the soup is bound with heavy cream and served piping hot over toasted bread. (See ROUX)

BIFF A LA LINDSTRÖM (Swedish) A type of meat patty that is composed of a mixture of ground beef, egg yolks, heavy cream, chopped onions and capers, mashed potatoes, salt, pepper, and diced pickled beets. The mixture is shaped into flat patties which are browned on both sides in hot butter and served garnished with onion rings. COMPATIBLE WINES: A red wine, e.g., Rioja, Barolo, Mâcon, Pinot Noir, Beaujolais, Nebbiolo.

BIGARADE/BIGARRADE, SAUCE (French) A sauce made from the juices of a cooked duck. These are reduced with oranges, lemons, Cognac, or Grand Marnier. An alternate sauce is composed by straining the roast duck juices, removing the fat, and then adding caramelized sugar *(gastrique)* which has been dissolved in vinegar. Then one proceeds to add the orange and lemon juice along with finely sliced orange and lemon rinds. The finest sauce, called *sauce bigarade,* is flavored with the pulp of the *bigarade* orange, the bitter orange from Seville that is much too acidic to be eaten raw. The juice of this orange is used in meat and poultry dishes, and the orange itself is used to make a perfectly delicious marmalade. The bigarade tree grows in Spain and in the West Indies. (See GASTRIQUE)

Young Duckling Bigarade or **Duckling à l'Orange** Roast duckling decorated with fresh orange segments and served glazed with the *sauce bigarade*. COMPATIBLE WINES: A red wine, e.g., St. Émilion, Talbot, Gruaud-Larose, Calon-Ségur, Cabernet Sauvignon; or a white wine, such as Vouvray, Graves, Saumur, Jesuitengarten, Tokay.

BIGOS (Polish) To prepare this hearty stew, mushrooms are dried and squeezed to remove the essence and then sliced. Salt pork and chopped onions are cooked in a large pot with the mushrooms, cubed poultry, pork, veal, sauerkraut, chunks of Polish sausage *(kiełbasa)*, Madeira wine, sugar, salt, and pepper. The stew is simmered covered until the meats are tender. It is that glorious type of stew that seems to taste better each time it is reheated. COMPATIBLE WINES: A white wine, e.g., Riesling, Orvieto, Brolio Blanc, Pinot Chardonnay, Sylvaner, Traminer.

BILLI BI (French) This soup, supposedly named after a William B. Leeds and later shortened to Billi Bi, is actually a bisque of mussels called *soupe au moules*. Well-cleaned mussels are simmered in white wine with shallots, onions, parsley, salt, pepper, cayenne, butter, bay leaf, and thyme. The mussels are reserved and the liquid is strained, brought to the boil, and removed from the heat. Beaten egg yolks and heavy cream are then added, and the soup is returned to the heat to thicken. The mussels are returned to the soup and the delicious dish is ready to be served. (See BISQUE)

BIRCHERMÜESLI (Swiss) A dish created by the famous nutritionist Dr. M. Bircher-Benner of Zürich, where his well-known clinic still flourishes. The dish is made from uncooked oatmeal (not the minute-type) that is moistened with cold milk, flavored with slivered almonds, and sweetened with either sugar or honey. Apples are grated into the mixture and heavy cream is added. Before serving, the dish is topped with whipped cream and grated nuts. The *Birchermüesli* can be varied by using other fruits and other kinds of nutmeats. The nutritious dish is eaten as a breakfast, a midday snack, or as a delicious dessert.

BIRD'S NEST SOUP (Chinese) This speciality, called *yin waw* in Chinese, is made from the disgorged dried secretions of the Salangan swallow, which the birds use to hold their nests together. It was during times of famine that the practical and imaginative Chinese discovered that not only were sharks' fins and carps' tongues edible and nutritious, but that swallows' nests were as well.

Frequently, the birds' nests are made into a sweet dessert, but the soup is more popular. Due to the great difficulty involved in obtaining the nests from cavern walls and precipitous cliffs, plus the subsequent pains taken to remove unwanted feathers from the very glutinous material, these nests demand high prices in Oriental stores.

The most costly is the whole bird's nest, not the chipped or ground-up variety, which resemble cellophane bags full of grated coconut. The soup is made by adding a nest to a rich chicken broth. Before serving, it is garnished with water chestnuts, minced cooked chicken, and egg white. (See AGAR-AGAR) COMPATIBLE BEVERAGES: Tea, sherry, Sauterne, saké.

BIRYANI (East Indian) This rice dish is similar to the well-known *pilaff* or *pilau,* with the exception that the rice of a *biryani* is partially cooked before it is added to the meat.

Chicken Biryani This dish originated with the Moguls, the nomadic Tartars of Mongolia who brought Persian eating customs with them, wedding rich Persian meats with rice. Pieces of chicken are marinated for many hours in a puréed mixture of ginger, garlic, onions, yogurt, lemon juice, and a variety of seasonings, such as cinnamon, cardamom seeds, coriander, cumin, mace, poppy seeds, bay leaf, peppercorns, and salt. The marinade and the chicken are brought to the boil and simmered for 15 minutes. Partially cooked rice is put over the chicken and streaked with saffron-flavored milk. This covered casserole is then baked for an hour and served garnished with raisins, almonds, chopped onions, and quartered hard-boiled eggs. A truly royal dish that takes time, care, and know-how. (See PILAFF) COMPATIBLE BEVERAGE: A fine black tea.

BISCOTTO (Italian) A twice-baked biscuit, wafer, or cookie. (See ZWIEBACK)

BISCUIT (French) A special type of bread that is cooked twice. The name stems from the medieval French word *bescuit* (*bes* meaning "twice," *cuit* meaning "cooked"). This is a very practical type of food to take when traveling, for it keeps very well. It is made from a pastry dough composed of flour, sugar, and eggs. In the United States, when unsweetened, these are called "crackers." (See ZWIEBACK)

BISCUIT TORTONI (Italian) This frozen dessert, though often classified as an ice cream, is really a *mousse.* First created by Signore B. Tortoni, a famous Italian restaurateur who thrived in Paris in the latter part of the eighteenth century, it consists of egg yolks and salt that are whipped into a hot sugar syrup until the mixture thickens. Sherry wine is then added, and the mixture is strained into heavy whipped cream. The rich, velvety mix is then poured into individual molds (sometimes paper casings), or into a single large mold. It is sprinkled with ground toasted almonds and chilled before serving. (See MOUSSE)

BISMARCK (German) Many dishes have been named for Otto von Bismarck, the greatest chancellor of the German Empire.

Bismarck Herring Having been scaled and cleaned and soaked overnight in vinegar, the herring are cut into fillets and alternately layered with sliced onions and seasonings. After a day or two, they are ready to be eaten.

Tournedos of Beef Bismarck These small fillets of beef are sautéed in fresh butter and garnished with stuffed potatoes. The potatoes are baked and the centers hollowed out. The potato mash is mixed with chopped mushrooms, heavy cream, and seasoning and spooned back into the potato hulls, topped with a poached egg, and coated with a sauce Hollandaise. (See HOLLANDAISE) COMPATIBLE WINES: A red wine, e.g., Chambertin, Pinot Noir, Fixin, Dôle, Barolo, La Tâche, Pommard, Talbot.

BISQUE (French) A thick puréed soup made from shellfish such as lobster, crab, or shrimp. The purée of shellfish is thinned with fish stock and bound with heavy cream. A touch of good Cognac and a sprinkling of chopped parsley and the soup is ready to be served. Sometimes, at table, sherry is offered as an optional added flavoring.

In the eighteenth century *bisques* were made from certain fowl, such as quail, pigeon, or chicken, but the fowl was not puréed. Usually it was served with bread soaking in the soup. Today, tomato soups made with plenty of rich, hot cream are called *bisques* as well.

BISTECCA ALLA PIZZAIOLA See PIZZAIOLA DI MANZO

BITKI (Russian/Polish) Meatballs composed of ground beef, chopped onions, salt, pepper, and breadcrumbs. Formed into balls, they are dusted with flour, fried, and served either with sour cream or a rich tomato sauce. In another variety of the *bitki,* chopped veal or lamb is mixed together with the chopped beef, and puréed anchovy is added to provide a tang. COMPATIBLE WINES: A red wine, e.g., Beaujolais, Zinfandel, Chianti, Dôle.

BIZCOCHO BORRACHO (Spanish) Marie Thérèsia, wife of Louis XIV and daughter of Philip IV of Spain, contributed not only chocolate to the French cuisine, but also the *bizcocho borracho*. This "drunken cake" is prepared from a simple batter—made from flour, separated eggs, butter, baking powder, and sugar, all laced with good brandy—that, when mixed and baked correctly, magically transforms itself into a light sponge cake. The French seized upon this treasure at once and rechristened it *biscuit au beurre.* The *bizcocho* is covered with a glaze made from sugar and sherry, and when cool, it is sprinkled with sugar and more sherry.

Bizcocho De Madrid A regular *bizcocho* batter is flavored with grated orange peel and brandy. The dough, shaped into twists and brushed with beaten egg yolks, is baked in a hot oven until done.

BLACHAN (Indonesian) A dried shrimp paste, used as a flavoring agent in the preparation of many Oriental dishes. (See BLATCHANG)

BLANCMANGE (French) This ancient pudding, meaning "white victuals," is said to have been born in Languedoc. It has as many variations as there are flavors: lemon, vanilla, coffee, almond, pistachio, hazelnut, strawberry, raspberry, honey. Or it can be flavored with rum or Kirsch or Grand Marnier liqueurs. To prepare this simple dessert, sweet and bitter almonds are blanched and then puréed in a mortar with a little water until a paste is formed. The paste is passed through a cloth several times to extract the almond milk, which is then heated with gelatin. After cooling, Kirsch or any other compatible liqueur or flavoring is added, and the pudding is poured into a mold and refrigerated. Prior to 1650, *blancmange* was used as a sauce with meats.

BLANQUETTE (French) The term *blanquette,* meaning "a sauce that coats thickly," refers to a *ragoût* of lamb, veal, chicken, or rabbit that is enriched with egg yolks and heavy cream and often garnished with small button mushrooms and onions. (See RAGOÛT)

Blanquette à l'Ancienne A method of preparing milk-fed veal or baby lamb. The meat is blanched then cooked in a white stock with root vegetables and herbs. Veal stock is poured into a white *roux*, and the sauce is finished with the addition of egg yolks and cream. The veal or lamb, white mushrooms, pearl onions, and chopped parsley are added last. (See ROUX) COMPATIBLE WINES: A white wine, e.g., Orvieto, Frascati, Rüdesheim, Anjou, Gewürztraminer, Sauvignon Blanc.

BLATCHANG (Japanese) A speciality prepared by drying prawns and shrimp in the sun, then pounding and grinding them with several kinds of pepper, and finally shaping this mass into the form of a large cheese. Fresh peppers, chopped gherkins, and onions or dates, apricots, quinces, and raisins are sometimes added as flavorings. COMPATIBLE BEVERAGES: Beer, ale, stout, tea.

BLEU, TRUITE AU The French discovered this extremely simple and delicately delicious method of preparing fresh-water trout. First, a live trout is stunned and quickly plunged into a boiling *court-bouillon* made with plenty of vinegar. The chemical reaction of the vinegar with the mucus protective covering of the fish produces a shimmering blue tint. The dish is complemented with boiled potatoes, sweet butter, and a tossed green salad. Any restaurant that serves its trout *bleu* must have a holding tank for the fish. The final gesture of *la truite au bleu* is that he appears on the diner's prewarmed plate curled into the form of a question mark. (See COURT-BOUILLON, FORELLE BLAU) COMPATIBLE WINES: A white wine, e.g., Chablis, Pouilly-Fuissé, Aigle, Soave, Pinot Chardonnay, Debro, Ockfener Bockstein.

BLINI This yeast pancake of Russian and Polish origin is made from buckwheat flour, yeast, butter, milk, and eggs. The mixture is left to stand until the yeast has worked a bit, and the batter is then cooked in butter in a hot pan. The pancakes are spread thickly with caviar and served with sour cream. (See BLINTZ, PANCAKE, PLÄTTAR, SUZETTE) COMPATIBLE WINES: A white wine, e.g., Chablis, Muscadet, Quincy, Debro, Soave, Verdicchio.

BLINTZ (Jewish) This is the Yiddish word, derived from *blini,* for a small pan-fried batter-cake that is rolled with a meat, potato, cheese, or fruit filling. The batter, made with egg, is rather thin. (See BLINI, CRÊPE, PANCAKE, PLÄTTAR, SUZETTE)

BLITZKUCHEN (German) This cake can be made *Blitz-schnell*—"lightning fast." After butter and sugar have been well creamed, egg yolks are beaten into the mixture. Then flour, salt, and baking powder are added alternately with milk that is flavored with vanilla. After beaten egg whites are folded in, the batter is poured into a pan and topped with a generous amount of sugar, cinnamon, and chopped walnuts. The cake is baked—*Blitz-schnell*—for a scant half-hour. (See KUCHEN)

BLOOD AS FOOD In the days of antiquity the Jews, the early Christians, and the Moslems all banned the eating of blood. On the other hand, Nordic people drank the blood of slain beasts such as bears and seals for ready nourishment, and today they still serve blood dishes such as black soup, black pudding, and paltbread. The French have their *boudin noir* and their *civets,* and the Irish enjoy *drisheen,* all made from animal blood. In the ninth century, a Chinese gentleman visiting an Arab land wrote that the Arabs pierced the blood vessels of their cattle to draw blood, which they consumed with milk. Even Marco Polo gave his account of how Mongol warriors of the thirteenth century traveled with a complement of eighteen horses—not only to provide the necessary change of mount, but also to obtain nourishment from the blood of these animals. By alternating the donor horses, the Mongols managed to sustain themselves en route without impairing either the health or the efficiency of their steeds. The blood was ingested raw because a fire might alert the enemy.

Today, in Tanzania, the towering herdsmen called the Masai subsist totally on a diet consisting of blood and milk while living and traveling with their herds of cattle. A leather strap is tightened around the cow's neck, causing the vein to swell with blood, then the jugular is pierced and enough blood is drained off as needed. The moment the leather thong is loosened, the wound is closed with a plug and the blood stops flowing. The Masai drink the blood uncooked.

The Laplanders of Finland also use animal blood, but they obtain it from the antlers of their domestic herds of reindeer. Ireland's national dish, *drisheen,* served in fine restaurants, can be made either from pig's or sheep's blood, but sometimes the blood of a goose is used. (See BOUDIN NOIR, BLUT UND ZUNGENWUST, CANARD À LA PRESSE, CIVET, CZARNINA, DRISHEEN, PALTBREAD, VERILETUT)

BLUT UND ZUNGENWURST (German) A blood sausage consisting of large chunks of pickled pork tongue, pork blood, kidneys, and hearts that are first cooked and then chopped up with bacon fat, spices, and herbs. These sausages are popularly served with sauerkraut and mashed potatoes and garnished with freshly grated horseradish. (See SAUERKRAUT, WURST) COMPATIBLE BEVERAGES: A good beer.

BOBOTIE (Malaysian) This minced meat dish is also popular with the Afrikaners of South Africa. It is composed of the finely chopped meat of game, sheep, or cattle mixed with soaked bread, cooked rice, or mashed sweet potatoes. Then, with the addition of eggs, butter, chopped onions, garlic, and a blend of curry powders and turmeric, all is placed in a shallow ovenproof dish and baked until it starts to brown. It is then removed from the heat, and after an egg-and-milk mixture and a few lemon leaves are added, the dish is returned to the oven and baked until done. COMPATIBLE BEVERAGES: Beer, ale, stout, tea.

BOCCONCINI (Italian) A stew composed of unfloured chunks of veal which are well browned in garlic-flavored olive oil and then simmered in a seasoned mixture of red wine (Chianti) and tomato sauce until fork-tender. COMPATIBLE WINES: A red wine, e.g., Chianti, Beaujolais, Zinfandel.

BOEUF (French) Beef.

BOEUF À LA MODE (French) As is the case with all classic dishes, stories vary as to the origin of this famous preparation. One claims that it originated with one "Papa" Duval, a Parisian butcher and restaurateur who in 1850 surprised his dining clientele with this beef dish. But then there was a restaurant called Le Boeuf à la Mode, situated on the rue Valois, and the speciality of the house was a larded pot roast braised in wine and brandy, richly garnished with fresh vegetables and flavored with herbs and spices. Soon the dish took on the name of the restaurant. However, in 1739 the famous chef Marin had already served *boeuf à la mode,* which was so inscribed by his contemporary, Menon, in his book, *La Cuisinière Bourgeoise.*

Whoever originated the dish, as served in restaurants today it consists of a bottom round or rump of beef that is first trimmed of all outer fat and then larded. The meat is left overnight in a marinade composed of red wine, nutmeg, pepper, brandy, and herbs. The following day the meat is removed from the marinade, patted dry, and browned in a mixture of olive oil and butter. The marinade is then added to the beef along with a veal knuckle; the pot is covered and simmered over very low heat for hours, or it can be baked. During the last hour of cooking, vegetables are added, including clove-studded onions. The veal knuckle is removed and the meat is served with the vegetables in the casserole with the broth. The dish is also excellent served cold. (See BOURGUIGNONNE) COMPATIBLE WINES: A red wine, e.g., Mercurey, Santenay, Côte Rôtie, Hermitage.

BO FAN Chinese for "potted rice," a simple *paella-type* dish, almost rustic in character, consisting of small pieces of beef, sausage, and poultry mixed with white rice. The rice is boiled in water, and before the cooking time elapses, the pieces of selected meats are placed on top of the rice to steam until done. (See PAELLA)

Gai Luk Bo Fan   For this Chinese dish, "chicken with potted rice," small pieces of chicken that have been marinated in soy sauce and wine are steamed together with ginger root and scallions with a quantity of white rice. COMPATIBLE WINES: A white wine, e.g., Sauterne, Riesling, saké, Anjou, Orvieto, Frascati.

BOGHAR (East Indian) A method of mixing the half-cooked part of a dish with the part that is almost completely cooked and finishing them together.

BOHÉMIENNE, À LA (French) Dishes so named were meant to honor the comic-opera *La Bohémienne,* by William Balfe, presented in 1869 in Paris.

Sauce Bohémienne   A mixture of egg yolks, salt, pepper, and vinegar is added to a cold *sauce Béchamel,* and then, as one makes *Mayonnaise,* oil is added gradually. The sauce is finished with tarragon vinegar. (See BÉCHAMEL, MAYONNAISE)

Pheasant à la Bohémienne   A pheasant is stuffed with goose liver and then is trussed up and baked in a casserole. Prior to serving, it is flamed with brandy. COMPATIBLE WINES: A red wine, e.g., Haut Brion, Pétrus, Kirwan, Côte Rôtie.

Brioche à la Bohémienne   Poached eggs garnished with a purée of goose liver and a fine *julienne* of ham that has been first cooked in Madeira wine are served in a warm *brioche.* (See BRIOCHE, JULIENNE)

BOK CHOY (Chinese) Chard cabbage, which looks like the result of a spring marriage between a Swiss chard and a celery stalk. It has long white stalks and dark green leaves. *Choy sum,* a smaller version, is more expensive and more delicate.

BOK YOU GUY (Chinese) A cut-up young spring chicken is simmered in water and soy sauce. When the chicken has cooked, cornstarch is thickened in water and added to the chicken to simmer together. The chicken dish is served with boiled white rice and raisins and sprinkled with peanuts and grated coconut. COMPATIBLE WINES: A white wine, e.g., Meursault, Chenin Blanc, Orvieto, Piesporter Goldtröpfchen, saké; or perhaps a red wine such as Beaujolais, Valpolicella, Zinfandel, Fleurie.

BOLLITO (Italian) Boiled.

Bollito de Gallina   Boiled chicken. COMPATIBLE WINES: A red wine, e.g., Valpolicella, Zinfandel, Médoc, St. Julien, Volnay, Nebbiolo.

Bollito di Manzo   If one wants boiled beef, this is what one looks for on an Italian menu. COMPATIBLE WINES: A red wine, e.g., Beaujolais, Brouilly, St. Estèphe, Nebbiolo, Barbera, Chinon.

Bollito Misto   A mixture of boiled meats and poultry, cooked and served in a rich vegetable broth made from onions, carrots, celery, and tomatoes. The French version is *pot-au-feu.* (See POT-AU-FEU) COMPATIBLE WINES: The same as for the *bollito di manzo.*

BOLOGNESE, ALLA (Italian) This tomato-and-meat sauce is served with all kinds of _pasta_ dishes. (See PASTA, RAGÙ)

BOMBAY DUCK A dried tropical fish, called _bombil_ or _bummaloe_ fish by the East Indians. Flavored with asafoetida and preserved in cans, it is served with curry dishes. (See ASAFOETIDA, HAWAIIAN SHRIMP CURRY)

BONAPARTE, BANANA FRITTERS (French) This was a great favorite of Emperor Napoleon while counting his days in exile on the desolate island of St. Helena. For the most part, the food on the island was dreadful, but bananas were plentiful and nutritious, so Napoleon's cook invented a new way of preparing them. First, the bananas were marinated in a mixture of rum and orange juice. They were then dipped into a batter of eggs and flour, and deep-fried until golden brown. A sauce of butter, sugar, and rum was poured over the bananas before serving. Napoleon was delighted.

BONNE FEMME (French) A phrase indicating that a dish has been cooked simply—that is, with vegetables and stock.

Sole Bonne Femme A dish of poached fillets of sole, prepared with shallots, parsley, white wine, mushrooms, fish stock, and cream. COMPATIBLE WINES: A white wine, e.g., Chablis, Meursault, Montrachet, Wehlener Sonnenuhr, Aigle, Riquewihr, Sauvignon Blanc, Orvieto.

Potage Bonne Femme A simple soup of vegetables cooked in beef or chicken stock.

Chicken Bonne Femme A chicken dish cooked in a "stewpot" as the "good housewife" might have prepared it. In this case the French have taken a young spring chicken and browned it in a pot with salt pork fat and butter together with small olive-shaped potatoes. Then the chicken, surrounded by the small potatoes, is baked in the oven until tender. COMPATIBLE WINES: A red wine, e.g., Margaux, St. Émilion, Pétrus, Beaujolais, Valpolicella, Zinfandel.

BONNEFOY, SAUCE (French) A sauce made by cooking chopped shallots, parsley, thyme, bay leaves, salt, and pepper in Sauterne wine until most of the wine has evaporated. With the addition of a _sauce velouté_, the sauce is again cooked, passed through a sieve, and enriched with fresh sweet butter and chopped tarragon. It is served with grilled fish and various white meats. (See VELOUTÉ)

BOOLA-BOOLA Although this soup is about as American as apple pie, it has nothing to do with the college song that has been popular at Yale University since 1901; nor has it any connection with the Seychelles Islands, contrary to whatever our English friends contend.

It seems that whenever a truly exceptional dish of unknown origin is discovered, those chefs who serve it time and again claim it to be their very own creation. So it is with this delectable soup, a happy blend of real turtle soup and a purée of green peas. This mixture is only brought to the simmer, never boiled, at which time a bit of sweet butter and an herb mixture of basil, majoram, rosemary, and thyme are added. It is then ladled into individual soup bowls, flavored with sherry, coated thickly with whipped cream, browned under the grill, and served. A fantastic soup! The French call it *potage boula boula gratiné.*

BORANI (Turkish) A meatless spinach stew cooked with chopped onions and tomatoes. COMPATIBLE WINES: A red wine, e.g., Beaujolais, Fleurie, Nebbiolo, Lambrusco, Savigny, Zinfandel, Petite Sirah.

Borani, Iranian Mushroom In Iran a *borani* is a mixture of vegetables and yogurt. This mushroom version is made by sautéing finely chopped onions in butter and, when tender, lemon juice and sliced mushrooms are added. Seasoned with salt and pepper, the dish is finished with the addition of yogurt and chopped fresh mint. This dish can be served as an appetizer, as a substitute for a salad, or to complement meat and poultry dishes.

BORC (Turkish) This Turkish version of the famous Russian *borsch,* commonly known as beet soup, is prepared by first sautéing chopped green peppers, celery, potatoes, and onions in butter, then simmering these vegetables in a beef stock with tomatoes, cabbage, garlic, and beets. Bay leaf and dill are added as flavoring. A dash of lemon juice is added just before serving and, instead of the traditional sour cream, yogurt is added to each bowl, or it is served on the side. (See BORSCH)

BORDELAISE, À LA When a French menu designates a dish as being *à la Bordelaise,* it means that the dish has been prepared with red wine.

Beef (Boeuf) à la Bordelaise A sirloin of beef is first marinated in red wine, then it is roasted and served with a sauce composed of the basic brown sauce plus some of the marinade. (See BROWN SAUCE) COMPATIBLE WINES: A red wine, e.g., Fixin, Chambertin, Nuits St. Georges, Barolo, Dôle, Mouton Rothschild, Pinot Noir.

Sauce Bordelaise To a mixture of finely minced shallots, ground pepper, thyme, and bay leaf, red wine is added. The whole is reduced and a *sauce demi-glace* is added. Before serving, the sauce is finished with the addition of lemon juice and beef marrow. The sauce is brought to the boil, topped with minced parsley, and served. (See DEMI-GLACE).

Cèpes à la Bordelaise For this mushroom (boletus variety) dish, after cleaning the mushrooms, the stalks are removed and chopped. Then the heads and chopped stalks are dried. Chopped shallots, ham, parsley, bay leaf, and mushroom stalks are then sautéed in hot olive oil. The mushroom caps are sautéed separately in oil and butter, set in the middle of the serving platter, and served surrounded with the ham garnish. (See CHAMPIGNONS, MUSHROOMS) COMPATIBLE WINES: A white wine, e.g., Frascati, Santenay, Chenin Blanc, Gewürztraminer.

BÖREKS (Turkish) Dumplings made from super-thin sheets of dough, called *yufka* by the Turks and *phyllo* by the Greeks. The dumplings are filled with meat, cheese, chicken, spinach, or the like. The French have adopted the *börek,* calling it *beurreck à la Turque.* The French version consists of Gruyère cheese wrapped in a paste, dipped in egg and breadcrumbs, and deep-fried. (See BANIROV BÖREG, PHYLLO, YUFKA)

Tartar Böreks Here, the dumplings are stuffed with seasoned chopped meat and cooked in boiling salted water. They are then drained and dried and served either topped with melted butter and paprika or with yogurt.

Cheese Böreks These dumplings are filled with a mixture of feta and cottage cheese, eggs, milk, parsley, and dill.

Chicken Böreks Cubed chicken is sautéed in butter then mixed with cooked onions, tomatoes, rosemary, salt, and pepper; this is used to stuff the dumplings.

COMPATIBLE WINES: A white wine, e.g., Sylvaner, Gewürztraminer, Lacrima Christi, Chenin Blanc.

BORJU PÖRKÖLT *Pörkölt,* literally "browned," is the Hungarian term used to designate a stew that can be prepared from any kind of meat, including game and poultry. *Borju pörkölt* is made with veal. Cubed veal is browned in oil with chopped onions and is then removed from the pot. After deglazing the pot with a bit of white wine, the veal and the onions, paprika, salt, and pepper are put into the pot together with chopped green peppers, small tomatoes, and crushed garlic. The stew is simmered slowly until the meat is tender. Boiled potatoes or egg noodles can be served with this stew. Or what could be better than the butter-fried *Spätzle*-like dumplings which the Hungarians call *galuska?* (See SPÄTZLE, GALUSKA) COMPATIBLE WINES: A white wine, e.g., Keknyelu, Graacher Himmelreich, Sauvignon Blanc, Gewürztraminer, Anjou, Vouvray; or if a red wine is preferred, Barbera, Zinfandel, Valpolicella, Santenay, Beaujolais, and Côte Rôtie are good choices.

BORRACHA, SALSA Mexicans describe this rather piquant sauce as being *borracha,* or "drunk," due to the amount of *pulque* present (*pulque* is the fermented sap of the agave or century plant which, when further distilled and aged, develops into the more powerful and better-known Tequila). The sauce is prepared by placing cleaned and blanched *pasilla* chilies into a blender together with fresh garlic and a bit of *pulque;* it is worked into a smooth paste. Then, little by little, olive oil is added, *Mayonnaise*-style. Salt and pepper to taste and more of the *pulque* is added to finish the sauce. (See CHILI, PULQUE, MAYONNAISE)

BORRACHO, POLLO (Spanish) This version of chicken in wine, literally "drunken chicken," is called *coq au vin* by the French. The Spanish use almonds and white wine to flavor their birds, whereas the French use garlic, morels, and usually red wine. Furthermore, the Spanish use hens, the French cocks. (See COQ AU VIN) COMPATIBLE WINES: A red wine, e.g., Premiat, Beaujolais, Valpolicella, Zinfandel, Côtes du Rhône, Moulin-à-Vent, Médoc, Fleurie.

BORSCH/BORSCHT/BORTCH/BARTCH Considered to be one of the finest soups in the world, this beet preparation comes from Russia and Poland and bears the honor of being the national soup of both countries. There are many variations, but *borsch* is traditionally made by simmering beets for hours in a meat stock with onions, caraway seeds, and cabbage. The whole is then passed through a sieve, and beetroot liquid is added together with liberal amounts of sour cream before serving. The soup is served either hot or cold. Either *bitki* (tiny meatballs) or *vatruschki* (small cheese tarts) are served as a garnish. (See BITKI, BORC, VATRUSCHKI)

BOSTON BAKED BEANS (American) In Colonial days, this dish was popular in Puritan households, where beans, pork, and molasses were abundant. The beans are soaked overnight in cold water, then drained and cooked in fresh water until the skins of the beans slip off easily. The beans are then put into a pot with scalded salt pork, salt, molasses, sugar, and enough water to cover. The beans are covered and cooked slowly for hours; for the last hour they are cooked uncovered. (See CASSOULET) COMPATIBLE WINES: A red wine, e.g., Margaux, Calon-Ségur, Pontet-Canet, Cabernet Sauvignon, Châteauneuf-du-Pape, Valpolicella, Zinfandel, Nebbiolo.

BOUCHÉE À LA REINE (French) A puff pastry made exactly like the *vol-au-vent* except for the size. The *bouchée* is much smaller; in fact, the word *bouchée* means "little mouthful." It holds such fillings as creamed mushrooms, sweetbreads, and chicken. It is served as an appetizer. (See PÂTE FEUILLETÉE, VOL-AU-VENT)

BOUDIN BLANC (French) A sausage made from ground pork and usually either veal or chicken or a combination of both. The ingredients are bound with eggs, breadcrumbs, and onions.

BOUDIN NOIR (French) This popular blood sausage, euphemistically called "black pudding," is served grilled and usually accompanied with mashed potatoes. (See BLOOD AS FOOD, DRISHEEN) COMPATIBLE WINES: A red wine, e.g., Beaujolais, Bourgueil, Chinon, Côte Rôtie, Lambrusco, Pinot Noir.

BOUILLABAISSE (French) Though often called a soup, *bouillabaisse* is really a stew, a one-dish meal. The name of the dish most probably derives from the phrase *bouille-abaissé,* meaning "boil, then reduce over low heat through evaporation." The true Marseilles *bouillabaisse* demands the inclusion of many local fish that are unobtainable elsewhere, but every good chef the world over has his own recipe, the most important ingredient being "freshness." Basically, the stew is composed of eel, haddock, sea bass, and red snapper, all cut into small pieces, plus lobster, mussels, leeks, onions, garlic, tomatoes, olive oil, bay leaf, thyme, celery, parsley, rosemary, saffron, fish stock, salt, pepper, and croutons. A good _rouille_ should always be served on the side. (See BOURRIDE, BURRIDA, ROUILLE) COMPATIBLE WINES: Muscadet, Chablis, Pouilly-Fuissé; if red wine is preferred, a Châteauneuf-du-Pape, Mercurey, or Côte Rôtie is recommended.

BOULA BOULA GRATINÉ, POTAGE See BOOLA-BOOLA

BOUQUET GARNI (French) A small culinary "nosegay" used to give aroma and flavor to wet-cooked dishes. The _bouquet garni_ is usually composed of parsley stalks, bay leaves, and thyme, all carefully bound together, but for certain dishes herbs such as chervil, tarragon, celery, basil, and rosemary are sometimes used as well. Of course, these aromatic clusters are removed before the dish is served. In English the _bouquet garni_ was once referred to as "an herbal faggot," but today, owing to the connotations carried by the word "faggot," the original French phrase has become standard, even in English.

BOUQUETIÈRE (French) A term designating that a variety of colorful and carefully chosen vegetables is served as a garnish. These vegetables are uniformly cut and tastefully arranged around the meat, and they are often coated with a _sauce Hollandaise._ (See CHIFFONADE, HOLLANDAISE, JARDINIÈRE, MACÉDOINE, PRINTANIÈRE)

Tournedos of Beef Bouquetière Small fillets of beef are cooked in butter, garnished with a _bouquetière_ of vegetables and served with a _sauce Madère._ (See MADÈRE) COMPATIBLE WINES: A red wine, e.g., Chambertin, Nuits St. Georges, Zinfandel, Pinot Noir, Richebourg, Saint Émilion.

BOURGEOISE, À LA (French) A term denoting that the dish is cooked in a very simple way: "citizen's style," similar to _bonne femme._

Bourgeoise Garnish Served with roasts, this garnish consists of tiny potatoes, glazed carrots, garlic, button onions, turnips, and diced bacon in a _sauce demi-glace._ (See BONNE FEMME, DEMI-GLACE)

BOURGUIGNONNE (French) The designation for a dish that is prepared with red wine.

Beef Bourguignonne A well-larded, thick piece of rump steak or pot roast is first browned and then cooked in red wine. It is served garnished with sautéed mushrooms and glazed onion. COMPATIBLE WINES: A red wine, e.g., Chambertin, Fixin, Pommard, Cabernet Sauvignon, Corton, Musigny.

Snails Bourguignonne Snails are first cooked in red wine then stuffed back into their shells, which have been filled with a _beurre composé_ of chopped shallots, parsley, and garlic. They are then baked in the oven. (See BEURRES COMPOSÉS) COMPATIBLE WINES: A red wine, e.g., Richebourg, Chambertin, Dôle, Nuits St. Georges, Saint Émilion, Musigny, Romanée-Conti, Pinot Noir.

BOURRIDE, LA (French) This famous fish stew, born in Provence, is a great favorite in Marseilles or with anyone who loves garlic in strength. *La bourride* is made with the same fish used to make the more famous *bouillabaisse:* red snapper, sea bass, cod, whiting, eel, lobster, etc. To prepare the dish, pieces of the fish are cooked in a rich fish stock flavored with garlic, tomatoes, leeks, onions, celery, pepper, and saffron. When done, the pieces of fish are removed and kept warm. Part of an *aïoli* (garlic *Mayonnaise*) is mixed with the fish stock; together they are simmered until the mixture is as thick as heavy cream. This sauce is poured over lightly toasted bread that has been placed in the bottom of a hot deep dish with morsels of the cooked fish on top. The rest of the *aïoli* is served separately. (See AÏOLI, BOUILLABAISSE) COMPATIBLE WINES: A red wine, e.g., Cahors, Côte Rôtie, Lambrusco; or a white wine, e.g., Orvieto, Gewürztraminer, Rüdesheim, Vouvray, Sauterne, Sauvignon Blanc.

BRABANÇONNE, À LA (French) A term for food prepared "in the style of Brabant," a province in Holland.

Brabançonne Garnish This garnish is composed of tartlets garnished with parboiled Brussels sprouts that are stewed in butter, covered with a *sauce Mornay,* and browned in the grill. It also includes potato *croquettes.* (See CROQUETTES, MORNAY)

Tournedos Brabançonne Small fillets of beef are fried in butter, seasoned, and served with the *Brabançonne* garnish. COMPATIBLE WINES: A red wine, e.g., Beaune, Chambertin, Aloxe-Corton, Pinot Noir, Mouton Rothschild, La Tâche, Richebourg, Haut Brion, Dôle, Chianti.

BRACIOLI (Italian) Individual slices of beef that are spread with a stuffing of choice, rolled up, and then braised. (See BALLOTINE, GALANTINE, MARHATEKERCS, PAUPIETTES, ROULADEN) COMPATIBLE WINES: A red wine, e.g., Chianti, Beaujolais, Côte Rôtie, Moulin-à-Vent, Châteauneuf-du-Pape, Nebbiolo, Zinfandel, Pinot Noir.

Bracioli di Castrato Mutton steaks, cut thin, are filled with minced garlic and onions then rolled and either fried or broiled. COMPATIBLE WINES: A red wine, e.g., Barolo, Nuits St. Georges, Fixin, La Tâche, Pommard, Pinot Noir, Dôle.

BRACIUOLA (Italian) Steak, usually veal or pork.

Braciuola de Maiale al Forno Pork chops, prepared Italian style. The chops are first dusted with flour then dipped in beaten egg, rolled in breadcrumbs, and sautéed in hot olive oil. When well browned and drained, the chops are placed in a pan with a bit of white wine and chopped onions and baked in a moderate oven. COMPATIBLE WINES: A red wine, e.g., Margaux, Côtes du Rhône, Zinfandel, Médoc, Bardolino, Valpolicella.

BRACIUOLINI DI MANZO (Italian) Flattened strips of round steak are topped with a mixture of chopped hard-boiled eggs, minced onions, breadcrumbs, parsley, and bacon bits—all flavored with salt, oregano, and a dash of red wine. The steaks are rolled, secured, and baked in the oven in a sauce composed of olive oil, tomato purée, and minced ripe olives. They are also called *brascioletti* or *bracioletti*. COMPATIBLE WINES: A red wine, e.g., Beaujolais, Châteauneuf-du-Pape, Côtes du Rhône, Chianti, Dôle, Ruby Cabernet, Petit Sirah, Bardolino.

BRADO FOGADA (East Indian) An attractive and delicious shrimp and spinach preparation. Freshly chopped spinach is briefly sautéed in only a dash of oil and soy sauce, to which chopped onions, lemon juice, and curry powder are added. The cooked shrimp are added last, and the ingredients are all stirred together. The dish is served garnished with chopped peanuts and slices of hard-boiled egg. COMPATIBLE BEVERAGES: Beer, ale, tea.

BRAMBOROVE KNEDLÍKY (Czech) Anyone who says potato dumplings can only be made in Germany has never tasted this Czechoslovakian version that puff up as large as tennis balls. First, and this is important, the potatoes used must have been boiled the day before. The potatoes are passed through a sieve into the flour, and eggs are added one at a time. After being well seasoned, the dumpling dough is kneaded, shaped into balls, and dropped into boiling salted water—or, better still, into a rich beef or chicken stock. What could be better to complement a fine pork roast or *Sauerbraten?* (See KARTOFFEL KLÖSSE, SAUERBRATEN)

BRANDADE (French) This delicious fish dish, created in Provence, is made from salt cod which is first boiled, then boned, cut into small bits, and quickly sautéed in olive oil with garlic and shallots. The sautéed fish is then ground up and pounded into a paste to which first olive oil is added, drop by drop, and then warm heavy cream, lemon juice, and seasonings. Rounds of bread, fried in butter and olive oil, are set in a dish or bowl, and the *brandade* is heaped on top. It can be served garnished with chopped truffles or surrounded with patties made from oysters, shrimp, or crayfish.

The French word *brandade* means "brandish." The city of Nimes in France is famous for its *brandade de morue.* The Italians liken their version of salt cod to Mont Blanc: they call it *baccalà Montebianco.* (See BACALAO, BACCALÀ) COMPATIBLE WINES: A white wine, e.g., Orvieto, Meursault, Sauvignon Blanc, Montrachet, Johannisberg, Riquewihr, Chenin Blanc.

BRASATO (Italian) Braised.
Brasato di Vitello al Barolo A pot roast of veal is marinated and then braised in red wine with herbs, butter, and ham fat. COMPATIBLE WINES: A red wine, e.g., Barolo, Valpolicella, Lambrusco, Beaujolais, Margaux, Châteauneuf-du-Pape, Côte Rôtie, Ruby Cabernet, Zinfandel.

BRASSERIE (French) Originally, this term designated a type of establishment where beer and cider were both made and sold. The German name was *Brauerei* (brewery). In days gone by, *brasseries* were the watering places for famous men of letters, politicians, and artists. Today a *brasserie* is not only a place to drink but a café or restaurant where food is also served.

BRATEN/GEBRATEN This German culinary term can be confusing. It often appears on menus as a general term encompassing all of the following methods of cooking: roasting, frying, baking, grilling, broiling, and at times it is also used to mean braising. Examples follow.

Leber Gebraten This is calf's liver that has been breaded and fried in butter.

Schweinebraten Here, the alternate form *braten* designates a roast, a pork roast.

Schmorbraten Here, the term is used to describe a pot roast that has been braised.

Sauerbraten A marinated beef pot roast, famous in Germany. (See SAUERBRATEN).

Hackbraten A German meat loaf, roasted in the oven.

Rostbraten A piece of pork or beef that is cut flat, rolled, tied, and roasted.

Rostbraten, Wiener This Austrian speciality is made from a cut of beef from the sirloin area. The meat is fried in butter and served Vienna-style, covered with fried onions.

Rostbraten, Zigeuner This beefsteak, also popular in Austria, is braised "gypsy-style" and served garnished with bacon and onions. COMPATIBLE WINES: A red wine, e.g., Beaujolais, Côte Rôtie, Chianti, Dôle, Pinot Noir, Egri Bikaver.

BRATWURST (German) This sausage is popular all over the world. Made from pork or from a mixture of veal and pork (the finest *Bratwurst* is made entirely of veal), the ground meat is seasoned with herbs and spices. The sausages are first placed in very hot water for a few minutes. They are then either fried in butter or grilled. Usually, *Bratwurst* is served with butter-rich mashed potatoes, sauerkraut, a purée of peas, a choice of fresh vegetables, and mustard. (See SAUERKRAUT) COMPATIBLE WINES: A white wine, e.g., Gewürztraminer, Anjou, Dézaley, Fendant, Johannisberg; or a red wine, e.g., Beaujolais, Valpolicella, Zinfandel, Petit Sirah.

BREADFRUIT When Captain Bligh was still sailing his ship, *The Bounty,* he introduced this Polynesian fruit to the islands of the Caribbean. Plain cooked breadfruit as a three-finger dip, however, is older than biblical history. This fruit comes from a tall tree native to the South Seas, and when baked, it truly resembles bread. It can also be boiled or fried.

Baked Breadfruit (Hawaiian) This speciality is made by first removing the stem and the core of the fruit, filling the cavity with butter and sugar, replacing the stem, and baking until done.

Breadfruit Poi After cooking the breadfruit in water until tender, it is skinned, cored, seeded, and then pounded and kneaded into a smooth paste. It is then passed through a sieve and left to ripen in the refrigerator for several days. It is served as a dip or pudding. (See POI). COMPATIBLE BEVERAGES: Tea.

BREDIE (Malaysian) This type of stew, popular in South Africa as well as Malaysia, is made by first sautéing chopped onions in oil or in *ghee,* then adding the meat or the fish of choice and cooking until well browned. A choice of vegetables plus red chilies, pumpkin, salt, ginger, and garlic are then added together with a fish, beef, mutton, or chicken broth, and the whole is cooked until done. (See GHEE) COMPATIBLE BEVERAGES: Beer, ale, stout, tea.

BRESSANE, SAUCE (French) This is basically a *sauce Espagnole* that is cooked with Madeira wine, orange juice, and a purée of chicken livers. The sauce is served with many chicken dishes. (See ESPAGNOLE)

BRETONNE, À LA (French) A culinary phrase meaning "in the style of Brittany," a province situated on the northwestern coast of France. The term usually implies that the dish is garnished with beans.

Potage à la Bretonne This rich soup, thick with white beans, is flavored with tomato purée, garnished with shredded leeks, celery, onions, mushrooms parings, and chervil, and served with fried croutons.

Bretonne, Sauce When this sauce from Brittany is to be served with meats, it is made from a *velouté* cooked with white wine, butter, and finely chopped onions, celery, and leeks. When prepared for use with fish dishes, it is made with a *fumet de poisson* that is enriched with cream and butter; chopped mushrooms are added. Remarkable that the sauce contains not one bean. (See FUMET, VELOUTÉ)

BRINJAUL (East Indian) Pickled *aubergine* (eggplant). Brinjaul is often prepared curried with rice or simply fried in fat.

BRIOCHE (French) This very light yeast cake is made in various shapes and sizes, one of which is similar to a ball with a small head on top. To make this *brioche,* two separate doughs are prepared: one is a mixture of flour, eggs, and butter; the other is just flour and yeast and water. Overnight, the yeast dough is allowed to rise; then the two doughs are joined and kneaded together. The dough is divided in two and, when ready for the oven, the larger ball of dough is placed into a buttered mold; the smaller piece of dough, the "head," is placed on top. The *brioche* is then baked in a medium oven.

Brioches may be served sweet or plain as an *hors d'oeuvre* or filled with chopped meats or poultry as an entrée; they may also be filled with fruit or even be made with grated cheese. A most practical pastry. (See BOHÉMIENNE, FOIE GRAS EN BRIOCHE, SAUCISSON CHAUD EN BROICHE)

BROCHET, QUENELLES DE (French) This is the culinary term for those exquisite pike dumplings that will transform a cook into a chef. The pike, skinned and boned, is first blended into a smooth purée into which egg whites and heavy cream are stirred. After seasoning with salt, white pepper, nutmeg, and cayenne pepper, the mixture is shaped with tablespoons into uniform ovals. The ovals are placed in a buttered flat pan half-filled with boiling fish stock; with the pan covered, they are simmered gently until done. The *quenelles* are then drained and served with a *sauce Vénitienne*. (See QUENELLE, VÉNITIENNE) COMPATIBLE WINES: A white wine, e.g., Montrachet, Meursault, Piesporter Goldtröpfchen, Graacher Himmelreich, Orvieto, Aigle, Pinot Chardonnay, Johannisberg.

BROCHETTE, EN (French) This term designates that method of cooking food over the fire "on a skewer." (See HUÎTRES EN BROCHETTE)

BRODO An Italian term for a simple "broth" or "bouillon." A beef broth would be a *brodo di manzo,* and a chicken broth, a *brodo di pollo.*

BROWN SAUCE (French) This basic sauce, the mother of all other brown sauces, is made from beef and veal bones, first well browned in the oven, then potted with boiling water and left to simmer. In yet another pot, chopped onions, carrots, and celery are dusted with flour and browned in fat; the vegetables are then added to the simmering bone stock. The stock, after being strained and flavored with garlic, peppercorns, a *bouquet garni,* and salt, is brought to a boil. This basic stock is kept on hand in the kitchen. It is periodically defatted and skimmed. Meat trimmings, bones, and leftovers are added from time to time. The entire stock pot is renewed once each month. (See BOUQUET GARNI)

BRUNEDE KARTOFLER (Danish) An unusual potato dish made by first browning sugar to a light caramel color. Small potatoes are cooked until tender, then drained, peeled, and placed in a heavy skillet sputtering with the caramelized sugar and butter. The potatoes are cooked until glazed and golden on all sides.

BRUNOISE (French) The word *brunoise* describes vegetables that are finely chopped or diced. Brunoise is a French district that is famous for its marvelous vegetables.

BRUNSWICK STEW (American) To some who live below the Mason-Dixon Line, Brunswick stew is a chicken dish, but the traditional version contains squirrel—plenty of grey squirrel. That little nut forager has been a ready dish for Southerners for many years.

There is a Brunswick county in Virginia and one in North Carolina, and both claim the stew as their very own creation. But one thing is certain: in the Deep South squirrels drop like manna from the sky for men and boys and their guns. To prepare the traditional stew, skinned and cleaned squirrels are cut into pieces, dredged in flour, and browned in bacon fat with plenty of chopped onions. The meat and onions are then transferred to another heavy pot, and with the addition of boiling water, tomato chunks, red and green peppers, parsley, thyme, and bay leaf, the entire mixture is simmered until the squirrel meat can be easily removed from the bone. Fresh lima beans, kernels of fresh corn, okra, chopped parsley, and Worcestershire sauce are added, and the whole is simmered until the vegetables are tender. (See WORCESTERSHIRE) COMPATIBLE WINES: A red wine, e.g., Nuits St. George, Dôle, Pinot Noir, Chianti, Cabernet Sauvignon.

BRUXELLES, CHOUX DE (Belgian) This term for the famous Brussels sprouts literally means "small cabbages of Belgium." Their flavor is best when they are small and firm. Usually, Brussels sprouts are steamed in a mixture of butter and very little water, after which they are flavored with nutmeg, salt, and pepper. After cooking, the sprouts should be crisp, really *al dente*. (See DENTE)

BUBLIKI (Russian) This is the name for the original bagel that was made famous in Russian song and rhyme and, when strung on strings, was sold at Russian fairs. A *bubliki* is said to bring luck. (See BAGEL)

BUL-KOGI (Korean) Often referred to as a Korean barbecue, *bul-kogi* is thinly sliced beef or chicken breast that is first marinated (a marinade of browned sesame seeds ground to a pulp and combined with sherry, onions, garlic, soy sauce, sesame oil, monosodium glutamate, and pepper) and then grilled over hot charcoal for half a minute on each side. It is served immediately. COMPATIBLE BEVERAGES: Beer, Sauterne, saké, tea.

BULLY BEEF (British) It was during the Second World War that the American G.I. was subjected at mealtime to a kind of creamed beef that he was served again and again until, at last, having had his fill of it, he baptized it "——— on a shingle." This described the despised beef to his satisfaction and allowed him to let off steam at the same time. Somewhat the same thing plagued the British soldier during the First World War. When the English Tommy found that he was destined to eat a salted, spiced, pressed beef, packed in cans, he euphemistically and with typical British reserve called it "bully beef." The word "bloody" is a no-no in polite English society. The more discreet claim is that the name was really derived from the French word *bouilli,* meaning "boiled." However, there is nothing boiled about the bloody bully beef. (See CORNED BEEF)

BÜNDNERFLEISCH (Swiss) A very special air-dried beef. (See GRISONS)

BURAKI (Polish) Beetroot. This is widely used as a vegetable, hot or cold, and is often served with sour cream. *Buraki* is also the base of many popular soups. (See BORSCH)

BURGHUL (Turkey) This cereal mainstay is also called *bulgur* or "cracked wheat," and because of its nutty flavor it is more popular than rice in this type of Middle Eastern cuisine.

BURGOO (American) Originally, in the early eighteenth century, *burgoo* was a rich porridge made from whatever could be amassed aboard the old sailing ships. It was later adopted by the hill people of Kentucky, who made it even thicker. The porridge included the meat of hens, squirrels, and pigs, as well as beef, lamb, and all root vegetables, herbs, and seasonings available. Gargantuan quantities—nearly one ton of beef, a quarter of a ton of chicken, a ton of potatoes—were served at great gatherings such as picnics, harvest festivals, church meetings, and hangings.

BURRIDA (Italian) A thick fish soup served in restaurants, made from various fish and seafood cooked in a fish stock flavored with white wine, onions, garlic, herbs, tomatoes, and often with saffron. (See CACCIUCCO, SAFFRON) COMPATIBLE WINES: A white wine, e.g., Soave, Sauvignon Blanc, Anjou, Riesling, Riquewihr.

BURRITOS (Mexican) These small *tortillas* are preheated then filled with various mixtures—hamburger meat, beans, tomatoes—and folded or rolled. (See TORTILLA) COMPATIBLE WINES: The wines served depend upon the fillings and the sauces used.

Burritos con Hamburguesa This culinary term means "little donkeys" and refers to flour *tortillas* that are filled with ground beef and chopped onions browned in oil, flavored with Tabasco sauce, garlic, tomatoes, and chili powder, and then rolled up to serve. (See TORTILLA) COMPATIBLE WINES: A red wine, e.g., Chianti, Rioja, Petit Sirah, Mercurey, Veltliner, Hermitage, Lambrusco, Nebbiolo.

BURRO, AL (Italian) This phrase refers to foods that are cooked or served with butter, especially *pasta* dishes. (See BEURRE, MEUNIÈRE, PASTA)

BUSHMAN'S RICE (Ugandan) White rice-like termites that are fried in butter and served with roast game dishes. In South Africa they are known as "white ants." They have a peculiarly sharp taste. Native Africans are not the only people with a taste for termites. The Japanese use them instead of nuts in chocolates. These chocolates make an interesting cocktail snack and provide an unusual topic for conversation.

BUTTERFLY SHRIMP The name "butterfly" comes from the form of the shrimp after it has been split almost all the way to the tail (the tail is left intact). Butterfly shrimp are dusted with flour and fried in a pan in hot oil. A tangy sauce composed of soy sauce, honey, salt, pepper, garlic, and brandy is served with the shrimp. COMPATIBLE BEVERAGES: Beer, ale, tea, saké, Sauterne.

CACALAUS (French) In this snail dish, which originated in Provence, cooked snails are perked up with a lively *aïoli* sauce or with a tomato sauce flavored with thyme, savory, and fennel. (See AÏOLI) COMPATIBLE WINES: A red wine, e.g., Mercurey, Chianti, Fleurie, Médoc, Valpolicella, Zinfandel, Côte Rôtie, St. Julien, Ruby Cabernet.

CACCIATORA, ALLA (Italian) This term, the counterpart of the French *à la chasseur,* means "hunter's style." The game or bird is browned in olive oil and then cooked in a sauce that incorporates tomatoes, scallions, mushrooms, onions, garlic, bay leaves, and red or white wine. One of the most popular is the *chicken cacciatora,* described below. The term *cacciatori* is not the plural of *cacciatora* but the name of a small Italian *salame.* (See CHASSEUR, SALAME)

Pollo alla Cacciatora This chicken dish always contains an abundance of mushrooms. The chicken is first disjointed, seasoned with salt and pepper, dusted with flour, and browned in olive oil. The chicken is then removed and white wine, vinegar, and chicken stock are added to the pot with chopped green peppers, onions, garlic, and tomatoes. After this mixture is brought to the boil, the chicken is returned to the pot and the contents are simmered until the chicken is tender. Just before serving, sliced mushrooms are added and cooked to blend with the other ingredients. COMPATIBLE WINES: A red wine, e.g., Beaujolais, Valpolicella, Zinfandel, Margaux, Médoc, Barolo, Nebbiolo, Santenay.

CACCIUCCO (Italian) A fish soup. The fish are cooked in red wine flavored with tomatoes and served garnished with garlic-flavored croutons. (See BOUILLABAISSE, BOURRIDE, BURRIDA) COMPATIBLE WINES: A red wine, e.g., Lambrusco, Valpolicella, Beaujolais, Zinfandel, Fleurie.

CAESAR SALAD This popular salad, said to be the creation of a chef named Cesar Cardini from Tijuana, Mexico, came into being during the Prohibition Era. Its elaborate preparation is usually done tableside in a restaurant. First, a large wooden salad bowl is rubbed with a clove of garlic. The addition of anchovy purée is optional. Then lemon juice is added together with black pepper, salt, mustard, olive oil and, finally, a shirred egg. Crisp romaine lettuce leaves are tossed in the mixture with fried bread croutons, and the salad is served with a sprinkling of grated Parmesan cheese.

CAJUN This word refers to those descendants of the former French colony in East Canada, called Acadia, who having been exiled by the British in 1755, settled in the region of St. Martinville in southern Louisiana, where they maintain a separate folk culture. It differs from the more common term *Créole:* the Cajuns did not come directly from France but from French ancestors in Canada. (See CRÉOLE)

Cajun Hachis A popular hash made from any meat that is cooked and then cut up and mixed with chopped hard-boiled eggs, sliced and sautéed green peppers, plus peeled and cooked new potatoes. Heavy cream is poured over the mixture, which is baked until quite firm. COMPATIBLE WINES: A red wine, e.g., Beaujolais, Lambrusco, Côte Rôtie, Zinfandel.

CALABAZA A type of squash native to the islands of the West Indies, where it is also referred to as "green pumpkin." It is quite large, has yellow flesh, and is sold by the slice or the wedge. It is added to soups or is served as a vegetable.

CALALOU (West Indian) This stew, popular in Créole cookery, originated in Martinique. The stew is composed of cooked pieces of pork, veal, beef, or fowl, which are simmered in a beef broth with fresh corn scraped from the cob. Minced garlic, peppers, okra, chopped celery, and a pinch of filé powder are added for flavor. *Calalou* is garnished with sliced cucumbers and parsley and served with white rice. (See FILÉ, OKRA) COMPATIBLE WINES: Either a red or a white wine would be appropriate, depending upon the kind of meat used in the dish.

CALAMAI/CALAMARI (Italian) Squid.

Calamai con Pomodoro Squid with tomatoes. When the aroma from the garlic cloves that have been simmering in olive oil has permeated the room, cut-up squid is added to the pot along with oregano, pepper, and sherry wine. After cooking for some 20 minutes, tomatoes and parsley are added, and the lot is cooked a few minutes more.

Chinese Squid For 24 hours the Chinese marinate the cut-up squid in a mixture of gin and ginger. Celery, cabbage, scallions, and mushrooms are sautéed in hot oil, fish stock is added, and the whole is cooked until the flavors meld. In a fresh pan the squid is sautéed in very hot oil. As soon as the squid is seized by the intense heat, the cooked vegetable mixture is added. Soy sauce and starch are added to the pan and heated until the mixture thickens. COMPATIBLE BEVERAGES: Beer, ale, saké.

Squid alla Catalana (Italian) Chopped onions, garlic, and parsley are cooked in olive oil until golden, then the cut-up squid and tomatoes are added. Pepper, saffron, cinnamon, bay leaf, and red wine complete the sauce, and the whole is simmered for two hours. The dish is then seasoned and served piping hot. COMPATIBLE WINES: A red wine, e.g., Valpolicella, Nebbiolo, Beaujolais, Veltliner, Zinfandel, Egri Bikaver.

CALDO VERDE (Portuguese) This popular soup, literally meaning "green soup," was so named because of the chopped green cabbage or kale from which it is made. Potatoes are added to thicken.

CALF'S HEAD VINAIGRETTE This calf's head preparation is popular throughout all European countries. The calf's head is thoroughly cleaned in several changes of water and then boiled in water with salt, pepper, chopped onions, lemon juice, and a *bouquet garni* until the meat becomes so tender that it nearly falls from the bone. The meat is removed from the bone, cut into pieces, with the exception of the tongue, and arranged in a mold with the tongue in the center. The stock is skimmed of all fat, heated, and then poured around the meat. It is set to cool, and when jelled, the dish is garnished with chopped hard-boiled eggs, gherkins, and capers. It is served with a *sauce vinaigrette*. (See BOUQUET GARNI, SÜLZE, VINAIGRETTE) COMPATIBLE BEVERAGES: Beer, ale, stout.

CALZONE (Italian) In the vernacular, this term means "a trouser leg," but in culinary parlance it refers to a crescent-shaped turnover that is stuffed with cheese, ham, salami, herbs, and spices and baked in the oven. COMPATIBLE WINES: A red wine, e.g., Chianti, Barbaresco, Lambrusco, Valpolicella, Beaujolais, Fleurie, Zinfandel, Petit Sirah, Nebbiolo.

CAMBACÉRÈS Although Jean-Jacques, the Duc de Cambacérès, held many high posts in the government of France (he was appointed Second Consul as well as Arch-Chancellor by Napoleon Bonaparte), this man is better known as one of the great epicures of all time. Cambacérès made himself personally responsible for the menus of his banquets and presided closely over the preparation of the food served. Anyone who arrived late to one of his great dinners was left outside and not invited a second time. He was adamant about maintaining complete silence while dining and expected his guests to conform to his idiosyncracy.

The respect Cambacérès held for good food and a fine table has done more to preserve his name for posterity than any of his political achievements. The proof lies in a soup and in two garnishes that bear his name.

Potage Cambacérès This soup is a delicious melding of two contrasting elements: a purée of crayfish and a cream of game.

Garnish for Fish This garnish is composed of a white wine sauce flavored with crayfish stock, crayfish tails, chopped mushrooms, and truffles. It is often served with salmon trout, and speaking of fish, Cambacérès once offered his guests two whole sturgeons, each weighing well over 300 pounds.

Garnish for Meat Dishes This garnish consists of a *sauce Madère* flavored with sliced black truffles, sliced mushrooms, and pitted olives.

CAMERONES, ARROZ CON (Mexican) To make this white rice and shrimp preparation, milk is added to a *roux,* which is then flavored with salt, pepper, and curry. Grated onions, chopped mushrooms, and cooked and peeled tiny shrimp are then added, stirred once, and removed from the fire. With a squeeze of lime juice, the shrimp sauce is ready to be served over boiled white rice. (See ROUX) COMPATIBLE WINES: A white wine, e.g., Sauterne, Anjou, saké, Chenin Blanc, Gewürztraminer, Graves, Aigle.

CANAPÉS In a cozy French living room or salon, a canapé would be the sofa or divan; but when speaking gastronomic French, canapés are delightful bite-sized tidbits—*hors d'oeuvre*—featuring anything from caviar and *foie gras* to delicacies made from fish, meat, or fowl. The canapé base may be crusty toast, a *barquette,* or a decorative cut of dark bread such as rye, sour dough, or pumpernickel. The Chinese originated the idea of serving appetizing tidbits before dinner, the Russians enlarged upon it, but the French refined it. (See BAR-QUETTES, FOIE GRAS, HORS D'OEUVRE)

CANARD À LA PRESSE (French) Preparing a *canard* (young duckling) *à la presse* entails first baking the duck briefly, then removing the legs and slicing the breast thinly. The breast slices are kept warm in a spiced red wine while the legs are grilled and the carcass put into a special duck press. The juices and blood that are forced out by the press are laced with brandy and spiced with cloves and mustard. After being heated, the liquid is poured over the grilled legs and breast slices to serve.

Parisian restaurants adopted the method of preparing *canard à la presse* from French peasants, who in their efforts to squeeze, pound, and twist as much juice as possible from their skinny ducks, finally resorted to smashing the carcasses with rocks. COMPATIBLE WINES: A red wine, e.g., Talbot, Valpolicella, Pommard, Côte Rôtie, Pomerol, Beaune, Châteauneuf-du-Pape, Cabernet Sauvignon, Pinot Noir.

CANARD À L'ORANGE (French) Roast duckling glazed with orange sauce. (See BIGARADE)

CANARD D'INDE (French-Créole) The name given to those ducks that were brought to Louisiana from Mexico and Brazil and were designated "Indian ducks."

CANDIED SWEET POTATO (American) This specialty, a delicious complement to ham steak dinners and southern-fried chicken, is prepared by boiling sweet potatoes in salted water, then removing the skins, slicing them, and arranging the slices in the bottom of a well-oiled, shallow earthenware dish. Meanwhile, brown sugar, water, and butter are cooked together, and after being flavored with lemon juice, the liquid is poured over the potato slices. The dish is baked in a medium oven and frequently basted with the caramelizing sauce. (See SOUTHERN-FRIED CHICKEN, SWEET POTATO)

CANETON À L'ORANGE (French) A young duckling braised and served with an orange-flavored sauce. (See BIGARADE, CANARD À L'ORANGE)

CANNELLONI (Italian) Literally, "little tubes." A good noodle dough—

made from flour, eggs, and water—is cut into wide strips and then cooked in boiling salted water. These cooked pieces of dough are chilled in cold water, drained, then cut into squares. Meanwhile, a meat filling composed of ground beef or pork, or a mixture of the two, is combined with chopped tomatoes, finely chopped onions, salt, oregano, paprika, and thyme and cooked in a pan. (Note that other fillings may be used as well. A mixture of chopped spinach, ricotta cheese, and egg yolks is a popular variation.) The squares of dough are covered with the filling of choice, rolled up pancake-style, and arranged side by side in a buttered casserole. Covered with a flour-thickened milk sauce and grated cheese, the *cannelloni* are baked until golden brown. (See PASTA) COMPATIBLE WINES: A red wine, e.g., Chianti, Bardolino, Beaujolais, Zinfandel.

CANNOLI (Italian) These Sicilian pastries are made from a rolled-out dough that is cut into segments, wrapped around small metal tubes, and deep-fried. When brown and crunchy, the pastries are filled with pastry cream or cheese (most often ricotta) flavored with chocolate bits, candied fruits, nuts, or liqueurs. *Cannoli* are not to be confused with *cannelloni,* which is a *pasta* dish served with a main course. (See CANNELLONI, PASTA)

CANTAL, SOUPE DE (French) An onion soup named for the hard Cantal cheese, produced in the mountainous region of Auvergne. This soup is so thick and rich with the cheese, chopped onions, and bread with which it is made that when a soup spoon is inserted in the center of a bowlful, the spoon will stand upright.

CANTONESE CUISINE This is probably the best known of all of China's regional cuisines because so many of the Cantonese people emigrated to Western countries. Cantonese cooking relies heavily on stir-fried dishes, the imaginative use of color, and the overall use of soy, *hoisin,* and plum sauces. The well-known egg roll and egg *foo yung* are native to Canton, which has the least greasy of all the regional cooking styles of China. (See CHINESE CUISINE, HOISIN, SOY SAUCE)

CAPERS The greenish flower buds of the caper bush, a shrub related to the mustard family. The bush is cultivated along the shores of the Mediterranean. Capers are pickled and widely used in sauces and as a garnish.

CAPILOTADE (French) A *ragoût* (stew) made from reheated poultry. A *ragoût* of meat is called *salmigondis.* (See RAGOÛT, SALMIGONDIS)
   Poulet en Capilotade Any cooked chicken—boiled, braised, or roasted—can be used to prepare this chicken hash. The meat is cut from the bone in slices and is simmered in a sauce, such as *Provençale, Portuguese, chasseur,* or *Italienne.* (See CHASSEUR, ITALIENNE, PORTUGUESE, PROVENÇALE) COMPATIBLE WINES: A red wine, e.g., Beaujolais, Santenay, Valpolicella, Zinfandel, Nebbiolo.

CAPON This is the best-eating, best-tasting chicken there is: a castrated young cock that is specially fed for the eight months it is allowed to live. The capon was first transformed from a wild Lothario to a placid, plump eunuch of the chicken yard by an imaginative surgeon of Old Rome. This gelded rooster is plump with well-marbled fat that is evenly distributed throughout the whole bird, rather than concentrated in certain sections of the body. A capon, well worth the roasting, should weigh from six to ten pounds. COMPATIBLE WINES: A red wine, e.g., Médoc, Beaujolais, Zinfandel, Mercurey, Volnay, Egri Bikaver, Pinot Noir.

CAPPELLETTI (Italian) See PASTA

CAPPUCCINO See ESPRESSO

CAPSICUM A genus of tropical herbs and shrubs of the nightshade family. Under this category one finds various kinds of peppers: bell peppers, which are red, yellow, or green; long green and red chili peppers; and of course the red peppers from which comes the famous Hungarian powdered capsicum known as "paprika."

There are nearly 200 varieties of the capsicum plant. The sweet peppers are served raw in salads or cooked and stuffed with any number of ingredients, including rice, onions, garlic, herbs, and/or finely chopped poultry and meat. Sweet peppers are also used to enhance the flavor of stews and casseroles. (See CHILI, PAPRIKA)

CARAMEL This is the culinary term given to burnt sugar. Caramel has many culinary uses. It can be used in the preparation of the liqueur-sauce that is used to coat *crêpes Suzette* or cooked fruits. Caramel is also used to coat puddings and custards, or it can be transformed into a firm but elastic candy. (See CRÈME CARAMEL, CRÈME BRÛLÉE, SUZETTE)

CARAWAY Caraway is an herb grown in Asia Minor, Europe, and in some parts of the United States. The herb has three parts: the leaves, the seeds, and the roots, each having its own distinctive flavor. The seeds are used to flavor rye breads, sauerkrauts, and stews. The leaves taste somewhat like the seeds, but the roots are sweet and delicate and can be eaten boiled as a vegetable. The roots are served buttered, just like parsnips. (See SAUERKRAUT)

CARBONARA, SPAGHETTI ALLA (Italian) A *pasta* dish featuring bacon or ham. To the meat, which has been cut into thin strips and cooked in butter, beaten eggs are added. Before the eggs begin to set, the mixture is poured onto the cooked *spaghetti* and folded in. To serve, grated Parmesan cheese is sprinkled over all. (See PASTA) COMPATIBLE WINES: A red wine, e.g. Chianti, Barolo, Beaujolais, Petit Sirah, Bardolino, Lambrusco, Zinfandel, Mercurey, Veltliner.

CARBONNADE À LA FLAMANDE (Flemish) Originally, the name was given to meat that was grilled over an open fire. Later it was used to denote various meat stews such as this Flemish beef dish. Cut into thin slices, the beef is seasoned. Together with chopped onions, garlic, thyme, parsley, and bay leaf, the beef is briefly sautéed in lard until brown. Brown sugar, vinegar, and flour are cooked into a *roux* to which beer and brown stock are added. This is strained over the beef and onions and baked in the oven. The dish is always served with boiled potatoes. (See ROUX) COMPATIBLE WINES: Beaujolais, Hermitage, Dôle, Chianti, but far better would be the same beer with which the *carbonnade* was cooked.

CARDAMOM Orientals refer to this aromatic condiment as "the seeds of paradise." In ancient Rome and Greece the seeds were used in the manufacture of perfumes, and they are said to have been known in Babylon and Ur 700 years before the time of Christ. During the Dark Ages, a man's wealth was determined to some degree by the amount and kind of spices he possessed. A pound of ginger would buy a sheep; a sack of cardamom or pepper was often worth a man's life. Cultivated in India, Ceylon, and Mexico, cardamom is a member of the ginger family. It is valued medicinally both as an antiseptic and as a stimulant, and in the kitchen cardamom is used to make Indian curries as well as to flavor tea, coffee, and cakes. It is also used in the production of liqueur.

CARDINAL, LOBSTER (French) The word "cardinal" describes the color of this dish, which resembles the red color of the robes worn by a cardinal of the Catholic Church. The dish consists of cubed cooked lobster meat that is mixed with a *sauce Américaine*, spooned back into the lobster shells, sprinkled with breadcrumbs, and browned in the grill. (See AMÉRICAINE) COMPATIBLE WINES: A white wine, e.g., Pouilly-Fumé, Sancerre, Montrachet, Riesling, Chenin Blanc.

CARDINAL, SAUCE (French) This lobster sauce has either a *sauce Béchamel* or a *velouté* as its base. This is added to a white fish stock and is then bound with lobster-butter, which gives the sauce its cardinal-red color. It is then flavored with truffle essence, anchovies, and tarragon. The sauce is served with fish. (See BÉCHAMEL, VELOUTÉ)

CARDINAL, SOLE (French) The preparation of this dish involves stuffing the sole with a forcemeat composed of pike mixed with lobster-butter. The stuffed fish is poached in a mixture of white wine and fish stock and is then served coated with a *sauce cardinal* and garnished with slices of lobster meat. The dish is named for the cardinal red color of the sauce. COMPATIBLE WINES: A white wine, e.g., Meursault, Montrachet, Pinot Chardonnay, Bernkasteler Doktor.

CARÊME, MARIE-ANTOINE Carême was the founder of *La Grande Cuisine Française,* the classic French style of cooking that is admired today throughout the world. Along with the French Revolution came Carême's great culinary revolution. This artist, writer, and extraordinarily gifted chef, one of the great innovators of the kitchen, led

French gastronomy into the nineteenth century and made the French culinary art sovereign throughout Europe.

Carême's father, having sired twenty-five children, had to get them out of the house as soon as possible. Marie-Antoine was no exception, so at the age of eight he was ousted from his home and was forced to work in a kitchen as a general runabout and pot washer. Yet this pot washer, in his time, fed the crowned heads of Europe and was on intimate terms with statesmen and philosphers. Carême was first employed by the famous pastry chef Bailly, for whom he created huge and intricate *pièces montées* of entire sections of Paris and famous monuments. Carême's works of art were made out of different doughs, preserved fruits, creams, and sherbets. While working for Bailly, he learned how to read, but only so he would be able to read every cookbook he could lay his hands on.

Carême did not always agree with what he read, and he decided that one day he would write the definitive book on French cuisine. A great egotist, he succeeded through those gifts that God gave him, but also in great part through his unflagging tenacity and dedication to perfection. Carême was the first to cut the theretofore huge menus down to merely soup, roast with vegetables, poached fish, roasted fowl, salad, pastries, and dessert. Carême began this menu simplification, but it was one of his great admirers who, at the end of the nineteenth century, actually brought the classic menu into usage. His name was Escoffier.

Carême's name lives on in the books he wrote and in the extraordinary dishes he created. He is thought to have been the greatest chef of all time, and by all accounts he was one of the most temperamental. But when kings and princes and noted statesmen were prompted to fight one another to keep Carême in their kitchens, who could care about his temper? As he lay dying, he sat upright in bed and gave one last order: "Shake the casserole." (See ESCOFFIER, TALLEYRAND)

Consommé Carême This double consommé (reduced consommé) made with chicken is garnished with sliced carrots, turnips, a *chiffonade* of lettuce, and asparagus tips. (See CHIFFONADE, CONSOMMÉ)

Tournedos Carême These small fillets of beef are sautéed in butter and served garnished with jumbo olives stuffed with finely chopped ham plus a *sauce Madère* and potato *croquettes*. (See CROQUETTES, MADÈRE) COMPATIBLE WINES: A red wine, e.g., Richebourg, Fixin, Cheval Blanc, Chambertin, Clos de la Roche, Aloxe-Corton, Zinfandel, Nuits St. Georges, Dôle.

CARIBBEAN PEPPERPOT (West Indian) This ancient Amerindian meat stew, which originated in Guyana, is prepared widely in the West Indies today. The main flavoring ingredient is the *cassareep,* which is flavored with salt, brown sugar, cinnamon, and cloves, and reduced through cooking to a thick brown syrup. The flavored *cassareep* works as a tenderizer and preservative, and as more meat is usually added to the stew pot each day, legend says that the preservative quality of the _cassareep_ will keep the same pot of food edible from one generation to the next.

The pepperpot is composed of pieces of chicken, cubed pork, salt beef, quartered calf's foot, segmented oxtail, hot peppers wrapped in cheesecloth, onions, salt, pepper, and the necessary flavored _cassareep_. The contents are covered with water and simmered until the meat is tender and the liquid quite thick. The hot peppers are removed, and the stew is served with boiled white rice. (See CASSAREEP) COMPATIBLE BEVERAGES: Beer, ale, tea.

CARMÉLITE, À LA (French) This culinary term honors the religious order of the Carmélites. These holy mendicant friars produced not only works of mystical theology but also many nonmeat dishes.

Crème à la Carmélite This cream of whiting soup is enriched with egg yolks and cream.

Oeufs à la Carmélite Eggs are hard-boiled, split, and the yolks removed. Fried chopped shallots, parsley, and sorrel are mashed into the egg yolks, stuffed into the white halves of the eggs, and baked.

Sauce Carmélite A _sauce Bourguignonne_ combined with finely chopped ham and onions—proof that even a mendicant monk sins a little (by using meat), but we will forgive him. (See BOURGUIGNONNE)

CARROZZA, MOZZARELLA IN (Italian) This imaginative egg creation rolls almost musically on the tongue when spoken in pure _Toscana_. The English translation, "cheese in a carriage," somehow does not have the same ring. However, the taste is the same when small squares of white bread, holding soft _mozzarella_ cheese between their slices, are dipped in an egg batter and deep-fried until golden brown. COMPATIBLE WINES: A red wine, e.g., Chianti, Barbaresco, Cahors, Savigny, Petit Sirah.

CARTOCCIO, AL (Italian) When a chef describes a dish as being prepared _al cartoccio,_ he is referring to a method of baking food wrapped in parchment.

Pesce al Cartoccio Any white-fleshed fish is flavored with a sautéed vegetable mixture, moistened with butter or oil, and baked in a special parchment. The French call food baked in this manner _en papillote_. (See PAPILLOTE) COMPATIBLE WINES: A white wine, e.g., Orvieto, Corton-Charlemagne, Verdicchio, Pinot Chardonnay.

CARUSO, SPAGHETTI (Italian) While the great tenor Enrico Caruso sang at the Metropolitan Opera in New York City, he managed to spread his patronage among various Italian restaurants within the city. One such honored him with a tomato-and-meat sauce that was served over mounds of steaming spaghetti and topped with sautéed chicken livers and mushrooms and grated Parmesan cheese. (See

PASTA, SPAGHETTI) COMPATIBLE WINES: A red wine, e.g., Chianti, Barolo, Valpolicella, Beaujolais, Ruby Cabernet.

CASA, DELLA (Italian) A restaurant term meaning "of the house," a special food preparation as done by that particular restaurant. *Alla casalinga* is an alternate term with the same meaning. (See HAUSART, NACH; MAISON, À LA)

CASANOVA, SAUCE (French) This sauce was named after one of the greatest lovers of all history because it contains a large proportion of eggs, which many claim to have aphrodisiac power. The sauce consists of a grated black truffle, chopped shallots, and the sieved whites and yolks of hard-boiled eggs—all of which are added to a *sauce Mayonnaise*. The sauce is served cold with cold cuts and cold fish dishes. (See APHRODISIACS, MAYONNAISE)

CASINO, OYSTERS Originally prepared at a casino situated in the bikini littoral of the Hamptons, on Long Island, New York, the oysters are placed on beds of rock salt in an ovenproof dish (besides being a good conductor of heat, the rock salt holds the oysters in their shells while cooking). The oysters are then covered with a blended mixture of butter, finely chopped shallots, green peppers, and parsley plus a seasoning of salt, lemon juice, and pepper. Finally, they are topped with strips of half-cooked bacon and broiled until the bacon turns brown and crisp. The oysters usually come to the table in the same ovenproof dish with an underliner. Clams casino are made in the same manner. COMPATIBLE WINES: A white wine, e.g., Meursault, Corton, Montrachet, Piesporter Goldtröpfchen, Aigle, Pinot Chardonnay, Soave, Quincy, Muscadet.

CASSAREEP (West Indian) The name given by the people of Guyana, Trinidad, Barbados, and other Caribbean islands to the boiled-down juice of the grated cassava root. The Caribbean pepperpot is one of the dishes that gets its distinctive flavor from the *cassareep* used in its preparation. (See CARIBBEAN PEPPERPOT, CASSAVA)

CASSATA Many ordinary Italian ice cream cakes are known by this name, but *cassata* ia also the name of a Sicilian cream cake composed of layers of sponge cake filled with a sweet riccota cheese filling.

Cassata Gelata A dessert made from various flavors of ice cream mixed with candied fruits and nuts. This is shaped like a dome and served in wedges.

CASSAVA This tropical vegetable—also called manioc, yucca, and farine—is native to the West Indies, South America, and the State of Florida in the United States. Cassava has a long tuberous root, a brown hairy skin, and its edible starchy flesh is white and rather hard. Tapioca and the unusual *cassareep* are both made from cassava. Cakes and breads are made from the dried meal of the grated root. Only the sweet cassava is available in the United States; the bitter variety is poisonous until it is cooked. (See CASSAREEP, MANIOC)

CASSIA The cassia tree is closely related to the cinnamon tree. Unlike cinnamon, however, which is obtained exclusively from the bark of the tree, the more pungent cassia is found in the leaves as well as the bark of the tree. The bark of the cassia tree is called "Chinese cinnamon." Cassia leaves are one of the main ingredients in the preparation of a fine Indian curry, and some species of the cassia are used medicinally as a cathartic. (See CURRY, KARI)

CASSOULET (French) Literally, "casserole." The name of a dried white-bean dish made with chunks of pork, mutton, goose, partridge, and sausages plus onions, white wine, garlic, goose fat, beef bouillon, and parsley. The best *cassoulet,* it is said, is baked in an earthenware vessel. This dish originated in France, in Languedoc at the foot of the Pyrenees. Although every chef feels free to create his very own *cassoulet,* there are three really great ones, which are described below. The common ingredient in every version of the revered *cassoulet*—and perhaps the most important—has always been time.

Cassoulet Castelnaudary This version uses pork rind, salted goose, small pork sausages, and beans.

Cassoulet Carcassonnais This version includes pork rind, pork, preserved goose, leg of lamb, partridge, country sausages, and beans.

Cassoulet Toulousaine Pork rind, pork, Toulouse sausages, and a large amount of preserved goose and beans are ingredients in this casserole.

COMPATIBLE WINES: A red wine, e.g., Margaux, Calon-Ségur, Pontet-Canet, Cabernet Sauvignon, Valpolicella, Zinfandel, Châteauneauf-du-Pape.

CASTAGNACCIO (Italian) This aromatic flat cake made from chestnut flour *(farina dolce)* comes from Florence. Flavored with rosemary, pignoli or walnuts, sugar, and milk, it is usually served with mounds of ricotta cheese. The name *castagnaccio* comes from the Italian word for chestnut, *castagna.*

CASTRATO (Italian) In culinary parlance the term refers to a castrated sheep, the meat of which is called "mutton." (See BRACIOLI DI CASTRATO)

CATSUP See KETCHUP

CAUL FAT The netlike web of fat that holds the pig's internal organs together. Caul fat is used in the kitchen to envelop pieces of lean meat. This does away with the basting chore: the caul bastes the meat continually and evenly as it cooks. (See CRÉPINETTES)

CÉDRAT (French) The citron, a thick-skinned yellow fruit resembling a lemon or lime but larger and less acidic. It grows in countries along the Mediterranean Sea. The *cédrat* has quite an aroma and is popularly used by pastry chefs and confectioners. (See CITRON)

CELERY CABBAGE Of all Chinese cabbages, this is the most delicate. It has an elongated head, wide green leaves, and ruffled edges. Known in Chinese as *pa-tsai.*

CÉLESTINE (French) See CONSOMMÉ

CELO RICE An old Persian rice preparation. *Patna* rice is washed thoroughly then placed in a flat dish with water just to cover; layers of white linen are placed over the top. Rock salt, placed on top of the linen, keeps it in place and also flavors the rice. After a few hours, the rice is washed again, blanched, and drained. The rice is then layered in a heavy pot with dabs of butter dotted over each layer. It is again covered with a linen cloth, and heat is applied from both the bottom and the top of the pot with charcoal embers. The rice rises, white and fragrant, doubled in size, ready to be served. Kingly, complicated, and good it is, but as outdated as Persia itself. Today, East Indian chefs use linen cloths to make a fluffy rice. (SEE PATNA)

CÈPE (French) A type of mushroom. (See BORDELAISE, CHAMPIGNONS)

CERVELAS (French) Because at one time this sausage was made with pig's brains, its name still refers to the word *cervelles,* French for "brains." Today, this short, fat, and richly garlic-flavored sausage is made with finely ground pork and pork fat.

CERVELAT (German) The name of this sausage is based on the French term for a somewhat similar pork sausage called *cervelas.* This highly spiced and smoked German *Wurst,* meant to be spread, is made from a fine paste of pork and beef fillets. The consumer must be wary of the practice of the budget-minded butcher who is sometimes apt to gather up all the bits and pieces of meat after a day's work and simply toss them into the *Cervelat* pile, to be made into sausage the following day.

Thüringer is a type of fresh *Cervelat. Holstein Cervelat* is a horse-shoe-shaped sausage made with coarsely chopped meat. *Goteberg,* a Swedish *Cervelat,* is made with coarsely chopped meat and is salty and smoked. (See CERVELAS, WURST)

CERVELLES (French) This term for "brains" can refer to the beef, calf, pork, or lamb variety. Brains are traditionally prepared by first soaking them in water then removing the membranes and tissues; when clean, the brains are simmered in a barely quivering *court-bouillon.* Brains can be served with brown butter or with *les sauces Mornay, financière, Madère, tomate,* or *piquante.* (See COURT-BOUILLON, FINANCIÈRE, MADÈRE, MORNAY, PIQUANTE, TOMATO) COMPATIBLE WINES: A white wine, e.g., Sancerre, Muscadet, Soave, Orvieto, Pinot Chardonnay, Anjou. Much depends upon the type of sauce used.

Cervelles aux Champignons For this dish, sliced mushrooms are cooked in butter. The soaked, cleaned, and blanched brains are added and cooked until brown and then removed. To serve, a mixture of cooked butter, chopped onions, and vinegar is poured over the brains. COMPATIBLE WINES: A white wine, e.g., Quincy, Muscadet, Chablis, Soave.

CEVICHE See SEVICHE

CHEVIZ SALÇASI (Turkish) A creamy walnut sauce made from chopped walnuts, breadcrumbs, garlic, salt, pepper, and paprika—all ground to a purée and mixed with a rich chicken stock. This is delightful with cold chicken or cold vegetable dishes.

CHAH GWA (Chinese) Tea melon. Westerners would consider this to be nothing more than a plain cucumber, which it resembles. The melon is pickled in a marinade of wine, spices, ginger, and honey and is used to garnish fish dishes as well as dishes of steamed beef and pork.

CHALLAH (Jewish) This bread, traditionally eaten at festive occasions, is made with yeast, sugar, saffron, eggs, shortening, salt, flour, and poppy seeds. The dough is left to rise twice, then it can be shaped into a loaf or buns, but most often the dough is separated into three parts, rolled into long, round strips, and braided. After rising again, it is baked. The *challah* of today most likely has its origin in the shewbreads mentioned in the Bible (Exodus 25:30).

CHAMBORD (French) The name comes from the famous Renaissance *château* of the same name, remembered not only for its unique stairway, built in separate overlapping spirals so that persons mounting would not meet those descending, but also because it was a great favorite of Louis XIV, Stanislaus I of Poland, and lastly the Duke of Bordeaux, to whom it was presented in 1821.

Sauce Chambord A mixture of red wine, fish stock, a *sauce demi-glace* and herbs that is reduced and strained to produce a regal sauce. Before serving with fish, the sauce is refined by whipping in a quantity of anchovy-butter. (See BEURRES COMPOSÉS, COMPOUND BUTTER, DEMI-GLACE)

Garniture Chambord A rich garnish consisting of fish *quenelles,* mushrooms, roe, shrimp, slices of truffle, *fleurons,* and the *sauce Chambord.* (See FLEURONS, QUENELLES)

Salmon Chambord A large salmon steak *(darne)* is carefully braised in a fish *fumet* made with either white or red wine. The salmon steak is drained, glazed in the oven, and finally served surrounded with the rich *Chambord garniture.* (See DARNE, FUMET) COMPATIBLE WINES: If a red wine is chosen, then a Gevry Chambertin, Chambolle Musigny, Bonnes Mares, Corton, Dôle; if white is preferred, then a Montrachet, Corton-Charlemagne, Meursault, or Bernkasteler Doktor.

CHAMBRER (French) The natural process of allowing a red wine's temperature to rise to that of the room *(chambre)* where it is being served. This must be effected slowly and naturally. Immersing the wine bottle in hot water to raise the tempertaure will ruin the aromatic bouquet of the wine. Any living thing that is subjected to extreme changes of temperature can die, and wine is no exception.

CHAMPENOISE, CHICKEN À LA The French take a small, plump chicken, stuff it *à la Champenoise,* cover it with larding bacon, then truss it. Chopped onions, carrots, and shallots are sautéed with bacon in a large pan. In a heavy skillet, the chicken is then browned well on all sides. Then, placed on top of the chopped vegetables with a calf's foot, chopped celery, and a half bottle of Champagne, the chicken is cooked covered over moderate heat until done. COMPATIBLE WINES: A red wine, e.g., Margaux, Figeac, Haut Brion, Côte Rôtie, Valpolicella, Zinfandel, Moulin-à-Vent, Champagne.

Champenoise, La Farce A speciality of the Champagne Province in France: a veritable Champagne stuffing. After browning chopped onions, garlic, and shallots, they are covered with Champagne and simmered slowly until the liquid is reduced to half. Pork sausage meat and chicken livers are ground and pounded together then passed through a sieve and added to the Champagne mixture. Salt, pepper, parsley, and spices are added as seasonings. An exquisite stuffing for chicken.

CHAMPIGNONS (French) Mushrooms. Looking back into history, we find that about 400 B.C. Hippocrates makes mention of the delicacy of the mushrooms that were so avidly consumed by the wealthy in Greece. The Greeks found this strange, wrinkled fungus in Egypt, where it was thought to possess nearly divine, magical powers because it had appeared in the land miraculously, overnight. But the Greeks refrained from worshiping the mushroom; being more practical, they ate it.

For the inexperienced, it is wise not to gather mushrooms indiscriminately but to rely on those varieties that are sold in vegetable markets or preserved in cans. Many of the innocent-looking mushrooms found in forests can be deadly. In Ancient Rome the easiest way to get rid of an enemy was to invite him to a disguised mushroom meal. In fact, the *amanita* family of mushrooms was and is as deadly as the infamous Borgia family. Like Lucrezia, these mushrooms are attractive and beautiful to behold, but they are also extremely poisonous. The poor can take heart that throughout history many of the rich and the aristocracy have succumbed to the poison of the mushroom: the list is endless, royal and sometimes amoral. Many debauched Roman emperors, Tiberius and Claudius included, were dispatched with the lowly, insignificant mushroom. In 1825, Alexander I of Russia died quite suddenly after eating poisonous mushrooms; even Pope Clement II and King Charles V of France fell victim to the fatal fungus.

Cèpe is the French term for the edible agaric mushroom, called *Steinpilz* in German. Together with the morel, the chanterelle, and the *funghi,* the *cèpe* is one of the tastiest and most popular of mushrooms. The chanterelle, called *girolle* by the French, is a cup-shaped mushroom with gills of deep yellow. It has a very short, stubby stalk. Of all mushroom varieties, it is the most easily identified. The chanterelle is imported in cans or in dried form. *Morilles* is the French word for "morels," a very expensive mushroom, much sought after for its fine flavor.

Gratin de Cèpes Farcis (French) To prepare this mushroom dish, mushroom caps are steamed in a heavy skillet and then dried in a warm oven. They are then filled with a stuffing composed of finely chopped mushroom stems, chopped pheasant or chicken meat, chicken livers, bacon, walnuts, and tarragon, all bound with breadcrumbs and egg yolks and flavored with a pinch of curry. The stuffed mushrooms are then brushed with butter, sprinkled with fresh breadcrumbs and grated Parmesan cheese, and baked.

Funghi In Umido (Italian) The chanterelle is used in this dish. First, garlic cloves and chopped mint are simmered in a pan and removed. Sliced mushrooms and bouillon are then added. The addition of plum tomatoes, lemon juice, and a dash of freshly ground black pepper produces a finished sauce for *polenta*. (See POLENTA)

Escalopes de Veau aux Morilles à la Crème For this meat preparation, veal cutlets are salted, peppered, and then dusted with flour and sautéed in butter over high heat. After the heat is reduced, the morels, white wine, heavy cream, and brown sauce are added, and the whole is simmered and served with a sprinkling of parsley. (See BROWN SAUCE) COMPATIBLE WINES: A white wine, e.g., Orvieto, Vouvray, Meursault, Schloss Vollrads, Aigle, Sauvignon Blanc.

CHAMPIGNONS, SAUCE AU (French) For this mushroom sauce, mushrooms are cooked in a mixture of boiling water, salt, and lemon juice. The mushroom caps are set aside while the cooking liquid is reduced to less than half. With the addition of a *sauce demi-glace,* the mushroom sauce is simmered, strained, and finally enriched with fresh butter and the mushroom caps. *Sauce au champignons* is served with steaks, chops, or chicken. (See DEMI-GLACE)

CHAMPVALLON, LAMB CHOPS (French) In preparing this extraordinarily delicious dish, after seasoning the lamb chops, they are browned on both sides in butter, placed in a casserole with chopped onions and enough white stock to cover, and set in the oven to bake. Toward the end of the cooking time, sliced potatoes are added. COMPATIBLE WINES: A red wine, e.g., Moulin-à-Vent, Calon-Ségur, Pontet-Canet, Zinfandel, Cabernet Sauvignon; or perhaps even a white Beaujolais or a Mâcon Blanc.

CHANTILLY (French) The city of Chantilly, in France, was not only famous for its remarkable lace work and fine porcelain but also for a heavy cream first produced at a dairy there. Therefore, the French gave the name *crème Chantilly* to whipped cream that has been sweetened with fine sugar and flavored with vanilla.

Chantilly, Sauce   There are two sauces that bear this name. One has a *sauce Mayonnaise* as its base; the other, a *sauce Béchamel*. Just the addition of whipped cream transforms each of them to *sauce Chantilly*.

CH'AO (Chinese) Stir-frying, a quick method of sautéing cut-up morsels of food in hot oil (usually sesame oil) in a wok (Chinese cooking utensil) over a very hot fire. The most suitable foods for stir-frying are the choice sections of pork, beef, and lamb; the tender white meat of poultry; the back meat of fish; shelled shrimp, prawns; and the youngest of vegetables. It is important that the fat be heated to the proper temperature before the food is added. All must be perfectly timed, and the foods to be cooked must be added in correct series. A stir-fried dish must be served the minute it is done. (See CHINESE CUISINE)

CH'AO MIEN (Chinese) Noodles that are first boiled then gathered into a bundle, the outside of which is lightly browned in oil, thus leaving the inside soft. This differs from the unauthentic American chow mein noodles, which are fried until each individual noodle strand is brittle. (See CHOW MEIN)

CHAPATTIS (East Indian) The dough of this favorite bread is made of whole wheat flour, salt, and water. The dough is cut into circles, flattened thin, and cooked in a skillet until lightly browned. The *chapattis* are used as receptacles for food, somewhat like the trenchers used in the Middle Ages.

CHAPON SALADE (French) *Chapon* refers to bread that has been rubbed with garlic and olive oil and sautéed in butter until brown. This salad, a Créole favorite made usually with chicory, is tossed together with *chapon* slices in a piquant dressing made from olive oil, wine vinegar, salt, and pepper.

CHARCUTIÈRE, CÔTES DE PORC (French) This pork chop dish is named in honor of the "pork-butcher," *le charcutier*. The French distinguish between the regular butcher and the pork-butcher, who sells only pork products, including bacon, ham, and various sausages. Pork chops are browned in a heavy skillet and then removed. In the same pan, a sauce is made from tomato paste, water, vinegar, thyme, garlic, and mustard. The chops are replaced, covered, and left to cook in the sauce for half an hour. Before serving, finely chopped pickles are strewn over the top. COMPATIBLE WINES: A red wine, e.g., Beaujolais, Mercurey, Hermitage, Côte Rôtie, Zinfandel; or a white Traminer, Sylvaner, Chalon, Chenin Blanc, Orvieto.

Charcutière, Sauce   This sauce, made by simply adding a *julienne* of tiny French pickles, called *cornichons,* to a *sauce Robert,* is served with pork dishes. (See CORNICHONS, JULIENNE, ROBERT)

CHARLOTTE RUSSE (French) A classic dessert prepared by lining a charlotte mold with finger biscuits then filling the mold with Bavarian cream and refrigerating it. Of course, it is served unmolded. (See BAVAROISE)

CHAROLAISE, À LA The area of Charolles, in France, is justly famous for its fine cattle, and this culinary term is used when referring to a fine beef dish that is richly garnished with *cauliflower Villroy* and pastry *barquettes* filled with a purée of turnips. (See BARQUETTES, VILLROY)

CHARQUI (Peruvian) Dried meat. At first, the Peruvians preserved only the meat of game animals by drying; but once the people began to raise cattle as well, beef became more generally used. The meat was boned then cut into slices and immersed in brine or covered with salt. The meat was then rolled into the skin of the animal to absorb the brine while stretched out in the sun to dry. It was when the English-speaking people tried to pronounce the word *charqui* that "jerked beef" was born, which is what it is called today. (See BÜNDNER-FLEISCH, GRISONS, JERKY, PEMMICAN, ROHSCHINKEN)

CHAR SIEW PAU (Chinese) A delicate Cantonese dumpling that comes to the diner's table filled with succulent roast pork.

CHARTREUSE (French) In 1084, *Chartreuse* referred to the wilderness where St. Bruno began the Carthusian Order, but in culinary parlance the term refers to casserole dishes prepared with fish, game, or with vegetables. It is also the name of a double beef consommé served garnished with cubed tomatoes, tiny spinach ravioli, and truffles as well as the name of a famous liqueur created by the Carthusian monks.

Faisan en Chartreuse A pheasant is browned well in the oven. Then, in a large casserole, the bird is encased in root vegetables and layers of blanched, well-seasoned leaves of cabbage plus sliced bacon and small sausages. The bird—enveloped *en chartreuse,* as the French would say—is then braised. COMPATIBLE WINES: A red wine, e.g., Pommard, Corton, Châteauneuf-du-Pape, Musigny, Dôle, Beaune.

Chartreuse Liqueur This famous French liqueur is still produced by the Carthusian monks, whose order was founded in the French Alps by St. Bruno. The recipe for this brandy-based liqueur remains a monastic secret to this day. When religious orders were banned in France in 1903, the good monks strapped on their sandals, hiked up their habits, and made for Tarragona in Spain. Although France, in the interim, produced an ersatz product, the Carthusians fixed all that when they were again allowed to return to Voiron, France, in 1930. Today, the liqueur is as good as ever it was—a bit more expensive perhaps, but just as good. It comes in two strengths: the green being the stronger, the yellow the sweeter. It is used to flavor creams and mousses.

CHA SHU (Chinese) A popular barbecued pork dish made by roasting a lean loin of pork that has been seasoned with salt, pepper, the five-spice essence, bamboo shoots, sugar, sherry, and soy sauce. While baking, the loin is constantly basted with this marinade mixed with the meat drippings. (See FIVE-SPICE ESSENCE) COMPATIBLE BEVERAGES: Beer, Sauterne, sherry, ale, saké.

CHA SOH JUHN (Korean) *Croquettes* made from finely chopped vegetables—such as potatoes, carrots, onions, and garlic—which are folded into a batter of eggs, soy sauce, water, and flour and then fried by the teaspoonful in hot oil until golden brown. The *croquettes* are served with a tangy dip made from a blend of soy sauce, wine vinegar, and sugar. Koreans dislike their food being mistaken for Japanese or Chinese, and *cha soh juhn* is definitely Korean. (See KOREAN CUISINE) COMPATIBLE BEVERAGES: Beer, ale, saké, Sauterne.

CHASSEUR (French) This term indicates that the food is being served "hunter's style"—that is, with plenty of mushrooms. Synonymous with *à la forestière*. (See CACCIATORA)

Veal Chasseur A browned breast of veal baked in white wine and beef stock with mushrooms and shallots. COMPATIBLE WINES: A white wine, e.g., Montrachet, Meursault, Orvieto, Bernkasteler Doktor, Graacher Himmelreich, Pouilly-Fumé, Riquewihr, Fendant, Frascati.

Sauce Chasseur This remarkable sauce is made from chopped mushrooms browned in butter, to which shallots, salt, pepper, white wine, a *sauce demi-glace,* and parsley are added and cooked together. *Sauce chasseur* goes excellently with a veal roast, with chicken, beef steaks, and it can do wonderful things to *pasta* dishes. (See DEMI-GLACE, PASTA)

CHÂTEAUBRIAND (French) A thick broiled fillet of beef named after the Vicomte Châteaubriand, a noted French writer of the Napoleonic Era. The Vicomte, however, was not actually the father of the fillet of beef that so proudly bears his name. It was his chef, Montmireil, who originally grilled this famous fillet between two inferior steaks in order to enhance its flavor and juiciness. Yet, today the Châteaubriand is grilled alone, every inch as thick as it ever was. Adequate to serve two or more persons, it is traditionally served with *château potatoes* and a rich *sauce Béarnaise.* (See BÉARNAISE, CHÂTEAU POTATOES) COMPATIBLE WINES: A red wine, e.g., Aloxe-Corton, Fixin, Chambertin, Dôle, Lafite Rothschild, Talbot, La Tâche, Richebourg, Cabernet Sauvignon, Barolo.

Châteaubriand, Sauce This rich brown sauce is made from a *sauce demi-glace* that is enriched with fresh butter and flavored with lemon juice, mushroom parings, red currant jelly, tarragon, cayenne pepper, and chopped parsley. It is served with grilled meats, especially with the famous fillet of beef bearing the same name.

CHÂTEAU POTATOES (French) *Château* is French for "castle," and this root vegetable dish does indeed have a regal elegance. Potato balls, cut out of raw potatoes into elongated olive shapes, are carefully baked in a mixture of oil, butter, and bouillon in a shallow pan. A good chef will take pains not to serve the potatoes swimming in the gravy of a meat course. He will offer them in an individual dish so that their own delectable flavor may be savored.

CHÂTELAINE (French) This archaic word for the mistress of a castle is derived from the custom of the *châtelaine,* who carried the keys of the castle suspended from her girdle.

Chicken Châtelaine A chicken is trussed, covered with slices of bacon, then slowly cooked in lots of butter, set on a bed of root vegetables in a heavy saucepan so that the chicken does not brown. The chicken is served garnished with artichoke hearts that are cooked in butter and covered with a *sauce Soubise.* (See SOUBISE) COMPATIBLE WINES: A white wine, e.g., Vouvray, Orvieto, Frascati, Anjou, Sylvaner, Rüdesheim, Verdicchio, Château-Grillet, Sauvignon Blanc.

CHAT, POTATO (East Indian) A rather spicy potato salad composed of diced boiled potatoes flavored with ground green chilies, chopped onions, coriander, tamarinds, and fresh lime juice. (See CHILI, CORIANDER, TAMARIND)

CHAUD-FROID, SAUCE (French) Literally "hot-cold," meaning the sauce was made "hot" but served "cold." When heavy cream, egg yolks, and a bit of aspic jelly are added to a *sauce velouté,* the result is a *sauce chaud-froid* to be served with cold dishes of eggs, white meat, poultry, and fish. The brown *chaud-froid,* used to coat cold meats, is made by adding aspic jelly, an essence of truffles, and Madeira to a *sauce demi-glace.* The *chaud-froid* is a gelatinous sauce favored by chefs not only to display buffet delicacies but to preserve them as well. (See DEMI-GLACE, VELOUTÉ)

Chaud-Froid de Volaille This French chicken dish came into being with somewhat the same expediency as did the famous *chicken Marengo.* It so happened that the Maréchal de Luxembourg had missed his dinner and bade his servant to bring out one of the dishes that had been prepared for him. His chef foraged furiously around the kitchen and finally presented his boss with a cold *fricassée* of chicken that had been standing so long that it had jellied in its own juices. The Maréchal ate it, was delighted, and a new dish was born. To prepare this French dish today, pieces of chicken are first boiled in a chicken-and-veal stock. The strained stock, flavored with herbs, spices, chopped mushrooms, and onions, is poured over the chicken, brought to a boil, and simmered. The broth is carefully defatted, and the pieces of chicken are placed in a casserole. After the sauce is reduced and left to cool, it is bound with egg yolks and slowly reheated. The sauce is cooled again. Half is immediately poured over the chicken in the casserole, and the other half is mixed first with an aspic jelly and then also added to the casserole. When served, the chicken, jellied and cold, is surrounded with multicolored diamond-shaped pieces of aspic fashioned into a decorative border. (See

MARENGO) COMPATIBLE WINES: A red wine, e.g., Beaujolais, Mercurey, Châteauneuf-du-Pape, Volnay, Moulin-à-Vent, Santenay, Margaux, Zinfandel, Valpolicella, Egri Bikaver.

CHAWAN-MUSHI (Japanese) A chicken-and-fish custard that is steamed and served in its own individual pot with a tight-fitting lid. Finely-chopped cooked chicken, shrimp, any white-fleshed fish, mushrooms, and string beans are folded into a custard made with eggs and chicken stock and flavored with salt, *mirin,* soy sauce, and monosodium glutamate. The dish is fully steamed. (See MIRIN, MONOSODIUM GLUTAMATE, SOY) COMPATIBLE WINES: A white wine, e.g., saké, Sauterne, Gewürztraminer, Frascati, Chenin Blanc.

CHAYOTE This popular food, botanically a fruit though commonly prepared as a cooked vegetable or mixed into a salad, is also known by the names *christophene, chocho,* and *choka.* The pear-shaped *chayote* is either green or white. Native to Mexico, it is crisp, much like the zucchini; it is best eaten when still only six inches long—in other words, it should not be left on the vine too long. Americans of the Southwest as well as people from the West Indies, Australia, and South America use the *chayote* extensively in their cuisines. To prepare, it is peeled, cut into quarters, and boiled in salted water until tender. It can be mashed and served with fresh butter or with any of the many Mexican chili sauces, or it may be served as a dessert. (See CHILI, PUDIM, RELLENOS)

CHERVIL This tasty herb, sometimes called "the gourmet's parsley" because of its greater delicateness than parsley, has been known to man since early Christian days. Pliny, the Roman author whose writings are full of anecdotal tidbits on food, claims that chervil was used "to comfort the old stomach of the aged." During the Middle Ages, its cooked roots were used to ward off the plague and to ease the pains of rheumatism. Pharmacists today advise taking chervil to cure hiccups.

Important in French and Italian cooking, chervil is used to flavor soups, sauces, and fish, and it enhances egg, cheese, and beef dishes. Chervil is best consumed fresh and therefore is rarely used to season any dish that demands long cooking. And when a chef says, *"fines herbes,"* he means parsley, tarragon, chives, and chervil. (See RAVIGOTE).

CHESTNUTS, ROASTED In the fall and winter, one finds chestnut vendors on street corners in many of our cities, and the intoxicating aroma of roasting chestnuts can make the right juices run. But roasted chestnuts generally are badly done in America. They crack apart, and because they are heated by fiery coals below, they often become bitter-black on one side and remain raw on the other. In China, however, the meat of the roasted chestnut is uniformly soft and fragrant. The secret to the Chinese success is roasting chestnuts in very hot sand that is constantly stirred. (See MARRONS)

CHEVALIÈRE, EGGS À LA (French) A method of serving poached eggs. Sliced mushrooms, chopped cockscombs, and kidneys, blended in a *sauce velouté,* are poured over poached eggs and baked in a pastry crust. The dish is garnished with cockscombs dipped in beaten eggs, covered with breadcrumbs, and sautéed.

CHEVREUIL, SAUCE (French) Named for the roe deer, or roebuck, one of the smallest and tastiest of all deer found in Europe, this sauce is prepared by cooking game trimmings in a *sauce poivrade.* The sauce is passed through a sieve, then red wine, cayenne pepper, and a bit of sugar are added. *Sauce chevreuil* is served with game, marinated domestic meats, and with roasts. (See POIVRADE)

CHEVREUSE, EGGS À LA (French) Preparation of this egg dish entails piping the circumference of a buttered ovenproof dish with a purée of white beans, filling the center with raw eggs and a liberal sprinkling of grated Parmesan cheese, and baking the dish until the eggs are just set.

CHIANG JEE YEH (Chinese) Ginger-flavored chicken wings. To prepare the dish, a thick slice of fresh ginger root, chicken wings, and garlic are put, in that order, into a wok sputtering with hot peanut oil. Soy sauce, salt, sugar, rice wine, and water are added, and all is left to simmer for a few minutes. The chicken is served on a bed of *bok choy* (Chinese cabbage). How foods are mixed and in what order, how spices and herbs are added and when—the foregoing are what determine the art of the Chinese cook and the quality of his kitchen. (See BOK CHOY, CHINESE CUISINE) COMPATIBLE WINES: A white wine, e.g., saké, dry sherry, Sylvaner, Orvieto, Riesling.

CHICHERRONES (Spanish) Crisply fried pork cracklings, sold in cans.

CHICKEN CHOP SUEY This Chinese-inspired dish is frequently served at buffet dinners and is a great favorite at wedding receptions. Bite-size pieces of raw chicken are browned in peanut oil. With the addition of water, celery, water chestnuts, mushrooms, bamboo shoots, and various Chinese greens and seasonings, all is covered and cooked for at least a quarter of an hour. A sauce made from soy sauce, cornstarch, sugar, brandy, and water is then stirred into the other ingredients over heat until thickened. The dish is usually complemented with fried noodles, *ch'ao mien.* (See CH'AO MIEN) COMPATIBLE WINES: A red wine, e.g., Santenay, Beaujolais, Médoc, Valpolicella, Moulin-à-Vent, Zinfandel, Egri Bikaver.

CHICKEN IN CLAY This method of roasting fowl dates back to the open cookery practiced by early man. Today, the bird is eviscerated and cleaned, richly buttered and flavored with herbs and spices, then wrapped in aluminum foil, covered with a layer of wet clay, and baked in a hot oven. When served in restaurants, the clay is carefully broken with a mallet at the diner's table, and one finds the chicken to be moist, perfectly cooked in its own juices to an almost trembling tenderness. The aroma will cause heads to turn and questions to be asked. COMPATIBLE WINES: A red wine, e.g., Valpolicella, Chianti, Beaujolais, Mercurey, Fleurie, Petit Sirah, Cahors, Nebbiolo.

CHICKPEAS This legume has been eaten by man since the days of antiquity. Popular in the Middle East, France, India, Italy, and in most Spanish-speaking nations, where they are commonly known as *garbanzos,* chickpeas are favorites in stews and in soups. In Morocco they are served with the traditional *couscous.* (See COUSCOUS, GARBANZOS, HUMMUS)

CHICONS GRATINÉS (French) This is the famous Belgian endive cooked *au gratin* (browned in the oven or grill). After braising the endive, milk and heavy cream are added to a *roux,* stirring constantly until the sauce is thick and smooth. Off the heat, grated Swiss Gruyère cheese is added and the mixture is seasoned with cayenne pepper and salt. This sauce is poured over the leaves of endive in a casserole. Fresh breadcrumbs are sprinkled over all, melted butter is added, and the dish is baked in a medium oven for half an hour. A delicious vegetable dish. (See GRATIN, ROUX)

CHICORÉE (French) Endive. (See CHICORY, ENDIVE)

CHICORY There are two types of chicory. One is a leafy, curly vegetable often used as a salad green. The second is a wild, bright blue-flowered perennial whose roots, when roasted, are used in the production of a coffee substitute. In France, many people prefer a coffee that is a dark blend of *chicorée* and the coffee bean. The vegetable-type chicory, known also as endive, has very little waste and is much used in salads in the United States. (See ENDIVE, WITLOOF)

CHIFFONADE This French culinary term refers to a method of cutting vegetables into fine strips or ribbons. It usually pertains to sorrel and lettuce being cut *à la julienne* and cooked in butter. The term can also define a special French salad dressing composed of a *sauce vinaigrette,* hard-boiled eggs, parsley, and beet root—all chopped fine. (See JULIENNE, VINAIGRETTE)

CHILE (Mexican) Chili.

CHILI When one speaks of chilies, one thinks immediately of Mexico, tasselled sombreros, clacking castanets, and twanging guitars. In all, there are about sixty-one different types of chilies, and it would appear that Mexico uses them all. Botanically speaking, chilies are capsicums, and they run the sizzling taste gamut from deceptively sweet through saucily piquant, pungent, and ultimately to really hot. It is hard to rely upon any chili because it can cross-fertilize at the snap of a chili pod, and what one expected to be a rather mild member of the clan suddenly stings the tongue with a fire that only floods of water can extinguish. (See CAPSICUM)
Red Chilies, Dried
   ancho: large and broad; highly-flavored; mild.

mulato: long; dark brown; pungent.

pasilla: long and thin; less flavorful than the above; piquant.

chipotl: small; bright red; full-flavored; extremely hot; sold fresh or pickled.

morita: as hot as the *chipotl* though smaller and a darker red; best when pickled.

pequin: very small; red; extremely hot.

With the exception of the very small, dried red chilies, which are merely crushed between the fingers, red chilies are washed, stemmed and seeded, and well soaked in warm water. Then they can be puréed in a blender. Powdered *ancho, mulato,* and *pasilla* chilies are also readily available, but they are quite different from the regular commercial chili powder, which contains other spices and herbs.

Green Chilies   One might surmise that the red chili would be hotter than its green sister; such is not the case. The green variety, sold either fresh or pickled, is searing hot.

serrano: small and tapering; green; quite hot; sold in cans.

jalapeño: larger than the above; green; quite hot, although the pickled mild *jalapeño* comes without the fire; sold canned.

largo: long and thin; pale green; has a delicate flavor but is hot.

poblana: small and thin; dark green; has a pleasant taste, usually mild; available fresh or canned.

In the case of fresh chilies, if the flavor of the hotter chilies is desired but one wants to lessen the hotness, the seeds should be removed. For canned chilies, the liquid should be washed away with water.

Green Chilies, Sweet

guero: medium-long and tapered; pale green; sold canned.

valenciano: deep green; sold fresh as "sweet green pepper" in markets.

Note: After handling chilies, always wash the hands with soap, because if by accident some of the chili juice is rubbed into the eyes, the pain can be devastating.

CHILI CON CARNE (Mexican)   This peppery meat-and-bean dish offers comforting warmth on a cold day. Chopped beef is simmered in salted water. Chopped chili peppers, onions, garlic, and oregano are added to the meat and simmered until thick. Cooked kidney beans are usually added at the end of the cooking period, and the *chili con carne* (chili with meat) is served in bowls. COMPATIBLE BEVERAGES: Beer, ale, or a rosé wine. *Note:* There are as many variations of *chili con carne* as there are chefs. Where one chef will add garlic, another prefers wine or cider vinegar, and *chili con carne* contests abound in western U.S.A.

CHILIPEPPER   This is the general term for the popular pepper from Mexico, where it is available in strengths ranging from very mild to eye-watering hot. The peppers can be yellow, brown, or deep red in color. They are used extensively in Mexican dishes. Note that chili powder is a blend of many different spices, much like curry, and has no relation to this pepper.

CHINESE CUISINE The Chinese cuisine is the oldest in man's history—and the most varied. China holds as high a place in world gastronomy as does France; in fact, in culinary matters China was the distinguished forerunner of France. The Chinese use more different types of food in more ways than any other people in the world. The Chinese epicure may normally limit himself to small services of from five to ten different dishes, but on more formal occasions he may partake of up to thirty. If a food is harshly flavored—very hot or peppery or otherwise extreme—it is avoided, even rejected; and most foods are limited to one type of flavoring.

China is an immense country, so it is hardly surprising that the cooking of the North differs markedly from the cooking of the South. Cantonese food, for instance, is finer, more easily digested than the heavy, fatty dishes prevalent in Shanghai. If hot food—that is, highly spiced food—is wanted, the Szechwan-type cooking is preferred.

All of the ingredients used in Chinese cooking are cut up into small pieces so they can easily be handled with chopsticks, and these foods are fried, boiled or stewed in a deep cooking pot called a "wok." The use of the wok is one of the most thrifty methods of cooking known to man because the heat is concentrated at the tapered point of the cooking utensil. The food is placed into the wok according to the determined cooking time, for most food is cooked in the same wok. (The canny Chinese never used an oven to cook their food because it was considered to be the most impractical and wasteful use of heat.) The rice served with most Chinese dishes is, of course, boiled separately, and various sauces are served as dips. In China a meal is considered to be one of the most sensuous pleasures relished by man, and it is respected as such. (See STIR-FRYING, WOK)

Chinese Condiments Pepper, salt, and soy sauce are commonly used in the preparation of Chinese foods, but they are rarely found on a Chinese dinner table. Their ubiquitous presence in Chinese-American restaurants should not reflect upon the chef's efficiency and know-how but be accepted as an imposition on Chinese cuisine of the American catsup-mustard-salt-and-pepper ritual. Szechwan-style restaurants feature a light soy sauce, a white vinegar, as well as a red-hot oil on their dining room tables, to be used with dumplings. However, the hot oil should be tempered with soy sauce the first time the adventurous diner tries it. (See SOYBEAN)

Chinese Food When a Chinese refers to meat, he invariably means pork because, in addition to being the most available, he considers it the most flavorful of meats. This Chinese love for pork is clearly illustrated, literally in black and white, in the Chinese calligraphic symbol for "home," which is formed by drawing a plump pig with a roof over its head.

All Chinese food is cut up to bite-size to enable the diner to pick up his food with chopsticks. Except for stews and soups, most food is cooked rather quickly to prevent the food from losing its nutritional value and its color from altering. Vegetables are always cooked crisp-to-the-tooth and thus retain their natural color. Sauces are most often served separately, in their own individual bowls, to be used at the discretion of the diner. In fact, the Chinese present each food preparation as an entity that should harmonize with the rest of the meal. Different foods are not served on one plate, where the nuances of taste can become lost in an amalgam of flavors. When wine is taken with Chinese food, it should be a white wine strong enough to match the food: a Hermitage Blanc, a sherry or Sauterne or a saké. Usually beer is preferable.

Chinese Hors d'Oeuvre The serving of *hors d'oeuvre* before dinner is not a custom followed by the Chinese. At a formal banquet one might find a huge platter of cold meats, seafood, and vinegared vegetables, but one would hardly find the mass of finger foods served at Chinese restaurants catering to the Western palate. The Chinese do serve a variety of foods called *dim sum,* which are eaten as snacks, as a luncheon, or even as a main course. (See DIM SUM)

Chinese Numerical Culinary Significance The Chinese cook is ever mindful of numbers connected with foods, other than those he is obliged to use in the measurement of foodstuffs. The frequent incidence of the use of numbers, coupled with the poetry and imagination used in titles for foods and dishes, adds to the fascination of the Chinese cuisine.

The accomplished Chinese chef knows that the Five Sacred Grains of the Orient are rice, wheat, barley, millet, and the soybean. He is also schooled in the ancient Taoist "five flavors" concept of the fourth century B.C., meant to infuse meals with both the complement and the contrast of such basic flavors as bitter, sour, salt, hot, and sweet. Numbers are also part of the names of many dishes, such as Eight-jewel Duck, Three-flavor Chicken, Five-spice Beef Stew, One Chicken—Three Flavors, and Eight-treasure Rice Pudding. There were five styles of early Chinese cooking: Peking, Honan, Szechwan, Canton, and Fukien. (See FIVE FLAVORS, FIVE-SPICE ESSENCE, RICE IN CHINA)

Chinese Parsley Known in Spanish-speaking communities as *cilantro,* and in India as *dhania,* Chinese parsley *(hsiang-ts'ai)* is actually fresh coriander. It can be grown from the coriander seed to a height of about ten inches; it is used as an herb or garnish. Because Chinese parsley has a richer flavor than ordinary parsley, the considerate host always asks if everybody likes it before adding it to food.

Chinese Restaurants Many Chinese restaurants in America have become Americanized. Restaurants have catered to the taste of the American to such an extent that a Chinese-American cooking style has developed. Chinese-American food is far different from authentic Chinese fare. Those desiring to sample real Chinese food, or, more accurately, to taste something that is as close to the "real thing" as one can get outside of China, would be wise to dine in those restaurants situated in the Chinatowns of America where the customers are, for the most part, Chinese. (See CANTONESE, FUKIEN, HONAN, PEKING, AND SZECHWAN CUISINES)

CHINGARA, À LA (French) The designation for a dish served with a garnish made from a *julienne* of ham, tongue, truffles, and mushrooms. (See JULIENNE, ZINGARA)

CHIPOLATA (Italian) This term was once used for a garnish of chestnuts, vegetables, diced pork, onions, and small spicy sausages. Today it refers to a small sausage made with onions. It can also refer to a small mild Italian onion or to a type of Créole stew served in New Orleans.

CHIRI-MUSHI (Japanese) A dish of steamed fish and eggs prepared with *kinugoshi,* a delicate soybean curd. A piece of the soybean curd is placed in each individual bowl; this is topped with an egg and a thin fillet of sole or whitefish. The bowls, placed on a rack in a Dutch oven, are steamed for a few minutes, until the egg is just firm and the fish flakes easily. *Chiri-mushi* is served flavored with *shoyu* and a slice of lemon. (See KINUGOSHI, SHOYU, TOFU) COMPATIBLE WINES: A white wine, e.g., Sauterne, saké, Graves, Chenin Blanc, Gewürztraminer.

CHIRIZU (Japanese) A spicy sauce served as a dip for *sashimi.* First, saké is heated and flamed. After cooling, it is mixed with grated radish *(daikon),* chopped scallions, lemon juice, soy sauce, monosodium glutamate (Ac'cent), and just a hint of the *hichimi togarishi* (a mixture of seven special spices). The *chirizu* sauce is served with *sashimi* dishes of striped bass, porgy, and fluke. (See DAIKON, HICHIMI TOGARISHI, SASHIMI) COMPATIBLE BEVERAGES: Beer, ale, saké.

CHISO (Japanese) A red herb, a prominent member of the mint family, the flavor of which seems like a fusion of parsley, coriander, cumin, and celery with just a touch of allspice. *Chiso* is served with both cold and hot foods. Its red dye is much sought after as a food coloring. (See ALLSPICE, PIMIENTO)

CHITTERLINGS The name used in the southern part of the United States for a type of rich sausage made from casings fashioned from pigs' intestines. The Russians serve them with sour cream, and the French boast of a delicious variety they call *les andouilles.* (See ANDOUILLES)

CHIVES A hardy plant *(Allium schoenoprasum)* of the lily family, with small, slender, hollow leaves having a mild onion odor. Chives can be found all over North America, even growing wildly between the busy lanes of New York freeways. Used to perk up soups, stews, and salads, chives are wonderful in potato salads and with fish or egg dishes. They are combined with cream cheese to make a tasty chive cheese. (See CHIVRY)

CHIVRY (French) This term refers to the chive and foods containing it.

Chivry, Sauce This classic French sauce is made from a reduction of a *sauce velouté* and white wine mixed with chopped shallots, parsley, chervil, tarragon, chives, and burnet, an herb related to the rose family. This is strained and finished with *chivry*-butter, also called *ravigote*-butter, composed of blanched parsley, chives, tarragon, and shallots, all of which are puréed and mixed with fresh butter. *Sauce chivry* can be served with chicken or eggs, or with fish if a fish stock is used to make the *sauce velouté*. (See VELOUTÉ)

CHO-CHO (Mexican) See CHAYOTE

CHOKA See CHAYOTE

CHOLENT (Jewish) See HAMIN

CHOP CHOY (Korean) This dish consists of a series of chopped ingredients which are sautéed briefly in hot oil. First, thin strips of sirloin are marinated in a mixture of soy sauce, garlic, onions, pepper, and toasted sesame seeds. In hot peanut oil in a wok, the beef is sautéed then removed. Chopped carrots and onions are likewise sautéed and removed. Then spinach, mushrooms, and bamboo shoots are chopped and sautéed. The beef, the carrots and onions, and a bit of the marinade is then added to the wok. Just before serving, cooked fine noodles are stirred into the mixture. (See VERMICELLI, WOK) COMPATIBLE WINES: A red wine, e.g., Beaujolais, Pinot Noir, Mercurey, Valpolicella, Fleurie, Veltliner, Châteauneuf-du-Pape.

CHOPPED LIVER See LEBER

CHOPSTICKS These eating utensils, about eight inches long, rectangular at the top and tapered at the business ends, are used by Chinese, Japanese, Koreans, Thais, and many other Asiatic people to pick up bits of food. Chopsticks are never made of metal because metal may react with the acids found in food and taint its taste. Although chopsticks are usually made out of wood, some of the more fancy ones are intricately carved out of bone or ivory. Bamboo is used as well.

Following Japanese chopstick etiquette, when taking food, such as *sukiyaki,* from a communal dish, the opposite ends of the chopsticks are used to transport the food to the diner's plate. The chopsticks are then reversed and used normally.

Chinese chopsticks were once referred to as *chu,* meaning "help in eating." Today, the Cantonese word *kuai-tse* is commonly used. According to Chinese etiquette, when eating noodles or any spaghetti-type food, it is improper to wind the food around the chopsticks as the Italians wind spaghetti around a fork. A reasonable amount of noodles should be raised to the mouth and then bitten off, allowing the rest to slip back into the bowl. The noodles may be sucked into the mouth; the accompanying slurping noise is never considered objectionable. On the contrary, the sound lets the host know that the diner is really enjoying his food. (See WARIBASHI)

CHOP SUEY (Chinese-American) There are many conflicting stories about the origin of this dish, but they all agree on one thing: chop suey is not Chinese; it is American. One legend tells of Chinese laborers who, while building the railroads that joined the eastern and western United States, were fed whatever bits and pieces that could be gathered; when the gathered foods were mixed with boiled rice, the resulting dish was called "chop suey." Another legend tells of the visiting Chinese diplomat who became so ill on American food that an aide, in desperation, fashioned for him a very simple dish of pork mixed with stir-fried celery and other vegetables. The aide called the dish "chop suey."

Today, the popular chop suey dish consists of bamboo shoots, bean sprouts, celery, and water chestnuts cooked together with chicken or pork and served accompanied with heaps of steamed white rice. COMPATIBLE WINES: A red wine, e.g., Beaujolais, Nebbiolo, Lambrusco, Valpolicella, Zinfandel.

CHORIZO (Spanish) A red sausage made from pork, pork liver, and pork fat, mixed with hot cayenne pepper, sweet red peppers, salt, juniper berries, and garlic. *Chorizos* are served in thick, souplike stews *(potées),* usually with *garbanzos* (chickpeas). (See CHICKPEAS, GARBANZOS, POTÉE)

CHORON, SAUCE (French) Named in honor of the composer Alexander Étienne Choron, this is simply a *sauce Béarnaise* blended with a concentrate of tomato purée. (See BÉARNAISE)

Tournedos Choron　Here, *tournedos* (small fillets of beef) are sautéed in clarified butter, placed on fried *croûtons,* and topped with a dollop of *sauce Choron.* The steaks are garnished with artichoke hearts stuffed with tiny peas and *pommes noisettes.* (See CROÛTONS, NOISETTE, TOURNEDOS) COMPATIBLE WINES: A red wine, e.g., Haut Brion, Kirwan, Dôle, St. Émilion, Margaux, Fixin, Chambertin, Chambolle-Musigny.

CHOU/CHOUX (French) The singular and plural form of "cabbage."

CHOUCROUTE (French) Sauerkraut.

Choucroute Garnie　This traditional Alsatian dish is served all over the world. It is basically sauerkraut that is cooked in white wine with ham, smoked goose, sausages, and bacon and served with heaps of boiled potatoes. The *choucroute* of Alsace, as the *garbure* of Béarn and the *cassoulet* of Languedoc, is a classic preparation. (See BIGOS, CASSOULET, GARBURE, SAUERKRAUT) COMPATIBLE WINES: A white wine, e.g., Gewürztraminer, Riquewihr, Fendant, Aigle, Ammerschwihr, Chenin Blanc, Alsheim, Orvieto, Frascati.

CHOW BAAK LOOK (Chinese) A sweet-and-sour shrimp dish made by adding large cooked shrimp to cubed onions, carrots and green peppers and stir-frying everything in oil together with chopped pineapple and a sweet-and-sour sauce. The dish is prepared in a matter of minutes. The sauce is composed of a mixture of catsup, soy sauce, vinegar, and crushed garlic; honey and pineapple juice are added as a delightful contrast, and cornstarch is added as a binder. COMPATIBLE BEVERAGES: Tea, saké.

CHOWDER Early French immigrants to Canada made a hearty soup called *chaudrée* from salt pork and fish. (*Chaudrée* derives from the Latin *calderia,* "caldron.") When the Breton-inspired *chaudrée* crossed the Canadian border and moved down the eastern seaboard of the United States, "chowder" American-style came into being. Maine, ever practical and plain, fostered a simple chowder using pure water, clams, salt pork, and, of course, potatoes. The dairy-rich state of Massachusettes chose to make its brand of chowder with milk, while the Manhattan and Connecticut versions added tomatoes. So, from Brittany in France to the Greek and Turkish shores of the Mediterranean, from the cold ports of Scandinavia to their counterparts in Canada and America, the recipes for various chowders became territorial, depending for their ingredients upon what was available in the locality. The main differences lie in the use of milk or tomatoes and various seasonings and herbs. Cooks having the same cooking utensils and same recipe produce vastly different results. How foods are mixed, in what order; how long they are cooked and at what temperature; how spices and herbs, eggs, and cream are added and when—all the foregoing determine not only the art of the cook but the quality of the dish. Chowder is a prime example. (See MANHATTAN CLAM CHOWDER, NEW ENGLAND CLAM CHOWDER)

CHOW MEIN (Chinese-American) This old standby of Chinese-American restaurants is, like chop suey, a very tasty catch-all dish. It is made of leftover meats, poultry, or seafood that is flavored with bean sprouts, water chestnuts, celery, or cabbage and cooked in oil and soy sauce. It is served over thin fried noodles. (See CH'AO MIEN)

CHOW YUK (Chinese) The term for any number of stir-fried dishes, one of which is ginger beef. This dish is prepared from thinly sliced cuts of beef that are fried together with shredded raw ginger in hot peanut oil. While stir-frying, a bit of water, cassava flour, sugar, and soy sauce are added. Oyster beef is another variation on the same theme, though this time an oyster sauce is used instead of the raw ginger. (See CASSAVA)

Gai Lan A *chow yuk* prepared with Chinese spinach.

Bok Choy A meat *chow yuk* made with Chinese cabbage. Garlic and onions are popular flavorings, though fruits, such as pineapple, plums, or lichee nuts are also used in *chow yuk* preparations. Sour fruit is used instead of vinegar.

Vegetable Chow Yuk For this dish, vegetables are cut to bite-size and braised in hot oil in a wok. The braising time is short, and always the wok remains uncovered.
COMPATIBLE BEVERAGES: Tea, sherry, saké, Sauterne.

CHOY SUM (Chinese) "Vegetable heart." Although said to be akin to the Chinese cabbage, *choy sum* must be allowed to grow to maturity before being harvested. Only the more delicate leaves from the inner part of the vegetable are used. (See BOK CHOY)

CHREMSLACH (Jewish) This fritter (singular, *chremsel*) is generally referred to in the plural form because many are made at one time. Traditionally served at Passover, they are prepared by soaking *matzos* in water, draining them, and then mixing in *matzo* meal (ground *matzo*), ground almonds, cinnamon, dried fruits, and sugar. Egg yolks are added to the batter and beaten egg whites are folded in. Some say that *chremslach* are best when baked in the oven, but the batter may also be dropped, a spoonful at a time, into hot fat and left to fry until brown on all sides. *Chremslach* are sometimes served sprinkled with sugar. (See MATZO, MATZO BREI)

CHRISTMAS PUDDING (English) This rich pudding is traditionally served in Britain at the close of a grand Christmas dinner. Originally, the dish was very thin in consistency, like a soup or a porridge, but today we think of a Christmas Pudding as being a solid mass of compressed fruits, nuts, eggs, and suet, flavored with various spices and good brandy. Tradition holds that a silver object, perhaps a ring or a coin, must be cooked in the pudding. Legend says whoever finds the coin will have luck in finances, and whoever finds the ring will hear wedding bells within the year. The pudding, decorated with sprigs of holly, is always carried to the festive table aflame with brandy. (See PLUM PUDDING)

CHRISTOPHENE See CHAYOTE

CHUTNEY (East Indian) The name of this popular relish is derived from the Hindi word *chatni*. Served with meat dishes, it is made from fruits or vegetables that are cooked with ginger, turmeric, sugar, cinnamon, and vinegar until thick. Indian chutneys are always freshly prepared to suit a particular dish. (See CINNAMON, GINGER, MANGO, NARIEL CHUTNEY, PINEAPPLE CHUTNEY, TURMERIC)

CHWIN GUEN (Chinese) See EGG ROLLS

CIBOULE (French) A type of onion, sometimes referred to as "scallion," and in Wales as "Welsh onion."

CIBOULETTES (French) Chives. (See CHIVES)

CIDER Cider is obtained from the fermentation of specially selected apples. In the United States, unfermented apple juice is used to produce a sweet cider that is free of alcohol, unless it is designated as "hard cider" or "applejack." Commercial cider is pasteurized, treated with preservatives, and often blended to equalize the sugar, malic acid, and tannin. In France the finest cider comes from Normandy and Brittany, where it is considered *le vin du pays*. Cider is also popular in Germany, Switzerland, and especially in Spain, where the *sidro* from Asturias is a tangy, sparkling type of cider, a product of both natural and artificial carbonation. While France has a fine apple brandy called Calvados, America has Applejack, both being hard ciders that are produced by allowing the fermentation of the apple juice to continue until all of the sugar has been converted into alcohol.

CILANTRO (Spanish) Chinese parsley.

CINNAMON This important spice, discovered by the Dutch in Ceylon in the sixteenth century, is obtained by drying the central part of the bark of the cinnamon tree. It is marketed either in stick or in a powdered form. Cinnamon and cassia, often confused, have been used since biblical times in the manufacture of perfumes and incense. True cinnamon is far more delicate in flavor than its more pungent sister, and it is widely used in the preparation of cakes, desserts, curries, and in various meat dishes. Today, true cinnamon grows only on the Island of Ceylon; this is a mild and delicate spice. The more pronounced cinnamon commonly used in cooking comes from China and the East Indies.

CIOPPINO (Italian-American) First concocted by Ligurian fishermen in San Francisco, California, this preparation consists of fish, shellfish, and tomatoes—all cooked together in a soup-stew and poured steaming over freshly buttered sourdough toast. COMPATIBLE WINES: A white wine, e.g., Chenin Blanc, Riesling, Orvieto, Frascati, Sauvignon Blanc, Volnay, Château Chalon.

CIPOLLA (Italian) Onions.

CIRCASSIAN CHICKEN (Turkish) Adopted from the cuisine of an ancient Caucasian race, the Circassians, whose beautiful women were treasured by the Turks as slaves, this dish is composed of cooked chicken, chopped into cubes and blended with finely ground walnuts, paprika, breadcrumbs, and chicken stock. COMPATIBLE WINES: A white wine, Orvieto, Sylvaner, Schloss Vollrads, Gewürztraminer, Tokay, Chenin Blanc, Neuchâtel, Johannisberg.

CITRON An ovate fruit that resembles a lemon but it is much larger and less acidic. A single citron can weigh up to twenty pounds. This fruit is said to have originated in the region between southern Arabia and western India. When the Jews fled from their Babylonian captivity, they brought the citron with them to Palestine and took pains to cultivate it. In fact, the rabbis used the citron in their rituals celebrating feasts such as Succoth, and they specified the size, color, and the freshness of the citrons to be used. In Corsica, the citron is used to make a liqueur called *cédratine,* but its main culinary use is relegated to its peel, which is cut up, glacéed, and used to flavor cakes and pastry. Glacé citron, known as *cédrat,* is green and has a tangy taste. (See CÉDRAT, GLACÉ)

CIVET (French) A game stew, usually rabbit, that has been first marinated in highly spiced red wine and then stewed with mixed vegetables, herbs, and mushrooms. The word *civet* is derived from another French word, *civette,* which means both "civet cat" and "chives." French gastronomes, with tongue-in-cheek and one eye on the purse, sometimes substituted the cat for the rabbit in making the stew, for does not the gay Parisienne, looking out of her attic window, refer to the tomcat balancing himself on the rain gutter outside as a "roof-rabbit"? One can readily tell if a rabbit is old: his teeth will be very long and yellow, even black, and his snout bristles will be turning white.

Civet de Lièvre The hare is cut up, marinated in cognac, red wine, oil, sliced onions, cloves, salt, and pepper. It is then stewed in a mixture of red wine, part of the marinade, salt pork, and crushed garlic; just before the dish has finished cooking, it is bound with the blood and crushed liver of the hare and served garnished with glazed onions and mushrooms. (See BLOOD AS FOOD, HASENPFEFFER) COMPATIBLE WINES: A red wine, e.g., Talbot, Haut Brion, Figeac, St. Émilion, Pétrus, Cabernet Sauvignon, Clos de la Roche, Pommard, Chambertin.

Civet, Canard en A duck stew made by cutting up a duck, browning the pieces in pork fat, then removing them and browning pearl onions in the pan. The duck pieces are sorted, and the less attractive ones are cooked with vegetables in a sauce of red wine, garlic, tomatoes, sugar, and ham and veal bones. The sauce is boiled, skimmed of fat, seasoned with pepper and salt and simmered for several hours. The reserved duck pieces are added to the strained sauce with Cognac and a *bouquet garni* and cooked over very low heat for another hour. The sauce is again defatted. The duck is served coated with the sauce. COMPATIBLE WINES: A red wine, e.g., Échézeaux, Pétrus, Cabernet Sauvignon, Fixin, Nuits St. Georges, Pommard.

CLABBER (Irish) Derived from the Gaelic word *clabar,* meaning "curds," this is a thick sour milk that has not separated into curds and whey: it curdled.

CLAFOUTIS (French) An open-faced cherry tart, a speciality of the Limousine district. A thick pastry dough is made from a blending of flour, eggs, sugar, Cognac, salt, and milk. The dough is pressed into a pie tin and filled with pitted cherries. After baking, the tart is dusted with powdered sugar.

CLAMART, À LA (French) In France, when one says *Clamart,* one thinks of the finest, the tiniest of peas. The phrase *à la Clamart* pertains to a garnish of hearts of artichokes filled with tiny French peas.

Selle d'Agneau Clamart   A saddle of lamb is roasted in the oven and served garnished with artichoke hearts stuffed with tiny peas. *Château potatoes* are often served with this dish. (See CHÂTEAU POTATOES) COMPATIBLE WINES: A red wine, e.g., Margaux, Pauillac, St. Estèphe, St. Julien, Beaujolais, Valpolicella, Zinfandel.

Ris de Veau Clamart   A dish of sweetbreads served with peas. The sweetbreads are cleaned, larded with pieces of bacon, placed on a bed of sliced carrots and onions, covered with bouillon, and baked in the oven. Of course, they are presented surrounded with the tiniest of green peas. COMPATIBLE WINES: A red wine, e.g., Mercurey, Margaux, Côte Rôtie, Beaujolais, Valpolicella, Zinfandel, Côtes du Rhône.

CLAM CHOWDER   See CHOWDER

CLAMS CASINO   See CASINO

CLARIFIED BUTTER   "Why clarified butter?" someone asks. The simple explanation is that butter that has been clarified will not burn, even when subjected to extreme heat. This is a great advantage when food must be fried quickly over high heat.

Clarified butter, called "drawn butter" in the United States (not to be confused with the drawn butter sauce), is prepared by slowly cooking butter over moderate heat. The scum that rises to the top is removed, and the clear butter beneath it is poured off through a muslin sieve. The cloudy white residue that remains in the bottom of the saucepan—that is, the whey, milk, and impurities—is the substance that will burn and must be disarded. Clarified butter is often added to sauces and to soups. (See DRAWN BUTTER, GHEE)

CLARIFY   The culinary process of removing unwanted fats and other matter from soups and sauces. To clarify a soup, the white of a raw egg is beaten into the liquid while slowly raising the temperature. After simmering the soup a short time, the undesired food particles will cling to the egg white, enabling the soup to be strained to a sparkling clarity. Butter may also be clarified. (See CLARIFIED BUTTER)

CLEAR-SIMMERING   (Chinese) Slow cooking in a clear liquid with no soy sauce.

CLOUD EARS   (Chinese) Another name for "wood ears" or *mook yee,* a favorite fungus used in Chinese cooking. (See MU-ER, WOOD EARS)

CLOUTER   (French) Literally, "to stud." The process of inserting pieces of bacon, tongue, or truffle into fowl, fish, sweetbreads, or veal by means of a skewer. It is a method similar to the larding process. (See BARD)

CLOVES   The dried flower buds of an East Indian tree belonging to the myrtle family. As fresh buds they are crimson, but they turn brown when dry. Cloves were first used in the manufacture of perfumes and breath fresheners. Chinese courtiers reeked so from raw garlic that they were required to fill their mouths with cloves when they addressed their emperor. (The problem could have easily been corrected, without the use of cloves, if the emperor had had a bit of the garlic himself.) Ground cloves are used in baked goods, chocolate pudding, spiced wines, hot drinks, stuffings, and stews and as a great flavoring for baked hams. This fragrant spice also grows on the islands of Madagascar and Zanzibar off the coast of Africa.

CLUB SANDWICH Created in the United States as an inexpensive, all-in-one luncheon for club members, this classic sandwich is composed of three slices of toasted white bread with two layers of filling. The first consists of slices of the breast of roast chicken on lettuce, the second of grilled bacon and thinly sliced tomatoes. The layers are spread with a rich *Mayonnaise*. The triple-decker sandwich is cut into four triangles and fastened with toothpicks, each topped with a pimiento-stuffed olive. Variations of this sandwich are as endless as the imagination of the chef. Raw onions, sliced chicken, chicken liver, cheese, liverwurst, bacon, tomatoes, and tongue may be substituted or added. (See MAYONNAISE)

CLUB STEAK A porterhouse steak from which the tenderloin has been removed.

COCHINEAL This important red dye was first thought to come from vegetable matter, but actually it is obtained from the female species of the scale insect, found on cactus plants in Mexico and Central America. After having painted her face calcimine white, the Virgin Queen Elizabeth would choose one of these tiny insects from her cosmetic etui, crack it open, and paint her lips carmine red. Formerly, this red-purple dye was used for wool, foodstuffs, liqueurs, and wines; but because it takes such large numbers of insects to produce but a little of the dye, the high cost forced the manufacturers to use chemicals instead.

COCIDO (Spanish) A meat and vegetable stew or soup.
  Cocido Español A thick Spanish soup made with either beef or with chicken and various mixed vegetables. COMPATIBLE WINES: A red wine, e.g., Rioja, Beaujolais, Pinot Noir, Valpolicella, Zinfandel, Margaux, Nebbiolo, Lambrusco.

COCK-A-LEEKIE SOUP Also spelled *cock-a-leeky* and *cockie leekie,* this chicken soup was born in Scotland. When Talleyrand fled to England during the French Revolution, he came to love the soup. It is said that after a good cockfight the loser was popped into a pot with a few leeks and offered to the spectators. Actually, veal bones, bay leaf, parsley, thyme, salt, pepper, and the tough bird are all placed in water in a pot and allowed to simmer for some hours. Before serving, the soup is defatted, the chicken boned, and a garnish of leeks, strips of chicken, and stewed prunes added.

COCKTAILS See SYMPOSIA

COCKTAIL SAUCE (French) This spicy sauce must be served quite cold. It is made from a _sauce Mayonnaise_ flavored with lemon juice instead of vinegar. To this, a tomato purée, Worcestershire sauce, gin, and lastly whipped cream are added. The sauce is served with a shrimp or crabmeat cocktail. A tangy substitute sauce can be made by simply blending tomato purée, a dash of Cognac, and a sprinkling of curry powder into heavy cream. (See MAYONNAISE)

COCONUT If one is marooned on a desert island where the coconut palm thrives, all is not lost. The meat is nutritious, and the coconut milk is wholesome and ever-cool because the shell acts as an insulator against the heat of the sun. Coconut milk is also thought to be a cure for indigestion. The roots of the tree can be ground up for use as coffee or as fuel, and its wood can be utilized to fashion furniture and stable dwellings. The shell of the coconut can be used as a cup, a bowl, or a plate. The meat of the nut, used for food, is called _copra._ In India the coconut is regarded as the Hindu symbol of prosperity and fertility, and it is referred to with reverence as _sriphala,_ the holy fruit. Coconut is used most by the East Indians in garnishes, such as _sambals_ and chutneys.

To be used as food, the coconut must first be drained of its water then baked for a short time in a very hot oven. Then, one blow or two with a mallet will easily remove the outer shell, leaving the meat covered with only a thin brown skin that can be peeled away with a knife. The delectable coconut milk is not the water that one hears sloshing about in the shell but the liquid that is obtained by squeezing the grated meat of the nut. (See NARIEL CHUTNEY, POL SAMBOLA)

COEUR À LA CRÈME (French) See FROMAGE BLANC

COFFEE See CHICORY, DEMITASSE, ESPRESSO

COLBERT During the reign of Louis XIV, two brothers, Charles and Jean-Baptiste Colbert de Croissy, brought great fame to their family through their unflagging service to the Crown. Charles ferreted out fraud, scaled down the public debt, forced the government to live within its means, and sponsored industry and the arts. Many dishes have come to bear the Colbert name.

Colbert, Sauce/Colbert Butter A butter _à la maître d'hôtel_ is stirred into a chicken or a meat glaze flavored with chopped parsley, tarragon, and lemon juice. (See MAÎTRE D'HÔTEL)

Sole Colbert The whole boned fish is floured, dipped in beaten egg, then in breadcrumbs, and deep fried. It is served filled with butter _à la maître d'hôtel._ (See MAÎTRE D'HÔTEL) COMPATIBLE WINES: A white wine, e.g., Chablis, Meursault, Soave, Verdicchio, Bernkasteler Doktor, Pinot Chardonnay, Dézaley, Debro, Sancerre, Montrachet.

COLE SLAW Often called "cold slaw," this salad, served chilled, is composed of finely shredded raw cabbage mixed with a rich _sauce Mayonnaise._ It is said to have come to America with the Dutch, who called it _kool sla,_ meaning "cabbage salad."

COLLARD GREENS (American South) A kind of kale, a hardy member of the cabbage family, with curled leaves.

COLLARED MEATS *The Queen's Closet Opened,* published in 1655, was very popular in seventeenth-century England. The closet referred to in the book is supposedly the culinary closet of Queen Henrietta Maria, a Medici and wife of Charles the First. This compendium is a collection of household hints and recipes for medicines (some horrible), pies, and sausages. The recipes are basically for meat pies and those for "collaring," or potting, meats. Collared meat was cut into long strips then rolled, tied, and cooked in a liquid heavy with spices. Rabbit, pork, beef, venison, and fish were all collared and still are. Meat to be processed this way was usually immersed in a pickling mixture full of saltpeter. It was a primitive sort of *ballotine.* The saltpeter (sodium nitrate) was used as it still is, to maintain the color. Today, it is used widely as a plant fertilizer. (See BALLOTINE)

COLLOP An Old English expression for an egg fried in grease. The term later came to refer to slices of meat. Our sirloin steaks would be called "beef collops" and pork chops would be called "pork collops." The term is still found in cookbooks and in many references to food, both technical and literary.

COLUMBA Made exactly like the *panettone* with the addition of toasted almonds, this cake is served in Italy at Eastertime. It commemorates the omen of two doves, *columbas,* whose propitious arrival in the city of Milan in 1176 was a sign for the Milanese forces to attack Frederick Barbarossa and to defeat him, thus saving Milan. (See KUGELHOPF, PANETTONE)

COLUMBO, LE (French) The name given by the natives of the Island of Martinique to a popular curry mixture composed of mustard seeds, toasted rice, garlic, hot peppers, saffron, coriander, and black pepper. It was introduced by migrant Hindu worders. The spices are finely ground, fried in oil, and readied for use by adding tamarind pulp. This curry is used to enhance the flavor of pork, lamb, and poultry dishes.

Columbo de Poulet This chicken curry dish from Martinique is prepared by frying a disjointed chicken in oil then transferring the pieces to an earthenware casserole. To this, *le columbo* curry is added together with white wine and various vegetables, such as eggplant, *chayote,* and taro. The dish is simmered, covered tightly, until the chicken is tender; prior to its being served, it is seasoned with salt, a squeeze of fresh lime juice, and a dash of Madeira wine. A *riz Créole* is usually served with the dish. (See CHAYOTE, RIZ CRÉOLE) COMPATIBLE WINES: A beer would be best; or a white wine, e.g., Sauterne, sherry, saké.

COMPANATICO (Italian) *Con,* meaning "with," and *pane,* meaning "bread," are joined to form the word *companatico,* which refers to any sandwich filling.

COMPÔTE (French) Stewed fruit. The fruit is cooked gently in a sugar syrup until tender. Frequently, a liqueur is added to the reduced syrup together with thinly sliced lemons and oranges and various spices.

COMPOUND BUTTER Fresh sweet butter blended with other foods, herbs, and spices. Compound butters may be combined with derivatives of the basic *velouté* and *Béchamel* sauces to develop flavors unobtainable by any other means. (See BÉCHAMEL, BEURRES COMPOSÉS, VELOUTÉ)

Colbert, Beurre A meat glaze and chopped fresh tarragon are added to a *maître d'hôtel* butter. Used to garnish any fish prepared *à la Colbert*. (See COLBERT, MAÎTRE D'HÔTEL)

Échalote, Beurre d' Minced shallots are blanched in boiling water then cooled and pressed almost dry in a muslin cloth. This is ground into fresh butter and strained through a fine sieve. This butter compound is used to enhance the flavor of many sauces, including *Bercy* and *ravigote*. (See BERCY, RAVIGOTE)

Estragon, Beurre d' Chopped tarragon is scalded, drained, pressed dry in a cloth, and puréed. To this mixture, fresh butter is added; the whole is strained through a fine sieve and preserved in the refrigerator. Great with chicken.

Gascogne, Beurre de This piquant sauce was born in what was once known as Gascony, the French Basque country that today is incorporated in the departments of Landes, Gers, Hautes-Pyrénées, and the Basses-Pyrénées. From the countryside that spawned the lusty musketeer d'Artagnan comes this equally lusty butter sauce composed of chopped and ground garlic blended with good pork fat, fresh butter, and a generous sprinkling of parsley. The *beurre de Gascogne* enhances the taste of beans, mushrooms, and lentils and gives zest to soups.

Homard, Beurre d' This lobster-butter is made by mashing the eggs and coral of the lobster and beating in fresh butter to develop a creamy mixture. The butter is served with fish soufflés, in fish sauces, with cold *hors d'oeuvre,* and with cold fish.

Manié, Beurre Butter and flour are kneaded together and the mixture is added to various sauces as a thickener. The *beurre manié* should be cooked together with the sauce long enough to remove the unwelcome taste of uncooked flour.

Meunière, Beurre à la Fresh butter is cooked until slightly golden in color. Lemon juice is then added and the butter is served over parsley-strewn fish.

Noir, Beurre Literally "black butter," made by cooking butter until quite brown and then adding vinegar, capers, and chopped parsley. *Beurre noir* is served with brains, and is delicious with poached ray. (See SKATE, STINGAREE AU BEURRE NOIR)

Pistache, Beurre de This pistachio-butter is made by blanching pistachio nuts to loosen the skins, cooling and cleaning them, then grinding them in a mortar and adding butter. Once it has been passed through a sieve, the sauce is finished.

CONCASSER (French) A process of skinning, chopping, and shredding tomatoes. When the tomatoes are seeded as well, they are called *tomates concassées.*

CONCHA (Spanish) The conch, a large mollusk belonging to the gastropod family and found on the sandy bottoms of shallow tropical waters. The extremely tough meat of this mollusk must be tenderized by pounding it before cooking. It is very popular in the West Indies, where it is used to make soups, stews, and salads. The heavy spiral shells of the conch, ranging in color from white to red, are used in the manufacture of ornaments, cameos, buttons, and even crude trumpets.

CONCHIGLIE (Italian) See PASTA, SCUNGILLI

CONDÉ (French) Prince Louis II de Condé had a penchant for hunting and a craving for rice. Accordingly, French chefs have named several creations after him.

Apricots Condé Apricots are poached in a sugar syrup, flavored with lemon, and served perched on top of boiled rice. They are coated with an apricot sauce and garnished with marinated cherries and angelica. (See ANGELICA)

Consommé Condé This consommé is made from a game stock and is garnished with a *julienne* of partridge fillets and small dumplings made from a bean purée. (See JULIENNE)

Crème Condé A thick soup made from a purée of red kidney beans that is flavored with red wine, onions, cloves, carrots, a *bouquet garni,* and a bit of diced fried bacon. Served with butter-fried croutons. (See BOUQUET GARNI)

CONEY ISLAND CHICKEN ALSACIENNE (American) New York's Coney Island would not be Coney Island without the ubiquitous "hot dog" (frankfurter sausage), nor would the German part of France, known as Alsace, live up to its Teutonic background without its traditional sauerkraut. When the two are joined together, the result is called "Coney Island Chicken Alsacienne," a euphemism for "a hot dog with kraut." COMPATIBLE BEVERAGES: A good cold beer.

CONFIT (French) The preserved meat of goose, duck, or pork, which after being cooked is covered with its own fat in hermetically-sealed cans or jars.

Confit d'Oie Preserved goose. Pieces of the goose, such as the legs, breasts, and wings, are preserved in rich goose fat in containers. A *cassoulet Toulousaine* or a *Carcassonnais* prepared without the *confit d'oie* would be just another pot of beans. (See CASSOULET)

CONGEE (Chinese) This thick gruel or porridge made from cooked rice will harmonize with almost any flavoring and with a variety of meats and seafood. It is similar to the East Indian *kedgeree.* (See KEDGEREE, RICE IN CHINA)

CONIGLIO SALVATICO (Italian) Wild hare.

Coniglio Salvatico in Salmi When a hare is cooked *in salmi,* it is twice cooked: first roasted, then braised. The hare is placed overnight in a spiced and herbed red wine pickling mixture. The following day the hare is dried, roasted, and then braised again, using the same marinade in which it was pickled. When the hare is done, it is removed to a serving dish. A mixture of white wine, anchovy paste, garlic, parsley, and vinegar is added to the pan, reduced by cooking, and poured over the *coniglio.* COMPATIBLE WINES: A red wine, e.g., Gevrey Chambertin, Corton, Chambolle-Musigny, Dôle, Pinot Noir, Vosne Romanée, Bonnes Mares, Pommard, Barolo.

CONSOMMÉ (French) A clear soup made from beef, chicken, or veal. The finished product—a soup that has been cooked and clarified, enriched and concentrated to its ultimate goodness—becomes "the consummate, the most perfect"—*le consommé!*

Andalouse A beef consommé with tomatoes, chopped beef, peppers, leeks, and carrots.

Belle-Hélène Chicken consommé made with thin slices of *crêpe.* (See CRÊPE)

Brunoise Any consommé made with diced vegetables. (See BRUNOISE)

Célestine A chicken consommé bound with tapioca and garnished with slices of rolled pancakes stuffed with minced and puréed chicken.

Chasseur A game consommé garnished with mushrooms.

Colbert A beef consommé with vegetables, egg white strips, and port wine. (See COLBERT)

Crécy, à la A chicken consommé bound with tapioca and garnished with a *brunoise* of carrots and chervil. (See BRUNOISE)

Diablotins A rich chicken consommé served with a garnish of fresh bread that is cut into decorative shapes then buttered, sprinkled with grated Parmesan cheese, and lightly browned in the grill.

Madrilène A beef consommé flavored with tomatoes and prepared with mixed vegetables and minced meat, egg whites, and egg shells. The soup is simmered, skimmed, and passed through a sieve. It is served garnished with croutons, chopped chives, diced tomatoes, and a dash of Madeira wine. In summer, *madrilène* is usually served jellied.

Milanese Cooked macaroni that has been cut into small rings, mixed with a *sauce Béchamel,* and thickened with egg yolk and grated cheese is formed into small cakes, rolled in breadcrumbs, and deep-fried. The cakes are served separately with a rich chicken consommé. (See BÉCHAMEL)

Mille-fanti (Italian) Raw egg that has been beaten with bread-crumbs, Parmesan cheese, and salt and pepper is poured through a sieve into boiling beef consommé and served piping hot.

Royale Any consommé garnished with cubed egg white.

CONTI (French) The Princess de Conti shared the bed and the affections of Henri IV for a time, during which she created, it is said, the puff paste and the *carré de mouton à la Conti*.

Carré de Mouton à la Conti ˙A rib of mutton, larded with pork fat, anchovies, shallots, and parsley, is placed in a pot and covered with white wine and beef stock. Flavored with bay leaves and tarragon, the meat is cooked until tender. The sauce is defatted, reduced, and served with the mutton, but separately. COMPATIBLE WINES: A white wine, e.g., Vouvray, Gewürztraminer, Mâcon Blanc, Sauterne, Champagne.

Conti, à la A dish so described is garnished with *croquettes* made of lentil purée and potato balls fried in butter. The garnish is served with small cuts of meat.

CONTORNI Many Italian restaurants list their side dishes, their vegetables, and salads under this heading. An alternate term is *legumi*.

COON A popular idiom for a type of oyster caught off the Florida coast. Also the name for a Cheddar-type cheese.

COPEAUX, POTATOES (French) A dish prepared by first peeling potatoes then paring them spiral-fashion into irregular ribbon shapes. They are then cooked, like *soufflé* potatoes, by first plunging them into a not-too-hot deep fat, which is heated gradually. When the potatoes start to rise to the surface, they are removed and drained. Prior to serving, the potatoes are again plunged into the deep fat, but this time a very hot fat. However, before they puff up, they are removed, drained, salted, and served. (See POMMES SOUFFLÉS)

COPPA (Italian) A very fine pork *salame*. (See SALAME)

COQ AU VIN (French) A rooster or cock cooked in red or white wine; today it is usually a chicken. The bird is cut into pieces and browned well in a mixture of oil, butter, and salt pork. Small pearl onions and mushrooms are added, and the whole is flamed with brandy. The chicken, covered with wine and meat stock, is set to simmer slowly until done. At the end, a *roux* is added to thicken the sauce. The chicken is served garnished with fried bread croutons in the shape of a heart. COMPATIBLE WINES: A red wine, e.g., Nuits St. Georges, Beaune, Chambertin, Dôle; or if a white wine was used in the cooking, a Riesling, Gewürztraminer, Johannisberg, Anjou, Chalon, Sauterne.

COQUILLE (French) Shell.

Coquilles St. Jacques   The _coquille_ (scallop shell) is venerated in France in honor of the holy Saint James, who, it is said, saved the life of a knight at sea. After having been duly baptized in the sea by Saint James, the knight emerged from the brine covered with these scallop shells. Today, religious Gallicians, wearing these shells draped over their shoulders, make an annual pilgrimage, on his name day, to the shrine of Saint James de Campostella in Spain. Of course, Jacques translates to James.

It seems that there are as many _coquille_ recipes as there are pilgrims. One way of preparing _coquilles St. Jacques_ involves removing the edible part of the scallops (the large muscle used to open and close the shell) from their shells, then washing them thoroughly and blanching them in boiling salted water. The scallops are then breaded, replaced in their shells, topped with garlic-butter and white wine, and baked with bits of bacon. They are served with a _sauce Mayonnaise_ and heavy cream. (See MAYONNAISE) WINES: See below.

Coquilles à la Dieppoise   Scallops are poached in white wine and a _court-bouillon._ To a _roux,_ fish stock plus the liquid from cooked mussels are added along with mussels, cooked shrimp, and scallops. This is then used to fill the scallop shells. The filling is covered with breadcrumbs, dotted with butter, and browned in the oven. WINES: See below.

Coquilles Frites   Raw scallops are dried, seasoned, rolled in beaten egg then in breadcrumbs, and deep-fried. They are served with chopped parsley and lemon slices. WINES: See below.

Coquilles à la Parisienne   Onions, shallots, and mushrooms are sautéed in butter to which parsley and breadcrumbs are added. This is cooked in a fish stock to a creamy consistency and is then spread in scallop shells. Topped with scallops and a _sauce Béchamel,_ the _coquilles_ are broiled and served piping hot. WINES: See below.

Coquilles à la Poulette   Finely chopped mushrooms are cooked in butter and seasoned with salt, pepper, and lemon juice. With the addition of breadcrumbs, this is then ground into a paste. The paste is placed into the scallop shells, covered with scallops and a _sauce poulette;_ covered with aluminum foil, it is baked in the oven. (See BÉCHAMEL, COURT-BOUILLON, POULETTE, ROUX)

COMPATIBLE WINES: A white wine, e.g., Meursault, Soave, Montrachet, Pouilly-Fuissé, Muscadet, Quincy, Sancerre, Piesporter Goldtröpfchen, Bernkasteler Doktor, Pinot Chardonnay.

CORAL   The mature ovaries of the lobster hen. Coral, green when raw but coral red when cooked, is used to make lobster-butter. (See BEURRES COMPOSÉS)

CORDON BLEU   Several stories tell of the origin of the famous _Cordon Bleu_ decoration, awarded for culinary excellence, and all are set during the reigns of the well-fed Louis of France. According to one version, the ribboned medallion was first created by Louis XV and pinned upon the ample bosom of his favorite mistress, Madame Du Barry, as a reward for her fine dinners. Since that time, this culinary decoration has been given as a sign of great praise to any female who has proved herself a skilled and respected cook. Another version of the origin of the *Cordon Bleu* tells of a cooking school run by Madame de Maintenon, the second wife of Louis XIV, where each young girl, upon her graduation, wore a blue ribbon as an emblem of her culinary accomplishment and expertise. Today, in Paris, a diploma from the *Cordon Bleu* cooking school on the rue Champ de Mars is considered to be one of the greatest references a chef can have.

Veal Cordon Bleu This is the name of an American garnish composed of a thin slice of ham and a slice of Gruyère cheese sandwiched between two veal cutlets, pounded thin, then dipped into beaten egg and covered with grated Parmesan cheese. This veal sandwich is allowed to ruminate for about a quarter of an hour and then is slowly sautéed in a mixture of olive oil and butter until golden brown on both sides. COMPATIBLE WINES: A white wine, e.g., Riesling, Sylvaner, Tokay, Anjou, Gewürztraminer, Riquewihr, Aigle, Orvieto, Frascati, Chenin Blanc.

CORIANDER This annual herb, native to Asia and to those countries bordering the Mediterranean, was first used by the Chinese in the fifth century B.C. It is used either whole, mostly to flavor fish dishes, or in powdered form to flavor cakes, cookies, and pastries. It is also used in sausages and Indian curries and is basic to all Chinese cooking. Coriander plays an important role in North African and in Mexican cooking as well. (See CHINESE CUISINE)

CORKSCREW A good corkscrew is essential to any *maître d'hôtel* as well as to anyone who enjoys drinking wine with his food without having the mess of a broken cork or having the cork pushed into the bottle. The one corkscrew that will extricate the cork without trouble is the screw with the "split helix." The tip of the screw should be curved, not straight. This type of corkscrew has a better bite and will always pull the cork out of the bottle intact.

CORN BREAD (American) Bread made from cornmeal is a great speciality of the South, and it seems that each southern state has its own individual recipe. Another variety of corn bread—a Jewish bread—takes its name from the common German word *Korn,* which means "grain," and it is actually made from rye flour. It is so delicious that one can make an entire meal of it. (See CORNMEAL, HOMINY, POLENTA)

CORNED BEEF Originally, the term "corn" meant "grains of salt," and today "corning" is the term used to describe the process of curing a brisket of beef by steeping it in a pickling solution. The beef is piled in layers and covered with a marinade containing sodium nitrate, sugar, and sodium nitrite. Originally, the meat was preserved by dry salting.

A complete curing of beef takes at least four weeks. When ready, the beef is covered with a mixture of boiling water and vinegar and simmered until tender. In England corned beef is known as "bully beef." (See BULLY BEEF) COMPATIBLE BEVERAGES: Beer, ale, stout.

CORNET (French) A small, conical pastry that is filled with cream. Our American ice cream cone would be a good example of *le vrai cornet.*

CORNICHONS (French) Very tiny sweet-sour pickles, better known as "gherkins." They are used in sauces and as a garnish. (See CHARCUTIÈRE)

CORNMEAL This product, made from corn kernels that have been dried and then ground, is used as a cereal and in bread and muffin baking. The best and most nutritious cornmeal, "stone-ground," does not have the flavorful germ removed during manufacture. Cornmeals from which the germ is removed are drier and more granular in texture. (See CORN BREAD, HOMINY, POLENTA)

CORN PONE (American South) *Pone* is an Algonquin Indian word referring to an original Indian bread made from maize (corn) flour. Today, corn pone is made in the Deep South from a batter composed of ground white cornmeal, salt, baking powder, bacon fat, and boiling water. The resulting batter, dropped by the spoonful onto a baking sheet, is baked in a hot oven.

COSTOLETTA (Italian) A cutlet or a chop of veal, pork, or mutton.

COTEAUX (French) The rather aesthetic term once used to classify those lovers of fine food who could identify the wine they were drinking at the first sip. Today, they are called *gastronomes.*

COTELETTE DE MOUTON À LA SOUBISE (French) When the very first Parisian restaurateur, Beauvilliers, was still working as chef to the Count of Provence, he created this dish to honor his master's dinner guest, the Prince of Soubise. He named the dish "lamb chops *à la Soubise,*" and because he knew that Soubise doted on onions, he made certain to use not just one onion but several pounds of onions in the preparation. To prepare the dish, half the onions are chopped fine and cooked in butter with chopped carrots, parsley, and scallions. Then, several double lamb chops are larded with ham and pork fat, set on top of the chopped vegetables, covered with bouillon and more pork fat, and baked in the oven for a quarter of an hour. In another pot, the rest of the onions, sliced thin, are fried in butter. They are then sprinkled with flour and cooked covered with bouillon until tender. These onions are ground to a pulp, pressed through a sieve, seasoned with salt and pepper, and, away from the heat, enriched with heavy cream. The double lamb chops are glazed in their own reduced cooking liquid and regally served, swimming in the rich, creamed onion purée. Soubise was delighted. COMPATIBLE WINES: A red wine, e.g., St. Julien, St. Estèphe, Pauillac, Carbonnieux, Olivier, Cabernet Sauvignon, Zinfandel, Côtes du Rhône, Egri Bikaver.

COTRIADE DE BRETON (French) Praising a Breton for his *bouillabaisse* would be much like telling a chef from Carcasson how much you enjoyed his Boston baked beans. This rich fish dish, created in Brittany, differs from the *bouillabaisse* of Provence in that it has not one shellfish in it. Instead, fish such as halibut, haddock, sea bass, cod, flounder, mackerel, and mullet are cut up and added to a mixture of potatoes, water, onions, garlic, bay leaves, thyme, majoram, parsley, salt, and pepper that has been brought to the boil. Now, all is simmered gently until the fish are just tender. The fish and potatoes are served separate from the thick fish broth, which is poured steaming over slices of French bread in a bowl. (See BOUILLABAISSE, CASSOULET) COMPATIBLE WINES: A white wine, e.g., Anjou, Chalon, Meursault, Gewürztraminer, Aigle, Dry Semillon, Sylvaner.

COULIBIAC See KOULIBIAC

COULIS (French) A rich meat sauce obtained from the juices that seep out from the meat as it roasts. Purées made from poultry, fish, or vegetables are also called *coulis.*

Coulis d'Écrevisses This French soup is made from crayfish that have been sautéed in a mixture of butter, seasoning, parsley, thyme, and a *mirepoix* and then flamed with brandy and slaked with a dry white wine. The meat is removed from the heads and the tails, half of which is puréed through a strainer with the rest of the mixture. The other half, the bits of the tail, is added to a *roux,* flavored with chopped onions and celery, and moistened with a rich consommé. It thickens to a cream soup consistency. The *sauce Espagnole* is one of the more famous descendants of the original *coulis.* (See ÉCREVISSE, ESPAGNOLE, MIREPOIX, ROUX)

Coulis de Tomates à la Provençale This is a thick French tomato sauce, and its affiliation with Provence means that it is amply flavored with garlic, onions, and herbs such as bay leaf, thyme, parsley plus the aromatic blend of fennel, coriander, and the costly saffron. It is served with broiled or boiled chicken, boiled beef, eggs, and *pasta* dishes. (See BASIL, CORIANDER, FENNEL, SAFFRON, THYME)

COUPE (French) A shallow cup made of glass, silver, or even stainless steel. The material takes second place to the form: the rather wide bowl must rest on a low stem. The *coupe* is usually used to serve cold desserts such as ice creams, sherbets, and fruit cocktails. (See JACQUES)

COURGETTES À LA ROMAINE (French) A dish of sliced zucchini which, after having been marinated in vinegar, parsley, and salt, are dipped in a batter and baked. *Courgettes* are served with a seasoned tomato sauce.

COURONNE (French) Literally, "crown." Used when referring to foods arranged in a ring as well as to describe a braided round loaf of French bread.

COURT-BOUILLON (French) Not a "short broth," but a tasty liquid composed of a variety of vegetables—onions, carrots, celery—plus vinegar or white wine and a mixture of herbs, salt, and pepper. It is used to give flavor to cooking fish, meat, and vegetables. Variations on the standard _court-bouillon_ are made specifically with vinegar as the liquid to cook pike or carp, with white wine as the liquid to cook salmon or trout, with red wine to cook carp or pike, and with milk to cook halibut, catfish, sole, or whiting.

COUSCOUS (North African) This French term stems from the Arabic word _kuskus,_ which in turn evolved from another Arabic word, _kaskasa,_ meaning "to pound, to make small." _Couscous_ (or _couscousso_) is an Arab dish that was adopted from the Chinese method of steaming rice or other cereal grains over cooking meat. Traditionally, the mush of wheat, corn, or millet seed is set in a perforated steamer over cooking meat.

> **Couscous de Maroc** In Morocco, a cereal grain (a byproduct of flour) a bit larger than the head of a pin is used. This grain is similar to the hard durum grain from which the best Italian _spaghetti_ and _macaroni_ are made. After the durum wheat is thoroughly cleaned, it is placed in a bowl and, by the spoonful, boiling water is added until the wheat swells up; all the while, the _couscous_ is kneaded with the hands. It is then cooked. Separately, either chicken or lamb is cooked into a stew. The _couscous_ is placed in the center of a large dish; and the meats, along with a sprinkling of the sauce, are placed on top of the mound of cooked grain. In Arab countries this dish is eaten with the right hand, specifically with the first two fingers and thumb. (The left hand is reserved; it is used for sanitary purposes, such as urinating.)

COVER CHARGE A fee levied by restaurants "to cover" the cost of tablecloths, napkins, cutlery, glasses, bread and butter, flowers, and other items. It has also become the custom for nightclubs and cafés, which offer entertainment as well as food and drink, to exact a cover charge for these professional services.

COZZE One of many Italian words for "mussels," this is often used on menus as a heading for a list of various mussel preparations.

> **Cozze alla Marinara** Mussels are steamed in an aromatic mixture of olive oil, white wine, and garlic. COMPATIBLE WINES: A white wine, e.g., Soave, Verdicchio, Chablis, Pouilly-Fumé, Muscadet, Pinot Chardonnay.

CRACKLING The browned, crisp rind of pork after the fat has been rendered out. It is popular in the southern part of the United States, where it is known as "cracklin." The term also refers to corn bread that contains this residue of hog fat. (See GRIBENES)

CRAPAUD (French) Although this word means "toad," the term is used in the French-speaking islands of the Caribbean to describe the large frogs found there. On the Island of Monserrat, the natives refer to *crapauds* as "mountain chickens." (See CRAPAUDINE)

CRAPAUDINE, SAUCE (French) To prepare this classic sauce, chopped mushrooms, mustard, and tarragon vinegar are added to a *sauce diable*. The term *crapaudine* is also used for a French method of preparing and cooking pigeons: they are split, opened, flattened, covered with butter, seasoned, and grilled.

The development of *crapaudine* from the word *crapaud* ("toad" in French) is another one of many culinary mysteries. In 1870, during the great famine in France, a noted chef, M. Thomas Génin, confessed that he served rats grilled *à la crapaudine,* calling them pigeons. Shortly thereafter, he formed the first cooks' union. Of course, the one accomplishment had nothing to do with the other. (See DIABLE)

CRÉCY (French) A word synonymous with carrots because the finest carrots in all France are grown in the Crécy district just outside Paris.

Purée à la Crécy This thick carrot soup is made by sautéing chopped onions in bacon fat then adding the onions, veal knuckles, parsley, leeks, celery, and the finest carrots together with spices, sugar, and herbs to a white stock. More chopped onions and rice are added, and the soup is simmered until the vegetables are tender. It is garnished with small croutons. The soup is also known as *potage à la Crécy.*

CRÈME À L'ANGLAISE (French) This sauce is named after the English, whom the French, after the Revolution, tried to emulate and to honor. Boiled milk, flavored with vanilla or any other flavoring, is slowly added to egg yolks that have been creamed with sugar. This mixture is stirred continuously over a low flame until it has thickened. It is then strained. It forms the base for all ice creams, and the famous Bavarian creams, and it is served with hot or cold desserts, such as puddings. (See BAVAROIS/BAVAROISE)

CRÈME BRÛLÉE (English) Although the name is French, meaning "burnt cream," this very old English dessert originated in Trinity College, Cambridge, and it is most important that the cream be cold and set before submitting it to the heat of the broiler. First, the cream is mixed with egg yolks, sugar, and vanilla and gently cooked until the custard thickens. Then the custard is poured into receptacles, either pie plates or smaller individual ramekins, and refrigerated. When cool enough and firm, the custard is covered with a layer of brown sugar and grilled until the sugar caramelizes. The plates are then returned to the refrigerator. The dessert is served cold. (See QUEIMADO CREME)

CRÈME CARAMEL (French) This famous dessert is made from a light custard prepared from a cooked mixture of egg yolks, sugar, and milk. Then a caramel is prepared and cooled at the bottom of the mold, and the custard is gradually blended in. The *crème caramel* is stirred over a bowl of crushed ice until it has cooled. It is kept refrigerated until served. (See CARAMEL, CRÈME BRÛLÉE, FLAN)

CRÈME CHANTILLY (French) See CHANTILLY

CRÈME PATISSIÈRE (French) A thick custard, sometimes called "baker's custard" or "pastry cream," used as a filling for cream puffs, *éclairs,* and for the famous *gâteau St. Honoré.* To prepare the custard, eggs are beaten into flour and, with the addition of sugar, whipped until smooth. Then, after adding milk and vanilla, the mixture is cooked in a double boiler until thick. (See ÉCLAIR, ST. HONORÉ)

CRÉOLE *Créole* refers to a style of cooking made world-famous by the early French and Spanish settlers of Louisiana and other Gulf States of the United States. These settlers were dubbed *Créoles* by the French and *Criollo* (literally, "native to the place") by the Spanish. Créole cooking has developed into what is considered the only true American cuisine.

Créole Sauce Chopped shallots, mushrooms, and green peppers are sautéed in butter then reduced in white wine, enriched with a *sauce Espagnole,* and topped with diced pimiento. (See CRÉOLE SAUCE II, ESPAGNOLE)

Créole Sauce II For this sauce, tomatoes are cooked in butter with garlic, thyme, bay leaf, salt, and cayenne pepper. With a bit of flour to bind, sautéed onions, peppers, and mushrooms are added.

Shrimp Créole Chopped onions, garlic, and green peppers are cooked in butter. Chopped tomatoes are added, and the vegetables are seasoned with salt, pepper, and paprika. After half an hour, shelled raw shrimp are added, just brought to the boil, and removed from the heat. The dish is served with heaps of gleaming steamed white rice.

Poached Eggs Créole Poached eggs are served on toast, napped with creamed chicken and a *sauce Béchamel* and browned in the grill. (See BÉCHAMEL)

Baked Fillets of Sole Créole A mixture of chopped onions, celery, and green peppers is cooked in butter, to which a dusting of flour and milk are added. Off of the heat, cooked crab meat and shrimp are added together with breadcrumbs, thyme, marjoram, parsley, salt, pepper, Worcestershire sauce, and a dash of Tabasco sauce. This filling is spread on each fillet of sole, which is rolled up and fastened with toothpicks, brushed with melted butter, seasoned, and baked for a few minutes. Then, covered with the *sauce Créole,* the fish is baked until tender. (See CRÉOLE SAUCE, TABASCO, WORCESTERSHIRE) COMPATIBLE WINES: A white wine, e.g., Orvieto, White Chianti, Pinot Chardonnay, Sauvignon Blanc, Frascati, Riesling, Sylvaner.

Baked Catfish à la Créole This Créole speciality, native to Louisiana, consists of a sauce of minced onions, tomatoes, green peppers plus *sauce Tabasco,* tomato purée, salt, and pepper poured over a skinned catfish. The fish is slowly baked until tender. (See TABASCO) COMPATIBLE WINES: A red wine, e.g., Beaujolais, Lambrusco, Côte Rôtie, Moulin-à-Vent, Médoc, Savigny, Mâcon, Ruby Cabernet, Zinfandel.

CRÉOLE CUISINE Born in New Orleans as early as 1750, the word *Créole* was used to define anything that originated in the French and Spanish colonies of America. Créole cuisine embraced the classical European style of cookery but added the herbs of the American Indian and spices from the West Indies. The actual preparation was done by the able hands of the African slaves. Créole dining always meant dining leisurely, for Créole food cannot be hurried. The Créole kitchen boasts of an excellence that is due to four basics: the stock, the *roux,* the herbs, and alcohol.

As a gastronomic center, New Orleans never lacked spirit, a spirit that often came in bottles whose contents enriched the Créole cooking pot. Créole food benefits most from that alcohol which is added after the heat has been turned off. Turtle soup, for instance, tastes best when sherry is added at the table, not in the kitchen; salad dressings made with wine instead of vinegar become more mellow; and fruits and desserts are served either marinated in fine liqueur or dramatically flambéed with it. Ultimately, Créole cookery is an American tradition marked by the use of okra and filé powder, influenced greatly by the African Negro and the people of the West Indies, France, and Spain. (See FILÉ, OKRA)

CRÉOLE JAMBALAYA (Créole) The Spanish brought *jambalaya* (closely related to the *paëlla*) to New Orleans. At the onset, because the name evolved from the Spanish word for ham, *jamón,* the dish was made only with ham. The Créoles, however, made it a classic by adding sausages, crabmeat, shrimp, chicken, and a variety of other foods. First, the ham, sausages, and green onions are sautéed in oil, with a bit of flour added at the end. Then, with the addition of water, shrimp, chicken, crabmeat, garlic, parsley, and tomatoes, the mixture is brought to a boil. Rice is stirred in and all is cooked until the rice is tender and the liquid is absorbed. The dish is served sprinkled with chopped fresh parsley. (See PAELLA) COMPATIBLE WINES: A red wine, e.g., Beaujolais, Côte Rôtie, Rioja, Chianti, Châteauneuf-du-Pape, Valpolicella, Zinfandel, Nebbiolo, Egri Bikaver.

CRÊPE (French) A very light pancake made from a mixture of eggs and flour. If they are to be sweet, sugar, butter, milk and cream are added; if they are to be savory, salt is required and the sugar is omitted. The latter can be filled with chopped poultry, shellfish, chopped meat, caviar, or various cheese mixtures. (See AEPFELPFANNKUCHEN, BLINI, BLINTZ, PANCAKE, PLÄTTAR, SUZETTE)

CRÉPINETTES (French) Small cakes composed of a mixture of highly seasoned ground meats (usually pork or sausage meat), truffles, garlic, chopped mushrooms, thick cream, plus other meats that are to be mixed with the pork, such as ham, chicken, or game. Pork, however, is the main ingredient. All the ingredients are kneaded together, wrapped in caul fat, and either fried, broiled, or baked to a golden turn. (See CAUL FAT) COMPATIBLE WINES: A red wine, e.g., Mâcon, Mercurey, Beaujolais, Châteauneuf-du-Pape, Côte Rôtie, Zinfandel, Petit Sirah.

CRESPELLE (Italian) Thin pancakes made from a batter of milk, flour, salt, water, eggs, and nutmeg. The batter is ladled into a fairly hot, buttered *crêpe* pan and fried on both sides. A German version of *crespelles,* called *Palatschinken,* are filled with fruit preserves and sprinkled with sugar. (See CRÊPE, PALATSCHINKEN)

CRESSON, POTAGE DE (French) A soup made from watercress that is cooked in boiling salted water together with sugar, pepper, and cubed potatoes. When the potatoes are tender, the mixture is puréed. The soup is again brought to the boil, chopped fresh watercress is added, and then off of the heat it is enriched with heavy cream and served.

Watercress in its raw state is frequently used to garnish broiled meats, but unfortunately it is most often left untouched on the diner's plate. This vegetable contains goodly amounts of iron, sulfur, calcium, and what is most important, iodine and vitamin C. It is delicious as a salad.

CREVETTES, SAUCE AUX (French) A classic sauce composed of a *velouté de poisson,* heavy cream, and a *fumet de poisson* that is reduced to half the original quantity. To this infusion a shrimp-butter is added. A dash of cayenne pepper and a sprinkling of finely-chopped cooked shrimp is added just before serving. This rich sauce is served with fish and shellfish. (See FUMET, VELOUTÉ DE POISSON)

CROISSANT (French) This flaky butter-rich roll was originally made by the Turks in honor of the crescent moon that has decorated the Turkish banner for centuries. But when the Ottomans were finally driven out of Austria, the excellent Viennese bakers made the *croissant* themselves, and they called it *Gipfel.* When Marie Antoinette became the Queen of Louis XVI, she brought the recipe for the *Gipfel* with her to France. Though the seed of the crescent roll was Turkish and the Austrians promoted it, it did not become the flaky pastry we know today until French bakers enriched the dough and developed the process of refrigerating the dough after each butter application and of folding (turning) and refolding the dough. (See GIPFEL)

CROMESQUI/KROMESKI Born in Poland but also a favorite in French kitchens, these *croquettes* are made from various foods. Chopped meats, fish, eggs, poultry, game, or liver—flavored with seasonings,

chopped mushrooms, and truffles and bound with a cream sauce—
are shaped into cones or balls. In France the custom is to dip the
cromesquis in batter, deep-fry them, and serve them as an *hors
d'oeuvre*. In Poland the mixtures are enveloped in thin *crêpes,* deep-
fried, and eaten as an entrée. COMPATIBLE WINES: A varied selection,
all depending upon the type of *cromesqui* served and the spiciness or
blandness of the sauce served with it. (See CRÊPE)

Oeufs en Cromesqui   French-fried eggs. Hard-boiled eggs are diced
then mixed with truffles and mushrooms and bound with a rich *sauce
Allemande.* They are then dipped in a batter and fried in deep fat.
(See ALLEMANDE) COMPATIBLE BEVERAGES: Beer.

CROQUANTE (French) Literally "crisp," but as a culinary term this
refers to a marzipan basket filled with ice cream or, in days gone by,
when the culinary art called for much sugar sculpture, the *croquante*
took the form of a huge table centerpiece composed of balls of flaky
pastry and trellised marzipan. (See ALMOND PASTE, MARZIPAN)

CROQUEMBOUCHE (French) This descriptive term means "crisp-in-
the-mouth," and that is exactly what these pastry balls are. The term
is also applied to orange segments, to grapes, and to cherries that
have been dipped into a sugar syrup and left to harden. The most
common, however, is the small *profiterole,* made from a *pâte à chou*
pastry, which is glazed with syrup and baked *au cassé,* "to the crack
stage." The red candied apples that children love so much fall into the
croquembouche category. (See PÂTE À CHOU, PROFITEROLE)

CROQUE MONSIEUR (French) A sandwich composed of a slice of ham
set between two slices of Gruyère cheese. The bread is buttered on one
side and the whole crustless sandwich is slowly fried in bubbling,
fresh butter until golden brown on both sides. Another method is to
deep-fry the sandwich in very hot fat. COMPATIBLE WINES: A white
wine, e.g., Sylvaner, Traminer, Riesling, Neuchâtel, Vouvray,
Frascati.

CROQUETTES This is the truly French way of deep-frying ground meat,
fish, or vegetables. The food is bound with egg yolk or with a *sauce
Béchamel* and appears on the plate cone-shaped and crisp.

Croquette Judic   Celery, egg yolks, carrots, beans, and mushrooms
are mixed with tomato sauce and fried.

Croquette Gorinflor   Roe, shrimp, egg yolks, truffles, and mushrooms are formed into *croquettes* and deep-fried.

Potato Croquettes   Chilled mashed potatoes are bound with egg
yolks, rolled in breadcrumbs, and deep-fried. (See DAUPHINOISE)

CROSTINI (Italian) Small slices of white bread which are served with
cheese, liver paste, anchovies, ham, *salame,* tomatoes, what-have-
you. The ingredients can be placed between the slices of bread and the
sandwich can then be toasted or fried, or they can be skewered and
toasted in the oven.

Crostini con Mozzarella e Acciughe Slices of white bread with crusts removed are made into small sandwiches with mozzarella cheese and anchovy fillets (one slice of cheese and one fillet per half-sandwich). The sandwiches are fried in butter on both sides, cut in half, and served immediately. As warm *hors d'oeuvre,* they are aromatic delights. (See HORS D'OEUVRE) COMPATIBLE WINES: A red wine, e.g., Chianti, Rioja, Dôle, Beaujolais, Valpolicella, Zinfandel, Santenay.

CROUSTADE (French) The word derives from *croûte* (crust) and literally translates to "pie." The *croustade* can be a pastry casing filled with the same ingredients used to fill a *vol-au-vent* and bound with a *Béchamel* or a *velouté* sauce. *Croustades* are also made from cooked noodles, boiled rice, mashed potatoes, or even of half of a hollowed-out loaf of crusty bread. They are baked until crisp and brown. (See BÉCHAMEL, VELOUTÉ, VOL-AU-VENT)

CROÛTE (French) A hard exterior or crust. The term can refer to the hard crust of bread or to pastry baked in the oven and filled with meat or fish—such as a *vol-au-vent* or a *pâté en croûte.* It can also refer to a piece of bread that is partially scooped out, filled with mushrooms or cheese, and baked. The Old French expression *casser la croûte* refers to the time when a loaf of bread really had a crust that was so thick and hard that one had to literally "break the crust" to eat it. Workers usually have their *casse-croûte* (break-of-the-crust) at ten in the morning, when they partake of bread, sausage, cheese, and a drop of wine to help them through the day. (See PÂTÉ, VOL-AU-VENT)

CROÛTONS (French) Bread cubes sautéed in butter or oil until golden brown.

CRUDA, SALSA This popular sauce, commonly seen on dining room tables in Mexico, consists of tomatoes, *serrano* chilies, onions, and coriander, all of which are chopped fine and seasoned with salt, pepper, and sugar to taste. The sauce is served cold with cooked meats, poultry, fish, and eggs. (See CHILI)

CRUDITÉS (French) Raw vegetables, often served cut into strips as a cocktail snack.

CRUMPET "Tea and crumpets" are popular in England as part of a light, mid-afternoon meal known in German-speaking Switzerland as *Z'vieri,* that is, "to eat a little something at four P.M." The crumpet, a typical English teacake, is round in shape, about a half-inch thick, with a top full of holes. It is served well toasted and thickly spread with gobs of fresh sweet butter.

CRYSTAL CHICKEN This is not only one of the most unusual of the Chinese chicken preparations but one of the most delicious. A young chicken, cut into bite-size pieces, is carefully placed in wildly boiling water that is full of aromatic herbs and spices. The chicken is boiled for barely one minute, then the heat is turned off, and the chicken is left covered in the hot water for three hours. The chicken absorbs all of the flavors of the herbs and spices and becomes so tender that even the eldest grandfather finds little difficulty in enjoying and digesting the succulent dish. COMPATIBLE WINES: A white wine, e.g., Graves, Montrachet, Schloss Vollrads, Orvieto, Nackenheim, Nierstein, Rüdesheim, Kientzheim.

CSÁRDÁS In any Hungarian restaurant or café, the crying strains of the *csárdás* will bring *gulyas,* paprika, and gypsies to mind. The gypsies, said to have come originally from Egypt via India, infused their fiery temperament into Hungarian music and its food. *Csárdás* means "a country inn."

CSIPETKE (Hungarian) A small dumpling made from flour, eggs, water, and salt. The dough is rolled into half-inch strips, from which small pieces are cut and cooked together with the goulash fifteen minutes before serving. (See GULYAS)

CSIRKE PAPRIKAS (Hungarian) "Chicken paprika." The bird is cut up and the pieces are carefully dredged in flour seasoned with salt and pepper. The chicken pieces are then sautéed until a golden brown in a bubbling mixture of butter and oil. The chicken is removed and minced garlic and onions are sautéed lightly in the same pan; paprika and chicken stock are then added. The pieces of chicken are returned to the pan and simmered. To this mixture heavy cream and sour cream are added. When cooked, the chicken is arranged on a large platter, covered with the cream sauce, and garnished with chopped parsley and a sprinkling of paprika. COMPATIBLE WINES: A white wine, e.g., Gewürztraminer, Piesporter Goldtröpfchen, Rüdesheim, Vouvray, Tokay, Szamorodni.

CUCCULLI (Italian) Small dumplings made from potatoes, nuts, and marjoram. The dumplings are breaded and fried until golden and crisp.

CUISINE BOURGEOISE (French) A cooking style that varies from region to region, based solely on local ingredients.

CUMBERLAND SAUCE (English) This traditional sauce is said to carry the name of the son of King George II of England, who was known as the Duke of Cumberland. The base of the sauce, red currant jelly, is dissolved over heat. Then, port wine, chopped shallots, the chopped rind of oranges and lemons plus mustard and cayenne pepper are added. After mixing together well, the sauce is allowed to chill; and when cool, chopped glacé cherries are added. The sauce is a favorite with game and cold meats.

CUMIN Native to those countries that border the Mediterranean Sea, cumin was used by the ancient Persians, the Egyptians, and the Hebrews. When pepper was hard to get and almost as dear as gold, the cooks of ancient Rome substituted cumin seed. Cumin enhances cheese, sausages, cookies, breads, meats, vegetables, fish, and game, thus covering many food categories. Powdered cumin is used in curry and in chili powder.

CURD When whole milk is subjected to the chemical action of rennet (a substance derived from the stomach of an animal, usually a calf), it coagulates and separates into two parts: a liquid called whey and a solid known as curd. Curd is similar to farmer's cheese or cottage cheese, and it can be combined with other foods such as eggs, or fruit, or even transformed into a deliciously rich cheesecake. (See BÄR-KRÄM, BAVAROIS, DAHI, RAHKA)

CURING The process of preserving meats or fish through salting, drying, or smoking.

CURNONSKY This name was adopted by M. Maurice-Edmond Sailland, the great French gastronome and writer. During the turn of the century, anything vaguely Russian was the rage in Paris, so Sailland took the Latin phrase *cur non,* meaning "why not," to which he added the Slavic *"sky"* to form "Curnonsky." *Cur non* was also the motto of Lafayette.

Because of his engrossing love for *La Table,* because of his good taste and knowledge of French gastronomy, and because his nose for fine wines was impeccable, Sailland was awarded the title *"Prince des Gastronomes."* When he died in 1956, the title did as well; it was forever abandoned, never to be passed on to a successor. In his declining years, Sailland is said to have been so heavy that he was unable to walk to his favorite restaurants: he had to be carried by six stout friends. At age 84, he leaned too far out of his window and fell to the Paris pavement, where he perished.

CURRANTS See BAR-LE-DUC

CURRIE, SAUCE AU (French) An adaptation of the Indian curry sauce, prepared by sautéing diced onions and apples in hot butter then adding curry powder and coconut milk. After the addition of the appropriate *sauce velouté,* the sauce is passed through a fine sieve and, just before serving, refined with a heavy cream. (See CURRY, VELOUTÉ)

CURRY To an East Indian, curry is not a specific powdered spice dispensed from a glass jar, but a special selection of spices chosen to complement an individual dish. Curry means "cookery" in the Tamil Indian vernacular, but throughout India it refers to sauces whose compositions are as different as are the sects of India.

Actually, the word "curry" is a vague and totally inaccurate description of Indian cookery. India lived under English rule for many years, and the Indian word *kari* (curry), meaning "a spicy leaf, a sauce," was mistakenly used by the English to refer to the whole of Indian cuisine.

Curry powder as we know it (which the Indians never use) is a packaged mixture of spices, such as fenugreek, cumin, coriander, red peppers, and turmeric. In India, curried spice mixtures vary with each dish being prepared.

The spices considered fundamental to a true curry are traditional: chilies are important for flavor; ginger must be present as an aid to digestion and for flavor; cloves, to lend their aromatic perfume; turmeric, for flavor and color; tamarind, for its acidic property; and garlic and onions for that inimitable flavor that has been honored by cultures and cuisines throughout history. Restaurants featuring the cuisine of northern India will use less hot curries to flavor food than will restaurants that cook southern-style, which use as many as thirty hot chilies. (See CLOVES, CORIANDER, CUMIN, GARAM MASALA, GINGER, FENUGREK, TAMARIND)

CUSCINETTI (Italian) Literally these are "tiny pillows," but any good Italian cook will tell you that this is the term for tiny cheese sandwiches that are cooked until a golden brown.

Cuscinetti al Prosciutto Small triangular sandwiches which are first filled with mozzarella cheese and ham, then dipped in milk, rolled in flour, and dipped into beaten egg before being fried on both sides in oil or bacon fat. COMPATIBLE WINES: A red wine, e.g., Chianti, Valpolicella, Rioja, Beaujolais, Zinfandel, Mâcon, Chinon, Pinot Noir, Châteauneuf-du-Pape.

CZARNINA (Polish) A tangy soup made from the rich broth and blood of a duck. It is flavored with cinnamon, mace, vinegar, salt, and pepper plus a garniture of sliced carrots, dumplings or egg noodles, and prunes. (See BLOOD AS FOOD)

CZECHOSLOVAKIAN CUISINE Pork and ham make up a great variety of Czech dishes, and though greatly influenced by the neighboring cuisines, especially that of Austria, the Czech cuisine proudly boasts of having created some of the finest dumplings *(knedliky)* and most succulent sausages in the world. Dumplings—light or heavy, small or large, sweet or tart—are served to accompany main courses or as desserts. Pork is used for the sausages. Of course, great praise must go to the beer brewed in Czechoslovakia, namely the Pilsner beer, which is touted as one of the finest lager beers in the world.

DAHI (East Indian) Milk curd. (See CURD)

DAHIBARA (East Indian) Lentils, cooked and then ground fine, mixed with yogurt, and fried until brown and crisp. Served as a snack.

DAIKON The term for a Japanese or Chinese radish, which is less sharp than the familiar red radish. Because it contains pepsin, it is often taken as a digestive or breath sweetener. The *daikon* can be preserved in a sweet-sour marinade for three months or more.

DAL This is not an Indian soup, despite its thin consistency when served in restaurants. It is the East Indian culinary term for lentils, dried beans, peas and chickpeas, which are puréed and always eaten with rice or with Indian breads *(poori, pappadum)*. It is either poured over the rice or placed beside it on the plate. Often the *dal* is served in a side dish, called a *katori*. *Tarka, bagar,* or *chhownk* are names given to various spice combinations which give zest to *dal* dishes by the infusion of mustard, cumin, fenugreek, asafoetida seeds, browned onions, or ginger. The selected spice combination is then cooked in hot oil or in *ghee* and poured over the cooked *dal*. (See ASAFOETIDA, FENUGREEK, GHEE, PAPPADUM, POORI)

DAMPFKNÖDEL (German) Yeast dumplings cooked in sugared milk and sweet butter and served with vanilla sugar and apricot purée or other fruit preserves.

DAMSON POCKETS These stuffed *ravioli*-type puffs come from Czechoslovakia, where so many pastry and dumpling delicacies are popular. First, grated potatoes, flour, salt, fat, lemon rind, and eggs are worked into an elastic dough. The dough is rolled out and cut into rounds. Then *damson*-butter (a purée of prunes worked into fresh butter) is placed in the center of each round. The edges are moistened, and one round of dough is placed on top of the other, sealing the fruit purée inside. These pockets are cooked in boiling salted water. When done, they are ladled out, well drained, and served sprinkled with powdered sugar.

DANOISE, CÔTELETTES DE SAUMON À LA (French) Salmon steaks that are richly spread with anchovy purée and fried in butter. The salmon is served with a white wine sauce flavored with grated cheese and with lobster-butter. COMPATIBLE WINES: A white wine, e.g., Muscadet, Quincy, Pouilly-Fumé, Meursault, Gewürztraminer, Soave, Pinot Chardonnay, Montrachet.

DANOISE, SAUCE (Danish) A rich sauce is made from a purée of tart apples blended with grated horseradish and heavy whipped cream. Usually served with cold fish. (See RAIFORT)

DARIOLE (French) A small cylindrical mold that is usually buttered,

lined with puff pastry, filled with *frangipane* cream flavored with slivered blanched almonds and Kirschwasser, and baked until golden brown. It is served sprinkled with fine sugar. *Dariole* is also the common name for a custard tart. (See FRANGIPANE)

DARNE (French) Literally, "slice." The term is used to define a thick fish steak cut from the center of the fish.

Darne de Saumon Grillé This savory salmon steak, grilled the French way, basted with gobs of fresh butter, is served with a rich *sauce Béarnaise.* (See BÉARNAISE) COMPATIBLE WINES: A red wine, e.g., Aloxe-Corton, Pommard, Échézeaux, Richebourg, Fixin, Dôle, Pinot Noir.

DARTOIS (French) Layers of puff pastry are filled with an almond cream or a *frangipane* cream, covered with another piece of pastry, brushed with egg, baked, and then iced with sugar and glazed. This name is also given to an *hors d'oeuvre* prepared by filling layers of puff pastry with any number of savory mixtures, such as a *salpicon* of *foie gras* and truffles in a *sauce demi-glace;* a forcemeat of pike with crayfish-butter; a *salpicon* of sweetbreads, truffles, and chopped vegetables blended in a *sauce velouté;* or a forcemeat of anchovy, tuna fish, or sardines. (See DEMI-GLACE, FOIE GRAS, FORCEMEATS, FRANGIPANE, SALPICON, VELOUTÉ)

DASHEEN A starchy tuber, considered a staple food in many tropical lands. In Polynesia it is called *taro;* in the West Indies, it is *eddo;* and it is known as *yautia* in Puerto Rico. A member of the calla lily family, it is prepared exactly like the potato. (See POI, TARO)

DASHI A fish stock used in the preparation of many Japanese dishes, including *tempura* sauce. (See OYAKO DOMBURI, TEMPURA)

DASHI KOMBU (Japanese) A rich fish stock flavored with dried kelp.

DAUBE, EN (French) A descriptive term for food that has been "very slowly cooked, stewed."

Boeuf en Daube This popular dish consists of a round of beef that is first cut into cubes and browned in salt pork. Beef stock and red wine are added and the meat is then baked very slowly for several hours together with onions, carrots, parsley, and spices. COMPATIBLE WINES: A red wine, e.g., Châteauneuf-du-Pape, Moulin-à-Vent, Beaujolais, Valpolicella, Chianti, Nebbiolo, Zinfandel, Ruby Cabernet, Côte Rôtie, Mercurey.

DAUMONT, À LA (French) Dishes so described are served with a garnish of mushroom caps cooked in butter, with crayfish tails, fish *quenelles,* and fried soft row bound with a *sauce Nantua.* The garnish is named after the famous French architect Daumet, who constructed the Palais de Justice in Paris. (See NANTUA, QUENELLES)

Sauce Daumont A sauce made by adding oyster liquid and lemon juice to a *sauce Hollandaise.* It is enriched with chopped mushrooms, truffles, and oysters. (See HOLLANDAISE)

Darne de Saumon Daumont Salmon steaks poached in white wine with chopped carrots, onions, parsley, thyme, salt and pepper. The fish steaks are served garnished with mushrooms, sliced truffles, and a *sauce Normande.* (See NORMANDE) COMPATIBLE WINES: A white wine, e.g., Meursault, Montrachet, Orvieto, Graacher Himmelreich, Johannisberg, Aigle, Graves.

DAUPHINE POTATOES (French) A classic dish made with a cream puff paste into which mashed potatoes, egg yolks, salt, and pepper are blended until the whole is light and fluffy. The mass is then rolled into a tubular shape on a floured board, cut into segments, dipped in egg yolk and crumbs, and deep-fried. A delightful change from the ordinary French fries. (See PÂTE À CHOU)

DAUPHINOISE, À LA (French) Anything prepared *à la Dauphinoise* relates to milk, cream, and cheese products from that mountainous region of France where the French and Swiss Alps meet.

Champignons à la Dauphinoise For this dish, button mushrooms are sautéed in bacon fat then seasoned with mixed herbs, salt and pepper, plus a quantity of chopped tomatoes and fresh cream. The mushrooms are removed from the pan and a mixture of egg yolks, lemon juice, and seasoning is added to the sauce. This is then poured over the mushrooms, which are served sprinkled with crisp bacon bits.

Potatoes à la Dauphinoise Alternately layered with thickly sliced potatoes and with grated Gruyère cheese seasoned with salt and pepper, this potato casserole is baked in the oven. Before the allotted cooking time has elapsed, a mixture of eggs and cream flavored with a dash of freshly ground nutmeg is added.

DECANTING In the best restaurants, when one takes a bottle of wine and, with the aid of a light or a candle set behind the bottle, slowly and carefully pours the wine into another bottle or decanter, being sure to prevent the sediment from passing into the new bottle, the process is called "decanting." The decanting of an old and gracious bottle of Bordeaux wine is a necessary ritual. It removes the bitter tannin sediment that is so distasteful when savoring a regal drop of this great wine. However, to decant a Zinfandel, for instance, would not only be ridiculous but quite pretentious, because only a well-aged wine, such as a red Bordeaux or one of the great Rhône wines, would develop this regal residue while lying on its side for ten years or more. Another advantage to decanting is that it aerates the wine, lending a mellowness to the taste.

DEGLAZING After browning meat over heat or baking a roast in the oven, the meat drippings and brown particles left in the bottom of the pan are removed by adding water, stock, or wine and then scraping and stirring the residue over heat. Before deglazing, the excess oil or fat must first be removed from the pan.

DÉGRAISSER (French) The process of degreasing or skimming off the fat that covers the surface of a stock or a sauce or even the juices that are left in the roasting pan. To degrease a sauce easily, one pours it through a sieve full of ice cubes, or allows the stock or sauce to chill in the refrigerator and then removes the fat which has conveniently solidified at the top.

DÉJEUNER This is the French term for "lunch," which was born in Paris during the Revolution to fill a need. Those poor, hungry *deputées,* who were then obliged to sit in session from 10 A.M. each day, provided a prosperous market for enterprising, new restaurateurs. Lunch for them was an opportunity to eat well and at the same time consummate a business deal. Luncheon was not a dinner. There was no soup, but a wide choice of cold preparations, such as *hors d'oeuvre,* egg dishes, oysters, chicken, vegetables, chops, fruit, desserts, tea and coffee—and, of course, there was wine. Luncheon seems to play much the same role in our lives today: it provides a break in the day to relax, to refresh one's self, and perhaps to close a deal on a full stomach.

DEL MESON (Spanish) See MAISON/DE LA MAISON

DELMONICO POTATOES The Swiss family Delmonico, starting with John, who was the first of the family to come to New York from his native canton of Ticino, followed by brother Peter, and on to the great nephew Lorenzo, is famous for having opened and successfully run a series of fine restaurants in New York City. The Delmonicos also created a fine potato dish. Raw potatoes are diced and cooked in salted water; then, with the addition of a bit of milk, they are sprinkled with breadcrumbs and browned.

DEMERSAL Fish that live at the bottom of the sea. Cod, haddock, sole, flounder, whiting, hake, ling, and bream are all examples of this type of fish. They swim and feed close to the sandy bottom and have but little fat.

DEMI-DEUIL, CHICKEN (French) This Gallic expression refers to a poached young chicken dressed in "half-mourning," as displayed by the bit of black truffle peeking out from under the skin. This tender chicken is served with boiled white rice and a *sauce suprême* and is decorated with *fleurons.* (See FLEURONS, SUPRÊME) COMPATIBLE WINES: A white wine, e.g., Meursault, Montrachet, Riesling, Sylvaner, Gewürztraminer, Orvieto, Chalon, Fendant, Chenin Blanc.

DEMIDOFF (French) A series of garnishes containing truffles. The richness of these garnishes reflects the grandeur of the Demidoffs, the Russian family for whom they were named. Prince Anatole Demidoff became the husband of Princess Mathilde, the daughter of Jerome Bonaparte. Dear Mathilde was rather plain, and in a short time a divorce took place, freeing Anatole to pursue his forte, that of becoming one of the most famous gastronomes of the Second Empire of France.

Poulet Sauté Demidoff A chicken that has been browned in sweet butter is flavored with finely chopped root vegetables, finely sliced truffles, and blanched parsley leaves. It is served with a *sauce Madère,* topped with fried onions rings. (See MADÈRE)

Poularde Demidoff A *poulard* (a chicken sterilized for fatness) is slowly browned in butter in the oven. It is then garnished with precooked turnips, carrots, onions, and celery. With the addition of a rich chicken broth, the bird is simmered in a *cocotte* until done. Truffles are added at the end of the cooking period. COMPATIBLE WINES: A red wine, e.g., Médoc, Mâcon, Beaujolais, Santenay, Volnay, Chinon, Châteauneuf-du-Pape, Valpolicella, Egri Bikaver, Zinfandel.

Potage Demidoff A soup is made from a rich purée of chicken that is garnished with a *julienne* of carrots, truffles, and mushrooms plus pearl onions. (See JULIENNE)

Sauce Demidoff This is simply a *sauce Madère* flavored with finely diced black truffles. (See MADÈRE)

DEMI-GLACE, SAUCE (French) This famous creation is made by enriching a carefully reduced *sauce Espagnole* with tomatoes, spices, and herbs and cooking it for hours, sometimes days, until it is so thick that it will glaze whatever it covers. The sauce becomes so thick that, for convenience, it can be rolled in wax paper and hung in the refrigerator. Pieces can then be chopped off as needed. When the sauce is reduced to a thick, viscous mass, it is called *glace de viande.* Well refrigerated, this will keep indefinitely. (See ESPAGNOLE, GLACE DE VIANDE)

DEMITASSE (French) The term means "half a cup," but refers to black coffee served in small cups after luncheon or dinner, often with a small slice of lemon peel floating on the top.

DENGAKU (Japanese) A dish made from fresh *tofu* (soybean curd) that is pressed to half an inch thickness and grilled until brown on both sides. The *tofu* is served coated with a thin layer of simmered red *miso.* (See MISO, TOFU) COMPATIBLE WINES: A white wine, e.g., saké, Graves, Traminer, Chenin Blanc, Sauterne, sherry.

DENTE, AL (Italian) A descriptive term indicating that a food has been medium-cooked, literally done "to the tooth"—that is, firm to the bite, chewy. The term is specifically used when referring to the various *pastas: ravioli, spaghetti, macaroni,* etc. (See MACARONI, PASTA, RAVIOLI, SPAGHETTI)

DENTELLE (French) A *crêpe* so thin that it resembles lace.

DERBY, POULARDE This English-inspired chicken preparation is truly French. While working in Lucerne with the famous Swiss *hôtelier* César Ritz, Escoffier created the dish for Edward VII, Prince of Wales. The bird is stuffed with a *farce* of boiled white rice, chopped goose liver, and diced black truffles. It is basted with butter then baked in the oven. The chicken is served garnished with whole black truffles poached in port wine and with slices of goose liver warmed in butter. The juices from the bird, deglazed with port wine and blended with a brown veal stock, are served with the chicken. (See ESCOFFIER, FARCE) COMPATIBLE WINES: A red wine, e.g., Margaux, Haut Brion, Saint Julien, Cheval Blanc, Gruaud-Larose, Beychevelle, Cabernet Sauvignon, Latour, Talbot.

DEVONSHIRE CREAM (English) This delicious, heavy, clotted cream is named for Devonshire County, in England, where it has been enjoyed in and on buns for hundreds of years. The cream is carefully skimmed from the top of scalded milk that is heated over a low fire. It is removed only when it has cooled completely. Delicious when served with various fruit preserves or with ginger, it is also utilized in the creation of a fine Turkish dessert, *emek kadayif.* (See EMEK KADAYIF)

DHANIA (East Indian) See CHINESE PARSLEY

DHUM (East Indian) Description for a food that has been cooked over wood and under glowing charcoal at the same time.

DIABLÉ (French) This "devilish" term describes any food that is highly seasoned or hot to the tongue.

DIABLE, SAUCE À LA (French) A sauce so highly seasoned that it carries the name of the devil himself. To prepare it, shallots are chopped and sautéed and then cooked in white wine. The liquid is reduced and, with the addition of a *demi-glace* and a bit of red wine, it is reduced again. The sauce is then bedeviled with the addition of cayenne pepper. The now-hot *sauce à la diable* is served with grilled fowl or leftover meats that call for a spicy pick-me-up. A substitute sauce, claimed to have been created by the great Escoffier, is a blend of tomatoes, vinegar, sugar, tamarinds, dates, mangoes, raisins, and spices. (See DEMI-GLACE, ESCOFFIER, TAMARIND)

DIABLOTINS (French) This term can refer to chocolates enveloped in foil with a motto enclosed, in the style of the Chinese fortune-cookie; or to a fruit-filled fritter; or to two popular soup garnishes. One garnish consists of small dumplings that are flavored with Parmesan cheese and strongly spiced with cayenne pepper. The dumplings, first poached and then browned in the grill, are served with soup or as an appetizer. The other garnish is made from small round slices of bread which, coated with a *sauce Béchamel* that is flavored with grated Parmesan cheese and cayenne pepper, are grilled until light brown. (See BÉCHAMEL, BEIGNETS, CONSOMMÉ)

DIABLOTKI (Polish) Thin toasted pieces of white bread are spread with a rather spicy paste consisting of egg yolks, butter, grated Parmesan cheese, and the paprika which gives these croutons their "devilish" name. Before serving, they are grilled until golden brown. (See

CROÛTONS) COMPATIBLE BEVERAGES: Beer, ale; or a red wine, e.g., Rioja, Chianti, Egri Bikaver, Beaujolais, Valpolicella, Lambrusco.

DIANE (French) The tomboy goddess of ancient Rome whom the Greeks called Artemis. She was regarded as the goddess of the hunt and the mistress of all animals.

Diane Sauce (French) Using the *sauce poivrade* as a base, game stock is added for flavoring and the mixture is bound with heavy cream and sweet butter. Served with meat dishes. (See POIVRADE)

Steak Diane No chef in France would consider serving this steak any more than a Swiss chef would think of serving a so-called "Swiss steak," if he even knew what that was supposed to be. Nevertheless, on many restaurant menus a "steak Diane" is meant to represent the French cuisine. The steak is usually prepared in the dining room in a large flat pan heated with an alcohol burner. Chopped onions and parsley are sautéed lightly. Mushrooms are added and cooked, and then all is pushed to a corner of the hot pan. A well-flattened fillet of beef is seasoned with salt, pepper, and English mustard and cooked on both sides in the hottest part of the large pan. After Worcestershire sauce has been added, the steak is covered with the onions and the mushrooms and set aside on a warm platter. A dash of red wine is cooked in the pan and poured over the steak. COMPATIBLE WINES: A red wine, e.g., Hermitage, Côte Rôtie, Pinot Noir, Barolo, Dôle, Chianti, Beaujolais.

DIAVOLO, POLLO ALLA (Italian) A barbecued chicken dish. Young broiling chickens are cut in half and placed in a pickling mixture composed of lemon juice, olive oil, ginger, onions, pepper, cloves, and parsley. The following day, the chicken halves are broiled over hot charcoal. COMPATIBLE WINES: A red wine, e.g., Nebbiolo, Valpolicella, Beaujolais, Zinfandel, Châteauneuf-du-Pape, Grignolino, Mercurey. (See FRA DIAVOLO)

DIEPPOISE, À LA (French) Dieppe is a French port on the English Channel, and the phrase *à la Dieppoise* refers to a fish dish or to some delicacy from the sea.

Garniture à la Dieppoise This is a rich fish *velouté* enhanced with shrimp tails, mussels, and mushrooms. The sauce is served with fish.

Sole à la Dieppoise Fillets of sole are poached in a white wine and a fish *fumet* and served garnished with the *garniture à la Dieppoise*. (See FUMET, VELOUTÉ) COMPATIBLE WINES: A white wine, e.g., Soave, Chablis, Muscadet, Quincy, Pouilly-Fuissé, Pinot Chardonnay, Riquewihr, Wehlener Sonnenuhr.

DIGESTIF This is another example of how delightfully the French use their language. They call a liqueur or cordial a *digestif* perhaps to comfort themselves with the idea that one imbibes, not for pleasure, but as an aid to digestion. *Vive la France!* What *bon vivant* would not rather stave off an upset stomach after a rich dinner by fortifying himself with a glass of Benedictine from France, a Kirschwasser from Germany, or a Strega or Fernet Branca from Italy than with baking soda or any of its bubbly commercial counterparts!

DIJON, MOUTARDE DE (French) The region of Dijon has been famous for centuries for having the finest mustard seeds grown in France, and its *Blanc de Dijon* variety, exported to all parts of the world, proves it. Unlike most mustards, the *Blanc de Dijon* mustard contains verjuice instead of vinegar. (See VERJUICE)

Sauce Dijonnaise Dijon mustard and hard-boiled egg yolks are seasoned with salt and pepper and whipped with oil and lemon juice to a *Mayonnaise* consistency. This sauce is popularly served with grilled fish of all kinds. (See MAYONNAISE)

DILL The dill plant, an annual herbaceous plant belonging to the carrot family, flourishes in all Mediterranean lands, in the Caucasus of Russia, in England, Germany, Holland, Rumania, India, Mexico, Canada, and the United States. The plant itself is aromatic from the bottom of the erect stem to the bright yellow flowers that splash their brilliance over rural countrysides. The fruit, called dill seed, has a slightly sharp taste, similar to caraway seed. Dill seeds are used whole or ground as a flavoring agent for soups, salads, meat and fish dishes, sauces, and of course pickles. It is used commercially in processing meats and sausages, including bologna.

DIM SUM (Chinese) While the Moslem culture reached its peak, while the Byzantine Empire thrived in Constantinople under the leadership of Basil II, the expanding tenth century brought with it not only the fall of Charlemagne's Empire but also the rise of feudalism and (a full three hundred years before Marco Polo was even welcomed by the great Kublai Khan) the creation of *dim sum* in the teahouses of the powerful Sung Dynasty in China. By setting the birth of this culinary creation parallel to its political counterparts in history, the enduring quality and influence of the great Chinese cuisine becomes vividly clear.

Today, *dim sum* (literally "to dot heart" or "to touch heart") are bite-size dumplings made from a mixture of wheat starch and tapioca flour or (the sweeter variety) flour, baking powder, milk, and sugar. Stuffed with forcemeats of fish or of meat, with vegetables, or even with fruits such as dates, these dumplings are steamed, deep-fried, or baked and served with a variety of food dips, often as a main course. The types of *dim sum* served are limited only by the imagination of the chef and the individual taste of the consumer. (See SHIN MAI)

DINDE The French believed that the turkey came from India and, as "from India" translates into *d'Inde* in French, the word *dinde* came to be used to designate the turkey hen.

The turkey came to Europe from Mexico in time to grace the royal nuptial tables of King Charles IX the day he wed the daughter of the

Emperor Maximillian in November of 1570. By 1600, the turkey had already travelled from Mexico to North America, where it has become almost a national fixture. The name of the bird came into being when the North American continent was settled. The native Indians introduced this bird, an ugly but tasty fowl, to the first English emigrants. They recognized it immediately as kin to the bird brought to England by the Turks. This was known as "turkey-fowl," so they called it the "turkey."

DIPLOMATE (French) The name given to several distinctly different dishes marked by their richness.

Diplomate, Sauce This rich French sauce consists of a *sauce Normande* enhanced with lobster-butter and garnished with chopped truffles and diced lobster meat. A dash of Cognac and a sprinkling of cayenne pepper finishes this favorite complement of fish dishes. (See NORMANDE)

Diplomate, Pudding This gratifying French dessert is made in a mold. Crystallized fruit is arranged in the mold, and the mold is then filled with alternate layers of sponge cake that has been saturated with Kirsch or some other favorite liqueur and with a vanilla-flavored Bavarian cream. Currants and seedless raisins, softened and swelled in warm syrup and rum, are strewn over each sponge cake layer with spoonfuls of apricot preserves. The mold is put on ice to set. When chilled, the pudding is served with a fruit sauce that is pepped up with a complementing liqueur. (See BAVAROIS)

Sole à la Diplomate The sole is boned then filled with a forcemeat of whiting, cream, and diced truffles. The stuffed sole is poached in a mixture of white wine and fish stock. The fish is served surrounded with a *salpicon* of lobster, coated with a *sauce diplomate,* and topped with bits of truffle in fish aspic. (See DIPLOMATE, FUMET, QUENELLE, SALPICON) COMPATIBLE WINES: A white wine, e.g., Chablis, Meursault, Quincy, Bernkasteler Doktor, Rüdesheim, Graacher Himmelreich, Pouilly-Fuissé.

DIVAN, CHICKEN (American) This chicken dish, a creation of the Divan Restaurant in New York City, is prepared by poaching the breasts of plump young chickens in a rich chicken broth until tender. The breasts are boned and placed in a casserole. A sauce made from a *roux* enriched with chicken broth is blended over low heat with grated Parmesan cheese, heavy cream, salt, and pepper. A thick *sauce Hollandaise* plus egg yolks and lemon juice are then added. After arranging precooked broccoli attractively over the chicken, the sauce is poured over all and the casserole is placed under the broiler until the top is delicately golden. (See HOLLANDAISE, ROUX) COMPATIBLE WINES: A white wine, e.g., Schloss Vollrads, Piesporter Goldtröpfchen, Graves, Vouvray, Tokay, Chalon, Sylvaner, Riquewihr, Johannisberg, Orvieto, Sauvignon Blanc.

DOBOS TORTE (Hungarian) This famous, rich, and oh so tasty cake is said to have been created by a pastry chef from Budapest named Joseph Dobos. Although every pastry chef seems to have his own individual recipe for this cake, the original calls for six individually-baked layers of sponge cake filled and iced with a light chocolate custard and coated with hard caramel. The cake, also a great favorite in Austria, must be cut into sections before the caramel hardens.

DODINE DE CANARD (French) A rich stew composed of duck meat, ham and veal bones, onions and garlic and other root vegetables, plus seasonings, herbs, and red wine. The dish is also known as *civet de canard* or *canard en civet*. (See CIVET) COMPATIBLE WINES: A red wine, e.g., Fixin, Dôle, Barolo, Nuits St. Georges, Calon-Ségur, Cabernet Sauvignon, Chambertin, Rioja.

DOLCE/DOLCI (Italian) Literally, "sweet." When found on a menu, the term means "desserts."

DOLCE E FORTE, SALSA (Italian) This sauce originated in ancient Roman times, when the lack of refrigeration demanded a strong, piquant sauce to cover up the disagreeable odor of rotting meat. Today this sauce is made from raisins and prunes that are cut up with brandied cherries, pignoli nuts, and candied fruit and stirred into a sugar sauce containing garlic and vinegar! It is served with game dishes such as venison, hare, and wild boar.

DOLCE RAVIOLI The *ravioli* are filled with ricotta or cottage cheese mixed with vanilla or apricot flavoring and egg yolks. The filled *ravioli* squares are fried in hot fat until golden and served dusted with powdered sugar.

DOLLAR FISH Commonly known as the butterfish (so named because of its high fat content), this fish is found along the Atlantic coast of North America. The dollar fish rides the summer waves and comes no longer than ten inches. It is best prepared by splitting the fish and then broiling or baking it with sweet butter. Its European cousin is the pomfret. COMPATIBLE WINES: A white wine, e.g., Sancerre, Pouilly-Fumé, Montrachet, Soave, Pinot Chardonnay, Dézaley, Chablis, Muscadet, Debro.

DOLLOP A soft mass or blob of any viscous food, such as sour cream, butter, jam, yogurt, or *pasta* or dumpling dough.

DOLMADES/DOLMADAKIA/DOLMATHES (Greek) Stuffed grape leaves, filled either with cooked rice and chopped meat or with a rice-and-herb stuffing flavored with an egg and lemon juice mixture. The fragrance that comes from a pot of cooking grape leaves is incomparable: it must be experienced. (See DOLMAS) COMPATIBLE WINES: A red wine, e.g., Saint Julien, Valpolicella, Mercurey, Beaujolais, Côte Rôtie, Zinfandel, Châteauneuf-du-Pape, Egri Bikaver.

DOLMAS (Turkish) The ancient Persians produced stuffed vegetables, and the early Greeks created the stuffed and rolled grape leaves. The early Turks, however, were known to make both. In addition to stuffing grape leaves, the Turks stuffed cabbage, eggplant, green peppers, squash, or artichokes with nuts, rice, onions, currants, diced meats, and the like. These stuffed vegetables, known throughout the culinary world as *dolmas* (from the Turkish *doldurmak,* meaning "to stuff"), are steamed, braised, or baked before serving. The dishes are flavored with the juice of fresh lemons, sour grapes, or plums, according to season. (See DOLMADES, YALANCI) COMPATIBLE BEVERAGES: Beer; the choice of wine depends upon the filling.

DOLPHIN Lord Byron's telling words in *Chile Harold's Pilgrimage* ("... Parting day dies like the dolphin whom each pang imbues with a new color as it gasps away/ the last still loveliest, till—t'is gone—and all is gray") echo my deepest feelings when confronted with the shocking fact that these delightful, almost human, mammals are slaughtered for their meat. The fact that they are caught during the months of May and June off the Carolinas seems to contradict the season that glorifies the rebirth of life. The dolphin is bled then skinned, and its fillets are broiled with almonds or poached or baked in white wine with shallots, onions, and butter. The baked version is commonly served in Créole country, New Orleans.

DOMBURI (Japanese) A soup composed of a rich fish stock flavored with soy sauce and *mirin.* (See MIRIN)

DOMINICAINE, À LA (French) A descriptive phrase for dishes served as those austere and contemplative monks of the religious order of Saint Dominic, the Dominicans, would have prepared them—that is, meatless. Although the Franciscans and the Dominicans were very much alike—in fact, St. Francis and St. Dominic met in Rome and became close friends—it was the Dominicans who abstained totally from meat, not the Franciscans, who so loved animals. The Dominicans obtained most of their protein from fish.

Timbale à la Dominicaine An herbed fish forcemeat is placed in a pastry dough lining an ovenproof mold. The dish is baked in a moderate oven and served with a lobster sauce. (See HOMARD, TIMBALE) COMPATIBLE WINES: A white wine, e.g., Chablis, Montrachet, Meursault, Muscadet, Pouilly-Fumé, Pinot Chardonnay, Soave, Debro.

DÖNER KEBAB (Turkish) The lamb for this *kebab* is not cut into cubes as is usual for this type of dish. Instead, it is cut into thick, long strips and entwined around a vertical spit. The spit is rotated just inches from a glowing charcoal fire, and the browning meat is continuously basted with a spicy sauce. When roasted to perfection, the meat is sliced off in thin layers. (See KEBAB, SHAMI KEBAB, SHASHLIK, SHISHKEBAB) COMPATIBLE BEVERAGES: Beer, ale, or tea.

DORÉE (French) A descriptive term for food that has been given a golden tint by frying, sautéing, or broiling.

Filet de Sole Dorée Fresh fillets of sole are dipped first in flour, then in cream, and finally in breadcrumbs. They are then fried in butter to a golden brown. A tomato-flavored *sauce Béarnaise* is served separately. (See BÉARNAISE) COMPATIBLE WINES: A white wine, e.g., Chablis, Soave, Corton-Charlemagne, Meursault, Pouilly-Fuissé, Piesporter Goldtröpfchen, Pinot Chardonnay, Montrachet, Muscadet.

DORIA (French) A term used to honor a famous Italian admiral, Andrea Doria, who lived during the sixteenth century and was prominent in the history of Genoa. The admiral must have loved cucumbers because the word *Doria,* in culinary parlance, has become synonymous with the vegetable.

Sole Doria Fillets of sole are sautéed *à la meunière* and served with cucumber balls sautéed in butter. (See MEUNIÈRE) COMPATIBLE WINES: A white wine, e.g., Chablis, Meursault, Quincy, Debro, Pouilly-Fumé, Aigle, Pinot Chardonnay.

Poulet Sauté Doria A cut-up young fryer is sautéed in butter and moistened with a *sauce demi-glace* flavored with lemon juice. The disjointed chicken is served with a garnish of sautéed cucumber balls. (See DEMI-GLACE) COMPATIBLE WINES: A red wine, e.g., Valpolicella, Zinfandel, Beaujolais, Margaux, Santenay, Côte Rôtie, Ruby Cabernet, Mercurey, Egri Bikaver.

DOUBLE CONSOMMÉ (French) This clear soup is a "clarified" or "twice-cooked" consommé. The rich clear broth obtained from cooking a good piece of beef together with the necessary vegetables is first defatted. Then, egg whites and crushed egg shells are whipped into the broth over high heat until the broth comes to the boil. After the consommé is left to simmer for an hour, it is carefully strained through a fine cloth and returned to the pan, where it is reheated and seasoned to taste with salt and pepper. When the soup has cooled, the fat is again removed, and egg whites and crushed egg shells are added to the cold stock, which is brought to the boil again. The consommé is then strained through two thicknesses of cheesecloth. The result is a liquid concentration of golden goodness that is fit for a king. (See CONSOMMÉ)

DOVER SOLE This tastiest of all soles, common to Europe, is named for the English seaport, Dover. The shape of the sole's body is a long, oval, and rather thick, with a width not equaling half of its length. The top is a reticulated dark brown and the bottom is white. The American flounder, almost completely round in shape, is also called a "sole," but this is a misnomer created by fish dealers who felt the "flounder" tag to be less marketable. Actually, American flounder do vary greatly in flavor and in texture. They are flatter than the Dover sole, not as meaty, and most often are not suitable when a recipe calls for sole.

The sole is one of the most accommodating of all fish. It can be served with a multitude of sauces; it can be poached; it can be broiled; it can even be fried; and in every case it holds its own and remains as delicate on the dinner plate as it was in the sea.

DOW FOO (Chinese) A bean cake. *Mung* or soy curd is allowed to ferment and then passed through a sieve. While still wet, it is cut into rectangular cakes. To the Chinese, *dow foo* is a type of cheese.

Bean Cake Chow Yuk For this dish, the bean cake is cubed, steam-cooked, and served with a sauce. (See MUNG, TOFU)

DRAWN BUTTER This is the term used in America for butter that has been defatted and cleared of all cloudy residue and impurities. (See CLARIFIED BUTTER)

Drawn Butter Sauce A mixture of flour and butter, moistened with water and seasoned with salt and pepper, is simmered in a double boiler until thick. Then, bit by bit, a nut of butter and lemon juice are added, being beaten continuously until the sauce turns almost white. It is strained before serving with vegetable dishes, meats, and fish of all kinds.

DRISHEEN (Irish) One of Ireland's traditional specialities, this is a type of blood pudding that looks much like a thick, long black sausage. The pudding is prepared from either pig's or lamb's blood which is first cooled then salted and strained. Heavy cream, mace, pepper, various herbs, and breadcrumbs to bind are added, and the ingredients are placed into a membrane casing and boiled. When the *drisheen* is served freshly made, it can be better than the finest French *boudin.* (See BLOOD AS FOOD, BLUT UND ZUNGENWURST, BOUDIN NOIR, CIVET, PALTBREAD) COMPATIBLE BEVERAGES: Stout, beer, Beaujolais, Pinot Noir, Châteauneuf-du-Pape, Chianti, Nebbiolo.

"DRUNKEN SHRIMP" These shrimp are called "drunken" by the inventive Chinese because they are marinated in liqueur, stock, and ginger and are said to veritably jump into your mouth as you eat them. If the shrimp are fresh, they have a bluish caste; the older (and staler) they are, the lighter or pinker they are in color.

DUBARRY The French have named more dishes after their mistresses than after their politicians, and the fine DuBarry garnish, made of cauliflower and served with meats and with soup, is no exception. Although the Countess DuBarry was a courtesan of illegitimate birth, like most prostitutes she was kind and generous; and because of the happiness she brought to Louis XV, long before she lost her head, she was immortalized with the lowly cauliflower.

DUCHESSE POTATOES (French) This puréed potato mixture is seasoned with salt, pepper, butter, and nutmeg and bound with egg yolks. It is then put into a pastry bag to be squeezed out into border designs for such dishes as *coquilles St. Jacques Mornay.* Or it may be made thicker and used to make potato *croquettes,* which are brushed with beaten egg and browned in the oven. (See COQUILLE)

DUGLÉRÉ, SAUCE (French) Invented by Chef Adolph Dugléré to please his customers at the Café Anglaise in Paris, this sauce is simply a *sauce poulette* to which diced tomatoes are added; the mixture is then cooked and enriched with butter. (See POULETTE)

Sole Dugléré Fillets of sole are poached in white wine with diced tomatoes, chopped onions, and parsley. The sauce is reduced, left to cool, and mixed with a *sauce Mayonnaise.* The fillets are coated with the sauce and served cold. When the sole is to be served hot, the fillets are cooked in a fish stock flavored with white wine, chopped shallots, parsley, onions, and tomatoes. They are then coated with the reduced stock. (See MAYONNAISE) COMPATIBLE WINES: A white wine, e.g., Sancerre, Soave, Muscadet, Pouilly-Fuissé, Aigle, Pinot Chardonnay, Debro, Verdicchio.

DUNG CHOY (Chinese) Shredded celery cabbage, heavily seasoned with crushed garlic and stored in glass jars. As it ferments in the jars, the cabbage takes on a briny flavor. Also known as "winter cabbage," this is used as a base for many dishes.

DUNG GOO (Chinese) A black mushroom, popular in Oriental cookery. The Japanese call it *shiitake.* (See SHIITAKE)

DUNG GWA See WINTER MELON

DURUM WHEAT A hard wheat that yields flour which produces the best Italian *pasta.* (See PASTA)

DUTCH CUISINE Holland has always been rightly famous for its fine dairy products, and the Hollander takes his food seriously. A hearty and robust people, the Dutch dine on thick soups and stews, pork, sausage, potato and cabbage dishes of all kinds; and they are very fond of herring, which they prefer to eat raw. Lobster, seafood, and fish dishes are plentiful, and because Indonesia was once a Dutch colony, many of the Indonesian dishes, such as *nasi goreng* and the famous *rijstafel,* found a second home in Holland. (See NASI GORENG, RIJSTAFEL)

DUXELLES (French) This creation of La Varenne, the great chef employed by the Marquis d'Uxelles in 1650, is a reduction of finely chopped mushrooms, parsley, onions, pepper, salt, paprika, and shallots in butter. It is used to flavor soups, sauces, and stuffings. La Varenne is said to have been the first great French cook of modern times, and his cookbook, *Le Cuisinier François,* published in 1650, is considered to be a primer of the French cuisine.

DZIRANOV UNGOUYZOV HAVGIT (Armenian) The use of nuts and dried fruits is common in Armenian cooking. For this egg dish, dried apricots are cooked in water and sugar until soft. Walnuts are browned in hot butter; then apricots are added, and eggs, beaten with cinnamon, are poured over the apricots. The pan is covered until the eggs have set.

EAU DE VIE (French) Literally, this means "water of life." *Eaux de vie* are white spirits and fruit liqueurs, many of which come from Alsace and Lorraine in France. Some are distilled only from the pits and stones of fruit. Kirschwasser, for example, is made from cherries, while Mirabelle, Quetsch, and Prunelle are all made from plums, and Marc is made from the distillation of the grape pressing. Other fruit liqueurs are made from berries—strawberry, raspberry, blackberry, elderberry—and they are all pure white distillates. Because of the enormous quantity of fruit necessary to make a bottle of genuine *eau de vie,* the price is naturally very high. Alcoholically *eaux de vie* are very strong, and their perfumes are exquisite.

EBI-IRI-SUMOMI (Japanese) A cucumber salad containing either crab meat or shrimp. Sliced cucumber is salted and drained of its water. The dry cucumber slices are then sprinkled with wine vinegar, and after a while the vinegar is drained off. The crab meat or cooked shrimp is added. Then a blend of soy sauce, monosodium glutamate, oil, salt, vinegar, and dill is poured over the salad. The top is decorated with hard-boiled egg slices and pineapple chunks. COMPATIBLE BEVERAGES: Tea.

ÉCARLATE, À L' (French) Literally meaning "scarlet," this marinade prescribed for beef or pork is composed of brine and saltpeter, which turns red when heated.

ÉCHALOTE, BEURRE D' (French) See COMPOUND BUTTER

ÉCLAIR (French) A delicate pastry made from a *pâte à chou* dough, filled with a *crème patissière* that is flavored with coffee, vanilla, or chocolate, and topped with an icing. Alternate fillings are heavy whipped cream, chestnut purée, or various fruits blended into a pastry cream. (See CRÈME PATISSIÈRE, PÂTE À CHOU)

ÉCOSSAISE, SAUCE This is a Scotch sauce as seen through the eyes of a French chef. He takes a *sauce Normande,* flavors it with chopped truffles and celery, and garnishes it with a *brunoise* of carrots. The basic Scotch sauce is made from the hard yolks of eggs, which are passed through a fine sieve and mixed into a *sauce Béchamel.* It is garnished with a *julienne* of egg whites and served with eggs, poultry, and variety meats. (See BRUNOISE, JULIENNE, NORMANDE)

Suprêmes de Volaille Écossaise Plump breasts of young chickens are poached in a rich chicken broth and served coated with the *sauce Écossaise.* (See SUPRÊMES DE VOLAILLE) COMPATIBLE WINES: A white wine, e.g., Schloss Vollrads, Rüdesheim, Vouvray, Tokay, Orvieto, Château-Grillet, Ammerschwihr.

ÉCREVISSE (French) Fresh-water crab, crayfish. (See COULIS)

EDAMAME (Japanese) Religions have always exercised a great influence in determining the foods people consume. As the ancient Israelites followed Moses, so did the Japanese follow the counsel of Buddha, who was an avowed vegetarian and a great advocate of the soybean, the lima bean, the black and the red bean, known as *azuki.* The *edamame* is a type of green soybean which can either be cooked in the pod or first shelled and then cooked together with rice. (See AZUKI)

EGG FOO YUNG (Chinese) See FU JUNG/FOO YUNG/FU YONG

EGGPLANT-BUTTER This favorite spread of the Moslem countries consists of the meat of a cooked eggplant mashed together with raw garlic, lemon juice, sesame oil, and salt, and garnished with pomegranate seeds or one or two spicy peppers. In Arabic this is known as *baba ghanouj.*

EGG ROLLS (Chinese) This stuffed pancake, known in Chinese as *chwin guen,* is also called "spring roll." The dough—made from a simple mixture of flour, salt, and water—is well kneaded and then rolled out paper-thin and filled with ground shrimp, chicken, prawns, ham, pork, etc., plus vegetables and mushrooms. The stuffed pancakes are fried until golden brown. Egg rolls can be served as an appetizer or as part of a main course. COMPATIBLE BEVERAGES: Beer, tea, saké, Sauterne.

ÉGYPTIENNE, À L' (French) A method of serving food according to what is considered to be the Egyptian style, which usually means using leeks, onions, eggplant, and rice to complement a meal.

Riz à l'Égyptienne To prepare this dish, a *salpicon* made from chicken livers, leeks, ham, and mushrooms is added to a *pilaff* of rice. (See PILAFF, SALPICON)

Eggplant à l'Égyptienne The eggplant is cooked in water then hollowed out; the pulp is puréed and mixed with chopped onions and cooked in oil. The skins, refilled with the pulp, are browned in the grill and served with sliced tomatoes and chopped parsley.

EI-KA-WU SALAD This is not Chinese. *Ei-Ka-Wu* stands for the Swiss-German terms *Eier* (eggs), *Käse* (cheese), and *Wurst* (sausage), which combine to make up this Swiss salad. Gruyère or Emmenthaler cheese is cut into cubes and, together with *Knackwurst,* sliced into rounds and mixed thoroughly in a sauce composed of sliced onions, grated fresh horseradish, wine vinegar, olive oil, mustard, basil, salt, and pepper. Just before serving, wedges of hard-boiled eggs are mixed in with the salad. COMPATIBLE BEVERAGES: Beer, ale, stout.

EINLAUF (German) A garnish for soups (usually clear soups), made from a batter of flour, eggs, salt, and water. This mixture is dropped, bit by bit, into a boiling soup. The pot is covered and the garnish allowed to "set" for a few minutes before the soup is served.

EISBEIN (German) A hearty dish made from a shank of pork that is first marinated in red wine then boiled and served with sauerkraut and boiled potatoes flavored with caraway seeds. (See SAUERKRAUT) COMPATIBLE WINES: A white wine, e.g., Rüdesheim, Johannisberg, Neuchâtel, Traminer, Kientzheim, Orvieto, Frascati, Gewürztraminer, Sauvignon Blanc.

EISWEIN (German) This word is found on the labels of unique white wines that are produced from fully-ripe "frozen" grapes. The grapes are harvested and pressed in this state at minus 20 degrees Fahrenheit. (See AUSLESE, BEERENAUSLESE, KABINETT, SPÄTLESE, TROCKEN-BEERENAUSLESE)

ÉMINCÉ (French) Literally "hash," but actually this is the process of mincing any meat in preparation for pan cooking. Meat so prepared is usually served with a sauce—a *chasseur, Italienne, poivrade,* or *vin blanc.* (See CHASSEUR, FOIE DE VEAU SAUTÉ, GESCHNETZELTES KALB-FLEISCH, ITALIENNE, POIVRADE, VIN BLANC)

EMPANADA (Spanish) A pastry turnover made from a dough of flour, salt, baking powder, water, and shortening. Cut into circles, the dough is filled with either savories or sweets, then folded over, pressed together, and deep-fried in hot oil to a golden brown. Sweet *empanadas* may be filled with candied fruits, jams, fruit preserves, freshly grated coconut, or raisins. Savory fillings can be composed of fish, meat, eggs, chopped onions, cheese, and chilies of all kinds. *Empanadas* are great favorites in Mexico as well as Spain.

Empanada de Mariscos This Spanish pie, made from seafood, onions, green peppers, and pimientos, is served in wedges like a *quiche.* (See PIMENTO/PIMIENTO, QUICHE LORRAINE) COMPATIBLE WINES: A white wine, e.g., Chablis, Meursault, Muscadet, Zeltlingen, Riquewihr, Quincy, Frascati, Orvieto, Chenin Blanc.

ENCHILADAS (Mexican) Pancakes, or *crêpes,* made from corn flour and filled with various mixtures, such as a combination of meat, beans, sausages, and vegetables. Another term for this preparation is *quesadilla.* (See BURRITOS, TORTILLA)

Enchiladas de Frijoles *Tortillas* stuffed with refried red beans are rolled up and fastened with toothpicks. They are fried in oil until brown, then baked, topped with sour cream. COMPATIBLE WINES: A red wine, e.g., Rioja, Petit Sirah, Pinot Noir, Fleurie, Beaujolais, Mercurey, Chianti, Nebbiolo, Barbaresco.

ENDIVE, BELGIAN (Belgium) There is much unnecessary confusion about what is "endive" and what is "chicory." It all goes back to our early English Colonial ancestry, who mistook the curly, bitter green chicory for endive. Endive, or more correctly Belgian endive, is grown from roots which produce white-headed, elongated, fleshy leaves from four to six inches wide which are pressed into a compact pointed head. Belgian endive salads are tastiest when served with a *vinaigrette* dressing. They can also be braised and served with a *sauce Hollandaise,* sweet butter, or a drawn butter sauce. (See CHICONS GRATINÉS, CHICORY, DRAWN BUTTER, HOLLANDAISE, VINAIGRETTE)

ENGLISH DRY MUSTARD This well-known, rather sharp mustard was created by a Mrs. Clemens in the eighteenth century by milling mustard seeds into a fine flour and then passing it through a fine sieve. Just a little water mixed into the dry mustard powder was enough to release such a fiery flavor that the Chinese readily adopted it for use in their hot sauces.

ENTRECÔTE (French) Literally meaning "between the ribs," this refers to that steak cut from the center of the loin of beef between the ribs.

Entrecôte à l'Anglaise A steak served with bacon and boiled potatoes to give it that English touch.

Entrecôte au Poivre A steak embedded with coarse pepper and either grilled or fried, and usually flamed with Cognac.

Entrecôte à la Forestière A steak served with mushrooms—morels, if possible.

Entrecôte Marchand de Vin A grilled steak napped with red wine and onion sauce.

Entrecôte Soubise A steak served with a thick onion sauce.

Entrecôte à la Béarnaise The steak is grilled, garnished with *château potatoes* and watercress plus a *sauce Béarnaise.* (See BÉARNAISE, CHÂTEAU)

Entrecôte à la Tyrolienne The steak is grilled, topped with fried onion rings, and surrounded with a purée of tomatoes cooked together with chopped onions and a breath of garlic.

COMPATIBLE WINES: A red wine, e.g., Chambertin, Fixin, Dôle, Cabernet Sauvignon, Latour, Barolo, La Tâche, Les Bonnes Mares, Richebourg, Romanée-Conti, Nuits St. Georges, Haut Brion.

ENTRÉE (French) As used today, this means the "main course" of a menu. When coined during the almost orgiastic days of the Grand Louis of France, whose dinners often consisted of from twenty to thirty different courses, it referred to those dishes which preceded the roast or game courses: the beginning or "the entry" to the main part of the meal. Sometimes there were as many as sixteen entrées, such as ribs of beef, saddles of mutton, partridge, aspics of game, *pâtés,* veal cutlets, or salmon steaks.

ENTREMESES (Spanish) Appetizers, usually consisting of tiny fried squid, meatballs, dried cod, sausages, anchovies, tuna, and cooked and raw vegetables in a spicy dressing. (See BACALAU) COMPATIBLE BEVERAGES: Beer, ale, stout, sherry, Sauterne.

ENTREMETS (French) This term (literally, "between dishes") once designated those foods served as "diversions" between courses of a grand dinner, which sometimes consisted of as many as thirty-two different courses. *Entremets,* customarily served to royalty during the early eighteenth century, might have included pheasant pie, *brioche, croquante,* eggs in gravy, artichokes, truffles, and ortolans. Today, when one finds the term on a French menu, it means "desserts." (See BRIOCHE, CROQUANTE, ORTOLAN)

EPICURE A person who enjoys and has a discriminating taste for all fine food and drink, named after the famous Greek philosopher Epicurus (342-270 B.C.).

ÉPICURIENNE, MOUSSELINES OF SQUAB (French) A dish of tiny, rich *mousselines* of pigeon that are poached in a white stock. To serve, the *mousselines* are arranged beneath a roasted breast of pigeon, and the whole is coated with a *fumet* made from the meat of the bird blended into a *sauce velouté.* (See FUMET, MOUSSELINE, VELOUTÉ) COMPATIBLE WINES: A red wine, e.g., Médoc, St. Julien, Hermitage, Musigny, Cabernet Sauvignon, Zinfandel, Valpolicella.

ERNESTINE POTATOES (French) After potatoes have been baked, the potato pulp is spooned out of the skins, mixed with a white wine sauce and the fresh roe from a herring, and then replaced in the skins and served piping hot.

ERWTENSOEP, DUTCH (Dutch) This national soup of Holland must be so thick that a spoon will stand upright, supported only by the tasty ingredients and tradition. The soup is prepared by cooking the following ingredients for several hours: split peas, water, salt, pig's feet, smoked bacon, white leeks, diced potatoes and celeriac (root celery), and pepper. The pig's feet and the bacon are removed from the pot, the meat cut from the bones and sliced; with sliced rounds of *Frankfurter Würstchen,* the meat is returned to the pot. The soup is best when left to stand overnight. Pumpernickel bread is usually served with this hearty, one-dish meal. (See FRANKFURTER WÜRST-CHEN, PUMPERNICKEL) COMPATIBLE WINES: A red wine, e.g., Côte Rôtie, Châteauneuf-du-Pape, Mercurey, Beaujolais, Ruby Cabernet, Barbaresco, Nebbiolo, Zinfandel, Valpolicella.

ESCABECHE (Spanish) The term, literally meaning "pickled," is used generally to designate fish, poultry, and game dishes that have been marinated. The dish *escabeche,* was probably adapted from the Malaysian *ingelegde,* which is also a South African favorite. *Escabeche* is made of fish—such as whiting, mullets, sardines and anchovies—which are first sautéed in boiling olive oil and then covered with a hot, highly seasoned marinade. (See ESCOVEITCHE, INGELEGDE) COMPATIBLE BEVERAGES: Beer, ale, stout.

ESCARGOTS (French) Snails. (See BOURGUIGNONNE)

ESCOFFIER, AUGUSTE (1847-1935) This great French chef came into the world at exactly the right time. He was born at Villeneuve-Loubet, a town so small it was not included on the maps of the area. Today, however, thanks to this little man, not only is the town well marked on the road between Cannes and Nice, but it boasts as well of having a great culinary museum founded by the tiny "Emperor of the World's Kitchens," a title given to Escoffier by the Kaiser Wilhelm of Germany.

At age thirteen, while working as a *commis-saucier* (sauce-boy) in his uncle's kitchen in Nice, Escoffier attended night school. At nineteen he arrived in Paris, where he became *sous-chef* of a fine restaurant called Le Petit Moulin Rouge. Within three years, he took the chef's hat at this same restaurant, but with the onset of the Franco-Prussian War Auguste was called to the colors. Some years after the war, in 1882, he met the enterprising Swiss *hôtelier* César Ritz, who made him his chef at the Grand National Hotel at Lucerne.

The talents and personalities of Ritz and Escoffier blended like eggs and butter, and a few years later they made the Carlton Hotel of London world-famous; there they were blessed by the patronage of the Prince of Wales. It is said that Escoffier was so inspired by Nelly Melba's singing of *Lohengrin* that he named the dessert *pêche Melba* after her. Escoffier denied ever having heard the great Australian diva sing, although he admitted to having named any number of his creations in her honor. (See MELBA)

ESCOVEITCHE FISH (West Indian) A version of the famous Spanish *escabeche*. It differs only in that garlic is added to the marinade. A grand lady of the Bahamas once offered me what she termed "a 'squeech' fish dish that will tantalize your taste buds." It did. (See ESCABECHE, INGELEGDE) COMPATIBLE WINES: A red wine, e.g., Fleurie, Veltliner, Côte Rôtie, Zinfandel.

ESPAGNOLA, OMELETTE À LA (Spanish) An omelette done "the Spanish way," which means cooking the omelette (composed of diced tomatoes, onions, potatoes, sausages, etc.) in a skillet until the omelette forms a crust on the bottom, then flipping it over to cook the other side. It is usually served cut in wedges. (See TORTILLA ESPAGNOLA) COMPATIBLE BEVERAGES: A good beer.

ESPAGNOLE, SAUCE (French) To prepare this famous sauce, a *mirepoix* of diced carrots and onions fried with bacon is added to a *roux*. Next, bacon fat, white wine, thyme, and bay leaf are added to the pan, simmered, and skimmed of fat. After straining the sauce by crushing the vegetables through a sieve, the sauce is cooked again for literally hours, from time to time skimming the fat off the surface. On the following day, a rich tomato purée is added, and the sauce is cooked further, periodically removing the fat from the surface. The sauce is then strained through muslin, and at last this grand sauce is ready to enhance any number of dishes and to stand as a base from which many other sauces spring. (See BORDELAISE, DEMI-GLACE, DIABLE, MIREPOIX, PÉRIGUEUX, PIQUANTE, PORTUGUESE)

ESPRESSO, CAFFÈ (Italian) This *demitasse* from Italy is made from darkly roasted, pulverized coffee that is made "expressly for the client" by forcing pressurized steam through the ground coffee. It is served in small cups, with a twist of lemon or orange peel if desired. Other *espressos* are laced with brandy, rum, or a liqueur of choice and spiced with cloves and cinnamon. (See DEMITASSE)

Espresso Cappuccino This is an *espresso* coffee served topped with whipped cream and dusted with finely grated chocolate, cinnamon, or orange rind.

ESTOUFFADE (French) Literally, "stew." Synonymous with both *daube* and *étuvée*. Beef is usually the meat used in an *estouffade*. (See DAUBE)

Estouffade de Boeuf To prepare this rump roast, the beef is well browned in butter together with small onions, cloves of garlic, a *bouquet garni,* salt and pepper, and a few pig's knuckles. With the addition of red wine, the pot is covered and the beef simmered slowly for hours. (See BOUQUET GARNI) COMPATIBLE WINES: A red wine, e.g., Pommard, Dôle, Chambertin, Chianti, Châteauneuf-du-Pape, Pinot Noir, Côte Rôtie, Fixin.

ESTRAGON (French) Tarragon.

ESTRAGON, BEURRE D' (French) See COMPOUND BUTTER

ÉTOUFFER (French) To cook under tight cover with but little moisture, literally "to stifle" or "to steam."

ÉTUVÉE See ESTOUFFADE

FA (Chinese) A method of precooking food, literally meaning "to develop." Because they are better preserved and thus more savory to the taste, a great many dried and salted foods are used by the Chinese. By *fa,* or parboiling, these foods are softened in preparation for further cooking.

FABADA ASTURIANA (Spanish) This Asturian speciality from the north of Spain is a stew of white beans and pork sausages seasoned with garlic, bits of salt beef, and ham. COMPATIBLE BEVERAGES: As the finest apples are grown in Asturia, the recommended drink is cider; or a white wine, e.g., Vouvray, Sauterne, Tokay, Sylvaner, Gewürztraminer, Riesling.

FAGARA (Chinese) A popular pepper grown in the Szechwan Province. A dish of peanuts that have been boiled with salt and *fagara* is a real taste treat. (See SZECHWAN CUISINE)

FAGGOT A small bundle of herbs used to flavor stews, soups, and sauces. The herbs are bound together so that they can easily be removed from the pot. (See BOUQUET GARNI)

FAGIOLI (Italian) Dried beans.
   Fagioli Toscana   This bean dish, popular in Florence, situated in the heart of Tuscany, is made with tuna fish and dried beans. COMPATIBLE WINES: A red wine, e.g., Chianti, Bardolino, Beaujolais, Ruby Cabernet, Margaux, Nebbiolo, Valpolicella, Zinfandel.

FA JU (Chinese) "Flower pepper," an aromatic, mild spice used in all types of Chinese cooking, especially the Szechwan. A member of the Rutaceae family, it grows in eastern Asia and is obtained from the red fruit of the Japanese or Chinese pepper shrub. Sometimes, chili peppers are erroneously referred to as "Szechwan pepper."

FANNY FARMER Although she cooked *pasta* to an indistinguishable mass of "goo" and called the famous French *tournedos* of beef "tornadoes," she served more sweetbreads and calf's brains than most restaurants do today, and her cookbook has sold more than four million copies to date. She also opened Miss Farmer's School of Cookery in Boston. Fanny later found time to write half a dozen more cookbooks. Today, one finds new editions of her work selling like hot cakes.

FARCE/FARCI (French) Stuffing/stuffed.
   Choux Farci   Scalded cabbage leaves are filled with a *farce* of bacon, chicken livers, mushrooms, onions, and parsley and simmered slowly on a bed of salt pork, onions, and carrots that has been flavored with thyme. (See CHOU/CHOUX)

FARCITO (Italian) "Stuffed" or "filled." (See RIPIENI)

FARFALETTE (Italian) See PASTA

FARFEL (Polish-Jewish) This soup garnish, also called "egg barley," consists of small, chopped-up grains of dough made from a mixture of flour, eggs, and salt. After thoroughly drying the minutely cut balls of dough, they are dropped into boiling soup. *Farfel* is also served as an accompaniment for meat dishes. It is first boiled then sautéed in oil in a heavy pan with finely chopped onions. (See FAUFAL)

Farfel Kugel Chopped onions and mushrooms are sautéed in *schmaltz,* to which pieces of *farfel* made from *matzo* flour, lemon juice, and *gribenes* are added. A rich chicken broth is poured over the ingredients and everything is cooked until all of the broth has been absorbed. Then the ingredients are poured into a greased casserole and baked in a medium oven. (See GRIBENES, KUGEL, SCHMALTZ)

FAUBONNE, POTAGE (French) This thick soup can be made from a white bean, a pea, or any other fine vegetable purée that is cooked gently in sweet butter and flavored with chervil. It can also be a purée of pheasant that is enriched with actual bits of the bird and a *julienne* of truffles. (See CHERVIL, JULIENNE)

FAUFAL (Arab) A cereal consisting of tiny balls of semolina, used in the preparation of the famous Moroccan *couscous*. (See COUSCOUS, FARFEL)

FAVA This bean of Asiatic origin, also called the "horse bean" or "butter bean," is usually eaten without the skin or hull, which is removed by blanching. Favas are served in salads in a puréed state, or to complement a meal as a warm vegetable. The small variety is called the "bell bean."

Fava Salad (Turkish) A rather unusual type of salad by Western standards, but delicious nonetheless. Shelled fava beans are soaked overnight in cold water, then drained and cooked in fresh water until soft enough to mash easily. After all the water has been absorbed, the beans are removed from the heat and mashed into a mixture of lemon juice, salt, oil, and sour cream. This purée is then smoothed out on a flat platter and allowed to cool. Garnished with dill, parsley, black olives, radishes, and scallions, the bean purée is served cut in wedges, like a cake.

FAVORITE (French) A garnish consisting of hearts of artichokes, served either with *tournedos* of beef or in a rich consommé thickened with tapioca. The latter is served with mushrooms and potato balls. (See TOURNEDOS)

FÉCULE/FECULA (French) A very fine flour, usually derived from potatoes. Also, a type of starch made from manioc and yams. Both are used to bind soups and sauces. (See MANIOC, YAM)

FEGATINI (Italian) *Fegato* means "liver," and *fegatini,* the diminutive form, means "little livers." Not surprisingly then, *fegatini* has come to mean "chicken livers." (See FEGATO)

FEGATO (Italian) Liver.

Fegato di Vitello al Marsala (Italian) Calf's liver is cut into slices, salted and dusted with flour, browned in hot butter, and removed from the pan. Diced ham, onions, leeks, and garlic are cooked in the still-hot pan; tomato purée, paprika, and chopped parsley are added. The sliced liver is returned to the pan, and the whole is given a quick hot bath with a dash of Marsala wine. The dish is served immediately with either rice or *pasta.* COMPATIBLE WINES: A white wine, e.g., Orvieto, Lacrima Christi, Vouvray, Graves; or red wine, e.g., Merlot, Valpolicella, Bardolino, Zinfandel, Egri Bikaver.

FELAFEL (Middle Eastern) A dish created by the Egyptian Christian Copts, who subsisted on it during the Lenten season, when meat was strictly forbidden. Today, these chickpea *croquettes* are made by adding boiling water to *burghul* or to wheat germ, then mixing in mashed cooked chickpeas, eggs, breadcrumbs, and a variety of spices and herbs. The mixture is formed into small balls and fried in hot oil until golden brown on both sides. Served hot, *felafel* makes a delicious appetizer. In Israel, stuffed into Arab bread, it is sold on street corners. (See BURGHUL)

FENNEL A tall plant with featherlike leaves. Its bright yellow flowers provide seeds used for flavoring. Another, more important variety is "Florence fennel," a thick low-growing plant native to Italy, where it is called *finocchio.* The bulbous stalks at the base of the stem are used in salads or as a cooked vegetable. To prepare to serve as a vegetable, the stalks are usually first braised and then sprinkled with grated cheese and melted butter and browned in the oven. Fennel has a distinctive licorice taste.

Sea Bass Flamed in Fennel The fennel flavor makes this Italian fish dish special. The whole bass is set overnight in a marinade of olive oil, wine vinegar, and chopped fennel. Long stalks of fennel are blanched, and when pliable, they are wrapped around the marinated bass and fastened with toothpicks. As the fish then bakes or broils, it is religiously basted with melted sweet butter. The bass, now enveloped in the crisp, dry fennel, is flamed with Pernod and served with small boiled potatoes. COMPATIBLE WINES: A white wine, e.g., Montrachet, Meursault, Quincy, Aigle, Sancerre, Graacher Himmelreich, Soave, Pinot Chardonnay.

FENUGREEK This annual Asiatic herb of the pea family is used to spice Indian dishes. The yellow and flat fenugreek seeds come sixteen to a pod, and because they are quite bitter, they are used with discretion. They do wonderful things to eggplant and potatoes. Just a touch of fenugreek will remind one of the taste of maple syrup. (See DAL)

FETA SOUFFLÉ (Greek) This _soufflé_ is made with the well-known feta cheese, produced from goat's or sheep's milk. This salty semisoft cheese tends to crumble, and it is usually kept fresh and moist in a brine solution.

To prepare the _soufflé_, a mixture of butter, flour, milk, pepper, and egg.yolks is cooked over moderate heat until it begins to thicken; then feta cheese, chives, and finely-minced cooked ham are stirred in and the mixture is set aside to cool. Beaten egg whites are folded into the batter and the _soufflé_ is baked in the oven until it has risen. And since a _soufflé_ waits for no man, it must be served immediately. COMPATIBLE WINES: A red wine, e.g., Retsina, Beaujolais, Fleurie, Châteauneuf-du-Pape, Pinot Noir, Valpolicella, Zinfandel, Egri Bikaver.

FETTUCINE One of the two Italian terms used to designate the long egg noodle; the other term is _tagliatelle_. (See PASTA)

Fettucine Alfredo The original Alfredo of Rome one day decided to put on a gastronomic performance at his famous restaurant by not only preparing the ordinary _fettucine al burro_ right in the dining room before his guests, but by adding heavy cream and grated cheese and mixing all with a gold-plated spoon and fork. The dish became a classic and Alfredo's name became immortalized. (See BURRO) COMPATIBLE WINES: A red wine, e.g., Chianti, Barbera, Nebbiolo, Beaujolais, Côtes du Rhône, Châteauneuf-du-Pape, Rioja, St. Julien, Pinot Noir.

FEUILLETAGE (French) An expansion of the word _feuille,_ meaning "leaf" or "sheet," _feuilletage_ is puff pastry dough (also called "puff paste"), prepared from a mixture of flour, salt, and water, which is well kneaded and rolled flat. Fresh, cool butter is added and the dough is given six turns, two at a time, and set in the refrigerator to chill between turns. Puff pastry dough, thus layered with butter, puffs up and becomes very light and flaky as it bakes.

Puff paste may be used to make sweet or savory pastries. These include the _mille-feuille_ (a pastry of "a thousand leaves" filled with whipped cream and either raspberry or strawberry jam); _Napoleons; friands_ (small sausages enclosed in puff pastry and baked); or tea pastries, called _feuillantines,_ which are brushed with egg white, sprinkled with finely granulated sugar, and baked. (See FRIAND, MILLE-FEUILLE, NAPOLEON)

FILÉ POWDER This condiment, often called "gumbo filé powder," is basic to Créole cookery. First created by the Choctow Indians from the dried leaves of the sassafras tree, filé powder is used as a thickening agent for gumbo dishes. _Filé,_ in French, means "to spin," and the gumbo can become stringy if it is boiled after the filé powder is added to the pot. The filé powder available in cans tends to lose its flavor. The best is always freshly made. (See CRÉOLE JAMBALAYA, GUMBO, OKRA)

FILET MIGNON (French) A small, choice cut of meat, sliced from the small end of the fillet of beef. *Filets mignons* are either pan-fried or broiled. COMPATIBLE WINES: A red wine, e.g., Fixin, Romanée-Conti, Chambertin, Haut Brion—the choice of wine really will depend upon the type of sauce served with the *filet mignon.*

FILOSES In Portugal, children look forward to these doughnuts on Shrove Tuesday, but they are a real treat on any other day of the week as well. Having steeped cinnamon in milk, a soft dough is formed by mixing the milk with flour, yeast, salt, sugar, melted butter, and eggs. After rising, the dough is dropped from a large spoon into deep fat and cooked until brown. Before serving, the doughnuts are rolled in honey and sugar. A delightful mouthful!

FINANCIÈRE, À LA (French) As the name implies, this is a rich garnish made from veal or poultry *quenelles* plus truffles, olives, cockscombs, kidneys, and mushrooms. It is also used as a filling for the *vol-au-vent.* (See QUENELLE, VOL-AU-VENT)

Ham à la Financière The ham is braised in Madeira wine, glazed, and then garnished *à la financière.* The braising liquid is reduced and poured over the ham. COMPATIBLE WINES: Montrachet, Muscadet, Anjou, Gewürztraminer, Vouvray, Tokay, Orvieto, Piesporter Goldtröpfchen, Wehlener Sonnenuhr.

FINES HERBES, SAUCE AUX (French) A popular sauce composed of *fresh* herbs—such as chopped parsley, chives, chervil, and tarragon—which are cooked in a dry white wine and strained. This sauce is served with boiled or poached fish. However, when a *sauce demi-glace* is added to this infusion and brought to a boil, with a quantity of finely chopped fresh herbs and a dash of lemon juice, the sauce can be served with chops and steaks. (See DEMI-LACE)

FINNAN HADDIE (Scottish) This delicious smoked haddock was named after Findon, the fishing village in Scotland that made the preparation famous. The haddock is cleaned, split and well salted, and left overnight. It is then hung up to dry and is cured by smoking.

Creamed Finnan Haddie The finnan haddie is cubed, covered with wildly boiling water, and left to stand for a few minutes; in other words, the fish is blanched. Butter and flour *(roux)* are blended in a pan, and when stirred to a smooth consistency, cream and milk are added. This cream sauce is seasoned with cayenne pepper, and the cubed fish is carefully mixed in and just warmed through. (See ROUX) COMPATIBLE WINES: A white wine, e.g., Orvieto, Frascati, Gewürztraminer, Graves, Sauvignon Blanc, Anjou, Sylvaner, Johannisberg, Aigle, Traminer.

FIOS D'OVOS (Portugese) This special method of using eggs in the making of sweets dates back to the convents of the early eighteenth century and the ingenuity of Catholic nuns. The nuns had time on their hands and the responsibility, now and then, of producing the most sumptuous foods possible for visiting Church dignitaries, bishops, royalty, and other travelers of importance. Among their creations were some marvelous original sweets, such as _fios d'ovos,_ "threads of eggs." This dish is prepared by piercing an egg shell and straining the egg yolks through the small hole into a boiling sugar syrup. They are used to decorate cakes and pastries.

FISKEPUDDING, NORWEGIAN The Norwegian diet is rich in fish, and the hearty people of Norway prepare fish in any number of unusual ways. This steamed fish pudding is a fine example of their culinary artistry and imagination. Fish fillets—usually cod, halibut, flounder, or sole—are cut up and then ground into a paste with salt, cornstarch, and mace. Cream and milk are slowly added, and the mixture is stirred vigorously until all the ingredients are well blended. The pudding is placed in a pan, which in turn is placed in hot water and baked in a moderate oven until a knife inserted comes out clean. Unmolded, the pudding is usually served with melted butter or with a fish sauce. COMPATIBLE WINES: A white wine, e.g., Orvieto, Johannisberg, Fendant, Sylvaner, Gewürztraminer, Riesling, Meursault, Hermitage Blanc, Chenin Blanc, Riquewihr.

FIVE FLAVORS, THE PHILOSOPHY OF The Chinese concept of the Five Flavors—bitter, salty, sour, hot, sweet—was established in the fourth century, early in the Chinese _haute cuisine_. It basically stresses contrast as the essence of good menu planning. Successful restaurateurs and all good chefs follow this _table d'hôte_ maxim purely by instinct.

FIVE-SPICE ESSENCE A popluar Chinese seasoning powder composed of finely ground star anise, fennel, cinnamon, cloves, and Szechwan pepper. It is used to flavor red-cooked (using soy sauce) and roasted meat and poultry dishes. A substitute, consisting of cinnamon, cloves, aniseed, and thyme, is sometimes used. (See ANISE, CINNAMON, CLOVES, FAGARA, FENNEL, RED-COOKING, SZECHWAN)

FLÄDLI (Swiss-German) A type of _crêpe_ made from a mixture of eggs, milk, flour, and salt. When cooked into pancake form, it is sliced into strips and used as a garnish for clear soups, such as consommés and bouillons. (See CRÊPE)

FLAMANDE, ASPARAGUS À LA (Belgian) Although the Flemish and the French-speaking Belgians share a country that was guaranteed "perpetual neutrality" in 1839, these two groups have been at loggerheads, politically and economically, for generations. However, when it comes to food, they are in complete accord. This asparagus dish is a case in point. The fresh white asparagus are cleaned, tied together in bundles, set upright in salted water, and brought to a boil. In this way the tender tips are steamed while the stems are cooked in the water. The asparagus are served with a garnish of hard-boiled eggs and chopped parsley and a _sauce mousseline_. In the spring, the

Belgian fancy turns to platters of this asparagus dish and slices of ham. (See MOUSSELINE) COMPATIBLE WINES: A white wine, e.g., Aigle, Meursault, Montrachet, Anjou, Château Chalon, Orvieto, Hermitage Blanc, Riesling, Deidesheimer Kieselberg, Sauvignon Blanc.

FLAN In Spain, the *flan* is a national dessert (the French know it as *crème caramel;* Americans call it "caramel custard"). To prepare the dish, sugar and water are heated until the mixture is transformed into a golden syrup, which is subsequently poured into several individual ovenproof molds or into a single baking dish. Scalded milk is whipped together with eggs, sugar, and vanilla. This is poured over the caramel and, placed in pans of hot water, it is baked until a knife inserted emerges clean.

Another type of *flan,* which is really an open-faced tart, is made by filling a prebaked pastry shell with any of a number of alternatives: whipped cream flavored with rum and topped with cherries, apricots, or other fruit; a plain thick custard; a flavored cream covered with toasted nuts and gobs of whipped cream; berries and whipped cream; ice cream; or even a rich meringue over a lemon custard. It can also be made with a savory fillings: cheese, meats, or vegetables. (See CARAMEL, CRÈME CARAMEL)

FLANK Also referred to as "the skirt," this cut of beef comes from the hindquarter, below the loin. The flank can be quite tough and is best served stuffed, rolled, and braised. The larger part of the flank is frequently corned. For a London broil, a popular restaurant offering, the beef must be prime or choice if it is to be tender. (See CORNED BEEF)

FLAT CARS (Créole) A dish of thickly sliced choice pork chops that are heavily peppered and salted and then fried in pork fat. They are usually served with baked sweet potatoes. (See SWEET POTATO) COMPATIBLE WINES: A red wine, e.g., Chinon, Ruby Cabernet, Rioja, Beaujolais, Fleurie, Barbarola, Moulin-à-Vent, Côtes du Rhône, Zinfandel.

FLEURONS (French) A crescent-shaped flaky pastry garnish used to decorate roasts, poultry dishes, *pâtés* cooked in pastry, and various soups.

FLORENTINE, À LA (French) A term indicating that spinach is present in the dish. Catherine de Medici made many things popular at the Court of France. Among them was spinach, and in honor of her Italian roots she dubbed *Florentine* any dish containing that vegetable.

Filets de Sole Florentine Seasoned fillets of sole are cooked in butter and lemon juice. Then, set on a bed of blanched spinach, the fillets are covered with a *sauce Mornay* and browned in the grill. (See MORNAY) COMPATIBLE WINES: A white wine, e.g., Chablis, Pouilly-Fuissé, Montrachet, Pinot Chardonnay, Pouilly-Fumé, Muscadet, Piesporter Goldtröpfchen, Debro, Johannisberg.

FLUDEN (Jewish) The Yiddish equivalent of the German word _Fladen,_ meaning "a flat cake." In Swiss-German, this is called _Flädli._ The _Fluden_ is made by enveloping cheese or fruit and berries between two rectangles of an egg-yeast dough and then baking the filled pancakes in the oven. (See FLÄDLI)

FOIE DE VEAU AUX FINES HERBES (French) A dish of calf's liver that is served garnished with a sauce made with fresh herbs. The calf's liver is sliced, seasoned with salt and pepper, and then dredged in flour. It is then sautéed in hot butter for only a few minutes on each side, lest it be overcooked and tough. A _sauce aux fines herbes_ is served separately. (See FINES HERBES) COMPATIBLE WINES: A red wine, e.g., Margaux, Médoc, Mâcon, St. Julien, Cabernet Sauvignon, Châteauneuf-du-Pape, Côtes du Rhône, St. Estèphe.

FOIE DE VEAU PIQUÉ (French) _Piqué_ means "pricked, larded," and this phrase designates a larded calf's liver. First the liver is larded with pork fat strips, then it is pickled in an oil and vinegar marinade flavored with bay leaf, parsley, onions, and allspice. The following day the liver is well dried, seasoned with salt and pepper, and roasted with the marinated onion slices on top of the liver. The dish is garnished with baked tomatoes that are filled with sausage meat and breadcrumbs and topped with crisp bacon. COMPATIBLE WINES: A red wine, e.g., Kirwan, Pomerol, St. Émilion, Gruaud-Larose, Zinfandel, Cabernet Sauvignon, Médoc, Valpolicella, Figeac.

FOIE DE VEAU SAUTÉ, ÉMINCÉ DE (Swiss) A speciality made by first slicing calf's liver _very_ thin and then adding the almost minced liver to chopped shallots which are already cooking in very hot butter. After quickly sautéing the liver and seasoning and dusting it with flour, it is removed from the pan. A dash of dry white wine and beef bouillon are then poured into the pan and seasoned, and the liver is replaced and simmered for a short time. It is served immediately with white rice, buttered noodles, or _Spätzli._ (See SPÄTZLI) COMPATIBLE WINES: A white wine, e.g., Dézaley, Aigle, Montrachet, Meursault, Soave, Sauvignon Blanc, Wehlener Sonnenuhr, Bernkasteler Doktor, Johannisberg, Hermitage Blanc.

FOIE GRAS (French) A rather expensive liver paste, or _pâté,_ made from the livers of force-fed geese. The very first _pâté de foie gras_ (goose liver paste) is said to have been created in Strasbourg in 1765 by a Norman chef named Close. He enclosed the goose liver in a layer of chopped veal and minced pork fat and then encased it in finely decorated puff pastry. The high point of his inspiration came when he stuffed the goose liver with delicate black truffles.

Today, the finest _fois gras_ comes from Alsace, although that produced in Toulouse and in Périgueux is also much admired for its delicacy and flavor. The Périgord variety, called _foie gras truffé,_ is enriched with chopped black truffles. Hungary, Austria, and Czechoslovakia also make goose liver *pâtés,* but the French variety surpasses all.

The richness of *foie gras* demands that it be served as the first course of a meal, when the stomach is yet untainted by other food. Only then can the exquisite *foie gras* be appreciated. COMPATIBLE WINES: A white wine, e.g., Château d'Yquem (very cold!), Tokay d'Alsace, Gewürztraminer, Château-Grillet, Sauterne, Meursault.

FONDANT, GLACE AU (French) An icing made by cooking granulated sugar in water to the soft-ball stage (240 degrees F.) and then pouring it out on a cold hard surface (marble is best). There, it is worked and moved about with a spatula until the sugar has developed into a kind of granular paste. This is kneaded by hand until smooth. To be used as a cake glaze, this sugar paste is cooked until it liquefies, then it is quickly poured over the object or objects to be glazed, such as *petits fours. Fondant* is used in candymaking as well. (See PETITS FOURS)

FONDANTES, POTATOES (French) For this dish, potatoes are cut in the form of elongated olives and sautéed in butter. Lightly moistened with consommé, they are covered and cooked very gently so that when done, the potatoes are golden on the outside and still soft inside.

FONDS (French) Basic liquid foundations necessary for the preparation of sauces, glazes, soups, etc.

Fond Blanc The light-colored liquid or broth produced by the careful cooking of veal or fowl. This white broth is used in the preparation of white sauces, stews, and steamed poultry.

Fond Brun This dark brown broth is the result of cooking beef and beef bones, veal, and poultry together with root vegetables in butter. This basic stock is used in braising roasts of meat, to form the base of a multitude of brown sauces, and in cooking brown stews.

Fond du Gibier A game stock prepared from venison, pheasant, hare, etc., cooked with wine.

Fond du Poisson The fish stock is made by cooking the bones and trimmings of fish in dry white wine with onions, parsley, thyme, bay leaves, and lemon juice. It is used as the foundation of many compound sauces, such as *Normande, suprême,* and *vin blanc.* (See NORMANDE, SUPRÊME, VIN BLANC)

FONDS D'ARTICHAUTS GARNIS (French) Artichoke hearts as a garnish for cold or hot dishes. To complement cold dishes, the hearts, *fonds,* are simmered in a *court-bouillon,* drained, and then either filled with various vegetables, seasoned with vinegar or with *sauce Mayonnaise,* or filled with a veritable host of compound butters made from shrimp, crayfish, caviar, hard-boiled eggs, etc. When prepared as a garnish for hot dishes, they are named according to their fillings: *Argenteuil,* purée of asparagus; *Bretonne,* purée of kidney beans; *Conti,* a lentil purée; *Saint Germain,* a purée of peas. They can also simply be coated with various sauces: *Mornay, Hollan-*

daise, Soubise. (See ARGENTEUIL, CONTI, COURT-BOUILLON, HOLLAN-
DAISE, MAYONNAISE, MORNAY, SAINT GERMAIN, SOUBISE)

FONDUE This national dish of Switzerland is prepared in a fireproof
casserole or chafing dish set over an alcohol burner in the center of
the table. First, the cooking utensil is rubbed with raw garlic, then a
dry white wine is added and heated. Grated Gruyère cheese is melted
in the wine. A dash of Kirsch and a bit of cornstarch (optional)
finishes the cheese mixture. The *fondue* is eaten by piercing cubes of
bread with long forks and carefully dipping the bread chunks into the
melted cheese mixture. The unlucky one who allows his bread to fall
into the *fondue* must pay for the meal or buy the next bottle of Aigle
or Neuchâtel wine. (See FONDUE BOURGUIGNONNE; FONDUE, CHOCO-
LATE; FONDUE, FRENCH-STYLE; FONDUTA) COMPATIBLE WINES: A white
wine, e.g., Dézaley, Aigle, Neuchâtel, Orvieto, Riquewihr, Riesling,
Sauvignon Blanc.

FONDUE BOURGUIGNONNE (Swiss) This popular dish is made by
piercing long *fondue* forks into cubes of fillet of beef and frying them
in hot oil until well charred. Like cheese *fondue,* this communal Swiss
dish is eaten while sitting around a pot (a *caquelon*), which is kept
bubbling on an alcohol burner in the center of the dining table. When
cooked, the meat is seasoned with salt and pepper and dipped into
one of several sauces, which are served separately in small bowls. The
sauces include a tomato purée mixed with a *sauce Mayonnaise,* sour
cream, and paprika; a *sauce Hollandaise* flavored with lemon juice
and soy sauce; a brown sauce made from beef extract, red wine,
tarragon, sugar, oil, vinegar, and cayenne pepper; a *sauce Mayonnaise* flavored with mustard, anchovy paste, and chopped hard-
boiled eggs; and a sauce made from paprika, oil, vinegar, sour cream,
and chopped dill. A tossed mixed-green salad rounds out this meal.
(See FONDUE; FONDUE, CHOCOLATE; FONDUE, FRENCH-STYLE; FONDUTA;
HOLLANDAISE; MAYONNAISE) COMPATIBLE WINES: A red wine, e.g.,
Châteauneuf-du-Pape, Mercurey, Côtes du Rhône, Dôle, Zinfandel.

FONDUE, CHOCOLATE (Swiss) There are two rich dessert *fondues* that
make lovers of chocolate glow. The first is prepared by combining
semisweet chocolate, evaporated milk, and marshmallows and simmering all over low heat in a chafing dish until the sauce is melted and
smooth. The second concoction incorporates unsweetened chocolate
and sugar with milk, coffee, cream, or sweet sherry. This is stirred
over low heat; when the mixture is smooth, rum, vanilla, and salt are
added. For both methods, bits of banana, cherries, pineapple, oranges, or small squares of sponge cake, pierced on the tines of long
forks, are dipped into the chocolate sauce set out in a chafing dish in
the middle of the table. (See FONDUE; FONDUE, FRENCH-STYLE; FON-
DUTA)

FONDUE, FRENCH-STYLE The French follow the classic Swiss recipe for
the cheese *fondue*—up to a point. They heat diced Gruyère cheese

with a bit of butter and flour in a double boiler, then they add the necessary white wine, a few drops at a time. However, after the cheese and wine are well blended, they make the Gallic addition of egg yolks. The *fondue* is placed in a chafing dish at the center of the table. A bowl of cubed French bread is set beside it. Using long forks, the cubes of bread are dipped into the *fondue* mixture and transferred—ideally, without a drop or a dribble—to the diner's mouth. (See FONDUE; FONDUE, CHOCOLATE; FONDUTA) COMPATIBLE WINES: The same as for the traditional Swiss *fondue*.

FONDUTA This is Italy's answer to the Swiss *fondue*. The dish comes from the Piedmont region, and the native Fontina cheese is used as the chief ingredient. The cubed cheese is melted in milk then thickened with cream and eggs. It is enriched with finely grated white truffles. As with the other *fondues,* cubes of bread are dipped into the cheese and popped into the mouth. (See FONDUE; FONDUE, CHOCO-LATE; FONDUE, FRENCH-STYLE) COMPATIBLE WINES: A white wine, e.g., Orvieto, Frascati, Aigle, Beaune Blanc, Sauvignon Blanc, Gewürztraminer.

FORCEMEATS These are stuffings made from finely ground and seasoned pork, veal, poultry, fish, or game. They are bound with eggs, heavy cream, and breadcrumbs. Forcemeats are used to make *pâtés, galantines, ballotines,* and *quenelles.* (See BALLOTINES, GALANTINES, PANADA, PATÉ, QUENELLE)

FORELLE BLAU (German) Blue trout. (See BLEU, TRUITE AU)

FORESTIÈRE, À LA (French) A descriptive term synonymous with *à la chasseur.* Both terms indicate that mushrooms are used in the dish.

FORK In 1608, Thomas Coryat sang the praises of the excellent food he was served in Italy and Germany, and he spoke glowingly of a new invention: "that Italian neatness, the fork." However, most Englishmen ignored not only the fork but all foreign dishes as well. The French avowed that God made fingers before forks, and their gluttonous monarch, Louis XIV, backed them up by continuing to use his whole hand to bring food to his mouth right up until the day he died. The Italians and the Spanish were the first to use the fork at table in the sixteenth century. A hundred years later, the French decided to follow suit—that is, all except Loius XIV, who kept using his fingers right to the end.

FORNO, AL (Italian) Baked in the oven.

Lasagne al Forno Wide, flat *pasta* is layered alternately with slices of mozzarella cheese, grated Parmesan cheese, and a tomato sauce flavored with onions and seasoning. The dish is baked as a loaf. COMPATIBLE WINES: A red wine, e.g., Chianti, Beaujolais, Médoc, Valpolicella, Nebbiolo, Zinfandel, Ruby Cabernet, Egri Bikaver.

FORSHMARK (Russian) A welcome addition to any fine *zakouski,* this rich appetizer is made by mixing together finely chopped meat or poultry, minced salt herring fillets, mashed potatoes, finely chopped onions, butter, sour cream, breadcrumbs, and seasoning. Then egg yolks and beaten egg white are folded into the mixture. Finally, placed in a well-greased baking dish, the mixture is topped with grated cheese and breadcrumbs and baked. It is served with side dishes of sour cream and tomato sauce.

The cold variety is much simpler. To prepare, chopped hard-boiled eggs are mixed together with finely minced salt herring fillets, minced cooked roast beef or veal, onions, and capers. With the addition of olive oil and lemon juice, this mixture is refrigerated at least overnight. Served mounded on a serving plate, it is set off with complementing borders of slivered pickles and black olives. (See ZAKOUSKI) COMPATIBLE BEVERAGES: Vodka, of course.

FOUR, AU (French) Baked in the oven.

FOYOT, SAUCE (French) A creation of M. Foyot, the one-time chef to Louis-Phillipe who, when put out of work by the Revolution of 1848, proceeded as did many other displaced cooks: he opened his own restaurant. If the old axiom, "Measure the girth of the chef and you can rate the restaurant," holds true, then Foyot's restaurant must truly have been superb because when he died, a special coffin had to be constructed to hold his gargantuan corpse. Foyot's sauce is made by adding a concentrated meat glaze to a *sauce Béarnaise.*

Veal Chops Foyot Veal chops are placed on a bed of chopped onions and shallots. They are then covered with white wine and bouillon and sprinkled liberally with grated Parmesan cheese, breadcrumbs, and butter. The chops are tightly covered and baked in a medium oven until done. The *sauce Foyot* is served separately. (See BÉARNAISE) COMPATIBLE WINES: A red wine, e.g., Santenay, Mercurey, Côtes du Rhône, Hermitage, Valpolicella, Egri Bikaver, Zinfandel, Nebbiolo.

FRA DIAVOLO (Italian) Applied to a lobster preparation, this phrase, meaning "brother devil," was actually the name of a well-known Sicilian Robin Hood, who stole from the rich and gave to the poor but always saw to it that he had enough to take him to Capri for the weekend. He and his band did their work disguised as Franciscan friars, hence the name.

Fra Diavolo, Aragosta Also known as "lobster *fra diavolo,"* this popular method of cooking lobster entails first splitting and spreading the lobster wide open. Garlic is cooked in olive oil and, with the addition of tomatoes, parsley, oregano, red pepper seeds, and salt, all is simmered together until fused. The sauce is then poured over the split lobster, which is baked until tender. It is served very hot. COMPATIBLE WINES: A white wine, e.g., Orvieto, White Chianti,

Sylvaner, Johannisberg, Vouvray, Graves, Gewürztraminer, Frascati, Sauvignon Blanc, Riesling.

FRAÎCHE, CRÈME (French) This thick cream of distinctive flavor is made by adding sour cream, yogurt, or buttermilk to fresh heavy cream and heating it to a simmer (about 85 degrees F.). It is left to stand overnight in a warm room. It should then be stirred well and refrigerated. In France, heavy cream is allowed time to mature, and it is the natural fermentation which thickens the cream.

FRAIS (French) Cool.

FRAISES (French) Strawberries.

FRAMBOISE FARCIE, DINDE À LA (French) This ancient but tasty method of roasting a turkey follows La Varenne's old recipe, which calls for the bird to be stuffed with any favorite stuffing, basted with butter, and roasted for several hours. Every quarter-hour during the roasting, the turkey is basted with a special mixture composed of raspberry preserves, lemon juice, hot water, and lemon rind. The sauce, served with the bird, is made from the pan juices, which are flavored with vinegar and grated lemon peel and reduced. COMPATIBLE WINES: A red wine, e.g., St. Émilion, Médoc, Mâcon, Musigny, Beaujolais, Figeac, St. Julien, Valpolicella, Zinfandel, Cabernet Sauvignon.

FRAMBOISES (French) Raspberries.

FRANÇAISE, À LA (French) Applicable to so many dishes, this phrase simply means "done in the French style," usually the style peculiar to the region of France where the dish was originally conceived.

FRANGIPANE (Italian) Count Cesare Frangipani presented this special custard-cream dessert to Catherine de Médicis when she left Florence for Paris and the Court of Henry II. *Frangipane* is a thick pastry cream generously flavored with crushed macaroons. Powdered sugar, flour, whole eggs and additional yolks are blended together and cooked in milk. Gobs of sweet butter and crushed macaroons complete this delicious custard used also as a topping for small tarts. For use as a filling, *frangipane*—made of flour, egg yolks, crushed macaroons, butter, and milk—is cooked like a *pâte à chou*. Almonds can be substituted for the macaroons. (See CRÈME PATISSIÈRE, DARTOIS, PÂTE À CHOU)

FRANKFURTER GRÜNE-SOSSE (German) This green sauce, created in the city of Frankfurt, is a mixture of many fresh herbs, such as dill, chives, parsley, watercress, chervil, and borage, all finely chopped and stirred into a sugar-sweetened oil and vinegar dressing. German-style restaurants serve the sauce with meat and fish dishes and with hard-boiled eggs.

FRANKFURTER WÜRSTCHEN (German) This sausage, originally made in Frankfurt, Germany, today is known all over the globe. For many years in America, the frankfurter was called a "red hot," until one day a cartoonist by the name of Dorgan envisioned this elongated German sausage as a Dachshund, made a drawing of it, and dubbed it "hot dog."

Frankfurters are made not only from beef and pork, but also from chicken, turkey, bone, cereal—in fact, from any number of foodstuffs that can be legally stuffed into those thin skins—not to mention the fat. (Some of these sausages, containing 33 percent fat, have been called "fatfurters" by American consumer-advocate Ralph Nader.) When all of the preservatives are added to the rest of the questionable ingredients, we have a new breed of frankfurter that would have dismayed Antoine Feuchtwanger, who introduced them to America in 1883. Frankfurters are sold precooked. They are available loose, packaged, or in cans and require only to be warmed by being gently boiled, or they may be broiled.

FRAPPÉ (French) Used gastronomically, this means "mixed or beaten with shaved ice." The word is used to describe certain creams, fruits, and sweets. It is also used to describe an iced drink, such as the green crème de menthe liqueur, which is served poured over shaved ice and sipped through a straw.

FRASCATI, À LA (French) A garnish served with large cuts of meat. It consists of large mushrooms that are stuffed with various fillings, such as tiny asparagus tips or black truffles and goose liver. A _sauce demi-glace_ laced with port wine accompanies the garnish. (See DEMI-GLACE)

FRENCH CUISINE The French, together with the rest of the world, must thank Italy for having sowed the seed of culture in France during the Renaissance. This included the advancement of gastronomy due to the intermarriages of the royal houses of Europe. When Catherine de Médicis, the fourteen-year-old heiress of one of the richest and noblest families of Italy, arrived at the French Court to wed King Henry II, she brought with her the expertise of an entourage of excellent Italian cooks and diplomatic aides. This was the foundation of the French cuisine as we know it today. Louis XIV, in turn, dedicated himself not only to improving the art of cooking but also to increasing the pleasure of dining. In Paris, cafés began to flourish, serving coffee, tea, and chocolate for the first time to the public. Restaurants, too, began to serve more than just heavy soups.

After the French Revolution, the end of aristocracy prompted French chefs to open their own eating establishments, and the preeminence of the French table was established. Every person of quality and means had to have a French chef. The eighteenth century brought the French cuisine to its greatest glory with the achievements of the talented Carême, who was weaned away from France, first by the English prince regent and then by the czar of Russia, Alexander.

Later, the French culinary crown was passed to Escoffier, who was responsible for the dinner menu and table service as we know it today.

The French cuisine is based on sauces that were initially created to disguise the repulsive taste of rotting meat. Today, however, these same sauces are refined to enhance, contrast, and complement our food. And as a country rich in wine, France uses wine to advantage in its cooking.

There are three basic tenets that the best of French chefs follow religiously: first, only the finest of fresh ingredients must be used; second, food must be prepared artfully and skillfully; and lastly, adequate preparation time must be allotted. By following these tenets, the chef can please the senses of those he wishes to enchant. (See CARÊME; DUXELLES; LOUIS XIV; LOUIS XVIII; MARIN AND MENON; PARMENTIER; RESTAURANT, THE FIRST; TAILLEVANT)

FRENCH DRESSING This is an American term for the basic French salad dressing, the *sauce vinaigrette,* which consists of three parts olive oil to one part wine vinegar. Salt and pepper are added as seasonings, and the sauce is shaken vigorously in the bottle. The mixture should be chilled so that the oil-and-vinegar emulsion does not separate when used. Often, a bit of prepared mustard is added. This is the foundation for many other sauces, such as *rémoulade, ravigote,* and *gribiche.* (See GRIBICHE, RAVIGOTE, RÉMOULADE, VINAIGRETTE)

FRENCH SERVICE *Service à la Française,* the old traditional French method of table service, entailed splitting a huge menu (sometimes consisting of as many as thirty-two courses) into two or more parts and placing all of the dishes of the first part on the dinner table at the same time. Often, a melee ensued, with the more aggressive, or those blest with a longer reach, faring better than their more timid table partners. In the 1850s, the situation was alleviated by the introduction of Russian Service. (See RUSSIAN SERVICE)

FRENCH TOAST In spite of its Gallic title, French toast did not originate in France. The famous Platina of ancient Rome describes this happy marriage of eggs and bread in his culinary work *De Honesta Voluptate.* In France the dish is known as *pain perdu;* in German-speaking lands it is called *Arme Ritter,* which the English have adopted as "the poor knights of Windsor." Whatever the name, the dish is prepared by soaking slices of absorbent bread in a mixture of eggs and milk or cream, sautéing the slices in butter, and serving them liberally dusted with cinnamon and sugar. (See PAIN PERDU)

FRIAND (French) Literally, "dainty," referring to a small hot appetizer, including such foods as sausage meat, ham, or small bits of game enclosed in puff pastry and baked. (See PÂTE À CHOU)

FRIANDISES (French) On menus, this term is used to designate a small pastry or sweetmeat as being a delicacy worth noting. Often used for *petits fours.*

FRICADELLES (French) Meatballs made from freshly ground meat of all kinds that is mixed with milk-soaked breadcrumbs, eggs, salt, pepper, and nutmeg. This meat paste is rolled into balls, flattened and browned in pork fat, and then baked in the oven. *Fricadelles* are served with vegetables, French-fried potatoes, and a *sauce piquante.*

In Belgium, where the dish is called *fricandelles,* the meatballs are poached in a bouillon after frying. The Danes call it *frikadeller* and traditionally serve pickled beets and boiled potatoes with the dish. (See FRIKADELLER, PIQUANTE, POMMES FRITES) COMPATIBLE WINES: A red wine, e.g., Valpolicella, Beaujolais, Moulin-à-Vent, Mercurey, Fleurie, Dôle, Zinfandel, Hermitage, Petit Sirah, Egri Bikaver.

FRICANDEAU (French) A loin of veal that is first well larded with salt pork then braised and roasted. A favorite Cajun method is to braise the veal in a mixture of water and apricot purée. Other variations of this dish, named for their garnish, include *à la bouquetière,* served with mixed vegetables; *à la Clamart,* served with artichoke hearts filled with peas; *à la bourgeoise,* with carrots, glazed onions, and sliced bacon; *à la Florentine,* with leaf spinach; *à la Milanese,* with macaroni and cooked ham; *à l'oseille,* with sorrel and veal stock. (See BOUQUETIÈRE, BOURGEOISE, CAJUN, CLAMART, FLORENTINE, MILANESE) COMPATIBLE WINES: A red wine, e.g., Chianti, Valpolicella, Zinfandel, Médoc, Margaux, St. Julien, Ruby Cabernet.

FRICASSÉE (French) A descriptive word signifying that white meat or poultry has been browned and then cooked like a stew in a sauce made from white wine, flour, lemon juice, seasoning, and sometimes cream.

Chicken Fricassée Probably one of the most popular of *fricassées,* the cut-up chicken is fried in butter then covered with a white wine sauce that is thickened with a bit of flour and laced with lemon juice. The dish is then simmered. Before serving, the sauce is refined with heavy cream. COMPATIBLE WINES: A white wine, e.g., Bernkasteler Doktor, Orvieto, Ammerschwihr, Sauvignon Blanc, Sylvaner Gewürztraminer, Chalon, Frascati, Meursault.

Fricassée de Veau This veal dish, much like the famous *blanquette de veau,* calls for the veal breast to be cut into small pieces. The pieces are then lightly dusted with flour, seared in butter, and simmered in a seasoned white stock together with finely chopped onions, mushrooms, and celery. (See BLANQUETTE) COMPATIBLE WINES: A white wine, e.g., Sauterne, Riquewihr, Piesporter Goldtröpfchen, Graacher Himmelreich, Orvieto, Hermitage Blanc, Sauvignon Blanc, Montrachet, Anjou.

Fricassée de Grenouilles After being sautéed in butter, white wine and seasoning are added to the well-browned frogs' legs. The sauce of choice—*Béchamel,* Parmesan, *Mornay,* curry—is then thickened with cream or with egg yolks and added. (See BÉCHAMEL, CURRY, FRICASSÉE, FROG, MORNAY) COMPATIBLE WINES: A white wine, e.g., Orvieto, Sauvignon Blanc, Frascati, Aigle, Trebbiano, Gewürztraminer.

FRIED RICE (Chinese) Preparing this rice dish actually provides one of the best ways to clean out both the larder and the refrigerator at the same time—and always with a tasty result. To prepare the dish, beaten eggs mixed with chopped scallions, onions, garlic, ham, chicken, mushrooms, or what-have-you are all cooked in lard over a hot fire. Boiled white rice is then quickly added and vigorously stir-fried. COMPATIBLE BEVERAGES: Beer, ale.

FRIKADELLER (Danish) These hamburgers, or meat patties, which in German are called *Frikadellen,* differ from their American counterpart in that they are made not from beef but from a mixture of chopped veal and pork, flour, club soda, eggs, and seasoning. The mixture is formed into large ovals, and the patties are well browned in butter in a hot pan. *Frikadeller* are traditionally served with pickled beets and boiled potatoes. (See FRICADELLES) COMPATIBLE WINES: A red wine, e.g., Beaujolais, Châteauneuf-du-Pape, Rioja, Hermitage, Dôle, Chianti, Médoc, Bardolino, Zinfandel.

FRITTATA/FRITTATE (Italian) Many consider this egg preparation an omelette, but the *frittata* is neither stuffed nor rolled, and when finished it does not even resemble an omelette. Made from meat and vegetables that are fried and blended into a cooking egg mixture, it looks more like a low cake.

Frittata di Porri To prepare this *frittata,* leeks are cut into rings, sautéed in olive oil until tender, then mixed with the eggs and seasonings. This mixture is poured into a hot pan with olive oil, cooked until well set, and then turned out onto a plate. The dish can be served as an *antipasto* or with a salad as a light luncheon. (See ANTIPASTO) COMPATIBLE WINES: A red wine, e.g., Chianti, Barbaresco, Nebbiolo, Petit Sirah, Beaujolais, Mercurey, Margaux, Valpolicella, Zinfandel.

FRITTER The English word "fritter" is derived from the French words *frite, friture,* meaning "fried." The French, however, not wishing to emphasize the obvious, especially in the kitchen, instead use the word *beignet,* which is derived from *baigner,* "to soak." Fritters have been around ever since Apicius, the famous Roman gastronome, tantalized the taste buds of ancient Rome with his chickpea variety. Today, fritters are made from any palatable foods—leftover meats, fish, vegetables, cheese—which are dipped into a batter and deep-fried. Fritters consisting of fruits that have been dipped into batters flavored with a liqueur of choice can even be served as dessert. (See BEIGNET, CROMESQUI, FRITTO)

FRITTO (Italian) Any food that has been "deep-fried."

Pollo Fritto alla Toscana A disjointed young chicken that has been fried Tuscany-style, meaning that it has been marinated in a mixture of olive oil, lemon juice, and parsley then dusted with flour, dipped into beaten egg, and fried in olive oil. COMPATIBLE WINES: A red wine, e.g., Beaujolais, Santenay, Nebbiolo, Valpolicella, Moulin-à-Vent, Zinfandel, Margaux, Rioja, Premiat.

Fritto Misto This combination plate comes from the region of Turin, and its composition is limited only by human imagination. It can be a vegetarian's one-plate feast, a gourmet's banquet of richness, or a mariner's festive fish-fry. Traditionally, it is a tastefully arranged and colorful presentation of sweetbreads, kidney, calf's brains, and liver plus artichoke hearts, cheese, eggplant, zucchini, and cauliflower—all of which have been well seasoned and dipped individually in a batter and fried. The above is but one possible combination. The chef can choose from any number of delectable foods—chicken, fish, apples, veal, _gnocchi,_ various vegetables—and prepare them in the same fashion. (See GNOCCHI) COMPATIBLE WINES: A good rosé wine.

FROG Mark Twain made many varieties of this leaping amphibian famous in his literature, but the only ones used for food in America are the bullfrog and the leopard frog. In France, the much smaller green frog and mute frog are preferred. In both cases, when prepared as food, the body of the frog is discarded and only the thighs are used. The taste is similar to that of tender chicken meat. (See GRENOUILLES)

FROMAGE (French) Cheese.

FROMAGE BLANC (French) This most uncomplicated of French cheeses is made by allowing cow's milk to sour and then draining it like cottage cheese. When refined with cream and sweetened with sugar, it is called _fromage à la crème._ The name _coeur à la crème_ has evolved from the heart-shaped basket (_coeur_ means "heart") used to drain and ultimately shape the cheese.

FRUITS DE MER (French) See FRUTTI DI MARE

FRUMENTY (English) A pudding-type dish created in medieval England, where it was usually served at harvest time. The wheat is left to ferment in warm water overnight (from whence comes the word "frumenty"); it is strained and then, mixed with raisins, sugar, cinnamon, and other fruits, it is boiled in milk. In Scotland, oatmeal is used instead of wheat. To some puddings of this type, kippered herring, salt codfish, and smoked haddock are added, and these may be served alone or garnished with vegetables and fruits. In the Middle East, nut-studded frumenty-type puddings are made using bulgur wheat. (See BURGHUL)

FRUTTI DI MARE Ordering these "fruits of the sea" from an Italian bill of fare would send the waiter to the kitchen for seafood, such as clams, squid, mussels, oysters. This platter of seafood can be served raw, steamed, or fried.

FU (Japanese) When this dehydrated wheat cake is soaked in water, it swells to nearly six times its original size. *Fu* is used in the preparation of *miso shiru* and *sukiyaki* dishes. (See MISO SHIRU, SUKIYAKI)

FUGU This rather silly-looking fish, without much silliness at all, manages not only to blow itself up to the size of a volley ball when threatened, but also carries enough poison in its ovaries and liver to kill the imprudent who are unskilled in preparing this fish for a Japanese *sashimi* (a raw fish dinner). Japanese chefs must be specially licensed after passing strict examinations in the technique of cleaning and preparing the *fugu.*

This fish has many names; the Hawaiians call it *makimaki,* but in English it is known as a blowfish, globefish, puffer, porcupine fish, or balloonfish. The poison present in the fish is tetrodotoxin, and although the poison is concentrated in the liver, the roe, and the ovaries, there are traces of it in the flesh of the fish as well. The poison numbs the lips and tongue of the diner, thereby adding to the excitement of dining out on *fugu.* In addition to a feeling of numbness in the extremities, the symptoms of severe *fugu* poisoning include severe chills, dizziness, itchiness, and violent seizures of vomiting. If untreated, paralysis followed by death can result. *Fugu* is served raw with the appropriate *ponzu* sauce or hot as a stew. (See MAKIMAKI, PONZU, SASHIMI)

FU GWA (Chinese) The "bitter melon," also called the "balsam pear." At first glance this dark green melon might be mistaken for a rather wrinkled cucumber. Its bitterness changes that.

FU JUK (Chinese) See BEAN CURD

FU JUNG/FOO YUNG/FU YONG However it is spelled, this is the Chinese term for the omelette that originated in the subtle southern cooking of Canton. Most restaurant menus list the dish as "egg foo yung," which seems as superfluous as describing an omelette as an egg omelette. *Foo yung* can be served plain or mixed with chopped meats, seafood, or poultry and can be flavored with a variety of vegetables, such as bean sprouts, scallions, onions, coriander, parsley, mushrooms, and water chestnuts.

This popular dish, as made in China, demands that the ingredients be cooked separately: first the minced meat, then the celery and scallions, and at the end the soy sauce and sugar. Then, into the same pan, now quite empty, the egg mixture is poured to cook in hot lard until it is set but still moist. The other ingredients are placed in the center and the cooked eggs are folded over. However, in most restaurants the ingredients are all mixed into the egg batter at the outset, and the egg is fried like a pancake on both sides until golden. *Foo yung* can be eaten plain or with a sauce composed of chicken broth, soy sauce, salt, sugar, and cornstarch.

The term _foo yung_ as used in North China means "hibiscus." There, it is made by using only beaten egg whites. When combined with other foods, the beaten whites cause them to puff up to to resemble the hibiscus flower. (See HIBISCUS, WATER CHESTNUTS) COMPATIBLE BEVERAGES: Tea, sherry, beer, depending upon ingredients.

FUKASHI MANJU (Japanese) To make these cakes, _azuki_ beans (a red bean) are soaked, cooked in water, then mashed with sugar over low heat until a thick paste is formed. A dough is made from flour, water, baking powder, fat, and salt. Small balls made from this dough are flattened and filled with the bean paste, and the dough is pulled up to envelop the paste—much like the Mexican _tamale_—and like the _tamale,_ they are steamed in a covered utensil. (See TAMALE) COMPATIBLE BEVERAGES: Tea.

FUKIEN CUISINE Fukien, in the south of China, is known for its outstanding seafood and mushroom dishes. Generally, the food is soupy and light, with the exception of their red fermented bean sauce. Fukien is also celebrated for its chicken and pork specialities, made with sweet-tasting red rice paste. The finest soy sauce comes from the Fukien region.

FUKUSA SUSHI (Japanese) A thin omelette is filled with vinegared rice, shrimp, crabmeat, and vegetables. It is then wrapped and tied together with a strip of _nori,_ a type of seaweed known as laver or red laver. (See NORI) COMPATIBLE BEVERAGES: Beer, ale, saké, rosé wine.

FUMET (French) A highly reduced extract of fish, meat, poultry, or vegetables, obtained by stewing these foods in wine, water, or stock until the liquid becomes a concentrated essence. A _fumet_ adds flavor to soups, sauces, and stews.

Fumet de Poisson, made from fish, is mixed with wine to flavor fish and fish sauces.

Fumet de Gibier, made from game, is used to flavor sauces and game dishes.

Fumet de Volaille, made from chicken, is used to add flavor to poultry dishes.

Fumet de Champignons, made from mushrooms, is used to flavor sauces, meat, fish, and poultry dishes.

Fumet de Truffes, made from truffles, is used to flavor rich sauces.

Fumet de Légumes, made from vegetables, is used to add flavor to meat, fish, and poultry and to sauces.

FUNGHI (Italian) Mushrooms.

Funghi Porcini al Tegame It is the _porcini,_ the mint flavor, which makes this mushroom dish special. Chopped anchovies are cooked in olive oil, to which sliced mushrooms, both the heads and the stems, are added together with crushed garlic, chopped ripe tomatoes, and, finally, fresh mint and seasoning. The mushrooms are served encircled with toasted bread and topped with more chopped mint. (See CHAMPIGNONS, MUSHROOMS)

FYLLD KROPPKAKOR (Swedish) A delicious filled dumpling made from mashed potatoes that are thoroughly mixed with heavy cream, eggs, salt, sugar, nutmeg, flour, and baking powder. All of the foregoing is whipped into a rich batter, rolled into a ball and stuffed with a mixture of finely chopped bacon and onions that have been precooked and drained of all fat. The batter is closed over the filling and cooked in boiling salted water until done. A sauce can be made by blending a bit of the filling with heavy cream. The dish is great with lingonberries.

GAI CHOY (Chinese) A mustard cabbage, more delicate than mustard greens, though having much the same flavor. The cabbage consists of light green stalks, each of which is topped with a large green leaf.

GALANTINE (French) A term for meat or fowl that has been boned, stuffed, and rolled. After having been cooked, it is chilled, sliced, and served in its own jelly. The terms *ballotine* and *roulade* or *rouladen* have much the same meaning. (See BALLOTINE, ROULADE, ROULADEN)

Galantine de Porc A boned suckling pig is stuffed with chopped liver, ham, and tongue. It is then rolled up, sewn together, and braised in a veal stock with vegetables and white wine. COMPATIBLE WINES: A white wine, e.g., Pouilly-Fumé, Gewürztraminer, Riesling, Montrachet, Anjou, Chenin Blanc, Orvieto, Frascati; or a good rosé wine.

GALLEGO, POTE (Spanish) A rustic soup made from pork and vegetables. It hails from Galicia, the northwest region of Spain that is so Celtic that redheads abound. This hearty soup is composed of lima beans, onions, garlic, and chunks of bacon stewed together for an hour or so. Cabbage, turnip greens, bay leaf and pepper plus several pieces of shoulder ham are added and cooked for another half-hour. Before serving, small boiled potatoes are added. (See POTÉE) COMPATIBLE WINES: A red wine, e.g., Rioja, Chianti, Barolo, Valpolicella, Ruby Cabernet, Zinfandel, Lambrusco.

GALUSHKI (Ukrainian) These plump dumplings are made from flour, butter, eggs, salt, and—the ingredient that makes them uniquely Ukrainian—sour cream. Having been poached in a beef or chicken stock, they are served either with fresh sweet butter or with additional sour cream. (See GALUSKA, SPÄTZLE)

GALUSKA (Hungarian) This Magyar dumpling is as much a part of the basic Hungarian cuisine as *gulyas, paprikas,* and *salami.* A dumpling dough is made from flour, salt, and eggs. After resting for an hour, the dough is placed on a wet cutting board, and with a spatula or knife it is cut off in regular strips into rapidly-boiling salted water. When the dumplings rise to the surface, they are removed, completely drained of water, sautéed in sweet butter, and served. (See GALUSHKI, SPÄTZLE)

GAMBAS (Spanish) Prawns.

Gambas with Sherry Shelled prawns are marinated overnight in a mixture of lemon juice, olive oil, bay leaf, onions, garlic, salt, pepper, and parsley. They are then sautéed in butter, flavored with sherry, and served. COMPATIBLE WINES: A white wine, e.g., Muscadet, Chablis, Soave, Verdicchio, Frascati, Pouilly-Fumé, Pinot Chardonnay, Debro.

GANMO (Japanese) Deep-fried *tofu* balls made by kneading together finely minced carrots and cloud-ear mushrooms, toasted sesame seeds, and grated yam with *tofu* that has been flavored with *shoyu* and squeezed dry. Shaped into balls, they are deep-fried in hot oil until crisp. (See CLOUD EARS, SHOYU, TOFU)

GÄNSEBRATEN MIT SAUERKRAUT (German) A popular method of preparing roast goose—of course, with sauerkraut. For the stuffing, chopped onions are sautéed in goose fat until tender; then, together with juniper berries, caraway seeds, and white wine, they are brought to a boil. The well-seasoned goose is then stuffed with the now aromatic sauerkraut. It is then trussed and roasted for several hours until done. (See SAUERKRAUT) COMPATIBLE WINES: A white wine, e.g., Niersteiner, Graacher Himmelreich, Steinberger, Tokay Badacsonyi, Forster Jesuitengarten, Muscat d'Alsace, Vouvray.

GARAM MASALA (Indian) The western world knows this mélange of spices as "curry": a mixture of ground cloves, cinnamon, cumin, coriander, mace, ginger, turmeric, fenugreek, cardamom, and black pepper. In India, *garam masala* is specially ground to order, much like a special coffee blend is in Vienna. It is used to flavor meat and vegetables dishes of India and Pakistan. (See CURRY, KARI)

GARBANZO (Spanish) Chickpea. In India this legume is called *gam*. Besides India, Mexico, and the Phillipines, *garbanzos* are grown widely in southern Europe and the Middle East. (See CHICKPEAS)

GARBURE, LA (French) This soup, as nutritious and as filling as a *pot-au-feu,* is composed of cut-up cabbage that is blanched and drained. It is then placed on top of a layer of bacon, pickled pork, ham, veal knuckles, and a bit of boiled beef, plus chopped onions, carrots, and a *bouquet garni.* A layer of bacon is placed on top with water to cover, and the whole is simmered for a few hours. When done, the pork, ham, and veal are served separately. The cabbage is placed neatly at the bottom of a soup tureen, then layers of grated Gruyère and Parmesan cheese, bread, and cabbage are added alternately until the tureen is full. Topped with more grated cheese, the tureen is placed under the broiler to brown and the dish is served piping hot. There are many variations of *la garbure,* one of which adds preserved goose, but basically the differences lie in the amounts of the ingredients used. (See BOUQUET GARNI, POT-AU-FEU) COMPATIBLE WINES: A red wine, e.g., Beaujolais, Margaux, Valpolicella, Zinfandel, Arbois Rouge, Ruby Cabernet.

GARIBALDI, SAUCE (Italian) Named in honor of the famous Italian patriot, soldier, and monarchist Giuseppe Garibaldi, who was responsible for the conquest of Sicily, this sauce is made from the basic brown sauce, generously flavored with chopped garlic, capers, curry, mustard, and anchovy paste. It is served with fish or with meat dishes. (See BROWN SAUCE)

GARLIC Although garlic has always been a principle ingredient of the bourgeois cooking of those people who lived along the sunny shores of the Mediterranean, garlic did not become a part of the French _haute cuisine_ until the early nineteenth century. _Allium sativum,_ the scientific name for this great-grandfather of the lily family, is kin to the onion, the chive, the shallot and the leek; and as is the case with most great food discoveries, the origin of garlic is the subject of controversy.

Carolus Linnaeus, also known as Karl von Linné, the noted eighteenth-century Swedish botanist, claimed that garlic was born in Sicily, while his admirer and one-time student said that he found evidence that the ancient Mongols brought garlic from Kirghiz to China, where for centuries it was known to cooks as the magic _suan._ Herodotus, the famous Greek historian, wrote that the Egyptians, who built the wondrous pyramids, went on strike one day because they were not given their daily ration of garlic. Even the Bible illustrates that the Children of Israel, led by Moses in their flight from Egypt, wept for "the leeks, the onions, and the garlic" (Numbers 11:5). The socially fastidious have always relegated garlic to the lower classes, basically because of its smell, and have, until recent years, completely excluded it from their kitchens.

Today, in the south of France, the noonday meal is often called _aïoli_ because of the garlic _Mayonnaise_ that is always present on the dining tables during the winter months. More and more, one finds garlic bread and garlic-flavored sauces spicing up a multitude of the _pasta,_ pizza, and casserole dishes featured on American, Canadian, and British menus. However, garlic is beneficial to man therapeutically as well. During the reign of Henry II of France, doctors carried cloves of raw garlic on their persons to ward off illness and contagion. Medicinally, garlic has more virtues than vices; once cooked, however, it loses much of its therapeutic value. Ancient Greeks, who wagered at cock-fights, primed their favorite cocks with fresh, raw garlic to bring them to fighting fettle. Through the ages, garlic has proved itself not only to be a protection against diseases of the blood and of the heart, but also, by its effect in neutralizing malignant bacteria, to be the strongest natural antibiotic known to man. Medical science says very little about garlic's power to prevent disease because so little actual research has been done to date. Doctors state that they have no evidence to support the claims of garlic's medicinal value, only because they devote their time, studies, and energies to cure with drugs and surgery what might well have been prevented through the judicious application of diet and nutrition. (See AÏOLI, MAYONNAISE)

GARUM This is the sauce that the ancient Romans used instead of salt. It was made from small fish, the entrails of larger fish, plus a quantity of oysters which they covered with salt and set out in the sun for periods of several days. At this stage, it was referred to as _liquamen._ As this mass would ferment and putrefy, a liquid called *garum* would be drawn off. *Garum* had an overpowering odor, and the Romans tried to mask the smell by mixing it with honey, vinegar, oil, wine, and spices and herbs of all kinds. When the Chinese used soy sauce, the Romans reached for their *garum*. A small jar of the substance was even found among the ruins of Pompeii. One story says that this jar is reserved for a Chevalier de Tastevin Banquet scheduled for the year 2000.

GASCOGNE, BEURRE DE (French) See COMPOUND BUTTER

GASTRIQUE (French) A culinary term for "caramelized sugar" that has been dissolved in vinegar. (See BIGARADE)

GÂTEAU (French) Literally, "cake." In Great Britain the word is used when referring to a rather rich butter-sponge cake that is covered with a creamy icing, nuts, fruits, and preserves.

GAUFRES (French) These waffles, first created by La Varenne, the famous chef of Louis XIV, are made from a batter of flour, butter, sugar, eggs, baking soda or yeast, and vanilla flavoring. They are cooked until crisp between heated plates of heavy irons that are decorated with embossed patterns. The light, sweet waffles are sometimes served as *gaufres fourrées,* filled with cream or with custard. (See VARENNE)

GAUFRETTES, POMMES (French) With a special cutter, potatoes are cut wafer-thin into a decorative shape, and they are then deep-fried to a golden brown.

GAZPACHO (Spanish) Initially a gypsy soup from Andalusia, this tomato soup is made with much raw garlic plus peppers, a purée of tomatoes, cucumbers, mashed cooked egg yolks, onions, and olive oil. One of the most refreshing of all cold soups, the true *gazpacho* is served with cubed tomatoes, peppers, and cucumbers in separate bowls as a garnish.

GEBRATEN (German) See BRATEN

GEFILTE (GEFUELTE) FISH (Jewish) As the dish is popularly known today, this is a dumpling made with finely ground whitefish or pike, or both, seasoned with chopped onions and spices. The dumpling is carefully poached then served either hot or cold in the jelly obtained from the cooked fish. *Gefilte* ("stuffed") *fish* originally consisted of a fish forcemeat encased in a fish skin. COMPATIBLE WINES: A white wine, e.g., Orvieto, Frascati, Riesling, Sauterne, Neuchâtel, Anjou, Sauvignon Blanc, White Chianti.

GELATO (Italian) Ice cream. Tuscany is credited with having developed the first ice cream in Europe. Catherine de Médicis brought it to the Court of France together with the *tournedos, quenelles, filets mignons,* and the best chefs of Italy, plus the most beautiful table enamelled by Bernard Palessy, fine crystal glassware from Venice, and silver engraved by Benvenuto Cellini. After the darkness of the Middle Ages, it was the Florentine, Catherine, who brought the first light of the Italian Renaissance to France—and a part of it was ice cream.

GÉNEVOISE, SAUCE À LA (French) To prepare this classic sauce, a _mirepoix_ is steamed with the tail-ends, fins, skin, and bones of fish (usually salmon), to which a _sauce Espagnole_ and a red wine are added and reduced through cooking. The whole is strained, defatted, and then thinned with fish stock _(fumet)_. Fresh butter, anchovy paste, and finely diced mushrooms are added before serving. (See ESPAGNOLE, MIREPOIX)

Sea Trout à la Génevoise The trout, also called the sea salmon, is cut into steak slices, which are steamed in a well-seasoned fish stock. It is served with boiled potatoes, garnished with parsley, with the _sauce Génevoise_ served separately. COMPATIBLE WINES: A white wine, e.g., Meursault, Pouilly-Fumé, Dézaley, Soave, Verdicchio, Chenin Blanc, Pinot Chardonnay.

GÉNOISE (French) A style of cooking prevalent in Genoa and adapted by the French.

Génoise Cake This butter-rich sponge cake, the base for many variations done with fruits and creams, is prepared with equal parts of sugar, butter, eggs, and flour. The secret of this famous French cake, originated by Italian pastry chefs, is the careful whisking or beating of the sugar and egg mixture over heat until it has attained the correct "ribbon" texture. At this moment, the flour and vanilla flavoring are gently folded into the egg mixture. The preparation is allowed to cool and the fatty residue from clarified butter is added a bit at a time. The batter is poured into tins and baked. Variations include the _Génoise à l'abricot, Génoise au Moka,_ and the _Génoise à la Normande,_ which is made with thick apple jam and flavored with Calvados.

GÉNOISE, SAUCE (French) A sauce prepared by adding chopped mush-rooms, parsley, truffles, and shallots to a reduced fish stock that has been enriched with a _sauce Espagnole_. A bit more red wine, another reduction, and the addition of an anchovy essence and sweet butter finishes this classic sauce. It is served hot with fish dishes. (See ESPAGNOLE, GÉNÉVOISE)

Génoise, Sauce (cold) This alternate version is made with a purée of pistachio and almond nuts stirred into a cold _sauce Béchamel_. To this, egg yolks, salt, pepper, lemon juice, and olive oil—poured drop by drop as when making a _Mayonnaise_—are added. Just before serving, the sauce is flavored with a blend of chervil, parsley, and tarragon. The sauce is served with cold fish dishes. (See BÉCHAMEL, MAYONNAISE)

GEORGETTE (French) A culinary term derived from the name of a light fabric whose gossamer quality best describes the texture of various food concoctions.

Potage Georgette A purée of carrots and tomatoes is blended with tapioca which has been cooked in a white consommé. Sweet butter is added before serving.

Crème Georgette This rich soup consists of a *sauce velouté* that has been flavored with artichoke hearts and sago (palm flour), to which heavy cream has been added. (See VELOUTÉ)

GERIDES (Greek) Shrimp.

Baked Gerides Extra-large shrimp are cleaned then baked in olive oil that is seasoned with much pepper, bay leaves, and chopped fresh tomatoes. COMPATIBLE WINES: A white wine, e.g., Retsina, Soave, Pinot Chardonnay, Sancerre, Dézaley, Aigle, Gewürztraminer, Sylvaner.

GERMAN CUISINE Unlike the other cuisines of Europe, German cuisine was little influenced by the French. The German cuisine consists mainly of heavy and hearty plate-filling dishes. Meals usually start with a thick rib-sticking soup or a herring appetizer, followed by beef dishes that are stewed or potted *(Sauerbraten),* favorite roasts of pork and veal, and such succulent game dishes as wild boar and venison. German cookery boasts of a great variety of fine sausages famous the world over and a penchant for a sweet-sour flavoring for food; their fondness for sugar in salads is well known. Most main course dishes are accompanied with steaming platters of sauerkraut, potatoes, dumplings, or noodles. (See SAUERBRATEN, SAUSAGE)

GERSTENSUPPE (German/Swiss) A soup made from barley, *Gerste,* that is cooked in a rich beef broth together with root vegetables and milk.

GESCHNETZELTES KALBFLEISCH (Swiss) To prepare this speciality, finely sliced veal is browned in butter then set aside. A sauce of white wine, bouillon or veal broth, chopped shallots, and a touch of heavy cream is then prepared. The minced veal is warmed and served in this delectable sauce, complemented with either *Rösti potatoes* or *Spätzli.* (See RÖSTI, SPÄTZLE) COMPATIBLE WINES: A white wine, e.g., Dézaley, Aigle, Pouilly-Fumé, Johannisberg, Hermitage Blanc, Meursault, Orvieto, Anjou, Riquewihr, Schloss Vollrads, Graacher Himmelreich.

GHEE In India, the *ghee* used in cooking is actually made from various vegetable oils. The *usli ghee,* however, is the real clarified butter, made from buffalo or yak butter that is cooked, cooled, and strained. It is preferred to ordinary cow's butter, first because cow's butter is both hard to come by and costly, and second, because the *usli ghee,* when used in frying, does not sputter or burn.

Even as the monks and brothers in the monasteries of Europe kept the gastronomic art alive, so did the followers of Buddha bring their methods of cooking, their great spices and even _ghee_ from the yak to the peoples of Asia. _Ghee_ has many advantages over plain butter or oil: the principal one is taste; another is that it will not burn; and yet another, that it will keep almost indefinitely, even when left unrefrigerated. (See CLARIFIED BUTTER)

GHIVETCH (Slavic) A huge vegetable stew composed of a variety of vegetables prepared and cut to a size. The stew includes peas, lima beans, green beans, green peppers, white turnips, eggplant, squash, potatoes, carrots, celery, leeks, okra, garlic, tomatoes, cabbage, cauliflower, parsley, and onions, plus salt, thyme, pepper, and dill seed. The foregoing ingredients are first sautéed in olive oil, then bouillon is added to cover, the lid put on the pot, and all baked until tender. Before serving this stew, seedless white grapes are added. (See GIOUVETSI) COMPATIBLE WINES: A red wine, e.g., Médoc, Beaujolais, Fleurie, Côte Rôtie, Chianti.

GIGOT (French) Leg of lamb or of sheep.

Gigot à la Provençale à la Potpourri This leg of mutton stuffed with pickled pork is one of 400 recognized recipes of Provence. It is made by removing the bone and stuffing the cavity with a mixture of pickled pork, breadcrumbs moistened with milk, minced herbs, eggs, salt pork, and garlic. The meat is then browned in pork fat with chopped onions, carrots, and turnips. White wine and water are added and the mutton is simmered until done. The dish is usually served with fried eggplant, baked tomatoes, and boiled onions. COMPATIBLE WINES: A red wine, e.g., Côte Rôtie, Hermitage, Pontet-Canet, Cabernet Sauvignon, Mercurey, Latour, Mouton Rothschild, Kirwan, Pichon-Longueville, Calon-Ségur.

GINGER ROOT This hot, spicy vegetable is one of the mainstays of Oriental cooking, especially that of the Chinese and the Japanese. If ginger is meant to be used as a main part of the dish, young ginger, that which is available during the spring of the year, must be used. The older ginger is quite strong and is used sparingly to spice food. If the roots have thin, smooth, green skins, they are young and tender. Avoid those that have become brown and wrinkled.

The aesthetic Chinese cook uses ginger root with discretion, for it can easily overpower the food that it is meant to enhance, a crime in Chinese gastronomic circles. The experienced chef knows from experience that peeling the green or bulb ginger must be done with caution because it can burn the hands of the imprudent. Ground ginger will not impart the piquancy or the delicacy of the fresh root. As to keeping ginger, placed in a plastic bag and refrigerated, ginger will keep for weeks. It can also be stored peeled and covered with sherry wine. In India, ginger is stored in cool, dry sand, where it will keep unpeeled for several months. By boiling sliced ginger with several tablespoons of brown sugar in water, it can be taken in a hot drink as a remedy for an upset stomach.

GIOUVETSI (Greek) A staple meat dish consisting of lamb baked with tomatoes, onions, and garlic to which *pasta* is later added. COMPATIBLE WINES: A red wine, e.g., Beaujolais, Barbera, Zinfandel, Egri Bikaver, Chianti, Nebbiolo, Valpolicella, Pinot Noir.

GIPFEL (Austrian) See CROISSANT

GIROLLES See CHAMPIGNONS

GLACE (French) Ice cream.
   Glace au Four See ALASKA

GLACÉ (French) "Glazed" when referring to fruits covered with a syrup that hardens when cold. The term can also mean "iced," as in describing a frosted cake. Still another definition refers to a cut of meat that has been glazed in a hot oven by constantly basting the meat with its own thickening juices.
   Glace de Viande A meat glaze made by reducing a white stock *(fond blanc)* or a brown stock *(fond brun)* by slow, careful simmering until thick. (See FONDS, GLAZING)

GLAZING This term has two meanings: (1) subjecting a roast of meat to high heat and basting it until a glistening, golden brown crust is formed, and (2) coating pastries and cakes with an icing. The meat glaze is purely a stock which has been reduced to a glutinous consistency. With the proper infusion of cream or butter, a glaze can be used as a sauce.

GLUTTONY A gluttonous addiction to food, exotic and otherwise, together with other vices, undermined the physical, moral, and political structure of ancient Rome. And in more recent years gluttony was instrumental in bringing about the revolt of the French populace against the abuses of the Crown. Indirectly, it performed a service: it liberated chefs from the royal kitchens and gave birth to the *Haute Cuisine de France*. (See HAUTE CUISINE)

GNOCCHI (Italian) Potato dumplings made from mashed potatoes, egg yolks, flour, and salt—all kneaded together then rolled out and cut to size. These bits are then dropped into boiling salted water. Before serving, they are sprinkled with grated Parmesan cheese and melted sweet butter or tossed with a good *pesto*. *Gnocchi* are also made from semolina (durum wheat) or from white cornmeal. *Gnocchi* dishes are served as an appetizer or to complement the main course of a dinner. (See PESTO)
   Gnocchi alla Romana This particular Italian dumpling is said to have originated in Rome. The *gnocchi* are made from coarsely ground durum wheat, which the Italians call *semolina*. White cornmeal or farina can be substituted. To prepare the *gnocchi,* milk is brought to the boil and, after adding a dollop of butter and a pinch of salt, the semolina is slowly poured into the milk, which is stirred constantly until all has been absorbed. The batter is poured out onto

a flat baking sheet, left to cool, and then cut into small rounds and placed in a buttered ovenproof dish. Then, covered with melted butter and grated Parmesan cheese, the rounds are baked until crisp and brown. COMPATIBLE WINES: A red wine, e.g., Chianti, Beaujolais, Fleurie, Médoc, Côtes du Rhône, Châteauneuf-du-Pape, Egri Bikaver, Dôle, Mercurey, Nebbiolo, Barolo, Valpolicella, Zinfandel.

Gnocchi Verdi "Green dumplings." The *gnocchi* dough is made with finely chopped, cooked, and drained spinach, ricotta cheese, eggs, mashed potatoes, flour, Parmesan cheese, salt, nutmeg, and pepper. The dough is chilled in the refrigerator then formed into small balls and dropped into boiling salted water. Before serving, the *gnocchi* are drained, topped with melted butter, and put under the grill to brown. COMPATIBLE WINES: A red wine, e.g., Pinot Noir, Chianti, Barolo, Nebbiolo, Barbaresco, Lambrusco, Châteauneuf-du-Pape, Zinfandel, Valpolicella, Moulin-à-Vent.

GOBO This vegetable, closely resembling rhubarb leaves, is much used by the Japanese, but then only the very young roots. To Western cultures, this is known as burdock root, and it grows nearly everywhere with the insistence of a pesky weed. Though considered to be distinctively Japanese, the young shoots of this plant are also cooked as a vegetable in Scotland. At one time, a drink named "burdock ale" was made from the fermentation of the leaves and the roots of this plant.

GOHAN (Japanese) Rice that has been boiled in water.

Kuri Gohan Rice cooked together with parboiled chestnuts in water flavored with saké or dry sherry and salt.

Maze Gohan A delightful mixture of rice cooked with mushrooms, carrots, ginger, ginko nuts, celery, soy sauce, saké, and salt. Peas and cleaned shrimp are added and cooked together with the rice so that all ingredients are done at the same time. COMPATIBLE BEVERAGES: Saké, beer.

GOLDSTEIN, SCHNITZEL À LA (Austrian) See SCHNITZEL

GOMA JOYU (Japanese) String beans in a soy and sesame seed dressing. A *dashi* is combined with sugar, salt, Ac'cent (monosodium glutamate), saké, and soy sauce. Precooked string beans are then added. Saké is flamed and added to a paste made from ground and toasted sesame seeds together with sugar and soy sauce. The beans are then tossed in this sauce and served. (See SHABU SHABU)

GOOSEBERRY FOOL There is really nothing foolish about this excellent English pudding. The name comes from the French *fouler,* meaning "to press, trample, crush," and in this case one crushes the gooseberries to a pulp. Whole gooseberries are simmered in butter and sugar until the berries are tender. Then they are crushed and mixed with an equal amount of whipped heavy cream. The pudding is chilled overnight and served in individual bowls with ladyfingers or almond biscuits.

GORDA (Mexican) Literally "fat girl," this is a *tortilla* filled with refried beans and then deep-fried. The *gorda* is then drained, the crust pierced and filled with sour cream, and served. (See MESA, TORTILLA) COMPATIBLE WINES: Rioja, Beaujolais, Fleurie, Mercurey, Zinfandel, Ruby Cabernet, Nebbiolo, Valpolicella, Egri Bikaver.

GORINFLOR, CROQUETTE See CROQUETTES

GOTEBERG (Swedish) A sausage. (See CERVELAT)

GOUJON, EN (French) *Goujon* is the name of a very tiny freshwater fish found in France, but for this dish fillets of fish such as sole are sliced in long strips and dipped first in milk, then in flour, and deep-fried. Crisp and tasty, they are served garnished with fresh lemons as an hors d'oeuvre or as a luncheon with a green salad. A cold *sauce ravigote* or *rémoulade* go well with this dish. (See HORS D'OEUVRE, RAVIGOTE, RÉMOULADE) COMPATIBLE WINES: A white wine, e.g., Chablis, Muscadet, Soave, Chenin Blanc, Aigle.

GOURMAND This French word was once a term of esteem, considered to be a step above *gourmet,* and much used by Brillat-Savarin, the noted nineteenth-century gastronomist, politician, and author. He writes: " . . . not everyone can be a *gourmand.* You will find him among the financiers, the men of letters, the hierarchy of the clergy." All of which tends to make one believe that the *gourmand* of nineteenth-century France was no different than his counterpart today: a glutton, the true definition of the word.

GOURMET For all the richness of the English language, how strange to find that it lacks a word for *gemütlich,* from the German tongue, as well as a word comparable to *gourmet* from the French. In fact, the word *gourmet* has been adopted, as so many foreign words have, by desperate English lexicographers who have lost their patience, ingenuity, and imagination. A *gourmet* is a person of impeccable taste who is not only concerned with the quality of the food and wine he serves but also with the way the foods he chooses harmonize with each other, with the table setting, with the décor. However, definitions of words erode with common usage. Today the word is often used in a derogatory way.

GRANA (Italian) The hulled whole-kernel wheat often used in the baking of pastry. (See PASTIERA NAPOLETANA)

GRAND-MÈRE, RIS DE VEAU (French) Sweetbreads done simply, as grandma used to do them. Trimmed and well soaked in water, sweetbreads and chopped mushrooms are added to already-cooking cubed carrots, celery, and onions. With the addition of water, the lot is cooked until tender. Then, just before serving, egg yolks and cream are whisked together and poured over the sweetbreads and vegetables. Served with tiny fresh peas and small potatoes, the sweetbreads make a delightful dish. (See RIS DE VEAU, SWEETBREADS) COMPATIBLE WINES: A white wine, e.g., Orvieto, Gewürztraminer, Riquewihr, Anjou, Montrachet, Pinot Chardonnay, Hermitage Blanc.

GRAND SALETTE (French) See SALMIS

GRAND VENEUR, SADDLE OF VENISON (French) The phrase used to describe this saddle of venison dish means "great hunter," and the dish is aptly named. The saddle is soaked for several days in a spicy marinade of red wine, garlic, vinegar, cloves, thyme, bay leaves, and onions. The venison is then dried, buttered, seasoned, and roasted so that it remains pink on the inside. The marinade is cooked separately, and as it cooks, red currant jelly and Worcestershire sauce are added. Some versions add heavy cream at the end. The sauce is served apart. Traditionally, a purée of chestnuts is served with this dish. COMPATI BLE WINES: A red wine, e.g., La Tâche, Chambertin, Musigny, Clos de Vougeot, Hermitage, Richebourg; or a white wine, e.g., Rüdesheim, Tokay Szamorodni, Schloss Johannisberg.

GRANITA (Italian) Sherbet. (See GRANITÉ)

GRANITÉ, CHAMPAGNE (French) The Gallic version of the Italian *granita,* a type of sherbet. During those almost orgiastic feasts of the eighteenth century, when sometimes as many as sixty-four different dishes were served, something had to be offered at midpoint to relieve the strain on the stomach, *et voila!,* the *granité* was invented. The juice of lemons and oranges is added to a cold sugar syrup. Placed in the container of an ice cream freezer, this mixture is surrounded with crushed ice. The freezer should not be turned on or rotated because the *granité* should develop a granular texture. When frozen, Champagne is poured into a glass and then filled to the top with iced *granité.* (See SORBET)

GRASSE, POULARDE (French) This roast chicken dish goes back to the time of the famous Sun-King, Louis XIV of France, and his chef, La Varenne. First, a *pâté* is made from ground chicken livers and hard-boiled eggs. Sautéed chopped onions, salt, pepper, and enough butter to form a creamy texture are added. This paste is spread over a tender roasting chicken that has been stuffed with sautéed sliced mushrooms and with whole onions studded with cloves. The delicious bird is served with a complementary sauce of chopped mushrooms, the liver *pâté,* and broth added to the pan juices. (See LOUIS XIV, PATÉ, VARENNE) COMPATIBLE WINES: A red wine, e.g., Médoc, Graves, Beaujolais, Santenay, Mâcon, Chinon, Mercurey, Valpolicella, Bardolino, Zinfandel, Petit Sirah.

GRATIN (French) The crust formed on top of foods by baking or broiling.
    au gratin A French culinary term meaning "cooked brown," refer-

ring to those dishes that are dusted with grated cheese and/or breadcrumbs and crusted over under the grill.

GRATINÉES, POMMES DE TERRE (French) This potato dish can consist of buttered mashed potatoes that have been sprinkled with grated cheese and browned in the grill, or it can consist of whole baked potatoes that have been halved and the pulp removed from the shells and mashed with butter and seasoning. This potato pulp is returned to the potato shells, sprinkled with grated cheese, and browned under the grill.

GRATINERAD SLÄTVARSFILET (Swedish) A rather unusual, rich, tasty fillet of sole preparation. After the fillet has been lightly poached in white wine, it is removed to a warm place and the wine is reduced. In another pan, shelled shrimp and cooked lobster and crab meat are simmered in a dry vermouth until nearly all liquid has evaporated. The cooked shellfish are placed around the fillets of sole in a baking dish. A *beurre manié* is added to the fish stock and stirred to blend. Egg yolks are beaten into this mixture, then seasonings are added and the sauce is poured over the fish. As the crowning touch, a blanket of salted whipped cream is spread over the fish and browned under the broiler. (See BEURRE MANIÉ) COMPATIBLE WINES: A white wine, e.g., Quincy, Muscadet, Mersault, Iphofen, Pinot Chardonnay, Montrachet, Wehlener Sonnenuhr, Rüdesheim, Nierstein.

GRAVLAX (Swedish) A very fresh salmon is boned and cut in half lengthwise, then the flesh side of the fish is rubbed with salt, sugar, and pepper. Skin side down, the salmon is placed in a bowl and covered with fresh dill. The other half of the fish is placed over this, skin side up. Covered, the fish is left to marinate in the refrigerator for a few days. To serve, the skin is removed and the fish cut into thin slices and garnished with fresh chopped dill and *gravlaxas*. This dish has a cherished place in the Swedish *smörgåsbord*. (See SMÖR-GÅSBORD) COMPATIBLE BEVERAGES: Akvavit, beer, ale.

GRAVLAXAS, SAUCE (Swedish) A sauce prepared by mixing mustard, sugar, and wine vinegar into a paste. Slowly, olive oil is added while beating continuously, until the sauce is as thick as a *sauce Mayonnaise*. It is seasoned with salt, pepper, and fresh dill and served with the *gravlax*. (See GRAVLAX, MAYONNAISE)

GRAVY A gravy should never be confused with a sauce. Whereas a sauce can be made from a gravy, which is then enhanced with other ingredients, such as cream, liqueur, vinegar, vegetables, etc., a gravy is the result only of a cooking meat. By cooking, the meat exudes an essence, a juice composed of the blood and the fat from the meat, and this forms a gravy.

GRECQUE, À LA (French) In the Greek style. Foods cooked in a mixture of olive oil, wine, lemon juice, and a variety of herbs are said to be prepared *à la Grecque*. Many vegetable dishes are prepared in this fashion, such as eggplant, artichokes, and mushrooms.

GREEK CUISINE When a good Greek chef is told that Greek cooking is nothing more than an extension of the great Turkish cuisine, he will take off his white hat and start sharpening his blades. Of course, the cuisines have their similarities, which is natural, for Greece was dominated by Turkey for nearly 400 years, and the Ottoman influence was strongly felt. Even today that influence is gastronomically quite visible. The one great difference that exists between Greek and Turkish cooking is based on a religious belief: the Turks, being of the Islamic faith, use no wine or liquor in the preparation of their food. The Greeks, on the other hand, love wine and liquor and use it freely in their kitchens. Greeks have always favored lamb dishes and vine leaves stuffed with meat and rice. Their desserts are often very sweet. Honey and lemon-soaked pastries are popular, and the Greeks have a fondness for pistachio nuts, which they use as a cake decoration. The use of lemon juice is extensive—with fish, in soups, and with desserts.

GRENADINE A world-famous French syrup, red and sweet, made from the pomegranate, a thick-skinned reddish fruit berry that is the size of an orange and has many seeds in a pulp that is crimson in color and agreeably acidic to the taste. It is also used to make a liqueur and to flavor icings and ice cream.

GRENADINS (French) Fillets of veal or the white meat of turkey cut in rectangular or triangular shapes and then larded and braised.

GRENOUILLES, CUISSES DE (French) Frogs' legs. Although there are numerous methods of enhancing the taste of this delicacy—by adding sauces, herbs, vegetables, and condiments—the legs are almost always first sautéed in butter. One exception is the American "frogs' legs Dinah," which are boiled in white wine then flavored with mushrooms and curry.

Grenouilles Poulette, Cuisses de Frogs' legs in a cream sauce. As the tender meat from the frogs' legs is practically indistinguishable from that of very young, fried chicken, in the United States the frog has been dubbed "water chicken," and even "swamp pigeon." Nevertheless, when expertly cooked, frogs' legs can be quite a treat. This example is prepared by first cooking sliced mushrooms in butter then adding chopped shallots and the legs and sautéing them well on all sides. After dusting the legs with flour and seasoning with salt, pepper, and nutmeg, a dry white wine and a fish stock are added. After cooking for a few minutes, the legs are removed and a mixture of egg yolks and heavy cream is poured into the skillet and simmered until the sauce has thickened. The frogs' legs are replaced, warmed through in the cream sauce, and served with a coating of the sauce and a sprinkling of chopped parsley. (See FROG, POULETTE) COMPATIBLE WINES: A white wine, e.g., Château-Grillet, Château Chalon,

Sylvaner, Riquewihr, Beaune Blanc, Aigle, Sauvignon Blanc, Orvieto, Johannisberg.

GRIBENES/GRIEVEN (Jewish) This popular garnish is made by frying pieces of poultry (usually chicken) skin until brown and crisp. The crisp cracklings are used in the preparation of many dishes. (See CRACKLING, SCHMALTZ)

GRIBICHE, SAUCE (French) A *vinaigrette* made thick by the addition of chopped capers and gherkins, mixed with chopped herbs and pounded hard-boiled eggs. The sauce is served with cold fish and cold meat dishes. (See VINAIGRETTE)

Calf's Head Gribiche A poached calf's head is sliced and served with hard-boiled eggs, slices of tongue, and the *sauce gribiche*. COMPATIBLE BEVERAGES: Beer.

GRIMALDI, FILET DE SOLE (French) A sole dish named in honor of Giovanni Francesco Grimaldi, the famous Italian painter and architect of seventeenth-century Italy. Fillets of sole are rolled, then poached in white wine sauce and served on a bed of spaghetti, topped with *sauce Nantua* and finely sliced truffles. (See NANTUA, WHITE WINE SAUCE) COMPATIBLE WINES: A white wine, e.g., Chablis, Muscadet, Montrachet, Meursault, Bernkasteler Doktor, Pinot Chardonnay, Piesporter Goldtröpfchen, Sancerre.

GRISONS, VIAND DE (Swiss) The Swiss-French name for a very special dried beef that is processed by being alternately marinated and then dried in the rarefied atmosphere of the Alps in the Canton of Grisons, in eastern Switzerland. Called *Bündnerfleisch* by Swiss-Germans, the beef must be cured at 1,500 meters or higher in small wooden huts that have slatted sides, which permit the air to circulate freely. The lean, dried Burgundy-red beef is served sliced very thin, in twirls, and garnished with gherkins, olives, and parsley, and always with a peppermill at hand. (See BÜNDNERFLEISCH) COMPATIBLE WINES: A red wine, e.g., Veltliner, Beaujolais, Valpolicella, Moulin-à-Vent, Egri Bikaver, Zinfandel, Côte Rôtie.

GRISSINI (Italian) The term for those hard-baked, crunchy breadsticks found right next to the grated Parmesan cheese on the tables of most Italian restaurants. First created in the year 1679 by Antonio Brunero, a native of Turin, Italy, the breadsticks are baked from a simple dough composed of wheat flour, vegetable oil, and yeast. Sesame seeds, cheese, garlic, and other flavorings are sometimes added.

GROSEILLES, SAUCE (French) A dessert sauce made by flavoring red currant preserves with Kirschwasser and binding it with arrowroot. (See BAR-LE-DUC)

GUACAMOLE (Mexican) This avocado preparation may be served as a sauce or as a salad. For both, avocados are peeled, mashed, and mixed with peeled and chopped tomatoes, chopped onions, and *serrano* chilies plus coriander, salt, pepper, and sugar. *Guacamole* makes an excellent dip at cocktail time. (See CHILI)

GUAYABATE (Mexican) A fruit paste *(ate)* made from the fruit of the guava tree, which is grown in most tropical countries. The greenish-yellow fruit, round or oblong in shape, can be eaten fresh, stewed, or puréed, or it can be made into jam or jelly.

To prepare the *guayabate,* the guavas are seeded, cooked until soft, and then puréed. The seeds are cooked in cool water and this is then mixed with the purée and cooked over low heat. After removal from the heat, the purée is whipped into a heavy paste, poured into a loaf pan, and set to cool. (See ATES)

GÜERO, SALSA DE CHILE (Mexican) This popular sauce takes its name from the *güero,* a relatively mild, pale green chili. The sauce is made by first blanching the *güero,* then removing the stem and the seeds, and, finally, placing it in a blender with chopped onions, garlic, parsley, tomatoes, and a *serrano* chili. Salt, pepper, and sugar are added to season. After blending, the mixture is cooked in hot oil for a few minutes to fuse the ingredients. Delicious served hot with scrambled eggs or served cold to perk up the taste of cold fish or chicken. (See CHILI)

GUGELHUPF An alternate spelling for *Kugelhopf.* (See KUGELHOPF)

GULAB JAMUN (East Indian) This snack, delectable served either with an aromatic black tea or with cocktails, is prepared by fashioning balls of dough from a mixture of flour, baking powder, and water and frying them in butter until golden brown. Several hours before serving, the *gulab jamun* are soaked in a sugar syrup made from a tart and juicy, purple plum-like fruit.

GULE AERTER (Danish) A thick and hearty yellow split-pea soup prepared by cooking a variety of vegetables together with salt pork and pig's feet. The meat from the pig's feet is served on the side.

GUL RECELI (Turkish) An exotic jam made by cooking rose petals and sugar until thick. Lemon juice is added and the sauce is left to cool. Once cool, it is stored in jars under refrigeration. *Gul receli* is spooned over ice cream, muffins, or pastry and is absolutely delicious on toasted cinnamon bread.

GULYAS/GOULASH (Hungarian) A stew made with plenty of paprika.

Beef Gulyas For over 150 years the Turks occupied both Hungary and Austria, and the Turks made a lasting impression on both cuisines. In fact, it was the Turks who brought paprika and sour cream to the Hungarian kitchens. Beef *gulyas* is prepared by adding garlic and paprika to a regular beef stew and, just before serving, stirring in scalded sour cream. COMPATIBLE WINES: A white wine, e.g., Szamorodni, Riquewihr, Gewürztraminer, Muscat d'Alsace, Sauterne, Graves, Riesling, Rüdesheim, Badacsonyi.

Gulyas Soup This stewlike peasant soup from Hungary will put meat on the bones and warm them at the same time. Chopped onions are sautéed until tender, then cubed beef or veal is added and well browned. After seasoning with paprika, salt, and caraway seeds, a beef bouillon is added to the pot and, together with garlic, green peppers, and tomatoes, all is cooked covered for about an hour. Cooked potatoes, cut into large cubes, are added before serving. An optional addition, to make the dish authentic, would be the addition of a half-dumpling, half-noodle called *csipetke*. (See CSIPETKE)

GUMBO/GOMBO (Créole) "He who once has eaten gumbo may look down disdainfully even upon the most genuine turtle soup." This statement, supposedly uttered by a Miss Frederika Bremer of Sweden while dining on gumbo in New Orleans in the year 1850, can be challenged. A real turtle soup is infinitely superior to any of its imitations. But the Créole gumbo can reap accolades on its own merits. The Créoles of New Orleans learned how to make their gumbo from the early Negro slaves who brought it with them from Africa, where it was called *grubombo*. Today, the term refers to a dish thickened with okra. The principal ingredient—chicken, fish, meat, etc.—will always identify the type of gumbo it is. Filé powder can also be added as a thickener. (See FILÉ POWDER, OKRA)

Gumbo, Shrimp This shrimp preparation was first made in Créole country—Louisiana, Mississippi, etc.—where gumbo is widely served. A *roux* is made from flour and bacon fat, to which a cooked mixture of tomatoes, tomato juice, seasonings, and okra is added, plus garlic and onions. The cooked shrimp are added and all is simmered together until done. With the sprinkling of filé powder, the shrimp gumbo is ladled out on heaping mounds of boiled rice in deep soup plates. (See FILÉ POWDER, OKRA) COMPATIBLE WINES: A white wine, e.g., Aigle, Orvieto, Anjou, Riesling, Gewürztraminer, Frascati, Chenin Blanc.

GTOGOWY, SOS (Polish) This "hawthorneberry sauce" is made by creaming butter and flour then adding hot bouillon, hawthorne-butter, and wine. Sugar is added to taste and the mixture is brought to the boil. The sauce goes well with game dishes. When served with veal dishes, sweet cream is added to the *roux* instead of bouillon and wine. (See HAWTHORNE-BUTTER, ROUX)

GWA (Chinese) Melon. Although the Chinese enjoy both the sweet melon and the savory type, only the latter is used in their cooking. In fact, many members of the gourd family are considered to be melons by the Chinese. (See CHAH GWA, DUNG GWA, FU GWA, MO GWA, PU LU GWA)

$\mathcal{H}$

HACKBRATEN (German) A large hamburger steak or a meat loaf. COMPATIBLE WINES: A red wine, e.g., Chianti, Beaujolais, Fleurie, Zinfandel, Ruby Cabernet, Barolo, Châteauneuf-du-Pape, Médoc, Valpolicella, Nebbiolo. (See BRATEN)

HAGGIS (Scottish) A traditional dish in which a sheep's stomach is stuffed with chopped organ meats—such as the heart, the lungs, and the liver of the sheep—as well as a quantity of fat, oatmeal, chopped parsley, and onion. All is highly seasoned with black and cayenne pepper, nutmeg, and salt. This stuffed paunch is tied securely, pricked to allow the gas to escape, and boiled in salted water for several hours. It is brought to the table surrounded with mashed potatoes and turnips. COMPATIBLE BEVERAGES: No real Scot would drink anything other than an aged Scotch whisky with a *haggis*.

HALVA/HALVAH (Turkish/Greek) A popular confection made by adding semolina flour to a syrup of sugar, milk, and water. Chopped almonds or pignoli nuts are sautéed in butter and added to the syrup mixture, and the whole is baked in the oven. As a dessert, *halva* is served flavored with cinnamon or topped with whipped cream.

HAMAGURI (Japanese) Clams.

Hamaguri Sakani Clams are removed from their shells and dropped into a boiling mixture of saké, water, and Ac'cent. After a few minutes, the clams are removed from the liquid and returned to their immaculately cleaned and scalded shells. They are served with fresh lemons. (See MONOSODIUM GLUTAMATE) COMPATIBLE WINES: A white wine, e.g., saké, Verdicchio, Chablis, Soave, Winkel, Rüdesheim.

HAMANTASCHEN (Jewish) Three-cornered pastries symbolizing the purse or the three-cornered hat worn by Haman, the wicked vizier of Persia who desired to exterminate the Jewish people. Queen Esther and her kinsman Mordecai thwarted the vizier's plan. The Jewish feast of Purim, which commemorates the downfall of Haman, is celebrated by eating these three-cornered pastries, which may be filled with poppy seeds, with raisins and nuts, with cheese, or with a rich prune-butter.

HAM CHOY (Chinese) Also referred to as Chinese sauerkraut, pickled cabbage, and mustard pickle, these are mustard greens which are pickled in a marinade of wine, salt, and sugar. These greens are a great favorite in soups and are also served with beef and pork dishes.

HAMIN (Jewish) This ancient Hebrew word meaning "hot" is synonymous with *cholent,* a rich stew thick with beans and other vegetables and spices. Rice and meat or fowl are sometimes added as well. *Hamin* is a favorite of observant Jews, who do not cook on the Sabbath. The dish can be prepared on Friday and be kept warm overnight in a slow oven. By noon on Saturday, when the hungry family returns home from synagogue services, the *hamin* is ready. (See CHOLENT) COMPATIBLE WINES: A red wine, e.g., Beaujolais, Rioja, Chianti, Fleurie, Zinfandel, Valpolicella.

HANGTOWN FRY An outlaw of the Old West of the United States, while being sentenced to hang, was once asked what he would like for his last meal. When he requested a large order of oysters plus scrambled eggs and bacon, the practical chef decided to throw all these foods together into one tasty omelette. That dish is still served today as "hangtown fry."

HAPUKAPSA SALAT (Estonian) A salad composed of sauerkraut mixed with chopped tart apples, sliced onions, salt, sugar, and dollops of sour cream.

HARICOTS (French) Beans.

HARIRA (East Indian) This concoction is also known as a "cobra cooler." As the deadly cobra is sacred to the Hindus, he is nourished on certain holy days with an offering of milk, set out for him in a bowl. The *harira* stems from this religious custom. It is made by grinding peppercorns together with sugar, cardamom seeds, seedless raisins, blanched almonds, and finally the milk. After being thoroughly mixed in a blender, the *harira* is strained and chilled before serving.

HARISSA (Moroccan) From North Africa comes this extremely hot sauce composed of dried hot chili peppers, garlic, cumin, caraway seeds, coriander, salt, and olive oil. It is served with *couscous*. (See COUSCOUS)

HAROSET (Jewish) Also spelled *charoseth* and *charoset,* this pastelike mixture of nuts and fruits moistened with wine is served at the Passover Seder service, at which the Exodus of the Jews from Egypt is recounted. The *haroset* symbolizes the mortar with which the Jewish slaves were forced to make bricks. The ingredients used for *haroset* vary in different parts of the world. In Europe, for instance, apples, walnuts, cinnamon, and wine are used, while the Yemenite Jew makes *haroset* from dates, figs, sesame seeds, ginger, almonds, hot peppers, and raisins. The Moroccan Jew will make his own slight variation with the addition of pine nuts; the Israeli will add orange juice and bananas; and in the Balkans, nutmeg and cinnamon are added to raisins, dates, and nuts.

HARUSAME (Japanese) Sometimes referred to as "cellophane noodles" because they are fine and transparent, these are actually bean threads fashioned from a paste of mung and bean starch. They are sold packed in small bundles. When cooked in a broth with meat and vegetables, the *harusame* are presoaked. When deep-fried, they increase greatly in volume and become crackling crisp. Like bean curd, *harusame* readily absorb the flavors of other foods. (See MUNG)

HARVARD BEETS Probably first made by a Harvard student (no one knows for sure), these pickled beets are rather frugally made by marinating cooked sliced beets in a sweet-sour concoction of vinegar and sugar. How much better they might have been had sliced onions, celery seed, and dry mustard been added to the marinade!

HASENPFEFFER (German) This popular dish was originally prepared from wild hare, which is much tastier than the domestic rabbit so often substituted today. The animal is cut into serving pieces and left to marinate in red wine for a day or two. The pieces are then dried, seasoned with salt and pepper, and placed in a pan to brown in bacon fat. After sautéing chopped garlic and shallots in bacon fat in another pot, red wine and chicken stock are added, plus brandy, currant jelly, and herbs. Then the pieces of meat and drained bacon are added to the pot to stew until done. Prior to removing the pot from the heat, the sauce is thickened with the blood of the hare or rabbit. Just a touch of lemon juice and the dish is ready to be served. COMPATIBLE WINES: A red wine, e.g., Chambertin, Aloxe-Corton, Chambolle-Musigny, Nuits St. Georges, Pinot Noir, Barolo, Haut Brion, Pétrus, Dôle.

HATCHING (Finnish) An old-fashioned method of slowly cooking foods by the heat of the same sturdy wood stoves once used to heat Finnish homes during their semiarctic winters. Today, this method—somewhat similar to stewing as well as to "crockery cookery"—entails slowly cooking foods in the oven's afterheat, the heat still present in the oven after the regular cooking has been done. When a dish is "hatched," the ingredients are cooked below the boiling point, which not only tenderizes the meat but retains its taste and nutritional value. Very little liquid is used, for the lid fits so tightly that no steam escapes. Heavy cast-iron pots or Dutch ovens are best for this kind of cooking.

HAUTE CUISINE (French) The cooking style of the French Court and of the nobility. The term was created by former chefs of royalty to advertise their new businesses: their restaurants. Today, defined categorically, *haute cuisine* is the finest restaurant food available, prepared by expert, diligent chefs who are dedicated to these culinary precepts: quality, suitability, moderation, harmony, patience, simplicity, and hospitality.

Quality means food that is absolutely fresh, totally nourishing, and attractive to the eye.

Suitability is food served in correct sequence, e.g., not caviar with cocoa or ice cream before roast beef; an *hors d'oeuvre* that will stimulate the taste buds, not cloy them.

Moderation means not overloading the platters with excessive amounts of food nor the glasses with more wine than is prudent.

Harmony in fine food is that food which is chosen to agree with the season of the year and is served with sauces and wines that enhance but do not overpower.

Patience means taking all the time necessary to do justice to the preparation, the cooking, and the service of the meal, making certain that it is nourishing, that there is a variety of textures in the foods and that they provide minerals, vitamins, proteins, and carbohydrates necessary to sustain the body.

Simplicity must never be omitted from *haute cuisine,* that simplicity that builds tastefully to the peak of the meal—the main course—and then retreats tactfully, ever conscious that the taste of what follows must accent what has gone before. Like an artistic piece of music or prose, it must have an unobtrusive beginning, a main theme leading to a climax, and then a denouement. There should be nothing superfluous, nothing that detracts from the *pièce de résistance.*

Aware that novelty and gimmicks have no place here, we proceed to the soul of *haute cuisine—***Hospitality.** To be able to really enjoy food that has been expertly and excellently prepared, to derive the greatest pleasure from it, human beings must be receptive to it in order to promote good digestion. This demands an atmosphere of civility, one that promotes relaxation and easy conversation.

HAWAIIAN CUISINE Few cuisines have had as many varied ethnic influences as the Hawaiian. It is a blending of Japanese, Chinese, Indian, Portuguese, and American cookery. Fish are naturally a favorite food but pork dishes (barbecued pig), leaves stuffed with fish and pork (*ti* leaves), plus chicken dishes flavored with coconut are also on most menus. *Poi,* a starchy paste made from the taro root, takes the place of bread and potatoes. (See POI, TARO)

HAWAIIAN SHRIMP CURRY (Hawaiian) A shrimp dish made with fresh coconut milk. First, onions and flour are cooked in melted butter to a paste consistency. With the addition of dairy milk, it is brought to the boil, and as it thickens, the coconut milk, shrimp, and seasonings—including lemon juice, ginger root, and curry powder—are added. The mixture is slowly cooked and when tender, the shrimp and curry sauce are poured into the center of a ring of cooked white rice. The following garnishes are served in individual small dishes: shredded fresh coconut, chopped hard-boiled eggs, finely chopped green peppers, peanuts, ripe green olives, pineapple chutney, pineapple pickle, orange marmalade, finely sliced onions fried crisp, and Bombay duck. (See BOMBAY DUCK) COMPATIBLE BEVERAGES: Tea, beer, saké.

HAWTHORNE-BUTTER (Polish) Hawthorne berries, or *larve* as they are called, are the tart fruit of a spiny shrub of the apple family. This mixture, which contains no real butter, is made from dark red hawthorne berries. After the berries are cleaned and pitted, they are sprinkled with sugar and left to stand covered for several days. When they have become soft enough to mash, the berries are pressed through a sieve and, together with an equal amount of sugar, simmered until thick.

HEAD CHEESE Although also called "souse," and in England "brawn," the name "head cheese" seems most apt because when this dish was created back in the Middle Ages, bits and pieces of meat and gelatin were enclosed in the head skin of the animal and cooked and served that way.

To prepare, chopped-up pig's head, the feet and the bones, even connective tissue and hides are all boiled in water with herbs and spices until the meat leaves the bones. After the stock is defatted and the boned meat finely chopped, the cleared stock is poured over the meat in a mold. It becomes jellied when cold and is served in slices with a spicy sauce, such as a mustard sauce. (See SÜLZE) COMPATIBLE BEVERAGES: Beer, ale.

HEDELMÄRAHKA (Finnish) A delightful fruit cream made from cheese curd that is ground fine or puréed and then blended with whipped cream, honey, and fresh berries or fruits—crushed raspberries or strawberries, chopped peaches with vanilla and orange juice, crushed pineapple, and the like. (See BÄRKRÄM, BAVAROIS)

HELSTEGT MØRBRAD MED SVESKER OG AEBLER (Danish) A tasty pork tenderloin that is pot-roasted, stuffed with such fruits as prunes and apples, and served with a cream sauce flavored with red currant jelly. COMPATIBLE WINES: A white wine, e.g., Sauterne, Tokay Szamorodni, Muscat d'Alsace, Riesling, Johannisberg, Nierstein, Forster Jesuitengarten.

HERBE ROYALE (French) See BASIL

HERO SANDWICH When it was created in New Orleans, there was nothing heroic about this sandwich. The holy nuns, in the confines of their convents, took the long loaves of French bread called _baguettes,_ sliced them lengthwise, and filled them with whatever they had stored in their larders. When young boys came a-begging, asking for a _pourboire,_ the good nuns handed out these sandwiches. In New Orleans today, these sandwiches are still available, but the name _pourboire_ has changed to "poor-boy sandwiches," our "heros."

HIBACHI (Japanese) A charcoal-burning brazier and grill, used for heating and for cooking.

HIBISCUS CHICKEN SLICES (Chinese) This dish, called _fu jung chi p'ien_ in Chinese, is delicate and unusual. Snow peas, water chestnuts, and the cooked white meat of a young chicken are all mixed with egg whites and poached in a mixture of white wine and sesame oil. When cooked, the food puffs up to resemble the hibiscus flower. (See FU JUNG, WATER CHESTNUT) COMPATIBLE WINES: A white wine, e.g., sherry, Sauterne, Orvieto, saké, Anjou.

HICHIMI TOGARISHI (Japanese) Like the Indian curry, this is a special spice mixture. Powdered hot mustard seed, sesame seed, pepper leaf, poppy seed, rape seed, hemp seed, and dried tangerine peel are blended together to make a tangy "seven-pepper spice." It is sold in small bottles in Oriental food stores. (See CHIRIZU)

HIMMEL UND ERDE KARTOFFEL The Germans found a heavenly way to prepare potatoes and consequently named the dish "heaven and earth." Cooked apples are puréed and mixed together with mashed potatoes seasoned with sugar, salt, and pepper. The dish is served with crisply cooked bacon bits strewn over the top.

HING (Chinese) See ASAFOETIDA

HIYAMUGI (Japanese) The term used for thin noodles when served cold.

HOISIN SAUCE (Chinese) A dark brown sauce thick with soybeans and flour and seasoned with sugar and many spices. (See PEKING DUCK)

HOLISHKES (Jewish) These sweet-and-sour cabbage rolls, which originated in Poland, are traditionally served by Jews at festive occasions. The cabbage head is blanched in boiling water and the leaves are removed, a leaf at a time. Each leaf is filled with a mixture of ground beef, grated onions, eggs, salt, and pepper then rolled up and fastened. The stuffed cabbage rolls are placed in a sweet-sour sauce composed of lemon juice, raisins, brown sugar, peppers, tomato purée, salt, and chopped onions and simmered until done. COMPATIBLE BEVERAGES: Tea or beer.

HOLLANDAISE, SAUCE (French) This basic sauce, from which all other rich butter sauces spring, is developed by slowly and carefully pouring melted sweet butter into a warm reduction of shallots, vinegar, and white wine. Egg yolks and seasoning are added as well, vigorously stirring all the while. At the end of the cooking time, just a hint of cayenne pepper and a dash of lemon juice complete this heavenly sauce. The consistency of the *sauce Hollandaise* and similar sauces can be controlled by either using more or less egg yolks or by applying more or less heat to the cooking of the eggs. The sauce is used to enhance the flavor of fish, egg, and vegetable dishes. (See MALTAISE, MOUSSELINE, NOISETTE, OYSTER HOLLANDAISE)

HOLSTEIN CERVELAT (German) See CERVELAT

HOLSTEIN, SCHNITZEL À LA See SCHNITZEL

HOMARD, BEURRE DE (French) See COMPOUND BUTTER

HOMARD, SAUCE (French) This sauce takes its name from the lobster coral that flavors it. Made by adding a lobster-butter (made from lobster coral) and a paprika-butter to a *velouté de poisson* that has been refined with heavy cream, the sauce is reserved for fish dishes and, certainly, for lobster. (See LOBSTER VELOUTÉ)

HOMINY (American South) A cereal made from corn that has been soaked then processed by machine to break up the grain. The bran and germ are sifted out, and what is left is dried and sold as "hominy." If the pieces are fairly large, the product is known as "samp" or "pearl hominy"; but when ground down to a coarse meal, the product is popularly known as "hominy grits," a cereal beloved in the southern United States. (See CORN BREAD, CORNMEAL, POLENTA)

HONAN CUISINE (Chinese) As the province of Honan is fed by the mighty Yellow River, its regional cuisine is replete with many fresh-water fish dishes, particularly sweet-and-sour specialities featuring carp. To confuse Hunan with Honan is understandable until one learns that Hunan cooking is closely allied to the hot-and-spicy style of its neighbor, Szechwan. (See CHINESE CUISINE, SZECHWAN CUISINE)

HOPPELPOPPEL (German) A synonym for *Mischgericht,* "a mixture of food," and a mixture so called always seems to incorporate eggs in some way. On a restaurant menu, the term refers to a type of pancake-omelette made with a harmonious hodgepodge of food. One such mixture consists of cubed beef that is sautéed in butter with bits of bacon then mixed with beaten eggs and fried pancake-style; another is an omelette made with chopped ham, minced onions, and fried potatoes. The term *Hoppelpoppel* also can refer to a hot punch composed of eggs and a liqueur, such as rum or brandy.

HOPPINJOHN This soul food preparation, popular in the Deep South of the United States, is composed of hog jowls and black-eyed peas. If eaten on New Year's Day, hoppinjohn is supposed to bring luck throughout the year. Fluffy white rice completes the dish. COMPATI-BLE WINES: A red wine, e.g., Côtes du Rhône, Mercurey, Beaujolais, Côte Rôtie, Zinfandel, Valpolicella, Médoc, Lambrusco, Bardolino.

HORS D'OEUVRE (French) This term (*les hors d'oeuvre* is the plural form) means "outside the meal" or "before the meal." As a menu term, *hors d'oeuvre* can designate the "first course" of a meal or refer to snacks served with cocktails.

HOTCHPOTCH (Dutch) This dish is just that—a hodgepodge—but a tasty one. The dish commemorates the lifting of the Siege of Leyden, when *Hotchpotch* was given to the starving people of the city. It is made from a flank steak that is first sautéed alone in butter and then sliced; onions, carrots, and potatoes are then added. When all is well cooked, the vegetables are all mashed together, seasoned with salt, pepper, and a bit of melted beef suet and served with the flank steak, sliced thin, on top. COMPATIBLE WINES: A red wine, e.g., Beaujolais,

Zinfandel, Fleurie, Côte Rôtie, Veltliner, Lambrusco, Petit Sirah, Valpolicella.

HO YAU (Chinese) A thick oyster sauce made from oyster extract, water, salt, cornstarch, and caramel coloring. Not at all fishy in taste, this sauce is used to enhance the flavor of meats and other sauces. It is also served as a dip. (See HUÎTRES)

HSIA (Chinese) Shrimp. The word for lobster, *lung-hsia,* bears the same connotation and means "dragon-shrimp," as does the Chinese expression *tui-hsia,* which means "paired shrimp."

HUEVOS ALLA FLAMENCO (Spanish) A gypsy-inspired dish made by breaking eggs into a simmering tomato sauce containing bits of ham and sausage. The dish is served surrounded with cooked peas and fried potatoes. (See CHORIZO) COMPATIBLE WINES: A white wine, e.g., Orvieto, Graves, Sylvaner, or Sauvignon Blanc, but beer would be best.

HUEVOS AL NIDO (Spanish) "Eggs in a nest" is yet another of the remarkable egg dishes made famous by the Spanish. The nest in this case is a hollowed-out tomato. The tomato pulp, mixed with peas, mushrooms, ham, breadcrumbs, and dry sherry, is spooned into the hollowed-out tomatoes. With an egg broken into each tomato and grated Parmesan cheese strewn over the top, the nests are first baked and then broiled until the cheese has browned. They are set off beautifully on top of mounds of boiled white rice. COMPATIBLE BEVERAGES: Beer, ale, Sauterne, sherry, saké.

HUI MEIN (Chinese) Noodles-in-gravy. Egg noodles are cooked *al dente* in boiling salted water. Green beans are blanched in the same water. Chopped onions, garlic, ginger, cubed cooked chicken, and the beans are sautéed in hot oil to which soy sauce and sherry are added. Chicken stock, brought to the boil, is thickened with butter, soy sauce, and cornstarch; then the noodles are added and cooked until warm. The bean-and-chicken mélange is served spooned over the noodles. (See DENTE) COMPATIBLE BEVERAGES: Beer, ale, sherry, saké.

HUÎTRES EN BROCHETTE (French) Detached oysters are quickly blanched in a mixture of their own juices and white wine, then the oysters are removed and the liquid is reduced. Egg yolk, salt, pepper, cream, and cornstarch are added to the reduced liquid and stirred over low heat until thick. It is strained and cooled. Oysters and pieces of bacon are alternately threaded on skewers then rolled in the chilled sauce, dusted with flour, dipped in a mixture of egg yolk, water, and oil, breaded, and finally deep-fried until golden brown. Mussels can be served the same way. COMPATIBLE WINES: A white wine, e.g., Chablis, Muscadet, Soave, Debro, Pouilly-Fuissé.

HUÎTRES, SAUCE AUX (French) An oyster sauce made by boiling the oysters in their own juice together with an herb bouquet. The oyster liquid is added to either a *sauce Normande* or a *sauce Béchamel,* with just a touch of lemon juice. The boiled oysters are now discarded and fresh ones are added to the sauce, which is usually served with boiled fish. (See BÉCHAMEL, HO YAU, NORMANDE)

HUMMUS (Middle Eastern) Also spelled *homus* and *humus,* this is the name given to both chickpeas and to a food dip composed of chickpeas, lemon juice, garlic, salt, and olive oil. Often *tahini* (a paste made from ground sesame seeds) is added and the dish is called *hummus bi tahini.* (See CHICKPEAS, GARBANZO, TAHINI) COMPATIBLE BEVERAGES: Arrack, beer.

HUNAN CUISINE See CHINESE CUISINE, HONAN CUISINE, SZECHWAN CUISINE

HUNGARIAN CUISINE For many years Austria and Hungary were one country, but the Hungarian cuisine remained distinctively free from the more reserved Austrian-Germanic influence by giving free reign to their national *gulyas* dishes. In like manner, they adopted the wild gypsy music rather than the staid waltz. (See HUNGARIAN STEWS)

HUNGARIAN STEWS

Gulyas A very thin stew composed of beef cut into one-inch cubes, browned with onions in hot oil, and cooked in a great quantity of beef stock.

Pörkölt This stew, literally meaning "browned," can be made from most any kind of meat, including chicken. The meat is cut a bit larger than the above mentioned, and it is braised in a small amount of stock. Beef is rarely used.

Paprikás This stew is cooked exactly as the *pörkölt,* in the same amount of stock, but at the end of the cooking time sour cream is added. Veal and chicken make the finest *paprikás* stews.

Tokány This stew, made from meat—any meat that is sliced thin— is cooked in very little broth, almost in its own juices. (See BORJU, GULYAS, RAGOÛT, SERTÉS, STEFADO, STEW)

COMPATIBLE WINES: For chicken and veal *gulyas,* a white wine, e.g., Badacsonyi, Nierstein, Oppenheim, Gewürztraminer, Graves, Sylvaner. For the beef *gulyas,* a red wine, e.g., Veltliner, Chianti, Bardolino, Ruby Cabernet, Egri Bikaver,Châteauneuf-du-Pape.

HUNG-SHU (Chinese) "Red-cooking," a method of slowly stewing food in a sauce composed mostly of soy. As the liquid boils, it evaporates, leaving the food reddish-brown from the preponderance of soy sauce. (See SOYBEAN, SOY SAUCE)

HÛNKAR BEĞENDI (Hungarian) See BEĞENDI

HUSH PUPPIES (American South) As the story goes, a group of southern hunters had gathered about the fire where their food was cooking.

The aroma of whatever was frying in the pan drove the hungry hunting dogs wild. To silence the howling and yapping, the hunters tossed balls of cornmeal batter into the hot grease of the frying pan, and when cooked, they threw the fried cornballs to the hounds with the gentle, "Hush, puppies!" Thus, the hush puppy was born. Children love them covered with honey or with molasses.

HUSKOVE KNEDLÍKY The Czechs are rightly proud of the many kinds of dumplings for which they are famous, but these "bread dumplings" head the list. The *knedliky* are made from a mixture of flour, salt, egg yolks, milk, and water. Cubed bread is added, and the dough, shaped like sausages, is simmered in water until done. When cooked, the sausage-shaped dumplings are sliced with a strong thread.

HUSSARDE, À LA (French) The brilliant horsemanship of the Hussars, the Hungarian cavalry, was matched by their brilliant red uniforms. A dish described as *à la Hussarde* will always have its fill of brilliant red tomatoes and lots of horseradish. The garnish called *Hussarde* consists of tomatoes and eggplant stuffed with a *sauce Soubise* plus mushrooms, *duchesse potatoes,* and grated fresh horseradish. It is served to complement large roasts. (See DUCHESSE, SOUBISE)

Hussarde, Sauce White wine is added to chopped shallots and onions and reduced. *Demi-glace,* tomato purée, raw ham, garlic, and herbs are added, simmered together, and strained. This sauce, garnished with grated horseradish, parsley, and chopped ham, is served with roasted and broiled meats.

ICE CREAM History tells us that ice cream was known as far back as the second century. In Rome it was referred to as *melca* by Galen. To the ancient Swiss, ice cream was a frozen milk that was shaken up in long jars until foamy and creamy. But it was not until 1413 that ice cream was served at a banquet, specifically at the coronation feast of the militant English monarch Henry V, and it was then called *creme frez.* The French influence, so plainly seen in the name, was due no doubt to the fact that Henry had a particular penchant for anything French, including certain parts of France that had once belonged to his ancestors. He proceeded to take those lands and, rascal that he was, after having trounced the French army at Agincourt, he took the French Princess Catherine as his wife.

It was not until 1660 that French gastronomes first took notice of such innovations as ices and sherbets. It was finally a Sicilian named Procopio who introduced them to Paris, but it took another whole century before ice cream and sherbets were accepted by the populace as desserts. Before Procopio came on the scene in 1533, Buontalenti, one of the cooks Catherine de Médicis brought with her to the French court, entranced the aristocracy—but only the aristocracy—with his fruited ices.

Egg yolks, fresh heavy cream, and natural flavorings are the essence of fine ice cream. (See ALASKA, BELLE HÉLÈNE, GELATO, GLACE, GRA- NITÉ, MELBA, MELLORINE, SORBET)

ICES These desserts are defined as fruit juices or purées of fruit that are blended with sugar syrup and frozen. The sherbet differs in that an Italian meringue (egg whites beaten into sugar syrup) or plain whipped egg whites are added to the pure fruit purée or juice and then frozen. (See GRANITÉ, SORBET)

ICHIBAN DASHI (Japanese) A basic soup stock used in the preparation of many meat, poultry, and fish dishes. First, *kombu,* a seaweed, is blanched in boiling water and removed; then *katsuobushi,* a dried bonito, finely grated, is simmered in the water. The stock is cleared and strained and served as a soup with various garnitures. (See DASHI, KATSUOBUSHI, KOMBU)

IKRA (Russian) Caviar. (See BELUGA)

IKRE (Rumanian-Jewish) This dish, also referred to as "poor-man's caviar," is composed of white carp roe mixed with oil and lemon juice and seasoned with salt and pepper to taste. The roe is served garnished with hard-boiled eggs and sliced onions. COMPATIBLE WINES: A white wine, e.g., Verdicchio, Soave, Debro, Sauvignon Blanc, Quincy.

IMAM BAYILDI (Turkish) Literally, "the Imam fainted." Legend says that after a certain Imam had ended his long fast during Ramadan, the delicious aroma of this dish so affected his senses that he fainted dead away. The dish consists of an eggplant stuffed with a meat or a vegetable mixture that is highly seasoned with herbs and spices. COMPATIBLE BEVERAGES: Tea or beer.

IMPÉRATRICE, À LA (French) A descriptive term for vanilla puddings that are made with candied fruits that have been soaked in Kirsch, rum, Grand Marnier, or the like.

Riz à l'Impératrice A delectable rice dish said to have been dedicated to both empresses, Josephine and Marie-Louise, of Austria. Although the plump Viennese empress had a sweet-tooth, it was Napoleon's bed partner, Josephine, who was the more food-loving of the two. But to whomever the *riz à l'impératrice* was dedicated, it is a royal dessert. The boiled rice is drained and placed in the oven to dry. It is then added to a mixture of cream, sugar, vanilla, and candied fruit that has been marinated in Kirsch and apricot preserves. After combining with a thick custard and whipped cream, the mixture is poured into a mold layered with red currant jelly. The dessert is set to chill, and *voilà*—a rice pudding so royal it can be served to an empress.

IMU (Polynesian/Hawaiian) A type of underground oven. Wood is set afire in a pit about four feet deep. Large cooking stones are placed on top of the burning wood, then large green fronds are placed evenly over the hot stones. Upon these leaves the food is placed. After being covered with more green fronds, damp cloths, and earth, the food is left to cook in this natural oven for several hours. When a huge animal, such as a whole pig, is to be cooked, hot stones are also placed within the carcass, and the carcass is sealed.

INDIAN CUISINE The use of spices in India evolved from the curative to the culinary, to the point where today Indian regional cooking uses spices more extensively than any other cuisine in the world. Indian cooking techniques are many and varied: currying or stewing, sautéing and pot roasting, steaming, braising, deep-frying, oven cooking, charcoal grilling, baking marinated foods, searing with *ghee* over high heat and glazing to finish, rolling and stuffing meats, and cooking food wrapped in leaves or in pastry. Meat and vegetables are not usually cooked in water; they are cut up and sautéed in *ghee,* with the result that the food retains much more of its vitamin and mineral content. Spicy pastes are widely used to blend with food or to surround it.

Although the knife and fork are both used in Indian cities, it is considered good manners to eat Moslem-style, with the right hand. In rural areas the knife and fork are not used. (See GHEE, RICE IN INDIA)

INDIAN PUDDING (American) This dish, created during Colonial days, is a refined version of the thick cornmeal-and-molasses mixture first offered to the early settlers by the Indians of the Northeast. Cornmeal, a bit at a time, is mixed with hot milk. Then, off the heat, sugar, baking soda, salt, and cinnamon are folded in together with molasses and more milk. The mixture is poured into a casserole, baked in a medium oven, and served warm covered with whipped cream and a sprinkling of freshly grated nutmeg.

INDIENNE, SAUCE À L' (French) A sauce made of chopped onions and apples sautéed in butter, to which curry, coconut milk, and a *sauce velouté* are added. After being passed through a sieve, the sauce is enriched with heavy cream. It is served with chicken, meat, and shellfish dishes. (See VELOUTÉ)

Another *sauce à l'Indienne* prepared by the French is an Indian salad sauce made by adding a pinch of curry powder and a handful of chopped hard-boiled egg to a regular sauce *vinaigrette*. (See VINAIGRETTE)

INDONESIAN CUISINE The culinary delights of Indonesia came to the Western world via the Netherlands, which ruled Indonesia as a colony and which today serves many Indonesian dishes *(rijstafel)* as their own. One of the most important foods in Indonesian cooking is garlic, which is mashed in great quantities and heated in oil with pepper, salt, and paprika to form a red paste. This paste is used to flavor nearly every dish. Rice is basic and pork, veal, beef, and chicken are often found on restaurant menus. Coconut, almost as important as garlic, is used both in cooking and as a beverage. Characteristic of Indonesian cooking is that a great variety of carefully prepared foods are served at once in small individual dishes, a kind of Oriental *smörgåsbord,* specially arranged to tantalize the taste buds with contrasting, aromatic, and complementary flavors. (See RIJSTAFEL, SMÖRGÅSBORD)

INFANT À L' (French) Poached fish—sole, halibut, turbotin, etc.—is said to be prepared in this manner when the poached fish is set upon a bed of mushroom purée and is then coated with a *sauce Mornay,* sprinkled with grated Gruyère and Parmesan cheese, and lightly browned under the broiler.

INGELEGDE This Malay dish, popular also in South Africa, is prepared by first frying fish in hot oil. Meanwhile, a mixture of sliced onions, red wine vinegar, salt, pepper, hot chilies, turmeric, curry powder, green ginger, brown sugar, and bay leaves is brought to a boil. After the scum and other impurities are removed, the boiled mixture is poured into a preserving jar over the crisply fried fish. (See ESCABECHE, ESCOVEITCHE) COMPATIBLE BEVERAGES: Beer, ale, stout.

INJERA (Ethiopian) A type of bread made from millet flour, which locally is called *teff.* The batter is left to ferment for a period of five days or more, at which time it is poured into a hot flat skillet. While frying, the escaping gas bubbles up the surface, making the bread appear pitted and pockmarked. Because of the long fermentation, the bread possesses a natural sour taste that is quite pleasant.

INSALATA MISTA (Italian) This phrase, found frequently on menus, means "a mixed (or combination) salad."

IRISH STEW This, the most famous and most popular dish ever to come from the Emerald Isle, is made from the boned breast and shoulder of mutton, cut into pieces. In a heavy saucepan, sliced potatoes and onions are alternately layered with the mutton, covered with water, and gently stewed. It is important to skim the fat periodically during the cooking. This glorious stew is sent to the table steaming hot. COMPATIBLE WINES: A red wine, e.g., Beaujolais, Pinot Noir, St. Émilion, Veltliner, Valpolicella, Zinfandel, Mâcon, Médoc, Châteauneuf-du-Pape, Hermitage.

ISABELLE, SWEETBREADS (French) A sweetbreads preparation named for that same Isabella, Ferdinand's queen, who smiled on Columbus and backed his foolhardy attempts to find a shortcut to the East Indies. The sweetbreads, stuffed with a mixture of a mushroom purée and black truffles and poached in a wine-flavored bouillon, are regally served on a bed of chicken *quenelles,* with chopped truffles, tongue, and pistachio nuts spread over the top. The dish is served with a *sauce Colbert.* (See COLBERT, QUENELLES) COMPATIBLE WINES: A white wine, e.g., Lacrima Christi, Traminer, Riquewihr, Vouvray, Johannisberg, Oppenheim, Alsheim, Chenin Blanc.

ISCAS (Portuguese) A favorite meat dish made from pork liver that has been sliced into strips, marinated in a mixture of wine, garlic, and herbs, then thoroughly drained, dried, and fried until crisp. The liver strips are usually served in a bowl with pickled vegetables, fried potatoes, and fresh watercress. Once fried, the crisp liver really looks like fishermen's "bait" (*iscas* in Portuguese). COMPATIBLE WINES: A red wine, e.g., Rioja, Beaujolais, Pinot Noir, Moulin-à-Vent, Zinfandel, Valpolicella, Fleurie, Nebbiolo.

ISINGLASS A refined type of gelatin, obtained from the dried bladders of such fish as the sturgeon. Today, animal gelatin, which is far easier to come by, has all but replaced the isinglass.

ITALIAN CUISINE Italian cooking as we know it today originated in the ancient cultures of Greece, Rome, and to a lesser degree the Orient. At a time when the rest of the civilized world was ravaged by barbarism and decimated by plague, Italy was instrumental in preserving the art of cookery. Ultimately the royal cooks of France profited by adopting the subtleties of Italian Renaissance cooking and claiming them as their own. However, the French added masses of sauces, broths, and extracts, which together with herbs and spices served to mask their foods. This the Italians did not agree with.

The Italian cuisine is not merely *minestrone, pasta asciutta,* and *scaloppine.* The great variety of Italian food is marked by regionally inspired dishes. Each province maintains its own traditions of cookery and has its own specialities, whether it be the *risi e bisi* or *scampi* of Venice; the *risotto* and *ossi bucchi* dishes of Milan; the redolent garlic-saturated *pesto* and fish soups of Genoa; the cheese dishes such as *fonduta,* the white truffles, and the *bagna cauda* of the Piedmont Alpine region; the *lasagne verdi* and tomato-rich *ragù,* the *tortellini* and *mortadella* of Bologna; the Chianti wine and the good beef and chestnut dishes of Tuscany; the famous *fettucine* and *saltimbocca* of Rome; the *pizza* of Naples; the *cassata, gelato,* and *spumone* of Sicily; or the *calzone* and *baccalà* of the southern regions of Apulia, Basicalata, and Calabria. Therefore, to call food "Italian" is a vast generalization; more definition is required. (See BACCALÀ, BAGNA CAUDA, CALZONE, CASSATA, FETTUCINE, FONDUTA, GELATO, LASAGNE VERDI, MINESTRONE, MORTADELLA, OSSI BUCCHI, PASTA ASCIUTTA, PESTO, PIZZA, RAGÙ, RISI E BISI, RISOTTO, SALTIMBOCCA, SCALOPPINE, SCAMPI, SPUMONE, TORTELLINI)

ITALIANSALAATTI (Finnish) Just the name of this salad might lead one to envision all sorts of aromatic vegetables and condiments relished by the citizens of Roma, Firenze, and Milano. But, in fact, this Finnish salad has very little to do with anything even vaguely Italian. The main ingredients of the dish—the meats and the vegetables, including veal, tongue, ham, potatoes, carrots, apples, a dill pickle, and fresh green peas—are all cooked and then chopped into uniformly-sized cubes. The salad is tossed in a dressing of egg yolks, mustard, and grated fresh horseradish to which oil is slowly added, plus lemon juice, salt, pepper, and ice water. The salad rests overnight in the refrigerator, and when ready to be served, it is enriched with freshly whipped cream.

ITALIENNE, À L' (French) A descriptive term referring to those dishes served with a garniture of an Italian-style *pasta*—such as *spaghetti, macaroni, linguini*—served as is or made into *croquettes* and filled with chopped artichoke hearts. The term can also mean that meat, fish, poultry, or vegetable dishes have been prepared with a fine *Duxelles* flavored with tomato paste and then served garnished with artichoke hearts and a *sauce Italienne.* (See DUXELLES, PASTA)

Sauce Italienne Although the French are ever eager to Gallicize any excellent dish, this classic sauce is totally French, in spite of the reference to Italy. One version of the sauce is composed of a *Duxelles* with chopped cooked ham, a *sauce demi-glace* and tomato, and just before serving, a touch of minced parsley, chervil, and tarragon. It is served with meat or fowl. Another version, which is served with grilled fish, is made exactly as the above but the ham is omitted and a special *sauce Espagnole* made with the addition of fish stock is substituted for the tomato *demi-glace.* (See DEMI-GLACE, DUXELLES, ESPAGNOLE)

Foie de Veau à l'Italienne Thin slices of calf's liver are seasoned, dusted with flour, and sautéed quickly in very hot oil and butter. The accompanying *sauce Italienne* can either be poured over the liver or served separately. (See ITALIENNE, VELOUTÉ) COMPATIBLE WINES: A red wine, e.g., Beaujolais, Mâcon, Margaux, Valpolicella, Zinfandel, Mercurey, Egri Bikaver.

IVOIRE, SAUCE (French) A sauce made by adding a strained chicken stock to a white *roux* and simmering the mixture with veal stock until thickened. After being strained and reduced, off the heat the mixture is enriched with scalded cream as it is stirred constantly. Egg yolks are briskly beaten into the mixture, then the sauce is passed through a sieve and is ready to be served with poached chicken or with sweetbreads. (See ROUX)

JACQUES, COUPE (French) A scoop of lemon and a scoop of strawberry ice cream are covered with mixed fresh fruits that have been marinated in Kirschwasser or some other liqueur. It is usually topped with a flavored whipped cream, and it is always served in a *coupe* (a stemmed glass). (See COUPE)

JAEGERSCHNITZEL (German) A speciality consisting of a fillet of pork that has been dipped in seasoned flour and pan-fried; a mushroom and wine sauce is then added. COMPATIBLE WINES: A white wine, e.g., Piesporter Goldtröpfchen, Sancerre, Schloss Vollrads, Meursault, Orvieto, Frascati, Gewürztraminer, Sylvaner, Johannisberg.

JAM The word "jam" is reserved for those liquid or "pourable" fruit preserves. The production of jam came to Europe from the Middle East, whose inhabitants first perfected the art of preserving fruit, and it came, as did many beneficial things, with the returning Crusaders. By the end of the Middle Ages, Europeans were producing such fruit delicacies as quince marmalade, musk-scented citrus jams, and jellies of many home grown fruits.

JAMBALAYA See CRÉOLE JAMBALAYA

JAMBON AU MADÈRE (French) Ham steaks prepared with Madeira wine. First, chopped onions are sautéed in butter and then simmered in a beef stock flavored with tomato purée. A *roux* is made and the onion mixture is added together with Madeira wine. Ham steaks are browned in a heavy pan, and the sauce is poured over them before serving. Leaf spinach cooked in butter is served on the side. (See MADÈRE, ROUX) COMPATIBLE WINES: A white wine, e.g., Orvieto, Frascati, Riquewihr, Hermitage Blanc, Aigle, Vouvray, Riesling.

JAO-TZE (Chinese) Dumpling "wrappers" that are filled with well-spiced and herbed ground meats. The dough is a simple one made from flour and water. It is well kneaded, left to rest, and then small balls of the dough are rolled flat into small rounds: these are the wrappers.

JAPANESE CUISINE Although closely related to Chinese cookery, which is considered to be one of the "original" cuisines of the world, Japanese food is more delicate, emphasizing clean, sharp, natural flavorings rather than the hot spices popular in regional Chinese cooking. Contrary to Chinese usage, many Japanese ingredients—especially fish, as in the *sashimi* dishes—are eaten uncooked, served with dip sauces to enhance the flavor. The Japanese consume more fish per capita than any other people in the world. This includes the deadly blowfish, the rather odd sea urchin, as well as such sea vegetables as the *nori* and *kombu*.

The Chinese tea-drinking ceremony has been refined by the Japanese. Every aspect of the ceremony has been stylized—from the correct method of pouring the hot water to how the tea bowl should be held. Highly formal, the tea service is a performance full of graceful simplicity and elegance that must be admired.

Gastronomy to the Japanese is an art dedicated to pleasing the palate and delighting the eye. Therefore, pains are taken to present the freshest of foods as tastefully as color and form will allow.

To a Japanese, the quality of a meal begins with how it looks. Food is served in small china dishes, and wooden chopsticks are preferred over metal utensils because the taste of metal in the mouth detracts from the taste of the food. Food is eaten from low tables or *tatami* mats. Diners recline on cushions around a large rectangular lacquered table, and the meal is served on individual trays with a bowl of soy sauce ever present. Japanese food is usually prepared tableside, on a small *hibachi*. Green tea or saké are served warm in small cups. A pickled food will usually finish the meal. (See CHOPSTICKS, FUGU, HIBACHI, KOMBU, NORI, OURSIN, SASHIMI, TATAMI)

JAPANESE-STYLE FRIED CHICKEN The distinctive flavor of this dish comes from its marinade. The boned and cubed chicken is placed in a mixture of soy sauce, sherry wine, lemon juice, fresh garlic cloves, ginger, and sugar. The chicken is left to marinate overnight, then enough cornstarch is added to the marinade to make a thin paste. The following day, the cubed chicken, covered with a coating of the paste, is placed into hot vegetable oil to cook until golden brown. Drained and served with white rice and a salad, this chicken provides a real taste experience. COMPATIBLE WINES: A white wine, e.g., Tokay, saké, Sauterne, Keknyelu, Graves, Orvieto, Chenin Blanc.

JAPONAISE, SALADE (French) This salad is referred to as Japanese because of the seafood it contains. Mussels are cooked in white wine, removed from their shells, and added to a potato salad flavored with a *julienne* of black truffles. A standard French dressing (three parts olive oil to one part vinegar) is also added for flavoring. The mussels and potatoes are then set decoratively atop a bed of lettuce leaves that have been tossed in the same dressing. This salad is often served as a first course. (See FRENCH DRESSING, JAPANESE CUISINE, JULIENNE)

JARDINIÈRE (French) The descriptive term for a dish served with "a variety of vegetables." The vegetables may be either boiled or glazed, but they are always cooked separately from the roasted, stewed, or braised meat or poultry that they garnish. (See BOUQUETIÈRE, CHIFFONADE, MACÉDOINE, PRINTANIER)

JERKY A word derived from the South American Indian term for sun and wind-dried strips of beef or buffalo meat. In Mexico, the dried strips are called *tasayo*. Cowboys and Eskimos always carried jerky with them as an energizer. At home, however, it was creamed and served on buns, biscuits, or with fried cornmeal cakes.

Today, jerky is a popular snack food in the United States. Made from round steak that has been stripped of fat and gristle and cut into strips, jerky is dried in ovens and sold in cellophane bags or in jars. (See BÜNDNERFLEISCH, CHARQUI, GRISONS, PEMMICAN, ROHSCHINKEN)

JERUSALEM ARTICHOKE A knobby tuber with a sweetish taste similar to that of the globe artichoke (the globe artichoke is what we commonly refer to as "artichoke"). The Jerusalem artichoke really has nothing to do with the holy city of Jerusalem. The origin of the name lies in the following: the Italians, knowing that the tuber really belongs to the sunflower family, logically named it *girasole*. The English, in turn, hearing the name, insisted on mispronouncing it, until with the passing of years it evolved into "Jerusalem." And it has remained so to this day.

JEWISH CUISINE Jewish cooking, for the most part, reflects the native cuisines of those lands where the Diaspora (the exiled Jews) resided for centuries, such as Germany, Poland, Russia, Bulgaria, Czechoslovakia, Hungary, Spain, Egypt, Tunisia, Persia, Syria. Each of these countries has left its stamp on Jewish cooking, whether it be the flaky Austrain *Strudels* stuffed with apples or cherries; the *gulyas* from Hungary, paprika-red and redolent with onions; from Russia, *kasha* and *blintzes* served with rich sour cream; from Germany, potato pancakes, sauerkraut, and *gefilte* fish; Polish pickled fish and *krupnik;* or the *bourekas* from Syria or the Arab *pita* bread. The only truly "Jewish" foods can be said to be those that are associated with the religion, that is, those foods served ritually to commemorate certain Jewish religious feasts. (See KOSHER FOOD)

JIA SHIANG HUNG SAU RO (Chinese) This is a pork dish that is red-cooked and served with bamboo shoots. A pork butt is cut into cubes and blanched in boiling water for a few minutes, after which the water is removed. Then the pork is simmered in a mixture of sherry, sliced ginger, and scallions for twenty minutes; then, with the addition of sugar, soy sauce, and cut-up bamboo shoots, it is simmered for another half-hour, until the pork is tender. (See HUNG-SHU, JOOK SOON, RED-COOKING)

JICAMA If it looks like a turnip but tastes like a water chestnut, it must be *jicama,* the brownish root the Mexicans prepare as one cooks a potato, either boiled or baked. The *jicama* may also be mixed with limes and oranges to make a refreshing salad.

JOLOFF, RICE (African) This rice preparation, which originated in Africa, actually in Nigeria, consists of morsels of chicken or of meat cooked together with rice. It is much like the Spanish *paella*. (See PAELLA) COMPATIBLE WINES: A red wine, e.g., Rioja, Beaujolais, Nebbiolo, Egri Bikaver, Valpolicella, Zinfandel, Veltliner, Margaux, Médoc.

JOOK SOON (Chinese) Bamboo shoots. They are preserved whole or thinly sliced in cans. Considered one of the most versatile plants, mature bamboo is used to make houses, furniture, rope, and paper. (See CHA-SHU, JIA SHIANG HUNG SAU RO, SUAN-LE-T'ANG)

JUBILÉ, CERISES (French) A cherry syrup is made by first simmering stoned cherries in a sugar syrup, removing the cherries, then reducing the syrup and adding cornstarch diluted with water to thicken. The cherries are then returned and the whole is flamed either with Grand Marnier or Kirsch and served plain or ladled over vanilla ice cream. With ballroom lights dimmed and with appropriate orchestral accompaniment, it is the banquet headwaiter's "showstopper" at weddings and Bar Mitzvahs.

JUDIC, CROQUETTE (French) See CROQUETTES

JUGGED HARE This hare preparation, the English equivalent of the *civet de lièvre,* demands that the animal be cut into pieces and marinated for a day or so in a red wine flavored with juniper berries. The pieces of meat are dried, well browned in bacon fat, then placed in a casserole together with chopped celery, onions, and carrots, all of which is flavored with allspice and lemon juice and covered with stock. The dish is baked for several hours. Before the cooking time has elapsed, the pounded liver and the blood of the hare are blended with heavy cream into the strained cooking stock; this is poured over the hare to serve. (See CIVET) COMPATIBLE WINES: A red wine, e.g., Richebourg, Pommard, Kirwan, Ausone, Fixin, Nuits St. Georges, Dôle, Pinot Noir, Cabernet Sauvignon.

JUIVE, CARP À LA (French) Carp cooked in the Jewish-style, as done by a French chef. The cleaned whole carp is cut into steaks and placed in a baking dish together with sautéed chopped onions blended into a *roux.* With fish stock, chopped celery, salt, and pepper added, plus a bit of white wine to cover, the fish is baked in a medium oven until done. To serve, the fish steaks are arranged on a large platter—steak next to steak—to resemble as much as possible the original fish. The delicious sauce is strained over the fish, which is left to cool overnight in the refrigerator. The following day, the fish is ready to be served, quite cold, with a tangy horseradish-cream sauce. (See ROUX) COMPATIBLE WINES: A white wine, e.g., Orvieto, Riquewihr, Gewürztraminer, Frascati, Riesling, Sauvignon Blanc, Anjou, Aigle, Debro.

JULEKAKE This "Christmas bread" is so favored in Norway that it is eaten the year 'round. A yeast dough is made from sugar, eggs, flour, milk, ground cardamom seeds, chopped citron, and seedless raisins. It makes a wonderful coffee cake. (See CARDAMOM, CITRON)

JULIENNE French chef Jean Julien is said to have introduced the *julienne* method of preparing vegetables, which involves cutting them uniformly into small, thin strips. The term is now applied to any food cut in this fashion.

KABINETT This German classification for wine of exceptional quality indicates that the vintner found the taste of a particular vintage and category of wine to be of such excellence that he keeps it stashed away in his very own personal *Kabinett,* to be brought out only for very special occasions. (See AUSLESE, BEERENAUSLESE, EISWEIN, SPÄTLESE, TROCKENBEERENAUSLESE)

KACZKA (Polish) Duck.

Kaczka Duszona z Kapusta Gerwona Duck braised in a casserole with red cabbage, onions, herbs, and plenty of red wine. COMPATIBLE WINES: A red wine, e.g., Talbot, Beychevelle, Cabernet Sauvignon, Zinfandel, Valpolicella, Bardolino, Dôle, Nebbiolo.

KADAYIF (Turkish) A dessert popular in Turkey and throughout the Middle East. Fine noodles are cooked in boiling water, drained, and placed in a shallow pan, where they are allowed to set. They are then cut into squares, covered with chopped hazelnuts, almonds, and honey, and baked in a medium oven. The squares can be eaten hot or cold.

Emek Kadayif This bread, cut into squares and cooked in caramel mixed with lemon juice and chopped cloves, is served topped with heavy cream that has been cooked until it has an almost butterlike consistency. (See DEVONSHIRE CREAM)

KADIN BUDU (Turkish) Literally the term means "a lady's thigh," but the dish is euphemistically referred to as "ladies' meatballs." These meat-and-rice burgers are made by mixing boiled rice with raw prime beef, parsley, and seasonings. This mixture is shaped into small oval dumplings, which are then cooked in boiling bouillon. When cool, they are dipped in beaten egg and fried in oil. COMPATIBLE WINES: A red wine, e.g., Beaujolais, Valpolicella, Moulin-à-Vent, Zinfandel, Ruby Cabernet, Cahors, Egri Bikaver, Châteauneuf-du-Pape.

KAERNEMAELKSKOLDSKAAL (Danish) This difficult-to-pronounce sour-milk soup entails no cooking. A real delight on a hot summer's day, it consists of egg yolks, sugar, lemon juice, lemon rind, vanilla, and buttermilk, which are whipped vigorously together until smooth. After being well chilled, the soup is served with gobs of whipped cream floating on top.

KAFFIR An African beer popular all the way from Aswan, in the north of the continent, down to the Cape. The word is Arabic for "unbeliever," a derogatory name given to those who drink the beer.

KAGIT KEBAB (Turkish) Cubed meat cooked *en papillote* (in a wax paper bag). (See PAPILLOTE)

KAISERSCHMARREN (Austrian) Legend says that as soon as raisins were added to this pancake, it was a dish fit for the *Kaiser,* Emperor Franz Josef. It is a simple preparation made with milk, salt, eggs, sugar, and raisins. Cooked in butter until golden brown, the pancake is then cut into long strips, dusted with powdered sugar, and served on hot plates.

KAISERSCHNITZEL NATUR (Austrian) An unbreaded veal cutlet served in a cream sauce flavored with paprika and lemon juice and garnished with black truffles and *Steinpilze* (agaric mushrooms, called *cèpes* in French). (See CHAMPIGNONS, SCHNITZEL)

KAKAVIA SOUP The national fish soup of Greece. The name stems from *kakave,* an earthenware pot used by Greek fishermen in ancient days to cook their fish. To make the soup, tiny fish, water, olive oil, onions, and tomatoes are simmered together then mashed through a sieve. To this base, large raw fish and lobster are added and cooked. The soup is flavored with garlic, bay leaf, parsley, and celery and garnished with croutons. COMPATIBLE WINES: A white wine, e.g., Muscadet, Chablis, Sancerre, Quincy, Debro, Verdicchio, Soave.

KAKI See PERSIMMON

KAKIAGE (Japanese) A dish consisting of finely minced shrimp, chopped scallions, and eggs, all of which is mixed together with flour and fried, pancake-style, in hot oil. *Kakiage* is served with white rice and a *soba tsuyu* sauce for dipping. (See SOBA TSUYU, TEMPURA) COMPATIBLE BEVERAGES: Tea, saké, beer, Sauterne.

KALB (German) Veal.

Kalbsbraten This boned leg of veal is filled with chopped onions, breadcrumbs, kidneys, and anchovies. It is then rolled, fastened, roasted, and served with hot sour cream.

Kalbshaxe The German counterpart of the Italian *osso buccho.* A veal shin is first browned then simmered slowly in white wine and meat stock together with root vegetables, parsley, cloves, bay leaf, and seasonings. (See OSSI BUCCHI)

Kalbsrouladen Thin slices of veal are covered with sautéed chopped mushrooms, onions, nutmeg, and seasoning. They are then rolled, tied, and simmered in veal stock flavored with tomato purée. (See BALLOTINE)

COMPATIBLE WINES: A white wine, e.g., Wehlener Sonnenuhr, Graacher Himmelreich, Soave, Vouvray, Traminer, Rüdesheim, Johannisberg, Keknyelu.

KALDOMAR (Swedish) A process of enveloping ground meats and other foods with cabbage leaves and thus cooking them. In the eighteenth century, while Charles of Sweden was held captive by the Turks, he became entranced with the taste of the Turkish *dolmas,* the stuffed grape leaves. As grape leaves were hard to come by in the cold

North country, the ingenious Swedes used cabbage leaves instead. To prepare the dish, a blending of ground beef and veal, chopped onions, cooked rice, allspice, pepper, and milk is placed neatly into blanched, supple cabbage leaves. The leaves are carefully rolled, and these rolls (also called "pigeons") are first sautéed in butter then drizzled with corn syrup and water and baked until done. The "pigeons" are served with a gravy made from the juices in the baking pan thickened with a bit of flour. (See DOLMADES, DOLMAS, HOLISHKES) COMPATIBLE WINES: A red wine, e.g., Côte Rôtie, Valpolicella, Beaujolais, Egri Bikaver; or a white wine, e.g., Orvieto, Riesling, Sylvaner, Nierstein, Johannisberg.

KALIA (Polish) A rich chicken broth is used as the base for this soup. The broth is flavored with pickled cucumber juice, celery root, and chopped carrots. It is served garnished with cubed chicken and parsley.

KALTESZAL (Polish) This soup, cooked in a double boiler, is made from beer, egg yolks, sugar, lemon juice, and cinnamon. It is served cold, flavored with rum and raisins. (See KALTSCHALE)

KALTSCHALE (German) Literally meaning "cold bowl," this soup is made from one or more fruits—such as oranges, strawberries, raspberries, blackberries—and their juices. The fruits are mixed with lemon juice, water, cinnamon, and cloves and brought to a boil. After simmering until soft, they are rubbed through a sieve and chilled overnight. The cold soup is served garnished with bits of fruit and dollops of whipped cream. Although this seems like a dessert, it is considered a soup, not only by the Germans and the Austrians but also by the Russians, the Israelis, and the Swiss. (See KALTESZAL)

KAMABOKO (Japanese) Usually served at a festive occasion, such as a wedding or a birthday celebration, this cooked fish cake is made by mixing chopped swordfish or shark with *ajinomoto* (monosodium glutamate), cornstarch, water, sugar, and salt. The mixture is formed into a cake and either steamed or broiled. It is brightly colored with red or green food dyes. (See MONOSODIUM GLUTAMATE) COMPATIBLE BEVERAGES: Tea, saké, rosé wine.

KAMPYO (Japanese) Strips of dried gourd, sold prepackaged. The strips are placed in water to soften before being used in soups and broths.

KANOM MAW GENG (Indonesian) Baked coconut. Shredded coconut is left in lukewarm water for a few minutes. Then the squeezed-out coconut meat is mixed with coconut milk, eggs, and sugar and poured out onto a flat baking dish. It is baked until the top browns lightly and then is turned out to eat as a warm pudding or cold with sour cherries that have been marinated in rum and sugar. Sweet biscuits complete this Indonesian dessert.

KANTEN (Japanese) Agar-agar, a gelatinous substance obtained from certain seaweed. It is usually sold in stick form. *Kanten* is also the name of a Japanese dessert similar to the American gelatin dessert. To prepare, the *kanten* sticks are washed, squeezed dry, then shredded into small pieces and soaked until soft. The strips are then cooked until completely dissolved. With the addition of sugar, salt, and flavorings (such as vanilla or almond), the mass is left to cook, after which it is cut into decorative shapes. This dessert is eaten with the fingers. (See AGAR-AGAR)

KÁPOSZTÁS LIBA (Hungarian) A dish of goose meat and sauerkraut, cooked together *gulyas*-style, which means that paprika has in some way been artfully blended into the sour cream that is added to the dish. To prepare, onions, sauerkraut, and paprika are sautéed in goose fat; after the addition of goose stock, the cubed breast of goose, and garlic, the pot is covered and simmered for several hours. When done, a bit of the cooking liquid is mixed into sour cream and this, in turn, is stirred into the pot. This hearty dish is usually complemented with boiled potatoes. (See GULYAS, HUNGARIAN CUISINE, HUNGARIAN STEWS) COMPATIBLE WINES: A white wine, e.g., Sauterne, Tokay, Keknyelu, Graves, Hermitage Blanc, Schloss Vollrads, Johannisberg, Rüdesheim, Nierstein.

Káposztás Töltelék A cabbage preparation used to fill the flaky Hungarian pastries known as *rétes (Strudels)*. The cabbage is first grated then tossed with salt in a large bowl. It is left to stand for some time then squeezed dry. Bacon fat is rendered in a heavy pan in which sugar is allowed to caramelize. The cabbage is then cooked in the caramel until brown. Seasoned with pepper and salt, the cabbage is chilled before being used to fill the pastries. (See RÉTES, STRUDEL)

KAPUSTA CZARWONA DUSZONA (Polish) Red cabbage cooked with beef stock, bacon, caraway seeds, and lemon juice. At the end, red wine is added.

KARHI (East Indian) A rather thick, highly seasoned gruel composed of a mixture of chickpea flour, buttermilk, and water. This is added to spices, onion seeds, and dry peppers that have previously been cooked in oil. The mixture is simmered for an hour and flavored with lemon juice. *Pakoris* are placed in the soup just prior to its service. Usually, boiled white rice, a vegetable, and some sort of relish accompany this dish. (See PAKORIS) COMPATIBLE BEVERAGES: Tea or beer.

KARI/KARA (East Indian) These colloquial terms were used by the English to refer to "curry." The leaves of this Asiatic shrub have the aromatic flavor of curry without the accompanying bite. *Kari* leaves are used to season vegetables, fruit, and fish when just a light semblance of curry is needed. Because the leaves lose their flavor when dried, they are not sold in that form. (See CURRY, GARAM MASALA)

KARLSBAD, ROULADE OF VEAL (Czech) This roast veal dish is named in honor of Karlsbad, one of the most famous health spas in all of Europe. The veal, cut from the shoulder, is pounded, seasoned, then covered with slices of bacon and ham, scrambled eggs, and a relish made from chopped pickles. The veal is then rolled, fastened, and browned well in butter. Finally, the _roulade_ is roasted in a medium oven; it is periodically basted with the juice from the roast mixed with a bit of white wine. (See ROULADE) COMPATIBLE WINES: A white wine, e.g., Anjou, Orvieto, Zeltlinger Himmelreich, Piesporter Goldtröpfchen, Gewürztraminer, Riquewihr, Hermitage Blanc, Chenin Blanc.

KARTOFFEL KLÖSSE (German) Potato dumplings made from potatoes that have been cooked the day before, peeled, riced, and left uncovered to dry out. The dried potatoes, mixed with butter, salt, nutmeg, eggs, and flour, are formed into small balls with well-floured hands. These balls of dough are then dropped into boiling salted water and cooked until they have risen to the surface. They are then removed and rolled in toasted breadcrumbs. Before serving, they are sautéed in sweet butter. (See KLÖSSE)

KARTOFFELPUFFER (German) For this potato dish, grated potatoes are squeezed dry of all water then mixed with grated onions, eggs, flour, salt and pepper. Spoonfuls of the mixture are dropped into hot clarified butter and fried until brown on both sides. These _Kartoffelpuffer_ (potato puffs) are served with applesauce, usually accompanying roast pork and sausage dinners.

KASHA This food from Eastern Europe—Poland, Russia, and vicinity—is known in English as buckwheat groats. Available in various grades—fine, medium, and coarse—it is a nourishing food that can be prepared in many ways. _Kasha_ can be cooked in boiling water then drained and baked together with grated carrots, chopped onions, butter, and seasoning. This dish goes well with all manner of lamb dishes, makes an excellent stuffing for fish, meat, or poultry, or can be served as a garnish with many soups. It is also sometimes used as a filling for _kreplach, knishes,_ and _pirozhki._ (See KNISH, KREPLACH, PIROG)

Gurievskaya Kasha (Russian) For this sweet form of _kasha,_ buckwheat flour is simmered in honeyed milk for a few minutes; then, off the heat, eggs and butter are stirred in. This mixture is then layered in a pastry-lined pan alternately with chopped walnuts, candied fruits, and apricot preserves until the pan is filled. Sprinkled with finely grated, fresh breadcrumbs, the _kasha_ dish is baked until done.

Varnitchkes Kasha (Russian-Jewish) Buckwheat groats are first coated with egg yolk and then browned in a heavy pan. Finely chopped mushrooms and onions, salt, and pepper are added and lightly sautéed together with the groats. Then a hot chicken or beef stock is slowly added, stirring constantly until the groats are soft and cooked. Then cooked noodles are added, often the bow-tie variety. With butter or *schmaltz* drizzled over the top, the dish is placed under the broiler. (See SCHMALTZ)

KASHRUT The word *kosher* (*kasher* in Hebrew), meaning "fit, suitable," refers to the dietary laws by which observant Jews abide. (See KOSHER FOOD)

KASSAWA In Africa, this is the accepted spelling for cassava, a member of the manihot family. (See CASSAVA)

KASSELER RIPPCHEN (German) A method of preparing smoked spareribs or a loin of pork, made famous in Kassel, the capital of Hessen on the Fulda. To prepare the ribs in this way, they are first well browned. Then, in a roast pan with a bit of stock, sliced onions, and soup greens, the ribs are flavored with rosemary and roasted. A sauce is made by slaking the pan juices with white wine or with sour cream, binding it with flour, and adding salt, pepper, and a dash of Kirschwasser to flavor. The ribs are usually served with mashed potatoes, red cabbage, or sauerkraut. COMPATIBLE WINES: A white wine, e.g., Rüdesheim, Nierstein, Riesling, Vouvray, Graves, Gewürztraminer.

KATSUDON (Japanese) An omelette prepared by mixing finely chopped pork and onions with eggs. The cooked omelette is served over rice. COMPATIBLE BEVERAGES: Beer, tea, saké, rosé.

KATSUOBUSHI No Japanese kitchen is ever without *katsuobushi* (dried bonito, otherwise known as "skipjack tuna"). For the Japanese chef to serve cooked vegetables, a *dashi* soup stock, any dish using soybean curd, or even a rice dish without the delicate flavoring of *katsuobushi* (a slightly salty tuna fish flavor) would be unthinkable.

The drying, smoking, and fermentation of fresh bonito into the hard-textured, valuable, and most remarkable *katsuobushi* is a long, painstaking process. And to shave off or grate the extremely hard *katsuobushi* demands the use of a very sharp cutting tool. This amazing food product never spoils and is often presented as a gift to a grateful new bride. (See DASHI, SABABUSHI)

KEBAB Kebabs are said to have originated in the Caucasus, where the rugged mountain people impaled hunks of lamb on their swords and barbecued them over hot coals. The diner usually thinks of the *kebab* as consisting of pieces of meat cooked over charcoal and served with a spicy sauce. However, *kebabs* can be made from fish and vegetables as well as from meats. (See DÖNER KEBAB, SHAMI KEBAB, SHASHLIK, SHISHKEBAB) COMPATIBLE BEVERAGES: What one drinks depends largely upon the type of food cooked and the degree of spiciness of the accompanying sauce.

KEDGEREE (East Indian) This is the Anglicized version of the Hindustani word *kichri,* or *khitcherie,* which means "mishmash, hodgepodge." Indian white kedgeree is composed of white rice, *ghee,* and spices, whereas the yellow version is made with eggs and turmeric, which colors it yellow. Another version consists of layered flaked fish alternated with either mashed or sliced potatoes or with rice in a covered pan. Still another version consists of boiled rice, cooked pieces of fish—such as haddock, halibut, or cod—and chopped hard-boiled eggs, all carefully folded together. Then, with the addition of butter, heavy cream, salt, pepper, and nutmeg, the mixture is warmed and served. (See CONGEE)

KESHY YENA (South American) When the Dutch settled in the islands of the Netherland Antilles off of the coast of Venezuela in 1634, they brought their great cheeses, Edam and Gouda, with them. The natives of Curaçao, who speak Papiamento, a blending of the Afro-Spanish and Dutch languages, created _keshy yena_ by filling these cheeses with shrimp, beef, chicken, or fish and baking them.

Keshy Yena coe Cabaron Literally, "baked cheese stuffed with shrimp." A round Edam cheese is hollowed out and the slice cut off the top is reserved for use as a lid. The cheese shell and the lid are soaked in water while the scooped-out cheese is grated and stirred into a simmering mixture of chopped onions, tomatoes, salt, cayenne pepper, raisins, breadcrumbs, sweet pickles, black olives, and cooked minced shrimp. Beaten eggs are added to the thickening mixture and all is poured into the cheese shell, covered with the lid, and baked until the cheese becomes soft and bubbly. When served, it is cut into wedges. COMPATIBLE BEVERAGES: Beer, ale, stout, tea.

KETCHUP/CATSUP This thick, spicy, mushroom-based sauce has been known in England for centuries. The name probably is derived from the Chinese dialect term _koe tsiap,_ which was a type of fish-brine sauce similar to the ancient Roman _garum._ There are numerous varieties of ketchup used all over the world, including cranberry ketchup, cucumber ketchup, grape ketchup, and tomato ketchup. Tomato ketchup, the best known, is made by cooking chopped tomatoes and onions, and when tender, pressing them through a sieve. Then cinnamon, cloves, and garlic, tied in a cloth sack, are simmered in vinegar. The spiced vinegar is then added to the tomato purée and cooked together with sugar, salt, paprika, and cayenne pepper, stirring constantly until the sauce becomes quite thick. A Dr. William Kitchiner, who created the rather unusually-named "wow wow sauce," also turned his hand to a type of ketchup. He ignored the old tried-and-true mushroom and walnut ketchups to develop his own—one made of cockles and oysters and one made of brandy and lemon rind, which he named "pudding catsup." (See GARUM, WOW WOW)

KHARA MASALA (East Indian) A mixture of whole spices, such as black peppercorns, bay leaves, cardamom pods, cinnamon sticks, and red pepper. (See CURRY, GARAM MASALA)

KHEEMA WITH FRIED ONIONS (East Indian) After having fried a mixture of herbs, spices, chopped onions, and garlic in hot oil, the ground lamb *(kheema)* is added and browned. Yogurt, tomato purée, water, mace, nutmeg, salt, and cayenne are added, and the whole is brought to a boil. The pot is covered, and all is left to simmer for an hour. This frying and boiling process is called *bhoon.* When done, fried onion rings are added, and the dish is served either with a side dish of rice and spinach or one of potatoes flavored with asafoetida and cumin. (See ASAFOETIDA, BHOON, CUMIN) COMPATIBLE BEVERAGES: Tea, beer, ale.

KIANGSU COOKERY (Chinese) The type of cooking, done by the people of Kiangsu, probably the most prosperous province in China, is distinguished by the frequent use of sugar in salted and sour dishes.

KIBBEH (Middle Eastern) This might very well be called the hamburger of the Middle East. In Syrian and Lebanese kitchens, lamb and *burghul* (cracked wheat) are chopped and pounded into a paste and served raw. *Kibbeh* can also be baked in a shallow pan in layers, alternating with chopped lamb, onions, nuts, and cinnamon. A salad of chopped fresh cucumbers and a sauce composed of yogurt flavored with salt, garlic, and mint will complete the meal. COMPATIBLE BEVERAGES: Mint tea, beer, ale.

KIEŁBASA In Poland this is the generic term for sausage. However, in English-speaking countries the *kiełbasa* is more specifically a garlic-flavored sausage composed of both lean and fat pork made into rings about a foot and a half in length and an inch and a half thick. It is dried and smoked. Also known as "Polish sausage," it can be served either hot or cold.

Kiełbasa w. Polskim Sosie A sausage is simmered in beer and flavored with onions. Then, to a *roux,* a bit of the beer, salt, sugar, and vinegar are added. The warm sausage is served sliced with the thickened sauce poured over it, accompanied with boiled potatoes. COMPATIBLE BEVERAGES: Beer, ale, stout, or a good rosé wine.

KIEV, CHICKEN À LA (Russian) This chicken dish is so named because when the cooked chicken is pierced, the spouting butter is reminiscent of the spouting oil from the derricks in the Kiev region. To prepare the dish, raw breasts of plump chicken are cut in flat slices, seasoned, and covered with a layer of finely chopped mushrooms. Various herbs and crushed garlic are kneaded with cold butter; the butter is layered on each slice of chicken, which is then rolled and tied. When ordered in a restaurant, the chicken rolls are removed from the refrigerator, dipped first in beaten egg and then in breadcrumbs, and deep-fried a golden brown. The initial cut of the chicken by the diner should result in a geyser of golden melted butter. Today, unfortunately, it has become more expedient for restaurants to inject the butter into the already-cooked *galantines* of chicken just before serving them. The chicken is more succulent if the butter is inserted before cooking. (See GALANTINE) COMPATIBLE WINES: A white wine, e.g., Wehlener Sonnenuhr, Frascati, Vouvray, Gewürztraminer, Johannisberg, Montrachet.

KIM-CHEE A type of pickle served with most Korean dishes. Different vegetables are used to make *kim-chee* at different times of the year—cabbages, cucumbers, onions, turnips, parsnips, or whatever is available—but the overpowering character of the pickle is a spicy, sharp, sour odor. Some pickles are marinated for days, other for six months or more. The taste for *kim-chee* must be acquired.

One popular variety is made of a mixture of chopped pears, pine nuts, and red peppers, which is rolled into cabbage leaves which have been soaking in a special briny marinade for several hours, days, or often weeks. The tightly rolled-up leaves are packed in an earthenware crock and either set in a totally dark place or buried in the ground. After about three days, the *kim-chee* are ready to eat. They are usually served cold together with hot boiled rice.

KING, CHICKEN À LA (American) Stories about the origin of this dish abound. One tells how Mrs. Foxhall Keene first happened to suggest the dish to the chef at Delmonico's Restaurant in New York City, another how the chef at Claridge's in London named the dish after his father, J.R. King. There have also been confirmations of the dish having been born in Miami, or way out on the tip of Long Island, or, yes, even at the Waldorf Astoria in New York City. No one seems to know for sure when or where chicken à la king was first served, but it is prepared by cooking sliced mushrooms and green peppers in butter, to which a mixture of sherry, salt, cayenne pepper, and a cream sauce made by adding heavy cream and lemon juice to a *sauce Béchamel* is added. This is brought to a boil and then, off the heat, a mixture of egg yolks and cream is added. Lastly, diced cooked chicken is added and merely heated, not cooked. When served, the chicken and sauce are spooned over toast, and the final touch is the use of a bit of pimiento to decorate the top. (See BÉCHAMEL, PIMIENTO) COMPATIBLE WINES: A white wine, e.g., Meursault, Montrachet, Riquewihr, Ammerschwihr, Chenin Blanc, Pinot Chardonnay, Graves, Riesling, Orvieto.

KINUGOSHI (Japanese) Sold water-packed in rectangular cakes, this refined type of *tofu* is soft and silklike. It is too delicate for use in simmered, broiled, or stir-fried dishes. It is steamed. (See CHIRI-MUSHI, TOFU)

KIPPER To have "kippered herring" for breakfast is a real treat for an Englishman. The term "kipper" refers to herring that is split, salted, and smoked. The best kippers are pale copper in color. Kippers can be fried, grilled, poached, or even made into a mousse.

Kipper Mousse For this kipper appetizer, first an aspic jelly is made, then the kippers are gently poached in a solution of milk and water. The fish are skinned and boned, and the meat is chopped into cubes. About half of the aspic is stirred into a white sauce (flour, butter, and boiling milk), then the chopped kippers are added together with the poaching liquid. This is left to cool. Stiffly beaten whipped cream is folded into the cool fish jelly and placed in the refrigerator to set. Warm water is added to the other half of the aspic, and this is poured over the unmolded mousse to coat it. The dish is served garnished with a border of thinly sliced cucumbers.

KIRSCHENSUPPE (German) The term for two very special cherry soups. One is served hot and one cold. The hot soup is made with pitted cherries cooked in water with cinnamon and lemon peel. The cherries are then puréed and cooked together with red wine in which crushed cherry stones have been boiled. After boiling, the liquid is strained and thickened with potato flour. The soup is served hot with crushed *Zwieback* strewn over the top. The cold variation is made by simmering puréed cherries in a mixture of lemon juice and sherry. After being set to cool, cloves, ginger, and cinnamon are added. Light cream is folded into the creamy soup, which is then chilled until ready to serve. (See ZWIEBACK)

KIRSCHPFANNKUCHEN, BASLER (Swiss) This cherry pancake comes from the city of Basel, which is known not only as a port on the Rhine and as a pharmaceutical center but also for its juicy black cherries. The pancake is made by first soaking breakfast rolls in milk. Then, butter and sugar are creamed, egg yolks are added, and the mixture is poured over the milk-softened rolls. Then, grated almonds, flour, cinnamon, and baking powder are mixed in a bowl, into which the milk-softened rolls and stiffly beaten egg whites are stirred. Finally, pitted cherries and macaroon crumbs are added, and the whole mass is poured into a buttered mold and baked until done. This delectable pancake can be eaten hot or cold.

KISHKE (Jewish) In Russian, *kishka* means "intestine," and for this dish a beef intestine is stuffed with onion-flavored mashed potatoes, breadcrumbs, *schmaltz,* herbs, and spices. After blanching in boiling water, the intestine is dried and baked in oil together with coarsely sliced onions. *Kishke* complements such dishes as roast fowl and beef. (See SCHMALTZ)

KLÉBER, TOURNEDOS (French) A steak named in honor of a French general, Jean Baptiste Kléber, who did not die on the battlefield but was assassinated in Cairo. There is also a famous guide book of France named after him. This *tournedos,* a cut taken from the heart of a fillet of beef, is broiled and served with goose liver and coated with a truffle sauce. (See TOURNEDOS) COMPATIBLE WINES: A red wine, e.g., Talbot, Ausone, Mouton Rothschild, La Tâche, Richebourg, Échézeaux, Barolo, Dôle, Cabernet Sauvignon.

KLÖSSE (German) Also known as *Knödel,* these light, fluffy dumplings are a favorite accompaniment for a roast loin of pork or a *Sauerbraten.* (See KARTOFFEL KLÖSSE, KNÖDEL, SAUERBRATEN)

KMINOVA POLEVKA (Czech) A rather unusual soup made from caraway seeds. Paprika and caraway seeds are added to a golden *roux,* then water is added. After bringing the soup to a boil, it is simmered gently to extract the flavor from the caraway seeds. The soup is served garnished with croutons that have been fried in butter until golden. (See CROÛTONS, ROUX)

KNACKWURST/KNOCKWURST (German) A short, thick sausage made from ground pork, beef and pork fat, cumin seeds, salt, and just enough garlic to give it zest. These sausages are dried, smoked, and usually served after having been warmed in hot water but never boiled.

KNAIDLACH (Jewish) *Matzo* meal dumplings (*knaidel,* singular), usually served floating in rich, tasty chicken broth. Although some have suggested that the *knaidel* bears some relationship to the round stone (also called *knaidel*) which Moses supposedly used to smash the walls and free his people from Egyptian bondage, it would be more logical to trace the origin of the dumpling to the German *Knödel,* "dumpling." (See BRAMBOROVE KNEDLÍKY, HUSKOVE KNEDLÍKY, MATZO)

KNISH (Jewish) The *knish* originated in the Ukraine of Russia, where it is called *pirog.* It is made from mashed potatoes mixed with egg, a good dollop of *schmaltz* (rendered chicken fat), some salt and flour to form a stiff dough, which is cut into rounds and baked until brown. Variations stem from this basic recipe, such as first making a hollow in the *knish* then filling it with chopped leftover meats, liver, cheese, hard-boiled eggs, or chicken, each filling bound with a raw egg. Some are filled with *gribenes* (fried bits of poultry skin) or with *kasha.* There is even a sweet version made with a filling composed of chopped nuts, cinnamon, raisins, grated lemon peel, cheese, and raw eggs. Prior to baking, the sweet *knishes* are brushed with butter and dusted with cinnamon, sugar, and chopped nuts. (See GRIBENES, PIROG/PIROZHKI, RAVIOLI, SCHMALTZ, WONTON)

KNÖDEL (German) Dumpling. (See KLÖSSE, KNEDLÍKY, SPÄTZLE)

KOBE BEEF Although the Japanese people ate very little beef until the middle of the nineteenth century, today their *kobe* and *matsuzaka* cattle are so pampered, massaged, and fattened daily with good beer that they yield a well-marbled beef that is considered to be the most tender and tasty in the world.

KÖFTE (Turkish) In Central India, where this meatball originated, it is known as *kooftah.* These are balls of minced mutton or beef blended with onions, garlic, ginger, and other spices. An Anglo-Indian version consists of small *kooftahs* and a curry with pickled chilies, tomato paste, and lemon juice. (See FRIKADELLER, KÖTTBULLAR, NARGISI KOFTAS) COMPATIBLE BEVERAGES: Beer, ale, tea, rosé wine.

KOIMO (Japanese) A type of potato similar to the starchy, tuberous rootstock of the taro plant. After boiling, a mere squeeze will pop the *koimo* from their skins.

KÖKSISTER (Dutch) A rich pastry made from a yeast dough enriched with eggs and various spices, such as nutmeg, cloves, coriander, and cinnamon. The dough is rolled out flat, cut into strips, and deep-fried to a deep brown color. To serve, these crisp pastry batons are dipped in a syrup made from brown sugar, water, and cinnamon. *Köksister* is also a favorite in South Africa.

KOKTEYL BÖREĞI (Turkish) The Turkish term for *börek* sticks, made from *phyllo* pastry sheets that are brushed with melted butter, sprinkled with grated Parmesan cheese, then cut and rolled up into six-inch lengths. Placed side by side on a baking sheet and brushed with melted butter, the sticks are baked until golden brown. Delicious served at cocktail time. (See BÖREK, PHYLLO)

KOLATSCHEN (German) Small yeast cakes.

Finger Kolatschen An Austrian dessert consisting of a dough made from flour, honey, hazelnuts, figs, and lemon. The dough is formed into small balls, and when placed in the pan in the oven, a finger indentation is left in each one. After baking, these indentations are filled with raspberry, apricot, or any other fruit preserve. Even soft white cream cheese is used, sugared or plain.

KOMBU (Japanese) Dried kelp (seaweed).

Dashi Kombu This is about six inches wide, rather tough in texture, and is used to prepare the *dashi* soup stock. (See DASHI)

KOME (Japanese) Rice.

KÖNIGSBERGER KLOPSE (German) This speciality comes from the former capital of East Prussia, Königsberg, which since World War II has been renamed Kalinengrad. The city is now so very Russian that its present inhabitants are unfamiliar with *Klopse,* which are world famous.

Klopse are delectable meatballs made from finely ground veal and pork, which are slowly simmered in a rich beef bouillon until tender. A *roux* is made from pork fat and flour; to this, sour cream, egg yolks, lemon juice, salt, and pepper are added. The *Klopse* are then warmed in this sauce and served with either boiled potatoes or potato dumplings. (See ROUX) COMPATIBLE WINES: A white wine, e.g., Nierstein, Rüdesheim, Gewürztraminer, Sylvaner, Tokay, Johannisberg, Riesling, Orvieto, Frascati, Sauvignon Blanc.

KÖNIGSWURST (German) Known as "the sausage of the king" because of its delicate richness, this large sausage is made from ground chicken and partridge meat enhanced with finely chopped truffles and mushrooms, all bound with raw eggs and seasoned with mace, salt, pepper, and a dash of white wine. This "royal" sausage is cooked, allowed to cool, and served as an appetizer. COMPATIBLE BEVERAGES: Beer, ale, stout.

KONNYAKU (Japanese) A white root vegetable. Gelatinous and opaque, it is sold in blocks. Sliced *à la julienne* or cubed, it is cooked together with meat and other vegetables in a richly seasoned broth. (See JULIENNE)

KOORMAH (Arabian) See KORMA

KOPELO (Bulgarian) A cold eggplant purée, served as a salad course. The eggplant is first roasted in the oven until the skin turns black and begins to flake. Then the eggplant is peeled and the meat removed and placed into a mixing bowl, where it is ground to a pulp. Slowly, while constantly stirring, olive oil and vinegar are added plus crushed garlic, salt, and pepper. The salad is thoroughly chilled before serving.

KOPFSÜLZE (German) Head cheese. The head, bones, feet, and skin of a pig are covered with cold water then simmered with root vegetables and spices. When done, the meat is drained and cut into small pieces. It is left to cool and the resulting aspic is poured out and mixed with vegetables of different colors—carrots, onions, beets—cornichons, hard-boiled eggs, and dill pickles. This is all poured into a form together with the cooked pieces of pork and refrigerated. It is served cool in slices. (See HEAD CHEESE, SÜLZE) COMPATIBLE BEVERAGE: A good beer.

KOREAN CUISINE Korean cooking may be said to be akin to the Szechwan style of China, for Korean dishes are unusually hot and spicy. Garlic and hot chili peppers are used extensively. Meals begin with a hearty soup, with no appetizers served before, then like the Chinese, Koreans eat their food cut up into small pieces always served with boiled rice. The pickle *kim-chee,* a national relish, is served with every meal. Koreans often borrow what they consider to be the best of neighboring cuisines. Therefore, one finds Chinese noodles wedded to Japanese dishes and their own meat, vegetable, or fish dishes married to various Indian-type curry sauces.

KORMA (Arab) Sometimes called *koormah* or *quoarmah.* For this dish, meat (usually mutton or fowl) is marinated in a mixture of sour curd, onions, garlic, ginger, coriander, turmeric, pepper, ground poppy seeds, and ground almonds. The meat is then sautéed in *ghee* flavored with cloves, cinnamon, and salt. Sometimes a thick coconut cream is substituted for the *ghee. Korma* is served with boiled white rice. (See GHEE) COMPATIBLE BEVERAGES: Mint tea, beer.

KOSHER FOOD The word *kosher* (literally, "fit or proper") refers to food that is proper for the Jewish people to consume as set out in the laws of *kashrut* (the kosher dietary laws) in the Old Testament. Observant Jews are permitted to eat the following foods:

- The flesh of quadrupeds that chew their cud and have cloven hoofs;
- All fish that have fins and scales;
- Birds that are not scavengers or birds of prey;
- Only meat slaughtered by a *shochet,* a specially trained butcher.

It is against the law for Jews to eat blood or meats that have been cooked with milk or with anything derived from milk. In other words, a steak cannot be eaten topped with butter; cheese cannot close a meat meal; nor can milk be served as a beverage when meat is on the menu. The term "Jewish cuisine" refers to a conglomerate of dishes of *many* nations which have been adopted by the Jews while living in those lands. It can therefore be said that the only truly Jewish food is that prepared in accordance with the kosher dietary laws. There is a distinct difference between a restaurant that serves "Jewish" food and one that serves "kosher" food. (See JEWISH CUISINE)

KOSHI-AN (Japanese) Used in dessert fillings and in other confections, *koshi-an* consists of *azuki* beans that are first cooked and then ground into a paste. (See AZUKI, MANJU)

KOSHNIKES (Jewish) A Slavic term used by Jews to describe those *knishes* that are served filled with *kasha.* (See KASHA, KNISH)

KOTA METHISMÉNI (Greek) A dish of sautéed chicken breasts that have been well marinated in lemon juice, salt, and pepper and then simmered in brandy until the liquor has been absorbed. The breasts continue to simmer in half a cup of heavy cream. COMPATIBLE WINES: A white wine, e.g., Montrachet, Anjou, Graves, Riesling, Piesporter Goldtröpfchen, Orvieto, Frascati, Sauvignon Blanc.

KÖTTBULLAR (Swedish) *Kött* is Swedish for beef, and *köttbullar* are the famous Swedish meatballs. To prepare, ground round steak and pork are mixed with chopped onions, mashed potatoes, bread bits soaked in milk, eggs, salt, and pepper. The mixture is formed into small meatballs, which are then fried in hot butter until brown and removed. Flour, water, and sugar are added to the pan drippings and stirred to create a thick sauce. With the addition of heavy cream, the meatballs are replaced in the pan, simmered a moment, and served. (See KÖFTE, FRIKADELLER) COMPATIBLE WINES: A white wine, e.g., Traminer, Chenin Blanc, Corton Charlemagne, Dry Sauterne, Johannisberg, Orvieto, Schloss Vollrads.

KOULIBIAC (Russian) Also spelled *kulebyaka,* and in America and England written *coulibiac,* this speciality was actually introduced to Russia by German immigrants, who called it *Kohlgebäck.* It consists of rectangular sheets of puff pastry layered alternately with rice, meat, and sliced hard-boiled eggs. Another version is made with poached fillets of sole, salmon, or turbot alternated with a rich *Duxelles* plus herbes and spices and served topped with butter and chopped *viazega* (sturgeon marrow, taken from the backbone of the fish). After layering, the whole is covered with another sheet of puff pastry or with a *pâte à brioche* and baked until golden brown. (See BRIOCHE, DUXELLES, KOHLGEBÄCK) COMPATIBLE WINES: The choice of wine depends upon the fillings used.

KOYATOFU (Japanese) Dried soybean curd. This cheeselike high-protein food is pressed into three-inch cubes. When still fresh—that is, not dried—it is called *tofu.* (See TOFU)

KRÄUTERBUTTER (German) A much-used herb-butter, called *beurre à la maître d'hôtel* by the French. It is made by kneading together a mixture of sweet butter, lemon juice, a bit of Worcestershire sauce, salt, and various herbs—such as chives, parsley and chervil—and rolling the result in wax paper. It is stored in the refrigerator and pieces of it are chopped off as needed to garnish steaks and other meats coming from the grill. The addition of a grated hard cheese is optional. In Switzerland, sapsago cheese is used, a cheese made from skimmed milk and Swiss mountain clover. (See MAÎTRE D'HÔTEL)

KREPLACH (Jewish) Similar to the Italian *ravioli,* this traditional dish is made from a noodle dough that is cut into square shapes and filled with minced chicken, ground meats, cheese, or *kasha* (buckwheat). These stuffed squares of dough are poached in boiling salted water and served with soup. During the Middle Ages, *kreplach* dough was made sweet with honey, filled with fruit, and fried until a golden brown, much like a French *crêpe.* (See CRÊPE, KASHA, PIROG, RAVIOLI)

KRITHARAKI (Greek) Barley.

Kritharosoupa Already in Ancient Greece, barley was a staple food; it was made into porridge. Today, however, it is more refined. The barley is first cooked in a consommé flavored with celery and enriched with cream before serving.

KROGVÄRDENS SÄS (Swedish) This "innkeeper's sauce" is made by heating a mixture of butter, egg yolks, dry mustard, sugar and minced onions in a double boiler until thick and then flavoring it with chopped tarragon and pepper. The sauce is chilled before serving. It is used to enhance the flavor of boiled or steamed fish.

KROMESKI/KROMESKY See CROMESQUI

KRUMKAKER (Swedish) A type of pastry made from a batter of potato flour, ordinary wheat flour, eggs, butter, sugar, and water. The batter is baked in a special *krumkake* iron, which presses a lacelike design into the batter as it bakes it to a golden brown. As soon as the pastries are baked, while they are still pliant, they are carefully rolled around a conical form. When cool, these horns, or *krumkaker,* are filled with whipped cream mixed with apricot or raspberry preserves.

KRUPNIK The word *krupnik* sounds much like the name of a character from a Gogol novel, but the name really is derived from the Russian word *krupa,* "grain." *Krupnick,* a soup popular in Poland, is made by first "seizing" barley and chopped mushrooms in a heavy pot with hot butter. Then the pot is filled with hot bouillon. Diced potatoes, green beans, and a sprinkling of parsley are added at the end of the cooking period. When stewing beef and lamb, onions, tomatoes, and spices are added; this soup becomes a meal-in-itself. COMPATIBLE WINES: A red wine, e.g., Dôle, Pinot Noir, Chianti, Côte Rôtie, Valpolicella, Bardolino, Barolo, Mercurey.

KUCHEN (German) Cake.

KUCHENRAGOUT (German) A "whatever-there-is-in-the-kitchen stew," composed of various foodstuffs that surprisingly go very well together, such as pieces of young chicken, sweetbreads, meatballs made of veal forcemeat, mussels, and asparagus—all cooked together in a sauce of cream, butter, and eggs. COMPATIBLE WINES: A white wine, e.g., Riesling, Gewürztraminer, Piesporter Goldtröpfchen, Orvieto, Aigle, Chenin Blanc, Johannisberg.

KUGEL (Jewish) The word *Kugel,* German for "ball" or "cannonball," here refers to a type of pudding. One version is made from grated raw potatoes which are mixed with egg yolks, grated onions, baking powder, salt, and pepper. Whipped egg whites are folded into the potato mixture which, topped with breadcrumbs, is baked in the oven. Another version is made of noodles and vegetables and both are usually served with boiled or roasted meat. (See FARFEL)

KUGELHOPF (French) Also spelled *Guglhupf, Gougelhopf,* or even *Gugelhopf.* Though famous as an Alsatian yeast cake, culinary scribes insist that M. Eugène, the master chef to the Austrian minister, handed the recipe for the cake to Carême, who in the end was responsible for the cake's great popularity in France. The dough is made with flour, yeast, plenty of eggs and butter, and seedless raisins. The bundt pan into which the dough is placed is dotted up the sides and on the bottom with sliced blanched almonds. (See COLOMBA, PANETTONE)

KULEBYAKA (Russian) See KOULIBIAC

KULOLO (Hawaiian) See TARO

KUMQUAT This ornamental shrub of the rue family, closely related to the orange and other citrus fruits, is widely cultivated in China, Japan, and the United States. The small sweet-tart orange-colored fruits are eaten fresh or made into preserves. Kumquats are sold bottled in syrup or pickled in wine vinegar. They can be served with ice cream, and the fresh fruit is sometimes substituted for the orange as a garnish for braised duck.

KUROMAME (Japanese) Black beans.

KUSHIAGE (Japanese) The method of deep-frying foods that have been heavily coated with breadcrumbs.

LADY CURZON She was an elegant English noblewoman, the spouse of Lord Curzon, once Viceroy of India. When her name is included in the name of a dish, the presence of curry is indicated.

Poulet Lady Curzon (French) A young plump chicken, stuffed with boiled white rice, *foie gras,* and truffles, is well braised. When ready for the table, the bird is coated with a rich curry sauce composed of heavy cream and coconut milk. (See FOIE GRAS) COMPATIBLE BEVERAGES: Beer, ale, tea.

Potage Lady Curzon This soup, prepared from a turtle soup to which heavy cream flavored with curry and a touch of sherry is added, is served in cups, topped with whipped cream and sprinkled with paprika or curry powder.

LAFITTE, POULET SAUTÉ (French) A fried chicken dish named in honor of French banker and politician Jacques Lafitte, a contemporary of the famous Jewish banking family, the Rothschilds. A young chicken is disjointed, seasoned, and sautéed in butter until brown. Then, dusted with flour, the chicken is cooked until the flour has turned a light tan color. After adding chicken broth, red wine, mushrooms, and diced tomatoes *(concasser),* the dish is cooked until the flavors have melded. The chicken pieces are removed and the sauce is reduced, strained, and poured over the chicken. (See CON CASSER) COMPATIBLE WINES: Beaujolais, Valpolicella, Côte Rôtie, Margaux, Savigny, Fleurie, Mercurey, Zinfandel.

LAHMAJOON (Armenian) Also known as *missahatz,* this was originally Arabic (the name derives from the Arabic words *lachim,* "meat," and *ajin,* "pie"). A yeast dough is divided into small balls, which are then flattened and topped with a mixture of ground lamb, finely chopped onions, green peppers, tomatoes, parsley, mint, garlic, lemon juice, salt, and cayenne pepper. The pies are baked in a hot oven then browned under the broiler. They are topped with paprika or yogurt and served with a green salad. COMPATIBLE BEVERAGES: Beer, tea, saké, rosé wine.

LAMAZE, SAUCE (American) This cold sauce, the creation of a chef named Lamaze of Hollywood, California, and a favorite sauce of the great chef Albert Stockli, blends a *sauce Mayonnaise* with mustard, ketchup, chili sauce, and a bit of A-One sauce. To this is added finely chopped pimientos, celery, chives, green peppers, parsley, hard-boiled eggs, and grated fresh horseradish. Stockli, the chef whose imagination and know-how produced such great restaurants as New York's Forum of the Twelve Caesars, Four Seasons, Tower Suite, La Fonda del Sol, and La Trattoria, as well as the popular Zum Zum restaurants, served this sauce with seafood, eggs, or poultry and often as a salad dressing.

LANGOSTA (Spanish) Lobster.

LANGOSTINO (Spanish) Crawfish. (See LOBSTER)

LANGOUSTE (French) Crawfish. A large crustacean, although also called the "spiny" lobster, has not the meaty claws of the lobster but long, whip-like antennae instead. (See LOBSTER)

LAP CHONG (Chinese) Pork sausage. The Chinese have two favorite sausages: *lap chong,* made from finely ground pork mixed with spices, and *opp gang chong,* made from duck liver.

LAPÉROUSE, POULET SAUTÉ (French) A fried chicken dish named in honor of an eighteenth-century French navigator, Jean-François de Galaud, Comte de la Pérouse. The chicken is cut up, sautéed in butter, and removed from the pan. The pan is deglazed with brandy, then a mushroom purée bound with egg yolks and heavy cream is added. The sauce is poured over the chicken, which is glazed and served garnished with artichoke hearts filled with a mushroom purée. (See DEGLAZE) COMPATIBLE WINES: A white wine, e.g., Sauterne, Orvieto, Gewürztraminer, Graacher Himmelreich, Schloss Vollrads, Vouvray.

LAPIN (French) Rabbit.

LARD See BARD

LASAGNE (Italian) Large, rectangular strips of *pasta,* which are boiled in salted water until just tender. There is also a green *lasagne,* which is flavored with spinach, called *lasagne verde.*

Lasagne al Forno In this most popular method of serving *lasagne,* the cooked *pasta* strips are placed in a baking dish alternately with layers of sliced mozzarella cheese, a sauce *Béchamel,* a *ragù,* and lastly, more *pasta* strips. Grated Parmesan cheese is sprinkled over the top and the dish is baked. (See BÉCHAMEL, PASTA, RAGÙ) COMPATIBLE WINES: A red wine, e.g., Chianti, Egri Bikaver, Bardolino, Beaujolais, Zinfandel, Nebbiolo.

LASSI (East Indian) A yogurt diluted with water, which according to preference can be served salty, sweet, or spiced. The beverage is taken with Indian food.

LATKE (Jewish) Supposedly, this is the pancake which the wives of the Maccabees quickly cooked for their soldier-husbands as they prepared to drive the ancient Syrians from their land. Today, it is eaten during the Jewish holiday of Chanukah, the Feast of Lights, which commemorates this great victory. *Latkes* are prepared from grated raw potatoes mixed with raw eggs, flour, salt, and pepper. The resulting paste is formed into little patties and fried in hot oil. Grated cheese and onions are often added, and generally applesauce and sour cream are served on the side.

LA TZE CHI (Chinese) Chicken with peppers. This method of cooking chicken comes from the Szechwan Province, and there is nothing subtle about it. It is a very, very hot dish that truly reflects the inordinate love of pepper and hot food that these hardy people have. To prepare this taste treat, breasts of chicken are boiled, cooled, then cut into bite-size pieces. In another pot, very hot green peppers are blanched in scalding water then quickly sautéed in a hot skillet shining with peanut oil. With the addition of the chicken, salt, sugar, crushed garlic, some finely-chopped candied ginger, water, and the fine Szechwan pepper called *fagara,* the pot is covered and all the ingredients are cooked just long enough to meld this exotic contrast of flavors. COMPATIBLE BEVERAGES: Beer, ale, saké.

LAUREL LEAVES Laurel leaves, or bay leaves, come from the sweet bay tree, an evergreen of the laurel family, which grows in Mediterranean countries and in Turkey, Portugal, Mexico, and Guatamala. The tree produces yellow flowers and purple berries, and the smooth leaves, used as a spice, are dark green on the upper surface and a pale gray-green on the lower. The crushed leaves emit a fragrant aroma, though the taste is somewhat bitter. Laurel leaves, a must for any kitchen, are used to flavor game, poultry, fish, soups, and sauces, and they are basic to a good marinade.

LAVASH (Russian) A special bread from the Caucasus, that fertile belly of the Soviet Union that the Armenians, the Azerbaidzhanis, and the Georgians call home. The dough, a simple one—a mixture of water, yeast, sugar, salt, and flour—is left to rise twice before being shaped into ovals about 18 inches in diameter and baked. The bread—thin and crisp—is excellent served as a cracker with cocktails. When softened, it can be used to sandwich various cheeses and meats.

LEBER, GEBRATEN (German) Breaded and fried calf's liver.

LEBER, GEHACKTE (Jewish) These German words literally translate to "chopped liver," and chicken, lamb, veal or beef liver can be used to make this tasty dish. The livers are salted and broiled to just a pink stage to remove most of the blood. They are then chopped fine and mixed with *schmaltz* (rendered chicken fat), chopped raw or sautéed onions, hard-boiled eggs plus sugar, salt, and pepper to taste. Served as an appetizer, thin slices of rye and pumpernickel bread are served separately. (See SCHMALTZ) COMPATIBLE WINES: A white wine, e.g., Keknyleyu, Orvieto, Chenin Blanc, Gewürztraminer.

LEBERWURST (German) Liver sausage, prepared from pig's liver, fine pork, allspice, and various seasonings and herbs. Available either fresh or smoked.

LEBKUCHEN (German) This richly spiced cake, first produced in Nürnberg during the Middle Ages, is favored by Swiss, German, and Austrian children, especially at Christmastime. It is made from flour, salt, baking powder, ground cloves, cinnamon, and allspice mixed with honey, brown sugar, candied lemon peel, eggs, and nuts.

Lebkuchen is often baked in the form of little men or even small doll houses which are elaborately decorated with candied cherries and other fruits and almonds and walnuts galore. In America, the Pennsylvania Dutch kitchens are famous for their *Lebkuchen,* which is similar to gingerbread.

LECKERLI, BASLER (Swiss) Having originated in Basel, Switzerland's prosperous port on the Rhine, this is a rectangular cookie that is richly flavored with honey, almonds, candied lemon peel, cloves, nutmeg, and ginger. The *Leckerli* connoisseur will know at first taste whether the cookies have been laced with Kirschwasser, which the Baslers love.

LECZINSKA, MARIE Marie, the wife of Louis XV of France, saw to it that Vincent de la Chapelle, the chef to Louis, prepared certain dishes under her own guidance and sponsorship. Among these were the *bouchées,* called *à la reine* after her good self, as well as *consommé à la reine* and the *poulet à la reine.* (See BOUCHÉE, CONSOMMÉ, REINE)

Poulet à la Reine Marie Leczinska was determined to please King Louis with this chicken. The pieces of chicken, seasoned with salt, pepper, and paprika, are simmered in a tomato purée. A *roux* made with chopped onions, paprika, and heavy cream is added to the sauce just before serving. The chicken is coated with the sauce and encircled with *timbales* of puréed chicken. (See ROUX, TIMBALES) COMPATIBLE WINES: A red wine, e.g., Valpolicella, Beaujolais, Santenay, Médoc, Margaux, Egri Bikaver, Premiat, Cabernet Sauvignon; or a white wine, e.g., Meursault, Corton.

LEEK One of the most delicately flavored members of the onion family, the leek is very important to flavorful soups and stews. Leeks are excellent by themselves, boiled until just tender and served with melted butter and lemon juice. (See COCK-A-LEEKIE SOUP)

Leek and Cheese Pie The word "leek" brings to mind the brave Welshmen—those shepherds, farmers, and forest dwellers who, in fighting for king and country, wore huge leeks in their helmets to distinguish themselves from their enemies. Today, to commemorate their valiant efforts, on Saint David's Day the Welsh adorn their hats with leek leaves.

The leek has become the favorite food of the Welsh (legend says that the leek has given them such extraordinary singing voices), and for this truly Welsh dish pieces of broiled bacon together with chopped leeks that have been sautéed in butter are placed into a baked pie crust with a rich custard batter made from eggs, heavy cream, salt, pepper, nutmeg, and grated Parmesan cheese. The pie is baked in a moderate oven for an hour or until the blade of a knife comes out clean.

LEGUMI (Italian) Vegetables. (See CONTORNI)

LETTUCE Eaten in ancient Greece at the end of the meal, the Romans later adopted lettuce as well, but they ate it as an appetizer. For many centuries lettuce was so esteemed that only those of noble birth were allowed to eat it. Others were punished by flogging if caught with only a leaf in their hand. Lettuce is mainly used as a salad vegetable, but it can also be braised. There are many kinds of lettuce, including Bibb, romaine, iceberg, and head. A narcotic used as a substitute for opium is made from the thickened juices of a certain species of lettuce.

LEVER MED SUR GRÄDDE (Swedish) Liver with sour cream. After cleaning and drying, calf's liver is larded with strips of bacon, rolled in seasoned flour, and browned in pork fat. Then, covered with milk, the liver is simmered for an hour, at which time sour cream is added and warmed through. (See BOURGEOISE) COMPATIBLE WINES: A white wine, e.g., Tokay, Vouvray, Graves, Schloss Vollrads, Keknyelu, Sauterne, Wehlener Sonnenuhr, Riesling.

LIÉGEOISE, À LA (Belgian) Named after the city of Liège, a Belgian town near the German border, this classic method of Belgian cooking involves the use of juniper berries as a flavoring. Veal kidneys or small game birds such as quail or thrushes may be prepared in this manner. After being braised in butter flavored with juniper berries, the dish is flamed with gin, a liquor made from juniper berries.

LIHAMUREKEPIIRAS (Finnish) A meat loaf baked in a sour cream pastry shell. The pastry dough is made by working butter, salt, and flour together with eggs and sour cream to form a fine dough. This is rolled out flat and placed in a buttered loaf pan. The meat mixture— composed of chopped beef, pork, and veal—is mixed with chopped mushrooms, onions, and parsley and cooked in a skillet. After seasoning with salt and pepper and grated Cheddar cheese, the meat mixture is positioned in the center of the dough in the loaf pan, covered with another sheet of dough, and baked in a medium oven until the pastry turns a golden brown. The meat loaf is served in slices with bowls of sour cream and fresh lingonberries. COMPATIBLE WINES: A red wine, e.g., Beaujolais, Cahors, Zinfandel, Valpolicella, Fleurie, Petit Sirah, Châteauneuf-du-Pape, Egri Bikaver.

L'ÎLE FLOTTANTE (French) "The Floating Island" dessert is made by first poaching spoonfuls of stiffly beaten egg white in a vanilla-flavored milk. The poached whites are reserved and a custard is made by adding egg yolks to the same milk. The "island" is formed by pouring the custard into a dish with puffs of the egg white piled in the center topped with caramel. The dish is served cold.

LIMOUSINE, À LA (French) A descriptive phrase for dishes prepared in the style of the French city Limoges, so famous for its fine porcelain. *Limousine* means that chestnuts in some form are present in the dish.
Chou Rouge à la Limousine Red cabbage cooked in bouillon with bacon fat and garnished with braised chestnuts.
Potage Limousine This thick soup is made by enriching a purée of

chestnuts and celery with heavy cream. It is served with a garnish of croutons and diced celery.

LING AU (Chinese) The term for the lotus root, actually for the stem of the large aquatic plant which, in the Buddhist religion, embodies the Eternal Entity. The cooked lotus stem, usually cut crosswise, is crisp and crunchy, with a nutlike taste. However, nearly all of the plant can be utilized: the stamens as an astringent, the seeds as an aphrodisiac or in soups. The leaves are used as wrappers for rice, forcemeats, and vegetables. (See LING JI, LOTUS BUNS)

LING JI (Chinese) The seeds of the sacred lotus flower. Used in the preparation of Oriental sweet dishes. (See LING AU, LOTUS BUNS)

LINGUINI (Italian) See PASTA

LINZERTORTE (Austrian) This rich, crunchy, raspberry-filled cake originated in Linz, on the Danube. The spicy crust (flavored with cloves, cinnamon, lemon peel, and vanilla) is filled with a rich raspberry jam, topped with a latticework of strips of the same dough as the crust, and baked. The torte is sometimes served dusted with vanilla-flavored powdered sugar.

LIPTAUER, AUSTRIAN A favorite appetizer whose name was borrowed from the soft Hungarian cheese from the province of Liptauer. Since Liptauer cheese has but little flavor of its own—it is much like a cream or a pot cheese—it is served as an appetizer in one of two ways. One involves placing the cheese in the center of a plate and surrounding it with various garnishes, such as capers, chopped chives, chopped onions, mustard, chopped anchovies, ground pepper, and paprika. The other method entails mixing the above listed ingredients into the cheese and serving the flavored cheese surrounded with slices of pumpernickel or sourdough bread. (See PUMPERNICKEL) COMPATIBLE BEVERAGES: Beer, ale, stout, tea.

LIVOURNAISE, À LA (French) A style of cooking prevalent in the vicinity of Livorno, a coastal Italian town not too distant from Pisa, where the use of chestnuts and ham are predominant.

Pheasant à la Livournaise A pair of pheasants are filled with chopped mushrooms and chestnuts then placed in a casserole atop a bed of sliced ham and peeled whole mushrooms. Moistened with red wine, the pheasants are baked, tightly covered, in a moderate oven. A *sauce piquante* is served separately. (See PIQUANTE) COMPATIBLE WINES: A red wine, e.g., Margaux, Haut Brion, Échézeaux, La Tâche, Richebourg, St. Émilion, Calon-Ségur, Mouton Rothschild, Cabernet Sauvignon.

LIWANZEN (Czech) This egg dish is similar to the Swiss *Vogelheu* (bread chunks soaked in beaten egg and fried in butter), but here breakfast rolls are crumbed through a sieve and mixed with eggs, sugar, salt, lemon peel, milk, and butter. The batter is spooned into shallow muffin cups and baked. When the *liwanzen* become golden brown, they are removed from the oven, sprinkled with sugar and cinnamon, and served.

LOBSTER The early Puritan settlers in the United States regarded the lobster as an ugly beast and ate it begrudgingly. This abhorrence of the lobster existed until about 1850, when the spiny delicacy started to come into its own and actually became so popular that conservation laws were passed to limit its catch. The common lobster, found in the North Sea, is bright blue and smaller than its New England counterpart. The large prawns which the Italians call *scampi* are the lady lobsters that inhabit the North Sea and the Mediterranean. The spiny lobsters native to Spain and France, called *langoustes* and *langostinos* respectively, are clawless and are sought mostly for their meaty tails. The Maine lobster can only be taken after it is seven or eight years old. Age is determined by size. If left to fust for itself, a lobster could live to be fifty years old and weigh as much as fifty to sixty pounds.

Lobster is one of the few foods whose meat can be completely consumed, including the tamalley, or green liver, and the female lobster's ovaries, the coral roe, which is a real delicacy. We eat the lobster broiled or boiled, and the latter tends to be preferred by lobster connoisseurs who like their lobsters less dried out. It is said that plunging the live lobster into wildly boiling water causes the poor beast to tense up as soon as it feels the intense heat. The result is that the flesh becomes very tough to eat. Preferable is merely massaging the live lobster's head with the thumb, which puts it to sleep. This tends to relax the flesh, and when the spinal cord is severed, the lobster meat remains succulent and tender.

If the diner has a choice, he should always opt for the female of the species, whose meat is tastier than that of the male. Usually the female can be distinguished by the roe or coral that she carries, or look for the feelers on the underside of the lobster, at the point where the tail meets the upper body. If they are short, the lobster is male; if long, it is a succulent female.

The elegant restaurant service of a lobster prescribes that the lobster coral, the tail meat, and the claw meat be removed by competent restaurant personnel (if the diner so desires). The lobster meat should be cut to size and kept warm on a tableside burner in a pot swimming with sweet butter mixed with sherry. The lobster ritual also demands the service of a finger bowl with lukewarm water, half a lemon, and an extra napkin for each diner.

LO HAN CHAI (Chinese) This Cantonese dish, in its totally vegetarian composition, adheres closely to the dietary principles of Buddha. In fact, it is called "Buddha's delight" as well as "Arhat's feast" (Arhat is the term for one who has attained Nirvana). It is also called "monk's food." And what a delight this dish is to the vegetarian! Cabbage, bean thread, bean curd, mushrooms, celery cabbage, ginko nuts, tree fungi, seaweed, lotus root, bamboo shoots, and a myriad of other vegetables are tossed with fermented white bean curd to ready this dish for the table. COMPATIBLE BEVERAGES: Tea.

LOKMA (Turkish) A type of doughnut made from a dough composed of flour, butter, salt, yeast, and water. After the dough has risen, it is dropped by the teaspoonful into hot oil. When the small puff balls rise to the surface, they are removed at once. Then they are refried at a somewhat higher temperature until golden brown. The crisp pastry balls are then covered with a thick sugar syrup flavored with lemon, removed to a serving platter, and allowed to cool. They are served sprinkled with cinnamon and topped with vanilla-flavored whipped cream.

LONGE DE PORC À LA SAUCE ROBERT (French) This method of roasting a pork loin originated during the time of La Varenne, chef to Louis XIV. The loin is seasoned with salt, pepper, and sage and well roasted. Half an hour before it has finished roasting, the pan juices are removed and replaced with a rich *sauce Robert*. The pork loin finishes its cooking in this sauce. When done, the sauce is strained and served separately. (SEE ROBERT) COMPATIBLE WINES: A red wine, e.g., Figeac, Arbois, Cahors, Santenay, Mercurey, Beaujolais, Côtes du Rhône; or a full-bodied white wine, e.g., Traminer, Sauterne, Graves, Schloss Vollrads, Riesling, Johannisberg, Rüdesheim, Gewürztraminer, Tokay.

LOP CHONG (Chinese) A spiced sausage made of pork and flavored with rice wine and grated orange peel.

LOQUAT This small yellow fruit has been cultivated in Japan for centuries, but it is native to China. It is fuzzy, has a really refreshing flavor, and is tart and juicy.

LOTUS BUNS (Chinese) The exotic name of these buns comes from their shape: they look like half of a lotus leaf. They are made from a well-kneaded yeast dough that is flattened and then cut into rounds. The rounds of dough are brushed with vegetable oil so that they will not stick when folded. They are then steamed, not baked, and often served as a garnish with crisp Peking duck. (SEE PEKING DUCK, LING AU, LING JI)

LOT YOW (Chinese) "Hot oil," a condiment made by heating peanut oil, removing it from the heat, and then adding crushed hot peppers. After it has brewed long enough to cause the oil to turn red, the mixture is allowed to cool and then is strained to remove the pepper residue.

LOUIS XIV, THE SUN KING Louis was a gourmet, a gourmand, a veritable pig of a man who insisted on eating everything he could get his hands and greasy fingers on. He ended each meal with six to ten hard-boiled eggs, after having already consumed a dinner consisting of three soups, five entrées, three fowl, two fish dishes plus vegetables. He tasted roasts by the half dozen, tried a few *entremets* (usually vegetables), plunked a few rich desserts into his mouth, and then finished with the usual hard-boiled eggs. It is said that people traveled miles and miles just to watch their king eat in public; it was such a sight. At the palace, his food had to be carried such long distances through drafty halls and up steep stairways from the kitchens below that by the time the food arrived, it was usually quite cold. Then too, before he could eat anything, he had to wait for his food-tasters to go through their ritual.

It was probably because of his impotence that Louis ate like a pig, and if anyone sought to please him, the surest way would be with some new taste thrill. By the time he was forty, the king's teeth were completely rotten, and while pulling his last two teeth, Louis' inept doctors broke his royal jaw. When, at long last, death claimed him, doctors found that his intestines were twice as long as the average man's, probably to hold the oversized tapeworm he fed for years. Another Louis, the XVI, lost his life also because of food. As he was fleeing Paris, he insisted that he had to stop to eat. The revolutionaries caught up with him at Varenne, as he was downing his second chicken.

LOUIS XVIII A wild gourmet cook, this French monarch was far out when it came to roasting a stuffed partridge, for instance. He first lined the inside of the partridge with a patina of black truffles and *foie gras,* but that was not all. Before sewing up the already richly-stuffed partridge, he popped three plump ortolans inside. Louis once said of his brother, Louis XVI, "My brother eats the way he takes his wife." (See FOIE GRAS, ORTOLAN)

LOUIS, CRAB (American) When the name Louis is mentioned in relation to food, one immediately thinks of Louis XIV, the Gourmet King of France. However, this crab dish was made famous by the great tenor Enrico Caruso, who while dining at the Olympic Club in Seattle, Washington, ate so much of it that the restaurant had no more to serve. Having learned that the name of the chef was Louis, Caruso dubbed the salad, then and there, "crab Louis." The dressing that makes this crabmeat so outstanding is composed of a *sauce Mayonnaise* mixed with whipped cream, chili sauce, grated onions, chopped parsley, and a dash of cayenne pepper. (See MAYONNAISE) COMPATIBLE BEVERAGES: Beer, ale, cider.

LOX (Jewish) *Lox* is the Yiddish derivative of the German word *Lachs,* "salmon." But *lox,* as used in the United States, refers specifically to smoked salmon. Lox is served sliced with bagels and cream cheese; or, cut into pieces, it is an ingredient in the lox-eggs-and-onions dish so popular among Jews. (See GRAVLAX, NOVA SCOTIA)

LUCULLUS The name Lucullus is synonymous with elegance, leisure, good taste, and rich food. Lucullus, a Roman general, was better known for his great banquets than for his military prowess. He is said to have first brought cherries to Italy from Asia, and to posterity he has left the "Lucullan feast," any meal incorporating greatness, style, and fine taste in everything from the food to the accouterments.

Darne de Saumon Lucullus (French) Large salmon steaks are studded with truffles, braised in Champagne, and garnished with small molds filled with oysters, *barquettes* of roe, and a crayfish-butter sauce. COMPATIBLE WINES: A white wine, e.g., Champagne, Meursault, Montrachet, Muscadet, Pouilly-Fuissé, Orvieto, Vouvray, Bernkasteler Doktor.

Garniture Lucullus (French) A garnish composed of black truffles cooked whole in Madeira wine. The truffles are cored and then filled with a *quenelle* (forcemeat) of chicken and the chopped truffle centers. The garnish is usually served with sweetbreads and with poultry dishes. (See BARQUETTES, QUENELLE)

LUNGENSTRUDELSUPPE (Austrian) In Vienna this soup is prepared with lung. One of the glories of Viennese cooking is its great variety of dumplings, some of which are served in soups, others as *hors d'oeuvre,* and still others as desserts. The dumplings used in this soup are made from a dough that is rolled out as thin as possible then topped with a mixture of ground veal that has been precooked in butter with chopped onions and mixed with eggs, parsley, caraway seeds, marjoram, salt, and pepper. The meat mixture is rolled up into this rectangle of dough, which is then cut into small segments and cooked in a rich beef broth.

LUNG-HSIA (Chinese) See HSIA

LUTEFISK (Norwegian) A rather complicated, albeit popular, method of preparing codfish. *Torskfisk* (unsalted dry codfish) is cut into small pieces and covered with cold water that is changed religiously for eight days. On the ninth day, the fish is placed into a solution of potash lye mixed with fresh water. It is kept there for two days, after which it is set into fresh water for another two days. With appetites at their peak, at long last comes the easy part—the cooking. Simmered in boiling water until just done, the cod is served with boiled potatoes and split peas. This dry cod more than doubles its weight through the series of soakings. COMPATIBLE WINES: A white wine, e.g., Arbois, Riesling, Gewürztraminer, Sancerre, Quincy, Traminer, Sauvignon Blanc, Orvieto, Frascati, Pinot Grigio.

LYONNAISE, À LA The sweet and mild onions grown there raise the standard of food in Lyon to great heights, as does garlic in Provence and the more discreet cousin, the shallot, in Anjou. To honor the city of Lyon and the part onions play in its cooking, French gastronomes have dubbed many of their creations *Lyonnaise*.

Tripe à la Lyonnaise Precooked tripe is added to chopped onions that have been browned in a mixture of soy sauce and bacon fat then sprinkled with wine vinegar and chopped parsley and simmered together. COMPATIBLE WINES: A red wine, e.g., Veltliner, Hermitage, Beaujolais, Mercurey, Margaux, Mâcon, Valpolicella, Zinfandel.

Lyonnaise Potatoes   Boiled potatoes are cut into cubes and sautéed in butter in one frying pan while lots of chopped onions are cooked in like manner in another pan. The onions are then mixed into the crackling potatoes and cooked together.

Lyonnaise, Sauce   This sauce, born in Lyon, is composed of chopped onions fried in sweet butter then cooked in white wine with a drop of vinegar. This is reduced to half and a *sauce demi-glace* is added. (See DEMI-GLACE)

LYULYA KEBAB (Russian) The Greeks, Romans, Arabs, and the Turks have all left their mark on the history, the culture, and the cuisine of the rich region of the Soviet Union known as the Caucasus. As this part of Russia overflows with an abundance of fine fresh foods, it is only natural that such traditional dishes as *shashlik, tabaka, dolmas,* and *kebabs*—for which Turkey is so famous—took root in this area. This *kebab* is made from ground lamb combined with grated onions, chopped parsley, oregano, salt, and pepper, all kneaded together until smooth. The meat mixture is then shaped into elongated, sausagelike forms, which are then pierced with flat-edged skewers and broiled over charcoal. The *kebabs* are garnished with fresh tomatoes, scallions, parsley, and lemon wedges and served traditionally on *lavash* bread. (See DOLMAS, KEBAB, LAVASH, SHASHLIK, SHISHKEBAB) COMPATIBLE WINES: A red wine, e.g., Châteauneuf-du-Pape, Barolo, Beaujolais, Chianti, Médoc, Egri Bikaver.

MACAIRE, POMMES DE TERRE (French) This potato dish, named in honor of a French knight of the era of Charles V, has three versions, all made from the scooped-out pulp of freshly baked potatoes. The first involves seasoning the pulp with salt, pepper, and nutmeg, spreading it on the bottom of a heavy pan containing very hot clarified butter, and browning it well on both sides. The second involves spreading the seasoned pulp of baked potatoes over the bottom of an earthenware dish containing clarified butter then baking it in a hot oven until the top is brown. Yet another method involves returning the well-seasoned, butter-rich potato pulp to the empty skins and baking them topped with breadcrumbs. (See CLARIFIED BUTTER)

MACARONI (Italian) The English word for the Italian *maccheroni,* a *pasta* made in long tube shapes but often cut into pieces and marketed as "elbow macaroni." When cut diagonally into shorter tubes, they are called *penna.* (See PASTA)

MACE A surprising thing happens when, in the process of ripening, the nutmeg splits: it then exposes to view a small red aril which is known commercially as mace. Mace is used to flavor oyster stews, cherry pies, chocolate dishes, fish sauces, stuffings, and marinades.

MACÉDOINE (French) This term refers to ancient Macedonia, which was cut up into small states and, since early times, has been a veritable "salad bowl" of nations. Culinarily, the term refers to either fruits or vegetables cut up into small pieces and made into a salad. The fruit salad is flavored with liqueurs, such as Kirsch and Grand Marnier, and the vegetable salad is seasoned with a *sauce Mayonnaise* or a *vinaigrette.* (See MAYONNAISE, VINAIGRETTE)

MADÈRE, SAUCE (French) A classic sauce known for the amount of Madeira wine it contains. First, a *sauce demi-glace* is reduced, to which a quantity of sliced mushrooms is added along with the clarified and defatted juices from any roast together with the Madeira wine (See DEMI-GLACE). Classically used in sauces, stews, and casseroles, there are many varieties of Madeira wine:

> *Sercial:* Pale, dry, nutty. The aperitif Madeira.
> *Verdelho:* Medium-dry, all-purpose. Good with soup or melon.
> *Bual:* Rich, medium-sweet. A dessert wine. Good with fruits.
> *Malmsey:* Sweet, rich, full-bodied, very fragrant, deep brown in color. Served with cheese, fruit, nuts, coffee, strawberries and cream.
> *Rainwater:* The indefinite term used to refer to a medium-dry Madeira blended especially for the United States.

MADRILEÑA, COCIDO (Spanish) This stew from Madrid is made from a breast of beef and ham, which are cut into cubes and browned with onions in hot oil. With the addition of water, marrow bones, and soaked dried peas, the stew is brought to a boil. It is simmered, defatted, and the bones are removed. Then celery, carrots, onions, leeks, and potatoes are cubed and added with fresh garlic. Before the cooking period has elapsed, pork sausages, green beans, and sliced tomatoes are added to the stew. It is usually served with white rice. COMPATIBLE WINES: A red wine, e.g., Rioja, Beaujolais, Chianti, Châteauneuf-du-Pape, Dôle, Mercurey, Bardolino, Nebbiolo, Pinot Noir.

MADRILÈNE (French) See CONSOMMÉ

MAHLEPI From Iran and Syria comes this spice derived from the black cherry kernel. The spice is used to flavor a New Year's cake of raised yeast dough called _vasilopeta_. It is traditionally served in Greece during the holiday season.

MA HO (Thai) An appetizer made from ground pork, coriander root, chopped roasted peanuts, and a shrimp sauce called _nam pla_. The mixture is rolled into small balls, deep-fried, and then served in the halves of peaches, tangerines, and plums. (See NAM PLA) COMPATIBLE BEVERAGES: Tea, cider, saké.

MAI JING (Chinese) See MONOSODIUM GLUTAMATE

MAISON/DE LA MAISON (French) A term used by restaurateurs to designate a dish that is considered to be a speciality of the "house," a dish that the chef is particularly proud of, such as a _pâté maison, cassoulet maison,_ or _mousse à l'orange maison._ The equivalent in Spanish is _del meson;_ in German, _nach Hausart._

MAÎTRE D'HÔTEL (French) This title originally referred to the steward responsible to the host of a large house or castle for the personnel and the general upkeep of the estate. In Italy he was known as the _major domo._ Today, the term _maître d' hôtel_ designates the head authority in the dining rooms of fine restaurants the world over.

Maître d'Hôtel Butter Butter that has been creamed with parsley, salt and pepper, and a dash of lemon juice. It is kept refrigerated and served with grilled meats and fish. (See COMPOUND BUTTER)

Entrecôte Maître d'Hôtel This steak, cut from the sirloin or the rib, is grilled and served with a sprig of green parsley and a good dollop of the _maître d'hôtel_ butter set in the center of the steak. COMPATIBLE WINES: A red wine, e.g., La Tâche, Fixin, Richebourg, Chambertin, Dôle, Barolo, Pinot Noir.

MAJPASTETOM (Hungarian) A chicken liver _pâté._ After the cut-up liver has rested in the refrigerator overnight, it is sautéed in garlic-flavored butter in a hot pan. With the addition of salt and pepper, the liver is flamed with brandy. Then butter, bouillon, lemon juice, and milk-soaked white bread are puréed in a blender with the chicken liver. The *pâté* is then pressed into a suitable mold and placed in the refrigerator to set. COMPATIBLE WINES: A white wine, e.g., Orvieto, Gewürztraminer, Riesling, Piesporter Goldtröpfchen, Sauterne, Chenin Blanc, Fendant.

MAKIMAKI (Hawaiian) See FUGU

MAKIZUSHI, NORI (Japanese) A dish composed of flavored rice, *shi-itake* (mushrooms), *kampyo* (gourd), green beans, carrots, and bits of tuna fish, all rolled into *nori* (thin sheets of seaweed). A *sudare* (a bamboo mat) is usually used to help form the roll, and after having had time to set, the long *nori* roll is cut into serving segments and placed decoratively on the diner's plate. COMPATIBLE WINES: A white wine, e.g., saké, sherry, Sauterne.

MAKOUNUCHI (Japanese) In this type of Japanese service, found in some restaurants, a partitioned tray holding a varied assortment of hot and cold foods is used. These trays are also called *teishoku*.

MALANGA Y YUCA (Spanish) Used in Mexico and in the Islands of the Caribbean, this phrase describes the farinaceous roots of the cassava and yucca plants, which are prepared, cooked, and eaten like po-tatoes. After having been cooked in boiling salted water until tender, these tubers are saturated with the *mojo de ajo* sauce and served. (See MOJO DE AJO)

MALTAISE, SAUCE (French) To prepare this tangy sauce, the red juice of blood oranges and grated orange rind are added to a fine *sauce Hollandaise*. *Sauce Maltaise* is named to honor the Island of Malta, where blood oranges abound. The sauce can do wonderful things to cooked fresh asparagus.

MALVA This leafy green plant, a member of the mallow family, which includes okra, is used in Mexico as a nutritious thickener for soups. Dietary experts have proven this to be the most nutritious leaf plant in the world of vegetables.

MAMALIGA/MAMALIGGE See POLENTA

MANDARIN PANCAKE (Chinese) A "mandarin" was a high official of China under the Empire. Mandarin is also the main dialect of Chinese, spoken in about ninety percent of the mainland, most notably in Peking. The imperial rulers made their residence in this city, and the best in food and cuisine was reserved for them. This Chinese pancake, therefore, has something of a regal heritage. It is made from a simple flour and water dough that is kneaded into a roll and then cut into small rounds. These rounds, flattened thin, are then well oiled and sandwiched together in pairs. The double pancakes are then sautéed on both sides in a large skillet until they puff up. When cooked, the pancakes are pulled apart. They are popularly served with Peking duck or with the various *moo-shu* dishes. (See MOO-SHU, PEKING DUCK)

MANGO CHUTNEY (East Indian) To prepare this condiment, chopped mangoes are salted and allowed to stand overnight. The mangoes are then cooked in a mixture of vinegar, sugar, chopped almonds, orange and lemon peel, raisins, ginger, salt, garlic, red peppers, and onions until thick. Mango chutney is served with curry dishes.

MANHATTAN CLAM CHOWDER (American) Salt pork and onions, both finely chopped, are cooked together. Cubed potatoes, fish stock or chicken stock, and seasonings are added; and when the potatoes are almost done, sliced cooked tomatoes and chopped clams are put into the pot and the lot is brought to a slow simmer. (See CHOWDER, NEW ENGLAND CLAM CHOWDER)

MANICOTTI (Italian) Literally, "little muffs." *Manicotti* are made from a basic *pasta* dough composed of semolina (hard wheat), eggs, salt, olive oil, and water. The dough is rolled out and cut into three-inch squares. After drying under a cloth for an hour or so, the squares are cooked in boiling salted water. Removed and drained, they are cooled before filling. The *manicotti* are usually stuffed with ricotta cheese, ground meat, or chopped vegetable mixtures and then baked with a sauce. (See PASTA)

MANIÉ, BEURRE (French) See COMPOUND BUTTER

MANIOC Also called cassava, this plant was first seen growing in Haiti. From there it was brought to Africa, where it has since thrived. Manioc is the source of the starchy tapioca. (See CASSAVA)

MANJU (Japanese) A dessert of small cakes filled with *koshi-an* (sweetened bean paste). The dough is formed from flour, eggs, baking powder, milk, sugar, and salt. Balls of the dough are flattened, filled with *koshi-an,* and folded into an envelope shape. The envelopes are placed on a cheesecloth, set on a rack over boiling water, and steamed until done. They can also be filled with fruit preserves.

Another version involves brushing the envelopes with a mixture of egg yolk and cream, sprinkling them with poppy seeds, and baking until done. These cakes are usually served at tea time, for as a dinner dessert the Japanese prefers a cold slice of melon, a juicy ripe peach, an orange, fresh berries, or a ripe persimmon. (See KOSHI-AN)

MANZO (Italian) Beef.

MARAÎCHÈRE, À LA (French) This term refers to any food preparation that utilizes the freshest of vegetables available from the local "vegetable gardener." In culinary parlance it describes, for example, a garnish composed of small braised onions, salsify, artichokes, carrots, and stuffed braised cucumbers. This garnish is usually served with roasts of meat, with braised meats, or even with fried eggs.

MARASCHINO, SAUCE (Italian) A sweet sauce composed of heavy cream, maraschino liqueur, and powdered sugar, all whipped to a stiff froth. The sauce is served with tutti-frutti ice cream. (See TUTTI-FRUTTI)

MARBREZ, OEUFS (French) Minced hard-boiled eggs are the base of this layered and molded dish. Half of the amount of eggs is riced, mixed with salt, pepper, and mustard, and bound with a *sauce Mayonnaise*. The hard-boiled yolks of the other half are minced and combined with puréed anchovies and *sauce Mayonnaise*. Lastly, the remaining whites are riced and mixed with finely chopped onions, salt, and again, the *Mayonnaise*. These egg mixtures are then alternately layered into a well-buttered mold, starting with the egg white mixture. Each layer of eggs is pressed firmly into the mold and set to cool. It is festively served unmolded, garnished with anchovy fillets and a rather regal sauce composed of sour cream and Beluga caviar. (See BELUGA, MAYONNAISE) COMPATIBLE BEVERAGES: Beer, cider.

MARCHAND DE VIN, SAUCE (French) *Marchand de vin* means "wine dealer," and this sauce is a reduction of red wine together with chopped shallots and chives, a *bouquet garni* (thyme, parsley, and cloves tied together with bay leaves), spices, garlic, and a dollop of *sauce demi-glace*. After the reduced sauce is simmered for a time, it is passed through a sieve; and just before serving, poached beef marrow, cut into cubes, is added with minced parsley and lemon juice. This sauce is served with pan-fried steaks, broiled steaks, fillets of beef, *filets mignon,* and large roasts of beef. (See BOUQUET GARNI, DEMI-GLACE, FILET MIGNON)

MARENGO, CHICKEN À LA (Swiss) Flushed from his victory over the Austrian troops at Marengo, Napoleon wanted to celebrate immediately with a fine dinner. However, his Swiss chef, Dunand, had lost his food wagons during the battle, so he was forced to scrounge and forage for whatever food was available in the vicinity. Dunand turned up a few chickens, some tomatoes, garlic, olive oil, and eggs. After simmering pieces of browned chicken in a mixture of the four latter ingredients, he flamed them with Cognac, added a bit of white wine, and presented the chicken, surrounded with a ring of fried eggs just for good measure. Napoleon loved it and Dunand was elated. Today, black truffles and crawfish are new additions to the formula that fêted a French victory in 1800, but the creation is Dunand's. COMPATIBLE WINES: A white wine, e.g., Vouvray, Johannisberg, Schloss Vollrads, Riesling, Sylvaner, Gewürztraminer, Sauterne, Graves.

MARGARINE In France, in the year 1869, a small man—gray, already stooped—entered the French patent office for the tenth time. His name was Mège-Mouriés, and he had invented margarine. The year before, Napoleon III needed something other than butter to feed his Imperial Navy, because butter spoiled so readily. He therefore held a contest. There was but one contestant: Mège-Mouriés.

It was not until 1874 that margarine was produced commercially, but due to complaints lodged by the butter producers and the board of health, the Academy of Sciences issued a report against the use of margarine. Consequently, the people of France went back to butter.

But today, enriched with vitamins A and D and because of its low cholesterol content, margarine has become the more popular. However, when the richness and the unequalled taste of butter are necessary to the perfection of a dish, no chef will use margarine.

MARGHERITA (Italian) This *grande dame* was Queen-Mother to Victor Emanuel III of Italy, and many culinary creations have been named in her honor.

Pears Regina Margherita Ripe pears are peeled and cored and then gently simmered in a mixture of water, sugar, and vanilla until the flavors have been absorbed. After draining the pears, a thick custard, known in France as *crème patissière* and in Italy as *pasticciera,* well flavored with a high-proof rum, is poured into the centers of the pears. (See CRÈME PATISSIÈRE)

Pasta Margherita A dessert prepared by carefully heating whole eggs plus additional egg yolks together with sugar and vanilla and beating the mixture until thick and velvety. Both a pastry flour and a potato flour are then added to the egg mixture, a bit at a time, constantly stirring; and at the end of the cooking period, melted butter is folded into the custard. This rich batter is then baked, first at a high heat then at a lower one, for about an hour.

MARGUERY (French) One of the great Parisian restaurants of Victorian days, the Marguery was situated on the Boulevard Bonne-Nouvelle. Created on the premises of this restaurant was an exquisite fish sauce of the same name. Composed of white wine, cooked mussels, mushrooms, shrimp, egg yolks, and heavy cream, the sauce is also known as *Dieppoise.* (See DIEPPOISE)

Marguery, Filets de Sole M. Mangin of the restaurant Marguery created this sole dish. The fillets are poached in a fish *fumet* that includes the essence of mussels that have been cooked in white wine. The fillets are then coated with the *fumet,* which has been bound with egg yolks and butter. After being glazed in the grill, the fillets of sole are served encircled with mussels and shrimp tails. (See FUMET) COMPATIBLE WINES: A white wine, e.g., Chablis, Meursault, Montrachet, Pouilly-Fuissé, Soave, Wehlener Sonnenuhr, Debro.

MARHATEKERCS (Hungarian) *Rouladen, galantines, ballotines, paupiettes, braciole,* and these *marhatekercs* are all preparations made by stuffing boned and flattened meats with various fillings, then rolling and braising the stuffed rolls in the oven. For the *marhatekercs,* the Hungarians use the top round, which they fill with chopped onions and ground pork that have been cooked together with eggs, salt, marjoram, pepper, sour cream, and enough breadcrumbs to bind. The beef rectangles are spread with this mixture, rolled up, tied, and browned in hot oil. Then the beef rolls are simmered in a casserole filled halfway with a beef stock flavored with paprika, caraway seeds, and garlic. As in many Hungarian dishes, a quantity of sour cream is folded into the beef broth, and this is poured over the *marhatekercs* when served. (See BRACIOLE, BALLOTINE, GALANTINE, PAUPIETTE, ROULADEN) COMPATIBLE WINES: A red wine, e.g., Santenay, Valpolicella, Beaujolais, Lambrusco, Egri Bikaver, Szekszárdi Vörös, Zinfandel.

MARIE LOUISE (French) The second wife of Napoleon I has been immortalized by the various culinary creations named after her.

Crème Marie Louise A rich cream of chicken soup is thickened with barley flour and served garnished with beans, green peas, sliced carrots, and macaroni.

Garniture Marie Louise Hearts of artichokes, filled with grilled mushrooms and coated with a *sauce soubise,* are served with *noisette potatoes* as a garnish for roasts. (See NOISETTE, SOUBISE)

MARINADE A spiced liquid mixture used to pickle various vegetables, fish, or meats—including game and fowl—in order to flavor and tenderize them. Marinades usually contain a combination of two or more of the following: wine, olive oil, vinegar, lemon juice, bay leaves, onions, thyme, parsley, cloves, garlic, salt, and pepper. Foods may be marinated for periods ranging from minutes to weeks. The acidic quality of the marinade is the most important ingredient in respect to toughness and to taste. (See BEIZE, PICKLING, SAUER BRATEN, HASENPFEFFER)

Marinade à Chaud This term refers to a precooked marinade used to pickle cuts of venison. It is made by first cooking a variety of vegetables and seasonings in olive oil. Then, after adding wine, vinegar, and water, the whole mixture is brought to a boil and simmered until all the flavors have blended. The marinade is cooled before being poured over the choice cuts of venison, such as the legs or the saddle.

MARIN/MENON In eighteenth-century France, these two gastronomes combed the provinces and rural regions to come up with their imaginative recipes. They were the first cooking experts to show the middle class how to dine like a prince with but one cook in the kitchen—*maman.* Marin, for instance, stated quite openly that he could not possibly hope to please everyone, so he chose recipes to please himself. He knew, as most successful publishers do, that if you want to sell your cookbooks, then cater to provincial tastes. Marin, who was major-domo to the famous gourmet Marshall Soubise, was the first to suggest that the whole animal—the tail, the feet, the snout, the stomach, the ears—must be considered when preparing a meal. Marin was also the first to make a list of the most important sauces and their composition, including the first description of the *sauce Béchamel.* His contemporary, Menon, the most prolific cook of the eighteenth century, was also the author of at least fifteen cookbooks, including *Nouveau Traité de la Cuisine, La Cuisinière Bourgeoise,* and *Soupers de la Cour.* Menon was most clear and definite in the description of his recipes, and although personal information about this great gastronome is nonexistent, his name is ever associated with the greats of French cuisine. (See BÉCHAMEL, GOURMET, SOUBISE)

MARINARA SAUCE (Italian) The term means "sailor-style," and the sauce can be made either "red" or "white," that is, with tomatoes or without them. But ever basic to the sauce is garlic, oregano, wine, olive oil, salt, pepper, and vinegar.

Mussels Marinara Mussels cooked in a sauce composed of garlic, white wine, olive oil, oregano, vinegar, and parsley. After cooking, the mussels are left to cool in the sauce. The above is the classic description of the dish, but some restaurants will add tomato sauce as well. It is best to inquire. (See COZZE ALLA MARINARA) COMPATIBLE BEVERAGES: A rosé wine or a kir (white wine and black currant syrup).

Spaghetti Marinara Here, the same sauce used for the mussels *marinara,* with the addition of tomatoes, tomato purée, basil, sugar, and anchovies, is served over the *pasta.* The dish is served piping hot, liberally sprinkled with grated Romano cheese. (See PASTA) COMPATIBLE WINES: A red wine, e.g., Chianti, Bardolino, Margaux, Beaujolais, Pinot Noir.

MARINIÈRE, MOULES À LA (French) *Marinière,* derived from the word *marinier,* refers to "products of the sea," and here describes one of the most famous of French dishes. Mussels are first washed and thoroughly rinsed, then placed in a pan with chopped shallots, garlic, parsley, fresh butter, and white wine. The mussels are cooked covered until their shells have opened. Then, the mussels are removed from the shells, more butter is added to the sauce, and this is poured over the mussels with a sprinkling of freshly chopped parsley. (See BOUQUET GARNI, MOULES, POULETTE) COMPATIBLE WINES: A white wine, e.g., Soave, Verdicchio, Meursault, Graacher Himmelreich, Gewürztraminer, Muscadet, Quincy.

Sauce Marinière (French) A sauce is made by adding a reduction of the cooking liquid from a batch of fresh mussels to a *sauce Bercy,* then vigorously whipping egg yolks into the sauce over heat until the sauce becomes thick. *Sauce marinière* is served with white-fleshed fish and, of course, with mussels. (See BERCY)

MARJORAM A perennial herbaceous plant belonging to the mint family, the dried leaves and flowers of which are used to flavor foods. Marjoram has a fragrant aroma and a slightly bitter taste and is used, either whole or ground, to flavor soups, stews, lamb or mutton dishes, sausages, egg and vegetable dishes, and poultry dressings. Native to countries bordering the Mediterranean and those of western Asia, today marjoram is widely cultivated in most of Europe and in North and South America.

In ancient Rome, marjoram was considered to be the symbol of contentment and happiness; newlyweds were bedecked with garlands of it. Germans bear this out by their name for marjoram, *Wurstkraut,* "the saucy herb." They also call it *Majoran.*

MARKKLÖSSCHEN (German) Marrow dumplings made from a purée of beef marrow, breadcrumbs, egg yolks, and spices. Beaten egg white is folded in, and after the mixture is allowed to rest for a few minutes, it is dropped by the spoonful into a boiling, rich bouillon. When the *Klösschen* float to the top, they are removed.

MARQUISE, POULARDE À LA (French) To prepare a chicken *à la marquise,* the bird is brushed with a seafood-butter then seasoned and roasted with a bit of chicken broth in the pan. The fowl is constantly basted during the roasting with a mixture of the broth and more seafood-butter. The chicken is carved into pieces and served with a *sauce Béchamel* that has been enriched with heavy cream and flavored with a dash of Pernod. (See BÉCHAMEL) COMPATIBLE WINES: A white wine, e.g., Piesporter Goldtröpfchen, Orvieto, Schloss Vollrads, Sauterne, Rüdesheim, Sauvignon Blanc, Hermitage Blanc, Montrachet.

MARRONS (French) Chestnuts.

Purée de Marrons Chestnuts not only can be roasted, boiled, steamed, grilled, or mashed, but can be made into a succulent purée by cooking peeled chestnuts in a consommé with pieces of fennel, celery, and sugar. When tender, the chestnuts are drained, crushed, and rubbed through a sieve; then they are mixed with a bit of butter and a little of the cooking liquid. With the purée over low heat, enough milk is beaten into it to bring the chestnut purée to the consistency of mashed potatoes. Chestnut purées are used as a poultry stuffing, or they may be served with venison and with other game or as a dessert with plenty of whipped cream.

Marrons Glacés To prepare these glazed chestnuts, they are dipped into hot fat, then they are quickly removed and peeled. The peeled chestnuts are covered with veal stock, simmered until nearly tender, then removed. The stock is reduced to a glaze and the chestnuts are gently rolled in the glaze until they become glossy with the coating. Glazed chestnuts are used as a garnish for roasts of meat, especially game. (See CHESTNUTS, NESSELRODE)

MARYLAND, CHICKEN (American) A speciality of the State of Maryland, the disjointed chicken is cooked exactly as southern-fried chicken with this exception: after having fried the chicken and removed it from the pan, a bit of flour and a mixture of cream and milk is added to half of the remaining chicken fat and cooked until it is smooth and thick. The chicken is served coated with this seasoned cream sauce. (See SOUTHERN-FRIED CHICKEN) COMPATIBLE WINES: A white wine, e.g., Anjou, Vouvray, Gewürztraminer, Montrachet, Meursault, Johannisberg, Sauvignon Blanc, Orvieto, Sauterne.

MARZIPAN Spanish nuns often occupied themselves with the art of cooking. One such order cloistered in Toledo adopted the almond, a gift from their Moslem rulers, and with it created a type of sugared paste that was not only adaptable and practical but tasty as well. They named it *mazapan,* and its goodness is extolled today throughout the world. The paste we know as "marzipan"—a mixture of ground almonds, fine sugar, and egg whites—can be molded into as many shapes, forms, and filigrees as the dexterous sugar-baker can imagine or devise.

MASTIHA This condiment made from the sap of the mastrica tree is very sweet and almost exclusively used by Greeks. Bakers use it in their cakes and pastries, and it is also used pharmaceutically as an astringent.

MATELOTE, À LA (French) A fish stew mixed with a sauce composed of butter, bay leaves, garlic, pepper, red or white wine, and mushrooms. Most often this stew is prepared with fresh-water fish.

Matelote à la Normande A fish stew made from fish cooked in cider, flamed with Calvados, and bound with a *sauce velouté.* (See VELOUTÉ) COMPATIBLE WINES: Chablis, Meursault, Pinot Chardonnay, Muscadet, Debro.

MA-TI (Chinese) See WATER CHESTNUT

MATIGNON, À LA (French) This term refers to a vegetable, meat, and herb coating used to cover large joints of meat or fowl as they cook; the coating imparts its particular flavor and aroma to the food it covers. To prepare, carrots, onions, and celery are finely minced and mixed together with chopped ham, crushed bay leaves, and thyme. This is stewed slowly in sweet butter and, finally, splashed with Madeira wine.

MÄTI JA PAAHTOLEIPÄ (Finnish) A delicacy made from the roe (fish eggs) of pike, whitefish, or rainbow trout. Usually, the smallest roe is used because that seems to mix better with the rest of the ingredients. The roe is first frozen and then thawed (it then requires less salt). It is then soundly beaten to remove the membranes and other unwanted matter, which actually stick right to the beater. After the roe is lightly salted, it is whipped until airy and fluffy. Chopped onions and a combination of whipped cream and sour cream are then folded into the roe, which is chilled before serving. COMPATIBLE BEVERAGES: Ice-cold vodka, Akvavit, or a white Gewürztraminer, Fendant, Orvieto, Chenin Blanc.

MATSUTAKE (Japanese) A long-stemmed mushroom, imported from Japan either in cans or in a dried form.

MATSUZAKA (Japanese) See KOBE BEEF

MATZO (Jewish) Thin unleavened bread eaten by Jews during Passover, the holiday that commemorates the Exodus of the Jews from

Egypt. Because of its plainness and crispness, *matzo* makes an excellent partner for cheese.

Matzo Balls These dumplings are made by blending egg yolks with chicken fat, matzo meal, salt, ginger, and a bit of hot chicken broth, beating all well. Whipped egg whites are folded into the mixture, which is then refrigerated for an hour or so. Then the chilled *matzo* dough is formed into small balls, which are dropped into boiling salted water until done. Sometimes grated onions and potato flour are also added to the *matzo* dough. When cooked, the *matzo* balls are served with a rich chicken soup. (See KNAIDLACH)

Matzo Brei A thick fried pancake made from crumbled *matzo* that is softened and mixed with eggs, milk, and seasonings.

MAYONNAISE, SAUCE (French) There are many conflicting stories about the origin of this great sauce. Some claim that it was originally called *Bayonnaise* (after the city of Bayonne), *Moyeunasie* (from the Old French *moyeu,* meaning "egg yolk"), or *Mahonnaise* (because Port Mahon was captured by the Duc de Richelieu). Some even cite the claim of an Irish general named MacMahon, who insisted that the sauce was his own creation. From whichever source *Mayonnaise* comes, together with *sauce Béchamel* and *sauce Espagnole* it comprises the royal triumverate of sauces from which nearly all others flow. A mixture of egg yolks, vinegar, mustard, salt, and pepper is beaten until completely blended. Then olive oil is dribbled in, drop by drop, until the sauce starts gradually to thicken. Drops of cold water are added intermittently to lighten the sauce. With the last of the oil, a mixture of lemon juice and boiling water is added. This classic cold sauce is used with many dishes and is particularly tasteful when served with shrimp and lobster. (See AÏOLI, ANDALOUSE, BÉCHAMEL, ESPAGNOLE, ORIENTALE, RÉMOULADE, RUSSE)

MAZARIN Jules Mazarin, born in 1601, was a French statesman, a pseudo-cardinal of the Catholic Church, and one of the most astute gastronomes of his day. He was baptized Giulio Mazarini in Italy, but years later, while serving under the name Mazarin as Papal Nuncio at the French Court, he fell into the good graces of Cardinal Richelieu, whom he succeeded as minister. Although Mazarin had never been ordained a priest, at the insistence of Louis XIII he was raised to the office of cardinal. While Mazarin held sway in France, the great dinners he hosted rivalled any banquet at the royal palace. He knew how to live as statesman, cardinal, and as epicure.

Mazarin, à la The cardinal's name came to grace two different garnishes. One, used to complement meat dishes, consists of artichoke hearts stuffed with minced vegetables plus rice *croquettes, quenelles,* and mushrooms. The other garnish, served with fish, consists of pastry *barquettes* filled alternately with truffles and chopped shrimp in a shrimp-butter. (See BARQUETTE, CROQUETTE, QUENELLE)

Mazarin, Petites Pâtes à la The recipe for these small veal-and-bacon pastries appeared in print some eighty years after the death of the cardinal whose name they bear. They consist of puff pastry filled with a mixture of minced veal and bacon; chopped parsley, scallions, and basil; salt, pepper, and nutmeg—all bound with eggs and heavy cream. The filled and sealed pastries are baked in a hot oven until brown and tender.

MEDHU VADAI (East Indian) Deep-fried fritters made from lentil flour, chopped onions, and water.

MÉDIATRICE, LA (Créole) When a New Orleans husband had a wild night on the town and sorely needed something to pour oil on the stormy waters at home, he made every effort to present his seething spouse with *la médiatrice,* "the peacemaker." This special bread roll was hollowed out, brushed inside and out with sweet melted butter, and toasted in the oven until light brown. Three oysters, sautéed in hot butter until they puffed out a bit from the heat, were placed in the hot roll with a drop of Tabasco and hot light cream. The warmer the rolls were when the woman got them, the better was the wayward husband's reception.

MEDITERRANEAN CUISINE Since early times, the whole Mediterranean area has been the object of conquest. The Greeks, the Romans, and the Phoenicians took turns as invaders, plunderers, and occupiers of the northern coasts of Africa and the soft, warm belly of Europe. They brought with them their foods and their methods of cooking. In later years, the Arabs did likewise, as did the Turks. So the whole Mediterranean region has become, with the passing of time, a veritable gastronomic melting pot. The sweet and peppery quality of the dishes native to this area is characteristic. Meat and vegetable dishes are often served sweetened with honey and sugar. Mutton is preferred over all other meats, and *pilaffs* of rice are served with almost every dish. Yogurt is commonly served in sauces or as a garnish, and the most aromatic and flavorful of all vegetables, garlic and onions, take precedence over all others on Mediterranean shores from Tripoli to Gibraltar. (See GREEK CUISINE, PILAFF, TURKISH CUISINE)

MEDLAR The medlar tree is related to the rose family. For centuries it was grown in Europe for its acidic apple-shaped fruit, and it was brought to America in the eighteenth century by the Jesuits. An unusual aspect of this small fruit is that it is not picked until it has been touched by a good frost, for the reason that it is only edible after it has begun to decay. The medlar fruit is eaten fresh or is used to make preserves. In Italy, where medlars are very popular, they are called *nespola.* The Japanese medlar is known as the *loquat.*

MEERESFRÜCHTE (German) Seafood. (See FRUTTI DI MARE)

MEERRETTICHSOSSE (Viennese) A horseradish sauce is made by whisking freshly-grated horseradish, egg yolks, salt, and pepper together with cubed bread that has been soaked in milk. Then olive oil is added, drop by drop, until the sauce is as thick as a *Mayonnaise.* A dash of vinegar completes the sauce. (See DANOISE, MAYONNAISE, RAIFORT)

MEHLSUPPE, GEBRANNTE (German) A popular soup made with roasted or cooked flour. Finely chopped onions and leeks are cooked in butter, then the flour is added and cooked until light brown. An egg is added to bind a rich consommé with red wine and paprika. The soup is served garnished with butter-toasted croutons. A variation is made by substituting heavy cream, grated cheese, and nutmeg for the red wine, egg, and paprika. This soup is traditionally served during *Fastnacht,* the pre-Lenten carnival celebration so famous in Basel, Switzerland.

MELANZANE (Italian) Eggplant.

MELBA The celebrated opera star Dame Nelly Melba was not only fond of eating and eating well, but prominent enough in restaurant circles to cause many a chef to name a dish after her.

Sweetbreads Melba M. Julien, *maître d'hôtel* at the famous Lapérouse in Paris, created this dish in honor of Dame Melba. He cooked it right at her favorite table in the restaurant's sumptuous dining room. The sauce is simple enough: butter, English mustard, beef stock, salt, pepper, and lemon juice. One sweetbread is sliced and added to the sauce. Asparagus and puréed mushrooms complete the dinner. COMPATIBLE WINES: A white wine, e.g., Traminer, Soave, Sauterne, Bernkasteler Doktor, Nierstein, Rüdesheim, Tokay, Sauvignon Blanc.

Pêche Melba The peach possesses a great richness and a certain voluptuousness, as did the voice of the great Nelly Melba. Perhaps this is why the great Escoffier, while presiding over the kitchens of London's Savoy Hotel, was inspired to create his *pêche Melba,* a dessert consisting of ice cream covered with fresh peaches and raspberry preserves laced with Kirschwasser.

Melba Toast This method of preparing toast was devised by Escoffier while he worked for César Ritz, the famous Swiss *hôtelier.* Escoffier took an ordinary slice of toasted bread and cut it to make two very thin bread slices, which he then retoasted. At first, Escoffier named the result "Toast Marie" in honor of Mme. Ritz, but after conferring with his boss, Mme. Melba took precedence and the name thenceforth appeared on menus at the Savoy in London as "Toast Melba."

MENU Derived from the Latin *minitus,* meaning "small, detailed," this term describes a detailed list of prepared dishes served at a meal. The menu was first fashioned in France as an *écriteau* (Old French, *escriteau*), a notice-board that hung on the wall of an eating establishment for the benefit of both the service personnel and the diners.

Later, small facsimilies of this large menu were made for use at each table until, ultimately, each diner was provided with his own individual bill of fare.

Many a menu is a work to be treasured, not only as a remembrance of the festive occasion it commemorates or of the excellence of the food served, but for the talent of the calligrapher who has transformed a piece of plain parchment into art. (The Forum of the Twelve Caesars had a menu that was not only beautiful to look at but so wittily descriptive, thanks to Joseph Baum, that today it is a collector's item.) Normally, the merit of a fine menu lies in the choice of foods offered, their sequential arrangement, and their suitability in respect to quality and season. Today, a menu indicates what food is available and, in restaurants, at what cost.

"To eat is a necessity, but to eat intelligently is an art," said La Rochefoucauld. An appetizer's function is to stimulate the right digestive juices to flow, and the soup that follows tends to condition the stomach; they both do much to ease the diner into the main course. The appetizer and soup should tease, not satiate, the appetite; and should the main course be swimming in a rich cream sauce, it would be imprudent and rather tasteless to precede it with a creamed or puréed soup. Likewise, if a _pasta_ is served as an appetizer, it would be wise to avoid a main course of _ziti_ or any similar starchy food. A well-composed menu will vary the texture, garnishes, sauces, flavors, and methods of preparation of a meal. Often, just the vivid description of a dish can conjure up the intoxicating taste pleasures that lie ahead.

Table d'Hôte Menu   This "table of the host" menu, featuring a complete meal at a fixed price, should be comprised of a nutritious series of dishes that complement each other. Because most of the food has been prepared before mealtime, this type of menu should be ready to be served as soon as the restaurant opens its doors to the public. Usually, a _table d'hôte_ menu affords the diner a choice of two or three appetizers and as many different soups; a meat, fish, or poultry selection is available as a main course; and there is a choice of two vegetables or a salad. A list of four desserts and a beverage of choice completes the menu. The _table d'hôte_ menu (also called a _prix fixe_ menu) is always cheaper than a comparable meal ordered from an _à la carte_ menu (see below). It is recommended as a pre-theater menu, for there should not be much waiting involved.

When hosting a party of six or more people at a restaurant, it is advisable to order in advance to assure good table service and the best food preparation possible. If you allow your guests to select their own menus, they will sometimes order then ask their neighbors what they have ordered and then proceed to change their minds twice after the disgruntled waiter has written the complete order on his pad. Then, too, if you order the dinner beforehand, you will be better able to select a suitable wine and have it chilled if necessary. On entering the restaurant, tip the headwaiter and have him arrange to have the food check brought to his desk for inconspicuous payment. He will not only watch over the detailed service of your meal, but he will respect you as a person of taste and tact.

À la Carte Menu This French term refers to those restaurant dishes that are prepared "at the moment" they are ordered. Each dish is individually priced, thereby allowing the diner to choose but a soup or perhaps a bit of good brie cheese, bread, and wine. There are times that the diner is really not disposed to fill himself with a whole dinner. It is a good idea in first-class restaurants to ask the captain or headwaiter to recommend a speciality of the house, which will, nine times out of ten, assure the diner of a fine meal, give an added boost to the captain's or headwaiter's ego, and at the same time, assure him of a good tip, should his advice prove sound.

Banquet Menu Banquet menus usually begin with a rich clear soup, followed sometimes by a fish course, then the main course with accompanying vegetables and salad (sometimes the salad is served as a separate course), and finally a dessert. If cheese is served, it should precede anything sweet. These formal dinners are served by teams of waiters, two to a team, immediately supervised by captains under the banquet headwaiter.

It is advisable, if wine and liquors are to be served, to have the headwaiter inform the host when a certain number of bottles of liquor or wine have been consumed; this will give the host some control over the size of the bill that is accumulating. The host (often the father-of-the-bride), to be sure of the liquor count, will put his personal mark on each bottle of liquor and wine before the banquet begins. Then it is a simple thing to get a correct count of the empty bottles at the end of the festivities. It is just good business.

MERLUZZO When looking for "cod" on an Italian bill of fare, you might find it listed as *merluzzo fritto,* "fried cod," or as *merluzzo gratia,* where fillets of cod are breaded and baked topped with a spread of anchovy purée and parsley. These are but two of the many cod preparations served in Italian restaurants. COMPATIBLE WINES: A white wine, e.g., Soave, Meursault, Pouilly-Fumé, Verdicchio, Frascati, Chenin Blanc.

MESA (Mexican) A type of cornmeal prepared by soaking corn in hot lime water overnight, then grinding it into the *mesa,* or corn flour, that is used to make *tortillas* and the many other *antojitos* (snacks). The lime present in the *mesa* is responsible, it is said, for the strong teeth of the native Mexican. (See ANTOJITOS, CORNMEAL, TORTILLAS)

MESHIMONO (Japanese) Rice dishes that are prepared with meat or with vegetables.

METIN SHURO (Ethiopian) A vegetable stew (a type of *wat*) composed of chickpeas, beans, and shallots spiced with cinnamon, nutmeg, pepper, and salt. (See WAT) COMPATIBLE BEVERAGES: Kaffir, beer, cider.

METTERNICH, SELLE DE VEAU (French) A saddle of veal dish named in honor of the great Austrian statesman, Prince Klemens Von Metternich, who was instrumental in securing the marriage of the Archduchess Marie Louise to Napoleon Bonaparte. In fact, Metternich was so important a diplomat and politician that the period 1815 to 1848 has been called the Age of Metternich. The dish named in his honor is prepared by browning in butter a saddle of veal together with root vegetables; white wine is then added. The saddle is then sliced half open and thin slices of black truffle are inserted between the pieces of veal together with a bit of *sauce Béchamel* flavored with paprika and lemon juice. The saddle is then closed, transferred to a huge platter, and covered with the rest of the cream sauce. It is browned in the grill before serving. (See BÉCHAMEL) COMPATIBLE WINES: A white wine, e.g., Vouvray, Riesling, Tokay, Sylvaner, Frascati, Brolio Blanco, Orvieto.

METTWURST (German) This smoked sausage, composed of lean pork meat flavored with spices and condiments, is of the general type known as *Streichwurst,* meaning "sausage that is meant to be spread." Although some *Mettwurste* are hard and require slicing, most are spreadable, and they are particularly excellent on good rye bread. (See BLUT UND LEBERWURST, CERVELAT, SAUSAGE)

METZELSUPPE (German) The term is dialectical, stemming from the German word *Metzger,* meaning "butcher." A *Metzelsuppe,* a "stuffed hog's belly," is a rural invention that has proved to be a culinary triumph. Once sampled, it can become addictive. In America, the dish is a great speciality of the Pennsylvania Dutch.

As first cousin to the famous Scotch *haggis,* the recipe for the *Metzelsuppe* is similar, but in the latter a hog's stomach is substituted for a sheep's. The freshly slaughtered hog's belly is stuffed with a mixture of diced potatoes, chopped parsley and onions, plus scads of sausage meat removed from their casings and salt and pepper to taste. After the stuffed pig's stomach is carefully sewn up, it is roasted for several hours. When ready to serve, it is crisp on the outside, and the stuffing on the inside is juicy and tender. For the stuffing, some use only pork sausage meat and add shredded cabbage and dried bread. (See HAGGIS) COMPATIBLE BEVERAGES: Beer.

MEULEMEESTER, OEUFS BELGES (Belgian) An *hors d'oeuvre* composed of shredded hard-boiled eggs that is mixed with heavy cream, chopped cooked shrimp, parsley, chervil, mustard, and grated Parmesan cheese. Poured into small ovenproof dishes, the egg mixture is baked in a fairly hot oven until the top is light brown. This egg dish also makes a delightful luncheon when accompanied with a tossed green salad. COMPATIBLE BEVERAGES: A beer would probably go best, but a red wine such as Beaujolais, Moulin-à-Vent, Fleurie, Zinfandel, or Mercurey is also good.

MEUNIÈRE, À LA (French) The descriptive phrase for any whole fish, fish fillet, or fish steak that is dusted with flour and sautéed in foaming sweet butter. When served, the fish is garnished with fresh herbs and a dash of lemon juice or a quarter of a fresh lemon.

Meunière, Beurre à la Butter is cooked just to the point of its turning brown and is then flavored with a dash of lemon juice and a bit of chopped parsley. The sauce is usually served over fish that has been cooked *à la meunière.*

Filets de Sole à la Meunière The delicate fillets of sole are seasoned with salt and pepper, dusted with flour, and sautéed on both sides in sweet butter. Before serving the sole, a dash of lemon juice is mixed into more sweet butter and poured over the fish. A slice of lemon is served as garnish. COMPATIBLE WINES: A white wine, e.g., Chablis, Meursault, Montrachet, Dézaley, Verdicchio, Soave, Debro, Wehlener Sonnenuhr, Pinot Chardonnay.

MEURETTE, EGGS (French) Eggs are gently poached in simmering red wine. The eggs are then served on triangles of toasted bread in tiny ramekins. A sauce composed of the wine thickened with flour and flavored with chopped onions, mushrooms, and bacon is served over the eggs. (See RAMEQUIN) COMPATIBLE WINES: A red wine, e.g., Beaujolais, Mâcon, Nebbiolo, Barolo, Moulin-à-Vent, Valpolicella, Zinfandel, Egri Bikaver.

MEXICANA, SALSA (Mexico) A basic piquant sauce. The following ingredients are chopped fine and cooked together: tomatoes, onions, celery, green and red chili peppers, olive oil, wine vinegar, salt, pepper, and coriander. The sauce can be served as a side dish with meats, eggs, *tacos,* vegetables, *enchiladas,* or *tamales.* (See EN-CHILADAS, TACOS, TAMALES)

MEZEDAKIA (Greek) Appetizers.

MEZZANI (Italian) See PASTA

MIDDLE EASTERN CUISINE A large segment of the population of the Middle East is Moslem. Moslem law forbids the eating of pork, so goat and kid, mutton and lamb, and chicken are used widely. Moslem cuisine is known for its flat loaves of thin hard bread *(pitis), dolmas* made of stuffed vine leaves, and *kebabs* of lamb barbecued on skewers. Syrupy coffee, yogurt, and sour milk are popular as beverages. The desserts consist mainly of figs and dates preserved in sugar and lemon juice with other fruits and plenty of honey and eggplant. (See DOLMAS, KEBAB)

MIGNARDISES (French) Also known as *friandises,* these are small sweet or savory delicacies. The term *mignardises* is often used to refer to *petits fours* and glazed fruits. (See FRIANDISES, PETITS FOURS)

MILANAISE (French) See CONSOMMÉ.

Milanaise Garniture (French) This garnish is made from a *julienne* of tongue, ham, mushrooms, and truffles—all sautéed in butter and deglazed with Madeira wine. These ingredients are added to *spaghetti* that is bound with tomato purée, grated Parmesan cheese, and butter. The garnish is served with veal cutlets. (See JULIENNE)

MILANESE, ALLA (Italian) A descriptive term for foods that are dusted with flour, dipped in egg yolk, then in breadcrumbs and grated Parmesan cheese, and fried in butter until golden.

Milanese, Calves' Sweetbreads alla Sweetbreads are a versatile food. They can be braised in either a white or a brown stock; they can be served grilled with various garnishes; or they can be poached, fried, grilled on skewers *(en brochette)*, or even souffléed. For this dish, the sweetbreads, having been properly soaked, blanched, and cooled, are cut into slices, dipped into cream and eggs, coated with grated Parmesan cheese and breadcrumbs, and cooked in clarified butter. The *Milanese* garnish includes cooked macaroni combined with minced ham, tongue, and mushrooms, sprinkled with grated Parmesan and Gruyère cheese. COMPATIBLE WINES: A white wine, e.g., Meursault, Graves, Saumur, Riesling, Sauvignon Blanc, Muscat d'Alsace.

Milanese, Salsa There are two sauces from Milan. The white sauce, based on a *sauce Allemande,* is flavored with tomato purée and pignoli nuts. The brown sauce is made from a *sauce demi-glace* mixed with a meat glaze and tomato purée and flavored with garlic and sautéed chopped mushrooms. (See ALLEMANDE, DEMI-GLACE)

MILLE-FANTI (Italian) See CONSOMMÉ

MILLE-FEUILLE (French) Literally meaning "a thousand leaves," this delicate pastry consists of layers of baked puff pastry tiered alternately with vanilla-flavored whipped cream and fruit preserves. The pastry is served iced lightly with *fondant.* (See FONDANT, NAPOLEON)

MINCEUR CUISINE A controversial innovation in French cooking that at its inception claimed to maintain the high standards and demands of fine French cuisine without using the great natural foodstuffs— such as butter, cream, oil, pork fat—that made the French kitchen exemplary. The French chefs responsible for introducing this cuisine are some of the greats: Michel Guérard, Paul Bocuse, and the Troisgros brothers, Jean and Pierre. Today the *minceur cuisine* and the *nouvelle cuisine* (the first meaning "slimming," the second "new") have come to espouse the same type of food preparation.

This style of preparation makes use of recent advances in kitchen technology (such as food processors, microwave ovens, and nonstick pans) to produce miniscule amounts of food which are set decorously on oversized plates. There is an overabundant use of purées. Tableside carving of meat and fowl and dining room salad preparation by captains and waiters is done away with. Food no longer comes from the kitchen on huge steaming platters, to be spooned and ladled onto the diner's plate at table, and table food-warmers are considered obsolete. All food comes plated, ready to be placed before the guest. Very much in the Japanese style, special attention is paid not only to the variety of tastes in a meal but also to the harmony of colors of the foods served.

This cuisine features quick-steamed vegetable dishes and low-calorie fish dishes. And although the cuisine has put forward a well-thought-out campaign to eliminate heavily floured sauces, to reduce cooking times, and to produce smaller menus, this has in no way reduced the size of the food checks. This all began in 1972-73, but today, as the first big surge of popularity has long since waned, only a few chefs clench their teeth and their pocketbooks and doggedly follow this fad.

MINESTRONE (Italian) Derived from *minestra,* meaning "soup," this, the national soup of Italy, is the "big soup." *Minestrone* is composed of a mass of uniformly cut vegetables—including onions, root celery, white beans, turnips, leeks, cabbage, and tomatoes—all first seared in pork fat then covered with bouillon and simmered until done. Served with macaroni or rice and dusted with grated Parmesan cheese, this makes a meal-in-itself. *Minestrone* usually tastes better on the following day. COMPATIBLE WINES: A red wine, e.g., Chianti, Nebbiolo, Beaujolais, Dôle, Veltliner, Pinot Noir, Egri Bikaver.

MIRABEAU (French) Named in honor of the famous French Revolutionary statesman and orator Comte de Honore Gabriel Requeti Mirabeau, this garnish is composed of pitted olives, anchovy fillets, and blanched tarragon leaves. It is served with small cuts of meat, such as broiled steaks.

Steak Mirabeau A rib or club steak is grilled and served decorated with fillets of anchovy and pitted olives and topped with an anchovy-butter. COMPATIBLE WINES: A red wine, e.g., Côte Rôtie, Mercurey, Beaujolais, Ruby Cabernet, Nebbiolo, Cahors, Châteauneuf-du-Pape.

MIREPOIX (French) Most generals and marshals of France died not on the battlefield fighting for God and Country but at the dinner table—one while reaching for his fifth helping of grilled salmon. Duke Maréchal Mirepoix, however, died in bed. But before doing so, he squeezed the best creations out of his cooks, one being the famed garniture *mirepoix,* named, of course, after the boss. When this Gallic mixture of cubed onions, carrots, celery, and pork is sautéed in hot butter and seasoned with thyme and bay leaves, it is used as a garnish, as an addition to a number of sauces, and as a flavorsome boost when braising meat or poultry. The pork, whether it be ham or bacon, may be excluded when the *mirepoix* is used with seafood or fish.

MIRIN This sweet saké (rice wine), often used in the preparation of Japanese dishes, is used for cooking only; it is never drunk. If a sherry or a white wine is used as a substitute, sugar is added. (See SAKÉ)

MIROTON (French) An innovative and tasty way of serving "yesterday's boiled beef." Sliced onions, sautéed in butter, are set in the bottom of an ovenproof dish. Overlapping slices of cooked beef are placed over the onions and covered with a *sauce Lyonnaise.* Breadcrumbs are sprinkled over all, and the dish is baked in the oven. (See LYONNAISE) COMPATIBLE WINES: A red wine, e.g., Médoc, Margaux, Mercurey, Côte Rôtie, Valpolicella, Ruby Cabernet.

MISO (Japanese) A fermented soybean paste used in the preparation of soup and as part of a marinade for vegetables and fish. The paste is often used to flavor the liquid in which food is boiled. There are two kinds of *miso:* the red, or *aka miso;* and the milder white, or *miso shiru.* (See MISO SHIRU)

MISO SHIRU (Japanese) A mild white soybean paste. Also, the name given to a favorite soup made from a mixture of *miso* and water, to which bits of dried fish, shellfish, and seaweed plus a flavoring of *daikon* (radish), spinach, watercress, and water dropwort are added. The water dropwort, a Eurasian herb of the rose family, lends a delightful fragrance to the soup. (See DAIKON, MISO)

MISSAHATZ (Armenian) See LAHMAJOON

MOCHI GOME (Japanese) The sweet glutinous rice that is the counterpart of the Chinese variety called *no-mi.* (See RICE IN CHINA)

MOCHIKO (Japanese) Used in the preparation of Japanese tea cakes, this rather sweet rice flour has a high gluten content. Gluten gives dough its elasticity.

MOCK-TURTLE SOUP (English) This soup is so called because its gelatinous quality makes it seem very much like a turtle soup. However, this soup is made from the meat of a calf's head. The meat is cut up and browned in fat with salt pork, veal knuckle, ham or bacon, and a bit of roast chicken. Chopped carrots, onions, and celery are added plus a good stock to cover. Herbs and Madeira wine are added for flavoring, and all is slowly simmered for several hours. Arrowroot is added to thicken, then the soup is strained, left to cool, and defatted. Mock turtle soup is served garnished with small cuts of the now gelatinous meat and with *quenelles* of forcemeat mixed with mashed hard-boiled egg yolks. (See QUENELLES)

MOCQUECHOU (Créole) There are conflicting stories about the origin of this traditional Louisianian dish. One story claims that it came from the Spanish *machica,* a dish of toasted cornmeal sweetened with sugar and flavored with spices. The Cajuns claim that the name refers to the phrase *moque chou,* "mock cabbage." Originally made from scraped corn and tomatoes simmered in water and butter, today the dish is enhanced with heavy cream, minced pimientos, onions, Tabasco sauce, and salt and pepper. This is all cooked in a heavy pot and served with warm French-type bread. COMPATIBLE WINES: A red wine, e.g., Rioja, Pinot Noir, Ruby Cabernet, Lambrusco, Beaujolais, Nebbiolo, Egri Bikaver, Zinfandel.

MOELLE, À LA (French) The designation for a dish served with beef marrow.

Steak à la Moelle A sirloin steak is grilled and served topped with a garniture of poached beef marrow. COMPATIBLE WINES: A red wine, e.g., Fixin, Pommard, Dôle, Beaune, Pinot Noir, Barolo, Nuit St. Georges, La Tâche.

MOGADOR Ever since the French bombarded the Moroccan seaport of Magador in 1884, French chefs, prompted perhaps by a certain guilt, have honored the city by naming certain culinary creations after it. These dishes contain truffles and goose liver.

Sauce Mogador This basic brown sauce is enriched by reducing it with a quantity of chopped black truffles and goose liver. (See BROWN SAUCE, FOIE GRAS)

Sweetbreads Mogador Again the goose liver is used, this time together with veal forcemeat to stuff sweetbreads. The stuffed sweetbreads are then braised and served garnished with stuffed olives and the *sauce Mogador*. COMPATIBLE WINES: A red wine, e.g., Margaux, Médoc, Valpolicella, Santenay, St. Julien, St. Émilion, Zinfandel, Fleurie.

MOGHLAI CHICKEN (East Indian) This complicated chicken speciality is most rewarding. First, a paste is made from chopped onions, ginger, and garlic. Then, sliced onions are fried in oil in a heavy pan and removed. Then, pieces of the chicken are browned in the same oil and likewise removed. Adding more oil to the pot, the onion paste and a mixture of spices—including cinnamon, bay leaves, cardamom pods, cloves, and cumin seeds—are quickly fried. Dry-roasted coriander, turmeric, and cayenne pepper are added alternately with yogurt, tomato sauce, and the browned pieces of chicken. All is simmered together. When the chicken is done, the browned onions and saffron milk are added. Pieces of *poori* (deep-fried whole wheat bread), relish, and white rice usually accompany this most tasty chicken dish. COMPATIBLE BEVERAGES: Beer, ale, cider, tea, or a rosé wine.

MO GWA (Chinese) The Cantonese term for "hair melon." Also called "Chinese watermelon," this white gourd is actually covered with a hairlike substance. Its delicate flesh is only found in Cantonese-style dishes.

MOJO DE AJO (Spanish) For this spicy sauce, raw garlic is ground into a paste. Lime juice, pepper, and salt are then added and the mixture is simmered in hot olive oil. The strained sauce is served with such dishes as suckling pig and *malanga y yuca.* (See MALANGA Y YUCA)

MOLASSES This food sweetener was probably first extracted from sugar cane by the early Chinese or by the East Indians. Until the early nineteenth century, it was the prime sweetener in America, used with everything from doughnuts and corn bread to puddings, griddle cakes, and pies. Molasses was a popular tonic given to children as a fortifier in the spring of the year, especially the "blackstrap" kind. Gleaned from the third pressing of the sugar cane, blackstrap has far less sugar than the ordinary type, as well as an amazing amount of iron, and it was used commercially as cattle feed and to produce alcohol. Early American kitchens were never without the large jar of molasses on the shelf. And there would be no Pennsylvania shoo-fly pie without it! (See SHOO-FLY PIE)

MOLE (Mexican) The name of this famous chili sauce derives from the Nahautl Aztec word *mollis,* meaning "a sauce made with chili." The method of cooking the mole is very similar to that used by the East Indians in the preparation of curry sauces. The chilies, tomatoes, nuts, and the herbs and spices are all ground into a thick purée and then cooked in salt pork, stirring constantly. The meat of choice—pork, chicken, beef, or veal—is cooked in another pot with a bit of beef stock, then the sauce and the meat are heated together.

Mole Poblano de Guajolote A dish of turkey cooked Puebla-style—that is, with chocolate—and as with all classics, a legend goes with this dish. It seems that the good sisters of the Convent of Santa Rosa were in a tizzy. An archbishop and a viceroy were both coming to the convent on the same day, and that brought up the eternal question, "What shall we serve for dinner?" The Indian girls at the convent had an answer: "Give them the turkey with spices and chocolate." The girls knew that under Aztec law they were strictly forbidden to eat of the wicked aphrodisiac called chocolate, but they remembered that chocolate was always reserved for royalty. Who could be more royal than an archbishop and a hungry viceroy? Well, the Indian girls saved the day with their suggestion; they allowed the nervous nuns to breath a sigh of relief and satisfied the hunger of two noble gentlemen with an unexpected taste treat.

To prepare this dish, a disjointed turkey is cooked in salted water. The pieces are then dried and browned in hot fat. In a blender, the following ingredients are whipped into a thick purée: onions, garlic, raisins, cloves, cinnamon, fresh coriander, anise, sesame seeds, *tortillas,* tomatoes, and three chilies—the *ancho,* the *pasilla,* and the *mulato.* To bind the flavors, this purée is cooked in hot fat then in turkey broth. Salt, pepper, and the chocolate are added and cooked, stirring until the chocolate has completely melted. This sauce is poured over the pieces of turkey and cooked covered in a casserole for a short time. The dish is strewn with toasted sesame seeds and served

with boiled white rice. (See CHILI, TORTILLAS) COMPATIBLE BEV-
ERAGES: Beer, tea.

MONÉGASQUE, ONIONS (French) This onion preparation comes from
the Principality of Monaco, famed for its gambling casino. Small
white onions are peeled, placed in a pan with water, olive oil, white
vinegar, salt, sugar, and pepper, then brought to a boil. The onions
are simmered until tender and then removed. To the liquid left in the
pan, tomato purée and seedless raisins are added and this is briskly
cooked down to a thick sauce. The sauce is poured over the onions,
which are then served sprinkled with chopped parsley with fowl or a
roast.

MONGOLE, POTAGE (French) A thick soup of equal parts tomatoes
and carrots, which are puréed to a smooth consistency. The soup is
garnished with a *julienne* of carrots. The connection of the dish with
Mongolia is unclear, for this area is basically a wasteland containing
the great Gobi Desert and the Altai mountain range. The Mongolians
subsist mainly on livestock and processed animal products. Agricultural produce is limited to a small valley of the Yellow River in the
South.

MONKEY BREAD See BAOBAB

MONOSODIUM GLUTAMATE Chinese cooks have used this exceptional
taste-enhancer for centuries. Strangely enough, except for a slight
saline flavor, it has very little taste of its own. The use of monosodium
glutamate is frowned upon by good Chinese chefs. If, for instance, a
cook has made an excellent chicken stock, he has no need for MSG,
as the term is often abbreviated. Cutting costs by diluting and
extending an inferior broth with water, and then atoning for the lack
of taste by adding MSG, will lower the quality of any kitchen. It
should be used with discretion. Monosodium glutamate is a salt
crystal with a formidable formula ($C_5H_8O_4NaN$). Some people display a strange physical reaction when consuming it together with
food: they experience headaches, dizziness, and sweating. The Chinese know MSG as *mai jing,* the Japanese as *ajinomoto.* Westerners
call it Ac'cent. (See AJINOMOTO)

MONT BLANC (French) This mountain of *crème Chantilly* rising in the
middle of a bordure composed of a purée of chestnuts cooked in
sweetened milk and flavored with rum or brandy, evokes, on a small
scale, the snowy summit of one of the highest mountain ranges in the
Alps. Such is the *Mont Blanc* of the fine *patissier.* (See CHANTILLY,
CHESTNUTS, MARRONS)

MONTMORENCY (French) Montmorency, a region located just outside
of Paris, is known for the excellent cherries grown there.
Roast Duck Montmorency Roast duck with cherries. The mainstay
of this dish, the sauce, is made by cooking vinegar and sugar in one
pan, and in another pan cooking butter and flour with the addition of
beef stock, orange and lemon juice and their grated rinds, plus cherry

juice and brandy. To finish the sauce, cherries which have been marinating in a mixture of lemon juice, brandy, and sugar are added. The sauce is poured over the pieces of roasted duck, and the rest of the sauce is served separately in a sauceboat. COMPATIBLE WINES: A white wine, e.g., Saumur, Tokay, Muscat d'Alsace, Sankt Alban, Nierstein, Piesporter Goldtröpfchen, Rüdesheim.

MOOK YEE (Chinese) See CLOUD EARS

MOO-SHU (Chinese) This popular pork dish, native to North China, derives its name from the yellow color of the scrambled eggs in the dish, a color similar to that of the cassia flower, called *moo-shoo*. The dish is prepared by first scrambling eggs lightly in a wok, until the eggs are just set. The eggs are quickly removed, then shredded pork is stir-fried in a wok with hot oil together with chopped tree ears *(mu-er)*, tiger lilies *(jin-zhen)*, and scallions. To this is added a sauce composed of soy sauce, sherry wine, sugar, salt, cornstarch, and the chopped-up scrambled eggs. The dish is usually garnished with Mandarin pancakes. Variations of this dish include *moo-shu* chicken and *moo-shu* beef. (See MANDARIN PANCAKE, MU-ER) COMPATIBLE BEVERAGES: Beer, tea, cider, saké.

MORILLES See CHAMPIGNONS

MORNAY, SAUCE (French) Legend tells us that one fine day the enterprising prime minister of France, Phillipe de Mornay, thought of adding butter and grated cheese to an ordinary *sauce Béchamel* and thus *sauce Mornay* was born. Yet another version states that it was created by a cook named Voiron, who dedicated the sauce to his former chef, named Mornay. The sauce can be served with fish, *pasta*, poultry, veal, vegetables, and with hot *hors d'oeuvre*. When made from a white stock, *sauce Mornay* is suitable to be served with eggs or with poultry; when made from a fish stock, it complements fish or shellfish dishes. (See BÉCHAMEL, HORS D'OEUVRE)

Sole Mornay Whether preparing the whole sole or only fillets, the fish is poached in a fish *fumet* with butter. The sole is then covered with a *sauce Mornay,* sprinkled with grated Gruyère or Parmesan cheese, and browned lightly in the broiler. (See FUMET) COMPATIBLE WINES: A white wine, e.g., Chablis, Aigle, Orvieto, Sauvignon Blanc.

MORTADELLA (Italian) The name of this large sausage, popularly known as *bologna* or "baloney sausage," is said to derive from *mortola,* the myrtle berry with which it is flavored. Of course, the finest *mortadella* still comes from Bologna, the gastronomic center of Italy. The original name of the sausage was *un mortaio della carne di maiale,* but this has been condensed to simply *mortadella.* Today, the *mortadella* is made from a mixture of puréed pork and beef that is larded, seasoned with salt and pepper and flavored with a dry white wine, myrtle berries, and coriander seeds. The mixture is cooked with steam. The "baloney sausages" are made from the meat of a pig's head, from tripe, pork, and veal—all blended with soya flour and colored with food dye.

MOSLEM CUISINE See MIDDLE EASTERN CUISINE

MOSTARDA DI FRUTTA DI CREMONA This very famous Italian mustard is made from various colored fruits which are pickled whole in mustard oil flavored with a sugar syrup. It is served with cold meats, poultry, and even in a mustard cream sauce to complement cooked shrimp.

MOSTOCCIOLI (Italian) See PASTA

MOULES This is the French word for the bivalve mollusks we know as mussels and which are much used as food. (See MARINIÈRE, POULETTE)

MOULES, SOUPE AU (French) See BILLI BI

MOUNTAIN OYSTERS This name, common in the western part of the United States, describes sheeps' testicles used for food. (See ANIMELLES)

MOUSSAKA (Greek/Turkish/Rumanian) Although the *moussaka* is said to be of Rumanian origin and the Turks claim it as their own, as do several other countries, it was the Greek kitchen that made it popular. This dish consisting of layers of succulent fried eggplant and ground lamb is flavored with tomato, oregano, and cinnamon, topped with *sauce Mornay,* and baked to a golden crustiness. It is served cut into squares. *Moussaka* can also be prepared with zucchini or potatoes as a base. (See MORNAY, PATLIKAN) COMPATIBLE WINES: A red wine, e.g., Côtes du Rhône, Beaujolais, Egri Bikaver, Zinfandel, Médoc, Rioja.

MOUSSE (French) Literally, *mousse* means "foam" or "froth," and in culinary parlance it refers to foods that are pounded, ground, or puréed and mixed with egg whites and heavy cream to an airy lightness. A *mousse* can be sweet or savory and can be served cold or hot. The savory varieties might include ham, smoked trout, salmon or mackerel, shellfish, poultry, or *foie gras.* Iced fruit *mousses* and jelly *mousses,* with or without cream, can be made as well. The sweet variety is made from chocolate or purées of apricots, peaches, apples, or other fruits. (See FOIE GRAS)

MOUSSELINE (French) A rich forcemeat made from finely ground, well-pounded meat, poultry, fish, game, or shellfish that is mixed with cream and the whites of eggs. *Mousselines* must be kept cold. (See ÉPICURIENNE)

Pommes Mousseline/Pommes de Terre Mousseline A rich potato purée is made from the pulp of baked potatoes. Seasoned with salt, pepper, and nutmeg, the purée is stirred over heat with the addition of egg yolks, butter, and whipped heavy cream. Formed into a dome shape and sprinkled with melted butter, the potato mass is glazed for a few minutes and served immediately.

Sauce Mousseline A delicate but rich sauce formed by folding egg yolks and heavy cream into the basic *sauce Hollandaise.* The sauce is served with fish, vegetable, or chicken dishes. (See HOLLANDAISE)

Mousseline of Chicken The French make this chicken forcemeat by first cubing and seasoning cooked chicken, then pounding and grinding it into a paste with egg whites. The paste is passed through a sieve and combined with heavy cream. Before serving, all is stirred over ice.

Mousseline of Chicken Alexandra Named to honor the delightful lady who was queen to Edward the VII of England, this dish consists of a *mousseline* of chicken that is formed into *quenelles* and poached. These *quenelles* then form a bed for cooked slices of chicken topped with truffles. Coated with a *sauce Mornay,* the dish is browned in the oven. In the midst of the *quenelles* a cluster of cooked asparagus is set like a floral centerpiece. (See MORNAY, QUENELLES)

Mousseline of Chicken Paprika *Quenelles* of chicken are poached, set on a platter, covered with a *sauce suprême,* and sprinkled with paprika. The *quenelles* are served garnished with small molds of *pilaff* rice and with tomatoes cooked in butter. (See PILAFF, QUENELLES, SUPRÊME) COMPATIBLE WINES: For both chicken dishes, a white wine, e.g., Schloss Vollrads, Sylvaner, Anjou, Vouvray, Piesporter Goldtröpfchen, Nierstein, Rüdesheim, Meursault.

MOUSSEUSE, SAUCE (French) The word *mousseuse,* meaning "foaming, frothy," is a suitable description for this rich sauce. It is made by seasoning a softened *beurre manié* with salt and lemon juice and, while whisking vigorously, adding cold water a drop at a time. Thick and frothy, the sauce is usually served with poached fish. (See BEURRE MANIÉ)

MOUTARDE, SAUCE (French) A piquant sauce made by adding mustard (from Dijon if possible) to a sleek, velvety *sauce Hollandaise.* It is served with fish and meat dishes. (See HOLLANDAISE)

MOZART GARNITURE (French) Named after the world-famous Austrian composer, Wolfgang Amadeus Mozart, this garnish consists of beef tongue, a poached egg, and a touch of black truffle served on top of *tournedos, filets mignons,* or *noisettes* of beef, lamb, mutton, or pork, surrounded by artichoke hearts filled with a purée of celery. A *sauce Colbert* is served separately. (See COLBERT, FILET MIGNON, NOISETTE, TOURNEDOS)

MOZZARELLA IN CARROZZA (Italian) See CARROZZA

MU-ER (Chinese) A black tree fungus—commonly called "tree ears," "wood ears," or "cloud ears"—which is often an ingredient in Szechwan and Mandarin dishes. Long thought to increase potency and to prolong life, the low incidence of coronary disease among the Chinese has been directly attributed to the inclusion of *mu-er* in much of the food they consume. Extensive laboratory studies and experimentation have proved *mu-er* to prevent blood clotting and atherosclerosis, conditions that lead to heart attacks and strokes. (See MOO-SHU, WOOD EARS)

MULLIATELLE (Italian) This highly spiced sausage from Naples is composed of the brains, the heart, and the lungs of a calf—all ground up, of course. The sausage is flavored with raw garlic and hot red peppers. It is usually broiled over charcoal.

MULLIGATAWNY SOUP (Anglo-Indian) This soup was born while India was still part of the British Commonwealth. The name is an Anglicized version of the Tamil words *milagu tannir,* "pepper water." Mulligatawny soup can be thin or thick, depending upon the ingredients used, for there are as many recipes for it as there are for chowders. Following one recipe, onions, celery, and ham are cubed, dusted with flour, and browned. With the addition of rice flour, all is covered with chicken stock and cooked with chopped chicken and sour apples. Seasoned with curry, bound with cream, and served with sliced chicken and rice, the soup makes a good luncheon.

Another method uses lamb chunks, rice, and chicken broth together with ginger, chickpea flour, garlic, and such spices as turmeric, cumin, coriander, and both black and cayenne pepper. COMPATIBLE BEVERAGES: Beer.

MÜNCHNER PRINZREGENTENTORTE (German) This regal chocolate cake is named for the Prince Regent of Munich. It uses baking powder as the leavening agent and is rich in eggs, butter, and chocolate. The cake is made in five separate cake tins by spreading a thin layer of the batter over each cake tin base. The five baked layers are topped with a rich chocolate cream made from butter, sugar, eggs, vanilla, and cocoa. They are carefully stacked, and the whole cake is covered with a chocolate-and-rum icing. The cake is chilled before serving. If you love chocolate, this is for you.

MUNG From this bean starch paste the Chinese make the translucent noodles that look so much like cellophane threads. If *mung* is unavailable, then cornstarch is used, but *mung* is preferred. The *mung* is made by allowing washed beans to ferment for a period of five days or more, using yeast as a catalyst. After rinsing and draining, the beans are ground into a purée, the fluid is extracted, and the mass is sieved to remove hulls and other unwanted particles. The residue, a starchy paste, is used by Chinese cooks to produce the *pasta.* (See HARUSAME)

MUNG BEAN (East Indian) Used chiefly in Indian cooking but popular in China as well, the mung bean is green and about half the size of the pea. The beans can be served cooked, or they can be ground up into a flour. They can also be germinated and the sprouts used in salads.

MURATABAK (Chinese) A type of *crêpe,* or pancake, that is served with eggs cooked with onions and with a curry sauce dip.

MURGA KORMA (East Indian) A famous curried chicken dish. To prepare, chopped onions and chili peppers are sautéed in hot peanut oil. The curry spice mixture _(garam masala)_ and a bit of water are then added and the contents are simmered together. After seasoning with salt, the diced chicken breasts are added with water, ground cardamom seeds, toasted coconut, walnuts, and yogurt; the whole is simmered over very low heat. To serve, the chili peppers are discarded, and the chicken and the spicy sauce are placed in the center of a hot plate, surrounded with shredded coconut and walnut halves. This dish is served with chutney and boiled rice. (See GARAM MASALA) COMPATIBLE BEVERAGES: Beer.

MURGHI CURRY The same as _murga korma._

MUSCOLI (Italian) Mussels. (See COZZE, MARINARA, MARINIÉRE)

MUSHIMONO (Japanese) This nonsweet custard, usually served as a main course, may contain a blend of fish, meats, shellfish, or vegetables. It is carefully steamed either in individual earthenware dishes or in a large communal bowl.

MUSHROOMS

Agaricus campestris The button mushroom, which has a mildly nutty taste and is one of the most commonly used in cooking.

Cantharellis cibarius A florally aromatic type of mushroom.

Boleti Called _cèpes_ by the French, these have a rooty taste. They are also known as "honeycomb mushrooms."

Morels The favorite of chefs, this species shows itself for only a two-week period. It is not only much in demand because of its elusiveness but because of its taste. The French call them _les morilles._

A correctly sautéed mushroom can enhance the flavor of foods and sauces like little else, but three important rules must be observed if one expects to extract the quintessence of the mushroom's glorious fragrance: (1) The mushroom must be completely dry, (2) the butter or oil must be very hot, and (3) the mushrooms must not be crowded together. If too many mushrooms are crammed into a pan, no matter how hot the pan may be or how much sweet butter is present, not only will the mushrooms brown improperly, but they will steam and shrink to shriveled lumps and the essential juices will evaporate their goodness into the air.

Each cuisine has its favorite ways of preparing mushrooms. The Italian cook will prepare them with crushed garlic, minced onions, tomato paste, oregano, and parsley, while the Russian prefers his mushrooms with a touch of paprika and gobs of sour cream, which goes for his Hungarian confrere as well. The cook native to the Côte d'Azur, in the south of France, will add chopped tomatoes, garlic, onions, parsley, oregano, and basil to his mushrooms. (See CHAMPIGNONS, DUXELLES)

MUSSALLAM MURGH (East Indian) A whole chicken is first marinated for several hours in a heavy paste of *garam masala,* garlic, ginger, turmeric, hot green chilies, salt, and yogurt. After the chicken is browned in hot oil, a thick purée of cooked onions, garlic, ginger, almonds, lemon juice, cardamom, cinnamon, nutmeg, and mace is packed around it. In a bit of water, the chicken is thus simmered and constantly basted until done. The chicken is served surrounded with hard-boiled eggs and accompanied with fried eggplant, green chutney, and a yogurt relish. (See GARAM MASALA, MURGA KORMA, TIKKA MURGH) COMPATIBLE BEVERAGES: Beer, ale, cider.

MUSTARD SEED Since biblical times, mustard has been used as a condiment and as a medicine, most often as a digestive stimulant and as the basic warming ingredient of a bath or a poultice. For centuries in India, the mustard seed was known to ward off evil spirits: anxious mothers sewed tiny mustard grains into the clothing of their children to protect them from demons. The elderly stuffed their pillows with them to avoid bad dreams. However, mustard seed is most important while in the kitchen. Of the many varieties, the black mustard, *brassica negra,* and the white mustard, *brassica alba,* are the finest. Fine chefs know the black mustard to be the more pungent and aromatic, though less hot than the yellow type. The young leaves of the mustard plant are used raw in salads or cooked as a green vegetable; they are very popular in the South of the United States, in India, where the greens are known as "leaf mustard," and in China, where they are known as *pok-choi.*

The estimable French mustard of Dijon, made with white wine, is one of the finest in the world. It is not as hot as either the English mustard or the German mustard. The Italians rightfully boast of a mustard marked *cremona,* which contains finely-chopped candied fruits.

In 1730, a woman named Clements, living in Lancashire, England, created the first mustard powder, or flour, which needed only the addition of a liquid such as water or wine to ready it for culinary use. She was able to keep her recipe secret for enough years to make herself a tidy fortune. Once she had sold the royal court of England, she was made.

Mustard has many culinary uses, adding its surprising flavor to cream sauces, leftover meats, egg dishes, and chicken, and it does wonderful things for the taste of ham, beef, and even fish. (See MOSTARDA DI FRUTTA, MOUTARDE, RAI KI MACCHI)

MYARJI PLOV (Caucasian) A delightful Azerbaidzhan *pilaff* of rice that is topped with a currant-flavored lamb stew. To prepare, cubed lamb is browned in hot butter and oil with chopped onions. Well seasoned with salt and pepper, the lamb is covered with a beef broth and simmered until tender. Dried currants, simmered in butter, are added to the stew, and all is cooked until most of the broth has been absorbed. The dish is served with a mound of steamed saffron-flavored rice. COMPATIBLE BEVERAGES: Beer, cider, tea.

NABEMONO (Japanese) A type of one-pot cookery which enables guests to help themselves from a bubbling pot filled with meat, vegetables, seafood, etc., right at the dinner table. The term also refers to a *fondue*-type service, where the guest actually cooks his own food in a rich boiling broth and then dips the food into a choice of sauces before eating it. Quite similar is the "Chinese fire-pot" from Canton, the "ten-varieties hot-pot" from Shanghai, and the "Mongolian fire-pot" from Peking. (See SHABU SHABU, SUKIYAKI, YOSENABE)

NACH HAUSART (German) See MAISON/DE LA MAISON

NAGE, À LA (French) Literally meaning "swimming," this term refers to those shellfish that are served in the same broth in which they were originally cooked. They can be eaten cold or hot.

NAMEKO (Japanese) A small mushroom, similar to the button mushroom.

NAM PLA (Thai) A condiment made from the fermented liquid of puréed salted shrimp. It is not spicy. (See GARUM, SOY SAUCE)

NAN (Indian/Pakistani) Another name for the flat, soft bread that is so often served with *chicken tandoori*. (See CHAPATIS, PAPPADUMS, PHULKAS, TANDOORI)

NANTAISE, À LA If a duck is listed on a French menu as *canard à la Nantaise*, the association of the fowl with the city of Nantes has nothing to do with its preparation and eventual service. *À la Nantaise* indicates that the duck has been drained of all blood before being cooked, in contradistinction to *à la Rouennaise*. (See ROUENNAISE)

NANTUA (French) The name of a town and of a lake in eastern France, near to the Swiss border. Culinarily, it denotes that a dish contains crayfish.

Ris de Veau Nantua Sweetbreads served in a rather special way—with crayfish. Cleaned and blanched sweetbreads are set on a bed of salt pork, carrots, and onions in the bottom of a well-buttered casserole. Seasoned with salt, pepper, and bay leaf, they are simmered for a few minutes. Then, with the addition of a chicken stock, the contents of the pot are brought to a boil. They are then braised in the oven, basting frequently. The sweetbreads are drained, set on a platter surrounded with crayfish, and coated with the strained sauce. COMPATIBLE WINES: A red wine, e.g., Mercurey, Côte Rôtie, Santenay, Margaux, Beaujolais, Mâcon Rouge, Zinfandel, Valpolicella, Veltliner, St. Julien.

Sauce Nantua A sauce made by reducing a *sauce Béchamel* and adding a *fumet* of crayfish, tomatoes, tomato purée, crayfish-butter, and heavy cream. The sauce is finished with a dash of brandy and a pinch of cayenne pepper. It is served with egg, fish, and shellfish dishes. (See BÉCHAMEL, FUMET)

NAPOLEON (French) Flaky layers of puff pastry filled with *crème patissière*. The pastry is topped with a light vanilla icing or powdered sugar and served in rectangular portions. (See CRÈME PATISSIÈRE)

NAPOLITAINE GARNITURE (French) Named for the port of Naples, this garnish of spaghetti mixed with tomatoes and tomato purée and topped with a generous amount of grated Parmesan cheese is served with meat dishes.

Napolitaine Ice Cream An Italian creation consisting of ice cream imaginatively frozen in three layers. Each ice cream layer is a different flavor and a different color.

Sauce Napolitaine This French sauce uses a *sauce demi-glace* as its base. This is cooked together with minced ham, a *bouquet garni,* chopped shallots, bay leaves, cloves, red currant jelly, thyme, and Madeira wine. The sauce is served with game dishes. (See BOUQUET GARNI, DEMI-GLACE, NEAPOLITAN)

NAPOLITANA, ALLA (Italian) A dish as it would be prepared in the city of Naples. "Naples" brings to mind the aroma of small tomatoes and crushed raw garlic simmering in olive oil—to be served with *pasta* dishes of all kinds, with toasted bread and cheese, with chicken, fish, and pizza.

Crostini alla Napolitana Bread that has been well toasted in olive oil and butter is placed on a baking sheet and covered with mozzarella cheese and a sauce composed of anchovies, garlic, parsley, tomatoes, and peppers. It is broiled until the cheese begins to melt. COMPATIBLE WINES: A red wine, e.g., Chianti, Barolo, Côte Rôtie, Pinot Noir, Egri Bikaver, Mâcon, Châteauneuf-du-Pape, Zinfandel, Rioja.

NAPPÉ (French) Coated with a sauce or with a jelly.

NARGISI KOFTAS (East Indian) A preparation of stuffed meatballs. *Koftas* means "meatballs," and *nargisi* is the Indian word for "narcissus," here pertaining to the yellow-white color of the eggs used to fill the meatballs. Ground beef is thoroughly mixed with yogurt, chopped Chinese parsley, and the following spices: ground cloves, cayenne pepper, cinnamon, mace, black pepper, cumin, and salt. The meat mixture is used to form individual round balls around whole hard-boiled eggs. These are carefully browned in hot vegetable oil flavored with cardamom pods and bay leaves. The meatballs are removed and a paste is made from onions, garlic, and ginger; this is stirred into the oil. Coriander, cumin, turmeric, yogurt, paprika, water, and tomato sauce are added to this mixture, then the meatballs are replaced and the covered pot is simmered for half an hour. The meatballs are served with heaps of steamed white rice. COMPATIBLE BEVERAGES: Beer, tea, ale, cider.

NARIEL CHUTNEY (East Indian) Shredded coconut and lemon juice are puréed and flavored with chopped fresh ginger, chili peppers, garlic cloves, and onions. The chutney is refrigerated until ready to serve with curried dishes. (See CHUTNEY)

NASI GORENG Dutch colonials have integrated Indonesian dishes into their own cuisine to such an extent that today these dishes are considered to be part of the traditional food of Holland. A good example is the *nasi goreng,* a kind of Indonesian *smörgåsbord* composed of sautéed pork, shrimp, chicken, crabmeat, and scallions; these foods are decorated with a *julienne* of fried egg, fried onions, and chopped chilies and served with fried rice. The dish is complemented with Chinese chili sauce and a soy sauce. (See JULIENNE, SMÖRGÅSBORD) COMPATIBLE BEVERAGES: Beer, tea, cider, rosé wine.

NATTO (Japanese) A preparation of soybeans. The soybeans are cooked and then allowed to ferment, during which time they develop a distinctive odor and flavor. When mashed, they become *natto.* Seasoned with salt, *natto* is added to rice dishes, served with *daikon* (a type of radish) or with soup. (See DAIKON)

NATUR SCHNITZEL (German) A veal cutlet that is cooked naturally, that is, unbreaded. (See SCHNITZEL)

NAVARIN (French) A stew made from mutton or lamb.

Navarin Printanier A spring lamb stew made with plenty of fresh vegetables: peas, onions, garlic, potatoes, string beans, parsley, chervil, and carrots. The finest *navarin* is effected by changing the pan that is used to brown the lamb, thereby removing the grease.

Navarin Provençale Peeled tomatoes and garlic added to the above *printanier* change it like magic to the *Provençale.*

COMPATIBLE WINES: A red wine, e.g., Mâcon, Margaux, St. Julien, Cabernet Sauvignon, Zinfandel, Valpolicella, Nebbiolo, Egri Bikaver, Médoc.

NEAPOLITAN SAUCE (Italian) The creation of Charles Elmé Francatelli, the Italian chief cook and *maître d'hôtel* to Queen Victoria, this sauce is made by melting red currant jelly and then vigorously whipping freshly grated horseradish into the warm jelly mixed with the drippings from the roast with which it is to be served plus a red wine. It is a variation of the *sauce Napolitaine,* which uses a *sauce demi-glace* as its base. Francatelli's essence is the horseradish, and it makes all the difference. (See DEMI-GLACE, NAPOLITAINE)

NÈGRE EN CHEMISE (French) Literally, "Negro in night-dress." A rather imaginative description for a combination of *crème Chantilly* and a chestnut purée. (See CHANTILLY)

NESSELRODE The French have made this name of a famous Russian count gastronomically synonymous with chestnuts when used to describe certain dishes. It was, however, Count Nesselrode's chef, Mouy, who created these dishes.

Pudding à la Nesselrode This delicious pudding—one might say ambrosia—is made by adding a velvety chestnut purée, currants, seedless raisins, candied orange rind, and candied cherries to an English custard. The dried fruits are macerated for a day or two in a cream sherry or sweet Madeira before they are used. An alternate version is composed of a chestnut purée plus vanilla ice cream flavored with Maraschino liqueur, candied fruits, raisins, and currants that have been soaked in liqueur and frozen. To serve, it is unmolded and topped with a *crème Chantilly* and *marrons glacées* (whipped cream and candied chestnuts).

NEWBURG SAUCE (American) Although this sauce was created at the famous Delmonico Restaurant in New York City, its paternity is one hundred percent French, having been sired by M. Pascal, the French chef of the great restaurant on 14th Street.

The sauce was originally named after a Mr. Wenburg, who was honored guest at the Delmonico until he had a row with the boss. Wenburg insisted that the sauce be renamed by reversing the first three letters: NEWburg instead of WENburg. The sauce, however, is the same.

Lobster Newburg Small pieces of cooked lobster are sautéed in butter. After sherry is added and boiled down, a fish stock and a *sauce velouté* is stirred in and simmered covered. With the lobster removed, the sauce is refined with heavy cream seasoned to taste; it is then put through a fine sieve and whisked over heat until thickened. Finally, the sauce is poured over the lobster served in a *timbale* or over toasted bread. (See VELOUTÉ) COMPATIBLE WINES: A white wine, e.g., Montrachet, Meursault, White Haut Brion, Corton-Charlemagne, Pinot Chardonnay, Orvieto, Szamorodni, Tokay, Vouvray, Nierstein, Rüdesheim.

NEW ENGLAND CLAM CHOWDER (American) Diced salt pork and cubed potatoes are cooked together. Chopped onions are added with a dusting of flour; then the clam juice, water, thyme, salt, and pepper are added and the liquid is brought to the simmer. After the sauce has cooked enough to blend the ingredients, chopped clams and heavy cream are added and the mixture is brought to the boil. The chowder is served piping hot with a dollop of fresh butter swimming in the center of each steaming bowl. (See CHOWDER)

NEW YORK SALAD (American) Were you to ask a Swiss for a Swiss steak, a citizen of Novgorod for a Russian dressing, or a native from Canton for a chop suey, you would probably get a dumb stare; or if something were presented, it would be radically different from what these culinary terms are usually taken to mean. The same holds true for the New York salad. New Yorkers are unfamiliar with it. However, in the Midwest, the South, and in the West of America, it is composed of head lettuce and chopped celery tossed with a light *sauce Mayonnaise* and topped with slices of hard-boiled eggs, olives, capers, and fillets of anchovy. Now, if one added slices of tongue and the white meat of chicken, the dish would immediately be recognized in every one of the five boroughs of New York as the "chef's salad." (See CHOP SUEY, MAYONNAISE, RUSSE)

NGAH CHOY (Chinese) The delicate white sprouts of the mung bean. (See MUNG BEAN)

NIÇOISE, À LA (French) A descriptive term for dishes served with a garniture composed of particular foods used by the chefs of the City of Nice, that famed Mediterranean resort on the southern coast of France, *le Midi.* This garnish usually includes garlic, tomatoes, anchovies, black olives, capers, and lemon juice.

Poireaux à la Niçoise This method of preparing leeks entails cutting them lengthwise and sautéing them in hot olive oil. With the addition of minced garlic, chopped tomatoes, black olives, lemon juice, anchovies, salt, and pepper, they are cooked a bit longer. The leeks are served with a sprinkling of chopped parsley and wedges of hard-boiled eggs.

NIGIRI-SUSHI (Japanese) A smoked fish and rice ball appetizer. Cooked rice is formed into balls then dipped into a mixture of soy sauce, vinegar, sugar, and salt. The balls of rice are then wrapped in the very thinly sliced smoked salmon and/or anchovies. COMPATIBLE BEVERAGES: Beer, tea, saké, cider, rosé.

NIMONO (Japanese) Foods that are simmered or boiled. Usually these foods are cooked in a rich beef, chicken, or fish stock *(dashi)* that can be flavored with any number of herbs, wines, and condiments, such as sugar, salt, soy sauce, *saké, miso,* or *mirin.* (See SAKÉ, MIRIN, MISO)

NISHIME (Japanese) A popular fish-and-vegetable dish composed of a plant of the aster family, called burdock, plus carrots, *daikon,* starch from the taro root, and seaweed. Dried fish, dried shrimp, or meat can be added to the dish. (See DAIKON)

NIVERNAISE, À LA (French) Foods garnished with root vegetables are often said to be prepared *à la Nivernaise,* after the province which supplies the finest root vegetables in France. The garnish is composed of carrots, turnips, onions, and boiled potatoes. The term can also denote a beef consommé flavored with onion and chervil, tiny balls of carrots and turnips, and decorated with cubes of egg white or custard. Or it may describe a sauce made from a *sauce Allemande* with tiny carrots and turnip balls. (See ALLEMANDE)

Tongue Nivernaise Beef tongue is braised in a bouillon flavored with onions and salt pork. Carrots sautéed in butter are added.

Poulet Nivernaise Chicken pieces are browned and then baked in white wine with onions, carrots, mushrooms, parsley, and spices. To finish, the chicken is placed under the grill while saffron and sour cream are added to the sauce and served with the dish. COMPATIBLE WINES: A white wine, e.g., Graves, Beaune Blanc, Corton-Charlemagne, Château-Grillet, Orvieto, Vouvray, Meursault, Aigle, Johannisberg, Piesporter Goldtröpfchen, Dry Sauterne, Anjou, Sylvaner.

NOCKERL, SALZBURGER (Austrian) Created in Salzburg, Mozart's birthplace, these creamy, light dumplings, almost like individual fluffy sweet *soufflés,* are specialities of the Austrian kitchen. The dish is made by carefully folding together beaten egg whites with egg yolks and sifted flour. This fluffy batter is then dropped by the spoonful into hot butter in a large pan and lightly browned on both sides. Served dusted with powdered sugar, they are delightful. Yet another version is a simple *soufflé* made by flavoring egg yolks with vanilla and lemon peel and then folding beaten egg whites into the mixture. Baked in the oven until lightly browned, the *soufflé* is sprinkled with powdered sugar and served at once.

NOHUT ERMESI (Turkish) A purée of chickpeas prepared with sesame oil, lemon juice, and crushed garlic.

NOIR, BEURRE (French) See COMPOUND BUTTER

NOISETTE (French) When used in culinary descriptions, this term refers to the hazelnut. Small, round choice morsels of meat are also often called *noisettes* because of their size.

Noisette-butter Butter that has been cooked until it has taken on the color of the hazelnut; however, should the term read explicitly "noisette of butter," it means then that the butter has been shaped like a hazelnut. The term *noisette* is more pertinently utilized to designate those dishes, usually desserts, that are flavored with hazelnuts.

Noisettes de Chevreuil aux Raisins Small venison slices with grapes. The sliced venison is sautéed in oil and butter; after seasoning, grape juice, brandy, and seedless grapes are added to the pan. As soon as the grapes have heated through, the dish is served. COMPATIBLE WINES: A red wine, e.g., St. Émilion, Talbot, Figeac, Fixin, Échézeaux, Chambolle-Musigny, Dôle, Cabernet Sauvignon, Chambertin.

Sauce Noisette A sauce prepared by adding hazelnut-butter to a *sauce Hollandaise.* It is served with most any type of boiled fish.(See HOLLANDAISE)

Pommes Noisette Potatoes cut into small ball shapes with a melon-ball cutter or similar tool and then browned in butter.

NOKI (Hungarian) Egg noodles.

NOODLES, "SWUNG" (Chinese) To produce these delicate noodles satisfactorily demands not only gastronomic artistry but great acrobatic skill as well. The sight of an adept Chinese chef in the process of forming these noodles from masses of glutinous dough is much like watching a vaudeville or music-hall turn done exquisitely. The flour must be high in gluten wheat, finely milled, with mung starch added. After the dough has been worked well and kneaded vigorously to develop the necessary gluten, it is shaped into a ball and allowed to rest for some twenty minutes or more. It is then rolled between well-floured hands to produce a long roll two inches in diameter. The elongated roll of dough is picked up by the two ends and swung like a jump rope in a circular arch until it has been stretched to a length of six feet. The ends are then put together and the process is repeated again, and again. A skillful "noodle-swinger" can make up to 128 separate strands in one session, and they are as round and as smooth as *vermicelli*. The feat calls for applause. (See VERMICELLI)

NORI (Japanese) Dried laver, a purplish-red seaweed used in Oriental cooking to cover rice balls, which are then served as a garnish. It also makes a pliable wrapper for rice rolls, such as *nori makizushi*. (See MAKIZUSHI)

NORMANDE, À LA (French) "In the Normandy style," pertaining to that regional cuisine known for its use of apples, cider, and the famous Calvados brandy, as well as for its seafood, its rich butter, and fresh thick cream. When used to describe dishes of meat and feathered game, the term indicates that the meat or game was cooked in cider and is served with a Calvados-laced sauce. When used to describe a poultry dish, it means that Calvados, cider, cream, and apples were used to cook and flavor the bird.

Côtes de Porc Sautées Normande A very tasty method of preparing pork chops cut from the loin. First, thick slices of tart apples are well dusted with flour and fried in a mixture of oil and butter until golden. Stoned prunes are wrapped in rashers of bacon and pierced with skewers. The pork chops are boned, flattened, dusted with flour, dipped in egg, covered with breadcrumbs, and sautéed in butter and oil. The apple slices are sprinkled with sugar and broiled on skewers together with the bacon-wrapped prunes. Each pork chop should then be regally served with a slice of the apple and a prune crowning the center of the chop. COMPATIBLE WINES: A red wine, e.g., Beaujolais, Zinfandel, Côte Rôtie, Moulin-à-Vent, Fleurie, Valpolicella, Mercurey, Margaux, Châteauneuf-du-Pape, Cabernet Sauvignon.

Crêpes Normande (French) Apple pancakes made with finely chopped apples mixed into an egg batter. They are served sprinkled with powdered sugar.

Filet de Sole Normande This rich method of cooking sole is common to the Normandy region of France. First, oysters and crayfish are poached in white wine. The fillets of sole are braised in a mixture of white wine and fish stock to which a garnish of mushrooms, mussels, oysters and crayfish are added. The fillets of sole are placed in the center of a platter, coated with a *sauce Normande* and surrounded with crayfish, mussels, oysters, and croutons. COMPATIBLE WINES: A white wine, e.g., Montrachet, Meursault, Corton-Charlemagne, Bernkastler Doktor, Soave, Pinot Chardonnay, Piesporter Goldtröpfchen, Johannisberg, Rüdesheim.

Sauce Normande A sauce made by combining a *fumet de poisson,* chopped mushrooms, oyster juice, a *velouté de poisson,* and heavy cream and then reducing the mixture to half. Away from the heat, more heavy cream, egg yolks and sweet butter are whipped into the sauce. *Sauce Normande* is served with sole, with other fine fish or with oysters. (See FUMET DE POISSON, VELOUTÉ DE POISSON)

Le Trou Normand The French word *trou* translates to "hole," but this seems to have little to do with *le trou Normand,* which is, in effect, a kind of *entremet,* a shot of potent liquor to be swallowed in one gulp. It is taken in the middle of a large meal as a *digestif* (an aid to digestion). *Le trou Normand* is always an *eau de vie* distilled from apples, which in Normandy is called Calvados. When a brandy other than Calvados is used, it is called *le trou de milieu* or *le coup de milieu.*

The drinking of a strong liquor during a large meal is a common custom in cold northern countries, such as Norway, Sweden, Finland, Denmark, and Russia. When the ancient Romans became so full of food during their orgiastic banquets that they feared they might burst, they used a feather; the French use *le trou Normande.* (See DIGESTIF, EAU DE VIE, ENTREMET, SMÖRGÅSBORD, SNAPSI)

Young Rabbit Normande The rabbit is cut up into pieces, dusted with flour, then browned in a mixture of oil and butter and simmered in cider until done. COMPATIBLE WINES: A red wine, e.g., Margaux, Médoc, Fleurie, Mâcon, Côte Rôtie, Châteauneuf-du-Pape, hard cider, Mercurey, Cabernet Sauvignon.

Sweetbreads Normande Sweetbreads are sautéed in butter and served in a rich cream sauce with apples. COMPATIBLE WINES: A red wine, e.g., Fleurie, Valpolicella, Zinfandel, Côtes du Rhône, Egri Bikaver, Premiat, Beaujolais.

Crêpe Normande A *crêpe* is filled with finely diced ham and apples, topped with chopped mushrooms and cream sauce, and grilled. (See CRÊPE) COMPATIBLE WINES: Barzac, Château d'Yquem, Champagne, Vouvray, Muscat d'Alsace, Forster Jesuitengarten, Badacsonyi.

NORVÉGIENNE (French) A dessert composed of ice cream enclosed within a sponge cake and covered with stiffly beaten egg whites. Just before serving, it is baked in a hot oven for a few minutes to brown the covering meringue. In America, the dessert is called "baked Alaska." (See ALASKA)

NOUGAT (French) A confection made with roasted almonds or walnuts mixed with honey and sugar. Of the two types of *nougat,* the most famous is the *white nougat* from the city of Montélimar. It is made from honey, sugar, orange blossom water, and stiffly beaten egg whites. After melting the sugar over heat with the other ingredients, the mass is left to cool and cut to size. The other *nougat,* called *caramel nougat,* is made by heating sugar to the caramel stage and then adding almonds or walnuts. Nougats are also made using hazelnuts, filberts, and pistachio nuts.

NOUILLES À L'ALSACIENNE (French) The Alsatians have a novel method of preparing egg noodles for the table. Using broad egg noodles, they blanch them for ten minutes in boiling salted water and then put them in a baking dish with alternate layers of grated Gruyère cheese. A handful of uncooked noodles are deep-fried in oil, strewn over the noodles in the baking dish, and dotted with bits of sweet butter. The dish is baked in a moderate oven.

NOUVELLE CUISINE (French) See MINCEUR CUISINE

NOVA SCOTIA An American idiom used in the delicatessen trade for "cold-smoked" salmon. As the name implies, the salmon once might have come from Nova Scotia, Canada, but so few salmon are caught there today that the term has come to include the Pacific Ocean variety as well. The term "cold-smoked" (dried with heat not above 90 degrees Fahrenheit) is the process that keeps the salmon solid enough to be cut into paper-thin slices. (See GRAVLAX, LOX)

NUDELTOPF (German) A noodle casserole made with cooked chicken bits and asparagus bound with a rich sauce made from heavy cream and eggs. It is baked in a medium oven.

NUOC-MAM (Indonesian) This equivalent of the well-known Chinese soy sauce, used to enhance the flavor of food, is made from fish.

NYMPHES (French) A euphemistic term for "frogs' legs." (See FROGS, GRENOUILLES)

O'BRIEN POTATOES (Irish) Although the identity of this O'Brien is uncertain, it is clear that he fried his diced potatoes with gobs of chopped onions and sweet green peppers.

OCHSENMAULSALAT (German) Literally, *Ochsen,* "ox"; *Maul,* "muzzle, snout." A jellied cold meat salad made with onions, vinegar, herbs, and spices. Much of the meat used is from the head of a steer or cow—hence the name. The salad is served in thick slices as an appetizer or as a luncheon dish. COMPATIBLE BEVERAGES: A good cold beer.

ODAMAKI MUSHI (Japanese) A type of custard that includes noodles, vegetable greens, or meat or fish. The noodle version consists of cooked *udon* (a thick white noodle made from wheat) that is seasoned with soy sauce and mixed with eggs, *dashi, mirin,* and chopped mushrooms. This mixture is spooned into small earthenware bowls, which are then covered with aluminum foil and steamed. It makes a delightful luncheon. (See DASHI, MIRIN, UDON) COMPATIBLE WINES: A white wine, e.g., saké, Sauterne, Graves, Sylvaner, Gewürztraminer, Anjou, Orvieto.

ODEN (Japanese) A stew made by layering small potatoes, turnips, sweet potatoes, and *daikon* (radish) in a *dashi* (soup) flavored with *kombu* (dried kelp) and bringing all to a boil. *Shoyu* (soy sauce), sugar, and saké are added with *agedashi* puffs (deep-fried soybean cakes filled with a mixture of finely minced cabbage, carrots, *shiitake* mushrooms, *daikon,* and bamboo shoots) plus *ganmo* balls. After simmering for twenty minutes, fresh *tofu* is placed on top and all is simmered again for half an hour. Removed from the heat, the pot is left to stand for a period of four hours. To serve, the stew is just brought to the simmer and is then served with side dishes of scallions, hot mustard, and pepper. (See AGEDASHI, DAIKON, DASHI, GANMO, KOMBU, SHIITAKE, SHOYU, TOFU) COMPATIBLE BEVERAGES: Warm saké or cold beer.

ODORI (Japanese) Literally meaning "still dancing," this refers to the ultimate in freshness when dining on raw fish—that is, consuming the fish, flecked with sauce, while it is still wriggling!

OEUF, L' (French) Egg.

Oeufs à la Neige (French) This is a classic and simple dessert. The whites of eggs are whipped until stiff and then carefully mixed with powdered sugar. With a spoon, these whites, now a meringue, are molded to egg shapes and carefully eased into a pan of boiling milk that has been sugared and flavored with vanilla. The meringues should be turned so that they poach evenly, and when firm, drained in a sieve. Egg yolks are added to the milk, and the mixture is heated to a *crème Anglaise* consistency. The egg-shaped meringues are placed in a large shallow dish with the English custard poured over them. The dessert is chilled before serving. (See ANGLAISE)

OIE, L' (French) Goose. (See CONFIT D'OIE)

OIGNON, SOUPE À L' (French) This famous onion soup has long been the traditional pick-me-up after a night on the town. To prepare the delicious restorative, thinly sliced onions are sautéed in butter and oil until limp. Then, having been seasoned with sugar, salt, and pepper, a hot beef bouillon is added together with a dry white wine. To serve, the hot soup is ladled into ovenproof bowls, topped with slices of toasted French bread, sprinkled with grated Gruyère cheese, and placed under a hot broiler until the top is golden and crusty. COMPATIBLE WINES: A red wine, e.g., Beaujolais, Valpolicella, Nebbiolo, Margaux, Médoc, Châteauneuf-du-Pape, Côte Rôtie, Zinfandel, Egri Bikaver, Pinot Noir.

OKRA This green vegetable is also called "gumbo." When young okra pods are firm, and when lightly cooked, they are agreeably crunchy and only slightly gelatinous. When the cooking of okra is prolonged, however, it becomes mushy or "gumbo" in consistency.

This vegetable, which grows abundantly in tropical climates, was known in ancient Egypt. It was first brought to America on slave ships. The Spanish word for okra is *quibombo;* the French word is *gombo.* In English, okra is also called ochro, ladyfinger, and bamie.

Gumbo Chicken Okra (Créole) For this dish from the bayou country of Louisiana, cut-up chicken and diced ham are sautéed in bacon fat until lightly browned and then removed. After chopped onion, trimmed fresh okra, thyme, parsley, Tabasco sauce, and tomatoes are brought to the simmer, the chicken and ham are returned. Water and salt are added and all is cooked for about an hour. The pot is removed from the heat and filé powder is stirred in. Chicken gumbo is usually served with steamed rice. (See FILÉ, GUMBO) COMPATIBLE WINES: A red wine, e.g., Petit Sirah, Beaujolais, Santenay, Côtes du Rhône, Valpolicella, Zinfandel.

OLLA PODRIDA A hearty Spanish stew containing almost everything the chef has in his kitchen. *Olla podrida* literally translates to "putrid pot" or "rotten pot." The French call it *pot-pourri,* but the Germans, who have a tendency to gild the lily, named it *Stinktopf,* meaning "stink-pot." In days of yore, this pot was never emptied, but added to daily. It remained hanging in the fireplace and was refreshed with new tidbits each day.

A good *olla* is a hearty feast, and today it is composed of *garbanzos* (chickpeas), bacon, salt beef, chicken, onions, and garlic—all cooked in water for four or five hours. The contents are then placed in a fresh pot with plenty of water plus lima beans, cabbage, carrots, blood sausage or *chorizo* (a sausage spiced with garlic and paprika), and veal-and-ham meatballs. It is seasoned with cinnamon and saffron. Potatoes are cooked separately. The vegetables are served separate from the meat and potatoes. To complement the gustatory giant, a sauce is made from garlic, pepper, and saffron plus a purée of tomatoes and potatoes—all mashed together with a flavoring of vinegar, parsley, and a rich bouillon. (See CHORIZO, GARBANZO) COMPATIBLE WINES: A red wine, e.g., Rioja, Hermitage, Egri Bikaver, Lambrusco, Valpolicella, Zinfandel, Mercurey, Veltliner, Côte Rôtie.

OMELETTE BAVEUSE See BAVEUX

OMELETTE NORVÉGIENNE See ALASKA

OMELETTE SURPRISE See ALASKA

ONIONS The onion is the oldest vegetable known to man. In Egypt, where first we hear of it, it had the same status as their gods. In fact, onions were held in such high esteem by the great Pharaohs themselves that they had them sealed into the sarcophagus to help pave the way into the next world. However, the onion was not native to Egypt. The Egyptians discovered the onion in Afghanistan and brought it home with them, as they did with all good things. The Egyptians not only esteemed the onion highly, but they swore by it and even worshiped it. The Hebrews, although slaves to the Egyptians, were more practical: they ate it. When Moses led his people out of Egypt across the Sinai, the Hebrews sadly deplored the loss not only of the onion but also of the great-grandfather of the whole onion family— garlic. The onion was then, and is today, used therapeutically as a medicine. It has been credited with having curative powers in the treatment of many illnesses: cirrhosis of the liver, ailments of the digestive tract, diseases of the blood, alcoholism, and even cancer of the liver. However questionable these claims may be, we must acknowledge the findings of the great Doctor Louis Pasteur. He firmly established the bacteria-inhibiting faculty of the onion, but like garlic, once boiled it loses its destructive power over malignant microbes. It can be said that the onion is one of the most beneficial vegetables to ever have graced man's table. And the exquisite flavor the onion imparts to food needs no clarification or certification.

The Critical Hungarian Onion "To know your onions" is one of the first precepts learned in becoming a fine Hungarian chef. In Hungary, perhaps above all other places, onions are most carefully, even religiously cooked, usually in lard or in pork fat, sometimes to just a translucent stage, other times to a light golden hue or even to shades of dark brown.

OPORTO, SAUCE (Portuguese) Chopped leeks and scallions are sautéed in sweet butter. With the addition of orange juice, the mixture is brought to a boil. Crushed pineapple, lemon juice, and port wine are added and simmered together to finish the sauce, which is served with poultry, pork, fish, and veal dishes.

OPP GANG CHONG (Chinese) See LAP CHONG

ORGEAT This emulsion of bitter and sweet almonds plus sugar, lemon peel, and water is a favorite ingredient in Swiss or Austrian pastries. It is also used with raw or with cooked fruit.

ORIENTALE, À L' (French) Any food described as _à l'Orientale_ is served with white rice and tomatoes and is flavored with plenty of saffron.

Orientale Garnish A garnish consisting of small tomatoes stuffed with a saffron-flavored _risotto,_ buttered okra, and sweet peppers. (See OKRA, RISOTTO, SAFFRON)

Sauce Orientale A _sauce Américaine_ is seasoned with curry and reduced. Away from the heat, the sauce is refined with heavy cream. (See AMÉRICAINE)

Sole à l'Orientale (Turkish) This version calls for chopped scallions and thinly sliced and seeded green peppers to be simmered in oil and water. Meanwhile, the fillets of sole are salted and peppered then folded and placed in a greased casserole. The cooked scallion-green pepper mixture is spread over the sole with slices of tomato and lemon. The fillets are baked.

(French) The French version first poaches the fillets of sole and serves them coated with a sauce Newburg with curry and boiled rice. COMPATIBLE WINES: A white wine, e.g., Meursault, Aigle, Soave, Dézaley, Pinot Chardonnay, Chablis, Muscadet, Pouilly-Fumé.

ORLOV/ORLOFF Prince Grigori Grigoryvich Orlov, the lover of Catherine II and the one who conspired and succeeded to put her on the Russian throne, was buttered-up by chefs trying to curry favor by naming many dishes after him. Russian royalty were the rage in Paris. (See CURNONSKY)

Tournedos or **Filet Mignon Orlov** Steaks are grilled and served decorated with latticed anchovies and dotted with pearl onions. A _sauce Madère_ is served separately. (See MADÈRE) COMPATIBLE WINES: A red wine, e.g., Fixin, Beaune, Aloxe-Corton, Chambertin, Nuits St. Georges, Haut Brion, Échézeaux, Dôle, Barolo.

Selle de Veau Prince Orlov This saddle of veal is first braised, then the fillets of veal are removed and then the saddle is reconstructed with sliced truffle placed between the veal slices with a _sauce Soubise._ Then, napped with a _sauce Mornay,_ the entire saddle is set to glaze in the broiler. The dish is accompanied with asparagus tips. (See MORNAY, SOUBISE) COMPATIBLE WINES: A white wine, e.g., Sylvaner, Wehlener Sonnenuhr, Gewürztraminer, Vouvray, Szamorodni, Château-Grillet, Johannisberg, Nierstein, Rüdesheim.

ORRECHIETTI (Italian) See PASTA

ORTOLAN The ortolan is a small European bunting which, despite its size, is very popular in France as a table delicacy; however, it is rarely found on a menu outside of France. Ortolans are either roasted on a spit or baked in their own fat, which is greatly esteemed. These tiny birds are never drawn before cooking, and they are devoured bones and all.

When the tiny ortolan is finally cooked in its own fat, it is probably the most humane treatment this poor bird has received from its captors. In parts of France, these birds are trapped in nets and fattened to bursting in cellars that are kept illuminated continuously so that the birds will not be able to tell day from night. Consequently, they eat and eat and eat. Mercifully, they are slain before they strangle in their own fat. Because of their exceptional flavor, the number of ortolans has greatly diminished, and the eating of them has somewhat the same air of decadence as that of the ancient Romans' penchant for hummingbird's tongues and the tiny brains of the pink flamingo. (See LOUIS XVIII)

ORZO (Greek) A popular barley-shaped *pasta* made from wheat flour. It is used in soups and salads and as an accompanying side dish. (See PASTA)

OSSI BUCCHI ALLA MILANESE (Italian) *Ossi bucchi* are veal shanks (*osso buccho* is singular). Here, veal shanks are prepared first *alla Milanese* and then stewed with herbs, vegetables, and white wine. Almost always, a *risotto* accompanies this dish. (See RISOTTO) COMPATIBLE WINES: A white wine, e.g., Orvieto, Brolio Bianco, Gewürztraminer, Vouvray, Anjou, Johannisberg, Frascati, Sauvignon Blanc, Riquewihr, Riesling.

OSTRICHE Upon first seeing this term on an Italian menu, one might be led to believe that the Italians have taken to eating ostriches. Such is not the case, and although the bird is edible, this is the Italian term for "oysters."

OSTRIGA SUPA (Yugoslavian) A delicious oyster soup made by first cooking chopped garlic and parsley with the bones, fins, and heads of fish in boiling water seasoned with salt, pepper, and bay leaves. The stock is strained and reheated with the addition of a dry white wine. Then away from the heat, lemon juice and raw oysters are added. The soup is served over toasted bread.

OTERO (French) The name of a famous Parisian dancer who made theatrical and romantic headlines around the turn of the century. Because of her beauty, she was known as *La Belle*.

Filets de Sole Otero Fillets of sole are seasoned, rolled and fastened, then poached in a mixture of white wine and fish stock. The poached rolls are placed in the hollowed-out shells of baked potatoes, covered with buttered mashed potatoes, sprinkled with grated Gruyère cheese and breadcrumbs, and browned in the grill. COMPATI-

BLE WINES: A white wine, e.g., Pouilly-Fuissé, Chablis, Muscadet, Meursault, Montrachet, Soave, Pinot Chardonnay, Debro, Aigle, Dézaley, Verdicchio, Randersacker.

OURSIN (French) This word has absolutely nothing to do with anyone's sins. It refers instead to a rather large marine "pin cushion" whose spines can rip open a foot if stepped upon accidentally at the beach. In English *oursins* are called "sea urchins," and in the West Indies they are referred to as "sea eggs." The creatures are plentiful along the Mediterranean Coast. On the east and west coasts of North America they are at their best from August to April, and as a cold-weather delicacy they reach their peak at Christmastime. The roe and the gonads are much sought after.

To remove the roe from the *oursin,* the creature must be handled carefully. An incision can be made around the bottom of the shell, and after the entrails have been removed, the delectable roe is in plain view to be scooped out. The male gonad has the finer texture, and eating it raw on French bread, with just a squirt of lemon juice, can be a real gastronomic experience. The sea urchins come in various colors—black, green, brown, and even purple. The taste for them must be acquired. COMPATIBLE WINES: A white wine, e.g., Muscadet, Quincy, Debro, Pinot Chardonnay, Verdicchio, Soave, Chablis.

OVOS A PORTUGUEZA (Portuguese) A unique method of serving eggs. First, raw garlic is heated in hot olive oil, and when it becomes light brown, it is removed. Thick fresh tomato slices are then placed into the oil, and after seasoning with salt and pepper, a fresh egg is broken into the center of each tomato slice. This tomato and egg concoction is baked in the oven until the white of the egg is set. COMPATIBLE BEVERAGES: Beer, cider, tea.

OYAKO DOMBURI (Japanese) A rice dish that combines a thinly sliced breast of chicken with sliced scallions and mushrooms, all of which are cooked in a hot *domburi* soup. A beaten egg flavored with a dash of *kona sansho* (powdered Japanese pepper) is eased onto the surface of the simmering soup and carefully cooked. Then this omelette, the soup, and the chicken are all poured over a bowl of steamed white rice and served. (See DOMBURI)

OYSTERS "Robert, don't use that knife. You must swallow your oysters whole," a mother was admonishing her son one evening while dining at the Four Seasons restaurant in New York City. "Your father and I just returned from Paris, and that's the way they are eaten. So, please, do not shame us here in this elegant restaurant." Of course, one can eat oysters any way one chooses, but the elongated Chingoteagues served to this young fellow should be cut up before being eaten. In fact, there was a small knife and fork set on the table exactly for that purpose.

The ancient Romans were the first to cultivate oysters in beds at

Brindisi. Oysters do not fare well in deep ocean waters; they flourish in bays and in river deltas, where the brine of the sea is correctly diluted with fresh water. In salty ocean water, the oyster is subject to the attack of starfish and other predators, as well as to disease.

Of the great number of species of oysters sold in volume on the world market, only four come from the fertile shores of North America: the Blue Point, the Cape Cod, the Chingoteague, and the Kent Island. But in total world production, the United States leads, producing more than 300,000 tons each year. In the British Isles the plate oyster is the Whitstable, the Colchester, the Pylefleet, and the Helford. The Olympia oyster is native to the Pacific shores of the United States.

The ideal way to eat an oyster is raw on the half shell, with just a splash of lemon juice, but many insist on smothering the oyster with a tomato cocktail sauce, horseradish, onions, and an unending array of spicy sauces, which mask the true flavor of the oyster. When oysters are to be cooked, they should be propped up in coarse salt (kosher salt) in muffin tins so that the oysters retain their juices. The salt does much to keep the shells warm.

It is not considered bad etiquette to submit shellfish to the smell test before eating or cooking them. If a bivalve opens a bit too readily, or if you find that a monovalve is a soggy, limp mass, get rid of them fast! If they smell bad, do not taste them, because just a sampling could be fatal. More gastrointestinal trouble, more fatalities are connected with spoiled seafood, in and out of restaurants, than any other food. Note, however, that there is no truth to the warning that danger and even possible death will result if one eats oysters during the months of May, June, July, and August. It is just that oysters do not taste their best until October, so the practical French spread this rumor simply to allow the oysters to spawn and frolic until they are ripe to eat in the fall. (See ROCKEFELLER) COMPATIBLE WINES: A white wine, e.g., Chablis, Muscadet, Quincy, Pouilly-Fuissé, Dézaley, Pinot Chardonnay, Verdicchio, Soave, Debro, Wiltinger Scharzhofberg, Iphofen, Sancerre, Montrachet.

Oysters Hollandaise (American) A sauce is made by first adding the juice from raw oysters to a *sauce Hollandaise*. The oysters are then cooked briefly in lightly salted water until they just begin to curl. They are then drained and added to the sauce, either whole or diced. This sauce, flavored with lemon juice and chopped parsley, will complement roast turkey, roast chicken, or poached fish dishes. (See HOLLANDAISE)

PAAN (Indian) The betel leaf, or *paan,* is similar to the ivy leaf, but the betel leaf is longer and will vary in taste from sweet to slightly bitter. In Indian cuisine, the *paan* is served wrapped around various ingredients: one is the *choona,* a white lime paste; another is called *katechu* or *kattha,* a red paste made from the bark of a tree. Mixed in with the pastes are chopped betel nuts. It is one of the essentials of Indian hospitality to offer a fine *paan* to guests after dinner. A simple *paan* can also mean a series of small, individual bowls filled with cardamom seeds, anise seeds, cloves, and sweet almonds. (See BETEL NUT)

PAËLLA (Spanish) One story claims that this traditional dish from Valencia gets its name from the large two-handed frying pan in which it is cooked. Another legend says that the dish was really created for a tiny, frail princess and was aptly called *paëlla,* "for her." As delectable as the *paëlla* is, considering the amount and the variety of foods that go into it one wonders just how frail and how tiny the beautiful princess was.

Spanish *paëlla* is a great mound of saffron-flavored rice decorated with pimientos and dotted throughout with mussels, clams, bits of chicken, shrimp, squid, sausages, cubed lamb, scallops, lobster meat, oysters, fish, and often the hearts of artichokes, green peas, asparagus, and tomatoes. COMPATIBLE WINES: A red wine, e.g., Rioja, Chianti, Beaujolais, Moulin-à-Vent, Zinfandel, Valpolicella, Egri Bikaver, Mercurey, St. Julien, Margaux.

PAGNOTTA DEL CACCIATORE (Italian) Game birds wrapped in a dough and baked until the birds are cooked and the dough is crisp and crusty. COMPATIBLE WINES: A red wine, e.g., Santenay, Fixin, Chambertin, Médoc, Côte Rôtie, Cabernet Sauvignon, Châteauneuf-du-Pape, Pommard.

PAILLARDE (French) A piece of meat that has been pounded flat before cooking. It takes its name from the Restaurant Paillard, situated at 38 Boulevard des Italiens, in Paris, where it is said to have originated. Edward VII, the Prince de Galles, the Khedive of Egypt, and King Carlos of Portugal took turns savoring the delicacies *chez* Paillard.

PAILLASSE (French) The layer of glowing charcoal embers, spread out on a grill, over which meat is cooked.

PAIN (French) Bread.

PAIN PERDU (French) Also known as "French toast," the dish is here dubbed "lost bread" because slices of plain white bread are camouflaged by first moistening them with vanilla-flavored milk, then tromping them in beaten egg yolk, and finally frying them in clarified butter. They are drained on absorbent paper and served sprinkled with powdered sugar.

PAISTETTU LOHI (Finnish) Delicately baked salmon steaks. There are foods that taste best when the least has been done to them: caviar is one of them, and salmon, trout, and sole have places high on the list. Here, the salmon is cut into thick steaks, brushed with salted butter, and baked for a few minutes in a medium oven. The steaks are then placed in the broiler, and with the heat turned to high, the steaks are broiled on both sides for just a few minutes. The salmon steaks must be served at once on warm plates, garnished with chopped parsely, fresh dill, and halves of fresh lemons. COMPATIBLE WINES: A white wine, e.g., Haut Brion Blanc, Meursault, Corton-Charlemagne, Pinot Chardonnay; or a red wine, e.g., Nuits St. Georges, Chambertin, Valpolicella, Zinfandel, Margaux.

PAK CHOI (Chinese) See CELERY CABBAGE

PAKORA (East Indian) Batter-fried vegetables. The batter is a blend of rice flour, baking powder, water, eggs, sesame seeds, and salt. The vegetables chosen are usually those that can easily be sliced and fried, such as potatoes, eggplant, and zucchini.

Chicken Pakora An appetizer composed of chickpea flour, ground chicken, ginger, cumin, onions, and garlic. This mixture is shaped into patties or small balls and deep-fried.

PAKORIS/BHAJIA (East Indian) Two kinds of fritters. The *bhajia* consists of uniformly sliced vegetables—such as cauliflower, peppers, onions rings, potatoes—dipped in a batter of chickpea flour, water, salt, turmeric, cumin, baking soda, and cayenne pepper, then fried in oil until brown. The plain *pakoris* fritter, made from the same batter but without the vegetables, is dropped from a teaspoon into hot fat.

PALACSINTA (Hungarian) This thin pancake is known to the Austrians as *Palatschinke*. A batter is made from flour, salt, eggs, milk, and butter; and just before cooking, enough soda is added to thin the batter. The pancakes are fried, one at a time, much like French *crêpes,* in a small frying pan. After having been browned on both sides, the pancakes are filled with various foods, such as pot cheese, calves' brains, chopped pork or veal, chopped ham. A dessert version is made by adding sugar to the batter and filling the cooked pancakes with a sweet filling. (See ARMENIAN PALACSINTA TORTE)

PALMENI (Russian) A thin dough stuffed with various *farces:* chopped cabbage, chopped grouse, ham, pork, rice, minced meats. They are prepared and cooked just like *ravioli.* (See FARCE/FARCI, RAVIOLI) COMPATIBLE WINES: The choice of wine depends upon the fillings used and the sauces served with the *palmeni.*

PALM, HEARTS OF Tender shoots of palm, available packed in lightly salted water in cans. In France they are known as *coeurs de palmier,* and in the French-speaking islands of the Caribbean they are called *chou palmist, chou coco,* and *chou glouglou.* Hearts of palm are prepared as vegetables with grated cheese or cream. They make delicious additions to salads or can be served alone as a salad.

PALTBREAD (Scandinavian) This black bread, popular in both Sweden and Finland, is made from a mixture of pork blood, rye flour, yeast, cloves, cinnamon, salt, ginger, and a dark "Bock" beer. The dough is kneaded, left to rise, then formed into flat, round cakes. It is allowed to rise again before being baked in a slow oven. Originally, this bread was baked with a hole in the center so that it could be suspended to dry out. When completely dry, this paltbread might be kept for more than a year if stored in a cold place.

PANADA (Spanish) Various flours, breadcrumbs, rice, or potatoes mixed with egg yolks. The mixture is used to make *quenelles.* (See QUENELLE)

PANCAKE As soon as primitive man ceased to be a nomadic hunter and settled down to live in communities as a seed grower, he made his first pancake: a simple mixture of ground meal moistened with water and cooked on a hot stone. Today every cuisine has its own pancake. Russia has the *blini;* France, the *crêpe;* Holland, *Pannekoeke;* Mexico, the *tortilla;* Switzerland, the Lenten *Fastnachtschuechli.*

Basically, a pancake is composed of eggs, flour, milk or water or beer, and a bit of oil or butter. The pancake batter, seasoned with either salt or sugar, pours with the consistency of a thick cream and is cooked in a hot lightly-greased heavy skillet. When light brown on one side, it is usually turned and cooked on the other side. The versatile pancake can be served flat, or rolled with lemon juice and honey, or folded. Filled or unfilled, sweet or plain, it can be served as an *hors d'oeuvre,* main course, or tasty dessert. (See AEPFELPFANNKUCHEN, BLINI, BLINTZ, CRÊPE, PLÄTTAR, SUZETTE, TORTILLA)

PANCH AMRIT (Indian) In the Hindi language, this term refers to the "five immortal nectars": honey, sugar, milk, yogurt, and clarified butter. (The well-known English magazine *Punch* got its name from this term.) It is interesting to note that two hundred years ago in India, honey and sugar were substituted for two former "immortal nectars," cow urine and cow dung. Cow urine (the cow is still considered sacred in India) is drunk even today. It is believed to endow the consumer with the strength and the blessings of the cow. And cow dung is considered not only sacred but also very practical when used as fuel.

PAN DE MUERTO In Mexico on All Soul's Day, November the second, the family makes an excursion to the local cemetery to visit their loved ones' graves. It is a kind of picnic-outing with the loving dead as spiritual participants. As the *pièce de résistance,* the *pan de muerto* ("bread of the dead") is served. This is a round coffee cake flavored with anise and orange-blossom water, and it has a rather special decoration. On top of the loaf is a cross made out of dough, baked in the pertinent form of tear drops and bones, and paradoxically, iced in pink. There is a kind of festive air about All Souls' Day. Vendors sell skulls made from candy with one's own name inscribed on it, presumably so that one may munch upon his own mortality.

PANEER This is the name of the only cheese that is indigenous to India. It is made simply by bringing whole milk to a boil and then adding fresh lemon juice. When the milk has curdled, it is strained through cheesecloth; all of the water is pressed out of the residue, which when solidified is cut into cubes or wedges and eaten as a cheese.

PANETTONE (Italian) "Tony's bread," a sweet bread *(pane)* baked by a man named Antonio in a Milanese bakery in the fifteenth century. (When something is good, there are countless stories and legends connected to its origin and that explanation seems as good as any.) *Panettone* is made from a simple yeast dough containing butter, sugar, eggs, salt, milk, plus seedless raisins, candied citron, and grated lemon peel. Most countries have their own version of this delicious fruit bread, which is delightful for breakfast. In Italy, it is a Christmas tradition. (See COLUMBO, KUGELHOPF)

PAPERISILLI (Finnish) Small salted herring, cooked and served in aluminum foil. The cleaned herring is soaked in milk overnight. Then, thoroughly dried, dotted with butter, and wrapped in aluminum foil, it is cooked in a hot heavy pan. The *paperisilli* can be taken as a snack or, when complemented with small boiled potatoes and pickled beets, it can be served as a luncheon dish. COMPATIBLE BEVERAGES: Cold vodka, beer.

PAPILLOTE (French) Meat or fish that is wrapped in wax paper or cooking parchment and baked in the oven.

Pompano en Papillote Poached pompano fillets are alternately layered with a mixture of spices and finely chopped vegetables. Then, with a dash of sherry wine, they are enclosed in buttered wax paper or parchment paper and baked. COMPATIBLE WINES: A white wine, e.g., Chablis, Muscadet, Ockfener Bockstein, Piesporter Goldtröpfchen, Johannisberg, Nierstein, Montrachet, Pouilly-Fuissé.

PAPPADUMS (East Indian) Pancake-like breads made of whole-wheat flour, salt, and water. In the north of India they are called *papars*. There are two varieties: one is made with crushed black pepper, and the other is plain. Both are deep-fried and served wafer-thin and crisp with meals. They are a great favorite at cocktail parties. (See CHAPATTIS, PULKA)

PAPRIKA This popular spice, made from the ripe fruit of the bonnet pepper, *capsicum tetragonum,* is available in various grades—sweet, semisweet, mildly pungent, pungent—and in colors ranging from a bright red to a brownish brick-red. Although Hungary produces an excellent paprika, America imports most of its paprika from Spain. These are classified as *dolce, agridolce,* and *picante,* respectively meaning sweet, semisweet, and piquant. Each of these, in turn, falls into three quality categories: extra, select, and common. The finest paprika has the reddest, richest color; when it has an orange or brownish cast, the quality of the spice is considered third rate. Only the cheaper quality has a hot taste. The best has a somewhat sweet, smoky flavor. Paprika adds flavor to meat and fish dishes, egg dishes, salads, marinades, and canapés. Commercially, it is used in the manufacture of sausages, catsup, sauces, and other prepared foods. Paprika is rich in vitamins A and C; in fact, it contains more vitamin C than any citrus fruit. (See CAPSICUM)

Chicken Paprikash (Hungarian) This famous chicken preparation, called *paprikás csirke* by the natives when made with sour cream and called *pörkölt* when made without it, consists of a cut-up chicken that is first dusted with flour and browned in bacon fat with chopped onions. Then, seasoned with salt, pepper, and paprika, it is stewed and basted with a bouillon. With the chicken removed from the pan, a sauce is made from the pan juices and a chicken *velouté* plus the optional sour cream. The chicken is served coated with the sauce and complemented with *noki* (egg dumplings) or boiled white rice. COMPATIBLE WINES: Château Carbonnieux, Vouvray, Orvieto, Johannisberg, Sylvaner, Bernkasteler Doktor, Badacsonyi, Leányka.

Paprikás Palacsinta (Hungarian) Pancakes filled with a mixture of finely diced veal that has been fried in bacon fat with chopped onions and sweet red paprika; the veal is then dusted with flour and fried again. The pancakes are filled with the veal mixture then rolled up, topped with sour cream, and baked in an ovenproof dish. COMPATIBLE WINES: A red wine, e.g., Beaujolais, Valpolicella, Zinfandel, Côte Rôtie, Margaux, Médoc, Egri Bikaver.

PARILLADA The Spanish term for an Argentine mixed grill composed of a variety of meats including short ribs, skirt steak, sweetbreads, kidneys, hearts, liver, black sausage, and a particular Argentine sausage. (See SKIRT STEAK, SWEETBREADS) COMPATIBLE WINES: A red wine, e.g., Rioja, Mercurey, Beaujolais, Mâcon, Zinfandel, Valpolicella, Rincón Famoso.

PARISIENNE, POTATOES (French) For this potato dish, raw potatoes are cut into ball shapes with a melon-ball cutter and sautéed in sweet butter and herbs.

PARKIN (English) A ginger and oatmeal cake from historic Yorkshire, in the north of England. Into a heavy batter composed of oatmeal, flour, sugar, ground ginger, salt, milk, and baking soda, a mixture of butter and molasses is added. The batter is poured into a flat baking pan, and when half-baked, it is topped with shredded almonds. Parkin is served cut into squares.

PARMENTIER (French) As a culinary term, this has become almost synonymous with potatoes. Antoine-Auguste Parmentier was a famous eighteenth-century French agronomist who was able to convince a suspicious French nation to accept the potato as food. His method was unique. Parmentier decided to use child psychology on the French by posting guards around the potato fields during the day but removing them as soon as the sun went down. Much like children forbidden to raid the cookie jar, the French invaded the fields at night and scooted home with sacks full of uprooted potatoes, which they would consume the next day. Every year, in August, potatoes planted on Parmentier's grave burst into flower to honor him. (See POTATOES)

PARMIGIANA, VEAL (Italian) This famous veal cutlet preparation originated in Milan then made its way to Naples. It was made popular in the United States by Italian-American restaurateurs. Imitations abound, with some restaurants using only breadcrumbs over the cutlet, others adding mozzarella or some other cheese, but *Parmigiana* means Parmesan cheese and nothing else.

The real veal *Parmigiana* is a flattened veal cutlet that is dipped in flour, then in beaten egg, and finally in a mixture of finely grated Parmesan cheese and breadcrumbs. The cutlet is sautéed in butter and oil. Before cooking the veal, a few cloves of garlic are simmered in the oil-and-butter mixture and removed. These cutlets, called *scallopine* in Italian, are often covered with a tomato sauce and thin slices of mozzarella cheese and heated in the oven or grill until the cheese melts. But classically, this is not a *Parmigiana*. (See SCALLOPINE, SCHNITZEL, WIENERSCHNITZEL) COMPATIBLE WINES: A white wine, e.g., Orvieto, Sauvignon Blanc, Château-Grillet, Fendant, Frascati.

PASHTET (Jewish) This dish, the name of which derives from the German word *Pasteten,* meaning "baked pastries," dates back to the eleventh century. The *pashtet* is made by browning ground beef together with chopped shallots and by mashing broiled chicken livers into a white wine. The beef and the chicken liver paste are mixed together and used as a filling for a puff pastry dough. The filled pastry, which is some ways resembles the *koulibiac,* is baked until light brown. (See KOULIBIAC) COMPATIBLE WINES: A white wine, e.g., Sauterne, Riesling, Graves, Johannisberg, Tokay, Sylvaner, Sauvignon Blanc.

PASTA (Italian) There are countless tales that describe how the first *pasta* was brought into Italy. Some say that a romatic Italian soldier plied a buxom Teutonic *Fraülein* with such flattery and sweet-nothings that she finally let the secret of the German noodle out of the bag. However, the story of Marco Polo's adventures in Asia are best documented, and more credence is given to his discovery of *pasta* while living among the Chinese some seven hundred years ago than to any of the other legends so often told.

Pasta is the Italian term for the dough from which all Italian noodles are made. Those made with eggs—including _ravioli, fettucini, ca-pelletti_, and _cannelloni_—are called _pasta all' uova. Spaghetti_ is made simply from durum wheat worked into a dough with water. _Pasta_ can be an addictive food, and fortunately there are more than a hundred different varieties from which to choose. The following is but a partial list:

acini de pepe Tiny round or square _pasta_, called "pepperkernels" because of their shape.

cannelloni Tubes of _pasta_, usually stuffed with meat or other ingredients.

cappelletti _Pasta_ shaped like "little hats," often filled with minced chicken.

conchiglie _Pasta_ shaped like "tiny sea shells."

farfallette Small and large ribbon-bow shapes, often called "butterflies."

fettucine Long egg noodles.

lasagne Egg noodles, made both medium-wide and wide; the largest of the flat _pastas._

linguini Narrow, plain noodles, called "little tongues."

macaroni/maccheroni _Pasta_ made in long tubes.

mafalde Twisted, long ribbon-noodles.

mezzani A smooth, tubular _pasta._

mostoccioli Smooth, tubular _pasta_ cut obliquely into two-and-a-half-inch lengths and referred to as "little mustaches."

orrechietti Little ear-shaped _pasta._

orzo Small barley-shaped _pasta._

pastina Tiny disks of _pasta_, used in soups.

pastina al uovo Same as _pastina_, but made with eggs.

perciatelli Tubular, long _pasta_, slightly larger than _spaghetti._

ravioli Very thin _pasta_, formed into squares and filled with finely chopped chicken, meat, or ricotta cheese.

rigati _Pasta_ that is ribbed and tubular.

rigatoni Ribbed, large tubular _pasta_, cut into three-inch segments.

spaghetti Long, thin strands of _pasta._

spaghettini Thin _spaghetti_, not as thin as _vermicelli._

tagliarini Very narrow egg noodles.

tagliatelle Another term for _fettucine._

tortellini Ring-shaped _pasta_ with ruffled outer edge.

tubettini Tiny tubular _pasta_, cut into small pieces. Used in soups.

vermicelli "Little worms," or very thin _spaghetti_, often twenty or thirty strands are twisted into a bow and knotted.

ziti Large tubular _pasta_, cut into three-inch segments.

PASTA ASCIUTTA Strictly speaking, *pasta asciutta* is the general Italian term for any "dry" pasta, as opposed to that which is "cooked."

Pasta Asciutta Marchigiania Having originated in the Marche Province of Italy on the Adriatic, this is a misnomer because this dish is really not a *pasta*. It is made from a bread dough that is thinly rolled, cut into thin strips, and left to rise. The strips are then cooked in boiling water and served with any of the sauces suitable for the regular *pasta* dishes.

PASTICCIERA (Italian) See CRÈME PATISSIÈRE, MARGHERITA

PASTIERA NAPOLETANA (Italian) This rich Neapolitan cheese cake is made from ricotta cheese mixed with *grana* (whole-kernel wheat), separated eggs, sugar, pastry cream, grated lemon and orange rind, candied citron, and cinnamon baked in a pie crust. (See CITRON, CRÈME PATISSIÈRE, GRANA)

PASTINA (Italian) See PASTA

PASTINA AL UOVO (Italian) See PASTA

PASTIRMA EGGS (Turkish) This egg dish takes its name from one of its ingredients—*pastirma,* a dried meat permeated with a tart paste heavy with garlic. This dish is prepared by sautéing chopped onions in butter then adding the tomato juice and the *pastirma,* sliced thin. Then, hollows are made in the thickening mixture and an egg is broken into each hollow. The eggs are seasoned and cooked until done. COMPATIBLE BEVERAGES: Beer, cider, tea.

PASTITSIO (Greek) A casserole of baked meat and macaroni, one of the finest examples of the heights that a simple macaroni dish can attain. The casserole consists of layers of cooked macaroni alternating with layers of meat bound together with a white, creamy cheese sauce. The meat layers are composed of beef, onions, tomato purée, red wine, nutmeg, salt, pepper, and cinnamon. Besides the cheese sauce, grated kefalotyri or Parmesan cheese is blended into the meat mixture together with breadcrumbs; some is held in reserve to be sprinkled over the top. The casserole is baked to a golden brown and is served cut into squares. COMPATIBLE WINES: A red wine; e.g., Rioja, Valpolicella, Lambrusco, Petit Sirah, Moulin-à-Vent, Chianti, Zinfandel, Mercurey.

PASTRAMI This Jewish delicacy is a refinement of its Armenian predecessor called *basterma,* which is a spicy, pepper-hot, marinated sirloin of beef. A good pastrami nestling between two hefty slices of sour-rye bread, covered with mustard, garnished with Kosher dill pickles, and washed down with steins of cool beer, is as Jewish as a *matzo* ball and just as tasty.

Pastrami is made from a brisket of beef that is covered with a mixture of garlic, peppercorns, salt, and coriander seeds. It is refrigerated overnight, allowing the spices to permeate the brisket. On the following day, a blend of brown sugar, oil, vinegar, and allspice is poured over the beef, and it is left to marinate for another day. After the pickling, the beef is dried, smoked, and ready to be enjoyed. (See BASTERMA, PASTIRMA) COMPATIBLE BEVERAGES: Beer.

PÂTÉ (French) Many people who want to dine *à la Française* like to begin their dinners with a fine *pâté:* a blending of various ground meats, flavored and baked. Originally, the terms *terrine* and *pâté* were only different in that a *terrine* is lined with pork or bacon fat whereas the classic *pâté* was always baked in a pastry crust, *en croûte*. Today, the term *pâté* is defined as a paste of ground meat or fish that is baked in a pan greased with pork fat or butter. A *galantine,* on the other hand, is the term given to a *pâté* that is made from a fowl or from a game bird and steamed. A *pâté* is a good gauge of a French chef's artistry, and along with the type of soup that is served, it indicates the quality of the meal to follow. (See FOIE GRAS) COMPATI-BLE WINES: A white wine, e.g., Gewürztraminer, Vouvray, Muscat d'Alsace, Champagne, Tokay, Forster Jesuitengarten, Sauterne.

PÂTE (French) Not to be confused with the aforementioned *pâté,* this is the general term for the "paste" formed by mixing flour with a liquid. It can refer to bread doughs, pastry, batters, and even *pasta*. (See PASTA)

Pâte à Chou Cream puff paste—a mixture of flour, butter, water, eggs, and flavorings—is cooked on top of the stove until a thick mass is formed. The paste may be used to make a variety of preparations. The *koulibiac,* fritters, *gnocchi,* and potatoes *à la Dauphine* are excellent examples of the versatile use of the *pâte à chou*. When used to make a dessert, sugar is sometimes added to the paste, and this then becomes the base for *beignets, profiteroles,* cream puffs, and *éclairs*. (See BEIGNETS, DAUPHINE, ÉCLAIRS, GNOCCHI, KOULIBIAC, PROF-ITEROLES)

Pâte à Brioche Made the same way as the *brioche* dough, this is used to fashion turnovers and pies. (See BRIOCHE)

Pâte Brisée A French short-crust pastry made with eggs, flour, butter, and water. Sometimes lard or vegetable shortening is sub-stituted for part of the butter.

Pâte Feuilletée See FEUILLETAGE

PATLIKAN MUSAKKA The *musakka* is one of Turkey's most popular dishes. In fact, it is so popular and so good that many countries have claimed it as their own. This *musakka* is made from sliced eggplant sautéed in butter and set in the bottom of a baking pan. With the addition of sautéed ground beef, tomatoes and onions, salt and pepper, and a bit of water, the whole is baked until the eggplant is tender. (See MOUSSAKA) COMPATIBLE WINES: A red wine, e.g., Egri Bikaver, Premiat, Médoc, Valpolicella, Zinfandel, Mercurey, Côtes du Rhône, Beaujolais.

PATNA RICE (East Indian) This long-grained rice is named after the town of Patna, which is in northeastern India, in the state of Bihar on the Ganges River. One of the best of the *patnas* is *basmati,* which is aged before it is cooked and consequently is so expensive that it is probably more easily obtained in New York than in Patna itself.

In India, there are special ceremonies to celebrate the planting and harvesting of rice. Rice is thrown at weddings as a symbol of fertility; and it has a place in Hindu religious rituals. Rice has been the staple food for Oriental people for centuries. However, the "instant" or "quick-cooking" rice is not acceptable, nor are the parboiled or partially cooked varieties, in which the nutrients are no longer present.

PA-TSAI (Chinese) See CELERY CABBAGE

PATTI, CONSOMMÉ ADELINA (French) A chicken consommé named after the famous Italian diva Patti, who was very fond of it. A rich chicken consommé is garnished with plain *royale* (baked and diced egg white), diced carrots, and with the one ingredient that tantalized the opera singer: puréed chestnuts.

PAUPIETTES (French) Thinly sliced pieces of meat or fish, or leaves of cabbage, are stuffed and then braised, baked, or stewed.

Paupiettes de Veau Thin slices of veal are stuffed with chopped mushrooms, a forcemeat of pork, truffles, peppers, and herbs. They are then rolled, fastened, and braised in a mixture of beef stock and wine. The *paupiettes* are served with an appropriate sauce: *Bourguignonne, bourgeoise,* etc. (See BOURGEOISE, BOURGUIGNONNE) COMPATIBLE WINES: A red wine, e.g., Beaujolais, Hermitage, Valpolicella, Zinfandel, Châteauneuf-du-Pape, St. Julien, Bardolino, Dôle, Pinot Noir.

PAVÉ (French) A cold pie or mousse that is jellied in a rectangular form. The sweet variety can be made from a chestnut purée or from chocolate, coffee, or fruits. The savory *pavés* are composed of cheese, sole, salmon, game, goose liver, and the like.

Pavé du Roi This regal *pavé* is made by baking goose liver, larded with black truffles, in a pastry dough. After a thorough chilling, port-flavored gelatin is inserted through a hole in the top of the baked pastry. The dish is rechilled before serving. COMPATIBLE WINES: A white wine, e.g., Tokay d'Alsace, Château d'Yquem, Sauterne, Meursault, Gewürztraminer, Vouvray.

Pavé de Foie Gras Lucullus Another name for the above.

PECÊNA HUSA SE ZELIM This is what the Czechoslovakians call their method of roasting a goose with sauerkraut. The sauerkraut is drained, soaked in water, then squeezed dry. Then, together with chopped onions, chopped apples, grated raw potatoes, salt, and caraway seeds, it is cooked in goose fat to blend the ingredients. The goose is generously seasoned with salt and pepper, then stuffed with the sauerkraut mixture, trussed, and baked the hours necessary to produce a tender, tasty bird. During the roasting period, the goose is basted constantly. When done, the sauerkraut is removed and served separately. (See STEKT GÅS) COMPATIBLE WINES: A white wine, e.g., Sauterne, Gewürztraminer, Muscat d'Alsace, Riesling, Vouvray, Ammerschwihr, Sauvignon Blanc.

PE'EPE'S (Polynesian) This is actually a Samoan word meaning "coconut cream," which is made by piercing the eyes of fresh coconuts, draining off the liquid, and scraping out the meat of the nut. The coconut meat is ground, and the liquid is extracted from it. This coconut cream can be seasoned with salt to cook vegetables, or flavored with lime or lemon juice when served with a purée of banana or papaya. When used as a dip for fish or breadfruit, chopped onions and lime juice are added. (See BREADFRUIT)

PEI DAN (Chinese) See THOUSAND-YEAR-OLD EGGS

PEKING CUISINE As the centuries-old capital of China, Peking was the residence of great emperors and aristocrats. And, as China's intellectual and cultural center, it also became the mecca for talented chefs who migrated from all corners of the vast country to ply their trade. Peking thus became the gastronomic center of China—what Paris is for French food—and it remains so to this day.

Peking food is light, though the many noodle dishes, breads, and dumplings reveal the preference for wheat flour over rice as the staple food of the region. Wine stocks are used in the preparation of many dishes, and the chefs of Peking have a penchant for sweet-sour dishes and the abundant use of garlic and scallions. (See CHINESE CUISINE)

PEKING DUCK This is probably the most famous speciality of the Peking cuisine. To prepare this delicacy, the duck's skin is made airtight and then is inflated away from the flesh until it is fairly taut. Then the duck is dipped into a mixture of water, honey, ginger root, and scallions and hung to dry. Garlic is blended with a mixture of soy sauce, sherry, brown sugar, and cloves; and the duck is rubbed, both inside and out, with this sauce. The duck is then dusted with red paprika and roasted on a rack. When the skin of the duck becomes crisp and crusty, it is removed and kept warm on a separate plate. The skinned duck is again basted, this time with honey and warm water, and replaced in the oven for a second roasting. The wings, the drumsticks, and the sliced breast of the duck are served on one dish and the skin on another, with a sauce on the side called _hoisin_. On one plate, we find Mandarin pancakes and on another, lotus buns.

The proper ritual of true Chinese service is to bring the uncooked duck out of the kitchen and show it to the guests. A nod of the head signifies that the duck meets with the guests' approval and that it is ready for the oven. While the duck roasts, the diners munch on

Chinese *hors d'oeuvre* and sip a little wine. In Chinese-American restaurants, Peking duck must be ordered a day in advance. (See HOISIN, HORS D'OEUVRE, LOTUS BUNS, MANDARIN) COMPATIBLE WINES: A white wine, e.g., saké, Sauterne, sherry, Gewürztraminer; or a rosé wine.

Peking Duck II   Peking duck is often served another way. The diner places a piece of the crisp skin, a slice of the duck, and a bit of chopped scallion and cucumber on a pancake that is seasoned with *hoisin* sauce. The pancake is rolled and eaten with the hands. The texture and taste contrasts make this a memorable dining experience.

Peking Duck Sauce   This sauce, used to complement the flavor of a Peking duck, is a mixture of *hoisin* sauce, grated orange rind, and sugar. Another sauce, available in cans and also served with the duck, is plum sauce, which is made from apricots, peaches, and plums mixed with sugar and vinegar. (See HOISIN, PEKING DUCK)

Peking Sauce   This sauce from Szechwan is a flavoring agent composed of a blend of *hoisin* sauce and brown-bean sauce. It should not be confused with the duck sauce which also bears the Peking tag.

PEMMICAN   This method of preserving meat by drying, used by American Indians, dates back to prehistoric days. The Indians pounded dry meat, usually venison, into a powder, then mixed it with bone-marrow fat (usually from a bear) that had been melted down to a buttery consistency with dried berries and vegetables. Early arctic explorers carried *pemmican* (dried meat and raisins) with them on their explorations, and it was said to have been fed to the hundreds of thousands of slaves who built the ancient Egyptian pyramids. (See BÜNDNERFLEISCH, CHARQUI, RÖHSCHINKEN)

PEPERONCINI (Italian)   A very small red sausage that is hot to the tongue and is served as part of a good *pizza*.

PEPERONI (Italian)   Bell peppers. Also, in the United States, a small sausage served on *pizza*. (See PIZZA)

Peperoni Ripieni   Stuffed peppers made by first toasting the peppers under the grill, then removing each stem and cutting out a circle from the top and removing both seeds and veins. The peppers are filled with chopped chicken, tomatoes, and anchovies and then closed by replacing the circular tops. Then the stuffed peppers are placed in a baking pan with a bit of olive oil. Topped with salt, paprika, and grated Parmesan cheese, they are baked until done.

PEPPER   The word "pepper" is derived from the Sanskrit word *pipali*. Cultivated in Burma and Assam, the pepper vine, the *piper negrum*, grows as tall as ten feet and produces berries that progress in color from green to red as the plant matures. When dried, the berries turn brown, even black. Green peppercorns are much hotter and juicier than the dried peppercorns. When the dark outer layer (the most aromatic part) of a peppercorn is removed by soaking, the white peppercorn is exposed, and for this there is great demand. *Lampong* pepper, considered to be by far the best, is grown in the Dutch East Indies. The Indian *Malabar* pepper is very costly because it is so difficult to come by.

Pepper has always been an expensive spice and very much in demand. In the Middle Ages, pepper was so highly esteemed that landlords preferred that rents be paid them in peppercorns. And going back a bit further, in 408 A.D., three thousand pounds of pepper was the sum paid to Alaric the barbarian to ransom Rome. No meager sum! The Crusaders brought much back to France with them, and of all the spices, pepper was the rarest. "As costly as pepper" was a phrase often heard. If one won a lawsuit at court, for example, it was customary to show gratitude to the judge by slipping him a large packet of pepper. Pepper was Columbus' ace-in-the-hole, and dangling it before the noses of the king and queen of Spain helped him acquire the necessary backing for his daring voyage to America. He was later jailed because he came back empty-handed.

Pepper is a healthful spice. It helps convert food into energy; it is a boon to salt-free dieters; it is an aid to digestion; and it stimulates the appetite. Of all the condiments known to man, with the possible exception of salt, pepper is the one most universally used. (See CAPSICUM)

PERCIATELLI (Italian) See PASTA

PÉRIGUEUX/PÉRIGOURDINE (French) All dishes so described include a garnish of black truffles. A fine distinction between *Périgueux* and *Périgourdine* is that the former truffle is chopped and the latter thinly sliced. This famous and expensive sauce enricher is snouted out in the south of France, near Périgueux, by greedy pigs who love truffles dearly. Once the truffle is located, however, the poor pig is pulled away from it and it is dug out of the ground. Today, dogs are also used for this purpose. The white truffle, found in Italy, is far less expensive but not quite so fine. (See TRUFFLE)

Tournedos, Sauce Périgueux Small fillets of beef are either sautéed in oil and butter or grilled and served with a brown sauce flavored with finely chopped black truffles. (For compatible wines see the following entry.)

Filet de Boeuf en Croûte Périgourdine This great fillet of beef is baked in a crust with black truffles and a black truffle sauce made with a purée of goose liver. COMPATIBLE WINES: A red wine, e.g., Chambertin, Fixin, Dôle, Romanée-Conti, Échézeaux, Nuits St. Georges, La Tâche, Pinot Noir.

PERSILLADE (French) A rather strong seasoning made by mincing together fresh parsley and raw garlic. This is usually added after the food has been cooked. It is also used to perk up the taste of leftover meats, especially beef, either sautéed or served cold as a salad.

PERSIMMON Of the many fruits relished by the Japanese, this Apple of the Orient, the persimmon, is one of the most popular. It can be dried and powdered and used to sweeten other foods; or it can be eaten fully ripe, when it is as sweet as sugar. When persimmons become overripe, they are frozen by the Japanese and transformed into a truly delicious sherbet-type dessert. The persimmon is cultivated in Europe and in America, but the Japanese variety, the *kaki,* which is grown also in France, is finest in flavor and aroma. It is used to make fruit preserves and fine jellies.

PESCE (Italian) Fish.

PESTO ALLA GENOVESE (Italian) This herb-and-cheese paste, which comes from Columbus' birthplace, Genoa, is made by pounding basil, parsley, garlic, pine nuts *(pignoli),* and Parmesan cheese into a pulp and then gradually adding olive oil, drop by drop, until a thick paste is formed. Walnuts may be substituted for the pine nuts. *Pesto* is served with hot *gnocchi* or *pasta* dishes, and it can do much to enhance the flavor of a *minestrone.* (See GNOCCHI, MINESTRONE, PASTA)

PETIT DUC (French) This is one of many names given to the son of Napoleon. Another was *L'Aiglon,* "the little eagle." The title *Petit Duc* came with the Austrian dukedom that was bestowed upon him by his illustrious father.
Filet de Boeuf Petit Duc   This fillet of beef is larded and set on a bed of finely chopped carrots, onions, and celery and moistened with Madeira wine. The fillet is then put into the oven, covered with melted butter, and allowed to cook gently. The roast is glazed and served with two garnishes: one consists of crisp rounds of puff pastry with asparagus tips in cream, the other of hearts of artichokes filled with truffles. (See L'AIGLON) COMPATIBLE WINES: A red wine, e.g., Chambertin, Fixin, Romanée-Conti, Aloxe-Corton, Calon-Ségur, Pomerole, Cabernet Sauvignon, Dôle, Nuits St. Georges.

PETITE MARMITE (French) The *marmite* is the small earthenware bowl in which this rich soup is served. Similar to the better-known *pot-au-feu,* this is a beef and chicken consommé garnished with carrots, turnips, leeks, cabbage, celery, and bits of beef marrow plus lean pieces of beef, oxtail, and chicken. The rich dish is served with French bread that is toasted and sprinkled with grated Gruyère cheese. (See GARBURE, POT-AU-FEU)

PETITS FOURS (French) Literally, "little ovens." In culinary parlance, this phrase refers to those tiny, delicate cakes that are no more than a mouthful and can be eaten with the fingers. The very first *petit four* was served all alone on a tremendous platter to one of the Louis of France while he was visiting a small landowner in the countryside. Everyone gasped in horror at this apparent effrontery, but the king was delighted with the tiny, exquisite cake and installed the creator in his royal kitchens at the palace. *Petits fours* are usually made from almond or butter cakes that are cut into decorative shapes and coated with various icings—from an apricot glaze to flavored *fondant* frostings. (See FONDANT)

PETS DE NONNE (French) These puffs of fried *chou* pastry are as right-ly famous for their crunchy lightness as they are for their rather quaint name, which means "a nun's farts." They were created by a tiny nun with deft hands and a lively imagination while she was cloistered in the ancient Abbaye de Marmoutier in Alsace. Often euphemistically referred to as *soupirs de nonne,* which translates to "a nun's sighs," these are properly served dusted with powdered sugar. (See PÂTE À CHOU)

PHILADELPHIA PEPPER POT (American) This old Berks County fa-vorite is a creation of the Quakers, who left the German Palatinate to settle in Pennsylvania around 1710. By the time of the American Revolution, the majority of the population of Pennsylvania, accord-ing to Ben Franklin, was so German that *"bitte schön"* and *"danke schön"* and *"Gesundheit"* were more commonly heard than "please," "thanks," and "I do hope you are well." It seems that more than one-third of the state of Pennsylvania was German-speaking. The enthu-siastic reports of the fine land and of freedom such as was never known prompted more Germans and many Swiss to follow their brethren and fill the counties of Northampton, Berks, Lancaster, Lehigh, Lebanon, and York with such religious sects as the Amish, the Mennonites, the Schwenkfelders, and the Dunkers (The Church of the Brethren), all known as the Pennsylvania Dutch (not Deutsch).

The pepper pot is made from two types of tripe, the honeycomb and the plain variety, which are boiled in water for eight hours. The tripe is removed, cut into small squares, and cooked for three more hours, this time with a meaty veal knuckle. After the broth is strained and the meat cut from the bones, bay leaves, onions, various herbs, salt, and cayenne pepper are added and cooked with cubed potatoes. With the addition of dumplings, which are cooked in the rich broth, to which has been added a sprinkling of chopped parsley, the dish is ready to be served. . . . *und schmeckt wunderbar!* COMPATIBLE WINES: A red wine, e.g., Beaujolais, Zinfandel, Valpolicella, Lambrusco, Médoc, Margaux, Petit Sirah, Egri Bikaver, Premiat, Mercurey, Côtes du Rhône.

Philadelphia Pepper Pot II Another version of the birth of the pepper pot was told at swank tea parties by Martha, wife to the father of his country, George Washington. She claimed that old George, while freezing at Valley Forge, was much concerned for his troops and ordered his cook to scrape up anything he could and make something hot for the men. Much like Napoleon's cook at Marengo, this wild-eyed chef took what tripe he could scrounge up and cooked them with enough peppercorns to make the broth hotter than its boiling temperature. The day was won, and some, said Martha, claimed that the success of the revolution was due to that pepper pot. (See MARENGO)

PHOENIX-TAILED SHRIMP (Chinese) This favorite is so called because when the shrimp are deep-fried, the tails, which are left on when the shrimp are shelled, turn a beautiful red color. Each shrimp is dipped into an egg-flour-water batter before it is fried. COMPATIBLE WINES: A white wine, e.g., Chablis, Meursault, Muscadet, Quincy, Soave, Pinot Chardonnay, Debro, Riquewihr, Aigle.

PHYLLO Paper-thin sheets (leaves) of pastry dough which the Greeks use to make *baklava* and other specialities. Austria and Hungary, who both boast of their *Strudel,* and rightly so, can thank the Turks for introducing this dough to their lands. When the Turks invaded the West, they brought *yufka* (which the Greeks call *phyllo*) to Europe. This pastry dough is sold wrapped in plastic packages containing from four to fifty sheets. The size varies with the manufacturer. These paper-thin sheets dry easily and can crumble and break if mishandled. *Phyllo* leaves, which are unsweetened, are also used to make savory pastries. (See BAGLAWA, BÖREKS, STRUDEL, YUFKA)

PIACERE, A (Italian) This phrase, meaning "done to your pleasure," is used by some restaurateurs who "go the extra mile" to please their guests by offering to serve certain foods—such as sole, shrimp, or veal cutlet—prepared in any way the diner might wish. This is as great a treat for the diner as it is a lovely gesture, but unfortunately it is so rarely done as to be unique. Today, tableside salad preparations where the diner can choose from various greens and a myriad of sauces fills the *a piacere* prescription.

PIATTI DEL GIORNO (Italian) "Dishes of the day," a term found on menus. Listed under this term there might be subcategories, such as: *carne,* meats; *arrosti,* roasted meats; *bolliti,* boiled meats; *alla griglia,* grilled; *piatti freddi,* cold dishes; or *specialita della casa,* the speciality of the house. (See BOLLITO)

PICADINHO COPACABANA (Brazilian) A hash does not always have to be nondescript or commonplace. This Brazilian variety, for example, can be quite an elegant presentation. Chopped cooked beef and pork are sautéed in oil together with finely chopped onions. To this meat mixture, one adds raisins, diced green peppers, tiny Italian tomatoes, a small hot pepper, a bit of sherry, chicken stock, and finely chopped garlic; this is allowed to simmer. When thoroughly cooked, the mixture is thickened by the addition of finely chopped blanched almonds and cornstarch that has been diluted in water. The mixture is carefully folded into a *crêpe,* topped with a *sauce Mornay,* and placed under the broiler until brown. (See CRÊPE, MORNAY) COMPATIBLE BEVERAGES: Beer.

PICCATA MILANESE This fillet of veal is pounded flat, seasoned, and then prepared in the style of Milan: dipped in flour and egg and sautéed in butter. Usually, a _risotto_ or _spaghetti_ is served as an accompaniment. (See RISOTTO, SPAGHETTI) COMPATIBLE WINES: A white wine, e.g., Orvieto, Vouvray, Sylvaner, Sauvignon Blanc, Hochheim, Johannisberg, Riesling.

PICKLING A method of preserving food, first used by the ancient Chinese and the Babylonians. It involves keeping food in brine (a salt solution), in sugar, in acidic liquids like vinegar, or in combinations of these. (See BEIZE, MARINADE, SAUERBRATEN)

PIECZEN HUSARSKA (Polish) Literally, "Hussar pot roast." The meat (beef, pork, veal, or game) is browned and then is either blanched in a boiling marinade or flavored with vodka and then simmered with onions and butter in a bit of water. When the meat is tender, it is cut into pockets and stuffed with grated onions, breadcrumbs, and butter. It is then tied up and simmered a bit longer. COMPATIBLE WINES: A red wine, e.g., Chianti, Egri Bikaver, Beaujolais, Valpolicella, Zinfandel, Premiat, Cabernet Sauvignon, Mercurey, Rioja.

PIÉMONTESE, À LA (French) Prepared in the style of the Piedmont region of northern Italy, which is bounded by France and Switzerland.

Garniture Piémontese Composed of a _risotto_ flavored with white truffles, this garnish is served with various poultry and meat dishes. (See RISOTTO)

Sauce Piémontese A _sauce velouté_ that is enriched with a veal stock flavored with anchovy-butter and chopped white truffles. (See VELOUTÉ)

PIGNATELLI, BEIGNETS (Italian) Crisp, crunchy nut-sized fritters that are served either as an _hors d'oeuvre_ or as a garnish for clear soups. They are made from a _pâte à chou_ mixed with chopped boiled ham and toasted slivered almonds. Small balls of this dough are deep-fried and drained. They are especially tangy when made with Parmesan cheese. (See PÂTE À CHOU)

PILAFF/PILAF/PILAW/PULLAU The _pilaff_ was born in Turkey, as were most of the classic Middle Eastern dishes. Considered the national dish of Turkey, it is made from rice seized in hot oil and butter with chopped onions and then covered with a good chicken stock. With the addition of meat, fish, poultry, game, vegetables, fruits, and nuts in a number of combinations, this dish is covered and baked. The dish has since been adopted by many nations: in Greece, where it is made with tomato paste, it is called _pilafi;_ in Poland it is called _pilaw;_ in India, where it is made with lamb, chicken, or fish, it is called _pullau._ (See PAELLA, SAADAA PULLAU)

PIMENTO/PIMIENTO These two words have spellings and pronunciations so much alike that they often cause confusion or error. For instance, when speaking of a "pimento-stuffed olive" one is in error because the *pimiento*, not the *pimento*, is the sweet pepper used to stuff olives. The *pimento* is the aromatic berry of a tree that grows in the West Indies; we also know it as "allspice." (See ALLSPICE)

PINEAPPLE CHUTNEY This condiment is popularly served with Hawaiian foods. Chunks of pineapple are simmered with chopped red peppers, crushed garlic, salt, chopped ginger and almonds, vinegar, brown sugar, and seedless raisins until the chutney is thick. It is served with meat and curry dishes of all kinds. (See CHUTNEY, MANGO CHUTNEY)

PINKELWURST Born in Bremen, Germany, this sausage is composed of smoked pork, bacon fat, oatmeal, and enough spices to make it rather piquant. This same sausage is also known by the name *Grützwurst* (in German, *Grütz* is the edible part of the oat kernel).

PINYIN (Chinese) The system of transliterating Mandarin Chinese into English to facilitate Western pronunciation of the Mandarin dialect. This system of transliteration is used on menus in many Chinese restaurants.

PIPÉRADE (French) An egg dish that originated in the Basque country of southern France. Finely chopped onions and garlic are tossed into a pan with hot olive oil, followed closely by chopped tomatoes, green peppers, and pimientos; a seasoning of rosemary, salt, and pepper are then added. As soon as the tomatoes and peppers are tender, the eggs are stirred into the mixture and cooked until they are softly scrambled *(baveuse)*. Served with a sprinkling of fresh chopped parsley, this makes a delightful luncheon dish. (See BAVEUX) COMPATIBLE BEVERAGES: Beer, ale, cider, rosé.

PIPIAN DE CAMERONES (Mexican) This dish of spicy shrimp is said to have originated in the ancient Aztec culture. Ground pumpkin seeds are added to cooked peeled shrimp and held in reserve. Then a combination of onions, garlic, coriander, tomatoes, *pequin* chilies, and pimientos are blended to a smooth purée, seasoned with salt, pepper, and sugar, and cooked in oil. The shrimp and ground pumpkin seeds are heated in the mixture and served with a dash of lemon juice. (See CHILI) COMPATIBLE BEVERAGES: Beer, ale.

PIQUANTE, SAUCE (French) A classic sauce made by browning chopped shallots and onions in butter with a bit of flour. After adding white wine and vinegar, the mixture is reduced, seasoned, and passed through a sieve; then chopped gherkins, parsley, and tarragon are added and cooked together. To finish the sauce, a bit of meat extract, brown sauce, or even the cooked residue of the meat are stirred in. The sauce is served with tripe and pork dishes. (See BROWN SAUCE)

PIRI-PIRI SAUCE (Portuguese) A spicy concoction of chopped hot chili peppers placed in an airtight bottle that is filled with olive oil and flavored with bay leaves and lemon rind. After marinating for a month, the sauce is used to perk up egg, fish, or poultry dishes.

PIROG/PIROSHKI (Russian) A yeast-dough pastry. The large ones are called _piroghi_ or _pirogi_ (plural of _pirog_), and the individual tart-size ones are called _piroshki_.

Piroghi Domeshny The dough is cut into rounds, and in the middle of each is placed a filling of finely chopped pork, sauerkraut, and onions moistened with sour cream. A second round of dough is placed over the first and the edges are sealed with egg yolk. The _piroghi_ are then cooked in boiling salted water and served coated with creamed onions. There are filling variations: cheese, whitefish, chopped veal, or various vegetables bound with a _sauce Béchamel_. When these fillings are used, the pastries are baked rather than boiled. COMPATIBLE WINES: The choice of wine depends upon the filling used.

PIRONA (Finnish) This traditional dish, also known as the "Karelian pork pot" (this refers to the Karelian Soviet Socialist Republic, situated north and east of Lake Onega; the majority of the population is Russian, although there are many Karelians, Lapps, and Finns as well), is cooked by the "hatching" method. Presoaked beans and peas are simmered in water in a heavy pot for several hours, until tender. Then, with the addition of barley, cubed pork, turnips, rutabaga, and potatoes, the pot is tightly covered and slow-baked (hatched) for several hours. (See HATCHING)

PISSALADIÈRE (Italian) This Neapolitan speciality is popular along the Riviera, especially in Provence, where it is spelled as here written. (The spelling suggests that it might have come from Portugal.) Bread dough is rounded to fit the pan and is topped with chopped onions, garlic, crushed anchovies; it is decorated with black olives. Baked to a delicate crustiness, this is a veritable _pizza Provençale_. (See PIZZA) COMPATIBLE WINES: A red wine, e.g., Chianti, Valpolicella, Bardolino, Beaujolais, Fleurie, Côte Rôtie, Dôle, Pinot Noir, Moulin-à-Vent.

PISSENLITS, SALADE DE (French) This dandelion salad might be considered a "wet-the-bed-salad," not only because of its literal translation _(piss-en-lits)_ but more pointedly because of the strong diuretic property of the underrated dandelion. Medicinally, the roots of this plant are valued more than its leafy growth. However, when destined to be used as a salad, the leaves should be picked before they mature, otherwise they will be too bitter. The leaves are blanched and kept in ice water until ready for use. Then the leaves are carefully dried and tossed in a dressing of olive oil, vinegar, salt, pepper, and a bit of mustard and mixed together with bread croutons that have been browned in olive oil flavored with fresh garlic.

PISTACHE, BEURRE DE (French) See COMPOUND BUTTER

PISTO (Spanish) A huge omelette that appears to include whatever one happened to find in the refrigerator, the vegetable bin, and the larder on a cold day in January. Among the ingredients might be cubed potatoes, cubed and browned pork, minced onions, peppers and garlic, fresh tomatoes, pimientos, shrimp, ham, and peas. This is all mixed in a egg mixture and cooked in an oversized skillet until done. (See ZUCCHINI) COMPATIBLE BEVERAGES: Beer, ale, cider, rose winé.

Pisto Mexicano The Mexican version of the Spanish omelette. In this case, it is prepared by first sautéing cubed ham in oil and then removing it. Chopped onions and peppers are simmered in tomato purée until tender. Beaten eggs are mixed with the cubed ham, to which the tomato-onion-pepper mixture is added and poured into a large heavy skillet to cook until set. COMPATIBLE BEVERAGES: Beer, ale, cider.

PISTOU The French may like to call this soup their very own, but it is as Italian in flavor, composition, and aroma as the *pesto* from which it springs. A combination of beans, potatoes, salt, onions, and leeks are cooked together in water until tender, then *vermicelli* is added. Garlic, basil, tomatoes, oil, and grated Gruyère cheese are pounded into a paste and added to the hot soup. (See PESTO, VERMICELLI)

PITA A Yugoslavian term for a *phyllo*-like, paper-thin pastry that is filled with cheese or spinach and served as a pie. This is also the name for a type of Middle Eastern flat "pocket" bread. (See PHYLLO, SPANAKOPITTA)

PITÉK (Hungarian) Short cakes made from a dough of sugar, butter, and flour in a one:two:three ratio. The pastry dough must be worked quickly, while all the ingredients are still cool, otherwise the butter will soften too much. The dough can be kept refrigerated until ready to be used. *Piték* cakes, usually rectangular and flat, can be filled with apples, apricots, peaches, or cheese, bound with a rich custard, covered with another pastry crust, and baked as a pie. The Hungarian apple variety is called *almás pite*.

PIZZA (Italian) Although the word *pizza* refers to any pie or cake, it has come to be used worldwide to refer to the popular Neapolitan pie usually topped with tomato sauce and a variety of garnishes. The *pizza* dough is made from flour, yeast, salt, sugar, water, and olive oil. After rising to double its size, it is flattened and rolled into a large circle, smeared with tomato sauce and dressed with any number of garnishes—including shrimp, anchovies, sausage, meatballs, garlic, green peppers, capers, tomatoes, sliced mushrooms, and Parmesan or mozzarella cheese. It is then sprinkled with herbs and olive oil and baked. COMPATIBLE BEVERAGES: Beer, ale, or a rosé wine, depending upon the spiciness of the ingredients.

PIZZAIOLA DI MANZO (Italian) A popular method of preparing steak, usually a T-bone or a sirloin of beef. The steak is first either fried or grilled. Then, the *pizzaiola,* a Neapolitan sauce consisting of chopped tomatoes cooked in olive oil that has been flavored with crushed garlic, is poured over the previously charred steak. The steak is sprinkled with fresh basil and, tightly covered, it is left to be seized by the heat for a few minutes. This is also called *bistecca alla pizzaiola.* COMPATIBLE WINES: A red wine, e.g., Chianti, Dôle, Barolo, Rioja, Nuits St. Georges, Pinto Noir, Mercurey, Châteauneuf-du-Pape, Egri Bikaver.

PLAKI (Turkish) Vegetables or fish cooked with onions, tomatoes, and olive oil. The dish is always served cold.

PLANTAINS Large green "cooking bananas" which grow in Mexico and in Central America. They should be baked or fried. Uncooked, they taste similar to raw turnip.

Plantains Cajun-style The plantains, popular in Louisiana, are mashed, fried, and then mixed with cayenne pepper, cinnamon, and nutmeg and served topped with cracklings. (See CRACKLING)

Plantains au Rhum The plantains are sliced in half then fried in butter and sprinkled with brown sugar, nutmeg, and cayenne pepper. Then, sprinkled with rum, they are browned lightly in the oven.

Banane Jaune, Sauce Blanche This French method of preparing plantains comes from the Island of Martinique and entails slicing the peeled plantains in half and simmering them in salted water until tender. They are then served coated with a thick *sauce Béchamel* flavored with nutmeg. (See BÉCHAMEL)

PLÄTTAR (Swedish) Small pancakes served as dessert. A thin batter is made from a blend of eggs, sugar, salt, milk, and flour. Cooked one after the other in a pan with hot butter, these small delicate pancakes are served with lingonberry, strawberry, or blueberry preserves. (See BLINI, BLINTZ, CRÊPE, PANCAKE, SUZETTE, TORTILLA)

PLATTENPUDDING (German) A pudding made from alternate layers of macaroons, raspberries, ladyfingers, and a rich custard.

PLUM PUDDING (English) Later called "Christmas pudding," this first appeared in England in the middle of the eighteenth century. Before then a plum porridge was eaten at Christmas, but this was a type of soup composed of a rich beef stock to which raisins, spices, currants, sugar, and a bottle of sherry and Bordeaux wine were added. (See CHRISTMAS PUDDING)

POËLÉ (French) A type of covered roast that is cooked entirely in butter (no other shortening is used) on a bed of sliced vegetables. Meats and poultry may be cooked in this fashion, and when earthenware cooking vessels are used, these dishes are referred to as *en casserole* or *en cocotte.* When game birds are *poëléed,* they are moistened with brandy; all other *poëléed* dishes are cooked in butter only. *Poëléed* roasts can be browned by uncovering the pot a half-hour before the allotted cooking time is up.

POI This vegetable paste is to the Polynesian what *pasta* is to the Italian. So popular in Hawaii, *poi* is prepared from the pulp of the taro root *(coco-yam, kalo, dasheen).* The pulp is cooked, pounded, strained, and left to ferment. Eaten unseasoned, *poi* is often served as a dip. There are three varieties of *poi:* the one, two, and three-finger types. The three-finger *poi* has the consistency of heavy catsup. *Poi* is grey, thick, and gooey and is served to complement other dishes, such as fish, meat, poultry, or tomatoes. (See POI COCKTAIL, TARO)

POI COCKTAIL (Hawaiian) A beverage made by stirring milk into *poi* until smooth. Salt, sugar, or nutmeg can be added according to taste. Chilled and well shaken, the liquid is poured into a tumbler filled with cracked ice. (See POI)

POISSON (French) Fish.

POIVRADE, SAUCE (French) This pungent sauce is named for the amount of peppercorns it contains. Chopped carrots, onions, and shallots are sautéed in butter together with bay leaves, cloves, and thyme. After adding red wine, red wine vinegar, crushed peppercorns, and a *sauce demi-glace,* it is simmered until all the ingredients have melded into an essence. The sauce is carefully strained before serving with venison or birds of game. It is important to add the peppercorns at the last moment lest they develop an acrid taste through overcooking. (See DEMI-GLACE)

POIVRE DE JAMAICA (French) See ALLSPICE

POIVRE, ENTRECÔTE AU (French) A peppered steak said to have been created by Leopold, prince of Bavaria, who ultimately became king of Belgium. His method of preparing the steak was to press coarsely ground pepper into the raw meat of both sides of the steak, even to salt it before cooking (salt draws out the blood), then broil it and serve it topped with melted butter. Another method uses white pepper only and douses the steak, after broiling it, with hot brandy. Yet another method calls for the surface of a thick steak to be scored using a special tomato knife having five small serrated blades; then the coarsely ground pepper and chopped parsley is pressed into the meat. Here the meat is not salted until it has been seared. The steak is then sautéed in a mixture of oil and butter in a heavy pan. COMPATIBLE WINES: A red wine, e.g., Fixin, Châteauneuf-du-Pape, Nuits St, Georges, Côtes du Rhône, Pinot Noir, Chianti, Margaux, Borolo, Dôle, Mâcon Rouge.

POJARSKI, CÔTELETTES DE SAUMON (French) Any food that is prepared *à la Pojarski* is sure to be minced, chopped, seasoned, and shaped into new forms before being cooked. These salmon cutlets are made by chopping up the salmon, mixing it with butter, breadcrumbs, and milk, seasoning it with salt, pepper, and nutmeg, then forming it into cutlets and sautéing them in butter until brown on both sides. A *sauce Bretonne* is served separately. (See BRETONNE) COMPATIBLE WINES: A white wine, e.g., Meursault, Montrachet, Pouilly-Fumé, Piesporter Goldtröpfchen, Aigle, Pinot Chardonnay, Soave.

Côtes de Veau Pojarski This French forcemeat is made from minced veal mixed with butter, breadcrumbs, cream, and eggs. After seasoning with salt and pepper and nutmeg, it is shaped into the form of veal chops and fried in butter. COMPATIBLE WINES: A white wine, e.g., Saumur, Aigle, Vouvray, Frascati, Bernkasteler Doktor, Gewürztraminer, Orvieto, Rüdesheim, Nierstein, Johannisberg, Sylvaner.

Suprêmes de Volaille Pojarski A *suprême* in French culinary parlance refers to plump and tender breasts of chicken that are first skinned then served in one of two ways: either "brown," meaning sautéed in butter, or "white," meaning that the breasts are poached in a rich chicken stock enriched with butter. These *Pojarski suprêmes* call for the breasts to be minced, mixed with breadcrumbs and cream and butter, seasoned with nutmeg, salt, and pepper, and then re-formed to the shape of the original breast. Dredged in flour, they are cooked in clarified butter and served at once. (See SUPRÊMES DE VOLAILLE) COMPATIBLE WINES: A white wine, e.g., Meursault, Orvieto, Vouvray, Johannisberg, Wehlener Sonnenuhr, Piesporter Goldtröpfchen, Graacher Himmelreich, Sauterne, Gewürztraminer.

POK-CHOI (Chinese) See MUSTARD SEED

PÖKÖLT, VEAL (Hungarian) *Pökölt* is Hungarian for "charred" or "browned." To prepare this veal dish, cubed onions are browned in rendered bacon fat and ground paprika is whipped into the sauce. Cubed veal and green peppers, cut into strips, are cooked in a mixture of bouillon, red wine, salt, and pepper in a covered pot with the onions. Just before serving, sour cream is mixed into the stew. Salads and buttered noodles are usually served with the dish, which is very similar to the unforgettable *gulyas*. (See GULYAS) COMPATIBLE WINES: A red wine, Margaux, Pétrus, Valpolicella, Cabernet Sauvignon, Mâcon, Zinfandel, St. Julien, Pomerole, Egri Bikaver.

POLEDWICA DUSZONA ZE SMIETANA (Polish) Beef tenderloin smothered in sour cream. The tenderloin is first larded, then broiled and basted with butter. Then the meat is placed in a casserole, covered with a mixture of sour cream and a bit of flour, and baked in a hot oven. COMPATIBLE WINES: A red wine, e.g., Fixin, Romanée-Conti, Nuits St. Georges, Dôle, Chambertin, Pinot Noir, Barolo, Chianti, Châteauneuf-du-Pape.

POLENTA (Italian) In ancient Rome, the forerunner of *polenta,* called *puls,* was considered to be the staple food of the empire. The dish consisted of chestnut flour, coarse wheat, millet, barley, and sorghum. Today, however, the hearty Italian *polenta* dish is made from corn flour, a cereal that was first brought to Italy from America some thirty years after Columbus discovered the New World. In 1530, corn was cultivated in Andalusia as cattle fodder.

It was not until the eighteenth century, in the northern provinces of Italy, in the Piedmont, that corn became a popular food. In fact, President Jefferson was so taken with the *polenta* he was served in Florence that he taught his own cook how to prepare it and served it frequently at the White House. Today, in northern Italy, no family is without its *polenta* pot.

Polenta is usually prepared by boiling white or yellow cornmeal in salted water. It can be refined with the addition of butter and cheese or with a meat and tomato sauce, and after being cooled, it is cut into rectangular shapes and either fried or baked. *Polenta* can be served simply as a gruel, with sausages, with herring, even with quail, or simply with rich milk poured over it. (See CORN BREAD, CORNMEAL, HOMINY) COMPATIBLE WINES: A red wine; e.g., Valpolicella, Lambrusco, Premiat, Egri Bikaver, Beaujolais, Zinfandel.

Mamaliga (Rumanian) A very thick porridge, almost a cake, made with corn flour. In Rumanian restaurants it is usually eaten in place of bread, with thick soups and stews. To prepare, corn flour is mixed with boiling water and stirred. When it begins to thicken, it is seasoned and left to simmer until done. *Mamaliga* is often served with egg dishes—fried, poached, or scrambled—or it is eaten with cheese or with sour cream. It is also a traditional Jewish dish (see below).

Mamaligge (Jewish) Corn flour is added to boiling salted water in the top of a double boiler and stirred well. It is cooked for half an hour. For a meat meal, *mamaligge* can be served with meat gravy; for a dairy meal, it can be served with pot cheese or with sour cream. A sweet variation is made by adding raisins, chopped almonds, pecans, or walnuts to the cornmeal cooking in salted water. This can then be served as is with sour cream or yogurt. Or it can be refrigerated, and when cold, cut into squares. These squares are dipped in beaten egg, rolled in a mixture of breadcrumbs and sesame seeds, and either fried in butter or baked in the oven. The *mamaligge* squares can be served with sour cream, yogurt, applesauce, maple syrup, or with berries of all kinds.

POLIPO Always an Italian favorite, "squid" are served in a great number of ways. These include *affogato,* meaning poached in white wine with tomatoes and herbs; *alla Luciana,* braised in oil with garlic, parsley, red peppers, tomatoes, and white wine; or *in humido,* a stew of small squid cooked in red wine with garlic, tomato and anchovy purées, parsley, and mushrooms. COMPATIBLE WINES: If a white wine is chosen, then Hermitage Blanc, Gewürztraminer, or Frascati; a red choice might include Beaujolais, Châteauneuf-du-Pape, Lambrusco, or Valpolicella.

POLISH KASHA The Poles simmer their buckwheat in a mixture of milk and butter. Eggs, sour cream, and more butter are then stirred into the mixture, which is set in a buttered mold and baked. It is usually served with heavy cream. (See KASHA)

POLLO A "chicken" in an Italian farmyard is always a *gallina,* but once cooked, it is called *pollo,* much as the English "pig" is usually "pork" by the time it reaches the dinner table.

POLLO (Spanish) Chicken.

Arroz con Pollo This is a meal-in-itself. The chicken is cut up, seasoned, and browned in oil. It is then added to a simmering mixture of chickpeas, tomatoes, pimientos, onions, seasoning, rice, and water. After having cooked for an hour or so, clams may be added. COMPATIBLE WINES: A red wine, e.g., Beaujolais, Fleurie, Valpolicella, Egri Bikaver, Grignolino.

PO LO JEE/PO LOH KAI (Chinese) Terms for chicken cooked with pineapple. The chicken breast is diced and dusted with cornstarch. Pineapple chunks are drained, set aside, and cornstarch is added to the juice. Then freshly minced ginger, green peppers, onions, and the diced chicken are stir-fried in hot vegetable oil in a wok (Chinese cooking utensil). Either rice wine or sherry, salt, and pineapple chunks are added plus the cornstarch and pineapple juice mixture. The wok is set over high heat and the mixture boiled until it clears. COMPATIBLE WINES: A white wine, e.g., rice wine, sherry, Sauterne.

POLONAISE, À LA (French) A dish so described is garnished with chopped hard-boiled eggs and chopped fresh parsley that have been mixed with breadcrumbs and fried in butter. This is served with salads or with cooked cauliflower. (See PANADA)

Polonaise, Sauce This sauce, made in honor of the great Polish people, consists of a veal stock simmered with butter, sour cream and lemon juice, grated horseradish, fennel, chives, shallots, pepper and, most important, the hard-boiled eggs, finely chopped. The sauce is served with fish, veal, and pork dishes as well as with cauliflower and other vegetables.

POLPETTE DI MANZO (Italian) These beef meatballs are made of twice-ground beef, seasoned with parsley, nutmeg, grated Parmesan cheese, and salt, and bound with moistened bread and eggs. The balls are flattened a bit, rolled in breadcrumbs, and fried in hot oil. COMPATIBLE WINES: A red wine, e.g., Chianti, Nebbiolo, Dôle, Beaujolais, Valpolicella, Zinfandel, Châteauneuf-du-Pape.

POLPETTINE (Italian) Tiny meatballs.

Polpettine alla Gremolada Beef, veal, and pork are ground fine and seasoned with nutmeg and with a mixture of chopped parsley, garlic, and lemon peel, which is called *gremolada*. Well kneaded, the meat is formed into tiny balls, which are then sautéed in olive oil.

Polpettine alla Napolitana The meatballs are made as the *gremolada* variety, except they are seasoned with chopped raisins and parsley instead of the *gremolada* mix; also, they are breaded before they are sautéed.

COMPATIBLE WINES: A red wine, e.g., Grumello, Inferno, Côte Rôtie, Zinfandel.

POLPETTONE (Italian) This is a meat loaf that is made with mozzarella and Romano cheese mixed with chopped beef and pork, eggs, and seasonings. It is also the name of a dish containing three different kinds of meat: fillets of beef and cutlets of pork and veal, all sliced thin and beaten flat. First, the fillet of beef is thoroughly massaged with a raw garlic clove; then it is seasoned and covered with a thin slice of ham. The veal slice is layered with finely chopped onions and tarragon. Lastly, the pork cutlet is coated with rosemary leaves and chopped egg. The meat slices are rolled up, fastened with toothpicks, and browned in butter. Then a mixture of white wine, tomato purée, and bouillon is poured over the *polpettones* and left to simmer. When done, the pot is removed from the heat, and grated Parmesan cheese, chopped mushrooms, and heavy cream finishes the sauce. COMPATIBLE WINES: A white wine, e.g., Orvieto, Frascati, Riquewihr, Vouvray, Johannisberg, Sauvignon Blanc.

POLPO (Italian) Octopus. Usually, only the smallest of the species is used for food.

POL SAMBOLA (East Indian) This *sambal* is made by mixing shredded coconut, chili powder, paprika, and grated lemon rind in a bowl with dried prawns or dried tuna fish. When ready to serve, lemon juice, finely grated onions, and coconut milk are added. This dish is served with many curry dishes. (See SAMBALS)

POMMES (French) Apples.

POMMES DE TERRE (French) Potatoes.

Pommes Frites French-fried potatoes, of which there are two types: *les pommes maltraitées* ("ill-treated potatoes") and the genuine article. The aforementioned *maltraitées* are usually cooked in oil that has been used and re-used for more than a week, and potatoes subjected to this indignity are greasy, hard, and most times oversalted. Tenderly treated French fries, on the other hand, are cut to a uniform size and then cooked in a moderately hot vegetable oil. As soon as the "fries" pop to the surface, they are removed. Then the oil is put over high heat; this time the potatoes are allowed to remain in the oil for but a few minutes and then are quickly removed and served at once, lightly salted.

Pommes Mousseline The baked, or sometimes boiled, potato is removed from its shell and mashed together with sweet butter, egg yolk, salt, pepper, nutmeg, and with that one important ingredient that makes the potato *mousseline:* whipped heavy cream. The mixture is stirred over heat. Then, dotted with butter, the potatoes are browned in the oven.

Pommes Soufflés Is there anything so simply satisfying to the palate as the magic, puffy crispiness of the souffléed potato? As most great inventions result from some quirk or accident, the banquet scheduled to celebrate the first railway line in France, linking Paris to Saint-Germaine, provided the scene for this great discovery. The presiding chef was informed that there would be a delay in the banquet because Louis-Phillipe and his queen were still en route; so the chef was forced to remove his already half-fried potatoes from the deep-fryer and allow them to drain and cool. *Quel malheur!* When the royal pair finally did arrive, the frustrated chef quickly threw the half-fried potatoes back into the deep fat and prayed that all would be well. He must have directed his prayer to a sympathetic saint because the potatoes that rose to the surface of the boiling fat were puffed up, light as air. The *pomme soufflé* was born! Today, the thin, oval slices of raw potato are first placed in ice water, then dried and dropped into hot oil until they pop up to the surface. After draining, they are dropped into a hotter batch of oil until puffed up with golden pride. They are then removed, drained, and served at once, sprinkled with salt.

POMODORO (Italian) Tomato.

POMODORO SALSA Literally "tomato sauce," which is widely used in all Italian cooking to enhance *pasta* dishes. Inasmuch as the word *pomo* means "apple," and *oro* is Italian for "gold," the first tomatoes to come to Italy must have been yellow. Today, this sauce is made from the ripest and reddest of tomatoes, small but deliciously aromatic. First, bacon, onions, celery, garlic, and carrots, all chopped fine, are cooked in olive oil in a heavy pan. Tomatoes, strained through a sieve, sweet basil, a touch of sugar, salt and pepper are added and cooked uncovered to a thick consistency. (See BOLOGNESE, RAGÙ, SUGO DI POMODORO)

POMPADOUR, FILETS DE SOLE Wives, courtiers, and mistresses all vied with each other for the favor of King Louis XIV by offering some new, exciting culinary concoction that was sure to please this glutton's jaded palate. One of his favorite mistresses, Mme. de Pompadour, invented several new dishes. Her fillets of sole were breaded, seasoned, buttered, and grilled. They were served with a *sauce Choron* and *château potatoes,* and Louis loved her all the more for it. (See CHÂTEAU, CHORON) COMPATIBLE WINES: A white wine, e.g., Pouilly-Fuissé, Chablis, Muscadet, Soave, Montrachet, Quincy, Bernkasteler Doktor, Meursault, Debro, Iphofen, Dézaley.

POMPANO (Spanish) Literally, "grape leaf." A flat, round fish found in the warm waters of the Gulf of Mexico and the South Atlantic. This fish swims in great schools all along the Florida coast and makes a truly delightful meal. The fish can be fried, poached in a white wine sauce, or served *en papillote.* (See PAPILLOTE)

PON PON CHICKEN (Chinese) This spicy chicken dish comes from Szechwan, where hot peppers are used in food to promote perspiration and the resultant lowering of the body temperature on a hot day. The dish is made from boiled chicken breasts, which are sliced into strips and then stirred into a zesty sauce. The sauce is composed of ground peanuts, sesame oil, soy sauce, wine vinegar, crushed red peppers, minced ginger root, cayenne peppers, and toasted ground peppercorns. The dish is served cold. COMPATIBLE BEVERAGES: Beer, ale, tea, cider.

PONZU (Japanese) A dip-sauce composed of lime juice and soy sauce, served with complementary bowls of *daikon* and chopped scallions. It can also be made by adding chicken stock and rice vinegar to the soy sauce mixed with lime or lemon juice. It is served with *sashimi.* (See DAIKON, SASHIMI)

POORI (East Indian) A bread made from whole wheat flour, salt, and warm water. After the dough is rolled out flat, it is deep-fried in hot oil until it puffs up.

POPPY SEED Poppy seed is the product of the opium poppy, which is native to Asia and cultivated as well in France, Holland, Denmark, Poland, Czechoslovakia, Yugoslavia, Turkey, England, Canada, and the United States. The powerful drug opium is derived from this flowering plant, but the seeds are not narcotic. The large flowers come in various brilliant colors, including red, white, purple, pink, and violet. The fruit is a large capsule holding kidney-shaped seeds which reflect the color of the flower: the white poppy has white seeds; the black contains seeds commonly called "blue," which are the ones used as the spice. Poppy seeds have a nutlike taste and are used to flavor cakes, pastries, cookies, breads, buns, rolls, and confections.

PORTOKALIA ME ELIÉS (Greek) This salad, made with oranges and black olives, provides delightful taste contrasts. The thinly sliced oranges are tossed with onions and pitted black olives in a well-seasoned salad sauce made of olive oil and lemon juice. Left to marinate in the refrigerator overnight, the oranges, onions, and olives are then arranged tastefully on a base of Boston lettuce leaves and served.

PORTO, SAUCE (French) A sauce made by reducing port wine, chopped shallots, and thyme then adding the zest and juice from oranges and lemons plus salt and cayenne pepper. After passing the mixture through a sieve, it is blended with a fine, thick veal stock. The English have their own version called Yorkshire. The sauce is served with meat, fowl, and *foie gras* (goose liver). (See FOIE GRAS, YORKSHIRE SAUCE)

PORTUGAISE, SAUCE (French) For this classic sauce, a tomato sauce is reduced with a veal stock and flavored with chopped garlic, onions, and parsley, and just before serving, it is refined with *sauce Espagnole*. (See ESPAGNOLE)

Filet de Boeuf Portugaise The fillet of beef is roasted and served garnished with *château potatoes* and with tomatoes stuffed with rice and chopped tomatoes. The *sauce Portugaise* is served separately. (See CHÂTEAU) COMPATIBLE WINES: A red wine, e.g., Fixin, Talbot, La Tâche, Châteauneuf-du-Pape, Pinot Noir, Dôle, Barolo, Pommard, Chambertin.

POTAGE (French) Originally, the word *potage* meant anything cooked in a pot, such as a stew *(pot au feu, petite marmite,* etc.). Today, the term refers to any thick soup which in itself constitutes a substantial meal. A good *bouillabaise* is a fine example. (See BISQUE, BOUIL-LABAISE, GARBURE, PETITE MARMITE, POT AU FEU, POTÉE)

POTAGE À LA CRÉCY (French) See CRÉCY

POTATOES This member of the nightshade family was first brought to Europe from the New World by the Spanish in the sixteenth century. At first, potatoes were considered strange and quite unpalatable as food. This fact was supported by the English, for when Sir Walter Raleigh proudly presented this new vegetable to the English court, it made everyone who ate it quite ill. It seems that the misinformed chef cooked not the tuber of the potato but the top greens, which are toxic. This was enough to put not only the English but most of the Western world off of the potato. Later, Sir Walter managed to convince his queen that the potato, when correctly cooked, was a very valuable food.

For a time, both the French and the German people were sure that the potato was definitely a poison and were wary about including it in their diet. How ironic that in twentieth-century Europe, and especially in Germany, it was the potato that kept people alive during two devastating World Wars.

France was the last European country to accept the potato. Fortunately for the French and for the world, the famous agronomist Parmentier learned to love the potato while he was a prisoner of war in Germany. His successful efforts to acquaint the French people with the goodness of the potato are honored today by the many great potato dishes that bear his name. The potato is one of the great staple foods of the world, without which we, as humans, would be far poorer and less nourished. (See PARMENTIER, POMMES DE TERRE)

Potato Chips An American Indian, George Crumb, while working as a chef at a Saratoga Springs resort hotel in upper New York State, was about to lose his Indian cool and dash into the dining room to scalp a guest who had just returned his French fries for the fifth time, saying that they were not thin enough. Finally, in desperation,

Crumb sliced another batch of potatoes, this time as thin as paper, and dropped them into the boiling oil. He served them and waited, but instead of complaints he received words of praise. Soon, everybody came to order Chef Crumb's special "Saratoga chips," as they were then called. Today they are served all over the world.

POT-AU-FEU (French) This is one of the national dishes of France, composed of boiled beef and a beef marrow bone cooked together for several hours with a variety of root vegetables, a *bouquet garni,* and seasonings in boiling water. First, the soup is eaten, then the beef is served with a garnish of capers, horseradish, mustard, gherkins, and vegetables. There are many versions of this dish, depending upon the locale. (See GARBURE, PETITE MARMITE)

POTÉE (French) This culinary term once referred to any foods that were cooked in heavy earthenware pots over fires in fireplaces. Today, however, the term is used to define a thick soup or stew for which pork is always used as the base. There are as many variations of this dish as there are chefs.

Alsace Potée Smoked ham and various vegetables are cooked together with garlic sausage and potatoes.

Auverne Potée The entire head of a pig, quartered, is cooked with bacon and ham, beans and potatoes.

Limousin Potée This central region of France, once a province, gives us its own *potée*. A piece of pickled pork (often called *petit-salé*) is first blanched in boiling water, then the boiling mixture is cleaned of all scum. Cabbage, smoked bacon, garlic, a *bouquet garni,* salt, pepper, turnips, carrots, and leeks are added and simmered for two or three hours. A half-hour before the cooking time has elapsed, potatoes are added. The dish is served garnished with grilled *chipolatas.* (See BOUQUET GARNI, CHIPOLATA)

Lorraine Potée This dish is considered *the* speciality of the province of Lorraine, once called Lothringen. To prepare the *potée,* a heavy pot is lined with plenty of pork cracklings, and with the addition of a half-cooked pork roast, blanched white cabbage, chopped carrots, turnips, and leeks, some beans, and a piece of smoked bacon, all is covered with a beef stock. Fitted with a tight lid, the *potée* is simmered for three hours. A quarter-hour before the dish has finished cooking, a piece of sausage and potatoes are added.

COMPATIBLE WINES: A red wine, e.g., Châteauneuf-du-Pape, Mercurey, Côte Rôtie, Zinfandel, Mâcon Rouge, Beaujolais, Margaux, Valpolicella, Egri Bikaver.

POTETES LEFSER (Norwegian) Rolled potato pancakes, a real Scandinavian treat. They are prepared from mashed potatoes which are mixed with butter and then chilled. When cool, enough flour is added to bind the mixture, which is then kneaded into a pliable dough and rolled out to form small, very thin pancakes. These are fried in butter over medium heat until lightly browned on both sides and are served with gobs of sweet butter, soft cheese, and lingonberry preserves.

POULARDE À LA POÊLE AUX TOMATES (French) "Chicken in a skillet with tomatoes." This method of cooking chicken with the flavorful tomato came about only because during the French Revolution the patriots of Provence brought the tomato with them to Paris. These citizens, members of the Legion of Marseille, not only induced the fearful Parisians to eat of the dreaded tomato but also to adopt their rousing marching song, which became the national anthem of France, *La Marseillaise.*

The dish is simple but tasty. A quartered chicken is seasoned, sautéed in oil and butter, and reserved. Then fresh tomatoes are peeled, diced, and lightly sautéed in sweet butter. With a dash of salt and pepper, some dry white wine, and grated onion, the pieces of chicken are replaced in the pan (called *poêle*) and warmed in the oven until all the flavors have blended. COMPATIBLE WINES: A red wine, e.g., Haut Brion, Talbot, Zinfandel, Valpolicella, Châteauneuf-du-Pape, St. Émilion, Cabernet Sauvignon.

POULE AU POT (French) President Herbert Hoover was not the first ruler to promise his constituents "a chicken in every pot" and then renege. Actually, a Frenchman, King Henry IV, is credited with having coined that phrase. He hoped that every Frenchman would be able to eat chicken every Sunday, but that never became reality. For this dish, a plump fowl is stuffed with a mixture of eggs, bread soaked in milk, chopped chicken liver, ham, garlic, and herbs. The stuffed bird, covered with slices of bacon and well trussed, is placed in boiling salted water and simmered until done together with chopped walnuts, leeks, onions, and herbs. COMPATIBLE WINES: A red wine, e.g., Juraçon, Beaujolais, Moulin-à-Vent, Fleurie, Valpolicella, Zinfandel, Nebbiolo, Egri Bikaver, Cabernet Sauvignon, Margaux, Médoc.

POULET (French) A chicken that is not more than three months old.

Poulet à la Reine   For this classic chicken dish, the bird is stuffed with a forcemeat consisting of chopped cooked chicken mixed with a *velouté* and bound with egg yolk. The stuffed bird is cooked in a veal or chicken stock and served on a platter surrounded with pastry *barquettes* filled with chicken purée, black truffles, and a *sauce Allemande.* (See ALLEMANDE, BARQUETTES, VELOUTÉ) COMPATIBLE WINES: A white wine, e.g., Piesporter Goldtröpfchen, Graacher Himmelreich, Nierstein, Rüdesheim, Montrachet, Graves, Meursault, Beaune Blanc, Sauvignon Blanc.

Poulet Poëlé au Riz   "Chicken pot roast with rice." To prepare the dish, a seasoned whole chicken is placed on a bed of sliced carrots and onions in a covered casserole. A good coating of butter is spread over the chicken, which is then baked in a moderate oven for an hour. The cover is then removed from the casserole to allow the chicken to brown for an extra half-hour or so. In another pot, chopped onions, diced bacon, and mushrooms are sautéed in butter, and the rice is folded into the mixture. A boiling rich chicken stock is poured over the rice mixture, which is then baked in the oven for some twenty minutes. The chicken is carved and served atop this delicious bed of rice, redolent with the flavor of mushrooms, onions, and bacon. (See POËLÉ) COMPATIBLE WINES: A red wine, e.g., Margaux, Beaujolais, Mâcon, Zinfandel, Côte Rôtie, St. Julien, Valpolicella, Châteauneuf-du-Pape.

POULETTE, SAUCE (French) A sauce made by reducing a *sauce Allemande,* adding to it the essence of cooked mushrooms, and then, off of the heat, enriching the sauce with sweet butter, lemon juice, and chopped parsley. (See ALLEMANDE)

Sweetbreads Poulette Sweetbreads, sliced then braised in a white stock, are served blanketed with the *sauce poulette.* COMPATIBLE WINES: A white wine, e.g., Meursault, Clos Blanc de Vougeot, Château Couhins, Haut Brion Blanc, Gewürztraminer, Johannisberg.

Moules à la Poulette The mussels, prepared *à la marinière,* are served in their shells with a *sauce poulette* that has been enriched with a bit of the cooking liquid from the mussels. (See MARINIÈRE) COMPATIBLE WINES: A white wine, e.g., Meursault, Quincy, Montrachet, Aigle, Gewürztraminer, Graacher Himmelreich, Muscadet, Pinot Chardonnay, Soave, Verdicchio.

POUSSIN (French) A young chicken, weighing about two and a half pounds, known in America as a "broiler." It should be cooked quickly to seal in the flavorful juices. It can be fried, grilled, or roasted with a stuffing composed of onions and breadcrumbs or chicken livers and mushrooms. The *poussin* can also be marinated in wine or in lemon juice and oil flavored with spices and herbs and then cooked.

PRAIRIE EEL When on a menu, this is a euphemism for rattlesnake. The name was given to the snake in the old frontier days, when food was scarce. Actually, rattlesnake steaks are delicious when grilled.

PRALIN (French) A much-used nut and sugar combination that is blended into custards, ices, mousses, cakes, and *soufflés.* To make a *pralin,* the nuts—almonds, walnuts, or hazelnuts—are browned in the oven and then added to a caramel made from sugar and vanilla. This mass is poured out onto a cold surface, preferably marble, where it can harden and cool. Finally, it is powdered in a mortar or in a blender.

Gâteau Praliné A cake consisting of layers of *Génoise* cake sandwiching a filling of powdered *pralin* that has been added to a buttercream. (See GÉNOISE)

PRASSÓPETA (Greek) A leek and meat pie. The white part of the leeks is cut into rounds and sautéed in butter with chopped beef or lamb. A mixture of white wine, nutmeg, pepper, and salt is added and simmered until the wine has evaporated. To a white sauce made with grated Kefalotry (a Greek cheese) or Parmesan cheese, a quantity of beaten eggs is added, into which the meat-leek combination is folded. A stack of well-buttered *phyllo* sheets is placed on a flat baking pan, then the leek and meat mixture is spread over them and covered with yet more *phyllo* sheets. The pie is then baked until the pastry leaves are puffed and golden brown. (See PHYLLO) COMPATIBLE WINES: A red wine, e.g., Valpolicella, Chianti, Beaujolais, Retsina, Chinon, Lambrusco, Ruby Cabernet, Zinfandel.

PRAWNS See SCAMPI

PRÉ-SALÉ This is a questionable phrase when found on an American menu. The French use the term to denote the salty, briny grass found near the sea, upon which certain cattle and sheep have fed.

Rack of Lamb Pré-Salé This rack of lamb, designated as being *pré-salé,* is either roasted or *poêléd* in its own stock or a thick, highly seasoned brown sauce. (See BROWN SAUCE, POÊLÉ) COMPATIBLE WINES: A red wine, e.g., Beaune, Châteauneuf-du-Pape, Mâcon, Margaux, Cabernet Sauvignon, Mercurey, Valpolicella, Zinfandel.

PRIMAVERA (Italian) Literally, "spring." In culinary parlance the term refers to the use of fresh spring vegetables, which give a dish its flavor and aroma.

Insalata Primavera A healthful Italian salad that is composed of fresh vegetables, cut to size, blanched, and then mixed with cooked rice and small pieces of cooked chicken and beef in a sauce of ricotta cheese and buttermilk, piquant with garlic. The choice of vegetables might include broccoli, diced tomatoes, spinach, carrots, and green beans.

Veal Primavera A number of fresh vegetables—such as squash, red peppers, zucchini, green beans, broccoli—are steamed separately. Scallops of veal are pounded paper-thin, cut into small rectangles, and sautéed with mushrooms, shallots, and garlic in hot clarified butter. To this, cooked *fettuccine,* the steamed vegetables, and a mixture of ricotta cheese and cream are added. The dish is served garnished with tomato sauce and lemon wedges. COMPATIBLE WINES: A white wine, e.g., Frascati, Lacrima Cristi, Orvieto, Brolio Bianco, Corton Charlemagne, Sauvignon Blanc.

PRINTANIER (French) Literally, "springlike." A descriptive term for a dish made with fresh green produce of spring.

Consommé aux Quenelles Printanier A rich chicken consommé that is cooked with carrots, turnips, tiny peas, small beans, and asparagus tips and garnished with small *quenelles* of chicken.(See QUENELLES)

Printanier-Butter This butter composite is made from early-season vegetables—such as carrots, beans, peas, and asparagus tips—

cooked, drained and pounded into a purée and then kneaded into sweet butter. It is served with meat and fish dishes.

Sauce Printanière This sauce is as green and fresh as the spring season its name glorifies. It is made from a *sauce Allemande* which is brought to a boil and to which a green-butter is added. The green-butter is composed of fresh spinach that has been finely chopped and subsequently puréed and cooked in water. It is then drained of all water, and the residue, a green coagulate of spinach *(vert d'épinard)* is whipped together with sweet butter. The sauce is served with chicken and egg dishes. (See ALLEMANDE)

PRIX FIXE See MENU

PROFESEN (Austria) A type of "French toast." This version is a sandwich made with jam. It is sprinkled lightly with white wine, dipped in beaten egg, and fried in butter on both sides until golden.

PROFITEROLES (French) Small, hollow pastries made with *pâte à chou* (cream puff pastry). The *pâte à chou* is put into a pastry bag, and small mounds about the size of chestnuts are squeezed out onto a baking sheet and baked until brown. When served with soups, *profiteroles* are often stuffed and various purées, such as a purée of *foie gras* mixed with cream, a purée of chicken, or one of vegetables. As a sweet pastry, they are filled with ice cream, jams, or pastry creams. They are also used to make the famous *gâteau Saint Honoré* as well as small cakes of the *éclair* type. *Profiteroles* may be covered with a rich chocolate sauce. The *croquembouches* are glazed with a sugar syrup. (See CROQUEMBOUCHE, FOIE GRAS, PÂTE À CHOU, SAINT HONORÉ, TAILLEVENT).

PROSCIUTTO DI PARMA This is the finest of all Italian hams, cured near the city of Parma by a process that includes the salting and drying of the ham in the pure, rarefied air found in high altitudes. It is usually served sliced paper-thin or used in various forms to heighten the taste of other foods. COMPATIBLE WINES: A white wine, e.g., Soave, Frascati, Lacrima Christi, Gewürztraminer, Vouvray, Johannisberg, Sylvaner, Gumpoldskirchner.

PROVENÇALE, À LA (French) Provence is a French maritime province that is famed for its wines, cuisine, and songs. When food is prepared *à la Provençale,* that is, in the style of that region, it usually means that garlic and olive oil are predominant.

Sauce Provençale This famous sauce is made by sautéing chopped onions in olive oil until they are translucent, then adding peeled and chopped tomatoes, crushed garlic, salt, and pepper. The mixture is then moistened with a dry white wine that is reduced and enriched with a good veal stock. A sprinkling of chopped parsley finishes the sauce.

Gigot d'Agneau Provençale A baby leg of lamb roasted with garlic, rosemary, thyme, bay leaves, and anchovies. COMPATIBLE WINES: A red wine, e.g., Fixin, Chambertin, Côte Rôtie, Hermitage, Valpolicella, Margaux, Latour, Mouton Rothschild, Lafite Rothschild, Zinfandel, Cabernet Sauvignon.

Côtelettes de Veau Provençale This French dish uses double-thick veal chops, lards them with anchovy fillets, then marinates them for several hours in a mixture of oil, vinegar, garlic, bay leaves, cloves, and oregano before browning them well in hot oil and butter. The chops are then placed in a pot or casserole with white wine, shallots, and parsley and baked in a medium oven until tender. COMPATIBLE WINES: A white wine, e.g., Johannisberg, Gewürztraminer, Graacher Himmelreich, Orvieto, Sauvignon Blanc, Fendant, Hermitage Blanc, Kenyelu, Oppenheim, Wehlener Sonnenuhr.

Cuisses de Grenouilles à la Provençale This classic dish of frogs' legs contains garlic—and plenty of it. First, the small legs are sautéed in hot olive oil. They are then seasoned with salt and pepper, removed, and kept warm. In the same pan, a mixture of minced garlic and chopped parsley is sautéed in hot butter. This is then poured over the frogs' legs, and they are quickly browned under a hot broiler and served at once. COMPATIBLE WINES: A white wine, e.g., Meursault, Montrachet, Neuchâtel, Aigle, Orvieto, Sauvignon Blanc, Hermitage Blanc, Corton Charlemagne, Anjou, Pouilly-Fumé.

PUDIM DE CHUCHU A pudding made from a Mexican squash called *chayote*. The *chayotes* are first peeled and halved and then boiled in salted water until tender. The seeds are removed and the vegetable is chopped up and mixed with grated Cheddar cheese, breadcrumbs, salt, pepper, butter, and egg yolks. Beaten egg whites are folded into the mixture, which is poured into a mold and baked. The pudding, usually served with a tomato sauce, is a delightful luncheon dish or a vegetable accompaniment for any meat, fish, or poultry dish. (See CHAYOTE) COMPATIBLE WINES: A red wine, e.g., Beaujolais, Rioja, Pinot Noir, Santenay, Valpolicella, Zinfandel, Egri Bikaver, Premiat, Mercurey, Fleurie.

PUFF PASTE See FEUILLETAGE

PU LA GWA (Chinese) A "bottle gourd melon." This pear-shaped melon is commonly used in soups and with beef, chicken, and pork dishes.

PULKA (East Indian) A whole-wheat bread made by frying the dough on a griddle to a toasty-brown color.

PULLAU See PILAFF

PULQUE (Mexican) A popular drink made from the fermented juice of the *maguey* (century) plant. The drink is made from the sap of the plant, and because of its low alcohol content (only 4 percent) it must be drunk at once, lest it spoil. While the adults enjoy *pulque,* the children drink the same juice of the maguey plant, but unfermented. This is called *aguamiel,* which means "honey water."

PULSE (East Indian) Dried vegetables—such as beans, peas, lentils, and chickpeas—commonly used in East Indian cookery.

PUMPERNICKEL Of the many stories relating to the origin of the name of this heavy black German bread, my favorite involves Napoleon's groom, his horse Nicole, and the hard black bread that was inevitably served to hungry soldiers. When once again he had to eat this hardtack bread, the groom exclaimed: *"C'est un pain pour Nicole!"* meaning that the bread is good for the horse, Nicole. With the passing of time, the phrase evolved from *"pain pour Nicole"* to "pumpernickel." Another story tells that the bread was first made in the town of Paderhorn. Because of the famine brought about by the Thirty Years' War, the authorities handed this bread free to the populace and, for some reason, gave it a Latin name, *bonum paniculum,* meaning "a good bread." Finally, the name was transformed into something more Germanic, "pumpernickel." This bread, also called *Schwartzbrot* (black bread), is made from rye flour that is unhusked plus yeast, salt, milk, and butter. It is wonderful served thinly sliced on a huge platter laden with various *hors d'oeuvre,* sausages, cheese, and, of course, plenty of butter.

PUPIK (Yiddish) The gizzard, or giblet, usually obtained from a chicken. It is cooked first in salted water and served spiced with pepper, paprika, and salt.

PU PUS (Polynesian) Bite-size pieces of sausage, chicken liver, beef, or seafood that are marinated and then grilled over charcoal. These delicacies are served with three dip sauces: (1) a mustard sauce made by heating white wine vinegar and dry mustard and whipping it to a creamy consistency, (2) a white wine sauce made by mixing dry mustard, mace, garlic, cinnamon, salt, cherry wine, and curry with a beef bouillon and cooking the mixture until smooth, (3) a curry sauce made by sautéing chopped onions and crushed garlic in butter then adding curry powder, salt, diced tart apples, and a chicken broth and cooking the mixture until thickened. COMPATIBLE BEVERAGES: Beer, ale, cider.

PUTANESCA, SALSA ALLA (Italian) This rather racy term defines a sauce as being made "in the style of the whore down the street, who puts everything she's got into it." This means tomato purée, tomatoes, capers, black olives, garlic, chopped onions, and parsley, all cooked in olive oil. It is served to perk up *pasta* dishes.

QUAGLIETTE DI VITELLO (Italian) A veal dish consisting of thin squares of veal seasoned with lemon juice, topped with ham, and rolled up in a slice of bacon. These veal birds are then skewered alternately with onions and bits of bread and baked in a hot oven. They are usually served on a bed of steaming herbed rice. *Quagliette* means "little quails." COMPATIBLE WINES: A white wine, e.g., Orvieto, Frascati, Pouilly-Fumé, Gewürztraminer, Sylvaner, Hermitage Blanc, Sauvigon Blanc, Château-Grillet.

QUEEN'S CHICKEN SALAD, A (English) This salad is said to have been the great favorite of the wife of Charles I of England, Queen Henrietta Maria. Cooked chicken is sliced into scallops and mixed with anchovy fillets with a touch of pepper, chopped celery, and a sauce made from a blend of vinegar and *sauce Mayonnaise.* The royal salad is served garnished with capers and sliced hard-boiled eggs. COMPATIBLE BEVERAGES: Beer, ale, stout.

QUEIMADO CREME (Portuguese) "Burnt cream," a type of custard dessert. The custard is made by mixing egg yolks, milk, cream, sugar, and vanilla and heating the mixture to the scalding point. It is then baked in a mold and turned out. Then, with a specially-designed hot filigreed iron, the custard is branded with a mixture of caramelized sugar and ground cinnamon. (See CRÈME BRÛLÉE)

QUENELLE (French) A forcemeat (farce, filling) made from chicken, fish, meat, or young game mixed with chopped onions, a *panada,* salt, pepper, and nutmeg plus a white sauce or heavy cream. The forcemeat is usually formed into dumplings and poached in wine or in stock. (See PANADA, WHITE SAUCE)

QUESADILLA See ENCHILADAS

QUICHE (French) An ancient dish created in the medieval kingdom of Lothringen, which was ruled by the Germans. (Later the French changed the name from Lothringen to Lorraine [Alsace-Lorraine]). The *quiche* was originally an open pie made from bread dough and various fillings. Today, the dish consists of an egg-cream mixture poured into a partially prebaked pie shell and baked in the oven until the custard is set.

There are many ways of flavoring the *quiche* custard: some use grated cheese, ham, or bacon, while others add seafood or finely chopped onions or other vegetables. All are delicious and make a wonderful luncheon complemented by a fresh green salad. Beware, however, of the budget-minded restaurateur who instructs his chef to skimp on the heavy cream and instead of the rich custard to use a flour-filled sauce that will form an unpleasant lump in the diner's stomach and a bulge in the restaurateur's billfold.

Quiche Lorraine For this most popular *quiche* of all, bacon strips are arranged in the bottom of the pastry shell together with Gruyère cheese. The shell is then filled with the egg mixture and baked until the custard is set.

COMPATIBLE WINES: A white wine, e.g., Pouilly-Fuissé, Muscadet, Sancerre, Soave, Dézaley, Pouilly-Fumé, Sauvignon Blanc, Gewürztraminer, Beaune Blanc, Anjou, Riesling.

RACHEL (French) A famous actress who trod the Parisian stage in the 1800s. Elizabeth Rachel Felix lives on today in the many dishes that have been named after her.

Filets de Sole Rachel The fillets are spread with a rich fish force-meat mixed with chopped truffles. These are folded and then poached in milk. The sole is served covered with a shrimp sauce and surrounded with asparagus tips and cooked shrimp. COMPATIBLE WINES: A white wine, e.g., Chablis, Soave, Montrachet, Graacher Himmelreich, Riquewihr, Debro, Château-Grillet, Sancerre, Quincy.

Garniture Rachel A rich garnish made up of hearts of artichokes that are simmered in butter with braised beef marrow, chopped parsley, and a red wine sauce. It is served with *tournedos, filets mignons,* and *noisettes* of beef.

Sauce Rachel A *sauce Normande* is flavored with lobster and a purée of anchovies. It is served with fish dishes. (See NORMANDE)

Tournedos Rachel These small steaks, cut from the end of a fillet of beef, are sautéed in butter and served on toasted bread slices that are well flavored with *glace de viande.* On the top of each steak, a cooked artichoke bottom should stand as a sentinel with a round of beef marrow right in its center. (See GLACE DE VIANDE, TOURNEDOS) COMPATIBLE WINES: A red wine, e.g., Talbot, Pomerole, Mouton-Rothschild, Calon-Ségur, Fixin, Nuits St. Georges, Cabernet Sauvignon, Dôle, Zinfandel, Barolo.

RACLETTE (Swiss) This speciality was born in the Canton of Valais, where the regal Matterhorn rises majestically over the town of Zermatt. The top of this cheese is heated until it becomes soft enough to scrape off, and in this melted state it is served with chopped onions and boiled potatoes. COMPATIBLE WINES: A white wine, e.g., Neuchâtel, Fendant, Gewürztraminer, Dézaley, Orvieto, Frascati, Hermitage Blanc, Johannisberg.

RAGOÛT (French) A type of stew containing pieces of meat, game, or poultry which are first lightly browned and then slowly simmered in a meat stock with a variety of vegetables, herbs, and spices. (See BORJU, GULYAS, HUNGARIAN STEWS, SERTÉS, STEFADO, STEW)

RAGÙ (Italian) This meat and tomato sauce, created in Bologna, is usually called *ragù Bolognese* or *sauce Bolognese.* It is made by cooking a mixture of chopped carrots, onions, celery, basil, and parsley in olive oil together with chopped beef and pork, red wine, tomato purée, bouillon, and plum tomatoes. It is served with *pasta* dishes. (See BOLOGNESE)

RAHKA (Finnish) Homemade curd. In this case, instead of whole milk, buttermilk is used. It is poured into an earthenware casserole and left in a 200-degree F. oven for several hours, during which time the curd will rise to the surface. It is then removed, sieved, drained of all liquid, and placed in a cheesecloth under a heavy weight and left overnight. The whey is used to make tasty breads and to give zest to soups.

RAHKAMAJONEESI (Finnish) A unique type of *sauce Mayonnaise* that is made with curd to which lemon juice, salt, mustard, and paprika are added. Then, just like any other *Mayonnaise,* the oil is added, a drop at a time, until the sauce becomes thick. The sauce is popular with smoked fish, with ham, and with salads. (See MAYONNAISE)

RAHMSUPPE (German) A "cream soup" made by adding veal stock and boiled milk to a *roux,* then flavoring it with onions, cloves, parsley, nutmeg, salt, cumin, and pepper and slowly simmering the mixture. After about an hour, the soup is strained, thickened with sour cream, and served over bread that has been fried in butter.

RAIFORT, SAUCE (French) A spicy sauce is prepared from grated fresh horseradish combined with lemon juice, salt, and pepper; this is then folded into whipped heavy cream. This sauce is served with cold fish, such as smoked whitefish, cod, or halibut, as well as with boiled and roasted joints of beef. (See DANOISE, MEERRETTICHSOSSE)

RAI KI MACCHI (East Indian) A fish or shrimp dish prepared with a spiced dry yogurt. The yogurt must be dehydrated by wrapping it in cheesecloth and letting the liquid drip through. Black mustard seeds (black mustard seed is not only more pungent and flavorful than the yellow, but it is also less hot) and seeded fresh green chilies are pulverized in a blender with a bit of vegetable oil; this is then mixed with the dry yogurt and placed in a double boiler to allow the flavors to fuse. The fish, preferably a white-meated variety similar to sole, is filleted and cut into strips, mixed with the spiced dry yogurt, and steamed in the double boiler until done. Peeled and deveined shrimp can also be prepared in this manner. COMPATIBLE BEVERAGES: Beer, ale, cider, tea.

RAITA (East Indian) A refreshing relish made from yogurt mixed with vegetables and spices.

    Raita Cucumber Fresh, cool yogurt is mixed with finely grated cucumber, roasted cumin, black pepper, salt, cayenne, and paprika. This relish is served together with chutney with nearly all Indian meals. (See CUMIN)

RAJAH'S TOAST (East Indian) A type of canapé made with toasted bread. A curried ham paste, sprinkled with a chutney of choice, is spread on buttered toast and grilled. (See CHUTNEY)

RAKI This is the national drink of Turkey, prepared from a distillate of grapes flavored with aniseed. It is drunk diluted with water and turns a cloudy white, much like the French Pernod and Pastis, which are similarly flavored. When a Turk refers to "lion's milk," he means

Raki, which is supposed to stimulate something like the roar of a lion if one drinks enough of it.

RAMEQUIN (French) This word ("ramekin" in English) has many definitions. Originally, it was a baked cheese. It is also a small pastry that is filled with a mixture of grated cheese, butter, eggs, and pepper and baked. The word *ramequins* (plural) also refers to small earthenware baking dishes that may be filled with *soufflé* mixtures or with eggs, cheese, or any other foods that are mixed with a sauce or a *chou;* the filled *ramequins* are baked in the oven. (See PÂTE À CHOU)

Ramequin Suisse (Swiss) A cheese dish made by bringing milk to a boil and then, off of the heat, adding flour, grated cheese, and egg yolks. Egg whites are beaten stiff and folded into the mixture. Heavy cream and cottage cheese are blended together, poured over the cheese custard, and baked until set. COMPATIBLE WINES: A red wine, e.g., Dôle, Chianti, Châteauneuf-du-Pape, Fixin, Hermitage, Pommard, Pinot Noir, Barolo, Nebbiolo, Valpolicella.

RAREBIT This late-night supper dish, popularly known as "Welsh rarebit," and often erroneously called "rabbit," was born in a Welsh abbey. An imaginative monk poured his wine over a piece of toasted bread, crumbled the mild Caerphilly cheese over the top, and held it before the blazing fire until the cheese melted. Today, the English have adopted the rarebit, making it with a similar cheese from Somerset County. As this type of cheese is quite bland, many rarebit lovers prefer to use a Cheddar or another cheese with more spunk. Today, beer is used instead of wine. The beer is mixed with butter, grated cheese, milk, pepper, and salt. The mixture is cooked into a thick mass and served over freshly-made toast. In the United States, because American beer is so weak, sherry is sometimes substituted for the beer.

In the year 1814, Antoine Beauvilliers, whose Grande Taverne de Londres was the first real restaurant in France, served his *lapin Gallois,* the French version of "Welsh rarebit." Beauvilliers was also the first in Paris to offer the English creation "ket chop," or catsup, which had been adapted from the Chinese original, which was made from mushrooms and walnuts. COMPATIBLE BEVERAGES: Beer is recommended, but either red or white wine may also be drunk.

RATATOUILLE NIÇOISE (French) A vegetable stew, born in Nice, composed of onions and garlic that are cooked in olive oil with the addition of sliced eggplant, zucchini, red or green peppers, and tomatoes. All is flavored with basil, rosemary, and thyme and garnished with black olives. The addition of a bit of white wine is optional. This dish can be served hot with grated Parmesan cheese or cold with toast and lemon quarters. COMPATIBLE WINES: A red wine, e.g., Veltliner, Beaujolais, Mercurey, Chianti, Egri Bikaver, Premiat, Pinot Noir, Ruby Cabernet.

RAVIGOTE-BUTTER See CHIVRY

RAVIGOTE, SAUCE A classic French sauce made from a *sauce velouté* with the addition of chopped onions, chives, tarragon, and chervil plus a reduced mixture of white stock and vinegar. This sauce is served with poultry, sweetbreads, and brains. The cold *sauce ravigote* is a mixture of oil, vinegar, raw and hardboiled eggs, capers, parsley, chervil, tarragon, chopped onions, and gherkins. This sauce is served chilled with cold boiled beef, calf's head, fish, chicken, or tripe. (See VELOUTÉ)

RAVIOLI (Italian) Small filled casings of *pasta* dough, usually square. When filled with cheese, herbs, and seasonings, they are called *ravioli all Caprese;* when filled with chopped veal, sweetbreads, calf's liver, eggs, spinach, and Parmesan cheese, they are called *ravioli alla Genovese.* In Turino, however, as soon as the *ravioli* are filled with fillings other than the traditional ricotta cheese and spinach, the name changes to *agnolotti.* (See PASTA) COMPATIBLE WINES: A red wine, e.g., Chianti, Nebbiolo, Beaujolais, Valpolicella, Barolo, Dôle.

RED-COOKING (Chinese) This method (*hung-shu* in Chinese) of browning food in soy sauce, either by sautéing the food in a wok or by braising it in a covered pot, changes the color of the food to a deep red, almost brown. The sauce is saved and can be used again and again; more soy sauce and water are added to the "master sauce" as they evaporate. (See FIVE-SPICE ESSENCE, SOY SAUCE)

RÉGENCE (French) The Regency Period (1715-1723) encompasses the time when France was ruled by the regency of Phillipe, the Duke of Orleans. The era, as well as the sauces and garnitures of the day, were rich, full of the cream of life.

Sauce Régence A *sauce demi-glace* mixed with the essence of black truffles and white wine is reduced and flavored with finely minced shallots. (See DEMI-GLACE)

Régence Garniture For meat dishes: a *sauce Allemande* is mixed with sliced *foie gras,* button mushrooms, cockscombs, and chicken *quenelles* made with truffles. For fish dishes: a *sauce Normande* is mixed with poached oysters, roe, mushrooms, truffles, and *quenelles* of fish. (See ALLEMANDE, FOIE GRAS, NORMANDE, QUENELLES)

Sauce Régence When the French add white wine, fish stock, finely chopped mushrooms, and black truffles to a *sauce Normande,* the resulting sauce, to be used with fish, is called *Régence.* However, when the same wine, mushrooms, and truffles are added to a *demi-glace,* the sauce is used to complement fowl. (See DEMI-GLACE, NORMANDE)

Potage Crème Régence To prepare this rich soup, a purée of *foie gras* is whipped into a cream of chicken soup. After garnishing with thin slices of tongue and a *julienne* of chicken breast, a dash of Kümmel (a liqueur flavored with caraway seeds and cumin) finishes the soup. (See FOIE GRAS, JULIENNE)

Poularde à la Régence A chicken, stuffed with pieces of bacon fat, is braised in brown butter and served surrounded with braised sweetbreads, cooked black truffles *au Madère,* and *quenelles* of chicken and prawns cooked in bouillon. The chicken is served coated with the *sauce Régence.* (See MADÈRE, QUENELLES) COMPATIBLE WINES: A red wine, e.g., Beaujolais, Zinfandel, Mecurey, Margaux, Mâcon, Médoc, St. Julien, Côte Rôtie, Bardolino, Valpolicella, Fleurie.

REH (German) Deer.

Rehrücken This is the German term for a saddle of venison. To prepare it, the meat is marinated in a pickling solution composed of red wine, cloves, root vegetables, bay leaves, pepper, and salt. The saddle is drained, dried, and roasted, and sour cream is added to the meat gravy. The dish is served with copious amounts of currant jelly. COMPATIBLE WINES: A red wine, e.g., Pétrus, Talbot, Cabernet Sauvignon, St. Émilion, Vougeot, Musigny, Richebourg, Chambertin, Bonnes Mares.

REINE, À LA (French) This phrase is meant to honor the Queen of Navarre, the daughter of Catherine de Medici and Henry II of France. Any dish described as *à la reine* is made with a delicately plump chicken.

Potage à la Reine Puréed almonds and pistachio nuts are added to a rich chicken broth. The broth is flavored with thyme and bay leaf and enriched with heavy cream and egg yolks. Chicken *quenelles* are served as a garnish. (See QUENELLE)

Consommé à la Reine This chicken consomme is thickened with tapioca, flavored with chervil, and served with a garnish of plain *royale* and a *julienne* of chicken. (See JULIENNE, ROYALE)

REKESAUS (Norwegian) A shrimp sauce made by first adding a mixture of fish stock and milk to a *roux;* then, with the addition of butter, sour cream, salt, and pepper, cooked deveined shrimp plus a touch of dill are added as well. The sauce is served with boiled fish and always with the famous *fiskepudding.* (See FISKEPUDDING, ROUX)

RELIGIEUSE, EGGS À LA (French) During the Dark Ages only royalty and the religious—the monks, friars, and good nuns—were able to enjoy real food and drink. In fact, the Church was the first to cultivate the grape, and were it not for the Revolution, which robbed the various religious orders of their French vineyards, we would most probably be drinking a Château Dominican, a Château Franciscan, or perhaps a Trappist brût Champagne. Then, as now, it was necessary to have either much wealth or much leisure to indulge in viniculture and the art of gastronomy; therefore, the nuns and monks took the time to pursue new taste thrills, evidenced by the many fine recipes we have available to us today. Take this delightful egg dish: one coats the inside of a deep pie shell with a *pralin* and lets it dry. Then fresh eggs are carefully poached in boiling milk and sugar, drained, and then set in the shell with small pieces of pineapple placed between the poached eggs. Enough eggs to make custard to cover are then added to the poaching milk, thickened over low heat, then strained and poured over the poached eggs in the pie shell. The pie is placed in a slow oven until the custard is set and browned. *La religieuse* is also the name of the "crust" left in the bottom of a Swiss *fondue*. (See FONDUE, PRALIN)

Gâteau Religieuse This rich cake, which originated in Paris, is made by either stacking in the form of a large pyramid, a series of *éclairs* filled with coffee, vanilla, or chocolate creams, or by filling small round balls of *chou* pastry similarly and setting one on top of the other, also in the form of a pyramid. (See ÉCLAIRS, PÂTE À CHOU)

Religious Influence on Food Religious leaders have always acted as mentors and advisors to their people, not only with regard to matters of faith and morality but also with regard to food and drink. Just as Moses counseled the Israelites, and Mohammed the Arabs, so also did the great Buddha influence the cooking and choice of food for most of the people of Asia. When the Buddhist priests spread out from India to minister the Word of God, they took with them their cooking pots, bags of rice, and mortars and pestles. During the stifling Dark Ages of Europe, only royalty and the religious—the monks, friars, and nuns—kept the nearly lost art of gastronomy alive by enjoying good food and drink. As mentioned above, the Church was the first to commercially cultivate the grape. What would the world be like without Dom Pérignon's discovery of the second fermentation of white wine, whose natural effervescence we enjoy today as Champagne?

RELLENOS, CHAYOTES The *chayote* is a type of squash native to Mexico. To make this dish, the *chayotes* are first boiled, then the flesh is scooped out and mixed with breadcrumbs, Cheddar cheese, eggs, salt, and pepper. The flesh is then returned to the shells. When the shells are filled, more breadcrumbs mixed with grated Parmesan cheese are liberally sprinkled over the tops of the *chayotes,* and they are browned under the broiler. (See CHAYOTE, PUDIM DE CHUCHU) COMPATIBLE WINES: A red wine, e.g., Chianti, Rioja, Côte Rôtie, Beaujolais, Zinfandel, Nebbiolo.

RELLENOS, CHILES (Mexican) A popular stuffed-pepper dish. The *poblana* chili is preferred for this dish, although the green bell pepper can be substituted. The *poblana* chili is first held with a long fork over a flame until the skin blisters; it is then wrapped in a damp cloth, and after a short while the skin can easily be peeled off. The stems and the seeds are removed. A filling called a *picadillo*— made from ground veal and pork cooked in oil with chopped onions, garlic, tomatoes, *jalapeño* chilies, raisins, and olives and spiced with cinnamon, cloves, and pepper—is set aside. The prepared *poblana* chilies are then dipped into a mixture of egg yolks and whipped egg whites and deep-fried to a golden brown. Filled with the *picadillo* meat mixture and

topped with a rich tomato sauce, they are a tasty treat. (See CHILIES)
COMPATIBLE BEVERAGES: Beer, ale, cider.

RÉMOULADE, SAUCE (French) To a good *sauce Mayonnaise,* one adds
dry mustard, anchovies, capers, parsley, garlic, chopped hard-boiled
eggs, lemon juice, and white wine. The result: *une sauce rémoulade!*

Shrimp Rémoulade Cleaned shrimp are boiled in salted water with
bay leaf, celery, parsley, and peppercorns. They are chilled and served
with the *sauce rémoulade.* (See RÉMOULADE) COMPATIBLE WINES: A
white wine, e.g., Chablis, Muscadet, Sancerre, Quincy, Montrachet,
Debro, Verdicchio, Soave, Pinot Chardonnay, Steinwein, Iphofen,
Gumpoldskirchner.

RENAISSANCE, À LA (French) This term refers to two separate garnishes. One consists of deviled vegetables sautéed in sweet butter, to
be served with poultry. The other garnish, served with meat dishes, is
composed of artichoke hearts stuffed with cooked vegetables and
served with a rich *sauce Hollandaise* and new potatoes. (See HOLLAN-
DAISE)

RENKON (Japanese) The lotus root, a vegetable used in all of Asia. The
Gautama Buddha, who founded the Buddhist religion, is often
represented by a carving showing him seated on a large lotus flower
or holding one in his hand. Even non-Buddhists consider the lotus,
with its many seeds, to be the epitome of fertility; just to eat of it
promises many offsprings. In the days of antiquity, the fruit of the
lotus plant was used to make bread and a fermented drink. The lotus
of classical literature is identified as the jujube of the buckthorn
family, which when made into wine brought the utter contentment
and forgetfulness associated with the legendary "Lotus-eaters." We
know the lotus as the water lily. Its rather nondescript root is thinly
sliced in salads or consumed boiled or fried. When cut diagonally, the
circle of five holes (the slice of the lotus) presented to the cook is
stuffed with glutinous rice and served as a dessert. It is sold fresh or in
cans and should be refrigerated.

RESTAURANT, THE FIRST In 1765 in Paris, M. Boulanger added an
extra dish of pig's feet to his regular menu of hot soups, and with this
act he created the very first restaurant. At the same time, he incited *les
traiteurs,* who dealt with ready-cooked meats, to bring suit against
him. Boulanger not only won the suit but also got enough publicity to
bring his name and his pig's feet to the attention of King Louis XV. So
it happened that for the first time at Boulanger's the diner was offered
a choice of *restaurantes* (restoratives), whereas the inns of that time
served only one dish.

In 1782, Antoine Beauvilliers introduced the first real restaurant, as
we know it today, to the citizens of Paris. Beauvillier's restaurant was
not a copy of Boulanger's. Rather, Beauvillier was influenced by the
English across the Channel, who had been dining out for several

decades. In gratitude, Beauvillier made a very fine gesture. He named his new restaurant La Grande Taverne de Londres. It was Boulanger, however, who first named his eating place a "restaurant," meaning a place to restore oneself with food.

RESTAURATIONSBROT A type of "open-faced sandwich" served in German restaurants. It is made from cold cuts (the best of sausages) and served with a varied garnish: pickles, tomatoes, anchovies, olives, lettuce, etc. COMPATIBLE BEVERAGES: A good cold beer or a rosé wine.

RÉTES (Hungarian) Equivalent to the very famous Austrian *Strudel,* this is an equally fine, flaky pastry that envelops fruits, nuts, cheese, and even cabbage. (See KÁPOSZTÁS, STRUDEL)

RETSINA This famous Greek wine is, strangely enough, full of resin. In ancient times, before corks and bottles were available, the Greeks had to store their wines in goat skins and had to use pitch pine to seal them. The Greeks became so accustomed to the resinous taste that, in spite of the invention of bottles and corks, even today they continue to add resin to their wines. Retsina wine can be white, red, or rosé. It is usually served chilled, often mixed with soda or with seltzer water, but the taste for it must be acquired.

REUBEN'S SANDWICHES After failing three times, Reuben persevered and finally opened his famous restaurant on 82nd and Broadway in New York City. And if the Earl of Sandwich created the convenient and satisfying sandwich, it was Reuben who transformed it into a real meal and chef José Baños who prepared it.

Famous Reuben's Sandwich Ham, turkey, Swiss cheese, cole slaw, and Russian dressing on rye bread.

Reuben's Superior Ham, turkey, sliced hard-boiled egg, sliced tomatoes, and thinly sliced onion on rye.

The Jack Benny Sliced tongue, turkey, Swiss cheese, cole slaw, and Russian dressing on rye.

The Walter Winchell Sturgeon, Swiss cheese, and sliced dill pickles on rye.

The Ed Sullivan Chopped chicken liver, turkey, cole slaw, and Russian dressing on rye.

The Barbara Stanwyck Sliced corned beef, bacon, and melted Swiss cheese on toasted rye.

The bread slices were always cut on the bias so that the ingredients were well displayed. Reuben demanded that every sandwich be neatly trimmed. COMPATIBLE BEVERAGES: Good cold beer, ale, or stout.

REVANI (Turkish) A popular and simple dessert made from flour, farina, and eggs. The dessert is served covered with syrup.

REYNIÈRE, GRIMODE DE LA He was a most unattractive man. One could say that he was really ugly: rotund, bent over, with hands so deformed that he wrote only with great difficulty. But write he did, and, mysogynist that he was, French culinary history is grateful that he turned his sensual appetites to gastronomy.

Côtes de Veau Hachées Grimode de la Reynière   Meat, taken from the veal chop bones, is finely ground. After being mixed with milk-soaked breadcrumbs, chopped truffles, and seasoning, the meat is returned to the bone and shaped to look like the original veal chop form. These chops are then dipped in egg, breaded, and fried in clarified butter. The dish is served garnished with asparagus tips, and the chops are sprinkled with *noisette*-butter. (See CLARIFIED BUTTER, NOISETTE)

RHINE WINE GLASSES   In quality restaurants it is considered *de rigueur* to serve the aromatic Burgundy and Bordeaux wines in glasses with large, generous bowls; and the thinner the crystal and deeper the bowl, the better the wines seem to taste. The Rhine wine glass, however, has quite another form. It is long-stemmed, and the bowl of the glass is tinted green. Many feel that the reason for this tinting is to differentiate from the Moselle glass, which also has a long stem. The truth is that the wine which first came from the fertile Rhine valley in Germany was not clear but always looked cloudy. This caused many people to think twice before drinking it. So, to mask the disturbing cloudiness, a new green glass was prescribed whenever Rhine wine was served. Today, the problem no longer exists: German Rhine wine is as clear as a French Chablis or a Swiss Aigle, but the long-stemmed green glass is still used.

RICCI (Italian)   Sea urchins. (See OURSINS)

RICE   Rice, the staple food of Asia, was grown and eaten in Siam in the fourth millenium B.C. Then, in the third millenium, it became known in regions below the Yangste River in China. But it was not until the Middle Ages that Europe first tasted rice.

More than politics, more than religion, food customs throughout history permeated countries by invasion, conquest, and occupation. And the customs often remained even after the invader was no longer present in the country as a national. Rice came to Portugal, Spain, and Italy when the Arabs, at the peak of their great culture, invaded and conquered them. Today, the only European country to grow rice is Italy. Rice, such a universal food, is flavored differently in nearly every area of the world that it is eaten. Examples:

> *New Orleans:* Tomato, okra, Créole seasonings.
> *India:* Garlic, onion, curry powder or paste.
> *Italy:* Garlic, oregano, marjoram, grated cheese.
> *Mexico:* Garlic, onion, chili, pimiento.
> *Spain:* Garlic, saffron.
> *Minnesota:* Salt added to natural rice, baked to harden into an ersatz "wild rice."

Rice in China   The Chinese people eat rice three times a day, and they actually use the term "rice" (*fan* in Chinese) to mean "meal." There are two kinds of rice used. The long-grained type is easier to cook than the other, the oval-grained. There is also a special glutinous variety of rice, called *no-mi,* which is reserved for dessert dishes. (See CONGEE)

Rice, Japanese-style   The Japanese cook rice in four basic ways:

> *Sushi:* This is steamed rice mixed with vinegar and formed into various decorative shapes with seafood, eggs, and vegetables in order to please the eye as well as tantalize the taste buds.
> *Domburi:* This is a large bowl of steamed white rice served with *yakitori* or *tempura* dishes and doused with a hot, rich, clear soup.
> *Boiled:* The most common method of serving rice—boiled plain, without salt.
> *In broth:* This method entails cooking rice in *dashi,* together with vegetables, meat, or fish. (See DASHI, TEMPURA, YAKITORI)

Rice in India   India boasts over a thousand different varieties of rice. This fact is not all that unusual because rice has been growing in India for the past 3,000 years, and in China for 5,000 years. In Indian cookery, the long-grained nonglutinous rice (each grain cooks separately from the other) is the best to accompany a meal; it is called *patna.* (The *basmati* and the *almora* varieties are also long-grained and nonglutinous).

The Indian chef serves five different rice preparations: (1) plain boiled rice, (2) plain steamed rice, (3) buttered rice, (4) the *pullau* dish, incorporating cooked rice that is first sautéed in *ghee* and then cooked in a stock, (5) the *byrani,* which is flavored and colored with saffron and is full of spices and has twice as much butter and twice as much meat or fish as any of the *pullaus.* An Indian will never eat parboiled or partially cooked rice (the "instant" or "quick-cooking" variety), for neither of them tastes like rice to an Indian, who eats nearly one pound of rice per day. (See PILAFF, TIL RICE)

RICHELIEU, À LA   (French) Richelieu was the Roman Catholic cardinal who really governed France from 1630 to 1639. The sauce bearing his name is composed of a rich *sauce Allemande* added to sautéed chopped onions and mixed with consommé, sugar, nutmeg, and pepper. After enriching the sauce with sweet butter and flavoring it with chopped chervil, it is ready to be served. The name *Richelieu* is also used to designate a garnish made from stuffed tomatoes, mushrooms, braised lettuce, and *château potatoes;* this is served with meat dishes. (See ALLEMANDE, CHÂTEAU)

Sole Richelieu   Another dish named to honor the famous, and often infamous, cardinal whose tenacity and ambition and quick mind brought him not only the post of minister to Louis XIII but also that of secretary of state. This particular sole dish is prepared exactly as the succulent *sole Colbert* except for the rich garnish. This sole is served on a bed of sliced truffles. (See COLBERT) COMPATIBLE WINES: A white wine, e.g., Chablis, Montrachet, Meursault, Soave, Sancerre, Quincy, Pinot Chardonnay, Debro, Riquewihr, Aigle, Dézaley.

RIFREDDI, COPPA (Italian) A meat loaf made with tuna fish, veal, salami, and *prosciutto* ham. (See PROSCIUTTO DI PARMA) COMPATIBLE WINES: A red wine, e.g., Chianti, Valpolicella, Zinfandel, Margaux, Médoc, Mâcon, Beaujolais, Fleurie, Mercurey, Egri Bikaver, Ruby Cabernet, Rioja.

RIGATI (Italian) See PASTA

RIGATONI (Italian) See PASTA

RIJSTAFEL (Dutch-Indonesian) Literally meaning "rice table," this creation is composed of various meat and vegetable dishes served with many different kinds of sausages and with a heaping bowl of boiled white rice. Some of the dishes that might make up a rich *rijstafel* are pork in soy sauce, eggs in a white sauce, stuffed omelette, sweet potatoes, roast pork on skewers, ribs in a sweet-and-sour sauce, fried bananas, vegetable curries, *sambals,* and fruit in a sweet-and-sour sauce topped with grated coconut. (See SAMBAL)

RILLETTES DE TOURS/ANGERS/LE MANS (French) A hearty country *pâté* made by melting leaf lard in a large pot and then adding (for Tours) the cubed pork shoulder, or (for Angers) the pork belly or breast, or (for Le Mans) the pork shoulder mixed with goose fat. A bit of water is added as well and the contents is cooked slowly until the meat nearly falls apart. The meat is removed, shredded, seasoned, and blended into the fat until a fine paste is formed. The mixture is packed into small terrines and sealed with melted pork or goose fat. The *rilletes* are kept refrigerated and served with French bread. (See PÂTÉ) COMPATIBLE WINES: A white wine, e.g., Champagne, Vouvray, Muscat d'Alsace, Johannisberg.

RIPIENI (Italian) Literally, "stuffed" or "filled." Another Italian term with the same meaning is *farcito,* which comes from the French word *farce.* (See FARCE)
Punta di Vitello al Forno Ripieni A roast brisket or breast of veal that is cooked stuffed with ground meat and herbs. COMPATIBLE WINES: A red wine, e.g., Zinfandel, Médoc, Valpolicella, Margaux, Beaujolais.

RIS DE VEAU (French) Sweetbreads.

RISI E BISI (Italian) This traditional dish used to be served at all official Venetian banquets. It is basically rice with green peas, minced onions, and ham or pork, all cooked in butter and moistened with a rich chicken broth and simmered gently until done. It is served strewn with grated Parmesan cheese. Although the dish is quite soupy, it is

always eaten with a fork. COMPATIBLE WINES: A red wine, e.g.,
Beaujolais, Médoc, Côte Rôtie, Hermitage, Veltliner, Rioja.

RISOTTO (Italian) A creamy rice dish containing chopped onions,
chicken stock, grated Parmesan cheese, and saffron. COMPATIBLE
WINES: A red wine, e.g., Chianti, Valpolicella, Barbaresco, Nebbiolo,
Cahors, Côte Rôtie, Margaux, Zinfandel.

Risotto alla Siciliana This rice preparation originated on the Island
of Sicily. After the rice has been cooked in boiling salted water,
chopped beef, chicken livers, and minced garlic are browned in olive
oil in another pan. Chopped mushrooms, tomato paste, and water
are added and this is seasoned with salt and pepper to taste. Butter
and grated Parmesan cheese are added to the well-drained rice. After
the meat and mushrooms are removed from the tomato sauce and
reserved, the sauce is added to the rice. The rice is mixed well and
formed into balls, into which the chopped meat, mushrooms, and
livers are stuffed. After dipping the rice balls in beaten egg, they are
rolled in breadcrumbs and fried a golden brown in hot olive oil.
COMPATIBLE WINES: A red wine, e.g., Chianti, Nebbiolo,
Châteauneuf-du-Pape, Lambrusco, Barolo, Dôle, Beaujolais, Ruby
Cabernet, Fleurie, Mâcon, Egri Bikaver.

RISSOLÉ POTATOES (French) *Rissolé* means "browned." To prepare
rissolé potatoes, a melon baller is used to scoop out raw potato balls.
The potato balls are cooked briefly in salted water, then drained, and
finally browned in hot butter. They are served seasoned with salt and
pepper. The noun *rissoles* refers to puff-paste forms filled either with
savory or sweet fillings.

RISTED LAKS MED KREMSAUS (Norwegian) Brook trout coated with
sour cream—a delight for lunch. The trout is salted, dusted with
flour, sautéed in oil and butter, and then served with a warm sour
cream sauce flavored with lemon juice. COMPATIBLE WINES: A white
wine, e.g., Gewürztraminer, Riquewihr, Orvieto, Chenin Blanc,
Frascati, Aigle, Graacher Himmelreich, Wehlener Sonnenuhr,
Szamorodni, Anjou.

RITZ, CHICKEN HASH À LA (American) Named after the Ritz-Carlton
Hotel in New York City, where the chef, Louis Diat, created it, the
dish is made up of two components: the hash itself and the sauce. To
prepare the hash, chicken is finely minced, mixed with heavy cream,
and simmered slowly until the cream is reduced. Then, to a *roux* in
another pan, milk is added with the chicken; after being mixed well
together, all is poured into a baking dish. Then, a sauce is made from
a *roux* to which hot milk is added, followed by sliced onions, beaten
egg yolks, butter, and grated Parmesan cheese. This sauce is poured
over the chicken hash, which is in turn placed under the broiler until
golden brown. (See ROUX) COMPATIBLE WINES: A white wine, e.g.,
Steinberger, Johannisberg, Sauterne, Traminer, Orvieto, Aigle,

Frascati, Sauvigon Blanc, Piesporter Goldtröpfchen, Nierstein, Rüdesheim.

RIZ CRÉOLE (French Créole) This method of cooking rice entails first washing the rice in several changes of water, then cooking the rice in three times the volume of water to rice. After rinsing in cold water, the rice is steamed dry.

ROBE DE CHAMBRE, POMMES À LA (French) This rather imaginative description of potatoes steamed in their own skins is delightfully French, translating literally to "potatoes in their dressing gowns."

ROBERT, SAUCE (French) There is much controversy concerning the true origin of the *sauce Robert*. Early in the seventeenth century, a Frenchman named Vinot stated adamantly that it was he who created this old French sauce and then proceeded to christen it with his own name, Robert. But as the author Rabelais had already referred to this sauce in one of his early pieces, Monsieur Vinot's claim can be disregarded. To add more spice to the sauce, the English claim that the Normans learned how to make the sauce while they were in Britain and brought it across the channel to France with them much later. Yet another version of the sauce was created by the culinary genius Escoffier, who bottled it for commercial use. Escoffier used a melding of tomatoes, vinegar, sugar, pimientos, and spices. Served with steaks, chops and with poultry, it is often found on cafeteria tables, right between the mustard and the catsup. The classic version is prepared by adding chopped onions to a *roux* and, with the addition of white wine, bouillon, and seasoning, allowing it to simmer. Prior to serving, a bit of mustard, tomato purée, and wine vinegar are added. This sauce is delicious served with broiled meats, especially pork, as well as with goose or turkey. A garnish of finely chopped gherkins is strewn over the top.

ROCKEFELLER, OYSTERS (American) When one of the diners at Antoine's Restaurant in New Orleans, rapt in ecstasy after having tasted this new oyster creation, said, "Why this is as rich as Rockefeller!" then "oysters Rockefeller" entered the annals of culinary history. The greatness of the dish lies in the garnish prepared for it. Raw spinach, parsley, celery, and onions are chopped fine and simmered in sweet butter with the addition of Tabasco sauce, breadcrumbs, and a drop of Pernod. A teaspoon of the mixture is placed on each oyster, which is then broiled in the oven. COMPATIBLE WINES: A white wine, e.g., Meursault, Muscadet, Montrachet, Pouilly-Fuissé, Debro, Johannisberg, Graacher Himmelreich, Sauvignon Blanc, Frascati, Aigle, Soave.

RØDKAAL (Danish) Red cabbage is made into a delicate vegetable dish by first shredding it, then blanching it in a mixture of vinegar, butter, sugar, salt, and water, and then braising the cabbage in the same liquid in the oven for several hours. Minutes before the dish is removed from the oven, current jelly and grated apples are added. *Rødkaal* is a delightful complement to a crisply roasted goose or a stuffed loin of pork. As an option, sliced onions can be added to the braising mixture.

ROGNONS DE VEAU FLAMBÉS À LA LIÉGEOISE (Belgian) This popular dish of flamed veal kidneys hails from the Ardennes district. After the kidneys have been trimmed and soaked overnight, they are dried, sliced, and cooked in a mixture of bacon fat and butter in a *cocotte* (a small earthenware saucepan). Seasoned with salt, pepper, and thyme, crushed juniper berries are added to the kidneys and they are flamed with a good gin. Covered, the kidneys are done in a half-hour. COMPATIBLE WINES: A red wine, e.g., Beaujolais, Mâcon, Mercurey, Beaune, Santenay, Chinon, Côte Rôtie, Médoc, Egri Bikaver, Zinfandel, Valpolicella, Ruby Cabernet, Nebbiolo.

RÖHSCHINKEN (Swiss) The German term for the special air-dried ham of Switzerland. Like the dried beef of the Grisons, called *Bündnerfleisch,* this ham is basted frequently with a secret marinade as it is dried in the thin air high in the Alpine huts of Switzerland. The French-Swiss, known as the Welsch, call this delicacy *jambon sechée.* (See BÜNDNERFLEISCH, CHARQUI, GRISONS, JERKY, PEMMICAN)

ROLLMOPS (German) This fresh herring preparation is known throughout the world. After the herring are cleaned and the heads and tails removed, the fish are soaked first in cold water and then in milk for several days. Split and boned, the herring fillets are covered with mustard, onions, capers, pickles, and peppercorns and then rolled and secured with toothpicks. The rolled fillets are placed in layers in a large nonmetallic bowl, then a cooked mixture of vinegar, sugar, peppercorns, juniper berries, bay leaves, and water is added and the herring are left to marinate for days. *Rollmops,* a traditional midnight snack on the Eve of St. Sylvester, New Year's Eve, are absolutely delicious served with sour cream. COMPATIBLE BEVERAGES: Beer, ale, stout.

ROMESCU, SAUCE (Spanish) This spicy, tangy sauce from Catalonia is composed of slivered almonds blended and ground together with chopped garlic, chopped tomatoes, chili peppers, and salt. To this paste, olive oil is added, bit by bit, alternating with wine vinegar to form a thick sauce. The sauce is served with shellfish, meat, and game.

ROOSTERS (Finnish) Probably meaning "roasters," this speciality of Savo, a province set in the middle of Finland, is a thick rye crust used to envelop meats, fish, or vegetables. Once filled, the dough is baked in the oven. It is quite similar to the Russian *koulibiac.* (See KOULIBIAC)

ROSSINI, TOURNEDOS (Italian) Giacomo Rossini, the great opera composer, left the world a rich musical legacy. But he was as great in the kitchen as he was at the keyboard, and he left us this culinary creation as well. Small and thick fillets of beef are sautéed in butter, topped with goose liver, truffles, and a *sauce Madère,* and served on fried bread. (See MADÈRE, TOURNEDOS) COMPATIBLE WINES: A red wine, e.g., Aloxe-Corton, Fixin, Chambertin, Pommard, Dôle, Échézeaux, Richebourg, Nuits St. Georges, Barolo, La Tâche.

ROSTBRATEN (German) A boneless cut of beef or pork loin that is roasted.

Wiener Rostbraten (Austrian) See BRATEN/GEBRATEN

Zigeuner Rostbraten (Swiss) A "gypsy" beef steak is highly seasoned, browned with chopped onions and bacon, then braised with cabbage and potatoes in a covered pot. COMPATIBLE WINES: A red wine, e.g., Dôle, Hermitage, Côte Rôtie, Mercurey, Pinot Noir, Châteauneuf-du-Pape, Rioja, Chianti.

RÖSTI (Swiss) Literally, "crisp and golden," this is a method of sautéing.

Rösti Potatoes Boiled potatoes that have been cooled, or plain raw potatoes, are shredded, seasoned, and cooked in hot butter in a heavy skillet. Pressed down flat, pancake-style, they are sautéed until brown and crisp and are then turned and browned on the other side.

Apple Rösti For this Swiss *Rösti,* sliced apples, onion, salt, cinnamon, and cloves are sautéed briefly in a hot pan. Then, slices of crusty rolls, eggs, milk, and sugar are added, and the dish is baked in the oven until crisp and golden. The first cookbook ever written by a woman—Faru Anna Weckerin from Aargau, Switzerland, in 1598—contains the first recipe for the *Rösti.* This dish—together with the Swiss *fondue;* the raclette, Emmenthaler and Gruyère cheeses; velvety milk chocolate; and the noted *Geschnetzeltes Kalbfleish*—rival the Matterhorn for what is truly Swiss. (See FONDUE, GESCHNETZELTES KALBFLEISCH, RACLETTE)

ROTHSCHILD (French) This name has been given to various creations in honor of the Baron de Rothschild.

Soufflé Rothschild To a mixture of flour, milk, sugar, and vanilla, one adds egg yolks and whites, candied fruit (cherries, pineapple, orange and lemon rind), and a dash of Danziger Goldwasser. Fresh strawberries are put on the *soufflé* after it has been baked.

Oysters Rothschild This oyster preparation was named after Nathan Rothschild, the financial wizard of the famous banking family. Fresh oysters are individually wrapped in rashers of bacon. The oysters, well seasoned, are pierced with skewers and broiled over charcoal. They are whimsically called "oysters on horseback." COMPATIBLE WINES: A white wine, e.g., Meursault, Montrachet, Pouilly-Fuissé, Pinot Chardonnay, Muscadet, Quincy, Debro, Soave, Gumpoldskirchner, Aigle.

ROTKOHL MIT SPECK (German) This red cabbage dish from Bavaria is prepared by first rendering bacon fat and sautéing chopped onions in the fat. A bit of flour plus vinegar and red wine are added. Shredded cabbage, caraway seeds, and diced tart apples are then added as well. After seasoning with salt and pepper, the cabbage is cooked until tender.

ROUENNAISE (French) When a diner sees this term on a menu, he immediately visualizes a plump, delectable duck, for it is in the city of Rouen where the very best ducks in France are to be found.

Sauce Rouennaise A sauce *Bordelaise* is brought to the boil. Then, off of the heat, a puréed duck's liver seasoned with salt and pepper is stirred into the sauce until blended. Many restaurants will substitute chicken liver for the duck liver, but the result is just not the same. This sauce is served with duck or with poached eggs. (See BORDELAISE)

Canard à la Rouennaise A stuffed duck is roasted in a hot oven. To serve, the legs are removed and grilled and the breast is cut into thin slivers. The *sauce Rouennaise* is poured over the sliced duck. Because the blood is not drained from the duck before it is cooked, the flesh is quite red and has a unique flavor, highly thought of by those who love duck. COMPATIBLE WINES: A red wine, e.g., Fixin, Volnay, Chambertin, Beaune, Pommard.

ROUILLE (French) A peppery garnish. A combination of red peppers and chili peppers is roasted until browned, and then, together with raw garlic and breadcrumbs, the mixture is chopped and mashed together with oil, into a paste. The garnish is served with the famous *bouillabaise.* (See BOUILLABAISE)

ROULADE (French) A culinary term that refers to a piece of meat (usually veal or pork but sometimes beef), that has been flattened, stuffed with a forcemeat, and rolled before cooking. (See BALLOTINE, GALANTINE, ROULADEN)

Roulade de Tête de Porc A whole pig's head is boned then filled with a dice of pig's tongue, bacon, various herbs and spices, and eggs. The head is rolled up and cooked in a jellied stock. COMPATIBLE WINES: A red wine, e.g., Côtes du Rhône, Beaujolais, Médoc; or a white wine, e.g., Traminer, Vouvray, Johannisberg, Gewürztraminer, Graves, Sauterne.

ROULADEN, BEEF (German) A popular speciality prepared by cutting rectangular slices of beef, pounding them as thin as possible, and then covering each thin rectangle with mustard, finely chopped bacon, diced pickles, and chopped onions. The beef slices are rolled up, secured with toothpicks, dusted with flour, and browned in a heavy skillet in hot butter. Once browned and seasoned with salt and pepper, the *Rouladen* are simmered in a beef bouillon. The dish is usually served with mounds of red cabbage and plenty of hot potato dumplings. COMPATIBLE WINES: A red wine, e.g., Arbois Rouge,

Beaujolais, Veltliner, Côte Rôtie, Moulin-à-Vent, Dôle, Petit Sirah, Mercurey, Egri Bikaver, Valpolicella, Zinfandel.

ROUX (French) A general term for equal portions of sweet butter and flour slowly cooked over low heat and used to thicken sauces and soups. Fats other than butter ae sometimes substituted. The color of the *roux* varies with the amount of time it is cooked.

Le roux brun is cooked long enough for it to take on color. Often the juices from a roast are added to the mixture. This *roux* is basic to the *sauce Espagnole* and the *demi-glace*.

Le roux blond is allowed to cook until it takes on a golden tint.

Le roux blanc is cooked for only a few minutes and is constantly stirred to prevent its changing color. This *roux* is the basis of the *Béchamels* and the *veloutés*. It is also used as a soup thickener.

Liquids are added to each of the *roux* above in measured quantities, to yield a sauce with the consistency desired—thin, medium, thick, etc. (See BÉCHAMEL, DEMI-GLACE, ESPAGNOLE, VELOUTÉ)

ROYALE (French) See CONSOMMÉ

RUMAKI (Polynesian) A *shishkebab* made by folding chicken livers around water chestnuts, then wrapping each one within a rasher of bacon and fastening it with toothpicks. These tidbits are marinated in a soy sauce flavored with fresh ginger and curry. They are later skewered and grilled over charcoal. *Rumaki* are served as appetizers. COMPATIBLE BEVERAGES: Cocktails, beer.

RUSSE, SAUCE À LA (French) This creation is made for those who can afford the luxury of adding the creamy interior of a lobster plus Beluga caviar and a touch of mustard to a *sauce Mayonnaise*. It is a treat served with fish dishes. Another version includes sharp chili sauce and chopped red and green peppers, which seems almost criminal when Iranian caviar must be added to it.

RUSSIAN CUISINE The Russian cuisine, with the exception of peasant cookery, did not begin until Catherine the Great mounted the Russian throne. Her great interest in the culture of the Western world influenced not only Russian art and politics, but cooking as well. For centuries, fine food in Russia was enjoyed only by the royalty, the aristocracy, the wealthy. Many dishes that originally were Polish, French, or Italian did, with the passing of time, take on new interpretations and become characteristically Russian. That meant, for the most part, the extensive use of sour cream *(smietena)*. The Russians use sour cream as freely as Americans use milk and butter. Today, heavy roasts, hearty stews, and pastry envelopes stuffed with everything from fish and cheese to meats and vegetables fill their menus. Of course, the greatest food treasure of Russia has always been the sturgeon and her caviar. (See SMITANE, PIROG/PIROZHKI)

RUSSIAN SERVICE Until 1810 or thereabouts, it had been the custom to set the whole dinner on the table at one time and let everyone help himself to whatever he wanted. A Russian nobleman of taste, one Prince Kurokine, changed all that. He was the czar's ambassador, and he is famous today not for his diplomacy and service to the Imperial Crown but for completely changing the manner of serving food at the dinner table. For the first time, dinner guests sat down to a table set with napkins, flowers, condiments, and perhaps silverware. The important innovation was that the food was brought to the table in courses, and after having been served, any extra food was returned to the kitchen. In 1856, writer-gastronome Urbain Dubois introduced the system to Paris. Until then even the kings of France had eaten their food cold more often than warm.

SAADAA PULLAO In India long ago, the divine sunbird Garuda, while transporting the nectar of the gods, a potion that guaranteed immortality, to his mother, allowed a drop to fall to the ground beneath. Garlic sprang from the ground exactly where the drop of immortality fell.

The marvelous seasoning capabilities of the garlic bulb are evidenced in this pullao of rice and lamb. As prepared, lamb shanks, cut into cubes, are first boiled; the resulting broth is skimmed. A cheesecloth bag filled with the following ingredients is boiled for an hour or more: half a dozen unpeeled bulbs of garlic, coriander, chopped onions, cloves, cinnamon sticks, cardamom, ginger root, and caraway seeds. The cheescloth bag is then removed, its juices squeezed into the broth, and the meat removed. The broth is reserved. In a large heavy casserole, chopped onions are sautéed in *ghee* together with cardamom pods, cloves, cumin seed, peppercorns, and the cubed lamb. After adding a bit of yogurt, the pot is covered and the ingredients simmered until the liquid has evaporated. Uncooked rice is stirred into the pot with enough of the broth to cover; the rice is simmered until tender. A fresh green salad complements this dish. (See GHEE, PILAFF) COMPATIBLE BEVERAGES: Beer, cider, tea.

SABAYON The French word for a velvety Italian custard. (See ZABAGLIONE)

Sabayon Mexicain This Mexican *sabayon* differs from the classic Italian version in that it is not cooked. Sugar, cocoa, and sherry are added to raw egg yolks. The egg whites, whipped until stiff, are carefully folded into the yolk mixture. This is then poured into appropriate tulip glasses and served with the tops lightly dusted with cinnamon.

SABLEFISH Most sablefish are really smoked Alaskan codfish. They appear salmon-colored from a vegetable dye. The sablefish is normally a grayish-blue or dull white color.

SACHERTORTE (Austrian) This rich cake first saw the light of day in Vienna. At the turn of the nineteenth century, Franz Sacher, Metternich's former chef, created this bit of chocolate ambrosia, which subsequently made his name and his restaurant world-famous. It consists of chocolate sponge cake cut into three layers, between which apricot preserves are thickly spread. The whole cake is then iced with velvet-like chocolate. Heaps of whipped cream are served separately. Who could resist it? This *Sachertorte* helped Johann Strauss make the word *gemütlich* synonymous with Vienna.

SAFFRON Saffron is produced from the dry stamens of the purple-colored autumn crocus (each crocus has three stamens), and it takes

250,000 crocus stamens to produce a pound of this most costly of all spices. Saffron is used to flavor the Italian *risotto Milanese,* the Spanish *paëlla,* and the French *bouillabaise.*

In culinary preparations, saffron can become offensive if an overpowering amount is used. It is meant to afford color, richness, and fullness, with but a breath of its own particular flavor. It should be added to a dish, like most other herbs and spices, just before the dish is served. (See BOUILLABAISE, PAËLLA, RISOTTO)

SAIGNANT (French) Literally, "bloody." The term refers to meats—such as steaks, game, or duck—cooked underdone or rare, which is the preferred way.

SAINT GERMAIN (French) Reference made to Saint Germain, a suburb of Paris, in the name of a dish indicates that fresh garden peas have been used in the preparation.

Tournedos Saint Germain Small fillets of beef are grilled, arranged on a bed of a purée of peas, and served coated with a *sauce Béarnaise.* They are usually served with glazed carrots and *Parisienne* potatoes. (See BÉARNAISE, PARISIENNE) COMPATIBLE WINES: A red wine, e.g., Talbot, Pommard, Fixin, Chambertin, Pétrus, Pinot Noir, Dôle, La Tâche, Richebourg, Aloxe-Corton, Nuits St. Georges.

ST. HONORÉ, GÂTEAU (French) Saint Honoré, the patron saint of all pastry cooks and bakers, is honored with this breath of exquisiteness. Only the base or bottom of the creation is "cake." The sides consist of light balls of cream puff pastry dipped in sugared syrup *(glacé).* The delectable filling is a rich cream custard (often whipped cream is used instead). (See CRÈME PATISSIÈRE, GLACÉ, PÂTE À CHOU)

ST. HUBERT He is the patron saint of hunters, and whenever his holy name is mentioned in connection with a French dish, it stands to reason that game must be an ingredient.

Salpicon St. Hubert A garnish composed of minced game, chopped black truffles, and mushrooms bound in a *sauce salmis.* (See SALMIS, SALPICON)

ST. MALO, SAUCE (French) The piquancy of this sauce is reminiscent of the corsairs of the seaport of St. Malo, those racy pirates licensed by the king of France to attack foreign ships. It is made by adding a shallot-butter to a *sauce au vin blanc* and then folding in a quantity of mustard and a purée of anchovies. Served with broiled fish. (See WHITE WINE SAUCE)

SAKÉ (Japanese) This wine—made from rice, malt, and water—is the traditional wine of Japan. It is served at weddings, but it is also offered ritually at the shrines of ancestors. Saké is yellow, rather sweet, and it is served warm, sometimes even hot, in dainty porcelain cups to complement a meal.

The custom of serving this wine heated began when an inferior saké was once presented, and to disguise its bad quality the wine was served warm. The custom has remained to this day. It is also considered impolite to pour your own saké. Each guest pours the saké for another. One drinks only when the host gives the signal. When the little cup is turned upside down, it is a sign that one has had his fill. The reason for the small size of the saké cup is to keep diners ever attentive, inasmuch as each diner is obligated to keep his dinner partner's cup full. A breach of this ritual would be tantamount to a shameful lack of table etiquette. (See MIRIN)

SALAME/SALAMI Although many countries manufacture this highly spiced, salted, and smoked sausage, it is basically an Italian speciality. It is eaten undercooked in very thin slices, and it seems that the thinner the slice, the better is the taste. Every province in Italy claims to have the best *salame:* Genoa, because of its predominance of beef over pork; Naples, because of the more equal proportions of pork and beef and the addition of chili powder, black pepper, garlic, and white wine; Florence, owing to the fennel flavor. An *antipasto* without *salame* is like an opera without music. (See ANTIPASTO) COMPATIBLE WINES: A red wine, e.g., Corvo, Bardolino, Valpolicella, Chianti, Zinfandel, Veltliner, Beaujolais, Mercurey, Egri Bikaver.

SALATA DE CREER (Russian) A salad made from the brains of a sheep or a calf. The brains are simmered in salted water then drained, cleaned, and placed in a bowl together with minced onions, pepper, and salt. While slowly adding olive oil and lemon juice alternately, the brains are worked into a creamy purée with a spoon. The entire mixture could well be puréed in a food blender. The salad is stored in the refrigerator until serving time.

SALISBURY STEAK (English) A common euphemism, often employed by pseudo-elegant restaurants, for a plain hamburger steak. Dr. James H. Salisbury was an English physician who recommended that hamburger steaks be eaten well-cooked. In 1888, Dr. Salisbury actually prescribed the hamburger for those of his patients suffering from such ailments as anemia, colitis, gout, rheumatism, and even arteriosclerosis. The steaks were tasty and easy to prepare and soon became very popular. They are found listed on menus everywhere. COMPATIBLE WINES: A red wine, e.g., Beaujolais, Petit Sirah, Moulin-à-Vent, Bardolino, Châteauneuf-du-Pape, Hermitage, Zinfandel, Valpolicella, Nebbiolo, Côtes du Rhône.

SALMIS Any game stew. The French, it seems, will make a *salmis* of anything wild that walks or flies, including such succulents as the *écureuil* (squirrel) or even the *corbeau* (crow). Perhaps the "four-and-twenty blackbirds baked into a pie" is not pure Mother Goose after all. Because a *salmis* entails both braising and roasting in its preparation, it is not, strictly speaking, a stew or a *ragoût*. (See RAGOÛT)

Sauce Salmis Finely chopped pieces of game are browned in butter, moistened with white or red wine, and reduced. After adding a *sauce demi-glace,* the sauce is reduced again and flavored with an essence of black truffles and mushrooms.

Salmigondis/Salmagundi   This Gallic culinary term has evolved from the *salmis* first concocted by a French chef named Gondi. The *salmisgondi* is a spicy combination of game, chicken, and fillets of anchovies mixed in a sauce composed of eggs, shallots, garlic, *fines herbes,* and a dry white wine. If the meat used is only poultry, the term changes to *capilotade.* In the sixteenth century a similar dish was called *grand sallett.* The word today is used to denote a stew made of leftover poultry, beef, or veal. Well prepared, it can be a satisfying savory dish.

Salmigondi Salad   A salad made from cubed chicken, lamb, or veal mixed with diced carrots, boiled potatoes, eggplant, peas, and beans—all marinated in a spicy blend of olive oil, tarragon vinegar, lemon juice, chopped onions, salt, and pepper. This mixture is drained and tossed with lettuce leaves or watercress in a *sauce Mayonnaise.* (See CAPILOTADE, FINES HERBES, SALMIS)

SALUMI (Italian)   General term for all sausages served cold and sliced.

SALPICON (French)   One or more ingredients diced and bound with a sauce.

SALSIFY   This is one of the most delightfully flavored root vegetables we have. Called the "oyster plant," it is supposed to taste somewhat like an oyster. Unfortunately, salsify is not very popular because of the amount of work entailed in preparing and cleaning it. Of the two varieties available, the black salsify, known as *scorzonera,* is preferred over its white sister. To serve salsify, the roots must be well scraped and cleaned then boiled in salted water until tender. After draining thoroughly and rubbing off the skin, melted sweet butter is poured over the vegetable. Salsify can be served with *sauce Béchamel* or covered with a cream sauce, grated cheese, and breadcrumbs and then browned in the oven. In Spanish *escorzo,* "serpent," is the term used for salsify, and the vegetable is taken as an antidote for snakebites.

SALTATE (Italian)   "Fried" or "sautéed."

SALTFISH AND AKEE (Caribbean)   This fish dish from the Island of Jamaica uses salt cod that has been well soaked in water, drained, and then simmered in more water. Just before it has finished cooking, fresh *akee* is added and the whole lot is drained and set aside. In another pot, onions are sautéed in pork fat together with chopped hot peppers, scallions, tomatoes, and thyme. Then, the flaked cod, the *akee,* and pork cracklings are added to the vegetables and heated to fuse the flavors. The pepperpot is served garnished with fresh tomato wedges, rashers of crisp bacon, and chopped parsley. (See AKEE, CRACKLING) COMPATIBLE WINES: A white wine, e.g., Muscadet, Orvieto, Sancerre, Soave, Pouily-Fuissé, Dézaley, Aigle, Traminer, Sauvignon Blanc.

SALTIMBOCCA (Italian) *Salt* (jump) *im* (in) *bocca* (mouth) means that the food is so tasty it literally "jumps into your mouth." Thin slices of veal are topped with sage and a thin slice of ham. The veal, rolled and held together with toothpicks, is floured, browned, and then slowly simmered in Marsala wine or in sweet sherry. (See PROSCIUTTO, SCALOPPINE) COMPATIBLE WINES: A white wine, e.g., Orvieto, Soave, Frascati, Sancerre, Fendant, Gewürztriminer, Riesling, Sauterne, Sauvignon Blanc.

SALT-WATER DUCK (Chinese) A duck is well massaged, both inside and out, with a mixture of salt and Szechwan pepper. The duck is then left to marinate for two or three days, after which it is rinsed and simmered in boiling water until done. Before serving, the duck is allowed to cool completely and is carved and served in segments. COMPATIBLE WINES: A white wine, e.g., saké, sherry, Sauterne; or a rosé.

SAMBALS (Indian) Leftover cooked vegetables mixed in a sauce of oil, onions, garlic, turmeric, cumin, ground chili peppers, and salt. The term is also used to designate dishes that accompany a curry dish.

SAMOSAS (East Indian) Appetizers made from dough that is formed into cones, filled either with minced vegetables or a meat filling, and then fried in hot oil until brown. The *samosas* are drained and served with a variety of chutneys, which are used as dips. The meat filling, called *kheema,* is a mixture of chopped beef or lamb, highly seasoned with garlic, onions, peppers, cloves, and various Indian spices.

SANS GÊNE A young French girl nicknamed *Sans Gêne,* meaning "free, without inhibitions," performed various and sundry tasks (such as his laundry and ironing) for the young Napoleon while he was still a military officer. The girl later became the wife of M. Lefebre, who was one day miraculously raised by General Napoleon to the rank of Maréchal. That very same day, a plate of eggs was named after the young lady.

Eggs Sans Gêne Poached eggs set on artichoke hearts are coated with a tarragon-flavored *sauce Bordelaise* and served with a garniture of beef marrow set on top. COMPATIBLE BEVERAGES: Beer.

SARAH BERNHARDT, FILET DE SOLE (French) A sole dish named after the world-famous Parisian actress Sarah Bernhardt who, it was said, once moved a whole restaurant full of diners to tears by merely reading the menu. The fillets of sole are rolled, seasoned, and poached in a *court-bouillon.* They are then served with a *sauce Vénitienne* plus a *julienne* of cooked carrots and truffles. (See COURT-BOUILLON, VÉNITIENNE) COMPATIBLE WINES: A white wine, e.g., Montrachet, Meursault, Rüdesheim, Hermitage Blanc, Orvieto, Fendant, Pouilly-Fumé, Nierstein, Johannisberg, Sauvignon Blanc.

SARMADES (Greek) Macedonian cabbage rolls stuffed with pork and cooked with sauerkraut. They can be served either before or together with the main course.

SARMI (Bulgarian) Stuffed grape leaves. The grape leaves are made pliable by soaking them in hot salted water. Pork is ground into a paste with rice and warm water, then a spoonful of the paste is placed in the center of each grape leaf. The leaves are rolled up and set side by side in a baking pan in the oven. Yogurt is served separately. The *sarmi* are served with game and roast pork dishes and with various stews. (See DOLMADES, DOLMAS, KALDOMAR)

SASHIMI To the uninitiated, a raw fish dinner might seem barbaric, but to the Japanese a *sashimi* is a real treat. This is the generic term for raw fish eaten with soy sauce and *wasabi* (green horseradish).

Sashimi, served in Japanese restaurants all over the world, is the traditional course in any formal banquet in Japan. The fish served must not have been taken from the water more than twelve hours before. Frozen fish is never served. The fish chosen for the *sashimi* are not opened, cleaned, or skinned until the minute they are to be served. If shellfish are to be used, then only the core, the heart of the meat, is used.

The true art of the *sashimi* lies in the cutting of the fish. Some fish, such as tuna or tile, are cubed *(kaku giri),* whereas the red snapper, striped bass, and porgy are cut into tissue-thin slices *(usu zukuri).* Quarter-inch-thick slices *(hira giri)* are cut from the more fragile fish, such as the weakfish or the corvine. Flounder and sole are cut into quarter-inch-wide strips *(itu zukuri),* and mollusks are served cut into small cubes.

A true *sashimi* will never smell fishy. It is always served with the accompanying bowls of soy sauce, slices of *daikon* (white radish), and *wasabi* (hot horseradish paste)—all to be mixed according to individual taste. The careful, colorful presentation of the *sashimi* is a joy to the eye, causing the right juices to flow even before the delicate fish are consumed. (See DAIKON, NIGIRI-SUSHI, SUSHI, WASABI) COMPATIBLE BEVERAGES: Saké, beer, rosé wine, Sauterne.

SATAY (Chinese) Small pieces of mutton, beef, and chicken are barbecued on a skewer then served with a sharp, piquant peanut sauce. A snack food.

SATE MANIS (Indonesian) Sweetly marinated beef cubes that are skewered and broiled. The sweet marinade is composed of brown sugar, soy sauce, lemon juice, minced garlic, chili powder, salt, and pepper. The broiled or barbecued beef is served coated with a thick sauce consisting of crushed garlic, dried chilies, *blanchan,* brown sugar, peanut butter, and coconut milk blended by cooking. (See BLANCHAN) COMPATIBLE BEVERAGES: Beer, ale, stout, cider.

SATSIVI (Caucasian) This sauce is most popular in Joseph Stalin's native Georgia. Chopped onions and garlic are sautéed in butter with a bit of flour. When lightly browned, a rich chicken broth is added and cooked together with wine vinegar, cinnamon, cloves, saffron, parsley, bay leaf, ground walnuts, salt, and pepper. The sauce is served with chicken and vegetable dishes.

SAUCES To quote the famous statesman, diplomat, and food connoisseur Talleyrand: "England has three sauces and three hundred and sixty religions, whereas France has three religions and three hundred and sixty sauces." A fine sauce must enhance the taste of the food with which it is served, either by complementing or by contrasting with the flavor of the dish. A sauce that overpowers is detrimental to the dish it is supposed to grace and uplift. If the cooking is always rich and heavy with sauces, the diner will quickly tire of it.

The ideal liaison for a fine sauce is a fresh egg yolk beaten into a cold stock and then slowly added, constantly stirring, to the rest of the stock as it heats up. When starchy products are used as sauce thickeners, the sauce is never so fine or light in texture.

SAUERBRATEN (German) This dish of marinated beef is best made from the bottom round of a prime steer. For five days or more, the beef is left to swim in a *Beize,* a marinade consisting of wine vinegar, red wine, onions, bay leaf, cloves, thyme, juniper berries, crushed garlic, salt, and peppercorns. When the beef is removed from the marinade, it is well dried and then seared in lard or bacon drippings. The marinade is reduced and added to the beef in another pot, where it is braised together with brown sugar, more chopped onions plus carrots, beef stock, tomato purée, and Worcestershire sauce. Before serving the beef, the Germans add a cup of sour cream. The Swiss add crumbled ginger snaps, homogenized beef blood, dill, and cayenne pepper instead of the cream. (See BEIZE) COMPATIBLE WINES: A red wine, e.g., Côte Rôtie, Beaujolais, Mercurey, Valpolicella, Veltliner, Egri Bikaver, Zinfandel, Fleurie, Margaux, Nebbiolo, Hermitage.

SAUERKRAUT The slaves who built the Great Wall of China were fed on cheap rice and cabbage, but when winter came, rice wine was added to the cabbage. This made it go sour, giving it a fascinating new flavor. When the Tartars invaded Europe, they brought this fermented cabbage dish with them, and it was the Austrians, not the Germans, who made the most of it. They still do to this day, by shredding cabbage, allowing it to ferment in salt, and then flavoring the sauerkraut with caraway seeds and juniper berries.

Choucroute Garnie See CHOUCROUTE

Sauerkraut à la Russe After cooking the sauerkraut in wine, the Russians add sour cream, chopped onions, and eggs. COMPATIBLE WINES: A white wine, e.g., Sylvaner, Neuchâtel, Schloss Vollrads, Piesporter Goldtröpfchen.

SAUSAGE Ground meat enclosed in either natural or artificial casings and eaten grilled, fried, or boiled. The casings are used to hold the finely chopped meat together to give the sausage form and as an aid to smoking them. When natural casings are used, there is no buildup of albumen on the outside of the sausages and, therefore, the sausages do not have to be skinned before eating.

Call it *Wurst* like the Germans; call it *saucisse* or *saucisson* with the French; give it the Italian name, *salumi,* the Polish title, *kiełbasa* or *sosiski;* or go all the way, go Hungarian with *kolbász;* but whatever its ethnic legacy, a fine sausage combined with cabbage, mashed potatoes, spinach, peppers, turnips, onions, or with baked beans can result in a most satisfactory meal. The ancestor of all these sausages came into being 3,000 years ago. Its Latin name was *salsus* (salted), but this sausage was made without the fiery spices and herbal taste enhancers which transform our present-day sausages into the following delicacies.

Italy, Hungary, and Germany are famed for their *salami.* The Italian variety is highly spiced and air-dried, whereas its German and Hungarian counterparts are smoked. Although *Leberwurst* and *Braunschweiger* are both types of German liver sausage, the *Braunschweiger* contains more pork liver and less pork meat than the *Leberwurst* and, coming either fresh or smoked, it is often used as a stuffing for roasts of fowl, pork, and crowns of lamb. Fine *Leberwurst,* on the other hand, can be so delectable that often a cost-conscious restaurateur will use an exquisite *Leberwurst* to fashion an ersatz *pâté de foie gras,* using *Mayonnaise* to give it smoothness and a liquor to give it tang.

Speaking of sausages, we must mention the *boudin blanc* and the *boudin noir,* which really sound more enticing in French than when translated respectively to "white pork pudding" and "blood pudding." The French can also boast of the fine *cervelas* and the *Lyonnaise* sausage made with pork, white pepper, garlic, salt, and, of all things, Curaçao. The French esteem for good sausage is summed up in the proverb, *"Ne pas attacher ton chien avec des saucisses"* or "Don't tie your dog to a leash of sausages."

In China, the *lap chong* sausage is steamed and served with rice or sliced as an *hors d'oeuvre,* or it can be stir-fried with other foods. (See ANDOUILLES, BOUDIN BLANC, BOUDIN NOIR, BLUT UND ZUNGENWURST, BRATWURST, CERVELAS, CERVELAT, CHIPOLATA, CHITTERLINGS, CHORIZOS, COPPA, CRÉPINETTES, DRISHEEN, FRANKFURTER, HAGGIS, HEAD CHEESE, KIEŁBASA, KISHKE, KNACKWURST, KÖNIGSWURST, KOPFSÜLZE, LAP CHONG, LEBERWURST, METTWURST, MORTADELLA, PEPERONI, PINKELWURST, SCHÜBLIG, SCHWARTENMAGEN, SÜLZE, WEISSWURST, WURST, ZAMPONE DI MODENA)

SAVARIN (French) A *baba*-type cake that is baked in a ring mold. The center of the cake is usually filled with whipped cream, cherries, or fruits flavored with a liqueur. The cake is named after the noted gastronome and writer Jean Anthelme Brillat-Savarin, the author of *La Physiologie du Goût*. (See BABA-AU-RHUM)

SAVOURY This culinary term is used in Great Britain to designate any small, highly seasoned dish that is served as a course at the end of a dinner, usually after the dessert. It prepares the palate for the liqueurs and brandies scheduled to follow. This category of foods includes such dishes as Welsh rarebit, raclette, soft roe, oysters and bacon, and spareribs. (See RACLETTE, RAREBIT)

SAVOYARDE, À LA (French) A reference to the harmonious blending of two foods—potatoes and Gruyère cheese—in the preparation of various dishes. The House of Savoy, an ancient dynasty of Western Europe, held sway over most of France, Italy, and Switzerland for many centuries. Therefore, many dishes using the Gruyère cheese of Switzerland bear the royal Savoy name, *Savoyarde.* Today, in the French department of Savoie, which shares its borders with Italy, a successful imitation of the Swiss cheese, called *Vacherin,* is produced.

Potatoes à la Savoyarde These potatoes are prepared just like the *Dauphinoise,* that is, sliced and cooked with grated Gruyère cheese. The difference lies in the use of stock instead of cream or milk. (See DAUPHINOISE)

Omelette à la Savoyarde Again, sautéed sliced potatoes join with Gruyère cheese, either to be used as a filling for an omelette or to be mixed with raw eggs to form a pancake-style omelette. COMPATIBLE BEVERAGES: Beer, cider.

Gratins Savoyarde These *gratins* ("grilled or baked to a golden crustiness") are baked in shallow round or oval ovenproof dishes, which are buttered and then layered with thinly sliced potatoes (or other ingredients, such as zucchini or eggplant), garlic, milk, and Gruyère cheese. This is topped with butter and more grated Gruyère, and the *gratins* are baked until the potatoes are tender. Before serving, the dish is placed under a hot grill for a few minutes to brown the top. COMPATIBLE WINES: A red wine, e.g., Fixin, Pommard, Chambertin, Nuits St. Georges, Dôle, Borolo, Zinfandel.

SCALLOPINE (Italian) Pieces of veal that have been pounded very thin. Also called *piccata.* (See PICCATA MILANESE)

con Fontina A veal cutlet topped with thinly sliced Fontina cheese.

al Marsala A breaded veal cutlet, flavored with Marsala wine.

alla Milanese The veal cutlet, pounded as thin as possible, is dipped in flour, then in beaten egg, and finally in freshly grated breadcrumbs mixed with grated Romano cheese. The cutlet is then sautéed in a heavy skillet in a mixture of olive oil and butter.

con Mozzarella The veal cutlet is topped with a thin slice of mozzarella cheese and lightly grilled.

al Prezzemolo A veal cutlet is doused with a white wine sauce and flavored with lemon, capers, and parsley. (See WHITE WINE SAUCE)

al Sugo This veal steak is pounded flat, browned in butter, seasoned with salt and pepper and nutmeg, then covered with white wine and simmered until tender. Just before serving, a squeeze of lemon juice gives the veal the right tang. The cooking liquid is often used as a sauce for the accompanying *pasta* dish.
COMPATIBLE WINES: A white wine, e.g., Vouvray, Frascati, Orvieto, Sauvignon Blanc, Sylvaner, Riquewihr, Anjou.

SCAMPI (Italian) Prawns or large shrimp (2 to 3 inches).

Scampi Bahamas After cooked and shelled prawns are sautéed in hot butter with chopped shallots, they are then flamed with Scotch whiskey. Sliced bananas and sliced pineapple are added, and the whole is simmered in heavy cream flavored with curry. The prawns are served in the center of a ring of steamed white rice and decorated with pignoli nuts (kernels of pine cones). COMPATIBLE BEVERAGES: Cider, Sauterne, or rosé wine.

Scampi alla Marinara Large shrimp "as a sailor might prepare them." Garlic is first sautéed in hot olive oil with quartered tomatoes, chopped oregano, chervil, salt, and pepper. After a short simmer, tomato purée, marjoram, paprika, and the shrimp are added and heated. The shrimp are then plated on a bed of cooked spaghetti, sprinkled with grated Parmesan cheese, and quickly browned under the grill. COMPATIBLE WINES: A white wine, e.g., Orvieto, Frascati, Vouvray, Anjou, Château Chalon, Sylvaner, Gewürztraminer, Sauvignon Blanc, Zeller Schwartze Katz, Naktarsch.

SCANDINAVIAN CUISINE (Norway/Sweden/Denmark) The cuisines of these great countries are noted for their marvelous use of fish, rich milk, buttermilk, cream, and butter. And for meat, lamb, pork, veal, and poultry are favorites. A variety of fresh vegetables is typically used to garnish a good Scandinavian meal, and the use of fruit soups is extensive. Scandinavians bake few cakes other than the ordinary coffee cakes and doughnuts, but cookies abound, full of rich butter. The *smörgåsbord* is a great favorite and the open-faced sandwiches called *smørrebrød* are famous. (See AEBELSKIVER, AEPPEL-FLÄSK, FISKPUDDING, GRAVLAXAS, KÖTTBULLAR, SILLBULLAR, SMÖRGÅSBORD, SMØRREBRØD)

SCANDINAVIAN OPEN-FACED SANDWICHES The open-faced sandwich is a speciality of all of the Scandinavian countries, and although more or less the same ingredients are used from country to country, each has its own name for them. In Sweden, the name is *smörgås;* in Norway, it is *smørbrød;* and in Denmark, it is called *smørrebrød.* (See SMØRREBRØD)

SCARPARIELLO, POLLO (Italian) The unusual legend of this chicken dish and its odd relation to "shoes" *(scarpe)* has been handed down by word of mouth from generation to generation. Following simple methods, the Italian vagabonds and "winos" used to trap, flay, and cook their birds. It is said that they used their shoes to kill the chickens whenever and wherever they happened upon them, plucked and dressed the birds on the spot, and quickly cooked them in wine. Today, the chickens are cut into serving pieces, salted and peppered and browned in a mixture of olive oil and butter, then flavored with lemon juice and finally simmered in white wine until tender. COMPATIBLE WINES: A white wine, e.g., Frascati, Orvieto, Montrachet, Sauvignon Blanc, Riesling, Gewürztraminer.

SCHLACHT PLATTE (German) The restaurant on whose menu this appears has a great treat to offer its patrons: a mammoth platter of freshly slaughtered pork meats. The platter usually consists of a hearty combination of German specialities, including boiled pork shank, *Bratwurst,* a juicy slice of *Kassler Rippchen* served with steaming mounds of sauerkraut, a purée of peas, and a potato dumpling or two. (See BRATWURST, KASSLER RIPPCHEN, SAUERKRAUT) COMPATIBLE WINES: A white wine, e.g., Riesling, Piesporter Goldtröpfchen, Graves, Rüdesheim, Gewürztraminer, Château Chalon, Riquewihr, Chenin Blanc, Orvieto, Frascati, Aigle, Naktarsch.

SCHLAG The German culinary term used by the Austrians, particularly in Vienna where it was born, for whipped cream mixed with vanilla sugar. The Viennese use *Schlag*—also called *Schlagober,* meaning "whipped over"—on anything from morning coffee to cakes, fruits, puddings, and chocolate. They even use dollops of *Schlagober* right on top of *Schlagober,* just to be sure that they haven't missed out on any. For a Viennese, there is always an excuse for having a *Schlag.* When the Frenchman calls for his Champagne with his last breath, the Viennese will whisper, *"Schlag, bitte."*

SCHLEMMERSCHNITTE (German) A type of "steak tartar" made of a slice of rye bread spread thickly with raw ground beef that has been mixed with raw egg, chopped raw onions, capers, and anchovies, and served garnished with caviar and sliced hard-boiled eggs. (See TARTARE) COMPATIBLE BEVERAGES: A good cold beer.

SCHMALTZ (Jewish) The result of carefully rendering chicken fat and chicken skins together with finely chopped onions. The crisp, browned pieces of chicken skin (cracklings) are called *gribenes* or *grieven,* and these are often used together with the *schmaltz* to prepare the popular Jewish delicacy *gehackte leber* (chopped liver).

The Yiddish word *schmaltz* is derived from the German *Schmalz,* which has an added colloquial meaning. For instance, if one says, *"Er hat Schmalz in der Stimme,"* it means, "He has a voice that is sentimentally mellow and rich," which is exactly what *schmaltz* means in a Jewish kitchen. (See GRIBENES, LEBER)

SCHMORBRATEN (German) See BRATEN/GEBRATEN

SCHNITZEL To break an old balloon, the *Schnitzel,* commonly known as the *Wienerschnitzel,* did not really originate in Vienna. It was created first in France, in a town called Vienne, and found its way to Andalusia in Spain, where it was known as *costoletta.* Then, during the reign of Carlos V, it was brought by the Spanish military to Italy. It was there, in Italy, in Milan to be exact, that Field Marshal Radetsky, in an account to his emperor, Franz Josef, praised the *scallopine Milanese* that he had feasted upon during the Italian campaign. Franz Josef was so delighted with this *Milanese* dish that he acclaimed it another Austrian triumph, and it was served in all of the fashionable restaurants in Vienna as the *Wienerschnitzel* we know today: a simple slice of veal, flattened thin, dipped in egg yolk, then breaded and quickly sautéed in butter. In Germany, however, a *Schnitzel* can also refer to a pork cutlet. (See KAISERSCHNITZEL)

Schnitzel à la Holstein This veal cutlet is prepared like the *Wienerschnitzel,* but it is garnished with a fried egg and an anchovy fillet.

Goldstein Schnitzel Made exactly as the *Wienerschnitzel* except that the breadcrumbs used must be freshly grated and untoasted. This makes all the difference in the taste of the dish.

COMPATIBLE WINES: A white wine, e.g., Gewürztraminer, Pouilly-Fumé, Gumpoldskirchner, Sylvaner, Hermitage, Johannisberg, Graacher Himmelreich, Orvieto, Chenin Blanc, Szamoradni.

SCHNITZ UND KNEPP (Pennsylvania Dutch) In German, this really translates to *Aepfelschnitten und Knoepfe,* meaning "apples and buttons." The dish was first introduced in 1690, about the time one Francis Daniel Pastorius settled in the area with his dedicated group of Mennonites. Today it still seems to be the rage in Pennsylvania Dutch Country as served at the Shartlesville Hotel, at the west end of Shartlesville. Dried apple slices are soaked in water overnight, and the following morning a small picnic ham or a few ham hocks are boiled for a few hours. Then the apples and the water in which they have been soaking are added to the ham and simmered for another hour. Then a dumpling batter rich with eggs is made, and the batter is dropped by the spoonful into the boiling liquid. When the dumplings float to the surface, they are removed and served together with the apples about the ham on a huge serving platter. COMPATIBLE WINES: A white wine, e.g., Vouvray, Saumur, Johannisberg Riesling, Gewürztraminer, Frascati.

SCHÜBLIG (Swiss) A long sausage made in the Canton of Sankt Gallen. It is composed of ground veal, herbs, and various condiments.

SCHWARTENMAGEN (German) A type of blood sausage made from pork meat that is mildly spiced and mixed with pork fat, blood, and gelatin and stuffed in the stomach of a pig. It is eaten cold.

SCHWARTZWÄLDER KIRSCHTORTE (German) This triple-layer pound cake created in the Black Forest has its first layer liberally sprinkled with Kirschwasser and spread with sugared sour cherries. The second layer is covered with a mixture of cream and gelatin, and the third and topmost layer is covered with whipped heavy cream and a generous sprinkling of flaked chocolate. The cake is refrigerated.

SCHWEINEBRATEN (German) See BRATEN/GEBRATEN

SCRAPPLE (Pennsylvania Dutch) As a true American regional speciality, the name of the dish derives from the scraps of the hog, which are scraped from the bone, stewed with meal, and pressed into cakes. Scrapple is called *Ponhaws* in the local Pennsylvania Dutch vernacular. (The "Dutch" in Pennsylvania Dutch has nothing whatever to do with Holland; it is an American convolution of *Deutsch,* the German word for "German." In the early eighteenth century the first Germans from the Platinate in Germany settled in eastern Pennsylvania. Over the years, a regional language—Pennsylvania *Deutsch*—developed.) Scrapple is made by cleaving a hog's head in two, removing the eyes and brains, and thoroughly cleaning the head before simmering it in boiling water until the meat falls from the bone. The meat is finely chopped, mixed with fine cornmeal, salt, pepper, and sage, and cooked into a soft pap. This is then pressed into buttered oblong bread tins and stored in the refrigerator. To serve, thin slices of the scrapple are cut off and fried in butter. It can be served for breakfast with eggs or as a side dish at dinner. Variations of the dish substitute either buckwheat or oatmeal for the cornmeal and utilize the heart, liver, and sweetbreads of the hog as well. COMPATIBLE WINES: A red wine, e.g., Côte Rôtie, Pinot Noir, Zinfandel, Châteauneuf-du-Pape, Valpolicella, Chianti, Bardolino, Nebbiolo, Beaujolais.

SCUNGILLI (Italian) Whelk, a thick spiral-shelled mollusk, distantly related to the conch and the abalone. The name, which comes from the ever-colorful Neapolitan dialect, is a corruption of the word *conchiglie.* To prepare as food, the meat is extracted from the shell, boiled, and served with a warm sauce. (See CONCHA)

Scungilli Marinara Chopped onions, garlic, and celery are browned in hot olive oil with whelks. The garlic is removed, and tomatoes, tomato purée, and salt are added and cooked together for a few minutes. Before serving the dish, a flavorful bouquet of oregano, bay leaves, basil, and hot pepper seeds are added. COMPATIBLE WINES: A white wine, e.g., Orvieto, Château Carbonnieux, Frascati, Sauvignon Blanc; or a good rosé wine.

SEAFOOD-BUTTER (French) This compound butter is made from equal amounts of lobster and shrimp ground up together with their shells. This is cooked, then sieved and kneaded into an equal amount of sweet butter. The sauce is served with seafood and fish dishes. (See COMPOUND BUTTER)

SEKIHAN/SEKI-HAN (Japanese) "Red rice." The red bean called the *azuki* is mixed with white rice and cooked together in a light broth flavored with sherry and soy sauce. (See AZUKI)

SEMMELKNÖDEL (Austrian) These dumplings are usually made from an Austrian-type roll called a *Semmel*. The rolls, which must be from the day before yesterday, are sliced and cubed then fried in bacon fat until crisp and brown. With the addition of flour, nutmeg, and salt, the cubed bread is then beaten with egg yolks and egg whites into a smooth, soft dough. The dough is rolled into small balls, dropped into boiling salted water, and drained. After mixing sour cream with the bacon fat residue, the dumplings are rolled in the mixture and are served with a roast or with a clear soup.

SEMOLINA The gritty, coarse, grainlike portion of wheat retained in the bolting machine after the fine flour has been passed through. This is the special durum, or hard wheat, from which the great Italian *pastas* are made. (See GNOCCHI, PASTA)

SENBEI (Japanese) Crackers made from rice. Crisp and delicately sweetened, they are delightful when served with an aromatic green tea.

SENEGALESE SOUP (Senegal/Ceylon/Sri Lanka) Somewhere, someone has surely coined a culinary adage that reads: "The birthright of a truly fine dish is claimed by many lands." So it is with this excellent curried cream-of-chicken soup. Since curry is rarely, if ever, used in Senegal (formerly part of French West Africa), one might logically conclude that the soup was born in Ceylon, which today is called Sri Lanka.

SENNEPSSOVS (Danish) A mustard sauce made by adding either fish stock or milk to a *roux* and then cooking the mixture slowly until the sauce is smooth and thick. To finish the sauce, dry mustard, sugar, salt, and pepper are added. Served with boiled fish. (See ROUX)

SERBET (Persian-Iranian) Sherbet. See SORBET.

SERRES During the reign of Henry IV, Olivier de Serres was instrumental in bringing fresh vegetables to the dining tables of France—and for that alone he should be sainted. He began growing the most beautiful crops of vegetables on a run-down farm, and he published books that made France "return to the soil."

SERTÉS PÖRKÖLT (Hungarian) A spicy pork stew flavored with paprika. Cubed pork shoulder is browned in hot oil. The pan is deglazed with beef stock to which salt, paprika, caraway seeds, sautéed chopped onions, and the cubes of pork are added; this is simmered together for a half-hour. Then chopped green peppers and tomatoes are added and cooked covered until the meat is tender. The Hungarian dumplings called *galuskas* are a welcome complement to the dish. (See GALUSKAS) COMPATIBLE WINES: A red wine, e.g., Beaujolais,

Mâcon, Mercurey, Médoc, Lambrusco; if a white wine is preferred, a Keknyelu, Sauterne, or Graacher Himmelreich is recommended.

SEVICHE (Mexican) This dish, also spelled *ceviche,* originated in the Polynesian Islands, and during the long transpacific crossing there were, of necessity, a few changes made, but all for the good. *Seviche* consists of cut-up mackerel or pompano arranged in a bowl, covered with fresh lime juice, and left to marinate overnight. Seeded chopped tomatoes and chopped onions are then mixed with a *jalapeño* chili, olive oil, vinegar, oregano, parsley, salt, and pepper; together with lime juice this is poured over the fish. This tasty fish appetizer is refrigerated until serving time. COMPATIBLE BEVERAGES: Beer, ale, stout, tea.

SFOGLIATELLI (Italian) Small pastries that are filled with either whipped cream and ice cream or with a sugared ricotta cheese mixed with candied fruits.

SHABU SHABU (Japanese) The name of this dish actually comes from the steaming sound of the food being cooked, which the Japanese hear as *"shabu, shabu."* The Swiss would describe the dish as a Chinese *fondue* served Japanese-fashion. A boiling chicken broth flavored with the inevitable *kombu* (dried kelp) is set in the center of the table. Then the meat—a good sirloin of beef, sliced thin—and the vegetables—rolled cabbage, spinach leaves, carrots, scallions, *tofu* (soybean curd), and mushrooms—are all simmered, a piece at a time, in the boiling broth. *Goma joyu,* a sesame paste, and a soy sauce are used as dips for the food. COMPATIBLE BEVERAGES: Saké, Sauterne, beer, tea, cider. (See GOMA JOYU)

SHAMI KEBAB (East Indian) A hamburger made from finely chopped beef that has been seasoned with cumin and hot peppers, formed into patties, and grilled. The dish is complemented with a tamarind gravy and a scarlet *kasundi* (hot onion relish). (See DÖNER KEBAB, KEBAB, SHASHLIK, SHISHKEBAB, TAMARIND) COMPATIBLE BEVERAGES: Beer, tea.

SHARK'S FIN SOUP This is called *yu-chi-tang* by the Chinese, who relish the shark more than they do fresh-water fish. Not only is the fin of the shark used in the preparation of this exotic soup, but also the tail. The shark's fin comes to the cook in a dried form, either with or without the impenetrably rough skin. The skinless fin is soaked in warm water; then, with the addition of bicarbonate of soda, it is simmered for several hours, until the fin has softened. The fin is then removed from what has become a rather thick broth ready for seasoning.

Shark's Fin Consommé To prepare this soup, the already-soft-ened shark's fin (actually, the dried cartilage from the fin) is cooked together with shredded celery-cabbage in either a clear chicken or beef stock that has been well seasoned with salt and Ac'cent.

SHARN LA TONG Whenever a Chinese chef decides to prepare a soup, he inevitably first reaches for a plump young chicken to make the stock. This sour soup is no exception. The chicken stock, together with dried mushrooms, dried shrimp, a *julienne* of pork and breast of chicken, bamboo shoots, and ginger, is all brought to the boil and left to simmer. With the addition of bean curd and chopped scallions, the soup is seasoned with vinegar, soy sauce, salt, pepper, and a cornstarch paste. When the soup has thickened, a beaten raw egg is added. The soup is served garnished with fresh scallions. (See JULIENNE)

SHASHLIK (Russian) These are succulent chunks of marinated lamb that are grilled on a skewer and often dramatically served in restaurants on flaming swords. Born in the Caucasus, where in early days the Tatar warriors barbecued their lamb by piercing it on their swords and placing it directly in their bonfires, the dish is traditionally served with onions, mushrooms, and tomatoes on a bed of boiled rice. (See SHISHKEBAB) COMPATIBLE WINES: A red wine, e.g., Chianti, Châteauneuf-du-Pape, Mercurey, Zinfandel, Ruby Cabernet, Côte Rôtie, Margaux, Egri Bikaver, Barolo, Médoc.

SHICHIMI TOGARASHI (Japanese) A hot seasoning made from a mixture of a very hot pepper, sesame seeds, ginger, and various other spices. It adds zest to noodle and meat dishes. (See UDON)

SHIGI YAKI (Japanese) To prepare this eggplant dish, the eggplant must first be treated as the Turks do their *beğendi,* which is to sear it well on all sides, then pare it and cut it into half-inch strips. The strips of eggplant, brushed with oil, are set out on a rack over a baking pan. They are subsequently grilled to a golden brown and served with a dip-sauce consisting of saké, sugar, and two different soybean pastes, one white and one red. This eggplant is often eaten *tsukemono-style,* that is, pickled and slightly sour. (See BEĞENDI, MISO, TSUKEMONO)

SHIITAKE (Japanese) The large black "tree mushroom," which is grown in water-logged tree stumps. These mushrooms are imported in a dried form. The stems are discarded as they are much too tough to eat.

SHIRATAKI (Japanese) This opaque noodle made from vegetable roots is quite thick and rubbery and must be rinsed several times in fresh water to remove its very fishy odor. Often served as a part of the *sukiyaki* dish. (See SUKIYAKI)

SHISHKEBAB (Arabic) *Shish* means "skewer." When Turkish soldiers in the field skewered chunks of freshly slaughtered lamb on their swords and roasted the meat over their bonfires, they called it *shishkebab,* "sword meat." Today this popular barbecue consists of bits of tender lamb that are marinated in a mixture of wine, lemon juice and olive oil, seasoned with oregano, and then grilled on skewers over hot coals. In Greece the dish is called *souvlakia.* (See DÖNER KEBAB, KEBAB, SHASHLIK) COMPATIBLE WINES: A red wine, e.g., Mâcon Rouge, Mercurey, Côtes du Rhône, Beaujolais, Margaux,

Médoc, St. Julien, Santenay, Zinfandel, Valpolicella, Nebbiolo, Cabernet Sauvignon.

SHIU MAI (Chinese) Steamed meat dumplings. A forcemeat is made from pork sausage, fresh pork, chopped water chestnuts, turnips, parsley, and scallions plus ginger, cornstarch, _teriyaki_ sauce (a mixture of sherry, soy sauce, and chicken broth), and sugar. A bit of this forcemeat is placed in the center of each round of _wonton_ dough, which is then gathered up around the filling. The dumplings are steamed on a rack over boiling water. They can be served with a dip made from a mixture of soy sauce and sesame oil. (See DIM SUM, TERIYAKI SAUCE, WONTON)

SHOGA (Japanese) Ginger root, a condiment prevalent in all Oriental cooking.

SHOO-FLY PIE "Let me show you what good is. . . ," says the Pennsylvania Dutch matron as she hurries to the kitchen to bring out a very special dessert: a molasses-rich crusty pie. One finds the pastry crust filled alternately with crumbs made from flour, sugar, nutmeg, cloves, ginger, butter, and salt and then a liquid mixture consisting of a blend of rich molasses, egg yolks, baking soda, and water. The pesky problem of having to extricate an unhappy insect from honey or molasses certainly makes the "shoo-fly" warning a logical one.

SHOYU (Japanese) An all-purpose soy sauce made from a mixture of soybeans and cereal flour left to ferment. The result tastes like sweetened soy sauce. Where wine might be used in cooking, _shoyu_ is selected. Chinese soy sauce, on the other hand, is not sweet and is used instead of salt.

SICILIENNE, À LA (French) See TOMATO

SIENA, PANFORTE ALLA A flat, hard, crunchy fruitcake from the Italian city of Siena. Toasted almonds and hazelnuts, cocoa, cinnamon, allspice, flour and grated orange, citron, and lemon peel are all mixed into a still-warm cooked mass of honey and sugar and baked in a medium oven.

SILAKKRULLAT (Finnish) Marinated rolled smelts. The fish are carefully butterflied then tightly rolled, skin side out, and set side by side, like little soldiers, in a pot. The marinade—water, sugar, salt, allspice, peppercorns, bay leaf—is brought to the boil and poured over the rolled smelts. After simmering for a short while, the pot is removed from the heat and left to cool. Chilled well before serving, the sauce will jell around the fish. Garnished with fresh dill, the smelts make a delightful appetizer. COMPATIBLE BEVERAGES: Iced vodka.

SILLBULLAR (Swedish) Herring balls. The herring is cleaned, soaked, and then ground finely with cooked meats, potatoes, and onions plus potato flour, pepper, heavy cream, and milk. This batter is rolled into small round balls _(bullar),_ which are then rolled in flour and fried in oil mixed with bacon drippings. The dish is served with a currant sauce, potatoes, and carrots. COMPATIBLE WINES: A white wine, e.g., Tokay, Rüdesheim, Johannisberg, Château Chalon, Sylvaner, Sauvignon Blanc.

SIRRA CHA This condiment can be found set out on almost every Thai dining table. The sauce is composed of the concentrated essence of the glutinous parts of fish bones added to ground chili peppers. It is an extremely hot sauce.

SKATE A fish, a member of the ray family, having large winglike pectoral fins that are edible. (See STINGAREE)

SKIRT STEAK Another name for meat that is cut from the flank of beef. It is often stuffed, rolled and tied together, then stewed in an herbed and spiced stock. (See PARILLADA, ROULADE)

SKORTHALIÁ (Greek) It was with garlic sauces such as this that the Greeks first conquered Rome. Only after they had assuaged Rome's physical hunger did the Greeks indoctrinate the Romans with their superior education. This strong sauce, made by mashing potatoes and garlic together with blanched almonds and then slowly adding olive oil and vinegar to the mixture, is usually served with fried eggplant or zucchini. In Bulgaria it is called *skordalia*. (See AÏOLI)

Skorthaliá me Yaourti This milder version of the garlicky *skorthaliá* is tamed somewhat by adding a goodly amount of yogurt to the basic sauce.

SKYR (Icelandic) A yogurt-like dessert that is served with sugar, cream, and blueberries. It is made by adding rennet to milk, allowing the fermentation to take place, and then straining the mass through a cloth sieve, thus removing the whey. This can be enriched by mixing in a raw egg or adding fruit. It can also be spiced with paprika, salt, and chopped onions and served as a spread for biscuits or rounds of toasted bread. (See YOGURT)

SLUMGULLION (American) In culinary parlance, this is the common name for any hash, stew, or salad that is made from leftovers.

Slumgullion Salad This cold salad is composed of cooked navy beans, kidney beans, garbanzos, black-eyed peas, and green beans mixed with shredded cabbage plus any pieces of leftover meat. A cold dressing made of *Mayonnaise,* sour cream, sugar, grated onions, and vinegar is poured over the salad before serving. (See MAYONNAISE)

SMÄRVARMT (Swedish) This is the series of various hot dishes, kept warm in chafing dishes, that comprise a richly laden *smörgåsbord* table. (See SMÖRGÅSBORD)

SMITANE, SAUCE (Russian) This sauce, adopted by all cuisines who know a good thing when they taste it, is made from grated onions that are sautéed in butter then moistened with white wine and reduced through cooking until all of the wine has evaporated. With the addition of sour cream, the sauce is brought to a boil, strained, and seasoned. It is a sauce that will enhance the taste of almost any food.

SMOOR-VIS (South African) Literally, "smothered" or "braised." One of the national dishes of South Africa, this fish dish is similar to the French _brandade._ The fish is first soaked in water to remove the salt. It is then skinned and boned. Chopped onions are sautéed in oil with hot chilies and cubed raw potatoes. The fish is flaked and slowly cooked together with the mixture until done. (See BRANDADE) COMPATIBLE BEVERAGES: Beer, ale, stout.

SMÖRGÅSBORD (Swedish) This traditionally rich and varied _hors d'oeuvre_ table began when country folk gathered for a seasonal feast. Each family would bring its own food, consisting of a sampling of whatever it could make best. All of the foods were arranged on a long _bord,_ or table, around which the guests would walk to fill their plates. Music and dance were an integral part of the festivities. On half of the long table of _hors d'oeuvre,_ platters of cold fish, cold meats, and vegetable salads were laid out. The other half of the table was laden with hot dishes, such as fish _au gratin,_ meatballs, and sautéed kidneys. A very strong liquor, called _snaps,_ was served, as well as much beer.

When dining from a _smörgåsbord_ table, one begins traditionally with the salty foods—the various kinds of herring with sauces. Then, after a change of plates, the other fish dishes, such as salmon and eel, are sampled, followed by a fresh plate for such dainties as jellied veal, ham, roast beef, calf's liver _pâté,_ and salads. The last raid of the _smörgåsbord_ is concentrated on the warm foods: meatballs, chicken, veal _lökdolmar_ (onions stuffed with seasoned chopped meat and baked), and similar preparations. And everywhere one hears the words _"Var sa god,"_ meaning "Please, be so good as to partake of the richness of our table."

SMØRREBRØD (Danish) "Buttered bread," a sandwich speciality that is a delight at lunchtime. The sandwiches consist of fresh smoked or salted fish plus meats, sausages, various egg preparations, salads, vegetables, and many types of cheese. The sandwiches are open-faced, topped with one or more ingredients. The bread must be firm and thinly sliced. Usually, square slices of dark bread _(rugbrot)_ are preferred, but pumpernickel or sour rye is also used. Important is the rich layer of sweet butter that first covers the bread. Then, placed decoratively over the butter one may find cooked fish, salami, cold meats, fresh tomato or cucumber slices, liver sausage, smoked salmon, cheese, and hard-boiled eggs. Garnishes used with the foregoing foods would include cold fried onions, raw egg yolks, tomatoes or radishes, sliced raw onions, dill or parsley, cooked aspic, cold scrambled eggs, pickled beets, anchovy fillets, pickles, relishes, asparagus tips, _sauce Mayonnaise,_ and marinated herring. (See

MAYONNAISE) COMPATIBLE BEVERAGES: Beer, ale, Akvavite, Snaps, Snapsi.

SNAPSI (Finnish) The traditional beverage, which we know as vodka, served with *smörgåsbord*. In Germany, a similar word, *Schnaps*, refers to any strong liquor. The American equivalent is "booze." When this chilled liquor hits the stomach, it explodes with satisfying warmth, acts as an aid to digestion, and brings cheer and merriment to the table. (See SMÖRGÅSBORD)

SNOW PEAS (Chinese) The pods of this favorite, called *syut dou,* do not have the parchment lining of the ordinary sweet pea. They are eaten pods and all.

SOBA NOODLE DISH (Japanese) A dish of brown buckwheat noodles, called *soba,* served with a spicy sauce. The noodles are cooked in boiling water and then are drained and left to cool. The accompanying sauce is made with *dashi,* sugar, and soy sauce cooked together. When served, *nori* is crumbled over the cold noodles. *Wasabi* paste, sliced scallions, grated ginger, and the sauce are placed in separate small bowls and served with the noodles. (See DASHI, NORI, WASABI) COMPATIBLE BEVERAGES: Beer, ale, tea.

SOBA TSUYU (Japanese) A dipping sauce composed of sweet saké or dry sherry mixed with soy sauce, dried bonita, and soup stock. A garnish of grated ginger root and *daikon* (radish) is mixed into the sauce. The sauce is used with *tempura* and many other Japanese dishes. (See DAIKON, TEMPURA)

SOFFRITTO (Italian) Literally "sautéed" or "slightly fried," a reference to those vegetables, such as chopped onions, parsley, and celery, that are cooked in olive oil or salt pork and used as a base for soups or for meat dishes.

SOFRITO (Spanish) The name of this basic tomato sauce is derived from the Spanish verb *sofreir,* which means "to sauté, to fry." Popular in Puerto Rico, it is prepared by first sautéing annatto seeds briefly in rendered pork fat then discarding them. Then garlic, onions, green peppers, coriander, oregano, the reserved salt pork dice, and pepper are added to the annatto-flavored fat and simmered together until their flavors have fused into a delicious sauce. After it has cooled, the sauce can be stored in covered jars in the refrigerator until needed. This should not be confused with the Italian *soffritto,* which is used as a base for soups and meat dishes. (See ANNATTO, SOFFRITTO)

SOGLIOLA (Italian) Another menu term for "sole." (See LINGUA)
    Sogliola Arrosto A whole sole baked in a mixture of olive oil, herbs, and dry white wine. COMPATIBLE WINES: Soave, Meursault, Orvieto, Muscadet.

SOLÖGA (Swedish) An appetizer consisting of a series of circles of food patterned around a fresh raw egg yolk set in the center of a plate.

Sológa translates to "eye of the sun," which in this case is represented by the egg yolk. The circles of food consist first of a ring of chopped anchovies, followed by a ring of chopped onions, then a ring of capers and one of chopped pickled beets; the outermost ring is chopped fresh parsley.

SOLYANKA (Russian) A soup composed of braised sauerkraut and parsley leaves added to a well-seasoned consommé made from ham.

SOMEN (Japanese) Thin wheat noodles. *Somen* is often served chilled in a cold *dashi* broth. (See DASHI)

SOMMELIER In days of yore, when the king wished to drink, his cupbearer made a sign to the *sommelier* (French for "wine butler"). The *sommelier* approached the king's table with a cup in one hand and wine in the other. To his right stood his assistant, who held ready a pitcher filled with water. The king's cup always had a hinged cover, which the cupbearer raised as the *sommelier* poured first the wine and then the water. The *sommelier* and the cupbearer both drank of the wine-water combination, then covered the cup. The king waited a reasonable time to see if the wine had any adverse effect, then he accepted his cup—still covered—and drank of its contents. For many years, the wine steward, or *sommelier,* was in complete charge of the ordering, storing, and serving of wines in fine restaurants all over the world. High-priced labor has all but eliminated the post of the *sommelier* from first-class restaurants, and today service captains have assumed his duties in the dining room.

SOM U MILERAMU (Yugoslav) Codfish baked in sour cream. Cod fillets are cooked in a mixture of water and dry white wine with salt, pepper, bay leaves, parsley, and onions. After blanching, the cod is removed and placed in a well-buttered ovenproof dish; it is then topped with chopped anchovies and covered with a blend of sour cream, flour, and the fish stock. After baking a scant quarter-hour in a moderate oven, the cod is ready for the table. COMPATIBLE WINES: A white wine, e.g., Gewürztraminer, Riquewihr, Chenin Blanc, Riesling, Fendant, Frascati, Orvieto, Anjou, Hermitage, Traminer, Szamoradni.

SOPA DE MIL INFANTES (Portuguese) "Soup of a thousand infants" is made from a mixture of egg yolks and breadcrumbs that is dropped a bit at a time into a boiling chicken broth that has already been enriched with egg whites, salt, pepper, and chervil.

SORBET (French) The name for this fruited ice comes directly from the Italian *sorbetto.* The Italians had learned of the dish from the Turks during the Crusades. The Turks called it *charbet,* and although the word derives from the Arabic *shariba,* meaning "to drink," it was the ancient Chinese, some 2,000 years ago, who first created what we today enjoy as sherbet. In 1660, *sorbets* and *granités* were introduced in Paris by a Sicilian named Procopio, but it took another 100 years for the French to accept this innovation. Today, the *sorbet* is a refreshing dessert made by whipping egg whites with a fruit-flavored sugar syrup and then adding a liqueur of choice: Kümmel, Grand Marnier, Williams Pear Brandy, etc. The *granité,* a fruited ice made without the meringue (egg whites), is a mixture of fruit, water, and sugar that is frozen before serving. (See GRANITÉ)

SOSATIE (Malaysian) From the word *sesate,* meaning "meat on a skewer." The Malays soak cubes of mutton overnight in a marinade of onions, curry powder, chilies, garlic, and tamarind juice. The next day, the marinated mutton cubes are skewered alternately with pieces of mutton fat and roasted over an open charcoal fire. The dish is served with boiled white rice and a sauce made by reducing the marinade. COMPATIBLE BEVERAGES: Beer, ale, tea, cider.

SOTO AYAMA (Indonesian) A curried chicken soup. Bite-size pieces of boiled chicken are cooked in a rich chicken broth that is highly seasoned with sautéed onions, garlic, ginger, hot chilies, a curry mixture, and *blanchan.* The soup is served garnished with *vermicelli,* chopped scallions, and chopped hard-boiled eggs. (See BLANCHAN, VERMICELLI)

SOUBISE, SAUCE (French) Because his heavy-handed chef, Bertrand, named this onion sauce after him, the Prince of Soubise has taken his place among the immortals of culinary magic. This sauce first requires that masses of chopped onions be simmered in butter. Flour and fish stock, white stock, or milk are then added. Dollops of heavy cream, nutmeg, and salt and pepper finish off the sauce in a heavenly fashion. *Sauce soubise* is served with eggs, veal, chicken, turkey, lamb, vegetables, and those dishes served gratinéed.

SOUFFLÉ (French) The *soufflé* can be compared to the delicate touch of love, for it too is warming and tender. The word *soufflé* is the past participle of the French verb *souffler,* meaning "to blow, to puff up," and when speaking of food the term is used as a verb-noun defining foodstuff that is served "puffed up."

Basically a *soufflé* consists of a purée of food that—off the heat—is bound with egg yolks, seasonings, and stiffly beaten egg whites. The preparation "puffs up" as it bakes in a moderate oven.

There are actually three kinds of *soufflés:*

- •The *entrée* or *hors d'oeuvre soufflé* may be made with vegetables, seafood, fish, game, ham, poultry, calf's liver, brains, or even a delicate cheese. This type of *soufflé* may be served as an appetizer or light main course, and it makes a wonderful luncheon treat.

- •The dessert *soufflé* is most often made with a base of finely puréed fruits or berries. To the purée is added sugared milk and a bit of flour. This may be perfumed with an essence of vanilla, almond, lemon, or orange or with a liqueur of choice. Dessert _soufflés_ are served warm in the same casseroles or _timbales_ in which they were baked. Their immediate service cannot be overemphasized, for once the _soufflé_ is ready it must be attended to like a woman in her tenth month of pregnancy. That is to say, the finished _soufflé_ must be delivered to the diner with professional dispatch and with the utmost care and respect.

●The _soufflé glacé,_ the "frozen _soufflé,_" differs from the other two types in that egg yolks, sugar, and milk are mixed together over heat. Then, only after cooling the mixture down, are stiffly beaten egg whites folded in. The preparation is refrigerated for several hours before being served topped with powdered sugar or crumbled macaroons. (See TIMBALE)

SOURDOUGH In the seventh century before the birth of Christ, sourdough was discovered quite by accident in Egypt, and later it was brought to Greece. Pliny the Elder writes that the Gauls and the Iberians produced a dough from skimmed beer, and the Greeks and the Italians did the same using fermented wine; but always a bit of the dough was saved from the previous day's baking to incorporate into a fresh batch. Even today, sourdough is made from the same kind of "starter" that was used by the Egyptians thousands of years ago. When Columbus sailed to the New World, he brought with him the first beneficial bacteria working away in sourdough. The service of sourdough bread on a restaurant table today is certainly the precursor of a fabulous meal.

SOUSE (Caribbean) Well-cooked pig's head and feet are cut up into pieces, marinated in lime juice, chili peppers, and salt, and served cold with a garnish of finely sliced cucumbers, chopped onions, and red and green sweet peppers. COMPATIBLE BEVERAGES: Beer, ale, tea, cider.

SOUTHERN-FRIED CHICKEN (American South) For this speciality of the Deep South, pieces of plump young chicken are transformed by frying into a succulent dining treat. Often, however, the disjointed chicken is immersed in some sort of batter and then tossed into a lazy cook's "deep-fry" composed of old fats and oils that have been simmering for days on end. This produces an unfortunate result. A properly "southern-fried" bird is cut into pieces, dredged in a well-seasoned flour, and carefully cooked in no more than a half-inch of vegetable oil flavored with just a trace of bacon fat. The chicken is carefully watched and turned again and again over moderate heat. Better to have a slightly overcooked chicken than a bloody one. The final color should be a rich golden brown, and the crust should be firm, brittle, tantalizingly crisp. The chicken should rightly be eaten with the fingers, and if you are seen licking your fingers, it is a great compliment to the chef. Southern-fried chicken is served with boiled rice and a crisp tossed salad. COMPATIBLE WINES: A red wine, e.g.,

Médoc, Beaujolais, Valpolicella, Santenay, Margaux, Zinfandel, Nebbiolo, Egri Bikaver, Mâcon, Hermitage, Moulin-à-Vent, Premiat.

SOUVAROV, À LA (French) Reference to a method of cooking feathered game as well as domestic birds. The birds are first half-cooked in a covered pot with plenty of butter, then they are transferred to an ovenproof casserole that is lined with truffles that have been simmered in Madeira. Game stock and butter are added, and the birds are baked. The cover of the casserole is completely sealed with a dough made from a mixture of flour and water. Pigeons, pheasants, quail, partridge, even chicken can be prepared in this manner.

Poularde à la Souvarov Chicken prepared in the *Souvarov* style. The chicken, stuffed with chopped goose liver and black truffles, seasoned with salt, herbs, spices, and brandy, is placed in a covered pan with butter and cooked until nearly done. The chicken is then placed in a casserole and covered with a sauce composed of Madeira wine, brown sauce, and black truffles. The lid is sealed in place with a paste of dough and water, and the chicken is baked until done. (See BROWN SAUCE, CHICKEN IN CLAY) COMPATIBLE WINES: A white wine, e.g., Montrachet, Meursault, Anjou, Schloss Vollrads, Wehlener Sonnenuhr, Rüdesheim, Orvieto, Steinberg, Chenin Blanc, Vouvray, Anjoy, Gewürztraminer.

SOUVLAKIA (Greek) See SHISHKEBAB

SOVANLI YUMURTA (Turkish) A particularly delicious method of preparing eggs with onions. Sliced onions are first sautéed in butter; then, with a mixture of water and sugar added to the pan, they are covered and left to simmer until the water is absorbed and the onions are translucent and tender. Whole raw eggs are spaced over the gleaming onion bed. With the addition of salt, water, and allspice, the eggs are covered and simmered until set. The dish makes a wonderful luncheon, but what a treat for brunch on a cold Sunday morning.

SOYBEAN As one of the sacred grains of the Orient, the nutritious soybean dates back to the year 2000 B.C. Together with rice, it is considered one of the staple foods of China. Of all the bean family, the soybean, ranging in color from green to yellow and black, is the most easily digested and the most protein-rich; in fact, it has almost the equivalent of animal protein. Soybeans are not only excellent substitutes for beef, pork, and lamb, but they are far cheaper and more readily available.

Soy Sauce Of the many Chinese seasonings, soy sauce is probably the best known to the Occidental world. This Chinese sauce, produced from the soybean, is usually fermented for periods of six months to two years or longer. The quality of the sauce varies with the aging time. The best grades are nearly like fine wines. Whereas soy sauce is used in China predominantly to salt food, Japanese soy sauce is on the sweet side.

The manufacture of soy sauce is a complicated process. First, wheat flour and a soybean paste are allowed to ferment. Salt and water are added and the fermentation continues in large vats set out in the sun. The very finest of soy sauces take as long as seven years to age to perfection. One of the best is called *ch'au yau,* but the one usually found in restaurants, "pearl sauce," does little to enhance the taste of food. It merely adds saltiness and color to the food it is intended to season. Soy sauce will rarely sour or develop mold. (See SOYBEAN)

SPAGHETTI (Italian) Many historians claim that Marco Polo brought *spaghetti*—probably the most popular of all *pastas*—with him from China. Others will swear on the golden fork and spoon of the renowned Alfredo di Roma that *spaghetti,* like other *pastas,* originated in Italy. Like its bigger cousin, *macaroni, spaghetti* is made from hard wheat and water that is mixed to a paste and dried in strings called *spaghi.* It is then cooked in a large amount of boiling salted water until it is *al dente,* "to the tooth," which usually takes about twelve minutes. The *spaghetti* is then drained and served with one of many different sauces. (See DENTE, PASTA)

Spaghetti al Burro Hot *spaghetti* mixed with melted butter and grated Parmesan cheese before serving.

Spaghetti all' Aglio e Olio Freshly made *spaghetti* mixed with garlic-flavored olive oil.

Spaghetti alla Bolognese Freshly made *spaghetti* served with *ragù Bolognese,* grated Parmesan cheese, and butter. (See RAGÙ)

Spaghetti alla Napoletana Freshly made *spaghetti* is first tossed in warm olive oil. A sauce made from chopped meat or chopped ham, garlic, celery, onions, and parsley—all chopped fine and cooked in tomato purée diluted with beef stock—is then added.

Spaghetti con Salsa Funghi The Italians love mushrooms almost as much as they love garlic and tomatoes, and they prove it by serving the ubiquitous *spaghetti* with a rich mushroom sauce. Finely sliced mushrooms are cooked in hot oil with chopped onions, to which sliced tomatoes are added. The mushrooms are removed, and in the same pan flour is lightly browned and slaked with milk. The mushroom-and-tomato mixture is returned to the pan; salt, oregano, basil, and red peppers are added, and the sauce is brought to the boil. This sauce is usually served in the center of a ring of freshly cooked *spaghetti* liberally sprinkled with grated Parmesan cheese. COMPATIBLE WINES: A red wine, e.g., Chianti, Beaujolais, Dôle, Fleurie, Valpolicella, Zinfandel, Pinot Noir, Ruby Cabernet, Barbaresco, Nebbiolo, Bardolino, Egri Bikaver.

SPAGHETTINI (Italian) See PASTA

SPANAKOPITTA (Greek) A spinach-filled pie, the crust of which is made with well-buttered *phyllo* pastry leaves. Chopped fresh spinach and onions are cooked for a few minutes in hot olive oil. The spinach and onions are transferred to a bowl and mixed with chopped parsley, feta cheese and cottage cheese, beaten eggs, and salt and pepper. This spinach-cheese mixture is spread into a pan that has been lined with the buttered *phyllo* pastry leaves. It is then covered with an equal number of *phyllo* leaves and baked until the leaves turn a golden brown. COMPATIBLE WINES: A red wine, e.g., Egri Bikaver, Beaujolais, Premiat, Valpolicella, Pinot Noir, Zinfandel.

SPANFERKEL (German) A suckling pig that has been crisply roasted on a spit or in the oven. COMPATIBLE WINES: A red wine, e.g., Beaujolais, Médoc, Côtes du Rhône, Côte Rôtie, Mercurey, Veltliner, Valpolicella, Chinon, Châteauneuf-du-Pape, Arbois, Figeac, St. Julien.

SPÄTLESE (German) The word *spät,* "late," is used here as a German vintner's term to describe a type of wine produced from grapes that came from a "late harvest," that is, from grapes that were left on the vine past the normal harvest time. This increases their sugar content. (See AUSLESE, BEERENAUSLESE, EISWEIN, KABINETT, TROCKENBEER-ENAUSLESE)

SPÄTZLE/SPÄTZLI (Swiss/German) A tiny dumpling whose batter—made from flour, eggs, milk, butter, and salt—is spoon-dropped into boiling water or stock. Often served with the Swiss minced veal in cream sauce and also with beef *Stroganoff.* (See GALUSHKI, GESCHNETZELTES KALBFLEISCH, STROGANOFF)

SPEZZATINO (Italina) A stew of cubed meat braised in a sauce.

Spezzatino alla Contadina Cubed veal cooked peasant woman-style (mushrooms, bacon, cooked in butter with Parmesan cheese) or braised in a sauce composed of a purée of anchovies, chopped olives, capers, chopped onions, tomato purée, bouillon, and finely grated Parmesan cheese. COMPATIBLE WINES: A red wine, e.g., Valpolicella, Chianti, Lambrusco, Egri Bikaver, Fleurie, Zinfandel, Moulin-à-Vent, Côtes du Rhône, Médoc, Margaux, Dôle, Pinot Noir.

SPICES The general term for seasonings that are obtained from the roots, the bark, the stems, the buds, the seeds, and even the fruit of aromatic trees and plants that grow in the tropics. They are used in the manufacture of certain medicines and to flavor wines and foods. "Herb" generally refers to the leafy part of the plant, whereas the term "spice" pertains to the seed, the fruit, or the root of the plant. Spices are available either whole or ground. They should always be stored in tightly capped containers because once the delicate oils in the spices are exposed to the air for a length of time, the wonderful aroma will be dissipated. Spices should always be used with a light hand, never so strong that they overpower the natural flavor of the foods they are meant to enhance.

Among ancient peoples—the Egyptians, the Babylonians, the Akkadians, the Sumerians, the Assyrians, the Jews—spices were used not only for food but for healing and to placate the gods (Exodus

30:23-25). Assyrian doctors versed in the medicinal powers of herbs and spices prescribed for their patients mixtures of cardamom, dill, cumin, fennel, thyme, saffron, and sesame, as well as garlic and onions, to treat various ailments.

During the Middle Ages, the consumption of spices increased steadily in Europe and in England; and owing to the great distances spices had to travel and the innumerable hands they had to pass through, their high cost put them out of reach of all but the very rich. Spices had become as dear as gold, and many a man was slain for the small packet of Malabar pepper he had on his person. As the preservation of food, up to that time, relied on drying, smoking, or salting, the influx of aromatic spices from the Orient proved a godsend, for it provided new methods of keeping and of flavoring food. During the devastating bubonic plague that ravaged Europe in the fourteenth century, various herbs and spices were used to prevent infection. Garlic was popular, as was rosemary, both because of their more-than-contrasting odors.

Those who lived in the Dark Ages were most conscious of their bad breath because their mouths were full of foul and rotting teeth. To sweeten the breath, they drank a concoction of rosemary, cloves, mace, cinnamon, and aniseed in the morning and again just before retiring for the night. In fact, bad breath was so prevalent that in later years married couples were forced to sleep with the wife's head at the husband's feet, to protect themselves from each other's halitosis. Many Orientals will rinse their mouths with water between courses, so that the lingering sharpness of the curry, used to flavor the main course, will not be there to ruin the taste of the sweet yet to be served.

It is not only which spices are used to flavor dishes but how and when in the course of food preparation they are used that gives dishes their special taste and attractiveness. Cumin, for example, if roasted crushed will give a very sharp, nutty taste to the food it is flavoring. However, whole cumin, cooked in hot fat, has a mild aroma and a gentle taste, much like licorice. Then there is uncooked cumin, which has the mildest taste of all. If the sharp, hot taste of a dried red pepper is desired, the pepper should be first browned in oil and then cooked with the food to be flavored. If the browned pepper is simply added to the already-cooked food, there will be no hot taste and the pepper flavor will be much more subtle. (See listings of individual spices for a description of their particular gastronomic use.)

SPIEDO, ALLA (Italian) Skewered on a spit and roasted.

Pollo alla Spiedo A young chicken that is broiled on a spit or skewered and baked in the oven. COMPATIBLE WINES: A red wine, e.g., Valpolicella, Beaujolais, Zinfandel, Fleurie, Médoc, Barolo, Nebbiolo, Margaux, Savigny, Santenay, Arbois, Cahors.

Spiedini alla Romana For this Roman speciality, chopped meat is mixed with grated Romano cheese, breadcrumbs, parsley, garlic, salt, and pepper and bound with eggs. The mixture is then formed into small oblong patties and set on a skewer alternately with squares of prosciutto ham, bread, and mozzarella cheese. The entire skewer is dipped in flour, then in beaten eggs and breadcrumbs, and fried in hot olive oil. COMPATIBLE WINES: A red wine, e.g., Bardolino, Nebbiolo, Chianti, Châteauneuf-du-Pape, Grumello, Lambrusco, Petit Sirah, Zinfandel, Valpolicella.

SPRING ROLLS (Chinese) See EGG ROLLS

SPUMONI (Italian) A dessert consisting of a layer of chocolate ice cream and a layer of vanilla ice cream, between which is sandwiched a layer of rum-flavored whipped cream that is dotted throughout with candied fruit and finely chopped nuts.

Spumoni al Craccante A regular *spumoni* ice cream, served topped with almonds that have been toasted and caramelized and ground very fine.

SQUID See CALAMARI

STAR ANISE This licorice-flavored fruit grows on a Chinese evergreen shrub *(Illicum verum)*. Its astral name comes from the eight-pointed star shape of its fruit clusters. It is also called the Chinese anise, and although it is similar in flavor to the ordinary aniseed, it comes from an entirely different botanical family. It forms an integral part of the favorite "five-spice essence," which is used in red-cooked and roasted meat and poultry dishes. (See FIVE-SPICE ESSENCE)

STEAK AND KIDNEY PIE A traditional English dish prepared by sautéing cut-up steak, kidneys, mushrooms, and chopped onions in hot clarified butter. With the addition of seasonings, flour, garlic, and beef stock, the ingredients are simmered until the meat is tender. The meat mixture is poured into a pie dish, covered with a lid of pastry, and baked in a moderate oven. Within a half-hour or less the treat is ready for the table, steaming and golden brown. COMPATIBLE WINES: A red wine, e.g., Chinon, Médoc, Mâcon, Beaune, Côte Rôtie, Calon-Ségur, Gruaud-Larose, St. Julien, Cabernet Sauvignon.

STEAK AND KIDNEY PUDDING When one thinks of English food, immediately several dishes come to mind: Yorkshire pudding, roastbeef, cock-a-leekie, roast leg of lamb, and steak and kidney pudding. This last dish is made by placing a stout piece of muslin in a bowl, dusting it well with flour, and fitting in a piece of dough large enough to hang over the rim of the bowl. Then slices of beef that have been dredged in flour and sliced onions that have been sautéed in butter are covered with beef stock, seasoned, and left to simmer. Veal kidneys are cut up, sautéed in butter, and seasoned. Together with the beef and the onions, the kidneys are arranged carefully in the bowl that has been lined with muslin and dough. The dough and muslin are drawn together, forming a sack, which is placed into boiling water and cooked for several hours. A good English mustard complements this dish. COMPATIBLE WINES: A red wine, e.g., Beaujolais, Mercurey, Mâcon, Châteauneuf-du-Pape, Pinot Noir, Dôle, Chianti, Côte Rôtie.

STEFADO (Greek) A favorite stew composed of hare, veal, or beef—actually whatever meat is at hand—cooked with stock, wine, onions, tomatoes, walnuts, and feta cheese. (See BORJU, GULYAS, HUNGARIAN STEWS, RAGOÛT, SERTÉS) COMPATIBLE WINES: A red wine, e.g., Nemean, Beaujolais, Mâcon, Margaux, Veltliner, Côte Rôtie, Fleurie, Nebbiolo, Egri Bikaver, Premiat.

STEINPILZ (German) The yellow boletus mushroom. (See CHAMPIGNONS.)

STEKT GÅS (Swedish) roast goose, a dish popular not only among Scandinavians but among the people of most Nordic countries, including Germany and Czechoslovakia. After the goose has been thoroughly rubbed, inside and out, with salt and pepper and seasoned with nutmeg and sage, the cavity is stuffed with pitted prunes that have been softened by precooking. Quartered apples are also added. The bird is rotated often, and after five to six hours of roasting with frequent basting, the goose is regally served surrounded with the prunes and apples. (See PECÊNA HUSA SE ZELIM) COMPATIBLE WINES: A white wine, e.g., Sauterne, Vouvray, Monbazillac, Forster Jesuitengarten, Muscat d'Alsace, Tokay.

STEW Two or more solid ingredients cooked in a liquid is called a stew; a compote of fruit, cooked in its own juices, is really a stew. The first stew preserved by the printed word can be found in the Book of Genesis where Esau, the hunter, and Jacob, the cook, were instrumental in preparing a stew of mutton made with lentils, onions, fat, and salt. (See BORJU, GULYAS, HUNGARIAN STEWS, SERTÉS, STEFADO, RAGOÛT)

STINGAREE (Créole) The term for a fish known as the ray, a flat-bottomed creature with a whiplike tail, armed with barbed spines, that seems to soar through the depths of all the seas of the world on tremendous wings. The huge manta ray spans twenty-two feet from one wing tip to the other, and it can weigh nearly two tons. The smaller variety, called the skate, is quite popular as food. Although closely related to the shark, the wings of the ray possess a highly edible white meat, similar in taste and texture to the sea scallop. The French love their *raie*, as do the Cajuns of Louisiana, who call them "stingaree" probably because of the sting in the fish's tail, which packs quite a wallop. (See SKATE)

Stingaree au Beurre Noir "Ray with brown butter." To prepare the dish, the wings of the ray are cut off and blanched in a boiling mixture of salted water and vinegar. The fish must be handled with care because the coarse skin can give a nasty cut. Removing the skin exposes a meat as white as snow. Then, butter is browned (but not burned) in a large pan; to this, chopped parsley and lemon juice are added. To serve, the hot butter sauce is poured directly over the fish and seasoned to taste. COMPATIBLE WINES: A white wine, e.g., Meursault, Montrachet, Pouilly-Fuissé, Quincy, Chablis, Pinot Chardonnay, Sancerre, Verdicchio, Soave, Pouilly-Fumé.

STIR-FRYING This method of cooking is endemic to the Chinese people. Stir-frying was begun in 600 B.C. by the Taoists under Lao-Tse, who believed that vegetables suffer from too much cooking. How right he was. Stir-frying necessitates cooking over high heat, usually in a wok, and this means that all of the ingredients for the dish must be prepared before the oil is hot. All of the food must be cut to the same size: if the meat is cubed, the other ingredients must also be cut into the same size cubes; and the same rule applies if the food is shredded or sliced. In this manner the foods all cook evenly. Naturally, if one food takes longer to cook, it should be started cooking before the other more tender foods are added. Some foods can be cooked separately and then joined together with a sauce at the end. The secret of fine stir-fried foods is the phrase *al dente,* "to the tooth"—that is, the food should be cooked just enough but never overcooked. (See CHINESE CUISINE, WOK)

STOLLEN, DRESDENER (German) This festive fruit loaf from historic Dresden is as famous as its English counterpart, the brandied fruitcake. To make the cake, candied fruit, including cherries, angelica, and lemon are marinated in warm rum along with raisins and currants. The dough is made with flour, sugar, yeast, milk, eggs, butter, grated lemon peel, and vanilla and almond extracts. It is kneaded well, and after flouring, the marinated fruit is pressed into the dough. After the dough has risen, it is rolled out into a rectangular shape, brushed with butter, and sprinkled with sugar. The dough, folded to form a loaf about a foot long, is left to rise again. Then, brushed with butter, the loaf is baked in the oven until brown and crusty. And like a devoted wife, the *Dresdener Stollen* improves with age.

STRACCIATELLA (Italian) A soup made by combining both a chicken and a beef consommé. Literally, the term *stracciatella* means "torn to shreds," and this is exactly how the mixture of eggs, flour, grated Parmesan cheese, and nutmeg appears when it is whisked into the boiling broth.

STRASBOURGEOISE, FILET DE BOEUF (French) A special roast tenderloin of beef dish. The beef is well larded and then roasted on a bed of vegetables until evenly browned. Then, with the addition of Madeira and a white wine, it is cooked until just rare. *Strasbourgeoise* indicates that goose liver is present. Slices of the liver are dusted with flour, browned in butter, then neatly placed between slices of the roasted tenderloin. The dish is then ready to be served. (See FOIE GRAS) COMPATIBLE WINES: A red wine, e.g., Pétrus,

Lascombes, La Tâche, Échézeaux, Fixin, Nuits St. Georges, St. Émilion, Dôle, Cabernet Sauvignon.

STRAWBERRIES À LA CUSSY (French) The Marquis Louis de Cussy, Napoleon's chief steward, not only chose his emperor's clothes, picked out his furniture, and sorted out those beauties who might have access to Napoleon's bed, but he also proved to be a discriminating gastronome. His strawberries, for example, were marinated in Champagne and sugar and served topped with heavy cream. Napoleon was very fond of de Cussy and his culinary creations.

STREUSELKUCHEN, SCHWÄBISCHER (German) *Streusel* is the term for the lumps that form when flour, sugar, and melted butter are mixed together in proper proportion. For this cake, a yeast dough is kneaded together, and when well risen, it is spread finger-thick on a buttered baking pan. The surface is then roughed up and pierced with a fork, and after the *Streusel* is equally distributed over the top, the cake is baked in a moderate oven.

STROGANOFF, BEEF À LA (Russian) Named after the general who is said to have first created it, this dish consists of cubed or thinly sliced fillets of beef. They are browned in butter and served in a sauce made from chopped onions, white wine, Worcestershire sauce and, the most important, sour cream. The dish is usually served with rice or with *Spätzle*. (See SPÄTZLE) COMPATIBLE WINES: A red wine, e.g., Margaux, Médoc, Valpolicella, Latour, St. Julien, Haut Brion, Calon-Ségur, Pontet-Canet, Mâcon.

STRUDEL This type of flaky pastry, so famous in Austria, was first brought to central Europe in the sixteenth century by the invading Turks. *Strudel* leaves, or *phyllo* pastry, must be so thin, Austrian pastry cooks claim, that the *Wiener Tagblatt* can be read through them.

Strudel dough is very much like noodle dough. After the dough has been kneaded, it must rest for an hour. Then it is rolled out on a board or a marble surface. With the hands, the dough is worked and stretched from the center outward; it is then restretched until very thin. The stretched dough is then covered with the filling of choice— apples, raspberries, cherries, apricots, cream cheese or cottage cheese—and rolled up and baked.

STUFATO (Italian) "Boiled" or "stewed."

Stufatino de Vitello Finocchio A veal stew made with fennel. After browning the breast of veal in olive oil with a mixture of root vegetables (including garlic) and bacon, tomato paste and a bouillon are added and the veal is cooked until tender. When the veal is almost done, the cooked fennel, cut into pieces, is added with sweet butter. The dish is served with boiled rice. COMPATIBLE WINES: A white wine, e.g., Orvieto, Frascati, Meursault, Johannisberg, Sylvaner, Wehlener Sonnenuhr, Riquewihr, Hermitage, Anjou, Montrachet, Sauvignon Blanc.

Stufato di Manzo e Patate A beef stew consisting of thin slices of meat (cut from the shin) that are simmered in a beef broth with bacon fat, onions, garlic, prosciutto ham, red wine, and potatoes. COMPATIBLE WINES: A red wine, e.g., Mâcon, Côte Rôtie, Mercurey, Chinon, Valpolicella, Zinfandel, Beaujolais.

STUFFED CABBAGE See HOLISHKES

SU (Japanese) Rice vinegar.

SUAN-LE-T'ANG (Chinese) This "sour-and-hot" chicken broth, made sour from white vinegar and thick with minced pork, wood ears, cornstarch, chopped bamboo shoots, eggs, and bean curd, is served piping hot. Before serving, a dash of sesame oil and a sprinkling of finely chopped scallions is added to each individual bowl of hot soup. (See JOOK SOON, TOFU, WOOD EARS)

SUBANKEN (Czechoslovakian) For this dish, potatoes are steamed and mashed. Seasoned flour is mixed into the mashed potatoes. The mixture is then cooked in a pan over very low heat. Dumplings are spooned off and cooked and then served either with browned onions and oil or with poppy seeds and sugar.

SUBGUM GAI TONG (Chinese) A chicken soup made by cooking diced chicken in a chicken broth with mushrooms, celery, water chestnuts, and bean sprouts. Before serving, an egg is beaten into the soup.

SUGAR In the year 500 B.C., King Darius of Persia first promoted the use of sugar. In 1230, a contingent of Jews from Maghreb was instrumental in introducing sugar into Sicily. But it was not until two hundred years later that sugar cane was planted by the Spanish in Madeira; still later, it was planted in America.

In the early days of its cultivation, sugar was taken only medicinally. Colbert, in France, was the first to realize that sugar could be used to enhance the taste of food and, indeed, to create entirely new sweet dishes. The first sugar refineries in France were established at Rouen, and American raw sugar was used. But in 1812, Delessert, a financier, founded a sugar factory in Passy, where he began making sugar from beets. Because of this accomplishment, Napoleon proclaimed him a baron.

SUGO DI POMODORO Francesco Leonardi, the first Italian cook of any importance to emerge after the Renaissance, was the first to record in print how the tomato was used to advantage in Italy. In fact, he was the first to combine the famous Italian *pasta* with the ill-used tomato. His early tomato sauce, made with small Italian tomatoes simmered together with chopped onions, garlic, and celery and seasoned with basil and parsley, is the same classic *sugo di pomodoro* that is served in fine Italian restaurants today. (See BOLOGNESE, POMODORO, RAGÙ)

SUISSE, SAUCE VERTE (Swiss) This excellent green sauce goes well with cold fish dishes. The color comes from the spinach, watercress, parsley, and tarragon used. These ingredients are first blanched, then drained and chopped very fine. Egg yolks, salt, pepper, dry mustard, and lemon juice are well beaten until combined. The green vegetables and herbs are added along with olive oil, drop by drop, until the sauce has a velvety texture. Glorious served with cold salmon.

SUKIYAKI (Pronounced *skee-ya-kee*) The Dutch introduced their version of this dish to the Japanese in the early seventeenth century. However, because the dish was a beef preparation, the Japanese would serve it only to foreigners. The Japanese detected vile and nauseating odors emanating both from the mouths and the bodies of those foreign businessmen with whom they had to come in contact. The odor was the result of a heavy meat diet, which produces an acid called butyric, a smelly substance stemming from animal fat. Of course, the foreigners had their own reaction to the Japanese: these same foreign businessmen felt that the Japanese girls they met reeked of fish!

Since the Japanese have finally accepted beef as a beneficial food, the odor problem seems to have disappeared. Today, *sukiyaki* is a Japanese way of quickly frying chicken, beef, or pork that has been cut up into small, bite-size pieces in a soy sauce mixture with vegetables and *vermicelli*. All ingredients are served crisp-to-the-tooth. The soy sauce mixture is composed of saké, soy sauce, broth, sugar, pepper, and Ac'cent. (See MONOSODIUM GLUTAMATE) COMPATIBLE BEVERAGES: Saké, tea, cider, a rosé wine, Sauterne.

SULTAN'S DELIGHT (Hungarian) See BEĞENDI

SÜLZE (German) Jellied meats. Bits of meat and finely chopped vegetables are cooked with wine, bouillon, lemon juice, various seasonings, and gelatin. When the mixture cools, it jells. It is served cut into slices. A favorite variation is made from calf's head. (See HEAD CHEESE)

SUMASHI (Japanese) A basic clear soup composed of *dashi kombu* and grated *katsoubushi*. The soup is strained and flavored with soy sauce. (See DASHI KOMBU, KATSOUBUSHI)

SUNOMONO (Japanese) A vegetable dish composed of finely sliced carrots, lotus root, and cucumbers—all marinated in a solution of vinegar, *shoyu,* sugar, and Ac'cent. It is often served with a festive *sukiyaki* dinner. (See SHOYU, SUKIYAKI)

SUPRÊME, SAUCE (French) A sauce made by cooking chopped mushrooms in a chicken *velouté*. Heavy cream is added just before serving. Served with various egg, poultry, and vegetable dishes. (See VELOUTÉ)

SUPRÊMES DE VOLAILLE These are the skinless, boneless, raw breasts of chicken, which in France are a great delicacy, cooked in various ways with assorted sauces and garnishes. Sometimes the wings are added.

Suprêmes de Volaille à la Milanaise Chicken breasts are rolled in flour then dipped in beaten egg, covered with a mixture of grated Parmesan cheese and breadcrumbs, and sautéed in clarified butter. (See CLARIFIED BUTTER)

Suprêmes de Volaille à la Crème Baked breasts of chicken are served in a sauce made of bouillon, white wine, and cream.

Suprêmes de Volaille Écossaise See ÉCOSSAISE

SURPRISE, OMELETTE (French) Call it *omelette surprise, omelette Norvégienne,* or *glace au four,* or by its American name, baked Alaska—this dessert is popular all over the world. In fact, it is so popular that a chef in Monte Carlo, another in a Chinese mission in Paris, and even an American physicist all claim to have invented it. This particular French version consists of a sponge cake base spread with a purée of apricots and generously sprinkled with Kirschwasser. Hard-frozen ice cream is set on top and covered with a meringue that has been sweetened with sugar and flavored with vanilla. The assembled dessert is placed into a hot oven until the meringue has delicately browned. The surprise for the uninitiated comes, no doubt, when the hot meringue is cut, exposing the frozen contrast of ice cream beneath. (See ALASKA)

SUSHI (Japanese) A popular rice preparation effected by boiling rice in water to which a piece of *kombu* (dried kelp) is added. The rice is served with a dressing composed of rice vinegar, sugar, salt, and sweet saké or Sherry wine poured over it. Japanese sandwiches can be made using this vinegared rice. The rice is mixed with any number of fish and vegetable variations, rolled in *nori* (dried laver seaweed), and cut into appropriate lengths. (See NIGIRI-SUSHI) COMPATIBLE BEVERAGES: Beer, saké, tea.

SUZETTE, CRÊPES No one is sure to which Suzette the enamoured French *maître d'hôtel* dedicated his famous *crêpes,* nor are we sure that she was dining with the rakish Prince of Wales at the time. We do know, however, that these dining room showpieces are brought to flaming prominence whenever an impression is to be made. A showpiece for any restaurant, these thin pancakes *(crêpes)* are simmered in a caramel, flavored with Cointreau, lemons, and oranges plus the oils from these fruits, and then flamed with Cognac. The preparation is always sure to fascinate, but as a dessert many consider the dish too heavy and much too sweet to follow a really good meal. (See BLINI, BLINTZ, CRÊPE, PANCAKE)

SVICKOVA PECENE NA SMETANE (Czechoslovakian) "A spicy pot roast" made from a sizable top round or flank steak that is first seared in hot fat and then set on a bed of bacon, onions, carrots, bay leaves, and seasoning in a large saucepan. It is then slowly cooked in a bit of bouillon and wine. The meat is removed, sliced, and kept warm while the sauce is strained, flavored with lemon juice and a bit of red wine, and brought to the boil. Off of the heat, the sauce is enriched with sour cream, and this is served over the roast. Bread dumplings are the usual accompaniment. (See HUSKOVE KNEDLÍKY) COMPATIBLE WINES: A red wine, e.g., Hermitage, Veltliner, Chianti, Cahors, Châteauneuf-du-Pape, Egri Bikaver, Beaujolais, Mercurey, Moulin-à-Vent, Pinot Noir.

SWEDISH MEATBALLS Sweden is known for her fine actresses, the Nobel prize, and her perfectly wonderful meatballs. Lean pork and beef is ground twice. Onions that have been cooked in butter and bread that has been soaked in milk are added to the meat. Finally, mashed potatoes, eggs, and seasonings are worked into the meat mixture, and meatballs are formed. After having been slowly browned in melted butter, the meatballs are removed. Off of the heat, a sauce is made by adding flour, water, sugar, and a bit of heavy cream to the pan juices. The meatballs are then returned to the pan and served with the sauce. COMPATIBLE WINES: A red wine, e.g., Valpolicella, Côtes du Rhône, Zinfandel, Egri Bikaver, Bardolino, Nebbiolo, Petit Sirah, Margaux, Médoc, St. Julien, Mercurey.

SWEETBREADS This word causes much confusion. The term actually refers to two separate glands found in animals: the thymus, found in the throat, and the other, called the "heart" sweetbread, located in the body proper, which is by far the best and most expensive of the two. "Heart" sweetbreads are rounded, whereas the thymus or "throat" sweetbreads are small and elongated in form.

The glands found in the throat of the suckling calf, used to suck milk, are largest when the calf is still feeding from its mother. They are often referred to as "milk glands"; in German they are called *Milken*. When referring to calf's sweetbreads (or veal sweetbreads), they are called *Kalbsmilken* or *Kalbsbrieschen*.

As food, calf's sweetbreads are preferred over all others, although those of the lamb and those of the pig are also eaten. Beef sweetbreads, however, are only prepared in stews together with other meats. Veal or lamb sweetbreads are versatile and satisfying as food but they must be well soaked and thoroughly cleaned of all membranes before cooking. They can be braised in either a white or a brown stock; they are served grilled with various garnishes; they can be poached, fried, or even souffléed. Although rich in protein, sweetbreads are also very delicate and should be used the day they are purchased. (See RIS DE VEAU) COMPATIBLE WINES: Depending upon the sauce and the method of cooking, either a full white Graves or Burgundy is recommended; or a light red, such as a Médoc, Margaux, or Santenay.

SWEET POTATO The sweet potato is native to the southern part of the United States and to the islands of the West Indies. Related to the morning glory, it grows on a vine and develops into an elongated, thick, sweet, and mealy tuberous root with yellow flesh. It is eaten as a vegetable. The sweet potato, often incorrectly called a yam (the yam, of African origin, is much larger), can be boiled and mashed to be used as a stuffing for a turkey, baked whole in hot ashes or in the oven, or even candied. The Chinese consider the sweet potato to be "a poor man's luxury," and as such it is commonly eaten between meals as a snack or a confection. (See CANDIED SWEET POTATO, YAM)

SZARY, SOS POLSKI (Polish) This sauce begins with a *roux*. Chopped blanched almonds, raisins, lemon juice, plain sugar and a caramelized sugar, plus a bit of red Malaga wine are added to the *roux* and simmered together. This thick sauce is served with carp or with fresh or smoked tongue.

SZECHWAN CUISINE (Chinese) Szechwan cooking is enriched and distinguished by the abundant use of many spices, chief of which is *fagara,* a piquant, rather discreet pepper. At first tasting it seems almost bland, but then all discretion is blown away, for suddenly there it is—strong and hot as an African sirocco—and if enough is taken, it can be as numbing to the tongue and mouth as novocaine. However, like garlic, the fire of *fagara* is much subdued when used in cooking, but the taste of the food cooked with it is—again as in the case of garlic—gloriously enhanced.

Naturally, the most characteristic Szechwan dishes are known for their vigor and zest; hot and sour dishes prevail. The Hunan, Chunking, Yunnan, and Chentu cuisines—all of which represent the West—are both influenced by Szechwan cooking and incorporated by the term "Szechwan style of cooking." (*See* CHINESE CUISINE, FAGARA)

SZEKELYGULYAS (Hungarian) Pork goulash with sauerkraut. The sauerkraut is drained and then cooked in bacon fat and wine. The stewing pork is cut into cubes and browned in bacon fat with chopped onions and paprika. Seasoned with salt and pepper, the meat is stewed over very low heat with just a bit of water in a covered pot. Then the pork and the sauerkraut are mixed together, flour and sour cream are poured over the contents of the pot, and the stew is cooked until blended. COMPATIBLE WINES: A white wine, e.g., Sylvaner, Gewürztraminer, Pinot Blanc, Frascati, Steinberger, Riesling, Badacsonyi, Muscat d'Alsace, Vouvray.

TABAKA (Georgian) This fried chicken dish is popular in the Caucasus region of southern Russia. A plump bird is cut along the breastbone but left intact. It is then pressed or beaten quite flat, massaged with salt, pepper, and raw garlic, and fried skin-side-down in hot clarified butter. The chicken is served either with boiled rice or with fried potatoes, garnished with fresh tomatoes and sliced pickled cucumbers. COMPATIBLE WINES: A red wine, e.g., Beaujolais, Fleurie, Valpolicella, Santenay, Petit Sirah, Savigny, Egri Bikaver, Zinfandel, St. Julien, Médoc.

TABASCO (Mexican) A spicy sauce developed in the state of Tabasco from a small, very red, exceedingly hot pepper. The sauce is aged in vats for several years before being sold commercially.

TABLE D'HÔTE (French) Literally, "the table of the host." As used today, this term refers to a bill of fare that offers a whole dinner, from soup to dessert, at a certain price *(prix fixe)*. The direct opposite, the *à la carte* menu, is one from which the diner can make up his own dinner from a variety of dishes. (See MENU)

TABLE MANNERS The dining customs that we observe tell much about us as people. The "correct" manner of chewing one's food with one's mouth closed dates back to primitive man, who believed that if he ate with his mouth open, his soul would leave the body and come under the power of his enemy. Primitive man always used his hand to cover his mouth while masticating food. For centuries, women were not permitted to dine with men. A woman was a sometime thing, used to bear children and tend to them, keep house, and prepare food. Charlemagne was the first to invite women to dine together with men, but only if they did not offend with nauseating body odors or with noxious perfumes. It was also at Charlemagne's table that, for the first time, people no longer ate with their fingers, but began to use the tip of the knife to spear food and bring it to their mouths. Cardinal Richelieu, however, insisted that only rounded knives be used at his dinner table: pointed knives frightened hosts. Breaking wind was frowned upon and guests were asked to leave the table to relieve themselves.

Erasmus of Rotterdam, famous humanist, priest, and scholar, also involved himself with table etiquette. As early as the sixteenth century, he writes, "Children should come to the table clean and in a merry mood; they should not rest their hands on their trenchers, nor drink more than two or three times during the meal (most drank wine diluted with water or thin beer); and they should wipe their lips with a napkin after each drink, especially if a common drinking-cup is used." It was customary for dinner guests to share their large wine goblets.

In Italy, books on table etiquette were already being read in 1265, and the most prestigious work, *The Fifty Courtesies of the Table,* published in 1480, instructed, "Do not stuff both cheeks with food. Do not keep the hand too long on the platter and put it in only when the other has withdrawn his hand from the dish." In 1620, however, when Anne of Austria became queen of France, she was often observed with both hands in the *ragoût,* up to the elbows.

The fork, an Italian invention, was first used in France by Henry III, but it was not in common use until the phlegmatic Louis XVI ascended the throne in 1774. Ironically, it was in large part due to his gargantuan appetite that this Louis was captured and ultimately guillotined.

"To make both ends meet," a phrase that originated during the reign of Henry IV of France, referred to the difficulty encountered while trying to tie the usual large napkin around one's neck. It was necessary, most times, to ask a neighbor to help in ". . . making both ends meet." Today, the phrase still refers to earning enough money to be able to sit down to a full table.

Both Arabs and Orientals, such as the Japanese, dine with their shoes off. But whereas the Orientals eat with chopsticks, the Arabs use neither cutlery nor chopsticks; they pick up their food with the first three fingers of the right hand. When an Arab was one day questioned about this rather bizarre custom, he replied: "I actually know where my hand has been before I sat down to dine with you. I wonder if you know who used your fork last." The Japanese consider their homes to be special places, reserved for family and intimates only. A Japanese would host a business associate quite regally—but in a restaurant, never at home.

It is said that sex and food somehow go together. In New Guinea, however, although couples are forbidden to eat together before they are married, it is perfectly all right for them to have sex.

Occidental habits have raised some eyebrows. For instance, some Americans firmly believe that it is crude and rude to push food onto the fork with the knife, although it is the accepted method of dining all over Europe. Europeans, on the other hand, think the American diner to be quite odd because he cuts his food with the right hand, as all civilized people should, but then he places the knife gingerly on the edge of the dinner plate and quickly switches the fork to the right hand to convey food to his mouth. Finnicky Europeans find it a waste of both motion and time.

When dining, we observe definite rules as to who should sit where and next to whom, as well as who should be served first, second, third, etc. First of all, the eldest should be served, then the ladies, and children always last, unless they are very young. If someone is being feted at the dinner, then, of course, he or she must be served first. As to children, a restaurant is no place for children who cannot behave properly. One can hardly enjoy a meal if at the next table a kid is standing on his chair, in full view of an admiring papa and mama, banging a spoon against the wall while making loud animal noises.

It is an American taboo is to be caught dining alone. This disturbs a lot of people and is considered a definite no-no. At lunchtime it is acceptable, but at dinner time people are considered really strange when observed to be enjoying a fine _pâté,_ followed by a roast duck with appropriate vintage wines, and topping all with a fine aged Cognac or Calvados. It is much like the consternation and dither displayed by married women when they learn that a strikingly handsome forty-year-old man is still a bachelor and somehow manages to enjoy life.

A part of restaurant etiquette that is often abused is that of the dinner party who have no intention of keeping their reservation for dinner, but who have not the common courtesy to voice their regrets by phone and advise the restaurant that they will not be able to come that night. This is gross inconsideration, not only for the restaurateur and the waiters, who keep looking at the empty table, but also for the party of five sitting at the bar for the past forty-five minutes who have come to dine, not to become inebriated while waiting for a table.

Cleaning the nails, applying cosmetics, smoking, and the picking of the teeth should all be avoided while seated at the dinner table. Needless to say, one's toiletry—including the care of the nails, hair, and face—should have been seen to long before one has sat down to dinner. To smoke _during_ dinner shows an utter lack of consideration for one's fellow diners. After dinner, the civilized person would inquire if his smoking will disturb anyone. As a matter of fact, some restaurateurs, proud of their food and their establishment, politely ask their patrons to refrain from smoking altogether.

There are times when that pesky caraway seed or kernel of corn lodged between the teeth can be so distressing that one just has to remove it to maintain his sanity—but never with a fork or knife. If one uses a toothpick, it should be used away from the table or with the mouth covered with a napkin. Speaking of napkins, there is nothing wrong, if necessary for protection, to wear a large napkin under the chin and draped over the dress or tie and vest. Ideally, the napkin should be used discreetly, placed over the lap and brought up to the face only when necessary.

Although one can still hold corn-on-the-cob with the fingers and not be considered a Philistine socially, some consider it better manners to use prongs inserted in each end of the ear of corn. Along the same lines, there are those who will not serve lamb chops, unless dressed in those dainty ruffled paper pantaloons, and who frown when poultry drumsticks and lobster are eaten by hand, although the latter is perfectly permissible, and in the case of broiled lobster, almost requisite.

Since the day man first learned to cook his food and began to live within a community, he has had to contend with problems rising out of his progressively civilized life. The solution came from a culture based on dignity, common courtesy, and politeness. The height of this refinement can be measured to some extent by the way we eat certain foods:

- Artichokes are always eaten with the fingers. When the heart of the artichoke is reached, the fuzzy, inedible part is scraped away and the balance is eaten with knife and fork. An artichoke is usually served with a dip-sauce.

- The soft ends of asparagus should be cut off and eaten with a fork and the stem-ends then picked up and eaten with the fingers.

- Baked potatoes should be halved, the insides buttered and seasoned, and eaten with a knife and fork, and to those who eat the skins as well I award five Michelin stars.

- Soft cheese should be spread with a butter knife or a salad knife, and when a hard cheese is served (perhaps with fruit), it should be eaten with a fork.

- Cherry tomatoes are always eaten with the fingers.

- Fruit should always be served with a sharp fruit knife, a fork, and a finger bowl. Raw apples and pears are quartered, cored, and eaten with the fingers. The skin may be cut away, but that is a crime against nutrition.

- One can hold the pantaloon end of a pork or lamb chop in the left hand and proceed to cut the meat from the bone with the right. But with a chop served without the protective paper tips, a knife and fork is a must.

- Lobster claws should be cracked in the kitchen and nutcrackers should be set next to the dinner plate. A shellfish fork is used to pick the meat from the claws, and the succulent meat from the tail should be removed and cut into bite-size pieces. The red roe and the green fatty part situated within the body of the lobster are choice bits and should not be discarded with the empty shells, for which a large receptacle should be provided. Napkins, finger bowls, and lemon wedges should be provided for the big clean-up after the meal.

- Pizza should be cut into wedges with a knife and be eaten with the fingers.

- Shrimp almost always pose a problem for the uninitiated. If they are tiny enough, they can be eaten whole, in one bite, with a shrimp fork; but if they are jumbo or prawns, they should be cut in two with the edge of the fork.

- Spaghetti should be twirled onto a fork whose tines are pressed tightly against the concave side of a spoon and then be eaten from the fork.

- Toxic or hot food must be removed from the mouth as quickly and unobtrusively as possible. A bad oyster can be deadly and should be spit out into a napkin. If food is scalding hot, one should drink cold water or beer—anything cold that is at hand.

- Hair, bugs, and foreign objects, when discovered in food, should immediately be brought to the attention of the waiter, captain, or manager of the restaurant, but not so loud that the voice can be heard four tables away. The food must be replaced.

Never push the plate away from you when finished eating; just cross the knife and fork on the plate. Do not call out for a waiter, using words such as "Hey you!" or "You there!" Either address him as "waiter," or if it is a woman, as "waitress," or ask for the name at the beginning of the meal. A first name always brings a quick response. When a woman is paying the food check, it is advisable for her to pay the tab at the headwaiter's desk or at some station away from the table to avoid embarrassment. It is much wiser to let the waiter know at the beginning of the meal if "separate checks" are to be given, or better still, have one person get each diner's share of the cost of the cost of the dinner and pay it all on one check.

Do not forget the chef in a restaurant. In commemoration of a great chef and late friend, Albert Stockli, let me cite an example. One evening at the Four Seasons Restaurant, a gentleman of a dinner party of eight asked me for the seemingly impossible: a plate of baked pork-and-beans. The Four Seasons had a rather extensive menu, as it still does, but unfortunately there was no pork-and-beans listed on the menu. In desperation, I entered the kitchen and asked the chef what I could possibly offer the man who had an appetite for a simple plate of baked beans. Chef Stockli told me not to worry. He would take care of him. He did. He sent out for some canned beans and worked the Stockli magic by adding *confit d'oie* (preserved goose) and morsels of well-roasted duck, pork, ham, and sausage, plus a few extra touches. The guest was overjoyed that he had decided to dine with us. He said that he never had pork-and-beans taste like that in all of his life. Of that, I was absolutely sure. When leaving, the diner tipped lavishly and asked if he had missed anyone. I tactfully reminded him of the chef in the hot kitchen and suddenly the man realized that it was Stockli who had gone the extra mile just to satisfy him that evening, and he asked if he might possibly see him. If, indeed, your meal is something very pleasurable, really "out-of-this-world," then by all means let the chef know that you are grateful for the pains he took to make your evening a memorable one. This type of restaurant courtesy occurs all too infrequently. (See CONFIT D'OIE, FORK, LOUIS XIV, PÂTÉ, WAITER SERVICE)

TABLES, DESCENDING Louis XIV, the Sun-King, reigned over France for 68 years, and with his death much about court life and politics had to change. Louis XV, for instance, hated the idea of allowing the public to watch him while he dined, as was the custom with his illustrious predecessor. Instead, he had a special table installed in his royal bedroom; like an elevator, the table descended to the kitchens below to bring up his dinner. What was really wondrous was that for the first time the king of France managed to get hot food. Ere this, by the time the royal servers brought the food up from the kitchens in the cellar, through one draughty corridor after another and up flights and flights of stairs, the soups, roasts, and sauces were lukewarm or even cold.

King Louis' plight of being served food cold is not unfamiliar to the modern-day restaurant diner. Many waiters today, although they do not have flights of stairs or draughty corridors to contend with, still manage to serve their guests cold food. Would it not be poetic justice if one day modern technology would expand on the descending-table idea utilized in 1785 by the Café Méchanique in Paris and thus insure the service of hot food without the use of waiters? At the Café Méchanique, food was ordered by writing a note to the cooks and placing it in the hollowed-out leg of the table, which then descended to the kitchens in the basement. Spectators would line up outside the café, noses pressed against the window panes, fascinated by the steaming hot food rising from the cellars on impeccably set elevator-tables—and not one waiter was to be seen. (See WAITER SERVICE)

TACOS (Mexican) These are *tortillas* fired in the form of a semicircle and served stuffed with various mixtures, such as chopped meat, sausage, or beans. In Mexico, *tacos* might be filled with such exotica as the delicate flesh of the iguana lizard or a finely chopped armadillo. In the mountainous regions of Hidalgo, one might be served the popular *tacos de gusano,* filled with the tasty maguey worm. Maguey is an agave plant, native to Mexico, from which *pulque* is made. (See PULQUE, TORTILLA)

TAFELSPITZ (Viennese) Literally, "the top-of-the-table." This was a great favorite of the Kaiser Franz Josef. It consists of a succulent boiled brisket of beef, served with both apple and horseradish sauces. The brisket of beef is cooked for hours in a beef broth made from beef knuckles, mushrooms, many root vegetables, plus parsley, tomatoes, herbs, and spices: a veritable *sauce Espagnole.* (See ESPAGNOLE, MEERRETTICHSAUCE) COMPATIBLE WINES: A red wine, e.g., Pommard,

Chambertin, Fixin, Talbot, Pétrus, Cabernet Sauvignon, St. Émilion, Châteauneuf-du-Pape.

TAGLIARINI (Italian) See PASTA

TAGLIATELLE (Italian) See FETTUCINE

TAHINA/TAHEEN/TAHENEH (Middle Eastern) This thin paste formed by crushing sesame seeds in a mill is served widely throughout the Middle East as an appetizer with Arab bread or combined with other ingredients in a salad. (See PITA)

TAILLEVENT His real name was Guillaume Tirel, famous in culinary history as the chef to such royalty as Charles IV, Philip VI, and Charles V, and also as one of the first great cooks to leave his recipes for posterity in a volume called, simply, _Le Viandier,_ "the meat cook." Tirel's nickname, Taillevent, probably referred to his rotund figure _(taille),_ which was as round in height as it was in width. Taillevent did not walk, he rolled. However, he brought himself up by his own bootstraps. While he was young, for many years he worked as _commis de cuisine_ (kitchen apprentice) in the kitchens of Queen Jeanne d'Evreaux. Subsequently, he was _esquire de cuisine_ for Philip de Valois, for the Dauphine de Vienne, and for the Duc de Normandie. Later, he was given the post of Esquire of all the Royal Kitchens of France by King Charles VI. This was in the year 1373, about the time that Taillevent completed _Le Viandier._ The book was not printed, however, until 1490.

Taillevent, who is said to have created the _profiteroles_— those fluffy, golden balls made from cream puff paste—fostered the heavy use of spices. And since in those days all food was eaten with a spoon, most of his dishes were ground to a puréed mass before they were served. (See PROFITEROLES)

TAKINOKO (Japanese) Bamboo shoots, a favorite Oriental food. They are eaten whole, shredded, or sliced into rounds. There are two types, the winter variety and the spring variety. The winter, being the tastier of the two, is naturally the more expensive. The flavor of the young bamboo shoot is very much like that of the artichoke. Of the canned shoots available, the unsalted are the finest. The texture of bamboo shoots give a crunchy, delicate contrast to Oriental dishes.

TALAWA (East Indian) Deep-frying.

TALLEYRAND (French) Historically, famous men and women have in time come to be called by only part of their full name—to wit, Napoleon, Voltaire, Escoffier, even Attila and Hitler. Charles-Maurice de Talleyrand-Périgord is another case in point. Talleyrand was considered such a grand connoisseur of fine food that he was dubbed "the first fork in France."

During his service as foreign minister to Napoleon, Talleyrand's first chef was Bouche and his culinary director was a man named Carême—a good start for any connoisseur. Talleyrand took as much care planning a dinner as he did a political ploy or the invasion of Mme. de Flahaut's boudoir. Even if this French statesman had not successfully made his mark as foreign minister under Napoleon and Louis XVII, even if he had not presided over the Concordat of 1801, even if he had not been dubbed Prince of Benevento, Talleyrand would still be famous today as the man who recognized the talents of Antoine Carême while he was still but an apprentice. It was Talleyrand who brought Carême into the dining salons of foreign monarchs whose policies and political secrets were important to France. Carême became a gastronomic James Bond. He attached himself to the Russian kitchens of the Czar Alexander, to the intimate banquet rooms of George IV of England, to the privy chambers of the Court of Vienna, as well as to the sumptuous dining rooms of the Baron de Rothschild, where the politically illustrious gathered to dine and relax and, from time to time, drop bits and pieces of valuable information.

Sauce Talleyrand A chicken *velouté* and a white stock are mixed and reduced. With the addition of heavy cream and Madeira, the sauce is garnished before service with finely chopped vegetables, truffles, and pickled tongue. (See VELOUTÉ)

Garniture Talleyrand A garnish made from elbow macaroni that is cooked and bound with Parmesan cheese and butter and then mixed with chopped goose liver, truffles, and sauce *Périgourdine*. It is served with *veal Talleyrand*. (See PÉRIGUEUX)

Veal Talleyrand Fillets of veal are stuffed with truffles then braised and served with the *garniture Talleyrand* and the braising stock. COMPATIBLE WINES: A red wine, e.g., Barbera, Chianti, Zinfandel, Valpolicella, Médoc.

Consommé Talleyrand A simple chicken consommé garnished with a *julienne* of truffles that have been cooked in sherry wine. (See JULIENNE)

TAMALES (Mexican) Thinking they were gods, the Aztec Indians first presented the *tamale* to the Spanish explorer Hernando Cortez and his men. This is probably the finest tribute that has ever been paid the *tamale*. This Mexican dough, which is far more elaborate than the *tortilla,* is made from *mesa* flour, a coarse cornmeal much like hominy. After the dough has been rolled out to about one-eighth-inch thickness and cut to size, a dollop of the filling of choice is placed in the center of the dough, which is then folded to enclose it. The filling can consist of a single food or a combination of foods such as chicken, ground beef, almonds, coconut, pork, and turkey. The *tamale* is wrapped in layers of corn husks or in the less traditional aluminum foil and steam-cooked on a special rack or colander. (See TORTILLA)

Tamales de Carne de Puerco *Tamales* are filled with diced cooked pork and steamed.

Tamales de Pollo Chickens are boiled, boned, and diced, then mixed to the consistency of a purée with crushed almonds, sesame seeds, chili peppers, onions, garlic, tomatoes, and spices. The *tamales* are then filled and steamed. COMPATIBLE WINES: A red wine, e.g., Rioja, Petit Sirah, Beaujolais, Médoc, Zinfandel, Lambrusco, Savigny.

TAMARIND (East Indian) The leaves, flowers, and pulp that surround the seeds of this Asiatic tree (the name is derived from the Arabic *tamr* and the Indian word *hind*) are great flavor enhancers. The leaves and flowers are used in India, and the pulp is used to make the tart chutneys and relishes so popular in East Indian cooking. Marco Polo claimed that the Indian *tamar-i-hind,* known as "the dried date of India," is so sour and tart that Malabar pirates made their captives swallow a mixture of tamarind and sea water, forcing them to vomit or to pass the entire contents of their stomachs, including any pearls they might have swallowed to prevent their being stolen.

Tamarind and Banana Chutney A sweet-sour chutney made with sugar, raisins, bananas, tamarind, salt, cumin seeds, and cayenne pepper.

Tamarind Juice This brown syrup, made from the pulp of the tamarind, is used much in Italian cooking as a substitute for lemon syrup.

TANDOOR (East Indian) A clay oven that is used to bake chicken, fish, meat, even bread. The top of the oven is open and, traditionally, coal and wood are used as the heat source. In 1947, after the partition of the Indian subcontinent, refugees crossed and recrossed borders freely. One small family from the former northwest frontier, having little more than guts and a *tandoor,* began serving chicken, meats, and fish from a small makeshift shack on the road to Delhi. Their cooking proved to be a great success and today, standing on the site of the former shack, is an air-conditioned restaurant. *Tandoori* cooking is now known the world over, and the *tandoor* has become the *rani* of the Indian kitchen.

Tandoori Chicken Chicken legs and breasts are skinned, slashed diagonally with a sharp blade, and marinated overnight in a highly seasoned mixture colored with an orange food dye. When the coals in the *tandoor* are hot, the chicken pieces are grilled. While grilling, they are basted from time to time with the marinade. When finished, the chicken is a cardinal red. It is usually served with several vegetable dishes, pickled small onions, and white rice or potatoes. For this spicy chicken dinner, beer or tea are recommended instead of wine.

TANSY The rather innocuous name of this powerful herb comes from the Greek *athanasia,* meaning "immortal." Used in ancient times both to embalm the dead and to preserve meats, this member of the aster family has an aromatic odor but a very bitter taste.

Tansy was adopted by the Church as the symbol of the Christian feast of Easter. In the seventeenth century, small yellow custard cakes, called "tansy cakes," were served on Easter Sunday. Tansy was also used as a tonic, taken in the spring to rejuvenate the body after a long, hard winter. During the early Colonial days in America, tansy was hung in food larders and in cupboards to repel insects; it performed the same service when rubbed on a person's skin. It was taken internally as an aid to digestion and to soothe the nerves; externally, it was used to treat infections of the skin and to alleviate the pain of muscular sprains. Today, tansy flavors salad dressings and omelettes and is rumored to be one of the secret ingredients of the famous French liqueur Chartreuse. (See CHARTREUSE)

TAPENADE (French) A type of *hors d'oeuvre* popular in Provence. Hard-boiled eggs are halved, the yolks are removed, and the whites reserved. The yolks are pounded together with finely chopped black olives, chopped anchovy fillets, dry mustard, and capers. When the mixture has the consistency of a pulp, olive oil is added, a bit at a time, until the mixture is as thick and smooth as a *sauce Mayonnaise*. With a pinch of pepper and a dash of brandy added, the purée is ready to be used as a stuffing for the whites. These stuffed whites are served as *tapenades*. (See MAYONNAISE)

TARAMA (Greek) Red caviar from pike.

TARATOR SALAD (Turkish-Bulgarian) This Bulgarian salad originated in Turkey. In Turkey today, the term *tarator* refers to a sauce (see below). The *tarator* salad is made from large green cucumbers that are chopped fine, sprinkled with salt, and left "to sweat" overnight in the refrigerator. The next day, the cucumbers are well drained of the accumulated water, and a mixture of crushed garlic, chopped walnuts, yogurt, and olive oil is added. The salad is always served well-chilled. Another version substitutes fresh mint and dill for the garlic, but much of the tang is then lost. The Spanish make a similar soup and call it *gazpacho*. (See GAZPACHO)

Tarator Sauce This Turkish sauce is made by blending pignoli nuts and water-soaked bread with olive oil, salt, garlic, and vinegar until smooth. The sauce is served with boiled vegetables.

TARDI (East Indian) A drink made from the fermentation of coconut milk and raisins. The popular name for it is "toddy." In northern countries, a "toddy" is a hot drink made with any liquor, hot water, sugar, and lemon and is usually taken to bring on a sweat to cure a cold and break a fever.

TARKA (East Indian) Searing food over high heat in clarified butter. (See GHEE)

TARO This plant of the arum family is cultivated throughout Polynesia and the tropics for its edible, starchy rootstocks. When the taro root is cooked and puréed, it looks very much like dehydrated mashed potatoes. In its natural state its color varies from steel blue to pink to purple. Using taro, the Hawaiians make a pudding called *kulolo*. The leaves of the plant are served as a green vegetable. Like the taro root, the leaves must be cooked for at least an hour to remove a peculiarly irritating taste. (See POI)

TARTARE, SAUCE (French) Cooked egg yolks are pounded to a paste and seasoned with salt and pepper. Olive oil is added until the mixture is *Mayonnaise*-like. Then, with the addition of wine, vinegar, chopped chives, shallots, onions, capers, gherkins, and olives, the sauce is finished, ready to be served with fried fish, brains, and cold cuts.

Tartar Steak or **Steak à la Tartare** This nourishing, spicy, raw meat dish comes from the Tatars, a Sunnite Moslem race. The name is derived from Tata, sometimes called Dada, a fierce fifth-century Mongolian tribe that had a great fondness for horse flesh. This steak dish is made from the fillet of beef or the sirloin, which is finely chopped, seasoned with salt and pepper, and served raw with an egg yolk nestling pertinently on the meat. On the side, chopped onions, capers, anchovies, and chopped parsley are served. This is the basic method of serving this raw steak, although each chef adds his own personal touches, such as Cognac, cream, curry, vinegar, and pickles. COMPATIBLE WINES: A red wine, e.g., Côte Rôtie, Hermitage, Veltliner, Petit Sirah, Bardolino, Dôle, Valpolicella, Zinfandel.

A Tartar Warning! Although a fine steak tartar is a real delicacy and very nutritious, one must be sure that the raw beef used to prepare the dish is absolutely fresh and free from contamination. A potential danger is a disease called beef tapeworm, which afflicts thousands of cows every year. Another organism that can be present in raw beef is a single-celled creature that is responsible for a disease called toxoplasmosis. A wise diner should know his restaurant, and a reputable house will always present the chopped raw beef to the diner before it is made into the steak tartar.

TAS KEBAB (Turkish) Chopped or ground meat that is pressed around a skewer with the hand and then broiled until done. Usually a binder, such as eggs, is used to hold the meat together. COMPATIBLE WINES: A red wine, e.g., Beaujolais, Mâcon, Petit Sirah, Margaux, St. Julien, Chianti, Rioja, Dôle, Egri Bikaver.

TASTE The most subtle flavors are not tasted by the tongue; they are detected by keen olfactory membranes as aromas enter the nasal cavity. The nose is far more sensitive and discerning than the tongue. The aroma of freshly baked bread, for instance, is far better than the first bite; the fragrance of freshly roasted, perking coffee will do more to tantalize the sensory glands than the first cup; and the delirium of frying bacon that wafts into a warm bedroom on a wintry Sunday morning is better remembered than the first forkful that is served with fried eggs a few minutes later.

Taste is developed. The young child, for instance, is conscious of sweet flavors, but then only at the very tip of the tongue. Other flavors only confuse him, and it is only with time and taste experience that the whole tongue, the throat, and the nasal passages become sensitive enough to distinguish the myriad flavors and aromas that are present in the dishes we enjoy. (See UNUSUAL TASTES)

TATAMI (Japanese) A type of bamboo mat, usually about six feet long and three feet wide, used for dining. The *tatami* may also be made from straw.

Tatami Dining The Japanese dines shoeless. He first goes to his knees and then sits with his legs folded under him. The dining mat, the *tatami,* is either directly on the floor or it is raised about a foot above the floor. Often, cushions are available to sit on.

TATLIST, YOGURT (Turkish) A yogurt cake made by first making a batter of yogurt, sugar, eggs, butter, flour, orange and lemon peel, and baking powder. After the cake is baked, a syrup of sugar, water, and lemon juice is poured over the cake, which has been cut into small squares. Placed in the refrigerator overnight, the cake is served the following day, sprinkled with pistachio nuts and topped with strawberries and gobs of whipped cream. (See YOGURT)

TEA The dried leaves of the *camellia sinensis,* a plant native to China, are steeped in hot water to make one of the most popular hot beverages: tea. An old Chinese legend says that the very first cup of tea came into being by accident. In 2700 B.C. an ancient philosopher, teacher, or emperor—accounts vary—was in the process of boiling water and was about to replenish the fire with some dry tea plant branches when some of the dry leaves fell into the pot. He drank the aromatic concoction and was delighted; tea was born.

Chinese Tea or **Ch'a** In the seventh century the Chinese named this beverage *ch'a* to differentiate it from those brewed drinks made from other plants and berries. Chinese teas vary as to quality, the best being a flowery orange pekoe, followed by broken orange pekoe, orange pekoe, pekoe, pekoe *souchong,* and *souchong* in order of grade. There are three sorts of tea: black or fermented; *oolong* or semi-fermented; and the green or unfermented. The finest Chinese green teas are the *Panyon* varieties, and the best *oolong* comes from Formosa, which we call Taiwan. There is another *oolong* from Foochow Province, but it does not have the fine quality of the Formosa type. *Oolong* teas are often blended with gardenia and jasmine petals to produce the "scented" or *Pouchong* teas.

Japanese Tea The Japanese also cherish their tea legends, such as the one concerning the holy Buddhist saint called Daruma, who, it is said, grew the very first tea plant in the sixth century—one century before the Chinese. To keep himself awake while meditating (a five-year meditation), he cut out his eyelids in desperation and cast them to the ground, where a green-leafed plant began to sprout. The leaves from this plant provided him with a brew (tea) that kept him awake to complete his long meditation. This is the Japanese and the Indian version of the birth of tea.

In Japan the tea ceremony, an ancient Chinese ritual, is still practiced today, and the ability to perform it is considered an important qualification for prospective Japanese brides. This tea ceremony sets forth correct procedures for pouring the water and holding the tea bowl, with emphasis placed on simplicity and harmony. The tea ceremony uses a special powdered green tea called *matcha,* which when whipped in hot water with a ceremonial bamboo whisk ultimately tastes rather bitter but refreshing. The finest green tea from Japan is called *mori.*

East Indian Tea   In spite of China's reluctance to share its secrets of tea production, tea plant seeds were smuggled into India by Chinese defectors. With the passing of time, tea planters came to learn that teas indigenous to India fared better than the Chinese varieties, and they therefore concentrated on growing native Indian tea. Today, Indian tea far outsells the Chinese variety, although India's tea crop is but half that of the Chinese. The Dutch brought tea from the Orient to Europe in the seventeenth century, and from Holland tea was introduced to England, where it soon ousted coffee as that country's most popular beverage.

English Tea   The English love their tea, respect and honor it with ritual brewing. First the ritual demands that the teapot be pre-warmed. Then allowing one teaspoon of black tea for each cup plus one for the pot, boiling water is poured over the tea leaves, which are allowed to steep for ten to fifteen minutes. A "tea cozy" is a must to cover the pot. Even the English soldier, when fatigued, preferred his "char" (tea) to any alcoholic pick-me-up. To cite an incident of the English "frenzy" for a four-o'clock tea, while fighting WWII in Italy, I happened to be driving a jeep through the high Appenines, and as I was rounding a curve on a steep incline, I was suddenly confronted with a huge English lorry parked right in the center of the road. My careening jeep screeched to a halt just before it was about to plunge down a precipitous incline. As I turned to give vent to my rage, I saw three "Tommies," seated coolly on the running board of the lorry, raise their cups to me and ask, almost in unison: "'ow about a bit o' tea, mate?" Black tea is usually drunk with milk and sugar, but it may also be taken neat with just lemon. Iced tea is a hot-weather favorite.

The United States   In America, nearly 90 percent of all tea consumed is the black tea imported from India or Ceylon. Black tea is stronger than other teas and goes under the following names: *Assam, Cachar, Darjeeling, Dijoya, Dooar, Ichang, Java, Madras, Nuwara, Sumatra,* and *Travancore.*

Green tea is usually served with highly flavored and fried food and also acts as an aid to digestion. It is a more effective stimulant than black tea. Black tea goes well with all seafood.

All in all, tea is considered to be one of the most satisfying and important beverages in the world. So important, in fact, that certain irate citizens one day in Boston Harbor made such a potent brew of an overtaxed British tea that the sparks from it still enkindle the flames of liberty in the hearts and minds of people all over the world; we call it America.

Tea Caddy (English) A corruption of the Indian word *kati,* a measure of weight, used by the English to describe a container for tea. Tea caddies are often divided into two sections, one for the green or Chinese tea, and the other for the black tea of India. It is also called a canister.

TEA SHERBET (French) A concoction prepared by making an infusion of green tea with the essence of bergamot (the oil obtained from the pear-shaped orange, the bergamot). Generous amounts of sugar and whipped cream are added to each portion. They are then frozen.

TEJFÖLÖS KAPOSZTA (Hungarian) Cabbage in sour cream flavored with dill. Shredded cabbage is cooked in boiling salted water with caraway seeds. The cabbage is removed when tender, and a *roux* is made using a bit of the cooking broth. Then, bit by bit, more of the cooking stock is added until a thin sauce develops. Sour cream is added, then the cabbage is added as well and all is reheated and served. (See ROUX)

TEL KADAYIF (Turkish) An extremely thin pastry dough that has been partially cooked and dried. Delicious sweet rolls can be made from this *kadayif* pastry. Filled with nuts, butter, sugar, and cinnamon and served topped with a lemon syrup, these pastries look like stuffed shredded wheat because they are made in long thin strands resembling *spaghetti.* The Greeks also have a word for it, *kataifi.* (See PHYLLO, STRUDEL)

TEMPURA (Japanese) This popular method of preparing deep-fried foods was introduced to the Orient by Saint Francis Xavier in the sixteenth century. He and his retinue of monks subsisted on these fritters while observing the Church's fast days, when eating meat was strictly forbidden. To prepare *tempura,* raw foods—shrimp, lobster, flounder, scallops, carrots, green peppers, string beans—are all cut up then dipped in a batter made of egg yolks, flour, oil, and water. They are then dropped into boiling oil until brown. A *tempura* sauce—a mixture of fish stock, soy sauce, saké, sugar, grated white radish, and powdered ginger—is served separately. COMPATIBLE BEVERAGES: Saké, tea, or a rosé wine.

Ice Cream Tempura If an enterprising chef can successfully cover ice cream with a meringue, bake it, flame it, and serve it as a flaming baked Alaska, it is not so farfetched an idea to deep-fry an ice cream ball. Batter-dipped, deep-fried ice cream balls are made by first freezing balls of ice cream, then rolling them in a mixture of cookie crumbs, cinnamon, and sugar, and then refreezing the balls until ready to serve. The frozen ice cream balls are deep-fried in hot oil for a minute and served topped with honey or fruit preserves and a dollop of freshly whipped _crème Chantilly._ Another method is to douse the fried ice cream ball with warm Grand Marnier and flame it at the table. (See ALASKA, CHANTILLY)

TENDRON (French) Literally, "gristle." This term refers to a cheap cut of veal or lamb, one that must be braised or stewed. The meat is usually cut from the section extending from the end of the rib to the breastbone or the shoulder of the animal.

TERBIYE One of Turkey's principal sauces, this is simply a mixture of fresh lemon juice and water. It is used to flavor soups, stews, and meat dishes. A variation, served with fish dishes and with meat _dolmas,_ uses chicken or meat stock instead of water. (See DOLMAS)

TERIYAKI (Japanese) A general term referring to a method of frying, grilling, or baking pieces of beef, poultry, or seafood that have been first marinated and then coated with a special _teriyaki_ sauce.

Beef Teriyaki After marinating small fillets of beef in _teriyaki_ sauce (see below), the steaks are either broiled (turning and recoating with the marinade), fried (topped with the marinade), or cubed and grilled on skewers with alternate pieces of pineapple and mushrooms (basted with the marinade). Dishes are served accompanied with a dip-sauce made from the marinade mixed with cornstarch. COMPATIBLE BEVERAGES: Beer, tea, rosé wine, or sparkling Burgundy.

Chicken Teriyaki Chicken breasts are marinated in _teriyaki_ sauce (see below), then either baked in the oven or, with the chicken cut into strips, stir-fried in a wok. COMPATIBLE BEVERAGES: The same as for the beef _teriyaki._

Teriyaki Sauce A mixture of sherry wine, soy sauce, sugar, ginger root, garlic, and lemon zest used as a marinade, coating, and a basting sauce for chicken, beef, and seafood.

TERRINE See PÂTÉ

TERRINE PAYSANNE (French) Literally a "peasant's pot," this predecessor of today's _boeuf Bourguignonne_ was the creation of Manon, a famous French cook and writer of the eighteenth century. The dish is made by first sautéing chopped shallots and cubed pieces of well-seasoned beef in bacon fat. The meat, together with shallots, bay leaves, thyme, garlic, parsley, and chopped celery, are placed in a baking casserole, covered with a mixture of red wine, brandy, and beef stock, and baked covered until the meat is fork-tender. COMPATIBLE WINES: A red wine, e.g., Pommard, Chambertin, Pinot Noir, Beaune, Mercurey, Barolo, Chianti, Dôle, Fixin.

TETRAZZINI, CHICKEN (Italian) A chicken preparation named in honor of the great Italian diva, Mme. Luisa Tetrazzini. She inspired a chef to boil a cut-up chicken, shred the meat, and add to it half the quantity of a rich chicken *velouté*. The other half of the *velouté* is added to cooked spaghetti and sautéed mushrooms. The shredded chicken is placed in the middle of the spaghetti-mushroom mixture, sprinkled liberally with grated Parmesan cheese, and baked in the oven until the chicken is brown and tender. COMPATIBLE WINES: A red wine, e.g., Margaux, Médoc, Valpolicella, Zinfandel, St. Julien, St. Émilion.

Note: There are several other dishes named *Tetrazzini*—one made with turkey, another with seafood. However, all have the same *Tetrazzini* base: a type of *pasta* mixed with cream and topped with grated cheese.

THAI CUISINE Thailand has a dual culinary heritage. Greatly influenced by China and India, the food of Thailand is cut into bite-size pieces and always served highly spiced with Indian-inspired curries. Often, all the dishes of a meal, including soups, are placed on the table at the same time. The Thai have a passion for coriander, and they sprinkle it freely over almost every dish they serve. Their favorite sauce, found on every table, is a creamy-textured concoction called *nam prik,* which is made from dried shrimp, garlic, and hot chilies. But the people of Thailand pride themselves on presenting their food in the most beautiful and attractive ways possible: their chefs will carve a decorative boat out of a melon, for example, and fill it with glistening marinated spheres of its own sweet flesh. Such food sculptures abound. Influenced early by Arab traders as well as the Chinese, the Indians, and the Polynesians, Thai cooking is an amalgam of a great many cuisines.

THERMIDOR, LOBSTER (French) This lobster dish was created by the owner of Chez Maire, a Parisian restaurant, in honor of the opening of a play entitled *Thermidor*. The play dealt with the fall of Robespierre and the subsequent Revolution of Thermidor (during the time of the French Revolution, the eleventh month of the Republican Calendar—July 19 to August 19—was called *Thermidor*). To prepare the dish, the meat of a lobster is cooked and chopped and then bound with a mixture of heavy cream, eggs, white wine, and cheese and flavored with shallots, tarragon, mustard, cayenne pepper, and grated Parmesan cheese. Replaced in the shell, it is glazed under the broiler. COMPATIBLE WINES: A white wine, e.g., Muscadet, Chablis, Pouilly-Fumé, Soave, Meursault, Pinot Chardonnay, Verdicchio, Debro.

THOUSAND-YEAR-OLD EGGS (Chinese) The name of this exotic type of egg is an exaggeration: the eggs are rarely more than two months old. The Chinese specially prepare these duck eggs by compacting them in a mass of ashes, tea, salt, and lime. Then, wrapped in rice husks, they are buried to allow the eggs to absorb the flavorings. Of course, the eggs are buried raw, but when at last they are removed from the earth and peeled, the eggs seem as solid as the flesh of an avocado pear. The exterior is blue-black, but the yolk has turned shades of green and blue and has a somewhat fishy taste. The eggs are served as an appetizer with pickled onions and ginger. The Chinese call them *pei dan.*

THÜRINGER (German) A sausage. (See CERVELAT)

THYME Any species of the genus *Thymus,* an aromatic herb or shrubby plant of the mint family. Lexicographers believe *Thymus* to be derived from an ancient Greek word meaning "to fumigate." As it was thought to be strongly antiseptic, thyme was often used in Greek and Roman homes to purify the air. Ancient Romans also used thyme as a stimulant whenever they felt depressed. How natural then for cooks to use thyme to perk up the taste of their dishes.

Of the many types of thyme, *Thymus vulgaris* is the most common and is widely used in soups and stews as a seasoning. It also yields a medicinal oil, called thymol, which was utilized as a battlefield antiseptic during World War I. The wild thyme, *Thymus serpyllum,* to which Shakespeare's Oberon makes poetic reference in the *Midsummer Night's Dream,* is the same Old World evergreen, naturalized in North America and popularly grown as ground cover. The plant is small and bushy, having dark green leaves and purple flowers.

In the kitchens of the world, dried thyme has nearly become a universal seasoning, used as freely as salt to enhance the taste of almost any food. There are many varieties of thyme (lemon, caraway, orange), and all have different mint-tinged flavors. The lemon thyme goes particularly well with fish dishes. The other varieties are used to complement meat, poultry, and vegetable dishes.

TIGANITES (Greek) These pastry puffs are a true delight. A mixture of water, butter, salt, and sugar is brought to a boil; then, with the addition of flour and baking soda and rum or Curaçao, the batter is stirred vigorously. Once removed from the heat, eggs are added, one at a time, and blended. The paste is dropped a teaspoon at a time into hot oil and cooked until brown on all sides. The puffs are served dusted liberally with vanilla-flavored powdered sugar.

TIISTAIKEITTO (Finnish) "Tuesday soup." The practical Finn bakes a beautiful ham on Sunday; he eats what is left over on Monday; and then, using the ham bone and whatever else is left, he cooks a thick, hearty soup on Tuesday. Ham bones and pork hocks are cooked for several hours. Barley is added, plus rutabaga, carrots, parsnips, potatoes, and celery seeds, and the ingredients are allowed to cook further. The ham bone is removed, and the meat from the pork hocks is cut up into small pieces and returned to the soup. A thickening paste of milk and flour is added with pepper and parsley, and the soup is ready to be served.

TIKKA MURGH (East Indian) A boneless chicken is first marinated for a day in a pickling mixture composed of garlic, ginger, lemon juice, salt, and pepper. It is then patted dry and barbecued over charcoal. A hot sauce is served separately. (See MURGHI, MUSSALLAM) COMPATIBLE BEVERAGES: Beer, ale, tea, cider.

TIL RICE This type of rice gives one the taste of ancient India. Sesame *(til)* rice is made by first toasting the sesame seeds in a hot dry skillet until golden brown. Then, with the pan off of the heat, salt and hot red chili peppers are stirred into the toasted seeds, and the whole lot is pulverized in a blender. When ready to serve, the ground spices are gently folded into hot boiled rice. The dish is usually complemented with melted butter and a side dish of unflavored yogurt. COMPATIBLE BEVERAGES: Beer, ale, saké.

TIMBALE (French) The name derives from the Arabic *atabal,* sometimes spelled *thabal,* meaning "small drum." In culinary parlance, the word is used to refer to a round mold made from metal or china or to any dish that is cooked or served in such a mold. Originally, the term described a food or mixture of foods cooked or served in a pastry crust: a *soufflé* or custard might fill a mold composed of baked *brioche-* or *Génoise*-type dough. (See BRIOCHE, GÉNOISE)

Timbale à la Parisienne After baking a *brioche* in a *Charlotte* mold, the inside is removed, leaving a shell of *brioche*. This is coated on the outside with apricot preserves, then it is filled with chopped pears, apples, and apricots that have been precooked in a vanilla syrup to which diced pineapple and raisins have been added. (See BRIOCHE, DOMINICAINE)

TINGA (Mexican) This stew, which originated in the Puebla, a mountainous agricultural region, is prepared of precooked meats and *chorizos,* cooked together with chopped onions, garlic, tomatoes, herbs, and most important, with the extremely hot *chipotl* chili. (See CHILI, CHORIZO) COMPATIBLE BEVERAGES: Nothing but a beer would go with this hot stew.

TIROPETES (Greek) Tiny triangles of *phyllo* pastry filled with a cheese and spinach mixture. These pastries, also known generally as *bourekia,* are served as an appetizer.

TKEMALI This sauce comes from the Soviet Republic of Georgia, situated on the Black Sea. To make the sauce, sour plums are cooked in boiling water. After draining the liquid and pitting the plums, ground garlic is added and blended until the mixture has the consistency of sour cream. Chopped basil, coriander, salt, and cayenne pepper are added, and the mixture is brought to the boil then allowed to cool. The sauce is served with *shashlik* or with *tabaka* (a boned, pressed, fried chicken). (See SHASHLIK, TABAKA)

TOFU (Japanese) Soybean curd. Extensively used in Japanese cooking, protein-rich *tofu* has a firm, custard-like texture. It is served as a soup garnish and with scrambled eggs; dusted with cornstarch, it may be deep-fried. Although _tofu_ has little flavor of its own, it sponges up other flavors quite readily. It can be sautéed, boiled, or broiled, and even made into a cheeseless cheesecake. (See ABURAGE, DENGAKU, KOYATOFU)

TOMATE CONCASSÉE (French) See CONCASSER

TOMATILLOS These small husk-covered green vegetables grow on low-hanging vines in Mexico. They look as if they might be related to the green cherry tomato, but they taste more like a sour plum, and the skin is so coarse that it must be removed before eating. _Tomatillos_ are most often an ingredient in Mexico's famous hot chili sauces.

TOMATO The tomato was once called the "love apple." Legend tells us that when Sir Walter Raleigh first presented the unusual tomato to Queen Elizabeth and she asked what it was, Raleigh's romantic reply was, "It is an apple of love, my Queen." The story could very well be true, for at that time the tomato was rumored to be as wicked an aphrodisiac as the cacao bean or the vanilla pod, all of which came from the New World. As far as accepting the tomato, the French were as wary and superstitious as the English, and it was not until the beautiful and charming Empress Eugénie introduced Spanish tomato dishes to France that the tomato became a part of the French cuisine.

Tomato Fondue (French) A garnish made by cooking chopped onions in butter and oil, then adding seeded and chopped tomatoes, salt, pepper, and a clove of garlic. With the addition of chopped parsley, this garnish is served hot with eggs, artichoke hearts, eggplant, and mushrooms. Chilled, it is used with cold _hors d'oeuvre_ and in the preparation of various sauces. (See ORIENTALE)

Tomato Sauce When the Spaniards conquered Mexico, they brought not only gold with them to Spain, but the tomato as well. This French sauce, adopted from the Italians and the Spanish, gives the final coup to most brown sauces and stews. The sauce is made by first cooking bacon and then adding tomatoes, onions, carrots, parsley, and garlic. This is dusted with flour and cooked together with a ham knuckle. To serve, the sauce is passed through a fine sieve and enriched with sweet butter. (See POMODORO SALSA)

Tomatoes, Stuffed The French, once they finally accepted the tomato as a delicious, mouthwatering vegetable, proceeded with their innovative minds to devise a tasty use for it. Here, firm, nearly ripe tomatoes have their centers removed and then become receptacles for various delicious stuffings.

> _à la Florentine:_ Of course, _Florentine_ means that spinach is present, and here it is chopped very fine and mixed with minced cooked chicken, chopped sautéed mushrooms, and seasonings. A light _sauce Mayonnaise_ serves as a binder. The tomatoes are stuffed with the mixture, then they are topped with grated Parmesan cheese and baked. (See MAYONNAISE)

à la Sicilienne: Here the tomatoes are stuffed with chopped sautéed onions, ground baked ham, basil, thyme, plus a dash of Madeira wine. These ingredients, bound with a light *sauce Mayonnaise,* are stuffed into the tomatoes, topped with breadcrumbs, and baked. (See MAYONNAISE)

à la Provençale: Provençale means that garlic is present. Here, the garlic is crushed and mixed with chopped sautéed mushrooms, a *panade,* nutmeg, salt, and pepper. The ingredients, are stuffed into the tomatoes, which are then topped with breadcrumbs, sprinkled with olive oil, and baked. These dishes are suitable as a first course or a light luncheon or as the accompaniment to the main course of a meal. (See PANADE)

TONNO (Italian) A term for "tuna," but when the fish is used as an addition to a dish or as part of a garnish, the term changes to *tonnato,* as when served with veal in the *tonnato vitello.* (See VITELLO)

Tonno alla Grilia Grilled tuna fish. The fish is cut into steaks, rubbed with oil, lightly seasoned, and rolled in a mixture of breadcrumbs, garlic, parsley, and mint. Then, topped with melted butter mixed with oil, the fish steaks are broiled until done. They should be served immediately with slices of fresh lemon. COMPATIBLE WINES: A white wine, e.g., Orvieto, Verdicchio, Soave, Frascati, Aigle, Pinot Chardonnay, Rüdesheim, Dézaley, Anjou, Gewürztraminer.

TOPFEN (German) When used as a prefix, this signifies that the dish in question contains cottage cheese.

Topfenknödel Dumplings made from cottage cheese, butter, eggs, flour, and fresh breadcrumbs. The mixture is rolled into balls and cooked in boiling salted water. After draining, the dumplings are browned in fresh butter. They can be served as a side dish or as a garnish in a soup. Sweet *Topfenknödel* is a variation made with cream cheese that is mixed with softened butter, sugar, eggs, and seedless raisins. Spoonfuls are placed in the center of small paper-thin rounds of dough, which are then folded and sealed. These are cooked in boiling water until tender. The dumplings are drained, dipped in melted butter, rolled in breadcrumbs, and sautéed in butter until golden brown. They are served with a sprinkling of cinnamon and sugar, with warm fruit preserves on the side.

Topfenpalatschinken (Austrian) Pancakes filled with a mixture of cottage cheese or cream cheese with lemon rind, vanilla, egg yolks, and raisins. The filled pancakes are rolled, topped with sour cream, and browned under the broiler. These pancakes can also be tiered, with the cheese mixture layered between each pancake, and then browned in the oven.

TOQUE BLANCHE, LA (French) The tall white hat worn by chefs the world over. Patterned after the priest's black one, the hat was originally worn by cooks in ancient Byzantine monasteries. In the Middle Ages, in order to escape from tyrannical overlords, many fine cooks hid in Greek Orthodox monasteries. The good monks never had it so good and they knew it; but to separate the goats from the sheep as it were, the cooks wore tall white hats instead of the ordinary black ones. Today, chefs commemorate these good men by wearing, as a proud badge of their office, their prototype of "the white plume," *la toque blanche*. Another story of the hat's mysterious origin claims that in 1950 B.C. the king of ancient Assyria gave his private cook the right to wear a headpiece similar to his own as material proof of his trust in him. Most kings feared being poisoned.

TORI TERIYAKI This is the Japanese answer to barbecued chicken. Boned chicken breasts and legs are dipped in a *teriyaki* sauce and then broiled, either over a charcoal grill (a hibachi) or in the oven. The chicken is basted continually with the sauce. When crisp and brown, the chicken is cut up into bite-size pieces and served covered with a *teriyaki* glaze composed of the sauce boiled down with sugar, water, and cornstarch. (See TERIYAKI SAUCE) COMPATIBLE BEVERAGES: Tea, Sauterne, saké, beer.

TORRONE (Italian) From the Latin word *torrere,* meaning "to toast" or "to roast." The term refers to a nougat made with honey, almonds, candied orange peel, grated lemon rind, egg whites, and sugar. A chocolate-flavored variation uses only hazelnuts, sugar, honey, and egg whites. Italians are famous for their confectionery.

TORT CU CREMA DE CASTANE (Rumanian) A rich chocolate cake. Of all peoples of the Balkans—including the amazing Greeks, Yugoslavians, Bulgarians, and the fiery Turks—the Rumanians are reputed to have the sweetest tooth. Count Dracula's sanguinary preference for all those "sweet young things" should be proof enough of that. However, more substantial proof is provided when we sink our teeth into this rich cake made from egg whites, sugar, cocoa, jam, and walnuts. The baked cake is cut in half and filled with a purée of chestnuts and butter mixed with sugar syrup, chocolate, and vanilla; egg yolks bind the filling together. Some of the filling is spread over the top of the cake. (See BENIZA)

TORTE (German) This is a difficult term to pin down with but one definition because it applies to many different types of cakes, as well as filled pies. In Germany, the word *Torte* immediately brings to mind a rich cake, at times layered with a filling, often covered with an icing, and many times served with whipped cream. (See LINZERTORTE, SACHERTORTE)

TORTELLINI (Italian) *Pasta* rings stuffed with a mixture of finely-chopped cooked chicken breasts, grated Parmesan cheese, egg yolks, grated lemon peel, nutmeg, salt, and pepper. The filled *pasta* rounds are then folded and secured and cooked in boiling salted water. They are then drained and served with a *sauce Bolognese*. In Yiddish these are called *kreplach;* in Russian, *pirozhki;* in most parts of Italy, they are called *ravioli;* but in Florence, Pisa, and Sienna—anywhere in Toscana—they are always called *tortellini.* (See BOLOGNESE, KREPLACH, PASTA, PIROG/PIROZHKI, RAVIOLI) COMPATIBLE WINES: A red wine, e.g., Valpolicella, Beaujolais, Zinfandel, Médoc, Margaux, Egri Bikaver.

TORTILLA (Spanish) An omelette. It can be plain or cooked together with bits of meat, vegetables, or seafood mixed in with the eggs. A real Spanish *tortilla (tortilla Espagnola)* should always contain loads of chopped onions and potatoes. In Mexico, however, a *tortilla* is made from *mesa* flour, salt, shortening, and warm water—all kneaded into a dough, flattened, and then cut into rounds. These rounds are cooked on both sides on a hot ungreased griddle until they are delicately browned. *Tortillas* are used instead of rolls and bread. They are necessary in the preparation of *enchiladas, tacos,* and *burritos.* (See BURRITOS, ENCHILADAS, MESA, TACOS, TOSTADAS)

TOSTADS (Mexican) *Tortillas* that are crisply fried to a golden brown in oil and then spread with various combinations of meats, poultry, or fish together with sauces, vegetables, and chilies. (See BURRITOS, ENCHILADAS, TACOS, TORTILLA)

TOSTONES DE PLATANO (Spanish) Slices of green plantains which are partly fried then crushed, flattened, and fried again on both sides until crisp and brown. They are popular in the Spanish-speaking islands of the West Indies, where they complement both meat and fish dishes. (See PLANTAINS)

TOURNEDOS Although these steaks were originally a Florentine specialty, they were introduced to the French court by Catherine de Médicis, and they have become French by adoption. *Tournedos* are thick slices of choice meat from the center of the whole fillet of beef. They are fried quickly (*tourne le dos,* "turn-the-back" and they are done) in a very hot pan in a blend of olive oil and butter or grilled. They are usually served on croutons and can be complemented with as many sauces and garnishes as Escoffier had at his fingertips: *Béarnaise, Bordelaise, Périgourdine, Rossini,* etc. (See BÉARNAISE, BORDELAISE, PÉRIGOURDINE, ROSSINI) COMPATIBLE WINES: A red wine, e.g., Chambertin, Beaune, Romanée-Conti, La Tâche, Fixin, Échézeaux, Richebourg, Haut Brion, Lafite Rothschild, Mouton Rothschild, Pinot Noir, Dôle, Aloxe-Corton.

TOURTIÈRE (French) From Landes, the Basque country of France, comes this tart made from thin sheets of pastry. The sheets are brushed with clarified butter, then filled with such fruits as thinly sliced pears and apples or chopped soaked prunes, and then baked until golden brown. This tart is also called a _croustade_. (See CROUSTADE, PHYLLO)

TOUTE-ÉPICE (French) See ALLSPICE

TRAHANA (Greek) A noodle made from a mixture of flour and yogurt and served in soups.

TREACLE (English) A term for molasses. Treacle is used to give a special sweetness and color to fruitcakes and gingerbread and to glaze baked hams and apples. (See MOLASSES)

TREE EARS See MU-ER

TRENCHERMAN A hearty eater. In medieval times, a "trencher"—a hard square of thick bread—was used as a plate from which knights ate their cuts of venison and beef. After the great banquets, the trenchers, soggy with the drippings from the roasted meats, were given to the poor of the community.

TRIPE Although in ordinary conversation "tripe" is used derogatorily to refer to something worthless or offensive, in culinary parlance it describes a highly valued food, specifically a part of the third stomach of the cow. Shakespeare tantalized the starving shrew, Katherine, by offering her tripe in iambic pentameter: "How say you to a fine tripe, finely broiled?"

Tripe à la Mode de Caen If this Norman city (Caen) depended for its culinary fame solely on this method of cooking tripe, that fame would be deserved. After the tripe is washed and carefully cleaned, it is cut into short strips. The bottom of a heavy pot is lined with thick slices of salt pork. Then carrots, sliced onions, a _bouquet garni_, leeks, minced celery, and chopped garlic plus the strips of tripe and a few ox feet are placed over the pork. Well seasoned with herbs, spices, salt, and pepper and covered with beef stock, cider, white wine, and apple brandy (Calvados), the pot is sealed with a rope of dough. Thus sealed, the tripe is baked for hours. Usually served in individual bowls, the tripe is complemented with boiled potatoes.

Cooked tripe may be sliced and then simmered in a _sauce poulette_, a _sauce piquante_, or a tomato sauce. Whenever tripe is served chilled as a salad, a _sauce ravigote_ or _vinaigrette_ is used as a dressing. (See PHILADELPHIA PEPPER POT, PIQUANTE, POULETTE, RAVIGOTE, TOMATO, VINAIGRETTE) COMPATIBLE WINES: A white wine, e.g., Sylvaner, Vouvray, Sauvignon Blanc, Orvieto, Château Olivier, Traminer, Szamorodni, Gewürztraminer, Hermitage Blanc, Frascati, Lacrima Christi.

TROCKENBEERENAUSLESE (German) A descriptive term for a rare white wine produced by a rather unique method of grape selection. By using a needle, only the almost-completely-dried-out grapes _(Trocken-Beeren-Auslese)_, those wrinkled grapes that have some-how managed to hang onto the vine until the very late fall of the year, only those are carefully picked. These grapes are afflicted with what is known in wine-growing districts as the "noble rot," *Edelfäule* in German. This is a kind of mold that drains most of the moisture from the grapes, leaving them very sweet indeed. The luscious, costly wine produced from these grapes is naturally not a dinner wine but one whose exquisiteness must be savored by drinking it alone, or if with a dessert, then something very special. (See AUSLESE, BEERENAUSLESE, EISWEIN, KABINETT, SPÄTLESE)

TRUFFLES Truffles were known to ancient Rome, but no one seemed to know exactly what they were or how to use them. Even medieval Baghdad relished their goodness; but in the land of the epicure, France, the natives did not know of their existence until the fourteenth century. They then extracted the truffles from a vinegar marinade, soaked them in hot water, and served the delicacy with mounds of sweet butter, like the steaming baked potato which followed much later.

The truffle is a fungus that has neither root, stem, nor seed and grows near to the roots of oak and chestnut trees in the south of France. There, it is snouted out of the ground by specially trained pigs and dogs. Truffles have also been found in the Kalahari Dessert in Botswana. The much-esteemed though less-expensive white truffle is found in Italy. Truffles cannot be cultivated, but their propagation can be stimulated by spreading soil taken from known truffle beds around the trunks of oak and chestnut trees—and then one must wait and pray. If patience and prayers work together with rain and sunlight, the truffles may appear in about five years' time, but they won't be ripe until ten years later.

This increasingly rare fungus, growing about a foot below its more common relative, the mushroom, has an aroma and taste that crowns it the prince of what is rare and delicate in the realm of food. The great French gourmet and author Brillat-Savarin went one step further, alleging that the black truffle possesses a great aphrodisiac power, but this has never been proved, not even by Louis XIV, who tried everything. Truffles come from Périgord in France, but tradition rarely allows their use by farmers of the region. They know what a truffle can do for a meal, but they hardly ever eat one.

Truffle Périgueux in Pastry This delicacy consists of a whole fresh truffle that is first marinated in Madeira wine, then covered with goose liver, wrapped in slices of *prosciutto* ham, and baked in a pastry dough for a half-hour. A sauce *Périgueux* is served separately. The truffle can also be served baked in clay. (See FOIE GRAS, PROSCIUTTO)

Truffles "sous le Cendre" "Truffles cooked in ashes," a dish that graced the highly imaginative menu of the Forum of the Twelve Caesars, once a great New York restaurant. Although this costly dish is rarely served today, it is a great delicacy. To prepare it, the truffles are cleaned, well seasoned with salt and pepper and a dash of Cognac, entirely enveloped in pastry, then baked in the oven. They are presented to the diner in the pastry. When the pastry is opened, the aroma is an almost sinfully pleasurable experience. COMPATIBLE WINES: A red wine, e.g., Haut Brion, Calon-Ségur, Kirwan, Talbot, Pomerol, Gruaud-Larose.

TSNI TCHAO SHRIMP PANCAKES (Chinese) The preparation begins by making a forcemeat of minced shrimp, chopped carrots, scallions, mushrooms, salt pork, coriander seeds, fennel, anise, cloves, cinnamon, salt, and pepper—all ground together and blended. This forcemeat is rolled into pancakes made from white rice. The stuffed pancakes are first baked in the oven and then deep-fried and drained. They are served with fried parsley or fried onions rings. COMPATIBLE BEVERAGES: Tea, beer, rosé wine, saké.

TSUKEMONO (Japanese) The general term for the pickle, which is served with most Japanese meals. The simplest pickles are made with salt brine; others use a more complicated marinade composed of various proportions of _miso,_ mustard, and soy sauce. (See MISO)

TSUNA HAMMU (Japanese) Sausages made from smoked, lean tuna fish.

TUBETTINI (Italian) See PASTA

TUI-HSIA (Chinese) See HSIA

TUNKE (German) A sauce or gravy.

TURMERIC This East Indian herb belongs to the ginger family. Its aromatic root stalk is used as a base for curries, as a yellow dye, and as a medicine. It is also one of the important ingredients in pickling mixtures. The turmeric root resembles the ginger root, but it is thinner and has a reddish color. It has, in fact, become an inexpensive substitute for saffron (rice can be colored saffron-yellow when boiled with it). Turmeric, with its slightly bitter and faintly resinous flavor, is one of the three basic spices used to flavor Oriental cooking, the other two being coriander and cumin. It is also used to flavor salad dressings, chutneys, mustards, kedgerees, and sweetmeats. (See KEDGEREE)

TURQUE, BEURRECK À LA (French) See BÖREKS

TUTTI-FRUTTI (Italian) A vanilla and pistachio ice cream that is mixed with water-ice and laced with various candied fruits, such as cherries, oranges, and angelica. It is served with a _sauce maraschino._ (See ICE CREAM, MARASCHINO, SORBET)

TWICE-COOKED MEAT (Chinese) This dish comes from the Szechwan Province, where strongly flavored foods are preferred. Here, a loin of pork is simmered for an hour. The bones are then removed and cooked separately to make a broth. After the meat has cooled, it is sliced and fried in hot lard with crushed garlic, soy jam (much like a thick brown bean sauce), scallions, and ginger. It is finished, Szechwan-style, with the addition of hot pepper and sugar. COMPATIBLE BEVERAGES: Beer, ale, tea, cider.

TYROLEAN CALF'S LIVER (Austrian) This method of cooking calf's liver comes from the Tyrolean Alps. Slices of calf's liver are dredged in flour then sautéed in hot bacon fat on both sides and removed from the pan. Chopped onions are sautéed until translucent, then vinegar is added and boiled until nearly all has evaporated. To the onion mixture a well-seasoned chicken stock is added, plus sour cream, a bit of flour, and chopped capers. The liver, placed in the sauce, is heated and served. COMPATIBLE WINES: A red wine, e.g., Mâcon, Margaux, St. Julien, Côte Rôtie, Zinfandel, Châteauneuf-du-Pape, Nebbiolo, Valpolicella, Médoc, Egri Bikaver, Santenay, St. Émilion.

Tyrolienne, Sauce In spite of its name, this French sauce has nothing whatever to do with Austria or with the Alps. It is simply a *sauce Béarnaise* made with olive oil instead of butter, to which a tomato purée is added. The sauce is served with broiled chicken.

TZIMMES (Jewish) This Yiddish term evolved from two German words, *zum Essen,* meaning "to dinner." The *Tzimmes* dish, which probably originated during medieval times, may be one of three distinctly different preparations: a sweet casserole of vegetables, a sweet casserole of vegetables in combination with fruits, a sweet casserole of vegetables and/or fruits with meat. Because *Tzimmes* is a sweet dish, it is served on Rosh Hashana, the Jewish New Year, when Jews express to each other their wishes for a sweet year.

Fruit and Vegetable Tzimmes This tasty casserole is made by first cooking sliced carrots and sweet potatoes in boiling water until tender. Then, after slicing the already cored and peeled apples, layers of sliced apples, carrots, and sweet potatoes are tiered in a casserole. Each layer is seasoned with honey, cinnamon, salt, pepper, and a bit of melted margarine. Enough water is added to cover, and the casserole is baked until the ingredients are tender. The casserole is uncovered and browned under the broiler. To make variations of this dish, one can add crushed pineapple or substitute pitted prunes for the apples.

$\mathscr{U}$

UDON (Japanese) A rather thick noodle made from white wheat flour.

Fried Udon The noodles are boiled, drained, then cooked in hot oil in a skillet or a wok. A dash of soy sauce is added just before removing the noodles from the pan. The dish is served sprinkled with chopped scallions and a dash of *togarishi*. (See SHICHIMI TOGARISHI)

UMIDO (Italian) Stewed or boiled meats.

Umido di Coniglio A rabbit stew made by sautéing the disjointed animal in hot olive oil with chopped onions that have been well seasoned with salt and pepper. When the pieces of meat have been well browned, tomatoes are added and the stew is cooked covered. Halfway through the stewing time, quartered potatoes are added with a bit of water, and the stew is cooked until the rabbit and the potatoes are tender. (See STUFATO) COMPATIBLE WINES: A red wine, e.g., Mâcon, Côte Rôtie, Mercurey, Chinon, Valpolicella, Zinfandel, Arbois Rouge, St. Julien, St. Émilion, Santenay, Cabernet Sauvignon.

UNUSUAL TASTES Diets around the world differ greatly according to climate, religion, transportation, tradition, heredity, locality, and superstition. Austrians, for instance, have avoided lamb dishes for centuries because their traditional enemy, the Turks, were big lamb-eaters during their occupation of Austria. The Greeks, on the other hand, although they share the same Austrian prejudice, have eaten plenty of lamb since the days Socrates walked the streets of Athens—and they still do. Many Asiatics, especially the Chinese, will not drink milk because as a people they lack the special enzyme lactase, which transforms the milk sugar, lactose, into the digestible dextrose. To drink milk would make them violently ill.

Sometimes the aversion to certain foods has more to do with class distinction than with any physical deficiency. A not-so-merry England, some years ago, fostered a dish called "umble-pie." It seems that the heart, the liver, the kidneys, the stomach, and the other entrails of animals were called "umbles" in Old England, and they were baked into pies. The pies were relegated to social inferiors and to the poor of the land.

Then there are some cultures, either out of necessity or geography, that relish particular foods that a neighboring nation considered disgusting. If the Australians relish kangaroo soup and the French delight in snails and frogs' legs, if the clever Japanese and the people of the Mediterranean love the gonads of the prickly sea urchins that the French call *oursins,* and if the Arabs have a penchant for sheeps' eyes and the lusty Italians devour *scungilli* by the pound, why is it odd to make a snack of crisply roasted grasshoppers and bumble bees, as the Japanese do for their cocktail parties? The Bantus of Africa, for instance, consider termites a very tasty food. These extremely handsome people entrap the termites right at the mound nests and prepare them roasted or fried; and when needed for future use, the termites are dried and ground into flour. They dine on gnats as well and have even baked them into pies to tempt the tourists. Locusts steer clear of Bantu land because these people know that locusts are a cheap source of protein, and before you can say, "Doctor Livingston, I presume," they are steamed, and after removing the unwanted wings and legs, they are fried to a crisp.

Even the great Escoffier, while a soldier at Metz, commented on unusual foodstuffs: "Horsemeat is delicious only when you are in a condition to appreciate it—and as to rat meat, it approaches in delicacy the taste of roast pig." Life in Paris during the Siege of 1821 was a horror. People ate everything they could put their hands on, including rats. A famous chef of the time, Thomas Génin, stated: "I have grilled rats as *pigeons à la crapaudine,* but more often as potted meat." (See CRAPAUDINE, ESCARGOTS, OURSINS, SCUNGILLI)

A typical Parisian menu from the Restaurant Voisin, where the great *hôtelier*-to-be César Ritz was working as a *stagiaire,* read:

Brochette de Foie de Caniche	Grilled Poodle Livers
Cuisse de St. Bernard Rôti	Roast Leg of St. Bernard
Selle de Lapin de Toit	Saddle of Roof-Rabbit (Cat)
Consommé d'Éléphant.	Elephant Consommé
Cuissot de Loup, ... *Sauce Chevreuil*	Haunch of Wild Wolf, Game Sauce
Rôti de Chat, Flanqué de Rats ..	Roast Pussy, Rat Garniture
Le Chameau Rôti à l'Anglaise ..	Roast Camel with Vegetables

URUCU See ANATTO

USLI GHEE (East Indian) Clarified butter. (See GHEE)

VACHERIN (French) This delightful dessert is made by squeezing rings of meringue out of a pastry bag. The rings are partially dried in the low heat of an oven and then placed one on top of the other, glued together with extra meringue, thus forming a kind of shell. This meringue shell is then returned to the oven until it becomes dry and hard. (See MERINGUE)

Vacherin à la Chantilly A *vacherin* filled with whipped cream flavored with vanilla and Kirschwasser (a white brandy made from cherries).

Vacherin Marron Glacé An ice cream dessert made with a chestnut purée and an almond-flavored meringue. Chestnuts are puréed; together with rum, vanilla, and raisins, they are added to ice cream that is rich with egg yolks and heavy cream. To form the *vacherins* (meringues), beaten egg whites with ground almonds and vanilla are baked halfway; while still pliable, they are formed into shells and baked again until they become dry and hard. These meringue shells are then glued to finger-thick pastry rounds with a caramel glaze. The *vacherins* are filled with the chestnut ice cream and served topped with sugared chestnut bits and *crème Chantilly*. (See CHANTILLY)

VALENCIANA, ENSALADA (Spanish) A salad from Valencia, where orange groves fill the countryside. To prepare this delicious salad, oranges, sweet red peppers, olives, and chicory are cut into fine strips. A clove of garlic is rubbed into a bit of salt in the salad bowl, and lettuce leaves and the rest of the ingredients are added. A *sauce Mayonnaise* is made from mashed hard-boiled egg yolks, salt, pepper, olive oil, and vinegar and sugar to taste. Whipped cream is folded into the mixture, and the dressing is poured over the salad, which is then tossed tableside. (See MAYONNAISE)

VALENCIENNE (French) Named after the town of Valence in Spain, this garnish is composed of rice and of both cubed and sliced cooked ham.

Chicken Valencienne The whole chicken is trussed, covered with slices of bacon, then cooked in clarified butter on a bed of root vegetables in a heavy saucepan; the chicken is not allowed to take on color. Surrounded with a *risotto* combined with diced cooked ham, the chicken is served with a tomato-flavored chicken stock that has been riched with heavy cream. (See CLARIFIED BUTTER, PAELLA, RISOTTO) COMPATIBLE WINES: A red wine, e.g., Margaux, Côte Rôtie, Beaujolais, Hermitage, Cabernet Sauvignon, Egri Bikaver, Valpolicella.

VANILLA BEAN Grown in Mexico, Java, and other tropical countries, this dried bean of the orchid is used for flavoring desserts such as puddings, custards, cakes, and ice cream. The extract of the bean is sold bottled.

Vanilla sugar Sugar flavored with vanilla. This can be made by placing one or two split vanilla beans in a tightly-covered jar containing granulated sugar. It is used to flavor desserts, pastries, and fresh berries.

VARENNE, LA François Pierre de la Varenne was head cook to the Marquis d'Uxelles. In honor of his master, La Varenne created a mixture of chopped mushrooms, onions, shallots, and parsley—all browned in butter; he named the mixture *Duxelles.* Today, this garnish is used extensively in fine kitchens all over the world. La Varenne's book, *Le Cuisinier François,* brought discipline and order to the culinary art. (See DUXELLES)

VARINIKI (Russian) This *ravioli*-type preparation consists of noodle dough filled with a stuffing: cottage cheese, cabbage, meats, etc. (See RAVIOLI)

VARNITCHKES, KASHA (Jewish) A combination of well-seasoned cooked buckwheat groats *(kasha),* sautéed chopped onions, and bow-tie shaped noodles. The mixture is tossed in hot chicken fat and topped with *gribenes* (chicken cracklings). (See GRIBENES, KASHA)

VATROUSHKI (Russian) These cream cheese tartlets are made of puff pastry that is filled with cream cheese seasoned with salt and sugar. They are often served as part of a *zakuski* or to garnish *borsch.* (See BORSCH, PÂTE À CHOU, ZAKUSKI)

VEAL AND RAISINS (Créole) Veal steaks are seasoned then dipped in beaten eggs and breadcrumbs and browned in a heavy pan. A sauce of bouillon, paprika, cream, and sugar is poured over the veal steaks. After being sprinkled liberally with raisins, they are baked in a moderate oven. COMPATIBLE WINES: A white wine, e.g., Chenin Blanc, Gewürztraminer, Riquewihr, Frascati, Orvieto, Meursault, Anjou, Graacher Himmelreich, Sylvaner.

VEAL VILLAGEOISE (French) Veal as prepared "in the small villages." The veal from the leg or from the loin is sliced as thin as possible, flattened with a mallet, and cut into rectangular pieces. These veal rectangles are filled with chopped boiled ham and Gruyère cheese and then rolled up, fastened with toothpicks, and browned in hot butter and oil. These *ballotines* or *roulades* of veal are then placed in a casserole with chopped shallots that have been precooked in butter. They are covered with white wine and beef bouillon and are baked in a medium oven. (See BALLOTINE, ROULADE) COMPATIBLE WINES: A white wine, e.g., Volnay, Piesporter Goldtröpfchen, Anjou, Riquewihr, Chenin Blanc, Aigle, Graacher Himmelreich, Sylvaner, Corton Charlemagne, Johannisberg, Orvieto.

VEGETABLE CHEESE See BEAN CURD

VELOUTÉ, SAUCE (French) This classic sauce is used as the base for many other fine sauces, including *Allemande, Normande, chaud-*

froid, and *poulette.* The word *velouté* is also used to describe certain thick soups.

Sauce velouté is similar to a *Béchamel* in that a *roux* (butter and flour) is mixed with cream; the blending in of a white stock—fish, veal, or chicken—and egg yolks makes it a *velouté.* As the sound of the word *velouté* implies, the sauce has, indeed, a velvety texture. (See ALLEMANDE, BÉCHAMEL, CHAUD-FROID, NORMANDE, POULETTE, ROUX)

Velouté de Poisson A basic fish sauce made from a *roux* to which a hot fish stock is added all at once and which is then rapidly whipped until creamy. It is served with fish dishes. Used as a base for many fish sauces.

Velouté Réduit, Sauté de Volaille This ancient dish dates back to the time of the famous gastronome Grimode de la Reynière, about 1803, when he advocated a *velouté réduit,* referring to a long, drawn-out cooking of a *velouté sauce.* Today, the sauce is completed much more quickly, but it equals that of the slow-handed Reynière. To prepare this classic, quartered fryers are flattened, seasoned, and sautéed in olive oil and butter. The chicken is not to take on color, so care must be taken in the sautéing. The thoroughly cooked pieces of chicken are then skinned and served swimming in a rich *sauce velouté* flavored with dry sherry wine. The chicken is garnished with sliced sautéed mushrooms and served with potato *croquettes* and a crisp green salad. (See CROQUETTES) COMPATIBLE WINES: A white wine, e.g., Orvieto, Piesporter Goldtröpfchen, Gewürztraminer, Corton Charlemagne, Meursault, Château-Grillet, Chenin Blanc, Keknyelu.

VENEZIANA, FEGATO ALLA (Italian) A well-known liver dish from the romantic city of gondolas, canals, and serenades—Venice. It is most important that the liver be sliced as thin as possible, but it is equally vital to the success of the dish that the liver be cooked neither too slowly nor too quickly. (If cooked too slowly, the dish would turn into a stew; if too quickly, the liver would become much too dry.) Chopped onions are heated in olive oil and butter until translucent, then the liver is sautéed until just tender. It is then seasoned with salt and pepper and chopped parsley. COMPATIBLE WINES: A red wine, e.g., Margaux, Latour, Haut Brion, Pétrus, Cabernet Sauvignon, Lafite Rothschild, Médoc, Valpolicella, Zinfandel.

VENISON Formerly, this term was used for the meat of any game animal. Today, however, it is used to designate the flesh of any type of deer, particularly fallow deer, roebuck, elk, antelope, red deer, or reindeer. The meat of the male is more flavorful than that of the female of the species, but the animal must not be more than three years old. The fillets, the haunch, and the loin make up the finest venison. (See CHEVREUIL, REH)

VÉNITIENNE, SAUCE (French) This green-colored sauce is so named after the Venetian penchant for lots and lots of green herbs. When used to complement fish dishes, the sauce consists of a white wine sauce mixed with a reduction of tarragon vinegar, chopped shallots, chives, and chervil, to which butter and egg yolks are added. Just before serving, lemon juice and freshly chopped parsley are added. However, with the substitution of chicken or veal stock for the fish stock in the white wine sauce, and with the addition of a *sauce Allemande,* the *sauce Vénitienne* is served with egg and chicken dishes as well. (See ALLEMANDE, WHITE WINE SAUCE)

VERDE, SALSA (Mexican) A "green sauce" made from green tomatoes, chopped onions, chopped *serrano* chilies, coriander, salt, and pepper—all blended together into a purée. The sauce is popularly served with meat and fish dishes. (See CHILI)

VERENIKIS (Jewish) Dumplings filled with various fruits, often with pitted cherries which have been precooked in lemon juice and sugar. With the edges of the dough carefully sealed, the dumplings are cooked in boiling water. When they float to the surface, they are removed, drained, and served warm with syrup and sour cream.

VERILETUT (Finnish) This rather unusual pancake is made with pork blood. The blood is strained into a bowl then aerated by beating it vigorously until it forms thin strings and becomes lighter in color. Then, with the addition of beer, fried onions, rye and barley flour, and eggs, all is beaten into a smooth batter. The batter is flavored with pepper, marjoram, and salt. Pancakes are prepared by pouring spoonfuls of the batter into a hot *crêpe* pan. The pancakes are sautéed on both sides until brown. They are served with lingonberry preserves and boiled potatoes. COMPATIBLE BEVERAGES: Beer, ale, stout.

VERMICELLI To the Italians this term refers to an extremely fine *pasta* that is usually served as a garnish with clear soups. The Chinese have a version of *vermicelli,* which they call *mein.* Although both the Italians and the Chinese agree that noodles should be eaten with a sauce or in a soup, they have never come to a meeting of minds on the subject of who invented the noodle. A plus for the Chinese could be the fact that they have been eating the noodle for thousands of years.

VÉRON, SAUCE (French) A sauce named to honor the amusing Doctor Véron—prolific journalist, boulevardier, and celebrated director of the Paris Opera—whose bent for the very best in food and drink was evidenced by the fine banquets he held each day of the week for his favored artistic friends. Two sauces are basic to the preparation of the *sauce Véron: sauce Normande* and *sauce Tyrolienne.* These are blended together then finished by adding a veal stock that has been flavored with anchovy paste and then reduced. The sauce is served with fish dishes. (See NORMANDE, TYROLIENNE)

VÉRONIQUE, À LA (French) A garnish of seedless white Muscat grapes, used mostly with fish or fowl dishes.
  Filet de Sole Véronique Whatever connection *Véronique,* or Ver-

onica, has with the large Muscat grapes used to make this sole dish has not been determined. The fillets of sole are folded, seasoned, and poached in a *fumet de poisson* (fish stock) composed of minced onions, lemon juice, white wine, the trimmings from the sole, and water. When cooked, the fillets are reserved, and the strained *fumet* is reduced and enriched with sweet butter. This, in turn, is poured over the fillets and quickly glazed under a hot broiler. Before grilling, the fillets of sole are encircled with clusters of skinned, seedless white grapes of the Muscat variety. Fillets of sole simply covered with a plain white sauce with grapes thrown on as a kind of afterthought is not a true *Véronique*. (See FUMET DE POISSON) COMPATIBLE WINES: A white wine, e.g., Muscadet, Chablis, Montrachet, Pouilly-Fuissé, Quincy, Wehlener Sonnenuhr, Mâcon Blanc, White Haut Brion, Pinot Chardonnay, Dézaley.

VERT-PRÉ (French) A green herb sauce made with peas and asparagus tips; it is served with light meats and with duckling. The term is also used to describe a garniture of shoestring potatoes and watercress that is served with broiled meats.

VIAZEGA (Russian) See KOULIBIAC

VICHYSSOISE SOUP (American) Created in America by a French chef named Diat, this soup is not known by that name in France. Its French counterpart, *potage Parisien,* was an old peasant soup. *Vichyssoise* soup is made from chicken stock, leeks, potatoes, onions, seasonings, and plenty of rich heavy cream. It is served ice cold, topped with chopped chives.

VILLAGEOISE See VEAL VILLAGEOISE

VILLROY (French) The most expedient way to curry the favor of French kings, whether they were the Henrys or the Louis, was through the stomach. The courtiers of that day learned the trick from the courtesans, and putting on aprons and toques, they plunged into sauces and soups and learned how to sauté, to roast, even to deep-fry. A Maréchal Villroy took the hint.

Poulet de Villroy Villroy, a Maréchal of France who lost every battle, determined to please his king by serving him a dish distinctively his own. He dropped his sword and took up spoon and bowl to invent a sauce that was to be served with chicken, quartered and cooked in a rich stock. The sauce is made by mashing hard-boiled egg yolks into sweet butter. The cooked pieces of chicken are then coated with this sauce, rolled in herbed breadcrumbs, and deep-fried. The king was delighted and Villroy was in ecstasy, and the chicken bearing his name is etched today in the archives of culinary history.

Sauce Villroy A *sauce Allemande* infused with an essence of truffles and a ham stock is reduced until it easily coats the back of a spoon. The sauce is served with vegetables. Instead of the essence of truffles, a tomato purée, onion purée, an essence of mushrooms, or a *mirepoix* may be substituted, depending upon the food to be served.

VINAIGRETTE, SAUCE (French) A basic *vinaigrette* is composed of salt, freshly ground pepper, and oil and vinegar in a 3 to 1 ratio. Often, chopped chervil, tarragon, parsley, and onions are added to the basic sauce. A *vinaigrette* is generally used to dress salads, in a marinade, to complement fish dishes, or it may be served with boiled beef.

VIN BLANC, SAUCE AU See WHITE WINE SAUCE

VIRGINIA BOILED DRESSING (American) This salad dressing originated in the South and has many variations. Egg yolks mixed with water and vinegar, mustard, sugar, and salt are cooked together in the top of a double boiler, stirring contantly until the mixture is thick. It is then left to cool and is enriched with sour cream. A variation, the Waltham dressing, is exactly the same, except that finely chopped hickory nuts are added at the end. The dressing is used to enhance the flavor of fruit salads, cole slaw, and potato salads.

VIROFLAY (French) Viroflay is a region near Versailles. When used to describe a dish, it indicates that spinach is present.

Oeufs Viroflay An egg dish. Small buttered molds are lined with cooked spinach, and a raw egg is set in the middle of each spinach-lined mold. After the molds are simmered in hot water, the egg mixture is unmolded onto rounds of toasted bread and served coated with a *sauce suprême*. (See SUPRÊME) COMPATIBLE BEVERAGES: Beer, cider.

VITELLO (Italian) Veal that has come from milk-fed calves. Veal is *the* meat of Italy, first because Italians prefer white meat to red; secondly because, with grazing land always at a premium in Italy, the calf rarely grows to be a full cow.

Vitello Tonnato A roast of veal served cold with a tuna fish sauce. A boneless veal roast, larded with anchovy fillets, is cooked in boiling water together with chopped onions, carrots, celery, parsley, bay leaves, salt, and pepper. When the meat is done, it is left to cool. A tuna fish sauce made by liquefying tuna, anchovy fillets, capers, and parsley with lemon juice and olive oil in a blender is poured over the thinly sliced veal when ready to serve. COMPATIBLE WINES: A white wine, e.g., Gewürztraminer, Aigle, Orvieto, Frascati, Chenin Blanc, Anjou, Brolio Bianco, Corton Charlemagne, Sylvaner, Szamorodni, Château-Grillet.

VIVANDIÈRE In days of yore in France, this was not a very respectable title for a young girl. A *vivandière* was a camp-follower. When armies had to forage for their own food, soldiers needed women to accompany them and to administer to their needs, and this, indeed, was a job for a *vivandière,* a young woman without shame.

Fish Vivandière Fish fillets are poached in a mixture of white wine and fish stock. Then, covered with a *Duxelles,* chopped tarragon, tomato purée, and chervil, the fillets are baked. (See DUXELLES) COMPATIBLE WINES: A white wine, e.g., Chablis, Meursault, Aigle, Muscadet, Riquewihr, Gewürztraminer, Sylvaner, Sauvignon Blanc, Piesporter Goldtröpfchen, Pouilly-Fumé.

VOLAILLE FLAMBÉES, CUISSES DE (French) Chicken legs flamed with brandy. The bones are removed from the chicken legs and the legs are stuffed with a mixture of chopped giblets, onions, liver, garlic, parsley, raisins, salt, and pepper. The legs are sewn up and marinated in white wine overnight. When ready to be cooked, the legs are dried and sautéed in butter until well browned. Then, placed in a shallow pan with more wine and butter, they are covered and baked in a moderate oven. The flaming to follow is quite a show. The legs are placed in the center of a platter. They are surrounded by a ring of boiled rice, mushrooms sautéed in butter, string beans, and carrots. Hot brandy is poured over the legs, which are flamed and served blazing to astonished and fascinated guests. COMPATIBLE WINES: A red wine, e.g., Margaux, Egri Bikaver, Premiat, Médoc, Cabernet Sauvignon, Valpolicella.

VOL-AU-VENT (French) Puff paste is rolled out to a quarter-of-an-inch thickness, and from it two rounds are cut. One round is placed on a moistened baking sheet. With a sharp knife, a circle of dough is cut and removed from the center of the other round, leaving a pastry circle. The circumference of the round on the baking sheet is moistened with water, and the pastry circle from the second round is placed on top of it. The top is brushed with beaten egg, then a circle is lightly cut around the inside diameter of the pastry circle, cutting into but not through the dough beneath. After cooking, this will form the lid. When the whole is baked, the pastry puffs up almost magically, forming a shell suitable for filling with sweetbreads, calf's brains, seafood, or chopped chicken in a white sauce (a *velouté* or a *sauce Béchamel*). (See BÉCHAMEL, BOUCHÉE À LA REINE, FEUILLETAGE, VELOUTÉ)

Vol-au-Vent à la Reine A *vol-au-vent* filled with a chicken and mushroom mixture. The filling is made from a *roux* to which a mixture of chicken stock, light cream, and egg yolks is added. After this is brought to a boil, the chopped chicken and mushrooms are added. (See ROUX) COMPATIBLE WINES: A white wine, e.g., Vouvray, Graves, Graacher Himmelreich, Aigle, Orvieto.

Vol-au-Vent aux Quenelles de Brochet Pike dumplings in patty shells. The pike dumplings, mixed with precooked mushrooms, are stuffed into the patty shells and served coated with a fish *velouté*. (See BROCHET, VELOUTÉ) COMPATIBLE WINES: A white wine, e.g., Montrachet Meursault, Pinot Chardonnay, Sauterne, Graacher Himmelreich, Szamorodni, Hermitage Blanc, Beaune Blanc.

Vol-au-Vent Duchesse Diced boiled chicken, mushrooms, and truffles are heated in a *sauce suprême* and then used to fill the *vol-au-vent*. (See SUPRÊME) COMPATIBLE WINES: The same white wines recommended for the *vol-au-vent à la reine*.

VOSPAPOUR (Armenian) A soup made with meat, dried apricots, and lentils. Beef and lamb are cubed and simmered in boiling salted water. The broth is clarified and the lentils are added. In another pan, cubed potatoes are sautéed in hot butter until golden brown. They are then added to the broth with chopped walnuts and dried apricots. After a half-hour's simmering, the broth is flavored with fresh tarragon and served piping hot.

WAITER SERVICE Maligned, elegant, underrated, overpaid, charming, rude, tactful, knowledgeable, willing, thieving—all of these terms have, at one time or another, been ascribed to the man or the woman in a restaurant who brings the diner his food from the kitchen and serves it. Actually, to be a good waiter one must have a pair of good feet, a strong back, graceful movement and balance, and more tact than an ambassador at the Court of Queen Victoria. In any first-class establishment, the diner should expect his waiter to be something of a linguist, able not only to describe the foreign dishes listed on the menu but to explain how the dishes are prepared and what they consist of.

The diner depends upon his waiter for a very basic human need: to be fed. If this need is frustrated through bad service, cold or bad food, an intolerable wait, indifference, or just plain rudeness, the diner will be put in a testy mood. The waiter must try to make the diner's meal as pleasant as possible. And while dealing with demands of the patrons in the dining room, the waiter must also cope with the demands of sweaty cooks in steaming kitchens. Often, he must prove his prowess as a philosopher who knows when and how to pour oil on stormy restaurant waters.

Fine restaurants usually have two waiters to a station of five or six tables. One takes care of the customer's needs in the dining room (cocktail service, cutlery and linen service, the crumbing and overall care of the table); the other, the "horse," brings the food order to the chef, and when it is ready, he carries the food to the table. There is a captain assigned to each station.

When the diner is seated, usually the first person with whom he comes in contact is the captain, who is responsible to the head waiter, or *maître d'hôtel,* for the service on his station. It is the table captain who presents the menus to the diners, takes the food orders, and generally coordinates and supervises service. The captain takes drink orders, opens and pours the wine, mixes salads, carves roasts of meat and poultry, bones fish, and does all *flambé* dishes. After being seated, the diner should ask the captain's name as well as that of his waiter. This helps insure that the diner will be promptly and diligently served.

When ready to tip, the diner should remember that the captain is not included in the fifteen to twenty percent tip afforded for service. All of this money goes to the waiters, unless otherwise stipulated on the check itself. If the captain has really done his job, been very attentive and performed extra services—such as carved a duck or pheasant, tossed a salad with a special dressing, carved roasts of meat and poultry, or entertained the dinner party with a regal *café diablo* or *crêpes à la Nero,* flaming of course—then five or ten percent of the total check is an adequate gratuity for the captain. If the diner wants to start a minor war behind the scenes of the restaurant, then let him tell the waiter, within earshot of the captain, that the captain is included in the waiter's tip. (See MAÎTRE D'HÔTEL, MENU)

WAKAME (Japanese) Dried seaweed. After soaking, it can be eaten with cucumbers, *miso,* and vinegar. In its dried state it is added to soups or served with *shoyu.* (See MISO, SHOYU)

WALDORF SALAD (American) This salad originated at the Waldorf Astoria Hotel in New York City. It consists of diced apples, chopped celery, and walnuts tossed with a thin *sauce Mayonnaise.* (See MAYONNAISE)

WALEWSKA, SOLE (French) The Polish Countess Walewska, the mistress of Napoleon who bore him a son, was honored by France and her chefs, who named this sole dish after her. The fillets are first poached in a *fumet;* they are then placed on a bed of sliced cooked lobster meat, flavored with truffles, coated with a *sauce Mornay,* and glazed under the broiler. (See FUMET DE POISSON, MORNAY, TRUFFLES) COMPATIBLE WINES: A white wine, e.g., Meursault, Beaune Blanc, Sylvaner, Ammerschwihr, Chenin Blanc, Gewürztraminer, Keknyelu, Orvieto.

Omelette Walewska This *omelette baveuse* is filled with diced cooked lobster, truffles, and chives. (See BAVEUSE) COMPATIBLE WINES: A white wine, e.g., Fendant, Orvieto, Dry Sauterne, Anjou, Kientzheim, Johannisberg.

WALTHAM DRESSING See VIRGINIA BOILED DRESSING

WARIBASHI (Japanese) The name for chopsticks that are disposed of after being used but once. The ordinary, everyday chopsticks are called *hashi.* (See CHOPSTICKS)

WASABE (Japanese) A fiery pastelike green horseradish that is mixed with soy sauce and served with *sushi* or *sashimi.* You will know when *wasabe* is present in the dish: it clears the sinus passages like nothing else. (See SASHIMI, SUSHI)

WAT (Ethiopian) A stew made from chicken, meats, and vegetables. (See METIN SHURU)

WATER CHESTNUT In Chinese this type of chestnut is called *mah tai,* "horse's hoof." It is so named because of its shape and color. Water chestnuts are fruits of aquatic plants that belong to the genus *trapa;* they are related to the primrose. In early days the American Indian collected another type of water chestnut, the water *chinquapin,* obtained from the nutlike seeds of the American lotus, *nelumbo lutea.* Chinese cooks use water chestnuts in steamed dishes to absorb what might be oversweet or oversalty.

WATERCRESS VICHYSSOISE (American) This is the creation of Albert

Stockli, the executive chef of Restaurant Associates, the one-time New York restaurant dynasty that in the 1950s and 1960s created a series of exciting eating places, one more imaginative than the other: the Four Seasons, Forum of the Twelve Caesars, Trattoria, Tower Suite, La Fonda del Sol, to name but a few. To prepare the soup, chopped potatoes, watercress, and leeks are cooked in chicken stock with a ham shank. When tender, the ham shank is removed and the vegetables are puréed. Sugar, salt, and pepper are used to flavor the puréed watercress, leeks, and potatoes; heavy cream is poured into the mixture, which is left to cool. Before serving, fresh watercress is finely chopped and strewn over the soup. Mr. Stockli also made this soup with almonds, carrots, and apples as substitutes for the watercress. (See CRESSON)

WATERZOOI (Belgian) This speciality can be made using fish or chicken.

Fish Waterzooi Either salt-water or fresh-water fish may be used in the preparation of this fish soup. Ocean fish such as halibut, eel, cod, and perch or fresh-water fish such as pike, bass, or carp would be appropriate. While mussels are steamed in salt water, in another pot a fish *fumet* is prepared from the bones and the skin of the fish. In the bottom of a buttered casserole, a bed of chopped vegetables is made from celery, carrots, onions, parsley, and mushrooms. These vegetables are glazed in a hot oven, and then the pieces of fish, together with the mussels, are arranged on top of the vegetables. The *fumet* is strained, thickened with egg yolks and flour, and made velvety with heavy cream that has been seasoned with nutmeg, salt, and pepper. This rich sauce is poured over the fish, and the casserole is then baked for a short time, until the fish is done. (See FUMET) COMPATIBLE WINES: A white wine, e.g., Meursault, Muscadet, Rüdesheim, Aigle, Frascati, Orvieto, Lacrima Christi, Sylvaner, Piesporter Goldtröpfchen, Graacher Himmelreich, Johannisberg, Nierstein, Dry Sauterne, Château Chalon, Sauvignon Blanc, Riquewihr.

Chicken Waterzooi This method of cooking chicken calls for the bird to be cut up, rubbed with lemon juice, and simmered in white wine with chopped onions, leeks, carrots, celery, herbs, and cloves. The chicken stock is strained and added to a white *roux* to which a well-seasoned mixture of eggs and cream is added. The meat is removed from the bones and, mixed together with the chopped vegetables, it is added to the creamy soup and served. (See ROUX) COMPATIBLE WINES: A white wine, e.g., Vouvray, Dry Sauterne, Szamorodni, Muscat d'Alsace, Johannisberg, Aigle, Zeller Schwartze Katz, Naktarsch, Fürst von Metternich, Chenin Blanc.

WEISSWURST (German) This famous sausage comes from the city in Bavaria where the best beer flows freely, where the *Oktoberfest* is a time of feasting, gaiety, and fun, and where the word *Gemütlichkeit* is synonymous with its name, Munich. The sausages, about six inches long, are made from finely ground veal, minced pork, milk-soaked white bread, nutmeg, salt, and pepper. The sausages are simmered in gently boiling water. They are often served with sauerkraut. COMPATIBLE WINES: A white wine, e.g., Aigle, Riesling, Sauterne, Sylvaner, Gewürztraminer, Riquewihr, Ammerschwihr, Sauvignon Blanc, Naktarsch, Liebfraumilch, Zeller Schwartze Katz.

WELLINGTON, BEEF (English) The Duke of Wellington is said to have requested that this beef dish be served at any dinner that he might host. While his proud English chef dubbed the preparation "Wellington steak," his Gallic counterpart across the Channel, still smarting from Napoleon's defeat, simply called the dish *filet de boeuf en croûte.* The fillet of beef is first well larded, then browned in butter, and finally wrapped in puff pastry. It is baked to a golden brown color and served with braised lettuce, tomatoes, and *château potatoes.* Variations call for either a fine *pâté* or for a layer of *Duxelles* blended with a forcemeat of chicken to cover the beef before it is wrapped in the puff pastry. (See CHÂTEAU, DUXELLES, PÂTÉ) COMPATIBLE WINES: A red wine, e.g., Chambertin, Échézeaux, Fixin, La Tâche, Lafite Rothschild, Dôle, Cabernet Sauvignon, Richebourg, Aloxe-Corton, Haut Brion.

WELSH RAREBIT A cheese dish from Wales. (See RAREBIT)

WHITE ANTS (South African) See BUSHMAN'S RICE

WHITE SAUCE This is probably one of the easiest French sauces to make, although care must be taken to use only the finest quality sweet butter. To prepare it, a good dollop of butter should be allowed to melt slowly in a pan—melt, not burn. Then, slowly, the flour should be added with salt and pepper. Constantly stirring the mixture, boiling water is added—but slowly, gradually—until the sauce is smooth. Away from the heat, the addition of an egg yolk and a dash of vinegar finishes the sauce. If a richer sauce is necessary, heavy cream is substituted for the water, and chopped scallions and parsley may be added. The sauce is served with potatoes, hard-boiled eggs, fish, poultry, or sweetbreads. (See IVOIRE)

WHITE WINE SAUCE (French) This famous sauce, *sauce au vin blanc,* has a variety of different recipes but the ingredients are the same. Basically, the sauce is a rich fish *velouté* to which fish stock bound with egg yolks and a dry white wine is added. Then, like the classic *sauce Hollandaise,* butter is added, a bit at a time, stirring constantly until the sauce has the right consistency. A variation, having no eggs, is made from a reduced fish stock flavored with white wine into which sweet butter is gradually whisked. The sauce, of course, is served with fish dishes. When chicken or veal stock is substituted for the fish stock, the sauce is served with various meat and poultry dishes. (See HOLLANDAISE)

WIENER BACKHENDL (Austrian) A speciality named after the *eins-*

swei-drei Stadt, Vienna. This *Backhendl* (chicken) is not an old layer, but a spring chicken cut into four parts, dusted with flour, dipped in egg and then in breadcrumbs and fried to a golden brown. It is served garnished with lemon wedges and a tossed green salad. The chicken's liver and stomach are also served, breaded and fried. COMPATIBLE WINES: A red wine, e.g., Valpolicella, Beaujolais, Egri Bikaver, Mercurey, Côte Rôtie, Médoc, Bardolino, Barbaresco, Nebbiolo, Zinfandel, Santenay, Cahors.

WIENER RAHMSTRUDEL (Austrian) A rich cream *Strudel,* a sumptuous dessert. Pieces of white bread are soaked in milk, put through a sieve, and mixed with butter, egg yolks, salt, vanilla, and grated lemon rind. This is puréed in a blender until smooth, then whipped egg whites and breadcrumbs are added. The mixture is formed into a long loaf and is then twisted to form a circle, which is placed on the bottom of a deep baking dish. After adding a mixture of eggs, milk, and sugar, the *Strudel* is baked in a moderate oven until a golden crust is formed. (See STRUDEL)

WIENER ROSTBRATEN An Austrian or, more exactly, a Viennese method of preparing a succulent beefsteak dish. The steaks are pounded flat then pan-fried in a mixture of oil and butter in a hot skillet. The steaks are served garnished with sliced onions which are fried to a crispness in butter. COMPATIBLE WINES: A red wine, e.g., Beaujolais, Pétrus, Pinot Noir, Châteauneuf-du-Pape, Valpolicella, Nebbiolo, Chianti, Dôle, Pommerol, Fixin, Échézeaux, Zinfandel.

WIENERSCHNITZEL This is the name given by the Viennese to the breaded veal cutlet. (See SCHNITZEL)

WILD RICE This culinary delicacy, *zizania aquatica,* grows in shallow water along the shores of ponds and muddy lakes. It is not a rice at all, but the seed of an aquatic grass. It grows wild in the northern United States and in southern Canada. There is another completely different variety which grows in the southern states.

Wild rice was one of the chief foods of the Indians who lived in the Great Lakes region of America. For centuries, the Sioux warred with the Ojibwa and Menominee tribes for control of the wild rice fields. Actually, the name of the Menominee tribe of Wisconsin was the same as the Indian word for wild rice, *menomin.* The Indians harvested the seeds by pulling the grain stalks out of the water and across their canoes; they then beat them with paddles to dislodge the seeds. The seeds were then sun-dried or parched over a low fire until the hulls cracked. In 1923, an inventor with an eye for wild rice profit created a machine that could harvest a ton-and-a-half of wild rice in an hour, but conservation authorities banned its use and had laws enacted which protected the Indians' traditions and their own manual methods of harvesting the grain. Today, the seed is harvested by the same primitive methods and commands a high price from the epicurean market.

The scarcity of wild rice and its distinctively nutty, slightly smoky taste keep the demand for it constant. It is delicious when stuffed into a roast loin of pork and excellent when served with game or with poultry, or even as a dish all by itself, perked up with onions, tomatoes, and green peppers. Wild rice was taken to China and Japan, and today a smaller species called "Manchurian wild rice" grows in Northeast Asia. It is prepared exactly like white rice but takes much longer to cook.

WINE SERVICE The accepted wine service protocol that should be observed in any first-class restaurant consists of the following:

- After the food order has been taken, the wine list is presented to the host of the dinner party.
- If a guest appears to be unsure of his selection of wine, it is proper for the captain to suggest a suitable wine.
- When the wine has been selected, the name of the wine and the table number is given to the waiter.
- The waiter is to bring the proper wine glasses with the wine and place them on the *guéridon* or service wagon.
- The captain presents the wine to the host, stating the name and vintage.
- The captain uncorks the wine, if red, to allow it to "breathe."
- The wine bottle should never be turned when cutting or removing the metal foil from the neck of the bottle.
- The foil is cut just below the neck and removed.
- The bottle neck and the top of the cork is cleaned with a napkin.
- The corkscrew is positioned into the center of the cork.
- Holding the neck of the bottle with one hand, the corkscrew is twisted slowly so as not to push the cork into the bottle.
- When the corkscrew has completely penetrated the cork, the cork is withdrawn with a steady, constant pressure.
- The inside lip of the bottle is wiped clean.
- The cork is unscrewed from the corkscrew.
- The captain inspects the cork. It should have the aroma of wine, not of cork.
- The cork is placed to the right of the person who ordered the wine, for his approval.
- If the host gives his approval, a very small amount of wine is poured into his wine glass to taste.
- At a sign of approval from the host, the wine is served first to the lady to the host's right, and then, continuing counterclockwise, to all the ladies. Then, also moving coun-

terclockwise, all the gentlemen are served. The host is served last.

- •Red wine—poured to one-third of the glass. Champagne—poured to three-fourths of the glass. White wine—poured to one-third of the glass. Rhine wine—poured to two-thirds of the glass.
- •After the wine has been poured, it is placed (if red) on the table in a holder or standing upright, or (if white) in a wine cooler.

WINTER MELON (Chinese) A round green-skinned melon whose white pulp tastes much like zucchini. It is never consumed raw; it is served cooked in soups or as a complement with a shrimp or chicken dish. In Chinese, the melon is called _dung gwa._

WITLOOF The Flemish name for a large-rooted variety of chicory for which Belgium is rightly famous. The Walloons (French-speaking Belgians) call it _chicon._ The leaf of this plant produces a delectable salad vegetable known the world over as Belgian endive. The root can be ground up to produce the rather bitter coffee-extender that is so popular with French and Spanish people.

The cultivation of the Belgian endive is a complicated process that involves two distinct plantings. The first is the cultivation of the rootstock, which is harvested before the first frost and is then replanted in special beds that are filled with heated fertilizer and covered with small "huts" to keep out the cold and the light. The crop of endive, grown in the dark, is beautifully white, formed of thick, fleshy leaves about four inches long and two inches wide, all compacted into a pointed head.

There are distinct differences between chicory, escarole, and what is known as Belgian endive. The chicory has narrow, finely cut, curly leaves; the escarole has a somewhat broader leaf and is less curly, but both have the same slightly bitter taste and crispness. The Belgian endive is a pointed, tightly compressed, snow-white vegetable whose topmost leaves are tinged with a yellow-green color. (See CHICONS, CHICORY, ENDIVE)

WOK (Chinese) This cooking utensil is probably one of the most versatile and economical ever concieved by man. It has a curved bottom, allowing the cook to use the least amount of oil and the absolute minimum amount of heat necessary. The wok can cook a tiny amount of food, as well as a banquet for six.

Woks can be made out of many metals and alloys, but the best is made from plain cast iron; it distributes the heat more evenly and heats much faster than woks made of other metals. After the wok has become well tempered, it will cook better with each succeeding use. As it can stir-fry, deep-fry, braise, poach, steam, yes, and even smoke foods, a more expedient helper in the kitchen would be hard to find. (See CHINESE CUISINE)

WONTON (Chinese) "A dumpling wrapper." The dough is made from a mixture of flour, egg, water, and salt. It is well kneaded in order to develop the gluten that will make the dough manageable and yet stiff enough to be rolled out paper-thin. The dough is cut into rectangular shapes and usually filled with various minced foods; whether plain or filled, they are called *wonton.* They are then steamed over or in a broth, or they may be deep-fried. Each cuisine seems to have developed its own version of the *wonton: gnocchi, ravioli* (Italian); *Klösse, Nockerl* (Austrian, German); *noques* (French); *Spätzli* (Swiss).

Wonton Soup A chicken broth flavored with celery is garnished with *wonton* that are stuffed with precooked minced pork, onions, and seasonings. Note that in China *wonton* is a snack, not a soup; and, in contrast to Western cultures, in China soups are always taken at the end of the meal.

WOOD EARS The ancient Romans called it by the Latin name, *Hirneola auricula-judae.* The French call it *l'oreille de Judas.* The English-speaking world dubbed this ebon-black, charred-looking mushroom "Jew's ears"; however, the more refined Chinese likened them to "cloud ears" or "wood ears." Before they are used, the mushrooms are cleaned of all dirt, pieces of wood, dried leaves, etc., by washing them in several changes of water. When cooked with dried tiger-lily buds, they prove to be a delicious treat and are quite inexpensive. (See MU-ER)

WORCESTERSHIRE SAUCE In spite of its title, this sauce was created in India. As everything in India was under British aegis for many decades, this Indian sauce was adopted and subsequently manufactured in Worcester, England. It has since returned to India, where it is manufactured as Worcestershire sauce. The sauce is composed of a spicy mixture of garlic, soya beans, tamarinds, onions, limes, anchovies, various spices, and vinegar. Today, it is a "must" when preparing a real "Bloody Mary," and it is served with steaks, chops, and with raw oysters.

WOW-WOW SAUCE An English gastronome, Dr. William Kitchiner, created this perky sauce with the doggy name. It is made of a brown *roux* mixed with bouillon, vinegar, mustard, and catsup, simmered until thick. To complete the sauce, parsley, pickles, and chopped walnuts are added. It is served with ham dishes and with roast loin of pork. (See KETCHUP, ROUX)

WURST Because Germany is considered the greatest sausage producer in the world, having more than 300 different varieties available—fresh, smoked, or in cans—the German word *Wurst* has become almost interchangeable with its English counterpart, sausage. (See BRATWURST, BLUT UND LEBERWURST, KNACKWURST, KÖNIGSWURST, METTWURST, PINKELWURST, WEISSWURST)

YAKI (Japensese) Grill.

>**Batayaki** A term indicating that a food has been broiled in butter.

>**Butter Yaki** A delightful meal cooked by each guest in an electric skillet set in the middle of the table. Thinly sliced beef, scallions, leeks, and Chinese cabbage leaves are cooked in hot butter and then dipped in a *ponzu* flavored with *daikon*. (See DAIKON, PONZU)

>**Okonomiyaki** A "personal" grill used by restaurant guests to broil their own food right at the table.

>**Teppanyaki** A metal grill that is used to broil meats and chicken. (See TERIYAKI, YAKITORI)

>**Yakimono** Charcoal-broiled foods. Meats or fish are marinated in a blend of soy sauce, *mirin,* grated ginger, and sugar. They are then skewered and grilled over hot coals. The famous beef dish *teriyaki* is prepared in this manner. Often, cut vegetables are skewered together with the meat or fish to fashion an Oriental *shishkebab*. (See MIRIN, SHISH KEBAB, TERIYAKI)

YAKITORI (Japanese) Skewered bits of chicken, chicken livers, and scallions, grilled over the white ash of a charcoal fire.

YALANCI (Turkish) Stuffed grapevine leaves; a type of *dolma*. To prepare the dish, grated onions are placed in a bowl and mixed together with rice, currants, pignoli nuts, mint, dill, parsley, lemon juice, oil, sugar, allspice, and salt. This stuffing is placed in the center of each of the grape leaves, which are then rolled, fastened with toothpicks, placed in a pot, and covered with a rich chicken broth. The stuffed vine leaves are cooked until the rice is tender. They are served cold as an appetizer, garnished with lemon wedges. (See DOLMAS) COMPATIBLE BEVERAGES: A good cold beer, ale, or cider.

YALAS CORBAST This is a Turkish soup made from a rich beef broth and yogurt. Crushed garlic is mixed with yogurt, salt, and pepper. This mixture, together with a little beef broth, is blended into a *roux,* a little at a time, and brought to a boil. After a short simmer, the soup is served piping hot in bowls garnished with fresh mint.

YAM Yams should never be confused with the orange-fleshed sweet potato; they belong to two different botanical families. The yam is the common name for the *Dioscoreaceae,* a family of tropical climbing herbs or shrubs whose fruit, often weighing thirty pounds or more, is used for human consumption and for feeding livestock. The flesh is white or yellow and has a nutlike taste and a potato-like texture. Yams are grown and used as food in the southern part of the United States, in the West Indies, in South America, and in South Africa, where it is known as "Hottentot bread" or the "tortoise plant." The yam is cooked as a potato. In Africa the yam is just not a food. To the natives, it is an object of deep emotion, an emotion similar to that which the Irish feel for the potato and the Chinese for their rice. These foods are all "survival foods." And they are prepared in numerous ways: they can be boiled; pureed; fried as *croquettes;* cooked layered with chopped onions, grated cheese, and breadcrumbs in a casserole; or even baked, flavored with cinnamon and sugar, to be served with game dishes. Yams, rice, and potatoes will adapt to any type of cooking. (See CANDIED SWEET POTATO, SWEET POTATO)

YANKEE COOKING The American Indians showed the first American settlers how to cook baked beans, proved to them what a wonderful food the wild turkey could be, and taught them when and how to trap the tremendous lobsters. Yankee food, from the beginning, was as frank and bold as the pioneering immigrants who came to tame the land and break the soil. There were no elegant sauces and garnishes; abundance alone seemed characteristic of all Colonial meals.

The Scandinavian, British, Dutch, and French settlers were the first to leave their mark on Yankee cookery. They adapted their own traditional dishes to the abundant produce at hand. Recipes for turkey, corn, lobster, the now-famous clam chowders, plus the pepper pot were all influenced by old-world dishes. For example, early Dutch and German immigrants, who had a penchant for sweet-sour foods, were instrumental in making sugar an integral part of American culture—to the point where today the American working man or woman with an hour for lunch will wash down a ketchup-coated hamburger with a Coca-Cola or a chocolate malted milk. Nevertheless, the integrity, tastiness, and baked-beans-and-apple-pie simplicity of good Yankee cooking causes one to rise after dinner, take a deep breath, and feel the glorious release that goes with the "aaah" that follows. (See AMERICAN CUISINE, BOSTON BAKED BEANS, BURGOO, CASSOULET, CHOWDER, CRÉOLE CUISINE, LOBSTER)

YAPRÁKIA ME YAOÚRTI AVGOLÉMENO (Greek) *Yaprákia* refers to grape leaves filled with rice, meat, and mint; *yaoúrti* is yogurt; and *avgolémeno* proves that lemon juice is present. Young lamb is twice ground and mixed well with chopped onions, salt, pepper, rice, mint, and a bit of water. The meat-and-rice filling is spooned into the grape leaves, which are then rolled up into small sausagelike forms. Set in the bottom of a heavy pot, the *yaprákias* are covered with a rich beef broth and cooked for several hours. The accompanying yogurt sauce, made by beating together a mixture of eggs, cornstarch, lemon juice, salt, pepper, and yogurt, is cooked over low heat until it thickens. The sauce can be served either directly over the *yaprákias* or separately in a bowl. (See DOLMAS) COMPATIBLE WINES: A white wine, e.g., Orvieto, Frascati, Sauvignon Blanc, Traminer, Hermitage Blanc, Neuchâtel, Fendant, Keknyelu, Szamarodni, Château Chalon, Dry Sauterne, Gewürztraminer.

YASSA CHICKEN (Sengalese) This speciality involves first boning the chicken and then, Chinese-style, allowing it to marinate overnight in a mixture of lemons, onions, pimientos, and hot peppers. The following day, the chicken is dried and grilled until crisp. The chicken is then simmered in the marinade and served with boiled white rice. COMPATIBLE BEVERAGES: Beer, ale, sparkling Burgundy, rosé, Sauterne, cider, tea.

YEMAS (Spanish) A Carmelite nun, one Santa Teresa de Avila, is said to have created this egg yolk confection. It is prepared by heating egg yolks in a sugar syrup; lemon juice and toasted almonds, ground fine, may be added. The mixture is cooled, shaped into balls, and rolled in sugar. It is gratifying to learn that even today in the walled-in town of Avila, in Old Castile, the nuns of the Convent of Encarnación continue to make *yemas* as round and as golden as those first made by the tiny Sister Teresa.

YIN WAW (Chinese) See BIRD'S NEST SOUP

YOGURT Yogurt is as common in a Turkish household as milk is in a Swiss chalet. Spelled *yoğurt* by the Turks, this dairy product is made by inoculating partially evaporated milk with a fermenting bacterium *(Lactobacillus bulgaricus)*, which thickens the milk. Yogurt is a favorite food not only in Turkey but also in the Balkan countries, as well as in Iran, Iraq, Afghanistan, and Russia.

When a food is as special as yogurt, all nations lay claim to having discovered it. The Turks, for instance, claim that when one of their nomadic ancestors got off of his camel to make camp and unloaded the leather gourd of milk from the back of his weary animal, he found that the heat of the day together with the movement of the camel had transformed the milk into something almost heaven-sent, which he promptly named *yoğurt*. However, many forms of fermented milk were originated by nomadic herdsmen in different parts of Asia and southeastern parts of Europe, and even in Scandanavia, Africa, and South America.

Only fresh milk or cream should be used to prepare yogurt. It is boiled, cooled, and then infused with the fermenting bacterium or an equal amount of already-made yogurt. This is kept in a warm place for a day or so in order to thicken.

Yogurt is good taken plain, as part of a dessert, as a sauce, or as an antidote for ptomaine poisoning. Yogurt is the great diplomat of the Indian cuisine; remaining tactfully in the background, it smooths the union of the sweet with the sour, the sharp with the bland, making all palatable.

Yoğurt Tatlist (Turkish) A simple dessert made by blending farina and yogurt with syrup. It is served with heavy cream and berries. (See SKYR, TATLIST)

Yoğurt Kebab (Turkish) This sandwich can be served as a main course. Garlic, salt, and yogurt are placed in a bowl. *Pita* (flat, unleavened bread) is browned on both sides in an oiled pan then covered with cooked tomatoes, a dollop of yogurt, paprika, and skewered pieces of lamb that were marinated overnight and then grilled. (See KEBAB, SHISHKEBAB, PITA) COMPATIBLE WINES: A red wine, e.g., Veltliner, Rioja, Retsina, Côtes du Rhône; or a rosé wine.

YOĞURTLU (Turkish) A round of *pita* bread is covered with yogurt, *köfte* (grilled spicy meatballs), and broiled chunks of lamb. Garnished with tomatoes, it is grilled just before serving. (See KÖFTE, PITA) COMPATIBLE WINES: A red wine, e.g., Côte Rôtie, Valpolicella, Médoc, Beaujolais, or Racki (Turkish date wine).

Yoğurt Salçasi Yogurt dishes and grilled meats are vital to Turkish cooking. This yogurt sauce is made by beating garlic and salt into yogurt; this is left in the refrigerator to mellow for days. The sauce is served with fried vegetables and fried meats.

YOKAN (Japanese) A favorite confection composed of ground *azuki* beans, sugar, and *kanten*. (See AZUKI, KANTEN)

YOKKO MEIN (Chinese) A culinary term, found on restaurant menus, meaning "an order of noodles." They are usually served in a clear broth.

YORKSHIRE PUDDING (English) A counterpart to France's *croûton,* or fried bread, which is served under beef to catch the flavorful juices. Yorkshire pudding is a thick baked pancake made from a mixture of flour, eggs, milk, nutmeg, salt, and pepper. It is most popularly served with a good English roast beef dinner. Originally, the batter was placed beneath the roast to catch the drippings while baking. Today, it is baked separately.

YORKSHIRE SAUCE (English) Prepared by adding red currant jelly and venison roast juices to a French *Porto* sauce, this popular sauce is served with joints of mutton and roasts of game. (See PORTO)

YOSENABE (Japanese) A casserole dish. Various kinds of seafood, bean curd, and vegetables are cooked in a casserole and served with a piquant sauce. COMPATIBLE BEVERAGES: Tea, saké, Sauterne.

YU-CHI-TANG (Chinese) See SHARK'S FIN SOUP

YUFKA (Turkish) Paper-thin sheets of pastry found all over the Middle East and used by the Turks to make *böreks*. (See BÖREKS, PHYLLO, STRUDEL)

YU-LANG-CHI (Chinese) A symphony of color and goodness is embodied by this dish of poached disjointed chicken served on a bed of buttered cooked broccoli and topped with strips of prosciutto ham and a sauce composed of soy sauce, the chicken stock used for poaching, and cornstarch. COMPATIBLE WINES: A white wine, e.g., Sauterne, saké, Gewürztraminer, Piesporter Goldtröpfchen, Graacher Himmelreich, Orvieto, Sauvignon Blanc.

YU TOE (Chinese) A fish maw (the dried stomach lining of a fish) used in soups because of its texture.

ZABAGLIONE (Italian) A velvety custard made from egg yolks, sugar, and usually Marsala wine, although any wine can be used. A liqueur of choice, such as Grand Marnier, apricot brandy, Curaçao, cherry brandy, or Izarra, is added to flavor the custard. Fresh fruit and whipped cream can also be added. A *zabaglione* can be served either hot or cold. In France this is called *sabayon.*

ZAKOUSKI/ZAKUSKI (Russian) This wild food assortment, the grandpapa of all *les hors d'oeuvre,* is served in individual bowls. The array of food may include radishes, caviar, anchovies, oysters, sardines, sausages, fish of all kinds, a multitude of cheeses, and pastries filled with a mousse of fish or of meat. And always, bottles and bottles of vodka are served to clear the way to the stomach. The foods are arranged on a large buffet table as a reception before a large banquet. COMPATIBLE WINES: Champagne and more Champagne, or a good rosé wine.

ZAMPONE (Italian) Literally, "big paw." This dish involves extracting the meat and the bone out of the pig's leg, then using the pork mixed with herbs, spices, or vegetables as a filling for the leg.

Zampone di Modena This speciality comes from the city of Modena in northern Italy. A pig's leg is stuffed with a fine forcemeat composed of minced pork, truffles, bacon, salt, and pepper. It is then cured and smoked. Before serving, the leg is soaked in water for ten hours; then it is simmered in a mixture of water and vinegar for several hours. It is usually served with beans or with black lentils. A real treat. COMPATIBLE WINES: A red wine, e.g., Chianti, Lambrusco, Mercurey, Beaujolais, Bardolino, Zinfandel, Médoc, Margaux, Egri Bikaver.

ZARZUELA DE MARISCOS (Spanish) A delicious seafood stew. To prepare, chopped onions, garlic, tomatoes, and ground almonds are cooked in hot olive oil with salt, pepper, and bay leaves. With the addition of clam juice, the mixture is brought to a boil; lobster, shrimp, and clams in their shells are then added. The pot is covered and simmered over low heat for just minutes. A dash of lemon juice and a sprinkling of chopped parsley finishes the dish. COMPATIBLE WINES: A white wine, e.g., Chablis, Pouilly-Fumé, Sancerre, Quincy, Muscadet, Soave, Verdicchio, Wehlener Sonnenuhr, Pinot Chardonnay.

Zarzuela de Pescado This is Catalonia's answer to the *bouillabaise* of Marseilles. Onions, pimiento, garlic, and tomatoes are sautéed in olive oil. To this preparation, sole, squid, monkfish, and halibut are added. Then comes the Catalonian touch: crushed almonds and white wine. (See BOUILLABAISE) COMPATIBLE WINES: The same white wines recommended for the *zarzuela de mariscos.*

ZENSAI (Japanese) Appetizers. The *zensai* is quite varied: stuffed mush-rooms, broiled oysters, shrimp on skewers, *sushi, sashimi,* and *teriyaki* strips barbecued on skewers. (See SUSHI, SASHIMI, TERIYAKI)

ZEYTINYAĞLI (Turkish) An identifying term for vegetable dishes pre-pared with olive oil, such as *zeytinyağli pirasa,* leeks cooked in olive oil; *zeytinyağli enginas,* artichokes cooked in olive oil; *zeytinyağli kereviz,* root celery cooked in olive oil.

Zeytinyağli Patlican Dolmasi The Turks make such a speciality of serving stuffed food that—much like the Chinese, who say, "If it moves, cook it!"—the Turkish adage might be, "If it's edible, stuff it!" This particular Turkish *dolma* consists of eggplants that are hollowed out and sautéed in olive oil. After filling the eggplant shells with a mixture of cooked rice and onions flavored with tomatoes, sugar, allspice, raisins, beef stock, mint leaves, dill, and parsley, they are wrapped in waxpaper and steamed on a rack in a heavy saucepan. (See DOLMAS) COMPATIBLE WINES: A red wine, e.g., Fleurie, Petit Sirah, Chianti, Valpolicella, Egri Bikaver; or a rosé wine.

ZINGARA, SAUCE (Italian) This sauce, along with several Florentine cooks, accompanied Catherine and Marie de Médicis to France. Since its arrival in France, the sauce has been called by many different names: *saingaraz, saingara, cingarat, gingara, Saint-Garat, singara,* and even *saupiquet!* This multinominal sauce is composed of chopped shallots, vinegar, *demi-glace,* chopped mushrooms, ham, truffles, and tongue. It is usually served with roast rabbit, ham steaks, veal cutlets, and chicken. In Germany, the sauce has yet another alias, *Zigeuner,* which means "gypsy," probably the most suitable name of all. (See DEMI-GLACE)

Veal Chops Zingara Veal chops are seasoned with salt and pa-prika and sautéed in butter. Slivers of sautéed ham are placed on top of each chop, and the top is coated with the *sauce zingara.* COMPATI BLE WINES: A red wine, e.g., Beaujolais, Zinfandel, Valpolicella, Savigny, Santenay, Nebbiolo.

ZITI (Italian) See PASTA

ZUCCHINI (Italian) A vegetable marrow, a tender squash which the French call *courgette.* Many nations have adopted this great food because of the variety of ways in which it can be prepared and served.

Zucchini alla Milanese This method of preparing zucchini, created in Milan, calls for the vegetables to be skinned and sliced, dipped in beaten egg and breadcrumbs, then fried. An alternate method is to marinate the zucchini, after they have been fried, in a mixture of vinegar, bay leaves, cloves, pepper, onions, carrots, and salt. Both methods ready the zucchini for a rich *antipasto.* (See ANTIPASTO)

Pisto la Mancha Español In Spain, a vegetable stew is called *pisto,* and in this particular stew zucchini plays a starring role. Chopped ham, garlic, and onions are sautéed in hot oil; then chopped

eggplant and sliced zucchini and chopped tomatoes and green peppers are added and cooked until tender. Beaten eggs and chopped
parsley are carefully stirred into the stew and simmered slowly until
the mixture is set. (See PISTO) COMPATIBLE WINES: A red wine, e.g.,
Rioja, Mercurey, Veltliner, Pinot Noir, Egri Bikaver, Chianti, Bardolino, Nebbiolo, Barbaresco, Valpolicella.

Zucchini Dolma with Meat and Rice (Caucasian) This speciality
from the richest agricultural region of the Soviet Union combines
ground lamb, grated onions, uncooked rice, and various herbs in a
beef broth that is well seasoned with salt and pepper. The mixture is
then used to stuff hollowed-out zucchinis. When filled, the tops are
replaced to seal the vegetables. Now enter the secret ingredient that
transforms this into something unique: a layer of peeled and finely
chopped quince is placed on the bottom of a heavy casserole, and the
stuffed zucchinis are bedded down side by side on top of the fragrant
quince. Covered with water, lemon juice, and more of the chopped
fruit, the zucchinis are simmered gently until tender. It is the tart
quince that makes this dish the mouthwatering taste sensation it has
always been. (See DOLMAS) COMPATIBLE WINES: A red wine, e.g.,
Rioja, Chianti, Pinot Noir, Dôle, Egri Bikaver, Mercurey,
Châteauneuf-du-Pape, Bardolino.

Zucchini Fritto (Italian) Fried squash. The dish can be prepared
two ways. One way is to deep-fry the zucchini in hot oil and serve it
drained and salted, like potato chips. The other method is to fry the
sliced zucchini in olive oil flavored with garlic. After cooking the
zucchini slices lightly on both sides, they are then put into the pan
again, seasoned with salt and pepper, and tossed in hot oil and served.
This is one of the most delicious of zucchini dishes.

Zucchini Ripieni The zucchini are cut lengthwise, seeded, and set
to soften in a pot of boiling water. The flesh of the zucchini is
removed, and together with chopped onions, tomatoes, and parsley it
is simmered in a pan with diced bacon, pork sausages, and garlic.
When warm, the zucchini shells are filled with this mixture, topped
with grated cheese and breadcrumbs, and baked. The baked shells are
served with an anchovy sauce. (See FRITTO, RIPIENI) COMPATIBLE
WINES: A red wine, Egri Bikaver, Premiat, Zinfandel, Valpolicella,
Beaujolais, Bardolino, Nebbiolo, Mâcon, Santenay, Côtes du
Rhône.

ZUPPA INGLESE (Italian) A rum cake topped with a custard cream and
slivered almonds. It was always so loved by the English tourists who
thronged to Italy that the Italians named it _zuppa,_ because it was so
"runny," and _inglese,_ in honor of those happy English who always
asked for it. It is very similar to the English "trifle."

ZUPPA PAVESE (Italian) This soup from Pavia in Lombardy consists of
a beef bouillon with poached eggs. The soup is usually served in small
individual bowls. Toasted bread is floated in the soup, grated Par-

mesan cheese is strewn over all, and the soup is placed under the broiler until the cheese is crusty. It is served piping hot.

ZWIEBACK (German) A type of toast or rusk that has been baked twice, as the words *zwei* (two) and *backen* (baked) imply. The dough is made from a mixture of flour, sugar, butter, milk, and yeast. After rising, the dough is cut into rounds, brushed with milk, and baked in a hot oven. When done and cool, the rounds are split in two and baked again, toasted side down, until the top is crisp and lightly browned. (See BISCOTTO)

ZWIEBELCREMESUPPE (Swiss-German) An onion soup that is enriched with eggs and heavy cream. Sliced onions are cooked in oil and butter until translucent; then, with the addition of scalded milk and cream, the soup is bound with beaten eggs. It is served piping hot, seasoned with nutmeg, salt, and pepper and garnished with rye croutons and chopped chives.

ZWIEBEL WÄHE (Swiss-German) An onion tart. Cooked onions are added to sweet butter and, away from the heat, a mixture of eggs and cream is stirred in. The mixture is seasoned then poured into pastry shells, dotted with crisp bacon bits, and baked. COMPATIBLE WINES: A red wine, e.g., Beaujolais, Veltliner, Valpolicella, Zinfandel, Nebbiolo, Egri Bikaver, Mercurey, Moulin-à-Vent, Châteauneuf-du-Pape, Fleurie.

Selected Bibliography

American Heritage Cookbook. New York: American Heritage Publishing Co., 1964.

Aresty, Esther B. *The Delectable Past.* New York: Simon & Schuster, 1967.

Aron, Jean-Paul. *The Art of Eating in France.* New York: Harper & Row, 1973.

Aubry, Ronald. *A Royal Chef's Notebook.* Surrey: Gresham Books, 1978.

AvRutick, Frances R. *The Complete Passover Cookbook.* New York: Jonathan David, 1981.

Beard, James. *Beard on Food.* New York: Alfred A. Knopf, 1978.

———. *Theory and Practice of Good Cooking.* New York: Alfred A. Knopf, 1977.

Booth, George C. *The Food and Drink of Mexico.* New York. Dover Publications, Inc., 1964.

Bridgewater, William, and Kurtz, Seymour. *The Columbia Encyclopedia.* New York: Columbia University Press, 1956.

Brown, Dale. *The Cooking of Scandinavia.* New York: Time-Life Books, 1968.

Browns, The. *The European Cookbook.* New York: Prentice-Hall, 1951.

Child, Julia, et al. *Mastering the Art of French Cooking,* Volumes I and II. New York: Alfred A. Knopf, 1961.

Claiborne, Craig. *International Cookbook.* New York: Harper & Row, 1971.

Claiborne, Craig, and Franey, Pierre. *Craig Claiborne's New New York Times Cookbook.* New York: Times Books, 1979.

Courtine, Robert. *The Hundred Glories of French Cooking.* New York: Farrar, Straus & Giroux, 1973.

Dallas, E.S. *Kettner's Book of the Table.* London: Centaur Press Ltd., 1968.

Davis, William Sterns. *Life on a Mediaeval Barony.* New York: Harper & Bros., 1923.

Derecskey, Susan. *The Hungarian Cookbook.* New York: Harper & Row, 1972.

Devore and White. *The Appetites of Man.* Garden City, New York: Doubleday, 1978.

Dictionnaire de l'Académie des Gastronomes. Editions Prisma. Paris, 1962.

Eren, Neset. *The Art of Turkish Cooking.* Garden City, New York: Doubleday, 1969.

Escoffier, A. *The Escoffier Cook Book.* New York: Crown, 1969.

Farb, Peter, and Armelagos, George. *Consuming Passions.* Boston: Houghton Mifflin Co., 1980.

Fisher, M.F.K. *The Cooking of Provincial France.* New York: Time-Life Books, 1968.

Fitzgibbon, Theodora. *Food of the Western World.* New York: Quadrangle, 1976.

Froud, Nina. *The International Jewish Cook Book.* New York: Stein & Day, 1972.

Garcia, Clarita. *Clarita's Cocina.* Garden City, New York: Doubleday, 1969.

Goldberg, Molly, and Waldo, Myra. *The Molly Goldberg Jewish Cookbook.* New York: Pyramid, 1961.

Gouy, Louis P. de. *The Gold Cook Book.* Philadelphia and New York: Chilton Co., 1947.

Grossinger, Jennie. *The Art of Jewish Cooking.* New York: Bantam Books, 1960.

Grüninger, Ursula. *Kiehnle Grund-Kochbuch.* Weil der Stadt, Germany: Walter Hädecke Verlag, 1975.

Guy, Christian. *The Illustrated History of French Cuisine.* New York: Orion Press, 1960.

Hahn, Emily. *The Cooking of China.* New York: Time-Life Books, 1968.

Hazan, Marcella. *Classic Italian Cooking.* New York: Alfred A. Knopf, 1976.

Hazelton, Nika. *The Belgian Cookbook.* New York: Atheneum, 1970.

Hering, Richard. *Hering's Lexicon der Küche.* Fachbuchverlag, Dr. Pfanneberg & Co., Giessen, Germany, 1963.

Howe, Robin. *Soups.* New York: Bonanza Books, 1967.

Käkönen, Ulla. *Natural Cooking the Finnish Way.* New York: Quadrangle, 1974.

Land, Mary. *New Orleans Cuisine.* Cranbury, New Jersey: A.S. Barnes & Co., Inc. 1969.

Lapidus, Dorothy Farris. *The Scrutable Feast.* New York: Dodd, Mead & Co., 1977.

Larsen, Egon. *Food.* London: Frederick Muller Ltd., 1977.

Lee, Calvin and Audry. *The Gourmet Chinese Regional Cookbook.* New York: G.P. Putnam & Sons., 1976.

Lo, Kenneth. *Peking Cooking.* New York: Panteheon Books, 1971.

Longstreet, Stephen and Ethel. *The Joys of Jewish Cooking.* New York: Weathervane, 1974.

Madhur, Jeffrey. *An Invitation to Indian Cooking*. New York: Vintage, 1973.

Marois, Gerald. *Cooking with a French Touch*. Garden City, New York: Doubleday, 1951.

McClane, A.J. *Encyclopedia of Fish Cookery*. New York: Holt, Rinehart & Winston, 1977.

Montagne, Prosper. *Larousse Gastronomique*. Paris: Larousse, 1938.

Nelson, Kay Shaw. *The Best of Western European Cooking*. New York: John Day & Co., 1976.

Ochorowicz-Monatowa, Marja. *Polish Cooking*. London: André Deutsch Ltd. 1969.

Oliver, Raymond. *Gastronomy of France*. Cleveland, Ohio: World Publishing Co., 1967.

Ortiz, Elizabeth Lambert. *The Book of Latin-American Cooking*. New York: Alfred A. Knopf, 1979.

———. *The Complete Book of Caribbean Cooking*. New York: M. Evans and Co., 1973.

Paterson, John. *The International Book of Wines*. London: Hamlyn Publishing Group Ltd., 1975.

Pearl, Anita May, and Kolatch, David, editor. *Completely Cheese: The Cheeselover's Companion*. New York: Jonathan David, 1978.

Pennsylvania Dutch Cook Book. Reading, Pa., Culinary Arts Press, 1936.

Perl, Lila. *Rice, Spice and Bitter Oranges*. Cleveland, Ohio: World Publishing Co., 1967.

Petits Propos Culinaires 5,6. London: Prospect Books, 1980.

The Picayune's Créole Cookbook. New York: Dover Publications, Inc., 1971.

Prentice, E. Parmelee. *Hunger and History*. Caldwell, Idaho: Caxton Printers Ltd., 1951.

Post, Laurens vand der. *First Catch Your Eland*. New York: William Morrow & Co., 1978.

Post, Elizabeth L. *The New Emily Post's Etiquette*. New York: Funk & Wagnalls, 1975.

Rao, Shivaji, and Devi Holkar, Shalini. *The Cooking of the Maharajas*. New York: Viking, 1975.

Reader's Digest Association, Inc. *Great People of the Bible and How They Lived*. Pleasantville, New York: Reader's Digest, 1974.

Root, Waverly. *The Cooking of Italy*. New York: Time-Life Books, 1968.

Saulnier, Louis. *Le Repertoire de la Cuisine*. Woodbury, New York: Barron's, 1976.

Shosteck, Patti. *A Lexicon of Jewish Cooking*. Chicago: Contemporary Books, 1979.

Simon, André L. *The Art of Good Living*. London: Michael Joseph Ltd., 1951.

Simon, André L., and Howe, Robin. *Dictionary of Gastronomy.* New York: McGraw-Hill, 1970.

Smith, Henry. *Master Dictionary of Food & Cookery & Menu Translator.* London: Practical Press Ltd., 1954.

Steinberg, Rafael. *Cooking of Japan.* New York: Time-Life Books, 1969.

Stewart, Katie. *The Joy of Eating.* Owings Mills, Maryland: Stemmer House, 1977.

Stockli, Albert. *Splendid Fare.* New York: Alfred A. Knopf, 1970.

Trager, James. *The Bellybook.* New York: Grossman, 1972.

Vence, Céline, and Courtine, R. *The Grand Masters of French Cuisine.* New York: G.P. Putnam & Sons, 1978.

Villefosse, René Heron de. *Histoire et Géographie Gourmandes de Paris.* Paris: Les Éditions de Paris, 1956.

Wallace, Forrest, and Cross, Gilbert. *The Game of Wine.* New York: Harper & Row, 1976.

Wechsberg, Joseph. *The Cooking of Vienna's Empire.* New York: Time-Life Books, 1968.

Wise, William H. *Wise Encyclopedia of Cookery.* New York: Wise & Co., 1949.

Yueh, Jean. *The Great Tastes of Chinese Cooking.* New York: New York Times Book Co., 1979.

About the Author

Ever since he graduated from the world-famous Swiss Hotel School in Lausanne in 1949, Norman Odya Krohn has been professionally engaged in some phase of the restaurant-hotel business. After a *stage* as *Kellner* under Hans Buol at the prestigious Hôtel Ascot in Zürich, he was employed as food and beverage manager at the Stadt-Casino in Basel.

Returning to America, Mr. Krohn obtained positions as restaurant captain, first at Lüchows, under restaurateur Jan Mitchel, and then at the plush Forum of the Twelve Caesars, both in New York City. Subsequently, under the aegis of Mr. Joseph Baum, Mr. Krohn presided as *maître d'hôtel* over the birth of one of New York's most elegant restaurants, The Four Seasons on Park Avenue.

Once again returning to Switzerland, Norman Krohn supervised the food service of two highly-rated restaurants at the Hotel Red-Ox in Basel, one of which was Chinese and the other, naturally, European. He returned to New York to serve as assistant banquet manager at the Delmonico Hotel, and he subsequently became general manager of Food Operations at the Philharmonic Café at Lincoln Center for the Performing Arts.

Mr. Krohn currently devotes himself to research and writing in the field of food.